落葉歸根

——東華三院華僑原籍安葬檔案選編 上冊

Fallen leaves returning to their roots :

A selection of archives on the bone repatriation service
of Tung Wah Group of Hospitals for overseas Chinese
(Book A)

東華三院檔案及歷史文化辦公室　編

中華書局

目錄

本書所選編三百封書信來自東華三院文物館館藏檔案「東華義莊文獻」的書信類別，是東華三院於二十世紀上半葉協助全球華人原籍安葬的重要歷史檔案。信件的數碼圖像已上載於「珍藏・分享——東華三院文物館檔案」（www.twmarchives.hk）網站與公眾分享，是次出版計劃把網站上三百封中文書信重新整理、翻譯及編目，以廣流傳。

信件涵蓋一九二〇及三〇年代，為方便有系統地閱覽，本書以先僑的西歸（去世）地區及書信數目多寡分成六個章節，順序為中南美洲、北美洲、亞洲、大洋洲、內地及香港和不知先友西歸地。上冊為圖輯，下冊為中文釋文及英文翻譯。

此外，信件中文釋文格式與字型均以原件為依據，部分字型與現今不同，釋文未予更改。人名、地方及機構名稱的翻譯使用本身的英文名字，其餘則使用廣東話輔以普通話併音。

The three hundred letters featured in these volumes were selected among the correspondences in the Tung Wah Coffin Home archives. A part of the collection of Tung Wah Museum, the Tung Wah Coffin Home archives contain important historical documents which shed light on Tung Wah's bone repatriation service for deceased Chinese in the first half of the 20th century. To share the archives with the public, digital images of the letters have been uploaded to the "Preserve and Share: Tung Wah Museum Archives" (www.twmarchives. hk) website. The publication of these volumes sets out to reorganize, translate (into English) and catalogue three hundred Chinese letters, thereby making them more accessible. The letters, which span a period of two decades – from the 1920s to 1930 – are divided into six chapters according to region (where the Chinese persons passed away) and the number of letters: Central and South America, North America, Asia, Oceania, Mainland and Hong Kong as well as Unknown Place of Death. Of the two volumes, Book A contains images of the letters, whereas the Chinese transcripts and English translation of the letters can be found in Book B. The format and use of words of the Chinese transcripts are based on the original historical documents – some of the words and phrases are different from contemporary usage. In the English translation, the original English names of persons, places and institutions, where available, are used. Otherwise, common Hong Kong Cantonese romanization and Putonghua pinyin are applied.

序一

東華三院

香港東華三院源自東華醫院。醫院於一八七〇年按法例成立，宗旨是為貧困華人提供中醫藥服務。醫院奠基時在地盤發現先人的骸骨，創院總理決定把他們安葬在港島西的一個義山。東華照顧沒有名字和身份的亡者之故事由此展開。

東華醫院發展迅速，為本地華人提供免費醫療、殯葬、賑災和教育服務。因着歷任董事局成員的環球商業網絡，東華醫院（一九三一年開始變為東華三院）延伸關顧至世界各地的華人。除賑災外，東華在海外華人去世後歸家的旅程中扮演重要角色。

十九世紀中葉由於中國政局混亂和經濟不景，另一方面美國加州於一八四八年發現金礦，大量廣東華人蜂擁到美國尋求改善生活。華人投身各種工作包括興建鐵路，例如一八六三至一八六九年的美國中央太平洋鐵路，過程中遇到種族歧視和生活挑戰。有些華人安身後在異鄉站穩下來，有些完成工作契約或致富後返鄉，不過有些華人死後回家的願望最終是由華人慈善組織基於同根心和鄉梓情協助達成的。這項生命中最後的安排讓亡者和家人獲得安慰。

全賴東華三院文物館保存一批東華義莊文獻，讓我們了解到海外華人對死後回國及與家庭團聚的熱切期望。東華抱着最大的仁愛之心，在香港接收遊子的棺骨及殫精竭慮地處理由人認領或將棺骨送回家鄉。可以想像，東華無論得到讚賞和稱謝，或遭到埋怨和投訴，都以極大的同理心和能力去完成任務。縱使通訊困難和資源有限，這項工作由十九世紀末至二十世紀中維持了六、七十年。至四十年代末，中華人民共和國成立產生新的政治形勢，其後香港與內地的水路交通中斷，東華為海外華人提供的原籍安葬服務結束。六十年代初，東華要在義莊地段興建醫院，不得不清理大量積存的棺骨；無人認領的棺骨最後葬在羅湖沙嶺墳場由東華建立的義塚。

為了研究原籍安葬服務的歷史和探索義莊文獻對香港、中國及世界的重要性，近年東華三院嘗試帶着海外華人組織昔日的來函重新聯絡他們現時的領導層。與此同時，我們聯繫江門五邑大學廣東僑鄉文化研究中心，與他們分享資料，讓大家從更多角度理解華人遷徙過程中的生命史。

適逢該中心與美國史丹福大學進行一項北美洲鐵路華工研究計劃，他們的學者認為有些鐵路華工可能一直留在北美洲至晚年，去世後由東華協助回鄉，因此東華保留的華人原籍安葬檔案便具有研究鐵路華工及其他華人落葉歸根歷史的價值。我們揀選了其中三百封上載於東華三院文物館屬網站的函件集結成書。這些函件足以反映這項服務無遠弗屆，複雜無比。我們希望是次合作為研究華人遷徙當中的中國文化以及文物保育的課題帶來啟示。

今天，東華三院董事局每年於清明節在東華義莊拜祭曾在義莊停留或現仍在義莊停留的先友。東華剛開展羅湖沙嶺墳場東華義塚的修復工程，並一直全心全意維護義莊和相關檔案，傳承年青一代。我衷心感謝一群東華三院文物館的義工，他們協助將義莊文獻數碼化、整理和將原件轉為中文文本，以及出版檔案的校對工作。由於我們有時難以閱讀和理解函件內容，也缺乏對華人遷徙歷史的知識，中文文本及英文翻譯可能有誤解、遺漏和出錯，希望讀者接受我們的不足，並不吝賜教，讓我們將來有機會更正。

東華三院於二〇二〇年慶祝成立一百五十周年。我希望獻上這本書作為我們推出各項慶祝活動的前奏。它提醒我們東華一個永恆的承諾——竭盡所能以愛心關顧有需要的人。

蔡榮星博士

東華三院二〇一九／二〇二〇年度主席

二〇一九年十一月一日

The Tung Wah Group of Hospitals

The Tung Wah Group of Hospitals in Hong Kong originated from the Tung Wah Hospital which was established by law in 1870 to provide Chinese medicine services for the destitute Chinese. When the foundation stone of the hospital was laid, the founding Directors found human remains in the site and decided to bury them in a free cemetery in the west of Hong Kong Island. The story of Tung Wah taking care of the nameless and faceless deceased began.

The hospital grew rapidly to serve local Chinese in providing free medical, burial, disaster relief and education services. With the global business network of successive Boards of Directors, the Tung Wah Hospital (and Tung Wah Group of Hospitals from 1931 onwards) extended its care for Chinese around the world. Besides disaster relief, Tung Wah played a significant role in the journey of Chinese returning home after death from overseas countries.

Because of political turmoil and economic hardship in China in the mid-19th century and the lure of gold in California, United States in 1848, many Chinese in Guangdong flocked to the United States to seek a better living. They faced racial discrimination and life challenges as they took up all sorts of job opportunities including building railroads, such as the Central Pacific Railroad in the United States from 1863 to 1869. Some Chinese were able to gain footing in the new land as they settled down, some went back to China having completed their work contracts or made a fortune, but there were some whose wishes of going home after death were fulfilled with the help of Chinese benevolent associations out of a strong sense of responsibility for fellow countrymen and fraternity care of the same hometown. The end-of-life arrangement brought comfort to the deceased and the living.

Thanks to the presence of a special collection of Tung Wah Coffin Home archives preserved by the Tung Wah Museum, we come to understand the yearning of overseas Chinese to return to the country and reunite with family after death. Tung Wah demonstrated utmost philanthropy to receive the remains of the sojourners in Hong Kong and devoted strenuous efforts to arrange for them to be claimed or send them to their hometown. It must have required great compassion and capabilities of Tung Wah to handle the logistics amidst praises and gratitude as well as lamentations and complaints. Although communication was difficult and resources limited, the mission last for about six or seven decades from the 19th century to mid-20th century. The bone repatriation service for overseas Chinese by Tung Wah ended in the late 1940s with a new political situation resulting from the founding of the People's Republic of China and the stoppage of water transportation link between Hong Kong and mainland China later. In the early 1960s, Tung Wah had to clear the backlog of remains in the coffin home for building a hospital in the lot. The unclaimed remains were eventually buried in the free cemetery established by Tung Wah in the Sandy Ridge Cemetery in Lo Wu.

In a bid to research into the legacy of the bone repatriation service and explore the importance of the coffin home archives to Hong Kong, China and the world, Tung Wah has been trying to reconnect with the present leaders of the overseas Chinese associations according to the letters their predecessors sent to us. At the same time, we establish rapport with the Guangdong Qiaoxiang Cultural Research Center of the Wuyi University in Jiangmen to share the information with them so that there could be more perspectives to understand the life history of Chinese in the migration. As the Center undertakes the Chinese Railroad Workers in North America Project with the Stanford University of the United States, their scholars consider that some workers might have stayed in North America till an old age and returned home after death via Tung Wah. Thus, the bone repatriation service archives preserved by Tung Wah are deemed important materials for academic research on the history of railroad workers and other overseas Chinese returning to the roots. We therefore selected 300 letters from the collection which had been uploaded on the Tung Wah Museum Archives website to compile the book. To a certain extent, the letters reflect the extent and complexity of the bone repatriation service. We hope the collaboration brings enlightenment to the academic study of Chinese culture in the Chinese migration and preservation of cultural heritage.

Today, the Board of Directors of Tung Wah pay annual respect in the coffin home on the Ching Ming Festival to those who once stayed and are still staying in the coffin home. Tung Wah has just initiated a restoration project to the Tung Wah free cemetery in Sandy Ridge Cemetery and has been preserving the coffin home and related archives with full dedication for passing onto our young generation. I wish to express my heartfelt thanks to the volunteers of the Tung Wah Museum who helped digitize, organize and transcribe the coffin home archives as well as proofread the archives in this publication project. Due to difficulties in reading and comprehending the content of the letters and our limited knowledge on Chinese migration history, there could be misinterpretations, omissions and errors in the Chinese text and English translations. We beg the pardon of our readers and hope they are generous enough to give us comment for our future rectification.

Tung Wah celebrates its 150th anniversary in 2020. I wish to present this book as a prelude to the celebration activities which we are going to launch. This book reminds us of our all-time pledge – that we spare no efforts to offer loving care to those in need.

Dr. TSOI Wing Sing, Ken
Chairman of Tung Wah Group of Hospitals, 2019/2020
1 November 2019

五邑大學廣東僑鄉文化研究中心

鴉片戰爭後中國與英國簽訂《南京條約》，香港被割讓予英國。其後，太平天國運動波及廣東，珠江三角洲的五邑地區又陷入土客械鬥，持續十數年，社會秩序紊亂，加上天災連連，人民生活艱難。在這樣的情況下，具有出洋傳統的五邑先僑以勞工身份出洋謀生，掀起了近代第一波移民高潮，香港成為他們遠走東南亞、北美洲、中南美洲、大洋洲、歐洲和非洲的出發港。這些赴外洋謀生的華工，秉承中華文化傳統，肩負養家立業的重擔，勤懇工作，任勞任怨，把積蓄寄回家鄉接濟家庭，為僑鄉的發展做出極大的貢獻。

這些謀職外洋的華工當中，不少人客死異鄉，為助死者達成落葉歸根、魂歸故里的願望，海內外善堂通力合作，建成了一張強有力的慈善網絡，把海外華僑的骸骨運回原籍安葬，這樣的活動一直持續了大半個世紀，是華僑歷史與文化研究領域中的重要議題。

香港不僅是早期華僑出國的必經之路，又是他們回國的中轉港，是連接家鄉與外洋的重要交通樞紐、資訊中心，也是僑匯中心。香港東華醫院（今天的東華三院）從建成至今，一直是香港最大的慈善機構，過去曾在大半個世紀以來，承擔了接收海外骸骨、建設義莊存放骸骨等服務。

因此，東華醫院的原籍安葬資料最能真實直觀反映這段歷史，彌足珍貴。

在東華醫院負責接收的骸骨當中，估計有部分來自美國和加拿大的骸骨都是當年建築鐵路的華工。適逢美國橫貫大陸鐵路通車一百五十周年，五邑大學廣東僑鄉文化研究中心與香港東華三院合作，從東華的原籍安葬文獻中選編三百封較為有代表性的信件結集出版。廣東僑鄉文化研究中心譚金花博士負責研究原籍安葬課題並撰寫研究報告，從居住國的撿骨到香港的轉運，再到家鄉認領或建設義塚安葬無人領取者，全面梳理原籍安葬的整個過程。

本書的出版，不僅是對學術界的重要貢獻——在研究華僑歷史、僑鄉文化等領域具有極高的文獻價值、學術價值和研究意義，而且，這也是對為建築鐵路、建設家鄉社會而付出努力的鐵路華工的紀念。

張國雄

五邑大學廣東僑鄉文化研究中心主任

二〇一九年九月一日

Guangdong Qiaoxiang Cultural Research Center, Wuyi University

After the First Opium War, China and Britain signed the Treaty of Nanking, which saw the cession of Hong Kong to Britain. Subsequently, the Taiping Rebellion spread to Guangdong province, whereas Wuyi (the Five Counties) in the Pearl River Delta was embroiled in the Punti-Hakka Clan Wars for more than ten years. Social unrest and repeated natural calamities made life extremely difficult for the people. Under these circumstances, people from the Wuyi area, who had a tradition of travelling overseas, left their hometown to earn a living abroad and started the first wave of emigration. Meanwhile, Hong Kong became the port of departure for those travelling to Southeast Asia, North America, Central and South America, Australia, Europe and Africa. These Chinese laborers upheld Chinese traditions. They took it upon themselves to support their families, they worked hard without complaining and sent their savings back home for their families, contributing immensely to the development of their hometown.

Many of the Chinese laborers died abroad. In order to help the deceased return to their roots and find eternal peace in their hometown, Chinese benevolent associations abroad worked together to build a strong charitable network undertaking bone repatriation for Chinese who passed away in foreign countries. These charitable deeds continued for almost a century and are an important topic in the research on the history and culture of overseas Chinese.

Hong Kong was not only a vital stop for Chinese leaving the country in the early days, but it was also the transit point for their return to China. It was a key transportation hub linking their hometown with foreign countries, an information hub as well as a center for overseas remittance. Meanwhile, since its founding, Tung Wah Hospital (now the Tung Wah Group of Hospitals) has been the largest charitable organization in Hong Kong. For more than a century, Tung Wah took the bones repatriated from abroad into its care, setting up a coffin home to provide temporary refuge for them. Thus, the bone repatriation information of Tung Wah can most faithfully reflect this chapter of history and is indeed invaluable.

Of the bones sent to Tung Wah Hospital from the United States and Canada, many belonged to Chinese laborers who built railroad tracks. As the first transcontinental railroad of the United States celebrates the 150th anniversary of its inauguration, the Guangdong Qiaoxiang Culture Research Center of Wuyi University has joined hands with Tung Wah Group of Hospitals in publishing 300 selected letters from the vast collection of bone repatriation documents in Tung Wah's archives. Dr. TAN Jinhua of the Guangdong Qiaoxiang Culture Research Center conducted extensive research into bone repatriation and composed a research article on the full process, covering the exhumation of bones in overseas countries, the stopover at Hong Kong, the claiming of bones by the deceased's families in their hometown and the building of communal graveyards for unclaimed bones.

The publication of this book is an immense contribution to the academia, offering exceptional historical, academic and research value for the study of the history of overseas Chinese compatriots and the culture of their hometown. At the same time, the book commemorates the Chinese laborers who devoted themselves to the construction of railroad tracks as well as the development of their hometown.

Zhang Guoxiong

Director of Guangdong Qiaoxiang Culture Research Center, Wuyi University

1 September 2019

中南美洲西歸先友

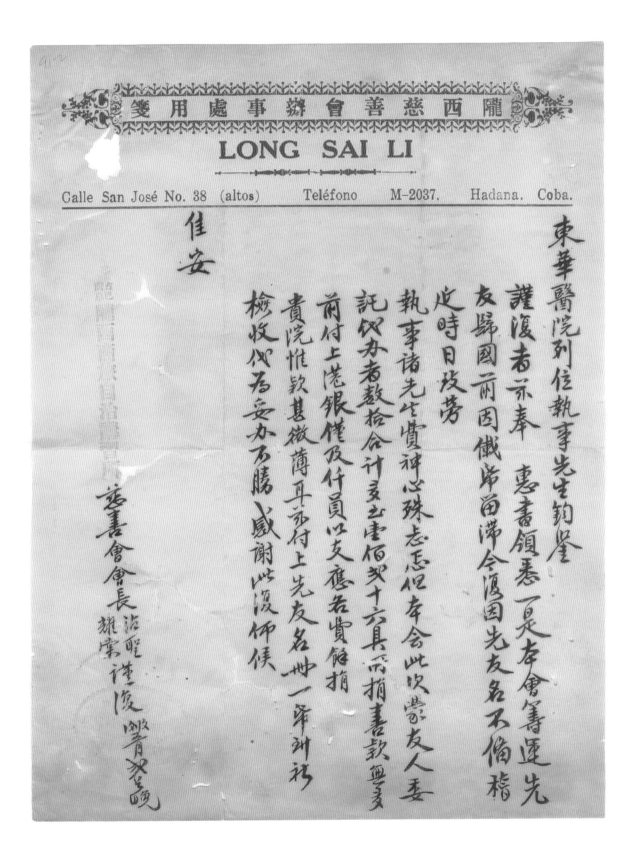

隴西慈善會辦事處用箋

LONG SAI LI

Calle San José No. 38 (altos)　　Teléfono　　M-2037,　　Hadana, Coba.

東華醫院列位執事先生鈞鑒

謹復者　示奉　惠書領悉　夏炅本會籌運先

友歸國前因俄患苗滯令渡固先友名不備稽

此時日攷勞

執事諸先生費神心殊志忌但本會此次蒙友人委

託代為暫拾合計共玖壹佰柒十六員亦捐書款並彙

前付上港銀僅及仟員以支應者賞餘捐

貴院惟欵甚微薄耳茲付上先友名世一華列衫

檢收代為妥為可膽　感謝此復仰候

佳安

慈善會會長　治暉謹復　齊棠　晚

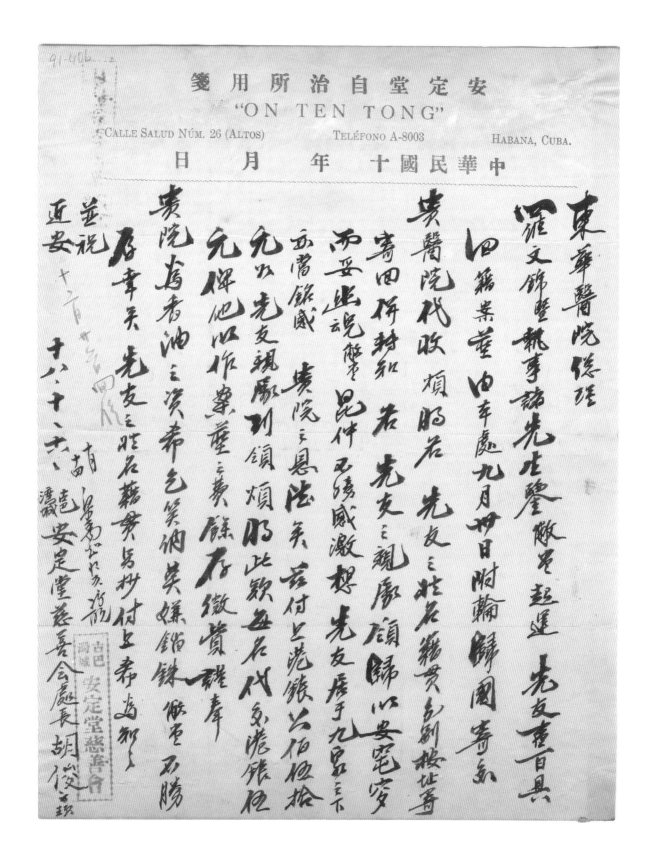

安定堂自治所用箋
"ON TEN TONG"
CALLE SALUD NÚM. 26 (ALTOS)　　　TELÉFONO A-8003　　　HABANA, CUBA.

中華民國十　年　月　日

東華醫院總理

羅文錦暨報事諸先生鑒　敬啓者逕　先生善百具

回籍荣董由本處九月廿日附輪歸國等气

貴醫院代收煩貴先友之親屬領歸以安宅穿

壽田俘轉和若　先友之親屬頌歸于九昌之下

兩要述說旅書　昆仲必绣感激想先友屡于九昌之下

亦當銘感　貴院之愚陛茇莙付上港銀六佰伍拾佰

免俾他以作樂華之費餘存徵賞諸拳

免以先友親屬刊領煩刵此頡每名代多港銀佰

貴院為香油之資希乞笑納其媒鎻鍊俄壹石膳

居等美先友之脏名藉贵另抄付上希為郵

善祝

近安　　　　　　　　　　　　十二月十八日　古巴灣城安定堂慈善會處長胡俊古璞

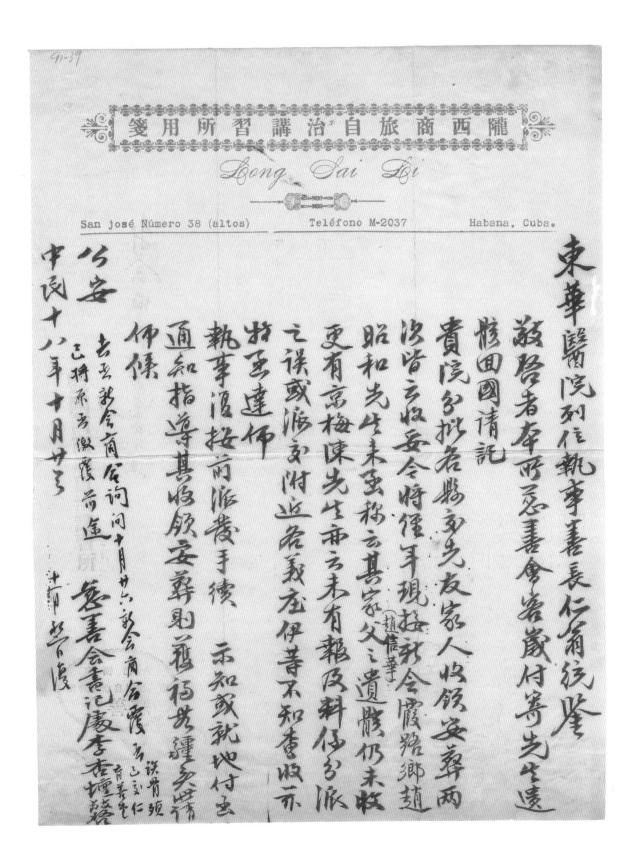

東華醫院列位執事善長仁翁統鑒

敬啟者奉　所屬惡善會善翁歲付壽先生遺

體囬國請託

貴院多抄各款寄先友家人收領安葬兩

沿省立收委令時僅年現接敝會囑辦鄉趙

昭和先生來函稱云甚家父之遺骸仍未收

更有高梅陳先生而云未有報及料俱分派

之誤或派安附近各義庄俾善不知查收示

對至達師

執事須按前派灑農手續　示知或就地付玉

通知指導其收領安葬覔覓福於種多善請

　仰俟

中民十八年十月廿三

　竹安

慈善會書記康李查壇敬

004〈頁一〉 古巴灣城黃江夏堂慈善會致東華醫院信件

1929 年 10 月 29 日

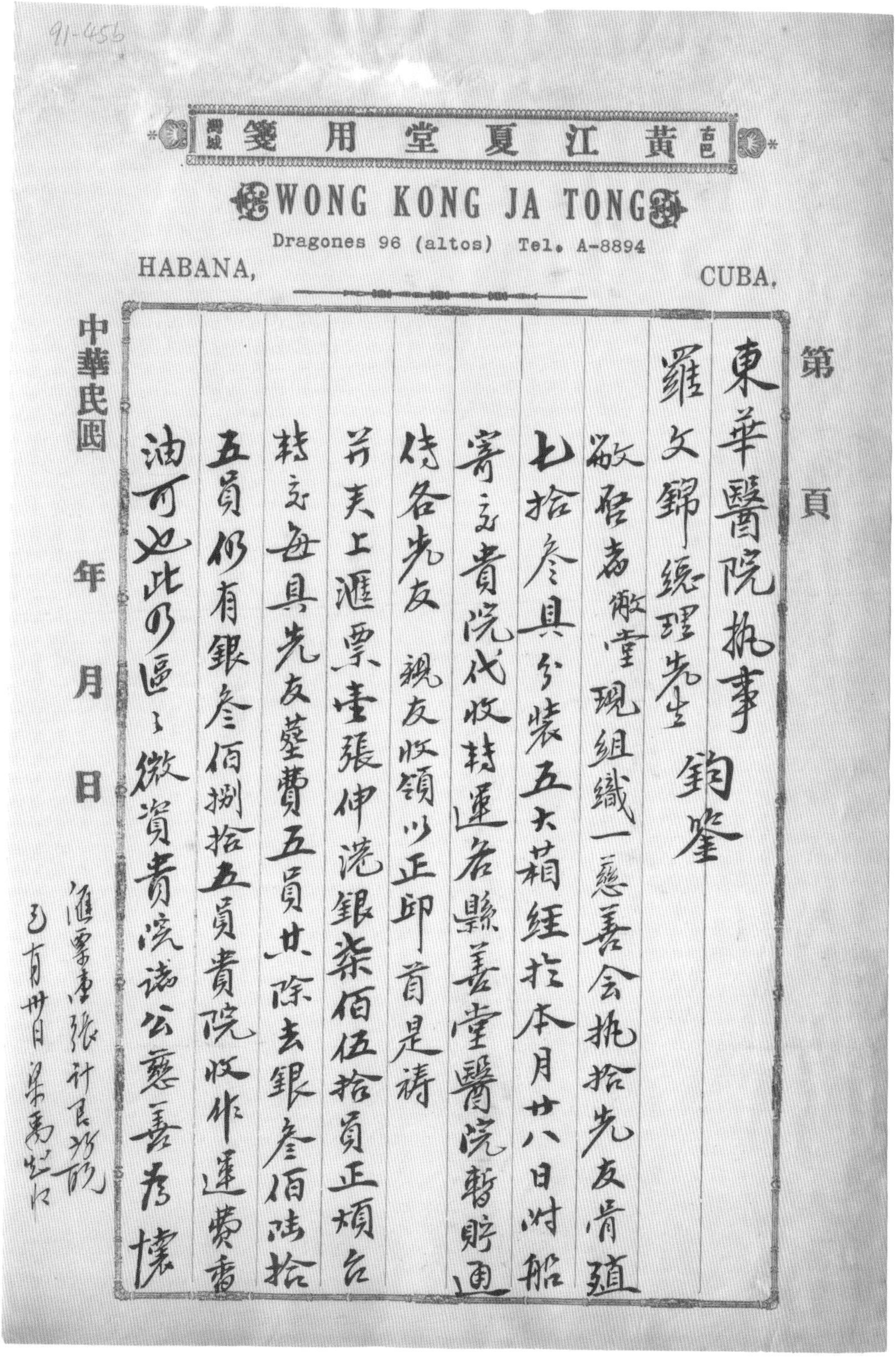

91-456

古巴 黃江夏堂用箋 灣城

WONG KONG JA TONG

Dragones 96 (altos) Tel. A-8894

HABANA, CUBA.

第 頁

東華醫院執事

羅文錦總理先生 鈞鑒

敬啟者 敝堂現組織一慈善会執拾先友骨殖

七拾叁具分裝五大箱經於本月廿八日附船

寄交貴院代收轉運各縣善堂醫院暫貯通

傳各先友 親友收領以正邱首是禱

并夫上滙票壹張伸港銀柒佰伍拾員正煩台

轉交每具先友塟費五員廿 除去銀叁佰陆拾

五員仍有銀叁佰捌拾五員貴院收作運費香

油可也此外區區微資貴院諸公慈善為懷

滙票壹張計艮[illegible]

十月卅日 梁禹[illegible]收

中華民國 年 月 日

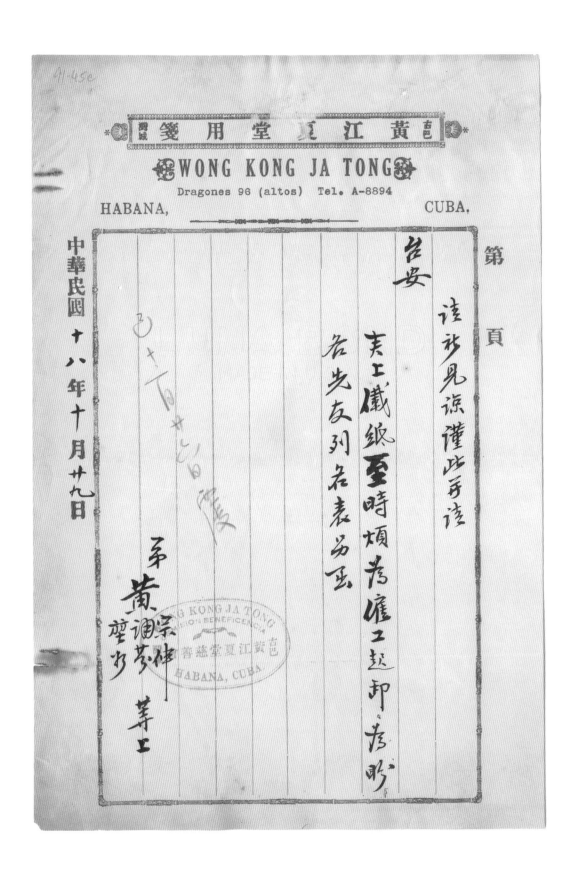

古巴 黃江夏堂用箋

WONG KONG JA TONG

Dragones 96 (altos)　Tel. A-8894

HABANA,　　　　　　　　CUBA,

第　頁

中華民國十八年十月廿九日

台安

諸祈見諒謹此手達

夫上儀紙至時煩為滙上趂郵寄晰

各先友列名表為盼

弟黃宗伸　　調芬　　璧步　莘　同具

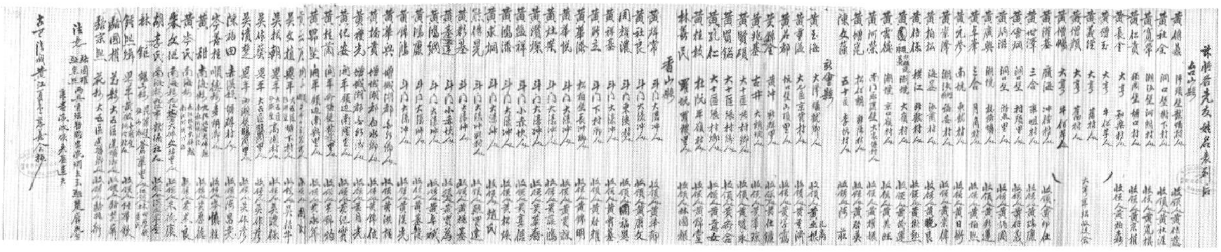

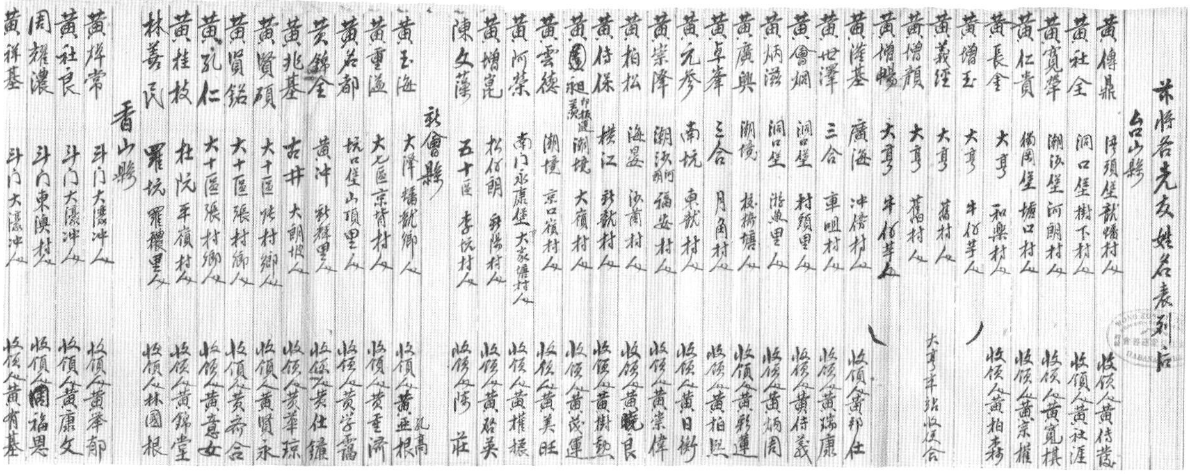

某埠各先友姓名表列后

台山縣

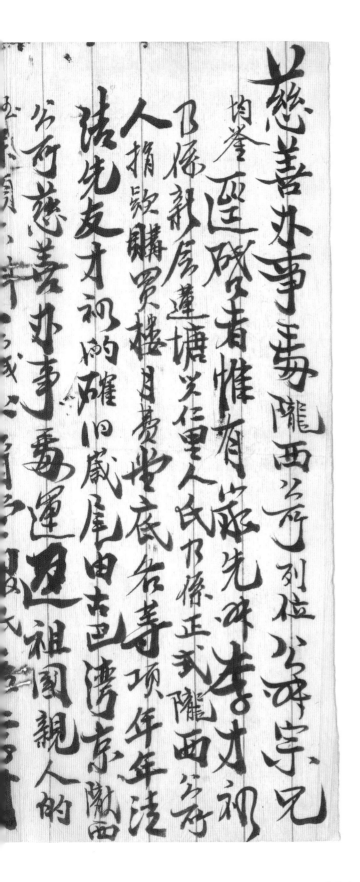

慈善辦事衆隴西公所列位公海宗兄

均鑒逕啟者惟有巖先祥孝才初

乃係新居蓮塘光仁里人氏乃係正武隴西公祠

人捐貲購買樓宇費用底名壽項年年逝

法先友才初的確係由古巴運京隴西

公所慈善辦事衆運迴祖國親人的

（91-516）

返祖國有𣏓𣏓𣏓不知由何埠運返祖國係由

古巴淳亮運返有乙元葬生費仁有埠奉還

乙州𣏓各先友葬費非係由古巴淳亲運返𣏓

各先友葬費清為乙馬有為親人有異不得

乙用商庄祖保保領若然一隙而手清𣏓各

𣏓友淫逺追究高港東華醫院新会城仁

育堂兩毒葬堂補回𣏓𣏓先友葬葬費柳

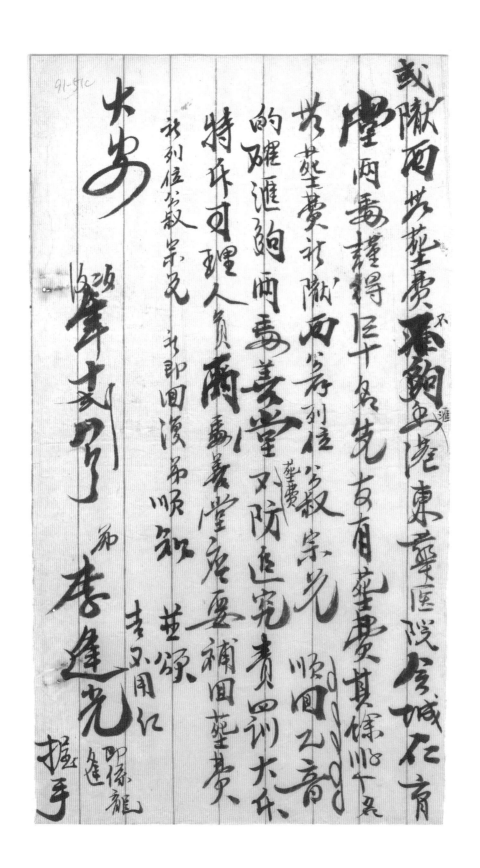

或瞞兩葬葬費運銷回港東華醫院金城在省
堂兩葬費謹得三十名先有有葬費其係州十名
芸葬費祈瞞兩岸列位公叔宗兄 順回乙首
的雕匯銷兩葬善堂不防追究責訓大衆
特乘可理人負兩葬善堂店要補回葬費
祈列位公叔宗兄即回復弟順知並頌
又用江即係龍逢

大安

弟 唐逢光 握手

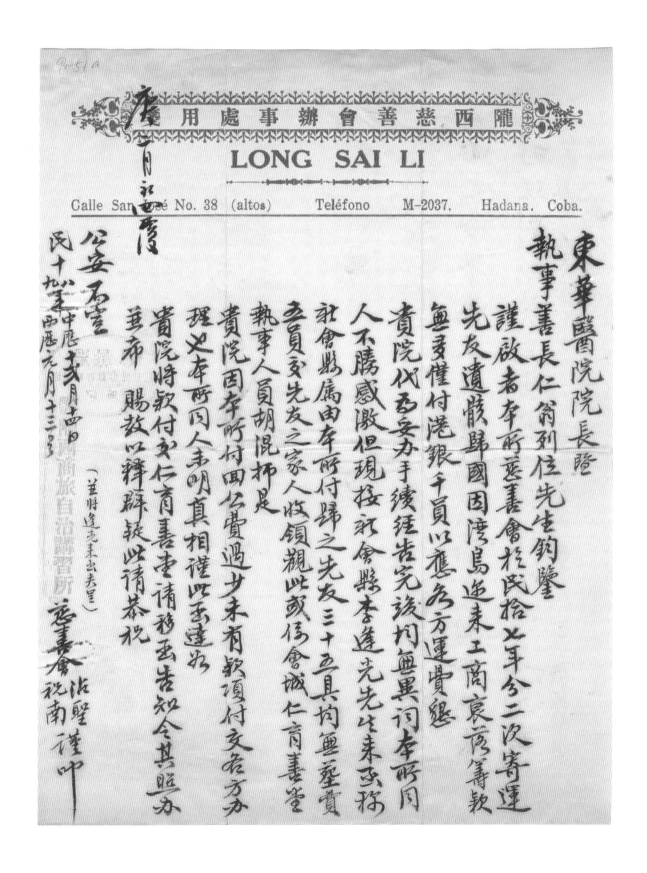

隴西慈善會辦事處用牋

LONG SAI LI

Calle San José No. 38 (altos)　Teléfono　M-2037.　Hadana. Coba.

東華醫院院長曁

執事善長仁翁列位先生鈞鑒

謹啟者本所慈善會於民拾之年分二次寄運

先友遺骸歸國固灣島運來工商衰彥籌欵

無奈僅付港銀千員以應各方運費總

貴院代西委辦手續經告完竣均無異詞本所同

人不勝感激但現接新會縣李逢先生來函稱

社會縣屬由本所付歸之先友三十五具均無墓費

五員交先友之家人收領觀此或俱會城仁育善堂

執事人員胡混抑是

貴院固本所付囘公費過少未有欵項付交咨方

理此本所同人未明真相謹此函達此

貴院將欵付交仁育善堂請移函告知令其照办

毋布　賜敎以釋疑此請茶祝

公安　不宣

民十九年西壓元月十三日

（並將逹先友名呈）

（中處古南旅自治辦習所）慈善委沈聖

祝南謹叩

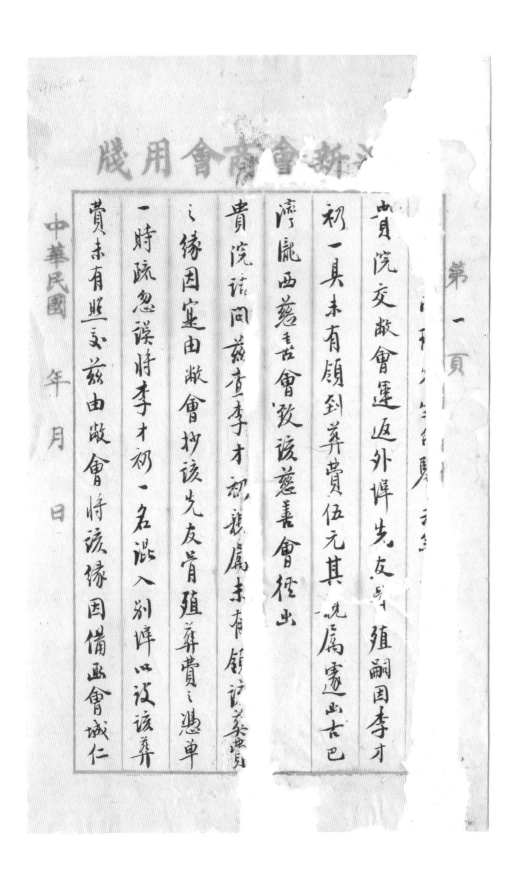

第一頁

貴院交敝會運返外埠先友等殮嗣因李才
初一具未有領到葬費伍元其先屬寄遷此吉巳
濟罷西慈善會致後慈善會經此
貴院諸問慈查李才初一龍屬未有領該葬費
之緣因寔由敝會抄該先友骨殖葬費之憑單
一時疏忽誤將李才初一名混入別埠以致該葬
貴未有照交敝由敝會將該緣因備函會會誠仁

僑港新會商會會用牋

第二頁

育善堂並請將葬費伍元補支李才初叚屬

照領以清手續用將情由函達

台端表白並希道歉希為

察照原諒為荷專泐順頌

台祺唯

照不宣

義務司理劉鯨芸

中華民國庚午年二月十六日

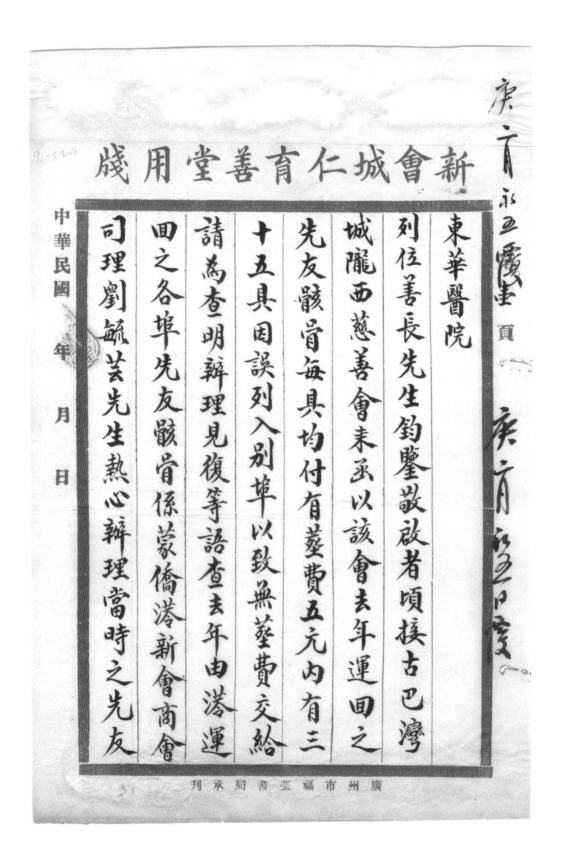

新會城仁育善堂用戔

東華醫院

列位善長先生鈞鑒敬者頃接古巴灣

城隴西慈善會來函以該會去年運回之

先友骸骨每具均付有蓋費五元內有三

十五具因誤列入別埠以致無蓋費交給

請為查明辦理見復等語查去年由港運

回之各埠先友骸骨係蒙僑港新會商會

司理劉毓芸先生熱心辦理當時之先友

中華民國　　年　　月　　日

廣州市福芸書局承刊

新會城仁育善堂用箋

第貳頁

姓名里居及由何處運回每具蓋費若干皆

蒙劉君列明寄下敝堂均依照來單點明始

行刊登告白名人認領至應給蓋費若干亦

照原單數目分給歷數十年辦理並無錯誤

此幫先友骨殖由劉君經手著陳洪記運返

計各埠先友骨殖二百四十六具照來人名

單點收有蓋費者祇得二百〇一具無蓋費

者占四十五具至古巴灣城隴西慈善會先

中華民國　年　月　日

廣州市福芸書局承刊

新會城仁育善堂用牋

第叄頁

友墓費照來單列明得十七具每具五元共墓
費八十五元內有李才祁一具照寄來人名單
係列入別埠且未有地名是以此具骸骨由
何處運回敝堂實不得而知今據該會來牋
所稱列入別埠而無墓費者相差至三十五
具之多顯有錯誤盍應盍請
示明以便轉致該會知照此帮先友骨殖
敝堂已代墊支運費港銀二百七十七元九毫

中華民國　　年　月　日

廣州市福芸書局承刊

新會城仁育善堂用牋

第四頁

而分給蓥費均照來單數目分給并無扣

減兹將去年劉毓芸先生經手列來之蓥

費進交清結單一紙附呈

察核竟此項蓥費如何差誤務請迅

賜查明詳為

示復以便轉復該會知照望勿有延是

所感盼專玆奉懇順頌

公祺

仁育堂同人敬叩

中華民國九年二月廿八日

廣州市蘆雲書局承刊

謹將劉毓芸先生經手先友骸骨葬費進支清單照列於後

進東藥醫院云來代收飛彼旅話埠中藥分所先友骸骨六具　　劈元

又云來代收運羅廣藥醫院先友骸骨三十二具　　劈元

又云來代收應李士彬單四邑積善堂先友骸骨四具　　收元

又云來代收墨國唐浔羅埠愛善堂先友骸骨二具　　廿元

又云來代收金山林崙埠中華會館先友骸骨一百里二具　　劈元

又云來代收金山芝城中華會館一具忱雲契伍根埠一具統　　八元

又云來代收古巴灣城隴西慈善會先友骸骨十具統　　沙元

　　芝美銀音叁拾乃元七厘九仙

支數列

支陳洪記運先友骸骨二百里五具舨腳作雲棺計　劈元　　劈元

支陳洪記運肉箱棺一具作雲殯丰計　劈元　　忱元

支陳洪記運骸骨士捰具丰　劈元　　忱元

支報閱十具丰　劈元　　劈元

支醫院工費

　　芝美銀弍百七十七元九厘

除支實存港銀惯元申紅毛四罗八十一元五厘四仙

　人貝初四貝列

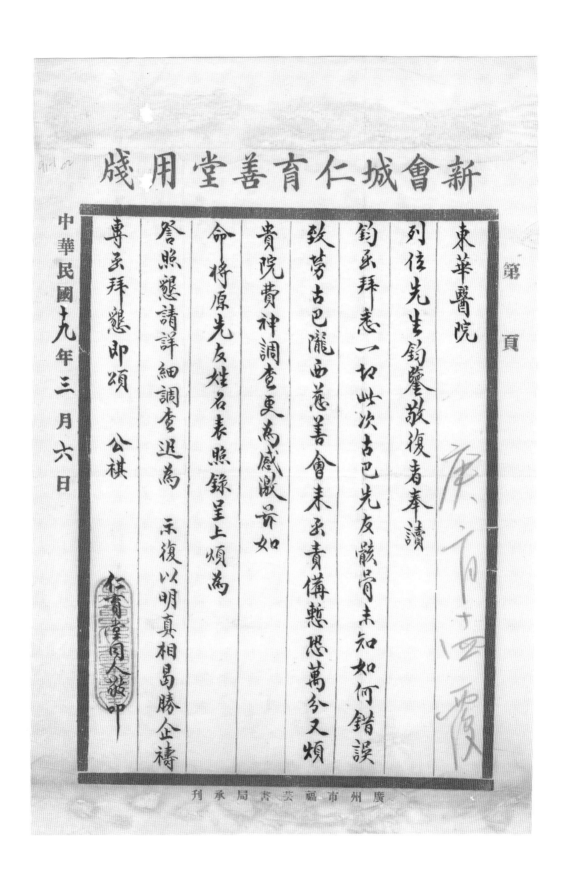

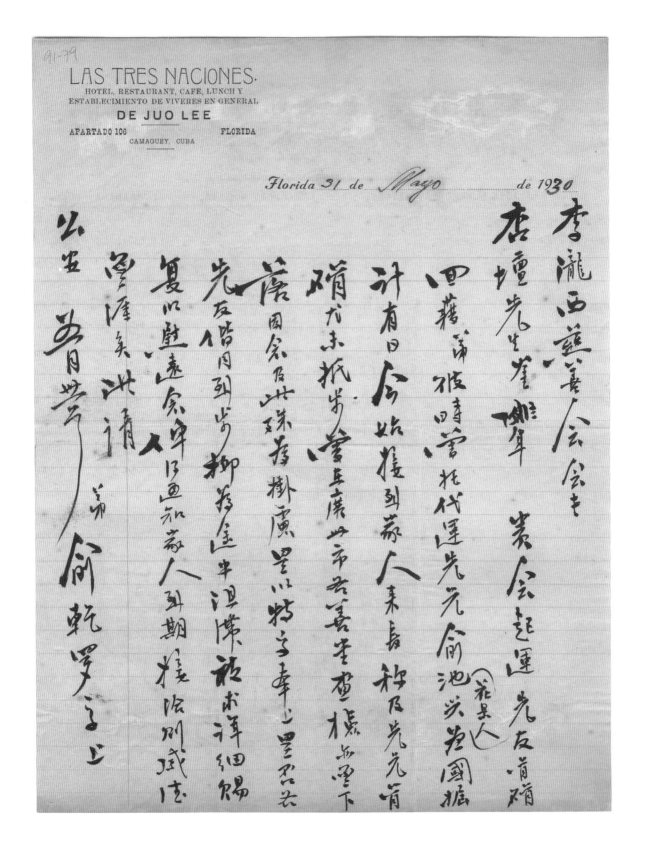

LAS TRES NACIONES.
HOTEL, RESTAURANT, CAFE, LUNCH Y
ESTABLECIMIENTO DE VIVERES EN GENERAL
DE JUO LEE
APARTADO 106　　　　FLORIDA
CAMAGUEY, CUBA

Florida 31 de _Mayo_ de 1930

李隴西慈善公会公鑒

　啟者　四藩市被回時當托代運先友俞池炎堂國揺（花县人）

李壇先生暨　貴會諸運先友喷嵧

　許有日今姑擱到茲人来長耜及先友喷

　喷尤未抵岁當至廣州省善善查檫尚望下

　廣固会在此珠荐掛廣曇以粘子奉以曇以去

　先友借月到岁柳矜金迨半淇悢話求详細鍚

　复以壁遠会年仍画知茲人到期摇洽刚戚传

　學滙美洪清

　少兄　賢月世界　　　　弟　俞乾罗学生七

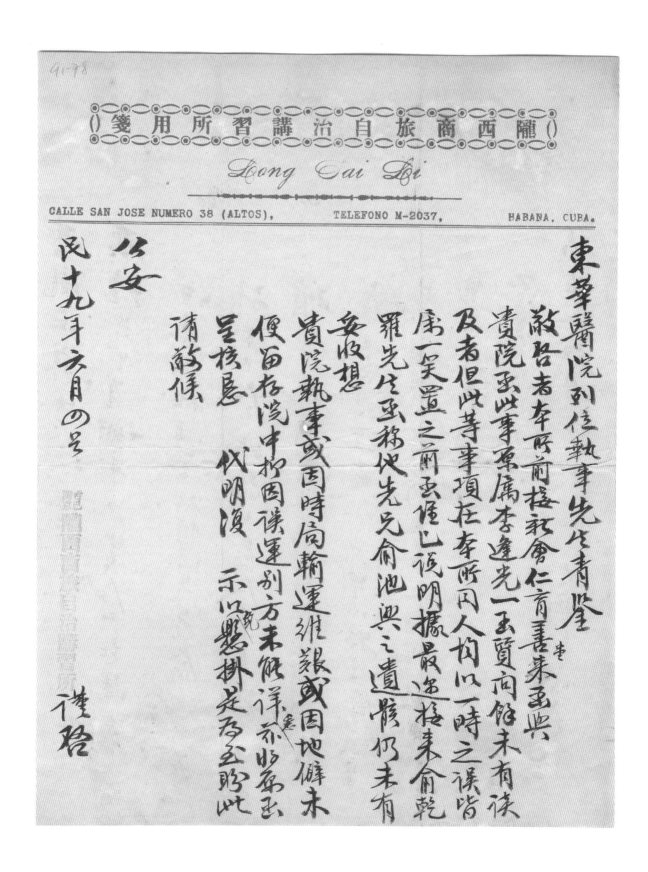

() 箋 用 所 習 講 治 自 旅 商 西 隴 ()

Long Sai Li

CALLE SAN JOSE NUMERO 38 (ALTOS), TELEFONO M-2037, HABANA, CUBA.

東華醫院列位執事先生青鑒

敬啓者本所前接敦會仁育善來函與
貴院承此事原屬李達光一玉賢向館未有誤
及者但此等事項在李所凡人均以一時之誤皆
屬一吳置之前玉惟已說明據最遠梅來俞乾
羅先生玉務他先兄俞池與之遺骸仍未有
妥收想
貴院執事或因時局輸運維艱或因地僻未
便由在院中抑因誤運別方未解詳亦明希示玉
呈核懇　代明覆　示以整挂是否玉妥此

叩安

請敬候

民十九年六月〇日

謹啓

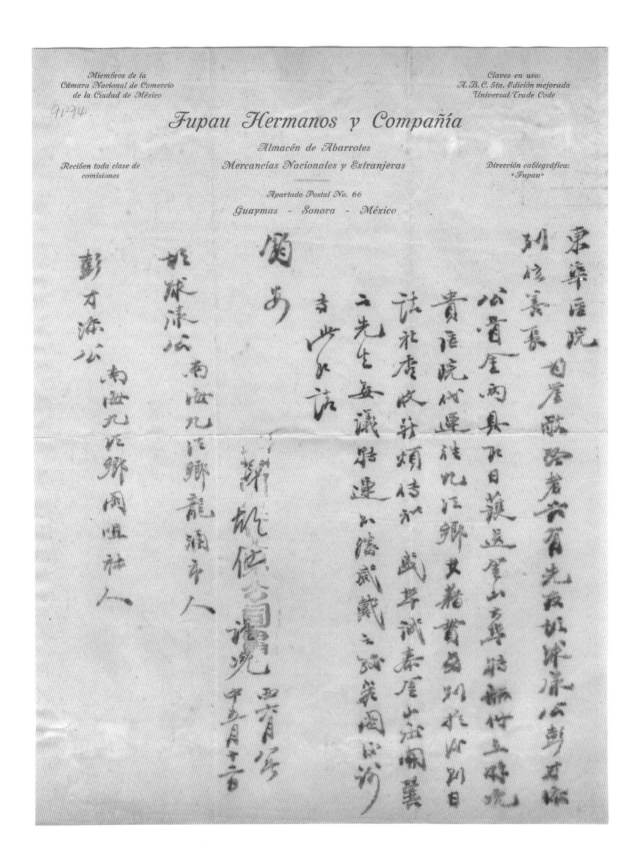

Miembros de la
Cámara Nacional de Comercio
de la Ciudad de México

Claves en uso:
A.B.C. 5ta. Edición mejorada
Universal Trade Code

Fupau Hermanos y Compañía

Almacén de Abarrotes

Reciben toda clase de
comisiones

Mercancías Nacionales y Extranjeras

Dirección cablegráfica:
"Fupau"

Apartado Postal No. 66

Guaymas - Sonora - México

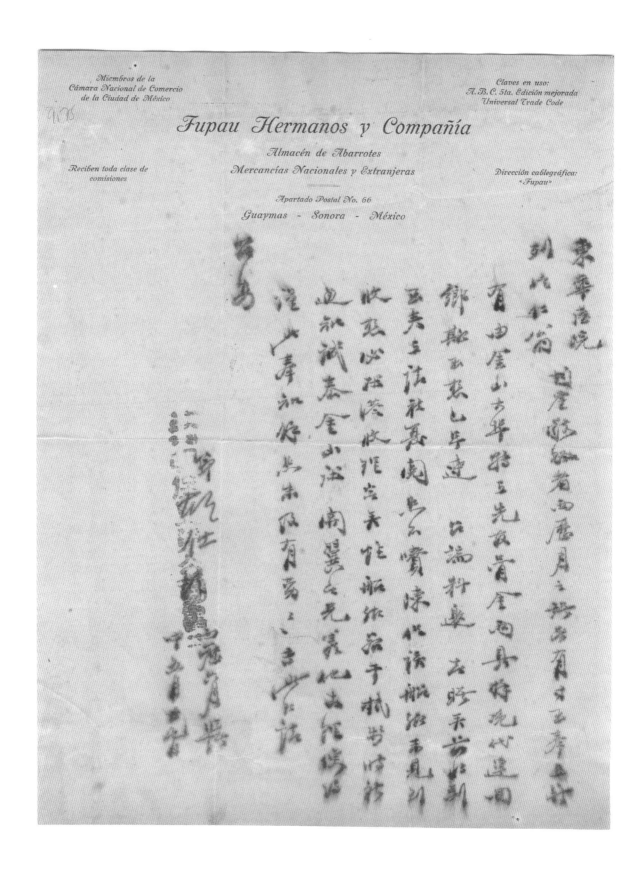

Miembros de la
Cámara Nacional de Comercio
de la Ciudad de México

Claves en uso:
A. B. C. 5ta. Edición mejorada
Universal Trade Code

Fupau Hermanos y Compañía

Almacén de Abarrotes
Mercancías Nacionales y Extranjeras

Reciben toda clase de
comisiones

Dirección cablegráfica:
"Fupau"

Apartado Postal No. 66
Guaymas - Sonora - México

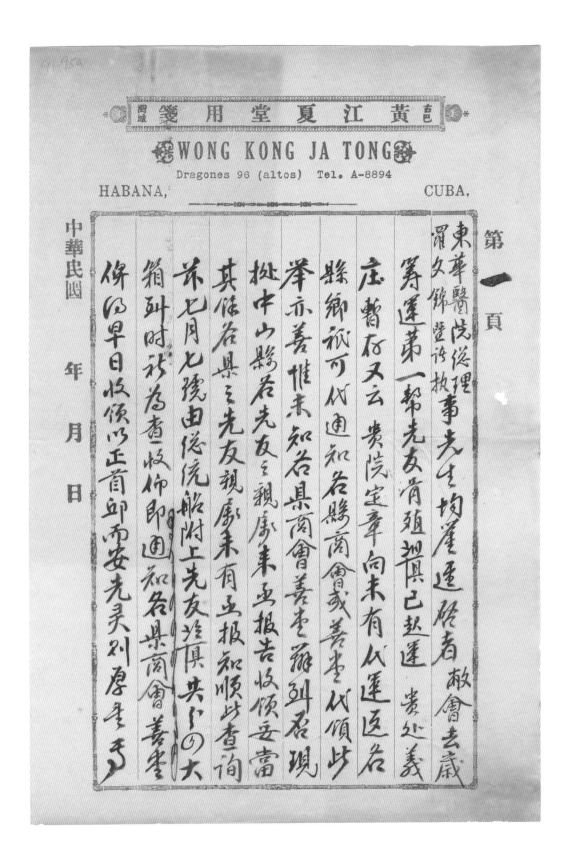

古邑 黃江夏堂 用箋 附城

WONG KONG JA TONG

Dragones 96 (altos)　Tel. A-8894

HABANA,　　　　　　　　CUBA.

第二頁

茶壽上县低壹修誤港銀陸佰大元斜時
孙查收隆盛具交回銀五元共收其係或
百套拾元以作艇脚至油等用是前希為
察納請早示知為盼统請

均安

菜弟先友各羊纸一修船纸或時查收可也

總理黃調樂
處長黃宗祥　仝顷
書記黃藜

中華民國九年七月七日

◎江夏堂慈善會啟事

為通啟事　本會籌運第二一得先友骨殖回國經已釘
裝妥當原定六月廿三日附輪歸國旋據護船公
司稱云是期貨物過多不能運儎是以改期於七月
初七日附輪並將各先友籍貫姓名詳列於下惟凡
其親友欲往中華義山致祭者請於初三日（即禮
拜四日）下午一時同往幸勿各玉望盼此佈
▲茲將先友籍貫姓名表列于后

黃傳烈　開平厚山堡咀頭村人
朱彌祥　中山東鎮西㯈鄉人
洪有德　中山東鎮西㯈鄉人
黃世遷　新會古井龜頭光龍里人
黃廷宗　台山三合銅鑼灣人
黃祕謂　台山三合銅鑼灣人
易子英　鶴山玉橋村人
黃堯　台山企嶺堡人
黃順傳　台山草骨剛盛平村人
吳章鑛　新會古井文樓鄉人
陸玲　勇鶴山十七堡那水村人
王攄皇　台山都斛南村山邊里人
楊濃　鶴山大凹鄉永興里人
黃金愆　開平百合風惢朗人

黃傳信　台山大塘堡安盛村人
林善實　新會北洋北合里人
黃作矩　台山那仁堡東邊頂人
黃宏熹　新會第十區張村鄉人
黃泗榮　台山三合鵝腔村人
黃雲灼　台山口嶺堡人
黃錫祥　台山南坑堡東逵村
黃達遠　新會古井大朗坡村
黃和世　台山洞口堡甘邊鄉人
黃榮享　台山草骨朗盛平村人
鍾周美　新會大澤鎮龍田鄉人
鍾德庚　新會大八區官田鄉人
楊紹熹　鶴山大凹鄉石樹里人
黃傳焜　字新會大七區沙富南薰里

呂紹文　新會大澤呂村人
呂北志　新會江門水南東海里人
呂傳昌　新會大澤呂村人
廖廷芳　台山公益區長塘舊村人
廖燦書　花縣蓮塘村人
黃滿誠　新會牛灣人
楊松榮　鶴山大凹鄉坑尾里人
楊弈青　新會仙洞太和里人
楊緒瑞　新會仙洞太和里人
馮天福　中山第八區黃梁鎮大蠔冲塘山里人
呂登統　新會大澤呂村人
黃潤德　台山企嶺堡永安村人
麥有爲　台山莘村磐石村人
黃佐德　台山企嶺堡永安村人
彭榮據　台山彭沙坑新龍村人
彭育民　台山彭沙坑新龍村人
何炎　恩平金汛堡錦定村人
趙不標　台山海晏都崙定村人
楊雲榮　鶴山大凹鄉石間里人
呂家榮　新會大澤呂村人

呂家傑　新會大澤呂村人
凌仲佑　新會河村亨美鄉人
廖撝光　台山冲蔞甫草洋村人
駱景林　花縣蓮塘村人
黃藉安　新會牛灣人
宋長　新會企嶺堡永安村人
黃義德　台山大凹曹坑村人
呂義挽　新會大澤呂村人
歐陽傍　中山東鎮四都歐陽昌村人
徐銘禎　蔴子村西堡人
黃詔德　台山企嶺堡永安村人
麥夢熊　台山莘村銀塘村人
葉明藻　台山筋坑君子坑新龍村人
彭劉氏　台山彭沙坑新龍村人
徐兆閏　新會仙洞接源里人
楊陸氏　鶴山古都獺山村人
黃衍圖　開平魁岡堡石灘村人
何章求　台山横江堡舊村人
黃昭棟　鶴山古都芸廖村人
楊弈博　鶴山大凹鄉里人

注意未註收領者因代報者一時忘記收領人

六月三十日

黃江夏堂慈善會謹啓

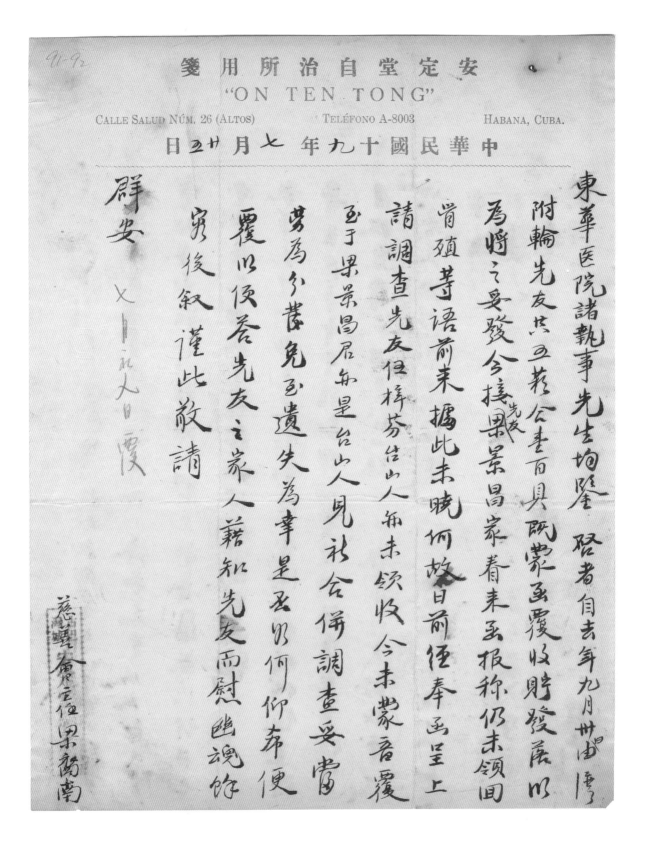

箋用所治自堂定安
"ON TEN TONG"
CALLE SALUD NÚM. 26 (ALTOS)　　TELÉFONO A-8003　　HABANA, CUBA.

中華民國十九年七月廿二日

東華醫院諸執事先生均鑒　啟者自去年九月廿四由灣

附輪先友共四葬公壼百具既蒙孟覆收貯發屍明

為將之受發令接眾景昌蒙眷來孟報稱仍未領回

嘗殮尋語前來攜此未曉何故日前經奉孟呈上

請調查先友但梓芬估山人亦未領收令未蒙音覆

至于梁景昌尼東是台山人見社會俾調查妥當

勞為分釁免至遺失為幸是乞明何仰奔便

覆明俾各先友之家人藉知先友而慰幽魂餘

窮後叙謹此敬請

群安　　　　　　　七月廿九日覆

慈善會主任梁蘭甫

安定堂自治⋯⋯

"ON TEN TONG"

CALLE SALUD NÚM. 26 (ALTOS)　　　TELÉFONO A-8003　　　HABANA, CUBA.

中華民國十九年七月廿八日

東華醫院諸執事先生鈞鑒　路云本堂慈善會恆于

去年九月間辦理先友歸國既蒙向顧一切欣慰曷勝

梁棕榮順德倫教人家屬來函報稱該等遺骸

銘感之中茲因疊接友先伍梓芬梁景昌俱是人

嘗殯至今日久仍未能收領東未曉將該等姓

名遺骸安置何屬抑構分各縣商會屬理旅之希

請追究向或誤會遺失迨即調查委旅先友伊

得歸原籍安歸樂土以慰幽魂便則含笑九泉

吾人等感佩莫名嗣後叙專此即請并候

　祺祉

　　計用

　　　伍梓芬　台山三十區平安村人莊在大二莇

　　　梁景昌台山松仔葫黄果村人莊在大二莇

　　　梁棕榮順德倫教人莊在大四莇

慈善會　梁喬南

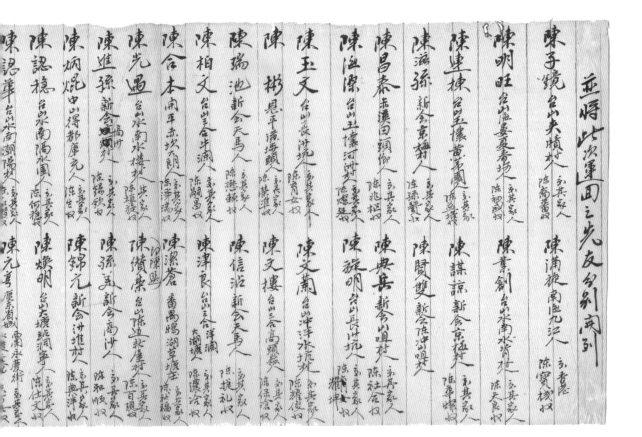

陳國美 恩平洲湖堡松塘人
陳光照 台山海晏洪文??人
陳光翼 台山冲蔞高嶺人
陳垂成 台山海晏大担人
陳國 台山三合北斗潮勝人
陳庭釗 南海九江大谷人
葉汝平 台山君子坑潮龍人
潘耳初 順德大良人
楊誠基 順德陳村人
余毓燧 台山桂水潮洞人

陳森彥 恩平洲湖堡松塘人
陳光添 台山冲蔞高嶺人
陳光勝 台山都斛東坑村人
陳彬 南海九江南方興教社人
陳文培 台山三合白石壞人
葉錦沛 台山筋坑順水村人
潘騰波 順德大良人
何伯懷 順德陳村人
趙鐵臻 台山浮石人

以上計列各先友之姓名籍貫佈
祈送回分發並每先友交港銀
五元其家人收以作葬費

劉顯祖之先友髮款送交乃七

民卅年即十九年八月十四號 陳穎川堂藝善会付

古巴 陳穎川堂書柬

CHANG ... SO CHUN TONG
DRAGONES NUM. 46 ALTOS
HABANA, CUBA

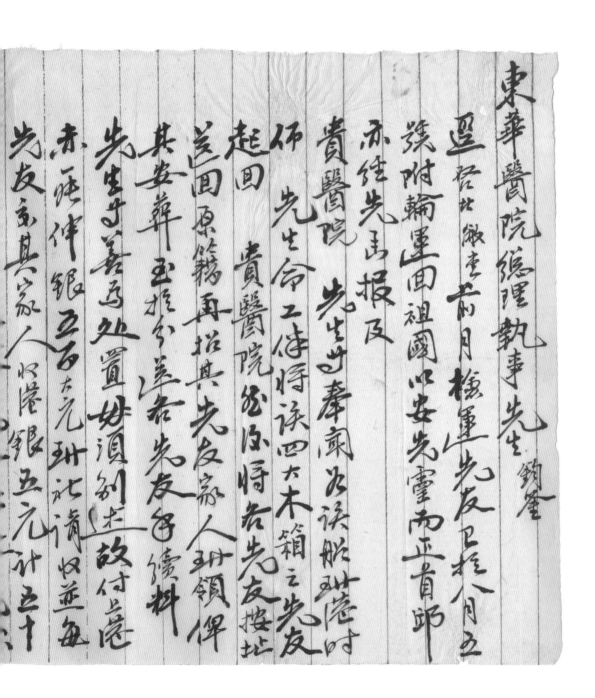

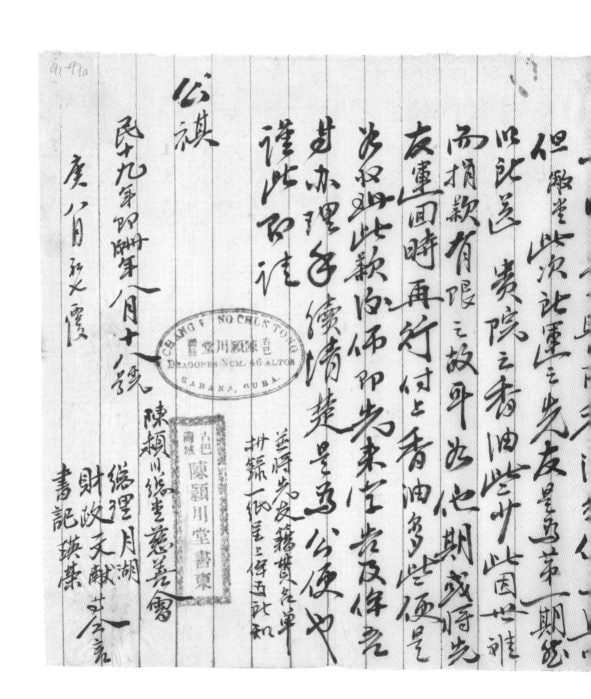

但敬啟者次批運至先友是為第一期能

照批送貴院之香油些少此因世難

而捐款有限之故再必他期或將先

友運回時再行付上香油多些便是

兹收到此款仍係即先來定岩及仔免

甚亦理子續清楚是為公便也

並將先友籍貫姓名單
抄錄一低呈上俾西此知

謹此即請

公祺

民十九年即卅九年八月十八號

庚八月弘火震

陳頴川總善慈善會

總理月湖

財政天獻

書記瑛葉　謹言

古巴
薄城　陳頴川堂書柬

CHANG YING CHUN TONG　陳頴川堂　古巴
DRAGONES NUM. 46 ALTOS
HABANA, CUBA

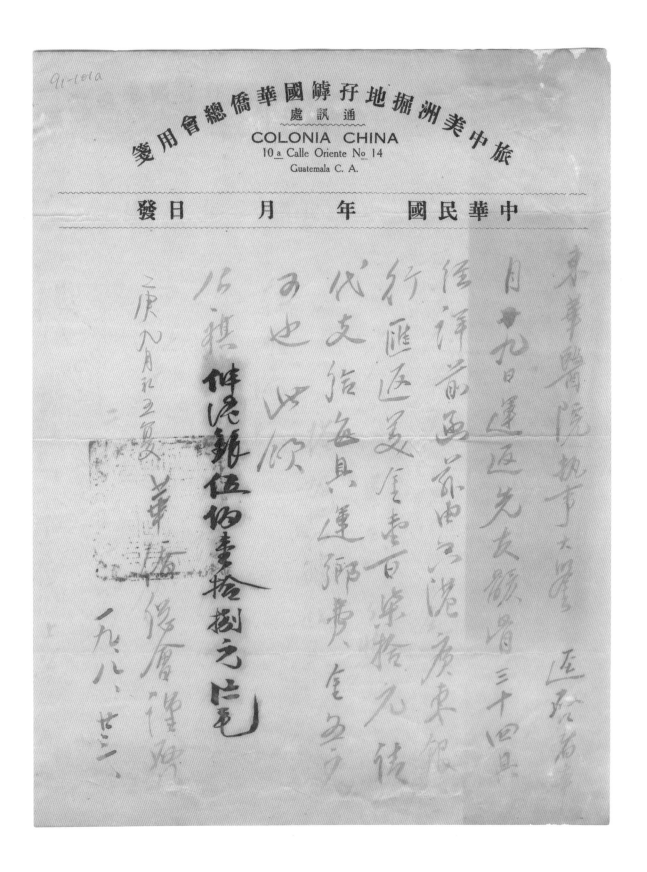

旅中美洲掘地孖罅國華僑總會用箋

通訊處

COLONIA CHINA

10 a Calle Oriente No. 14

Guatemala C. A.

中華民國　　年　　月　　日發

東華醫院執事大鑒 逕啟者

月九日遞返先友額增三十四具

逕詳前函由香港交廣東銀

行匯返及查每百幕捨元銀

代支結每具運鄉費壹毫半

而也 此候

仍祈 伴送報伍佰壹拾捌元正

庚九月初五夏

華僑 修倉謹理

一九八八、廿二

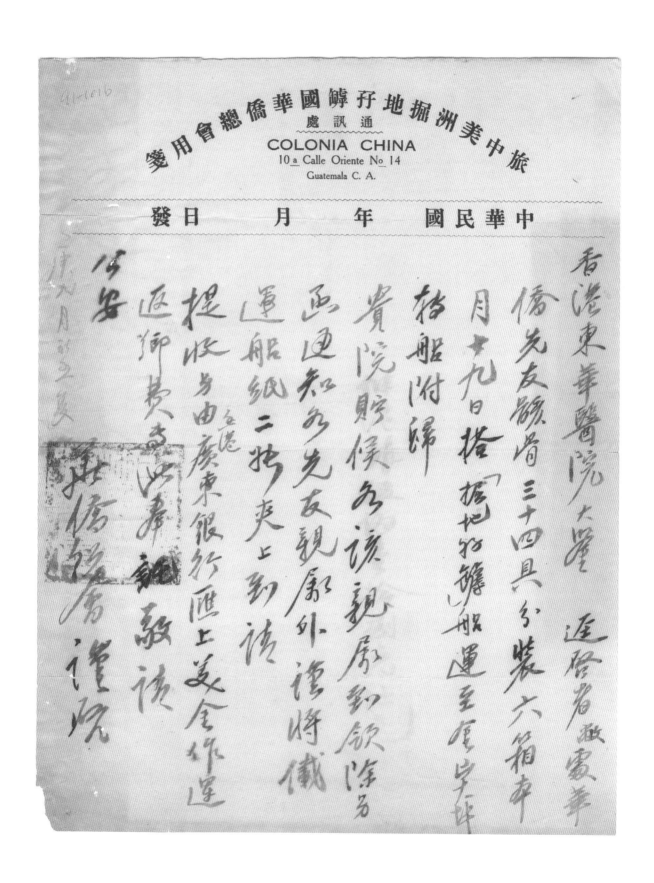

華僑國罅孖地掘洲美中旅 會總僑華國罅孖地掘洲美中旅
箋用會總僑華國罅孖地掘洲美中旅
通訊處
COLONIA CHINA
10a Calle Oriente No 14
Guatemala C. A.

發　日　月　年　國　民　華　中

香港東華醫院大鑒　逕啓者敬寰華

僑先友骸骨三十四具分裝六箱本

月十九日搭「搭地羅罅」船運至金岸省埠

轉船附歸

貴院貯候各該親屬勤領除号

函通知各先友親屬外謹將儀

運船紙二批夾上勤請

提收并由廣東銀於匯上美金作運

返師費壹仟肆百敬請

此佈即頌

台安

此僑總會謹啓

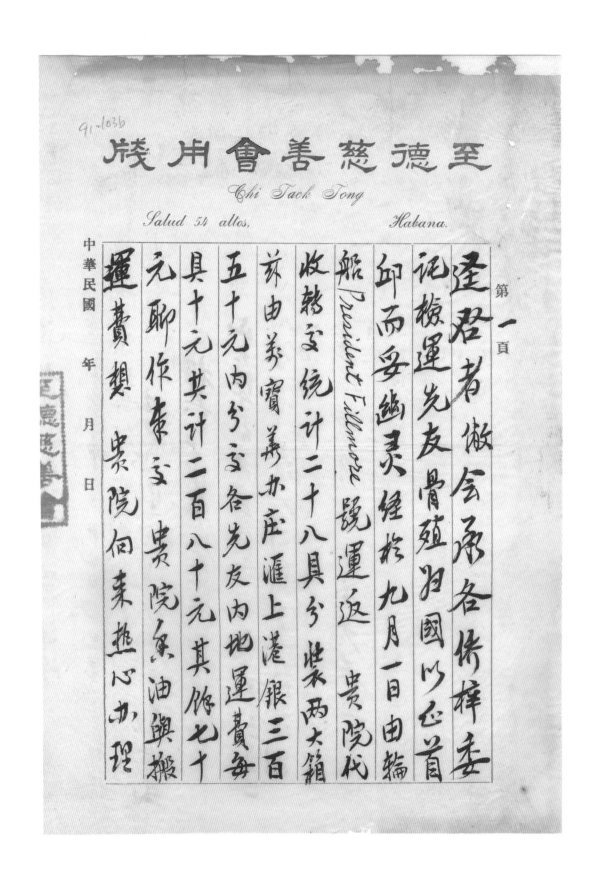

箋用會善慈德至

Chi Tack Tong

Salud 54 altos. Habana.

第一頁

逕啟者敝会承各僑梓委

記檢運先友骨殖归國以迺首

卯而妥幽泉經於九月一日由輪

船 President Fillmore 號運返貴院代

收轉交統計二十八具分裝兩大箱

茲由萍寶美办庄滙上港銀三百

五十元內分支各先友内地運費每

具十元共計二百八十元其餘七十

元聊作奉交貴院系油與搬

運費類 貴院伺来热心办理

中華民國 年 月 日

中南美洲西歸先友

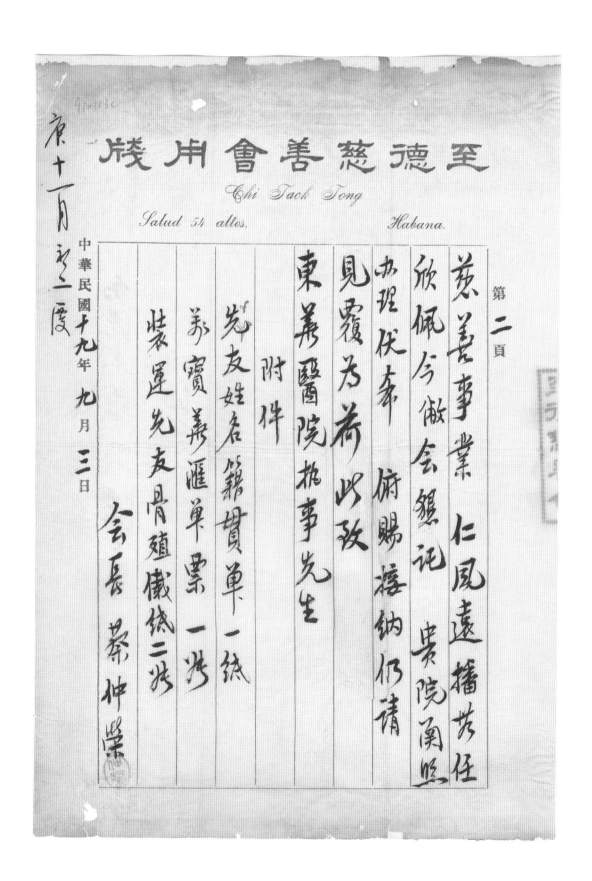

至德慈善會用牋

Chi Tack Tong

Salud 54 altos, Habana.

第二頁

慈善事業　仁風遠播芳任

欣佩今敬　會懇託貴院關照

辦理伏乞　俯賜接納仍請

見覆為荷此致

東華醫院執事先生

　　附件

先友姓名籍貫單一紙

華寶善匯單票一紙

裝運先友骨殖儀銀三折

會長蔡仲棠

中華民國十九年九月三日

京十百三厘

至德慈善會檢運先友骨殖名單

吳振濃　恩平烏石蓢人

吳奕銘　開平樓冈西頭新屋里人

周集和　中山縣神涌村人

周瑞棠　開平茅冈下洞橫坑里人

周奕棉　中山縣東鎮閬塘埔村人

周成付　開平茅冈西社人

周遵杖　開平茅冈西社人

周家儀　開平周坑調山人

蔡盛煜　台山橫嶺鄉人

蔡英寕　台山和安里人

蔡傑球　台山橫嶺鄉人

蔡維國　台山雙楼村人

蔡鴻鈞　台山橫嶺鄉人

蔡元燦　台山上蓮塘村人

蔡英亮　台山甫草村人

蔡文初　台山沙浦下蓮塘村人

曾孝南　南海九江大谷人

莫福純　恩平那西堡水流坪人

岑祝元　恩平大江堡石塘村人

歐陽池萬　中山縣大嶺鄉人

張培簡　開平羊蹄龍山東咸里人

李聖鑒　新會西十區河村鎮沙灣鄉人

李福有　新會西十區河村鎮沙灣鄉人

馮妣熾　鶴邑雅瑤羅涇坊人

高北樂　新會古井那伏鄉人

關聯太　南海九江北方沙咀四閘人

封德慈善會

91-103a

「內有先友骨殖三具乃曾武城旅所記西人
釘裝箱内非敝会經手
曾章南
曾社信曾南

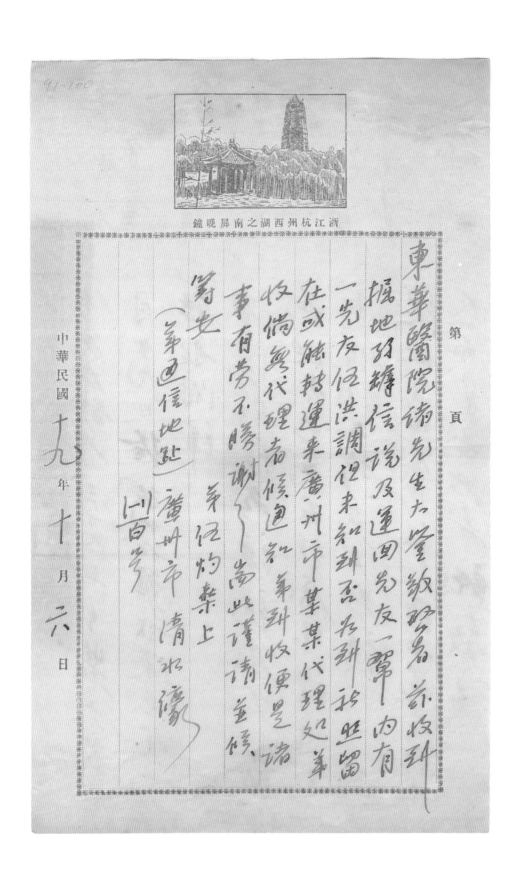

鐘晚屏南之湖西州杭江浙

第　頁

東華醫院諸先生大鑒敬啟者　茲收到

掘地移靈信一說及運回先友一幫內有

一先友係洪調但未知到否在別批留

在或能轉運來廣州市某某代理處　茲

收備無代理者候通知華到收便是諸

事有勞不勝謝之尚此謹請　董候

等安

華伍灼燊上

（華通信地址）廣州市清水濠

曾某

中華民國十九年十月六日

箋用所治自堂定安
"ON TEN TONG"

CALLE SALUD NÚM. 26 (ALTOS)　　　TELÉFONO A-8003　　　HABANA, CUBA.

日：十月十年九十國民華中

91-105a

東華醫院執事先生鑒 屬接大函領悉一是勿念悸

是數月前未得各先友親屬玉覆以何故未將裁答現

在台山先友果景昌伍梓芬之親屬來玉亦云收要誤

肖殖吳玉于順德籍吳棕榮先友尤未見覆以何據云

侯安屬置然因無地址是以遠屬在貴院義庄侯領善

特前來攜此吾人日久雜達完成工作當月前由敏堂給

与公玉一封交其親房藉作為憑挨此前往提領而安

歸土以盡吾人責任以見誤玉希為攜洽是託切聆

端此玫覆

　　台安

慈善會重信梁僑南上

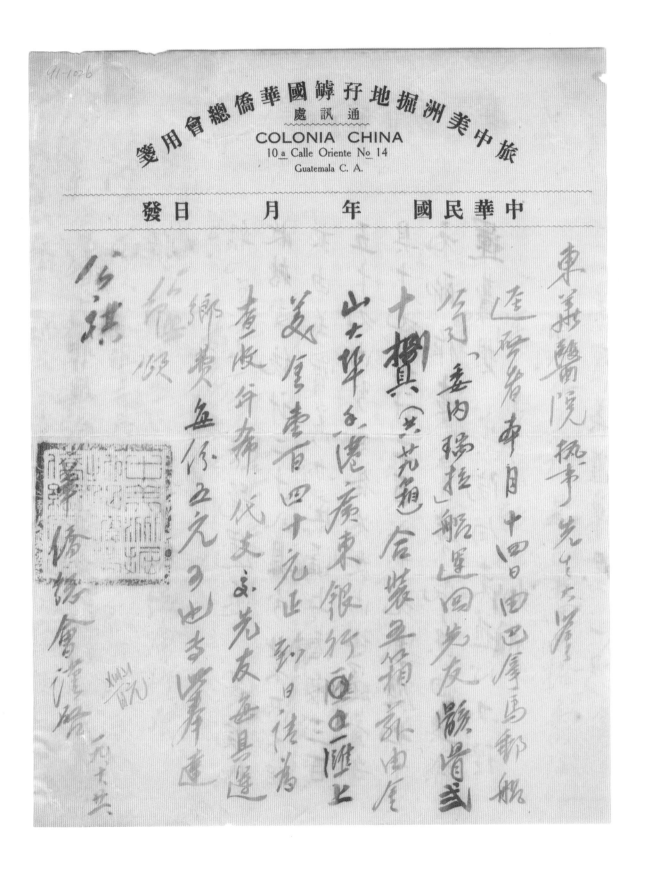

旅中美洲掘地孖罅國華僑總會用箋

通訊處

COLONIA CHINA

10 a Calle Oriente No 14

Guatemala C. A.

中華民國　年　月　日發

東華醫院執事先生大鑒

逕啟者本月十四日由巴度馬郵船

所以「垂內稱拉」船運回先友骸骨弍

十櫃（共花箱）合裝五箱茲由廈

山大埠各港廣東銀行匯上

美金壹百四十元正到日請為

查收舉辦代支亥先友葬具遷

鄉費無須立元亦也寺峰遠

令琪

佈候

中美掘地孖罅華僑總會謹啟

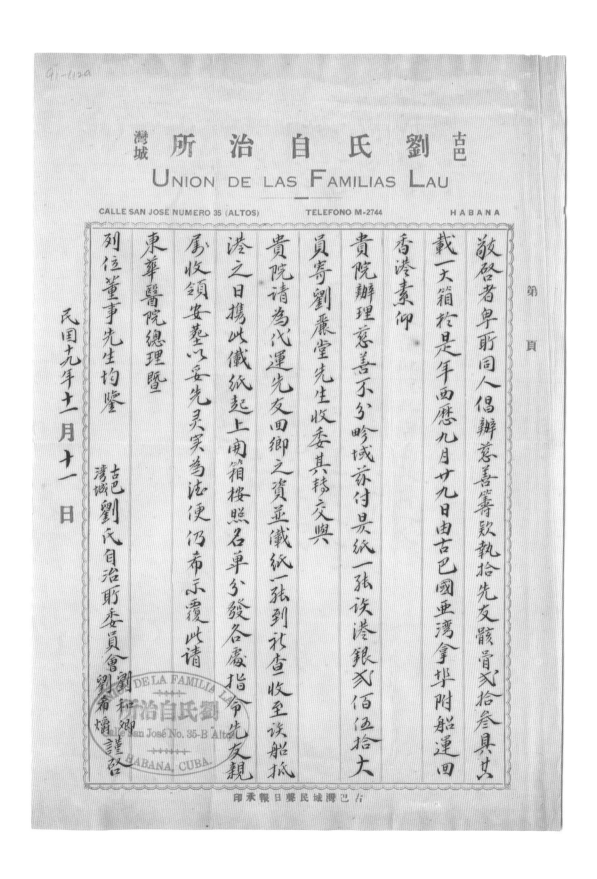

古巴 劉氏 自治 所 城灣

UNION DE LAS FAMILIAS LAU

CALLE SAN JOSÉ NUMERO 35 (ALTOS)　　　TELEFONO M-2744　　　HABANA

第頁

敬啟者卑邑同人倡辦慈善籌欵執拾先友骸骨共拾叁具其

載一天箱於是年西歷九月廿九日由古巴國亞灣拿埠附船運回

香港素仰

貴院辦理慈善不分畛域茲付員紙一張迻港銀弍佰伍拾大

員寄劉巖堂先生收委其轉交與

貴院請為代運先友回鄉之資並儀紙一張到社查收至該船抵

港之日攜此儀紙起上開箱模照名單分發各處指令先友親

屬收領安葬以妥先靈實為法便沿希示覆此請

東華醫院總理暨

列位董事先生均鑒

民國九年十二月十一日　　古巴灣城劉氏自治所委員會劉郷劉希燦謹啟

古巴灣城民聲日報承印

先友名單

鍾法進　廣東新會古井官田鄉人氏

劉維芳　廣東台山橫水鄉金紫里人氏

劉孔霖　廣東台山橫水鄉橫圳人氏

劉孔安　廣東台山橫水鄉中沙莘人氏

劉貴昌　廣東中山谿角鄉人氏

劉煜維　廣東台山橫水鄉上橫圳人氏

劉維芬　廣東新會牛灣龍蟠里人氏

吳賢鐸　廣東新會古井龍泉鄉人氏

劉維掌　廣東新會牛灣坑頭人氏永昌里

劉栢希　廣東新會牛灣坑頭鄉岐山里人氏

劉樹蕃　廣東台山橫水鄉龍塘村人氏

勞經漢　廣東開平長沙塘蕌畔堡崗背人氏

劉儒槐　廣東台山白虎頭鄉人氏

劉尊德　廣東台山白虎頭鄉人氏

劉希勻　廣東台山橫水龍安里人氏

劉銳希　廣東台山橫水鄉石鼓村人氏

劉惠維　廣東新會牛灣坑頭岐山里人氏

吳良晃　廣東新會古井龍泉鄉人氏

吳賢棣　廣東新會古井龍泉鄉人氏

吳煥英　廣東增城雅瑤塘邊坊人氏

劉生　廣東鶴山城綠合鄉人氏

古巴黎伯熙致東華醫院信件

1930 年 11 月 12 日

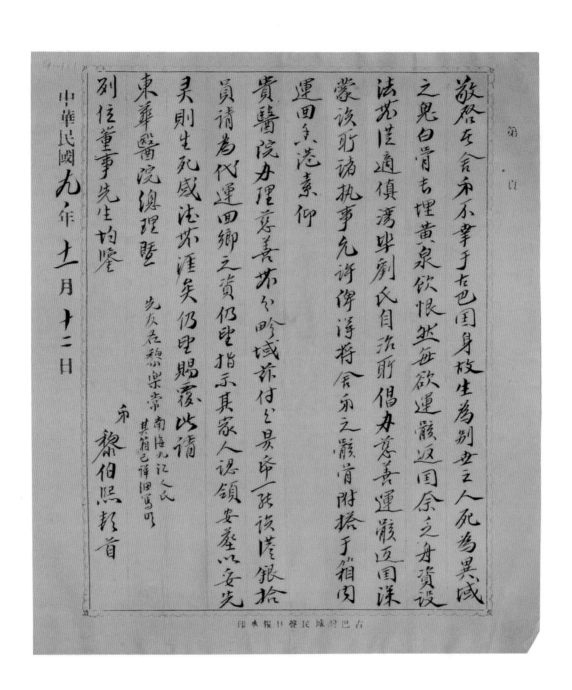

第一頁

敬啓者 金布不幸于古巴因身故生為別世之人死為異域

之鬼白骨吉埋黃泉飲恨然每欲運骸返国奈之舟資設

法苾遘值灣卑劉氏目洃所倡办慈善運骸返国謀

蒙該昕諸执事允許俾將 金命之骸骨附搭于箱内

運囙头港素仰

貴醫院办理慈善茅分畛域荻付公员帝一矼該港銀拾

員请為代運囙鄉之資仍望指示其家人認領安葬以妥先

灵則生死感沐誼汪洋矣仍祈賜覆此请

東華醫院總理臺

列位董事先生均鑒

中華民國九年十一月十二日

先友名黎榮常 南海先江人氏 其箱已諅囙寫明

布 黎伯熙頓首

古巴城僑民日報承印

東華醫院

貴執事先生大鑒

敬啟者　當西十月行事已之州函內云有南海西樵

藩美鄉吳順高貴人骨殖一荷乃由墨國文慎无竞坤

西人船務謹托代理由日本直吳輪船轉付返港亥

貴醫院　代收一節

　悭是亙來因日收芳理進兵強占東省九屬中國內地

乃外埠之國民芳不病心疾首憤芰蛮橫芳理之要求

這以吳順高誤葡骨殖收著誤西人代理停上由日本

輪船而付今改由美國輪船直付返港亥　貴醫院代收亥

但下日誤葡骨殖抵步未补劳重收是茂特此書知

补蔫諒之是荷

仍遙不敘專此順頌

夫安

民廿年　兄弟

墨國埠　協興隆書寄扎

設有輪列屯诗通知　文咸東朗

　　盂弄菜　電话二二五三九昂卜

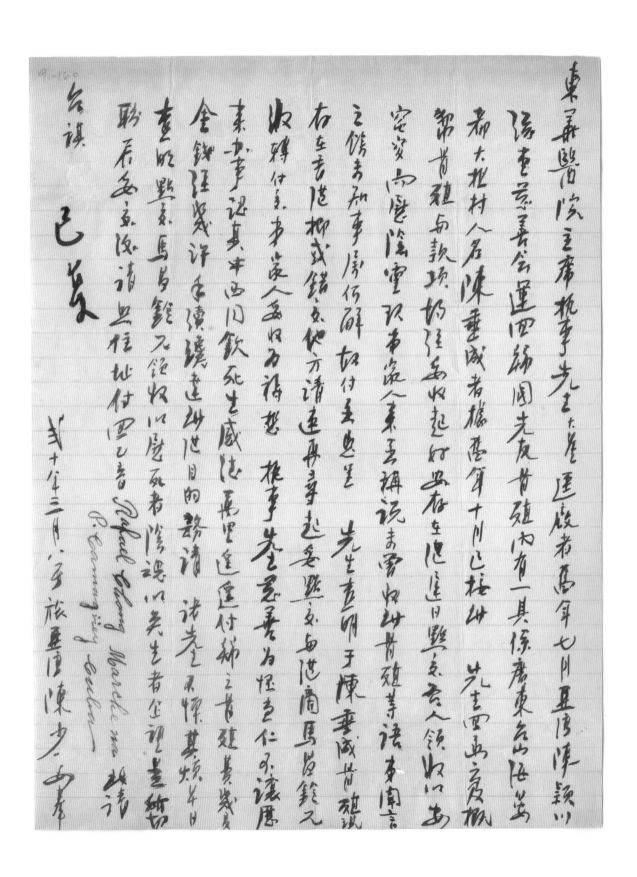

9-160

東華醫院主席板事先生大鑒 運啟者為舊年七月吾鄉東莞陳穎川

隆運意善會運回稱聞先友昔殖內有一具係廣東東莞縣

郝大批村人名陳垂咸者據歷年十月已抵埠　先生雲云有人領以安

窆貧而歷陰靈現本宗人素無掃說查實收此昔殖葬埋之言

之館查知事屬何解故付委真生　先生查明于陳垂咸昔殖說

右在吉港柳式錯系他方清運再事起委無點系故商馬昔鈴之

收轉件系某人為收為將懇　板事先善善為慎意仁不讓歷

素未事記真本西以飲死生感德運票運付稱之昔殖葬埋墓

金錢匯寄評查續逶運此世目的諮請　諸先者全祈善缮

查明點系馬昔鈴又領收以歷死者陰魂以死生者全祈善缮

聯屐無吝後請無信址付回乙音 Rafael Chang Marche na

台祺　巳菜　　　　　　　　　P Camaguey Cuban

　　　　　　　　　　　廿十年三月八年旅歪值陳少安頓

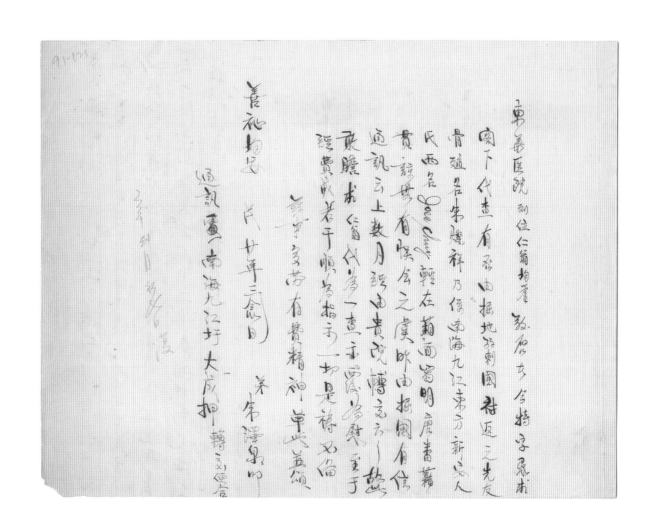

東華醫院列位仁翁均鑒 敬啟者今持字麻求

閣下代查 有盆由掘地新剌國得返之先友

骨道名朱煥祥乃係南海九江東方新圣人

氏 西名 Jose Chun 前在葡面富明廣書藉

貴 諸姐有隆舍之虞昨由掘國有信

通訊云上數月歸由貴院轉之云〜熱

竊膽求仁翁代爲一查未悉移尉至于

經費成者于順處拾来一切是禱又倘

寶有貴精神草此英頌

善祉均安 民 廿年三月廿日

通訊處〔南海九江圩大成押─轉〕

弟 朱澤泉叩

三年剳日收發

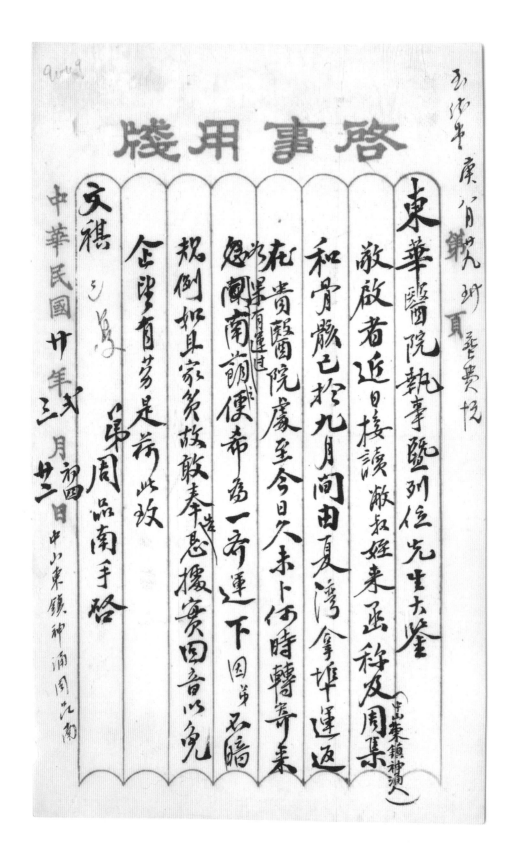

啓事用牋

東華醫院執事暨列位先生大鑒

敬啓者近日接讀敝姪來函稱及周集（中山隆鎮神涌人）

和骨骸已於九月間由夏灣拿埠運返

在貴醫院處至今日久未卜何時轉寄來

以果有運過懇煩南頭便希為一齊運下因弟不暗

聞南頭便希為一齊運下因弟不暗

規倒如其家貧故敢奉懇擾實因音以兔

企望有為是荷此啓

弟周品南手啓

中華民國廿年式三月初四廿三日

中山隆鎮神涌周品南

文祺

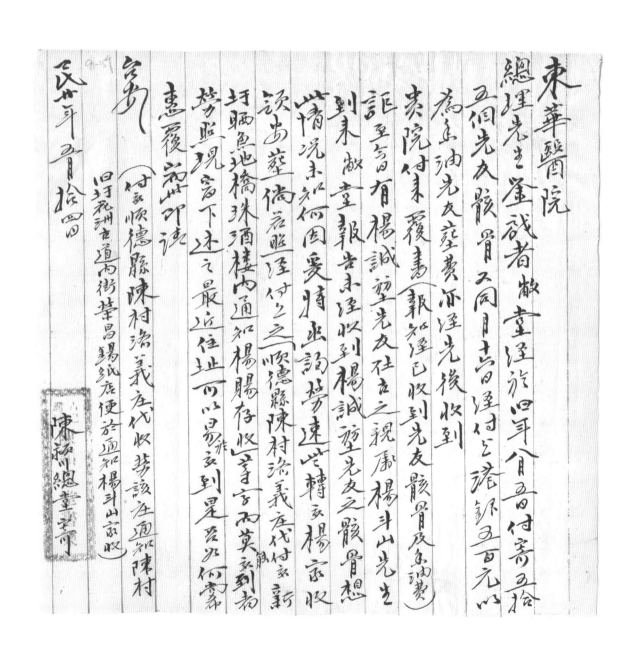

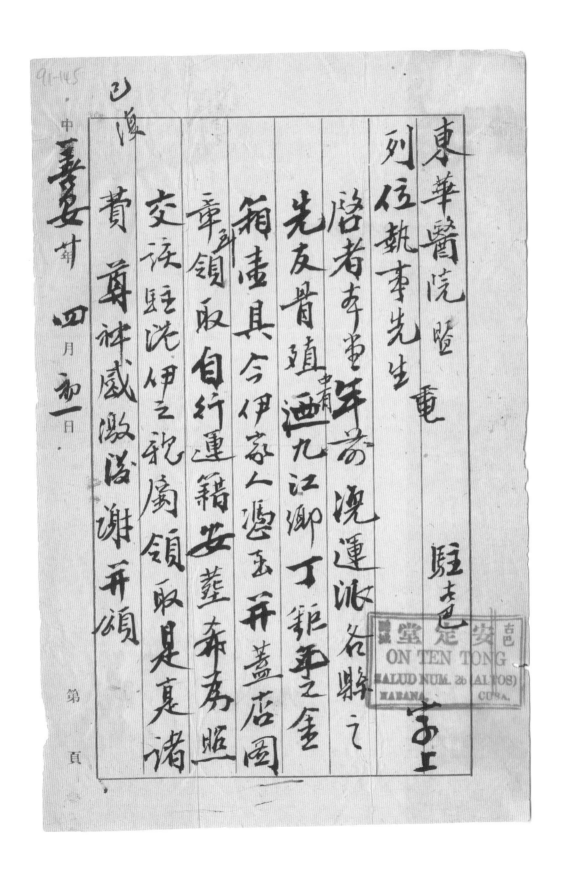

東華醫院暨
列位執事先生　駐古巴
敬啟者本堂年荷　况運派各縣之
先友骨殖酒九江卿丁銀年之金
箱盡具令伊家人灣玉開蓋店圖
章到領取自行運籍安葬希為照
交該駐洗伊之亁屬領取是萬諸
費尊神感洛謝并頌

己復

中華民國廿年四月初一日

安定堂 古巴
ON TEN TONG
SALUD NUM. 2b (ALTOS)
HABANA.　CUNA.
宇上

第　頁

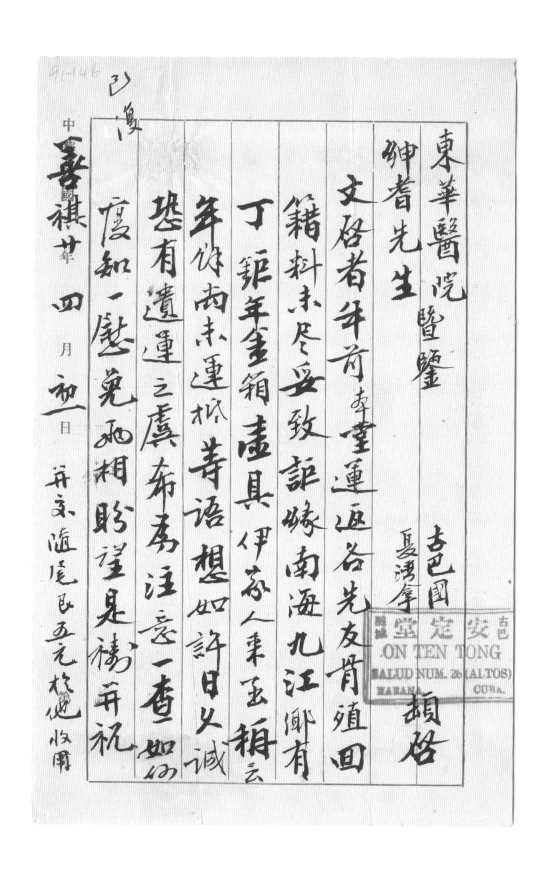

東華醫院醫鑑

紳耆先生

文啟者年前李壹運返各先友骨殖回

籍料未盡妥致訛嫁南海九江鄉有

丁鉅年金箱盡具伊茲人秉玉相云

年作雨末運柩壽語想如許日火誠

墊有遺運之虞布壽注意一查如何

庶知一慰兔兩相盼望是禱并祝

古巴國

長灣拿

頓啟

安定堂
ON TEN TONG
SALUD NUM. 26 (ALTOS)
HABANA   CUBA.

中華民國廿年 四月 初一日

并寄臨尾民五元於第俾收團

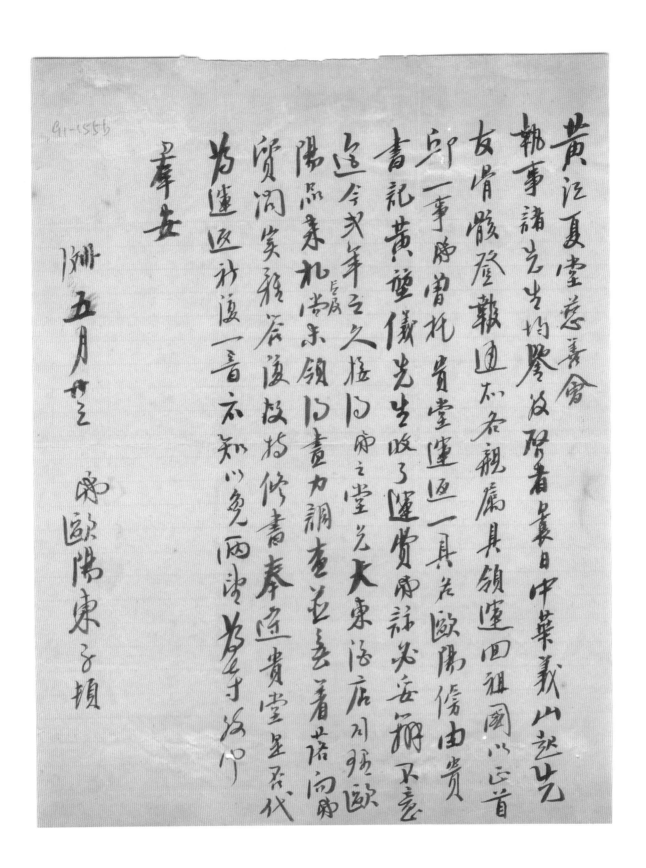

黃江夏堂慈善會

執事諸先生均鑒敬啟者裏日中華義山起兏

友骨骸登報通知各親屬具領運回祖國以正首

邱一事曾託貴堂運逕一其為歐陽僑由貴

書記黃堃儀先生收了運貴僑詳先安柵不意

迄今數年之久擱[以下小字:乙辰]府之堂兏大東治店列頻歐

陽點來扎領[以下小字:乙辰]盡力調查並去看落向爾

質洵笑雅荅後設措修書奉逕貴堂至今代

為運逕補返一音亦知以免兩法為免于法們

壽安

湔五月廿三

[印章] 歐陽東子頓

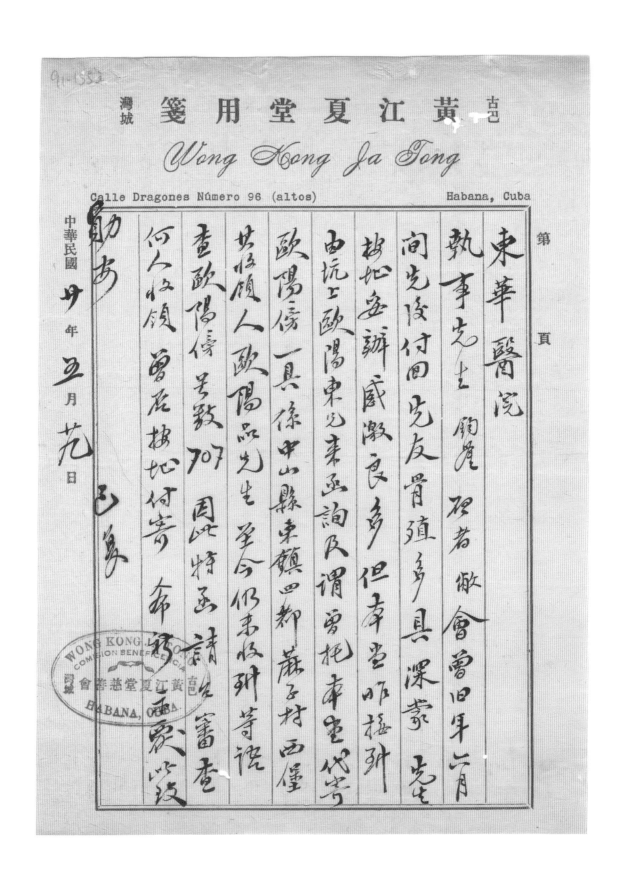

灣城　**笺用堂夏江黃**　古巴

Wong Kong Ja Tong

Calle Dragones Número 96 (altos)　　　　　　Habana, Cuba

東華醫院

執事先生鈞鑒 逕啟者 敝會曾日前二月

間先後付回先友骨殖多具 深蒙

由沅工歐陽東先素盂詢及謂曾託本堂代寄

歐陽傍一具 係中山縣東鎮四都巌子村西隆

其收領人歐陽品先生 至今仍未收到耑等說

查歐陽傍善敦707 因此特盂請台查審查

何人收領 曾店掛地付寄 希望

勷助

玉成

眾啟

第頁

中華民國廿年五月廿九日

（印章：WONG KONG JA TONG / COMISION BENEFICA / 灣城 會善慈堂夏江黃 古巴 / HABANA, CUBA.）

古巴灣城陳頴川總堂用箋
Chang Weng Chun Tong
Calle Rayo No. 15 (altos), Teléfono A-2939, Habana, Cuba.

第　頁

東華醫院主任先生義鑒敬啟者敝
堂去歲叨回之先友譽
貴院接收妥當經寄來字賜起感謝
良多禱必按址附回各縣著母親
屬領收無誤惟現接先弟來函稱
母親屬之先友骨石仍未收到來
字在處仍望以據情奉告以尚有
在港未運回各縣者請為留心妥辦
為感肅此奉請
義祺
　　陳頴川總堂總理月湖頓

中華民國二十年六月念四日

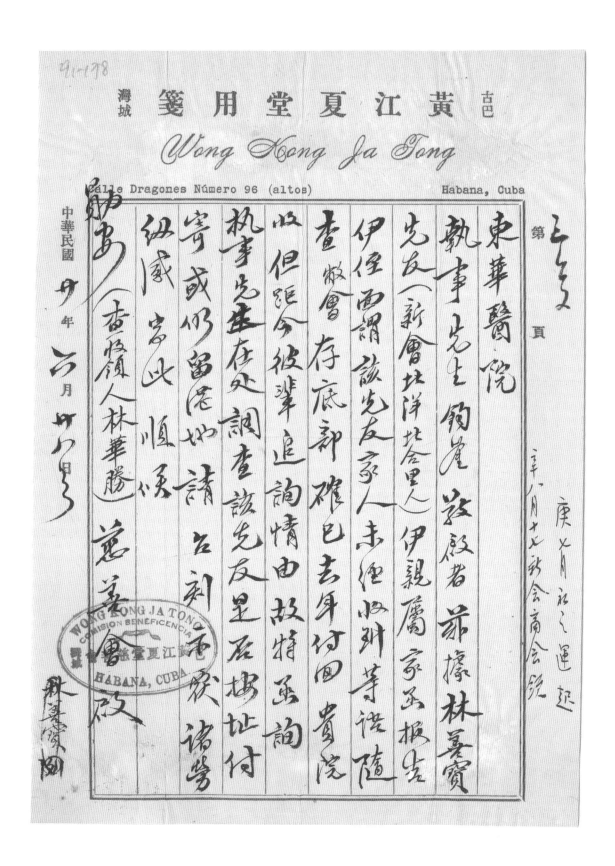

灣城　古巴　**籤用堂夏江黃**

Wong Kong Ja Tong

Calle Dragones Número 96 (altos)　　　　Habana, Cuba

東華醫院

執事先生鈞鑒　敬啟者　茲據林美寶

先友（新會址洋北合里人）伊親屬家兄振生

伊侄西賈該先友家人未經收訃等語隨

查敝會存底雖已去年付回貴院

收但距今彼輩追詢情由故特函詢

執事先生在處調查該先友

寧或仍留居此請台覆兩復諸荷址付

紕咸肅此順候

是否居此址付

臺安（查收領人林華勝）

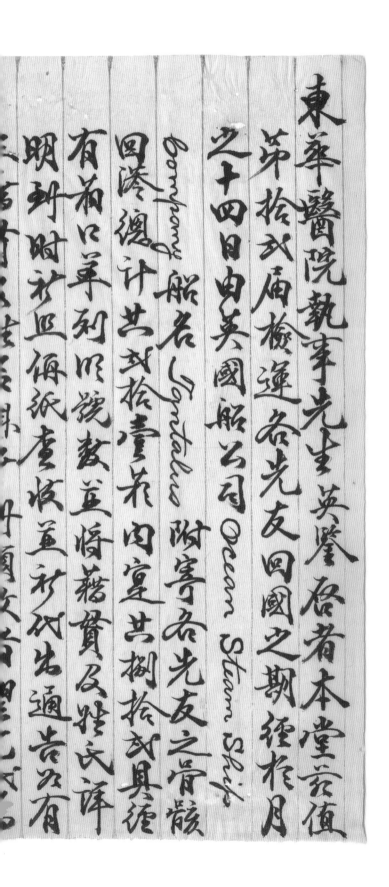

東華醫院執事先生英鑒 啟者本堂茲值

茲拾式届檢運各先友回國之期經於月

之二十四日由英國船公司 Ocean Steam Ship

回港總計共式拾壹萬内宣共捌拾式具經

明班附寄各先友之骨骸

有若口畢列所號数益將藉貫及雜民譯

明班附并每紙畫收益所代先通芸尔有

Company 船名 Tantalus 附寄各先友之骨骸

亦祈徽信録一節遲日列妥定必竟速推勞

仍為列印諒佰紙各体苦膏返港德興泰號

將單刃諒號將各体示斩时市即代為妥取

一切事闖慇善公孟諒必當仍石讓遠頌

仍德各量謹此車托若頌

義安

卿之月十五日　　巴拿馬三邑同善堂

總理接興號謹啟

茲將茅捨式届橋蓮先友相比華列呈

第壹號相內

馮棻球公同空比南海夏鄉　　盧夢凌公同矜海沙頭堡
厲有志公同矜南海居灣鄉　　厲湛　公同矜海居灣鄉

第式號相內

蘇溪公同怀　番禺鴻湖　　　莫佳公同怀　番禺
曹灼球公同矜　番禺居蓁鄉　蘇福秋公同矜　番禺

第叄號相內

黃加公同矜　番禺居蓁鄉　　黃炳會公同矜　番禺勤村
潘沈添公同矜順德冲鶴鄉　　黃吉甫公同矜　番禺基村

第四號相內

張西就公同矜十六田令村　　馮東海公同矜　花縣西壇村
溫祉記公同矜花縣西崗頭鄉　侯天保公同矜花縣上族村

第五號相內

侯養華公同矜花縣上族村　　廖炳乾公同矜　花縣
張右金公同矜花縣上族村　　張運章公同矜　花縣右逢村

第陸號相內

張雲清公同矜　花縣　　　　劉唇浦公同矜　縣大心塘
劉德和公同矜花縣大心塘　　林文楷公同矜　花縣

第柒號相內

遲月閏公同矜南海丹灶鄉　　潘湘公同矜　南海
崔港海公同矜南海沙頭　　　郭三公同矜　番禺

第捌號相內

馮紹文公同矜　南海朔村　　馮耀公同矜　南海朔村
區律金公同矜南海西雁　　　蔡海鑑公同矜南海大滿村

第九號相內

譚亮文公同矜書坑村柏水　　陳文湛公同矜大墾村
譚祥文公同矜上嶺白水　　　陳炳公同矜車州上澤圩

第拾號相內

芳迺長公同矜湖平長沙塘　　陳貽曉公同矜上澤圩
陳貽操公同矜吳賢坊　　　　陳享公同矜牛山村

吳述宏公祠佰柒碩退圓芽芳五區　蓮安里

吳廷姿公祠修碬　永乐村

弟十叁箥　祠內

黃金鏐公祠發　中山良都弟兄捐　張連公祠發　中山良都石歧

趙元兆公祠發乾會皐頭村　胡元慶公祠發升平歡會　廊培公祠發　鞏村束頭

弟十四箥　祠內

陳潔元公祠發　香山石岐　鄧潤炳公祠芽　塘樣坊多㮔杯

陳洪德公祠發　平安村　謝文敦公祠發　開平西門　蔡天球公祠芽　中山良都涌

弟十五箥　祠內

林寬公祠發　中山良都　陳在好公祠芽　中山涌都

伍任公祠發　中山涌都南村

弟十六箥　祠內

劉其興公祠修　鶴山四堡　黃栢鄉公祠發　香山戚門　金鳳昌公祠發　鶴山四堡

丘土萃公祠發　鶴山東坑堡　黃玉堂公祠發　中山石岐　鍾北興公祠發　鶴山縣

弟十七箥　祠內

李宗景公祠芽　中山谷鎮白石　古廷勝公祠發　中山菜郁　鍾祺公祠芽　香山谷鎮校

駱永煇公祠芽　中山石布郁　黃衣秀郁

弟十八箥　祠內

東門鍾氏公祠發　大布沙郁　梁讓明公祠發　香山菜村　林禹谷公祠發　邊海大菜鄉

毛學鑑公祠發　大布沙郁

弟十九箥　祠內

陳母劉氏同　香山束鎮校　楊纘鴻公祠芽　鶴山白水帶村　梁象英公祠發　沙涌鄉郁

甘天蓮公祠芽　邊海大菜郁石

弟廿箥　祠內

杜承基公祠發　鶴山縣　田寶泉公祠芽　鶴山縣

余社福公祠芽　鶴山縣

弟廿一箥　祠內

呂加堯公祠記　鶴山縣

東華醫院　執事先生　台照

附六月十五日　巴馬工邑同善堂謹上

二千七月十二九號收

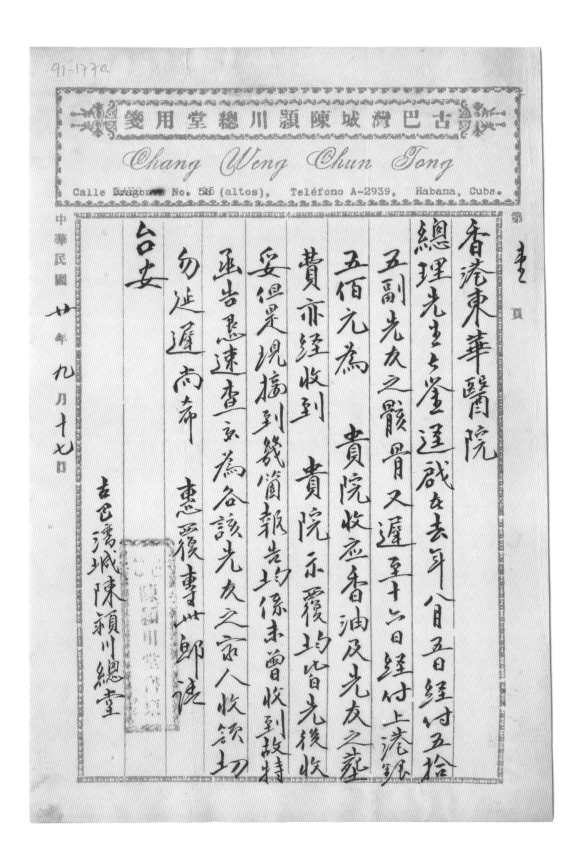

香港東華醫院

總理先生大鑒逕啟者去年八月五日經付五拾
五副先友之骸骨又遲至十二日經付上港銀
五佰元為　貴院收应香油及先友之塟
費亦經收到　貴院示覆均必先後收
安但是現搃到幾箇信報告均係未曾收到故特
正告惠速查亥為各該先友之家人收領切
勿延遲為荷　惠示覆專此郵谠

台安

中華民國廿年九月十七日

古巴灣城陳頴川總堂

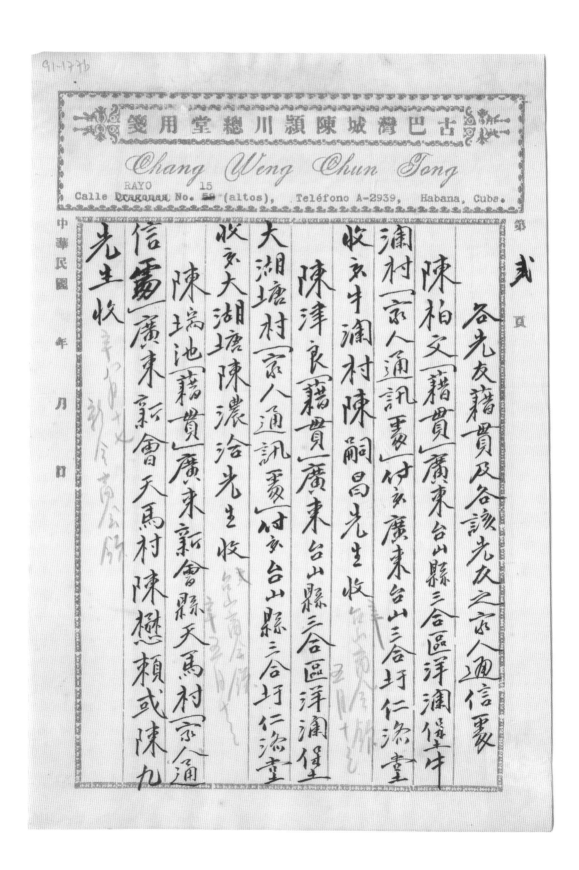

古巴灣城陳潁川總堂用箋

Chang Weng Chun Tong

RAYO Calle Dragones No. 58 (altos), Teléfono A-2939, Habana, Cuba.

第　參　頁

陳寅芳〔籍貫〕廣東台山縣新昌區冲洋堡

水坑村〔京人通信裏〕廣東台山縣新昌區冲洋
水坑村陳耀儉先生收

陳元亨〔籍貫〕廣東省城永慶二巷陳
誠德堂〔京人通信裏〕廣東省城永慶二巷

陳誠德堂陳阿女先生收
誠德堂〔籍貫〕廣東順德陳村〔京人通
楊誠垫〔籍貫〕廣東順德陳村〔京人通
信裏〕付交順德陳村渝義庄代收交陳村旧
圩花洲古道內街榮昌錫紙店轉交楊斗山先
生之京人收

中華民國　年　月　日

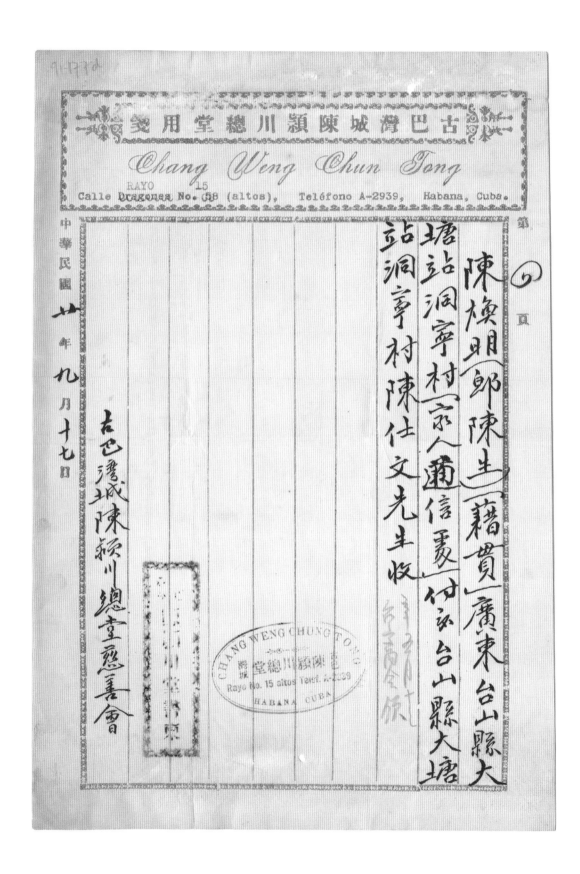

古巴灣城陳穎川總堂用箋

Chang Weng Chun Tong
RAYO 15
Calle Dragones No. 58 (altos), Teléfono A-2939, Habana, Cuba.

第　頁

陳煥明（邸陳生）籍貫廣東台山縣大
塘站洞寧村（宗人）通信處仲京台山縣大塘
站洞寧村陳仕文先生收

中華民國卅五年九月十七日

古巴灣城陳穎川總壹慈善會

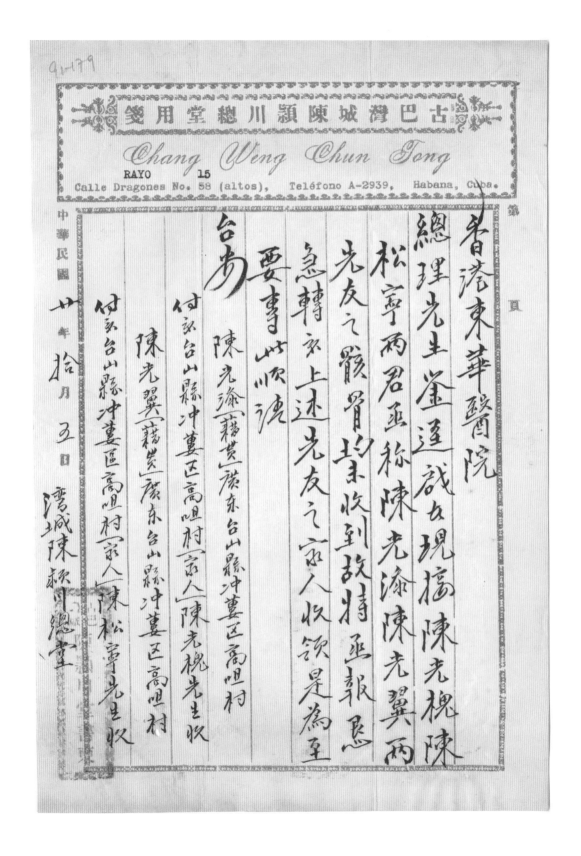

笺用堂總川潁陳城灣巴古

Chang Weng Chun Tong

RAYO 15

Calle Dragones No. 58 (altos), Teléfono A-2939, Habana, Cuba.

香港東華醫院

總理先生鈞鑒逕啟者現據陳光槐陳

松寧兩君函稱陳光滌陳光翼兩

先友之骸骨均未收到敬特函報思

急轉交上述先友之家人收領是為至

要事此順頌

台安

　　　付交台山縣冲蔞區高咀村〔宗人〕陳光槐先生收

　　陳光滌〔籍貫〕廣東台山縣冲蔞區高咀村

　　付交台山縣冲蔞區高咀村〔宗人〕陳光翼先生收

陳光翼〔籍貫〕廣東台山縣冲蔞區高咀村

　付交台山縣冲蔞區高咀村〔宗人〕陳松寧先生收

中華民國 廿年 拾月 五日

灣城陳潁川總堂

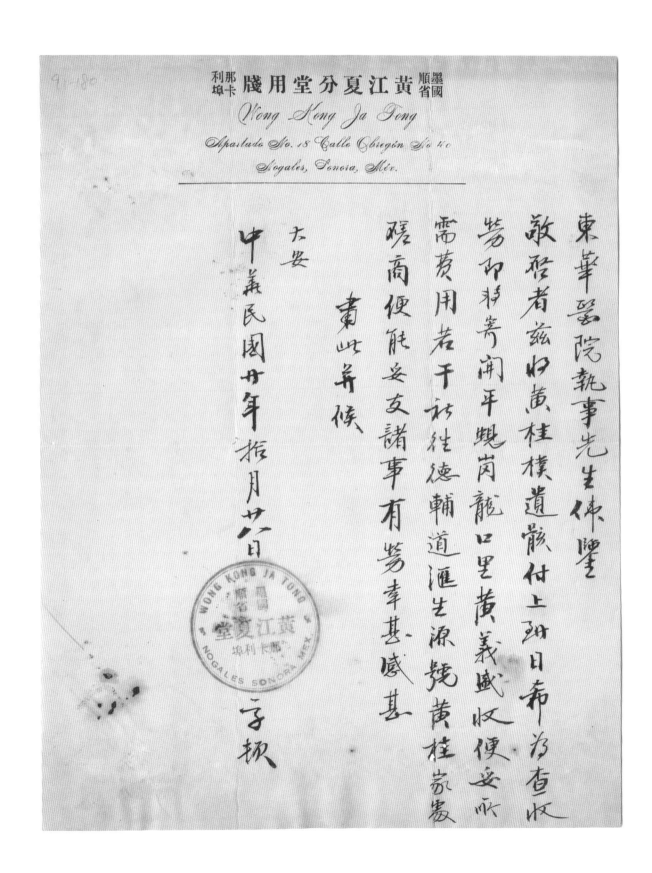

墨國
順省黃江夏分堂用牋
那卡利埠

Wong Kong Ja Tong

Apartado No. 18 Calle Obregon No. 40
Nogales, Sonora, Mex.

東華醫院執事先生偉鑒

敬啟者茲由黃桂橫道嚴付上班日希為查收
等所籌開平魁岡口里黃義盛收便妥派
需費用若干祈往德輔道滙生源魏黃桂蒙襄
磋商便能妥友諸事有等幸甚感甚

肅此奉候、

大安

中華民國廿年拾月廿八日

字頌

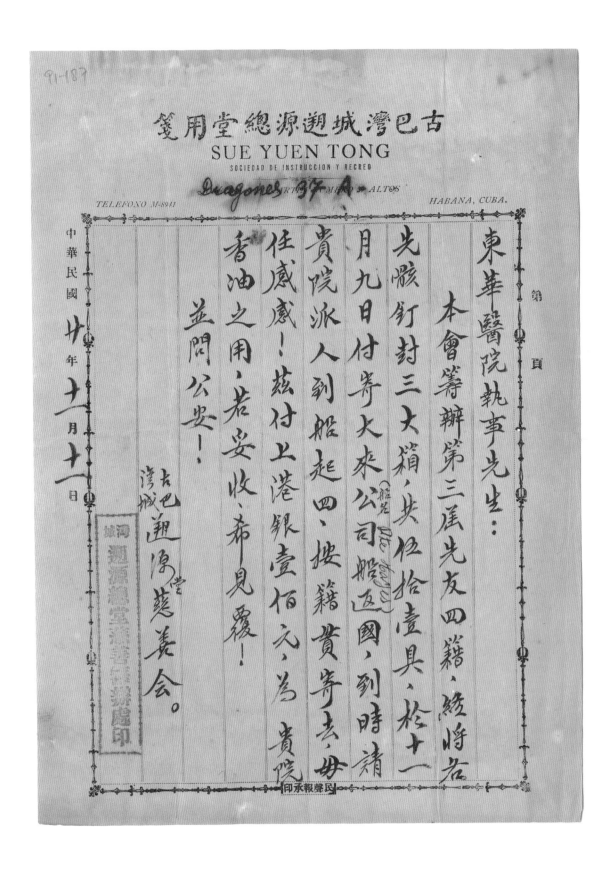

筬用堂總源遡城灣巴古

SUE YUEN TONG

SOCIEDAD DE INSTRUCCION Y RECREO

Dragones

TELEFONO M-8941　　　　HABANA, CUBA.

東華醫院執事先生：

　本會籌辦第三屆先友四籍、統將各
先骸釘封三大箱、共伍拾壹具、於十一
月九日付寄大來公司船返國、到時請
貴院派人到船起囬、按籍貴寄去、毋
任感感！茲付上港銀壹佰元、為貴院
香油之用、君妥收、希見覆！
　　並問公安！

　　　　　　　　古巴灣城遡源總堂慈善會。

中華民國 廿年 十一月 十一日

○溯源總堂慈善會啟事

本會經將是屆各先骸二執安，定於十一月九日付船歸國，並擬定每先骸給同葬費十元。○（港銀）茲為慎重起見，凡領先骸葬費者，要覓殷商盍章擔保，方准領取。○○

△茲將運歸之先骸姓名籍貫列左

（第一箱）

鄺有廣　台山嶺背長安村人
鄺修平　台山沖雲四龍里人
雷學積　台山張長邊人
雷維彩　台山塘面和樂村人
雷法昌　台山塘面坑尾人
雷祥維　台山大崗大洞村人
雷金女　台山大崗大洞村人
鄺乃衍　中山斗門小濠涌人

鄺敬銓　台山嶺背長安村人
鄺光仁　台山倉下人
雷維沛　台山塘面和樂村人
雷學滋　台山塘面曹岡人
雷從江　台山塘面龍岡村人
雷家嵩　台山大崗大洞村人
雷子榮　番禺銅村長巷人
容佑　新會官沖鳳鳴里人

（第二箱）

鄺煜堂　開平泮村太平里人
方艮錫　開平古宅龍岡人
方富濯　開平沙塘坑口村人
方北海　中山險都濠涌村人
方計來　中山南區人
鄺抱光　中山斗門小濠涌鄉人
鄺竻修　中山斗門小濠涌鄉人
譚業駿　中山斗門斜排村人

鄺永同　開平社邊四頭社寶華里人
何齊好　開平社邊中心社寶華里人
方弈鳳　開平古宅安榮里人
鄺飛雄　中山斗門小濠涌鄉人
鄺悅榮　中山斗門小濠涌鄉人
鄺保養　中山斗門小濠涌鄉人
莫裕興　中山斗門赤水坑村人
方寬　東莞人

（第叁箱）

雷龍廣　台山塘面三家村人
雷道基　台山公益區張邊村人
雷積勝　台山五十區洞頭人
鄺榮顯　台山嶺背人
鄺光詔　台山嶺背同與社人
黃新活　台山牛山區鳳岡村人
關鑾達　台山都斛豐江村人
雷瀚　台山人

雷有傳　台山塘面棠樣里人
雷宜斌　台山張良邊龍溪人
雷銳民　台山鎮口地維人
鄺琴光　台山沖雲順和人
郭耀林　台山筋坑逕常安村人
梁百濃　台山吉那區西廓高龍人
許大富　台山大塘橫坑村人
方喜　潮州人

十月廿三號

古京溯源總堂慈善會啟

△附啟

凡屬本堂之先骸，其在山埠者，要在本月三十日以前運出本灣，方得搭是屆運回，（歸落第三箱）運回保留至第四屆付歸。

茲定於十一月八日下午一點鐘，為公祭先友回籍之期，仰各先友親屬依期到中華義山虔祭一切，此啟

（各先友姓名籍貫，如有差錯，仰從速指正。）

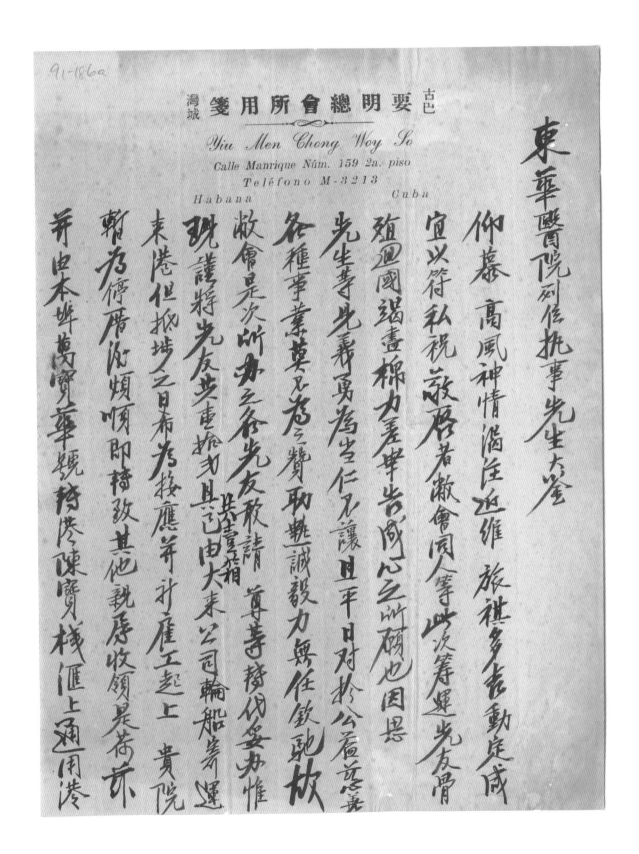

古巴
灣城 要明總會所用箋
Yiu Men Chong Woy So
Calle Manrique Núm. 159 2a. piso
Teléfono M-3213
Habana　　　　　　Cuba

東華醫院列位執事先生大鑒

仰慕 高風神情溜注延維 旅祺多吉動定咸

宜以符私祝 敬啟者敝會同人等此次籌運先友骨

殖迴國竭盡棉力蓋華崙同心之所願也因思

先生等先義勇為尚仁不讓且平日對於公益慈善

各種事業莫不為之贊助誠毅力無任欽馳故

現謹將先友步柩由其己由大來公司輪船寄運

敝會是次所辦共壹箱算善請代妥為惟

東港但撚垻之日希為接應其他數屇收領是荷苏

賴為停屇沿煩順即轉致 貴院

並由本埠萬寶華親替港陳寶亨棧滙上通用港

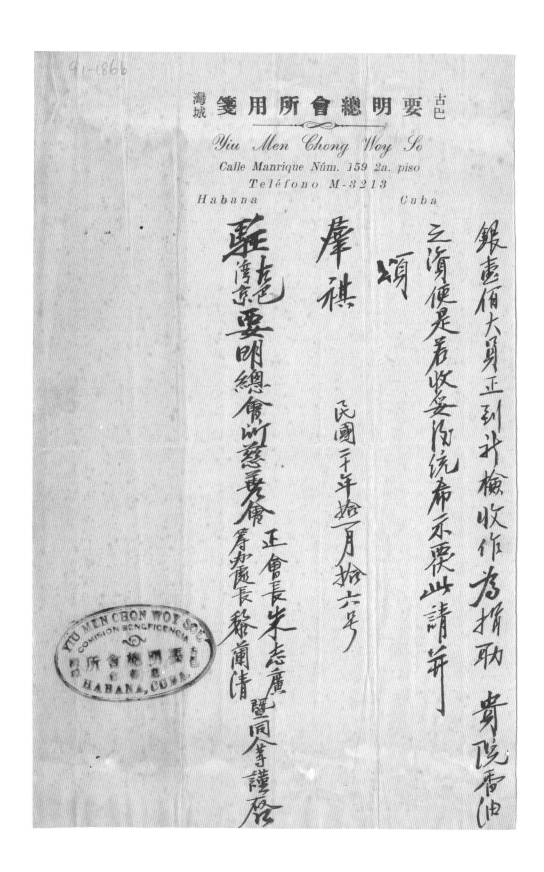

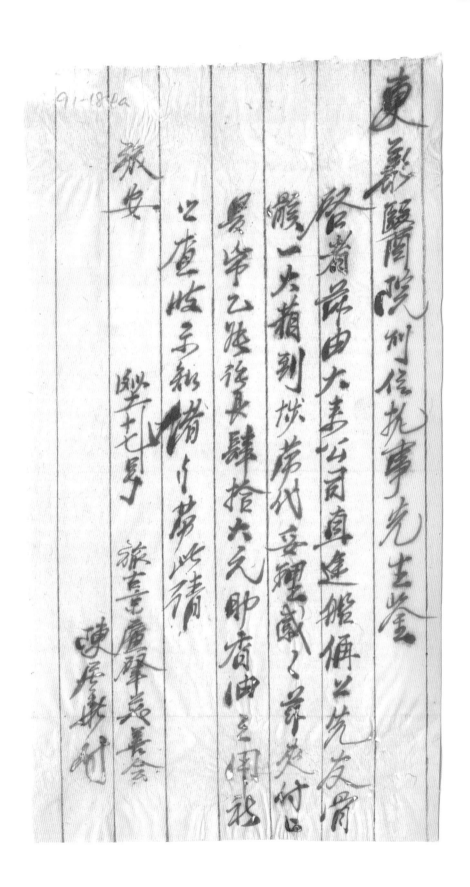

東華醫院列位善長仁翁暨事先生鑒

啟者茲由大吉公司直達船佩恂先友骨
骸一大箱刻狀蒙代妥理藏及葬費附上
最常之號經真肆拾大元即查由妥團友校

敬安

已煩收支並請惠予收

此請

旅古廣肇慈善會
陳屈薪叩

坐十七號

香港東華醫院列位先生大鑒 敬啓者 前由墨國民成李

祐水畢掛本年西歷元月廿八号啓行之輪船直夆付交

貴醫院先友昔骸一束 茲付昔骸俩紙正張經四沃水

畢代理西人當日隨南付工今時副俩紙套工但剄先清之

查叔出蒙代叔妾荮沅再桂寄玄南洵九江萬善堂玄錢行

西街致妾祥銀諢和便會妾工東灣大頂艮行横一張第

951号值邊艮四拾元剄专清之查叔將作代叔昔骸及轺寄之

雙用但口叔妾便笔示慰俱末信清之信雨西住址付末妾悞

滋事桂工慣神之妪也餇盅末妾丰一并候

台祺

（此数壬戌月彩九日此）

ㅗ门牌住址

瞰筆戎目 拾号　　　注墨國關海公司字密

Jase Juan y Cia

Apartado #18

Arriaga Chis, Mexico

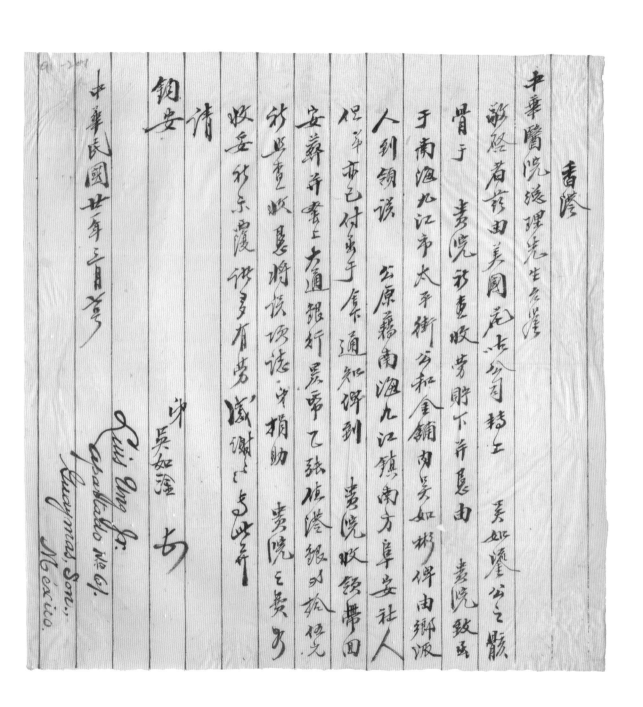

香港

中華醫院總理先生台鑒

敬啓者前由美國昆士公司轉工 吳如鑒公之骸

骨于 貴院茲查收勞賜下幷懇由 貴院致函

于南洛九江市太平街公和金舖內吳如彬俾由鄉派

人到領誤 公原籍南洛九江鎮南方卓安社人

但茅亦已付妥于倉通知得到 貴院收領帶回

安葬等費上大通銀行暨帝乙號碼港報对拾伍元

弟此畫收慈將誤理誌并捐助 貴院之費另

收妥祈示覆俾乡省省夥等有勞

　請

鈞安

　　　　弟吳如淦 安

中華民國廿年三月七日

Luis Ung Jr.
Caballero no 61.
Guaymas, Son.,
Mexico.

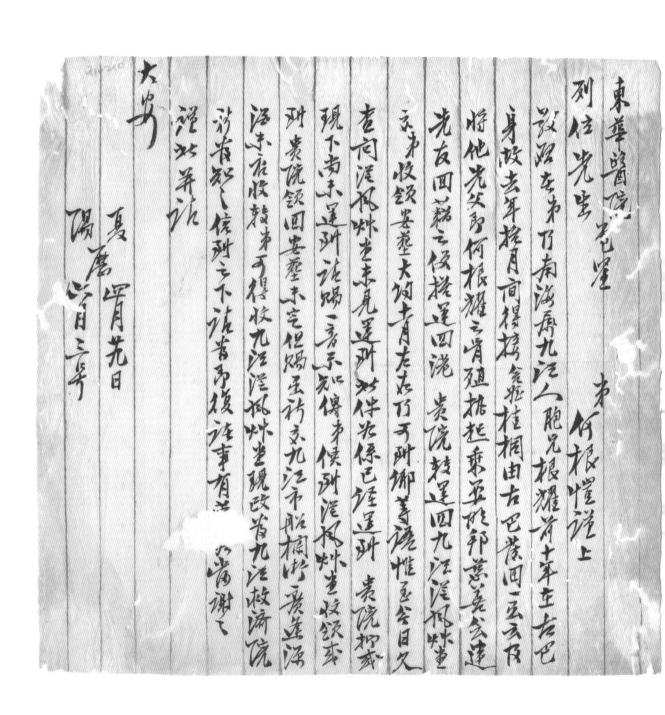

東華醫院

列位先生大鑒

　敬啟者弟乃南海喬九江人胞兄根耀前十年立古巴

身故去年拾月前得據來症桂桐由古巴蒙回一玉交及

將他先父勞何根耀之骨殖搭挺乘本於郵蒙差交送

先友回藉之候搭運回港　貴院轉運回九江郵蒙

弟收領妥產大約十肯本方干郵卿菁諳惟至今日久

查向港郵蒙未尽見運到　如伴發係已經運到　貴院郵蒙

現下尚未運到話賜一音示知傳令候到港郵蒙妥收領來

郵貴院領回妥產本宅倘玉葬京九江市貽棺術蒙差源

源未在收報本可得投九江港郵蒙妥現政省九江救濟院

荷者如之信附二不諳普舟後諸事有菁　　省謝

謹此草祝

大安

　夏暦肖芫日

陽暦肖三芫

何根愷謹上

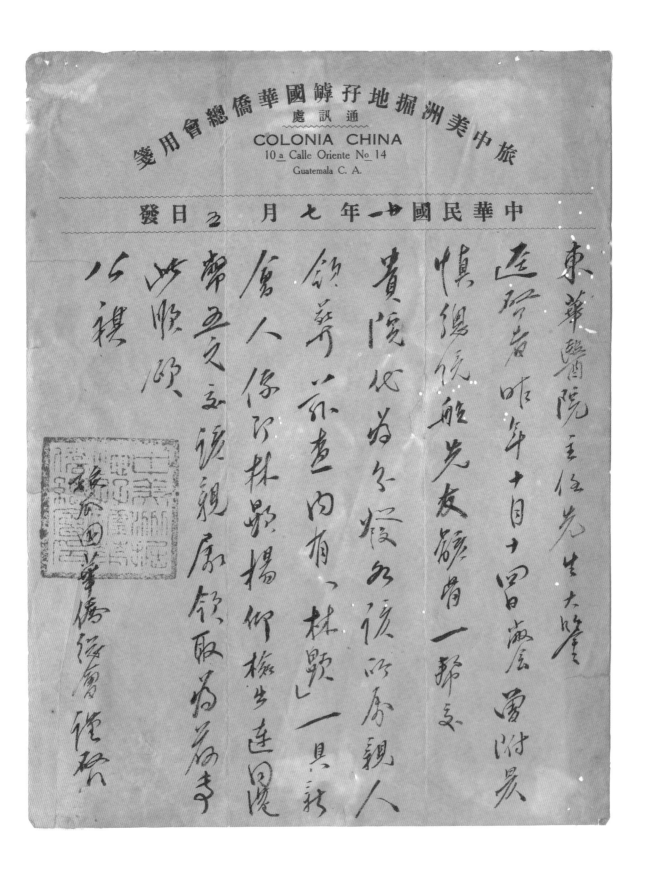

旅中美洲掘地孖罅國華僑總會用箋

通訊處

COLONIA CHINA
10_a_ Calle Oriente No_ 14
Guatemala C. A.

中華民國十一年七月之日發

東華醫院主任先生大鑒

逕啟者昨年十月十四日蔵扁曾附

慎記輪船先友體骨一部寄

貴院此為先疫名後所有親人

領葬並煮內有、林題」一具新

僑人保印林影揚仰檢出連回院

常互文之領原領取為荷希

此順頌

公祺

旅中美洲掘地孖罅國華僑總會謹啟

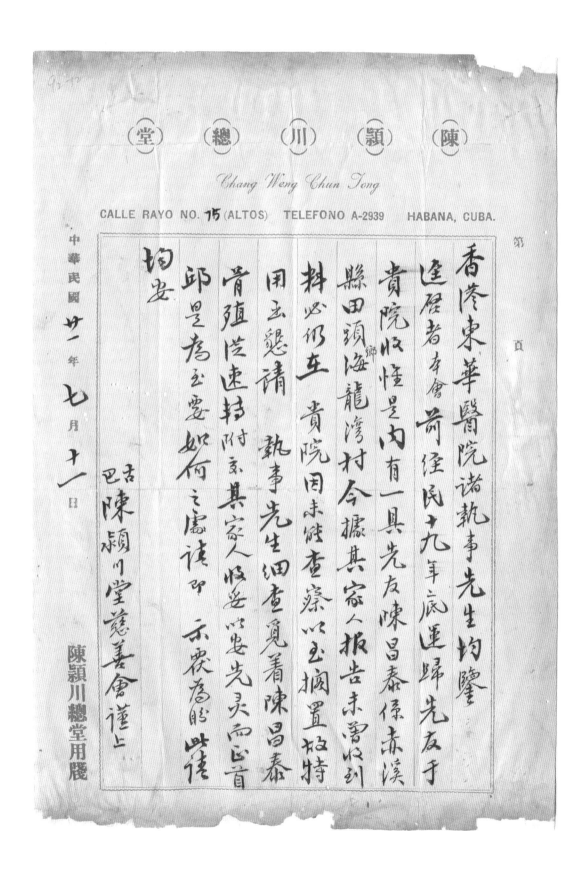

陳　頴　川　總　堂

Chang Weng Chun Tong

CALLE RAYO NO. 15 (ALTOS)　TELEFONO A-2939　HABANA, CUBA.

第

頁

香港東華醫院諸執事先生均鑒

逕啟者本會前經民十九年底運歸先友于

貴院收惟是內有一具先友陳昌泰係赤溪

縣田頭海龍灣村今據其家人報告未曾收到

料必仍在 貴院同未經查察以玉摘置故特

用玉懇請 執事先生細查覓着陳昌泰

骨殖涇速轉附京其家人收妥以妥先灵而正首

邱是為玉要如何之處請即示覆為盼

均安

中華民國廿一年

七月十一日

古巴陳頴川堂慈善會謹上

陳頴川總堂用牋

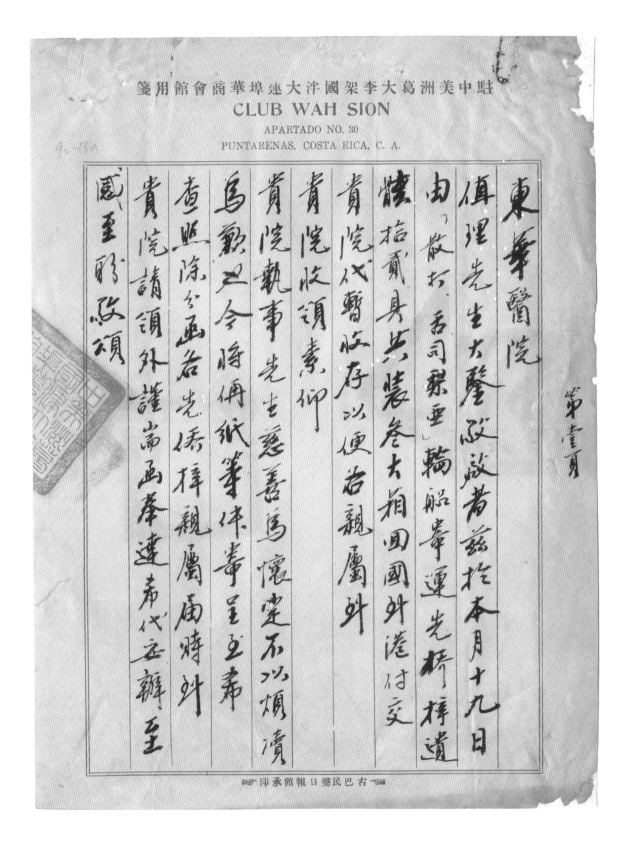

駐中美洲葛大架國泮大連埠華商會館用箋
CLUB WAH SION
APARTADO NO. 30
PUNTARENAS, COSTA RICA, C. A.

東華醫院

值理先生大鑒茲啟者茲於本月十九日

由敝埠吾司葉垂輪船韋運光橋樟遺

懷拾貳具其裝叁大箱回國外港付交

貴院代暫收存以便若親屬外

貴院收領素仰

貴院執事先生慈善為懷定不以煩瀆

為顧茲令將佈紙筆伴辈呈至希

查照除令函告光僑拜親屬屆時外

貴院請領外謹當函奉達希代為辦至

感毋勝盼敬頌

第壹頁

古巴民聲日報館承印

駐中美洲葛大李架國沰大連埠華商會館用箋
CLUB WAH SION
APARTADO NO. 30
PUNTARENAS, COSTA RICA, C. A.

93-136

公安

第貳月

沰大華商會館 正會長 陳培興
　　　　　　隨埠 書記 薛國慶

計開

卓玉泉公道骸一具
廣東中山縣第六區官樂鄉人氏寄
卓展宏鳥崧三君收　堂
　　　　　　　　第壹號箱

黃慶公道骸一具
廣東中山縣谷鎮白石環攔山村人氏煩寄
黃容保林啟維二君收
　　　　　　　第貳號箱

黃光喜公道骸一具
廣東中山縣谷鎮平湖村人氏煩寄
黃畔君收
　　　　　　第叁號箱

古巴民聲日報館承印

駐中美洲葛大李架國汴大連埠華商會館用箋
CLUB WAH SION
APARTADO NO. 30
PUNTARENAS, COSTA RICA, C. A.

第叁頁

林陳氏遺骸一具　第肆號歸箱
廣東中山縣谷鎮白石環獺山村人民頓亨
林菽維先生附

余良和公遺骸一身　第伍號歸箱
廣東台山縣平安村獲海運人民亨
余里和先生附

陳杜氏遺骸一具　第陸號歸箱
廣東中山縣谷都白石環人民頓亨
陳經鳳蕭鳳均鳳三位先生附

陳燦興公遺骸一具　第柒號歸箱
廣東中山縣谷鎮白石環下涌人民頓亨
陳經鳳蕭鳳均鳳三君

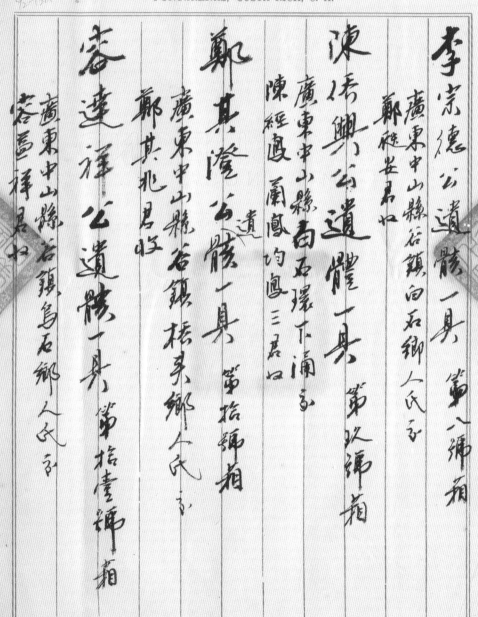

箋用館會商華埠連大汴國架李大葛洲美中駐
CLUB WAH SION
APARTADO NO. 30
PUNTARENAS, COSTA RICA, C. A.

李崇德公遺骸一具 第八歸箱
　廣東中山縣谷鎮向石鄉人氏子
　鄭祇莊君收

陳僑興公遺體一具 第玖歸箱
　廣東中山縣商石環下浦家
　陳經渡蘭鳳均返三君收

鄭其澄公遺骸一具 第拾歸箱
　廣東中山糖谷鎮橋美鄉人氏子
　鄭其兆君收

容達祥公遺體一具 第拾壹歸箱
　廣東中山縣谷鎮烏石鄉人氏子
　容喬祥君收

單鋒員

印承館報日聲民巴古

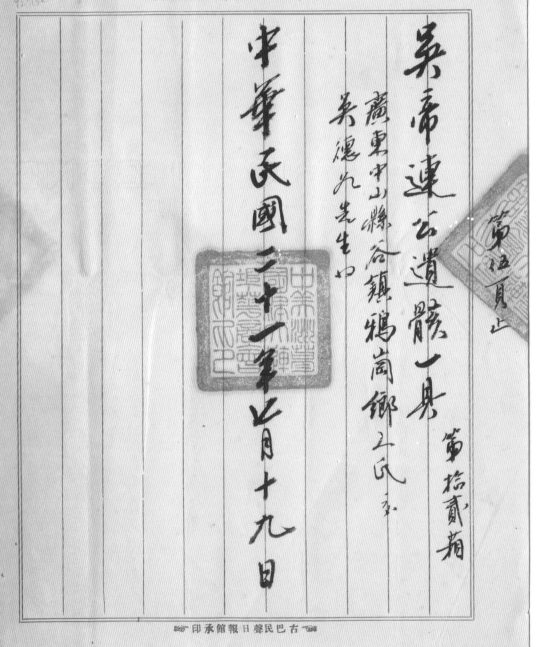

笺用館會商華埠連大汴國大架李大葛洲美中駐
CLUB WAH SION
APARTADO NO. 30
PUNTARENAS, COSTA RICA, C. A.

第拾貳箱

吳帝連公遺骸一具

廣東中山縣谷鎮鴉崗鄉上氏交

吳德九先生收

中華民國二十一年七月十九日

第捨貳箱止

古巴民聲日報館承印

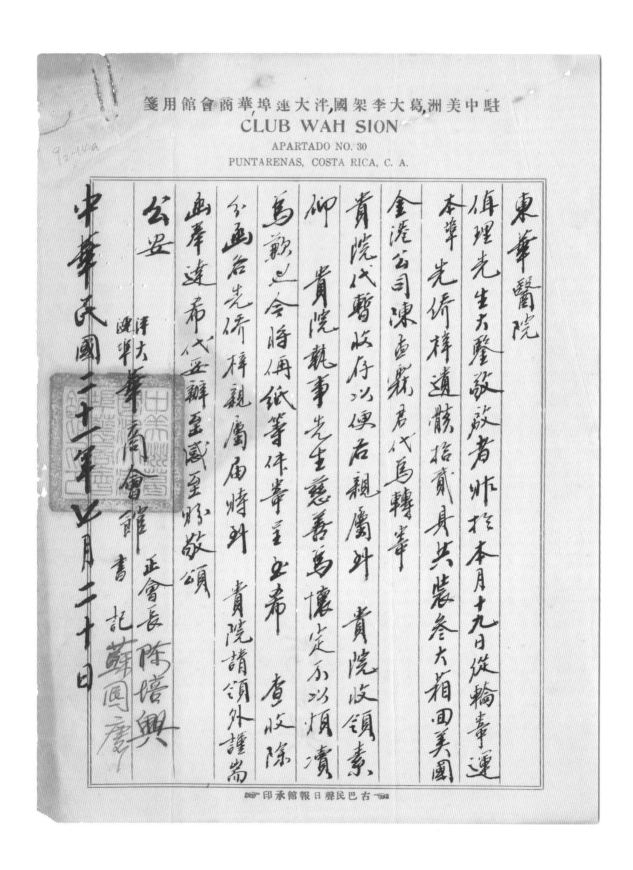

箋用館會商華埠連大泮,國架李大葛,洲美中駐
CLUB WAH SION
APARTADO NO. 30
PUNTARENAS, COSTA RICA, C. A.

東華醫院

偉理先生大鑒敬者昨接本月十九日從輪寄運

本埠先僑梓遺骸指貳身共裝叁大箱囬美國

金港公司陳畫霖君代為轉事

貴院代醫收存以便各親屬升 貴院收領素

仰 貴院董事先生慈善為懷定不以煩瀆

為 顧之今將俪紙筆件奉呈立希 查收除

兹函各先僑梓親屬届時料 貴院請領外謹此

函達希代妥辦至感至盼敬頌

公安

譯埠華僑商館書記

正會長 陳培興

蘇囬慶

中華民國二十一年七月二十日

印承館報日聲民巴右

箋用館會商華埠連大沰國架李大葛洲美中駐
CLUB WAH SION
APARTADO NO. 30
PUNTARENAS, COSTA RICA, C. A.

計開

卓玉泉公　廣東中山縣第六區貢塘鄉人民
　　　　　子卓慶芳　卓鳥芬二君收

黃慶公　第壹編箱
　　　廣東中山縣谷鎮白石環獺山村人民
　　　子黃蓉偲　林啟維二君收

黃先賣公　第貳編箱
　　　廣東中山縣谷鎮平湖村人民
　　　交黃群先生收

林陳氏　第肆編箱
　　　廣東中山縣谷鎮白石環獺山村人民
　　　交林啟維先生收

余良和公　第伍編箱
　　　廣東台山縣平妥村莊滙區人民
　　　交余良和先生收

陳杜氏　第陸編箱
　　　廣東中山縣谷都白石環下浦人民
　　　交陳經戲蘭戲均戲三君收

陳燦興公　第柒編箱
　　　廣東中山縣谷鎮白石環下浦人民
　　　交陳經戲蘭戲均戲三君收

李崇德公　第八編箱
　　　廣東中山縣谷鎮白石鄉人民
　　　交鄭継坒君收

陳僑興公　第玖編箱
　　　廣東中山縣白石環下浦人民
　　　交陳經鳳蘭鳳均鳳三君收

鄭其澄公　第拾編箱
　　　廣東中山縣石橋頭鄉人民
　　　交鄭其兆吉收

蓉達祥公　第拾壹編箱
　　　廣東中山縣谷鎮鳥石鄉大坪人民
　　　交蓉達祥君府上收

吳帝連公　第拾貳編箱
　　　廣東中山縣谷鎮鴉蘭鄉人民
　　　交吳德九君收

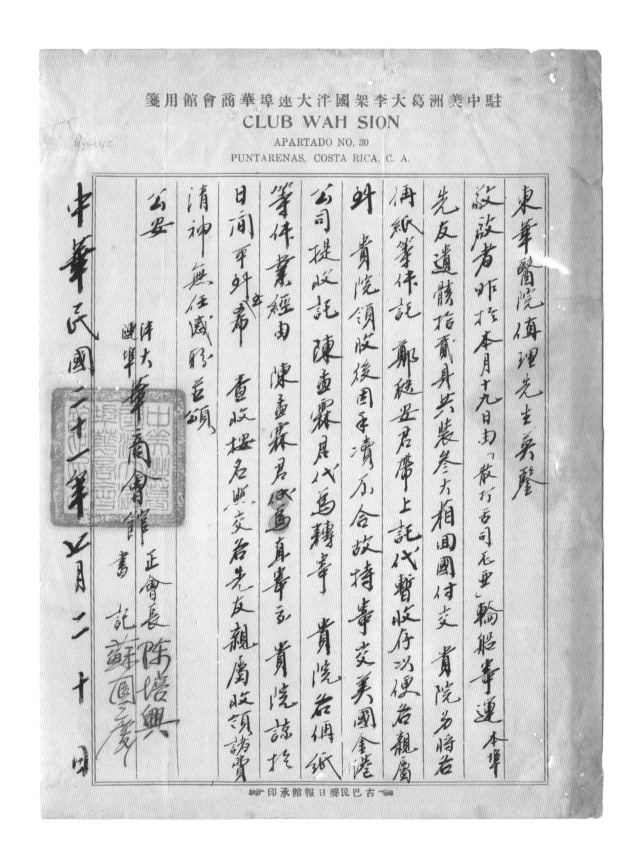

東華醫院倂理先生英鑒

敬啟者咋於本月十九日由「藪行吾司无亞」輪船幸運本華

先友遺骸拾貳具共裝叁大相囘囯付交 貴院為妥若

倂紙筆件託 郑穗委君帶上託代暫收存以便各親屬

斜 貴院領收後囘不濬示合故持幸交美國金港

公司提收託 陳垕霖君代為轉幸 貴院諒於

筆件業經由 陳垕霖君代為真幸言 貴院諒於

日前平幸外希 查收揭名與交各先友親屬收領諸費

清神無任感形盞頌

公安

泩大華囯商會館 書記 蘇囯之幸

正會長 陳培興

中華民囯二十一年 七月二十日

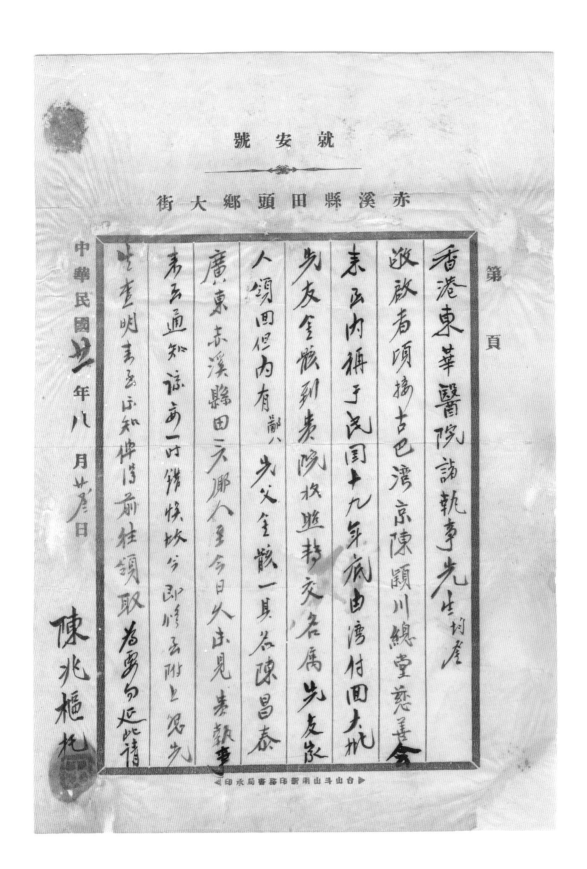

就安號

赤溪縣田頭鄉大街

第頁

香港東華醫院諸執事先生均鑒

敬啟者頃擒古巴灣京陳顯川總堂慈善會

來正內稱于民國十九年疯由灣付回大批

先友金骸到貴院核點轉交各屬先友眾

人領回但內有鄙人先父金骸一具為陳昌泰

廣東赤溪縣田頭鄉人至今日火未見壽歎事

壽至通知誤寄一時錯快坎今即修正附上恐先

生查明壽至示知俾得前往領取為要句延此情

中華民國卅一年八月廿六日

陳兆樞托

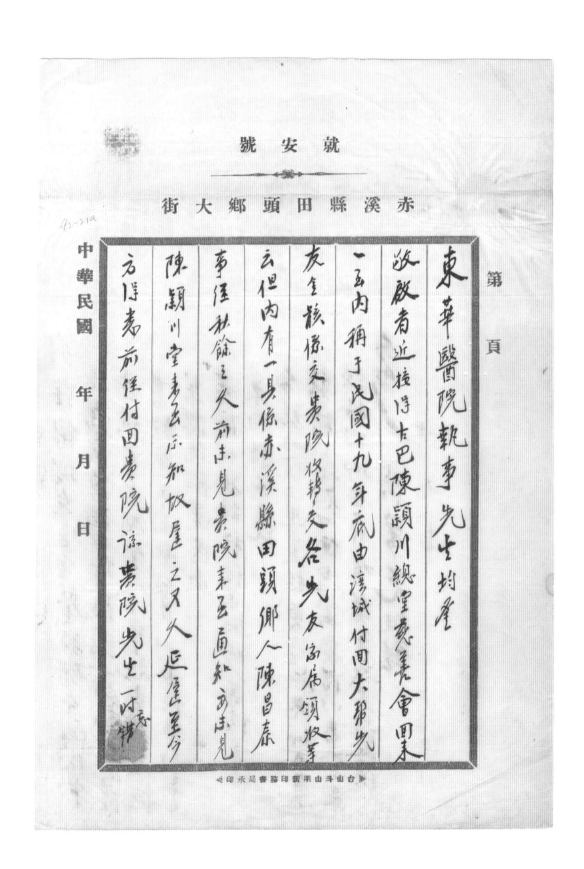

號 安 就

街 大 鄉 頭 田 縣 溪 赤

中華民國　年　月　日

東華醫院執事先生均鑒

敬啟者近接得古巴陳穎川總室惠寄會回未

一玉內稱于民國十九年底由灣城付回大鄔先

友金核係交貴院將轉交各先友家屬領收筆

云但內有一具係赤溪縣田頭鄉人陳昌泰

事經秋餘玉久前未見貴院寄玉匯知亦未見

陳穎川室寿玉示知故屋之又久延屋甚分

方保考前往付回貴院諒貴院先生一時忘

第頁

就安號

赤溪縣田頭鄉大街

兄長書玉通知今晨特瑪修玉奉上怨

貴執事先生見告即查明諒陳昌春核實

一具即書玉吉知偉傳前往領回以步光灵

廣初規貴執事先生皆躬身為懷逐

不以為部伏祈留心是禱謹此并候

第　頁

計開

又前付之一玉內挟湾京藐喜

會一玉諒查情枚美候

中華民國廿年八月廿九日

陳兆櫃托

◀台山斗山平新昌蓉印書局永印▶

尼架拉瓜國步路飛埠中華會館致東華醫院信件

1932 年 9 月 24 日

箋用館會華中埠飛路步國瓜拉架尼洲美中

CHINESE CLUB, BLUEFIELDS, NICARAGUA, C.A.

第頁

東華醫院執事諸公偉鑒逕啟者

敝會將歷年先友骸骨共六名裝成壽

莊由總統輪船寄交少社代收分運各埠

望得回視歸葬土儀尚祈玉成幸甚

諸公慷慨義舉遠大懷空能代籌為荷

因再玉達（另函夾有出口單）專為諸公川

草此奉請

善禧　計開　木牌一萬　共六名

鄭武琳　中山縣谷都平嵐鄉東隆

林鑑清　中山縣谷都平嵐鄉林佳

侯賢祖　中山縣谷都白石鄉

鄭文祿　中山縣烏石鄉

黃立禮　開平縣百合圩赤塘堡

鄭忠休　開平縣百合圩白沙窩屋

中華民國二十一年九月廿四日　中華會館付

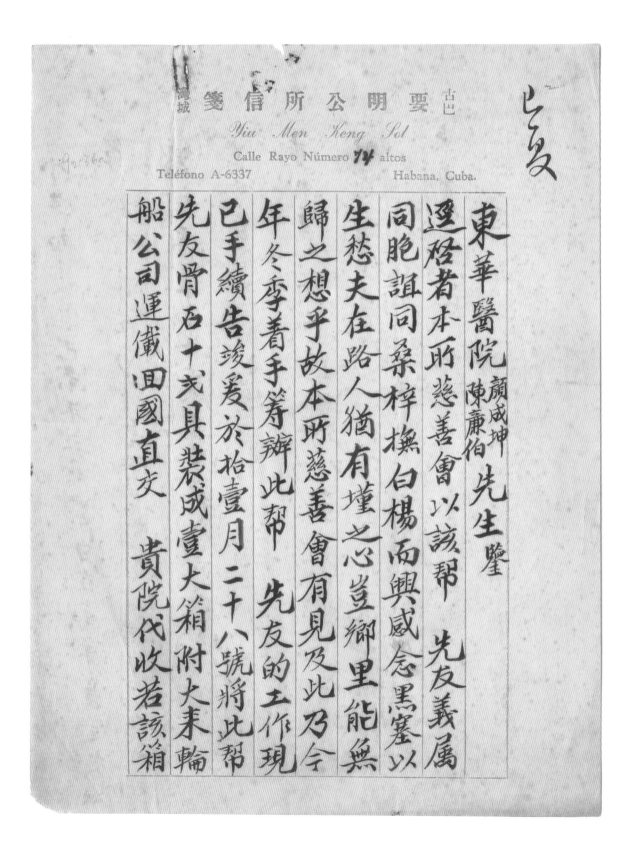

古巴
灣城 要明公所 信箋
Yiu Men Keng Sol
Calle Rayo Número 74 altos
Teléfono A-6337　　　　　Habana, Cuba.

東華醫院顏成坤 陳廉伯 先生鑒

逕啟者本所慈善會以該幫　先友義屬

同胞誼同桑梓撫白楊而興感念黑塞以

生慈夫在路人猶有壤之心豈鄉里能無

歸之想乎故本所慈善會有見及此乃今

年冬季著手籌辦此幫　先友的工作現

已手續告竣爰於拾壹月二十八號將此幫

先友骨石十戈具裝成壹大箱附大來輪

船公司運儀回國直交　貴院代收若該箱

要明公所信箋 城灣 古巴

Yiu Men Keng Sol

Calle Rayo Número 74 altos

Teléfono A-6337　　　　　　　Habana, Cuba.

先友骨石到時請　台轉達「永樂街十四號

怡來號暨「永和街十三號和興昌」兩號便能

料理轉寄伊親屬妥收也且即日由紐約銀

行購赤壹張值港幣伍拾元滙上乃作要

明公所慈善會捐助　貴院之微忱實不

成敬意用特函達希為查收復達則不勝

銘感矣此致順頌

旅祺

民．卅、青卅日　　要明公所慈善會謹上

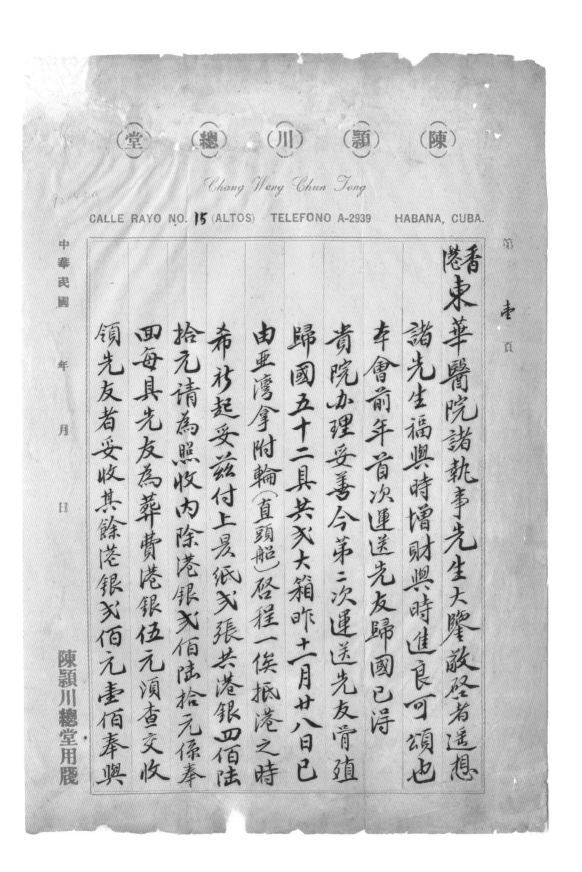

(堂) (總) (川) (潁) (陳)

Chang Weng Chun Tong

CALLE RAYO NO. 15 (ALTOS)　TELEFONO A-2939　HABANA, CUBA.

第壹頁

香港東華醫院諸執事先生大鑒敬啟者遙想

諸先生福興時增財興時進良可頌也

車會前年首次運送先友歸國已得

貴院辦理妥善今第二次運送先友骨殖

歸國五十二具共弍大箱昨十一月廿八日已

由亞灣拿附輪（直頭船）啟程一俟抵港之時

希於起妥茲付上晨紙弍張共港銀四佰陸

拾元請為照收內除港銀弍佰陸拾元係奉

回每具先友為葬費港銀伍元須查文收

領先友者妥收其餘港銀弍佰元壹佰奉興

中華民國　年　月　日

陳潁川總堂用箋

92-406

陳穎川總堂

Chang Weng Chun Tong

CALLE RAYO NO. 15 (ALTOS) TELEFONO A-2939 HABANA, CUBA.

第弍頁

貴院為香油資壹佰為分送各先友歸各
縣各鄉之費得以回籍以正首邱而安先靈
定當獲福靡既矣尤收到此銀信仰速示
覆免盈遠望是荷修未細及喃此並候
近祉

并付上往起先友之西文帋弍張祈注意收

古巴灣城陳穎川總堂慈善會謹上

中華民國二十一年十二月八日

CHANG WENG CHUN TONG 陳穎川總堂 Rayo No. 15 altos Telef. A-2939 HABANA CUBA

陳穎川總堂用牋

篆用館會華中埠飛路步國瓜拉架尼洲美中

CHINESE CLUB, BLUEFIELDS, NICARAGUA, C. A.

第頁

香港東華醫院執事先生均鑒

公啓者得接到去年志月廿日賜來大教得知一切

再查以寄名先梓苟之骨殖係由該房親人往尋覔

荷今查詢該八據云西鄭式琳鄭文祿二位先友

之骨殖係封埋在候賢祖之確內因當日當信立人

未知梗概是以未查詳明　致令列位賢心初見鄭式

琳文祿二位之親屬斟領時領可對他言明在候賢祖

之確內暨迷分給古人二親屬領四安葬以安寵

穿不緣墳神之王蕭此詩頌

　　　　　　　　　　公安

西曆一九三十三年二月　日

醫　中華會館

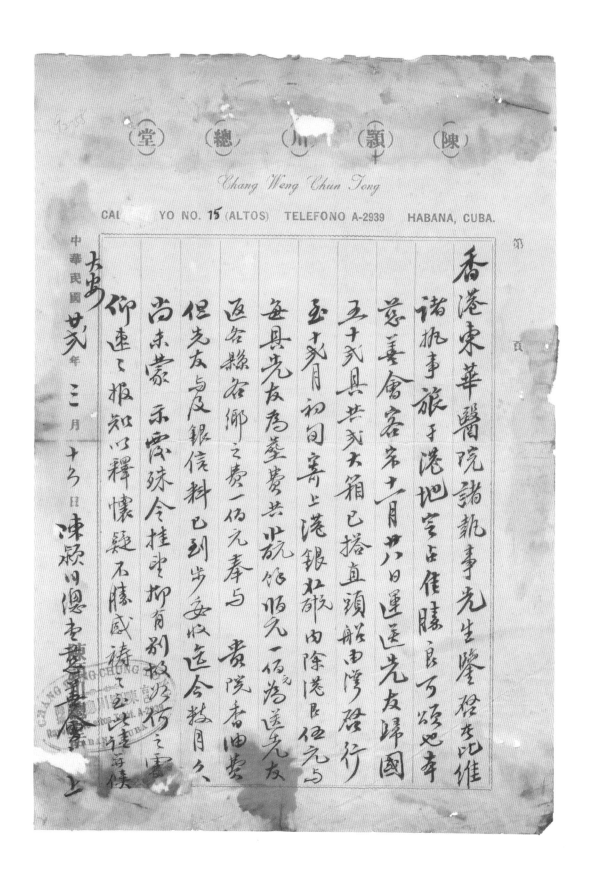

（堂）（總）（川）（潁）（陳）

Chang Weng Chun Tong

CAL___YO NO. 15 (ALTOS)　TELEFONO A-2939　HABANA, CUBA.

香港東華醫院諸執事先生鑒啓者此維

諸執事旅于港地定占佳勝良可頌也本

慈善會容第十月廿八日運運先友歸國

五十六員共六大箱已搭直頭艇由灣啓行

玉六月初旬寄上港銀社敝由除港民伍元与

無具先友為盤費共少航館佰元一佰送先友

迨各縣各鄉之費一佰元奉与　貴院香油費

但先友与友銀信料已到步妥收迄合扱目久

尚未蒙承需殊令挂望柳有别故好行之重

仰速丁報知以釋懷疑不勝感禱至此専此奉候

中華民國廿六年　三月　十六日　陳潁川總...慈善會書上

中國陳章烈致東華醫院信件

1933 年 6 月 25 日

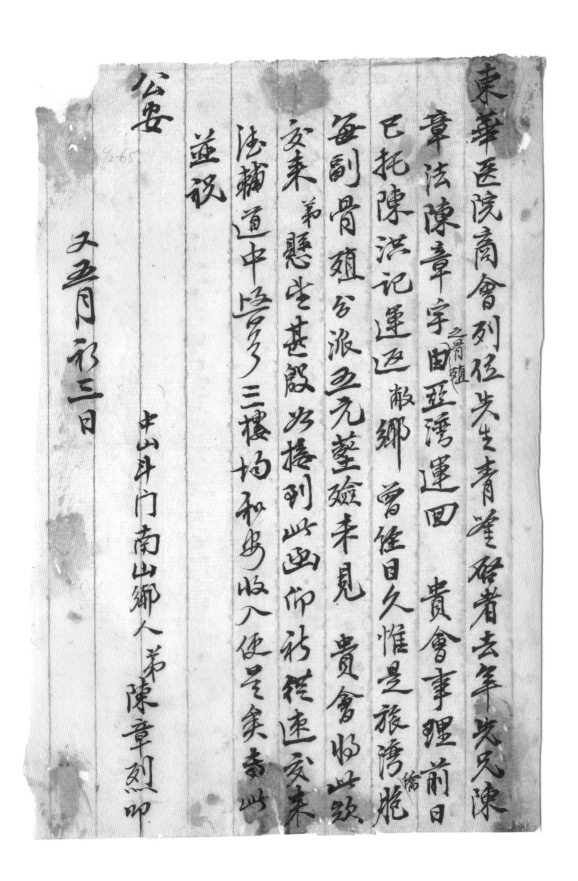

東華醫院商會列位先生青鋒諸君先兄陳

章法陳章宇之骨殖由亞灣運回　貴會事理前日

已托陳洪記運迴　敝鄉　曾隹日久惟是振灣艙僑

每副骨殖各派五元蓋蓋來見　貴會收此欵

安東　弟懸坐甚殷為捲列此函仰祈速交來

陸輔道中醫多三樓均和安收入便是矣專此

莊說

公安

又五月初三日　中山斗門南山鄉人弟陳章烈叩

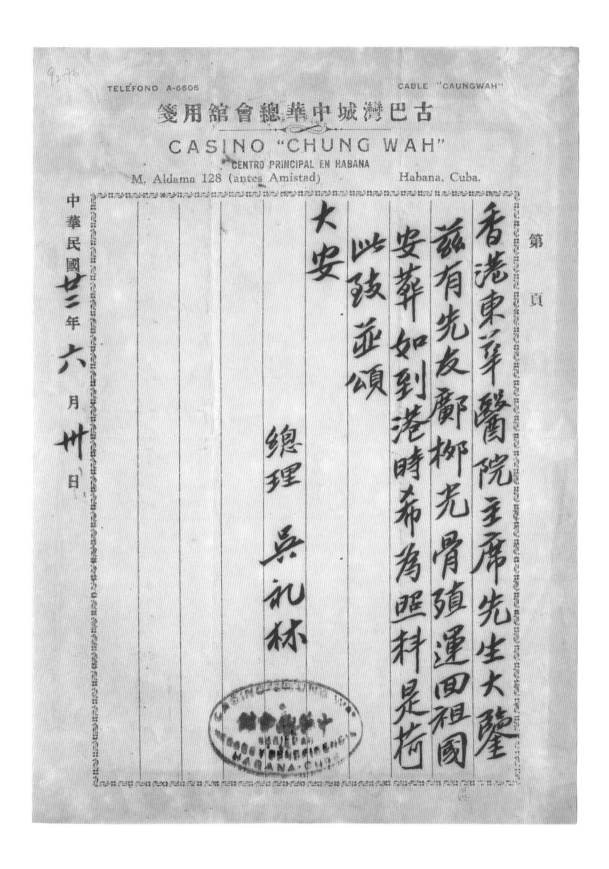

TELÉFONO A-6605　　　　　　　　CABLE "CAUNGWAH"

古巴灣城中華總會館用箋

CASINO "CHUNG WAH"
CENTRO PRINCIPAL EN HABANA
M. Aldama 128 (antes Amistad)　　　Habana, Cuba.

第頁

香港東華醫院主席先生大鑒

茲有先友鄺柳光骨殖運回祖國

安葬如到港時希為照料是荷

此致並頌

大安

總理 吳礼林

中華民國廿二年六月卅日

美國金山大埠廣利號致東華醫院信件

1933年10月28日

Telephone CHina 0017　　　　電話差拿〇〇一七號

金山大埠 廣利
都板街八百四十八號
Quong Lee & Company
848 GRANT AVENUE
SAN FRANCISCO, CALIF., U. S. A.

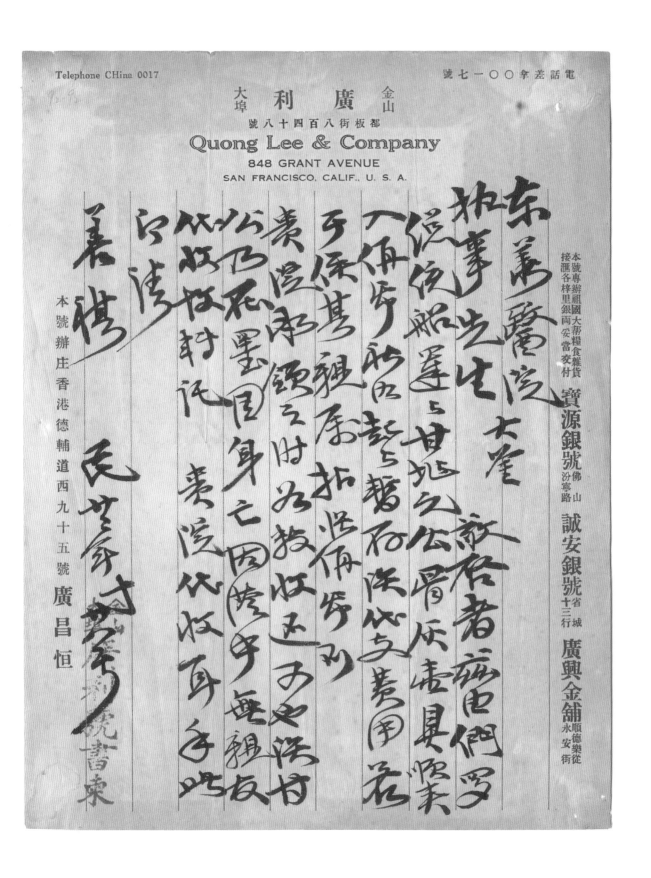

本號專辦祖國大帮糧食雜貨 接滙各梓里銀両妥當交付
寶源銀號 佛山汾寧路
誠安銀號 省城十三行
廣興金舖 順德樂從永安街

東華醫院 大鑒
執事先生 敬啟者 竊由[illegible]
院[illegible]船運乙甘[illegible]之位骨[illegible]具[illegible]
人[illegible]所因[illegible]暫存保[illegible]費用若
干保其親屬[illegible]
貴院承領之時[illegible]收[illegible]
公乃[illegible]身亡因[illegible]無親友
代收[illegible]託 貴院代收[illegible]
可[illegible]
善祺
民廿二年十月廿八日 廣利號書柬

本號辦庄香港德輔道西九十五號 廣昌恒

063
〈頁一〉

瓜地馬拉旅瓜華僑總會通告

1933年11月30日

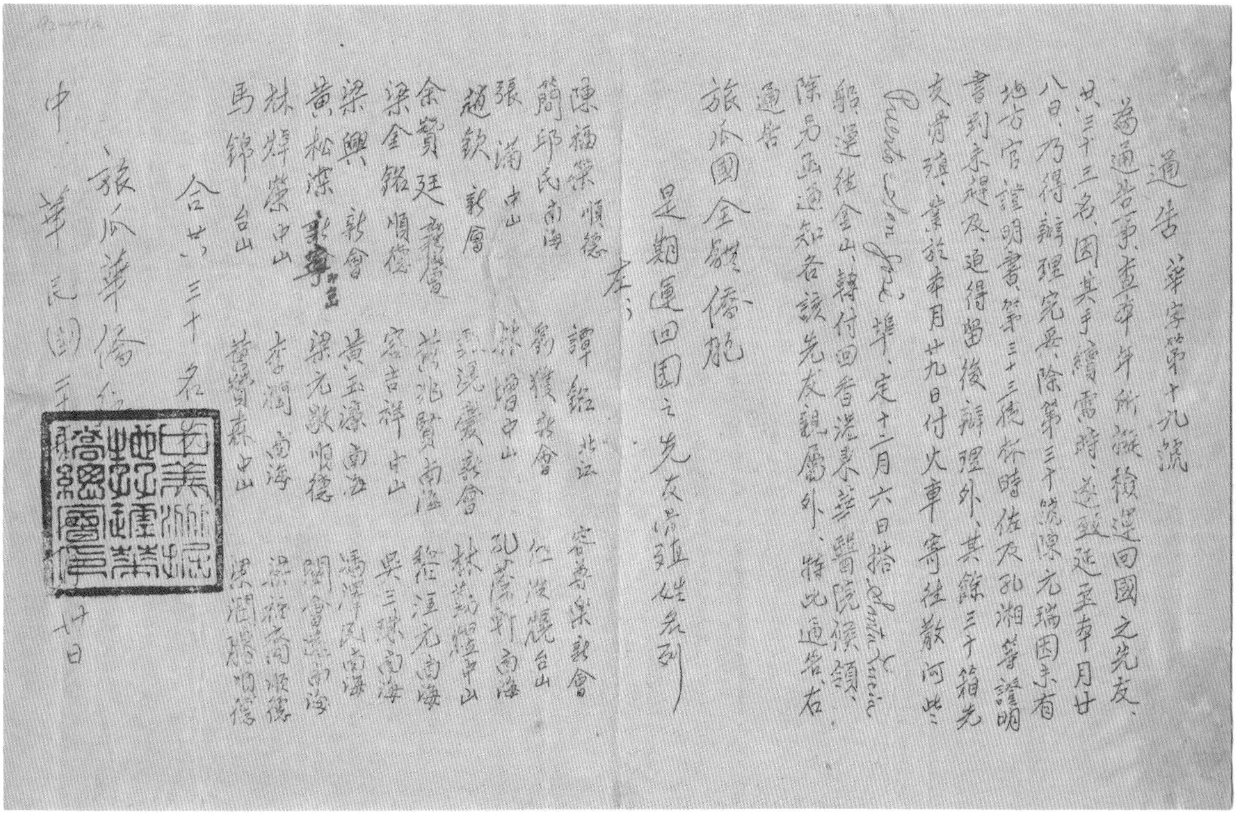
通告 華字第十九號

為通告事，查本年所擬檢運回國之先友，共三十三名，因其手續需時，遂致延至本月廿八日，乃得辦理完妥。除第三十號陳光瑞因未有地方官證明書，第三十三號林時佐及孔湘等證明書到未趕及，追得留後辦理外，其餘三十箱先友骨殖，業於本月廿九日付火車寄往散河些 Puerto San José 埠，定十二月六日搭船運往金山，轉付回香港東華醫院領，除另函通知各該先友親屬外，特此通告。右

通告

旅瓜國全體僑胞

是期運回國之先友芳名姓名列左：

陳福棠 順德
簡邱氏 南海
張滿 中山
趙欽 新會
余贊廷 新會
梁全銘 順德
梁興 新會
黃松深 新寧
林焯棠 中山
馬錦 台山
譚銘 北江
劉猴 新會
林增 中山
劉[illegible] 新會
黃兆賢 南海
容吉祥 中山
黃玉濂 南海
梁元啟 順德
李潤 南海
黃[illegible]森 中山
容帝樂 新會
伍[illegible] 台山
孔蔭軒 南海
林[illegible] 中山
羅渥元 南海
吳三[illegible] 南海
馮[illegible] 南海
關[illegible] 南海
梁[illegible] 順德
梁潤[illegible] 順德

合共三十名

旅瓜華僑總會

中華民國二十二年十一月卅日

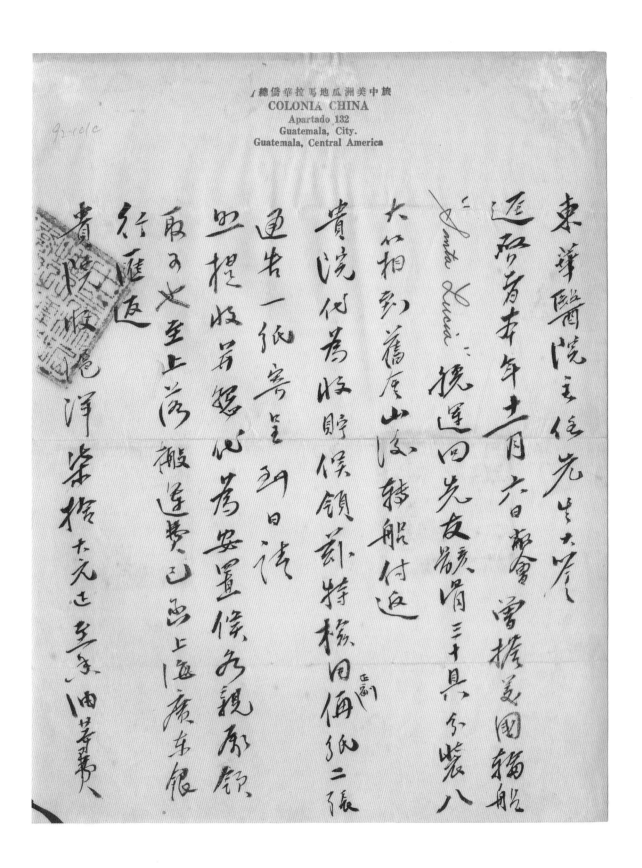

東華醫院主任先生大鑒

逕啓者本年十一月有幸曾搭美國輪船

Santa Lucia 揽運回先友骸骨三十具分裝八

大木箱到舊金山後轉船付運

貴院代為收貯候領並特檢回價紙二張

通告一紙寄呈到日請

即提收具憑心為安置候務祈原諒

再另文至上海搬運費已函上海廣東銀

行匯返

貴院棧租洋銀捌大元正至亲由華葬費

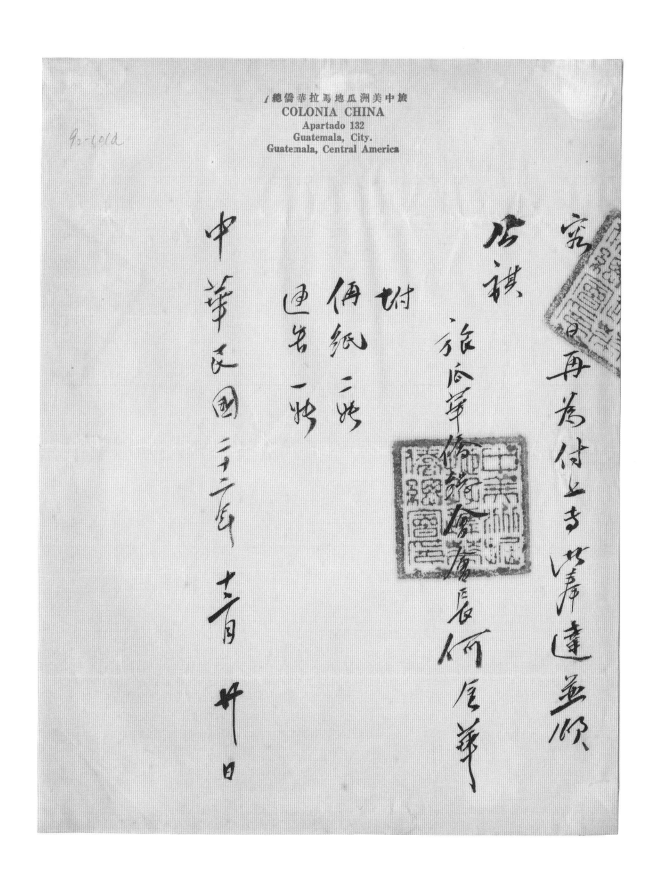

旅中美洲瓜地馬拉華僑總

COLONIA CHINA
Apartado 132
Guatemala, City.
Guatemala, Central America

敬再為付上寺災達善順、

公祺

旅瓜華僑總會會長 何信華

附

僑紙二件
匯名一件

中華民國三十二年六月廿日

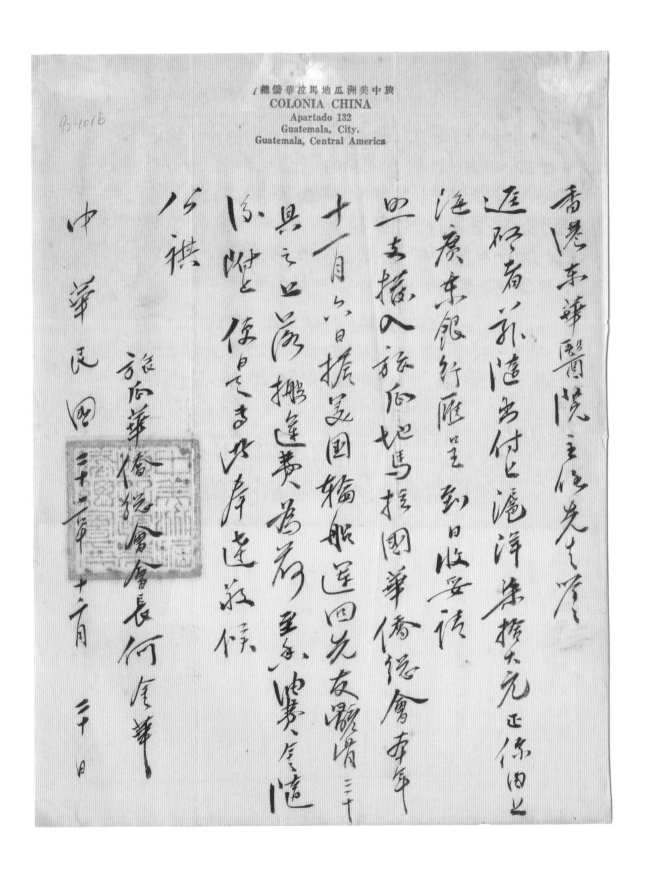

COLONIA CHINA
旅中美洲瓜地馬拉華僑總

Apartado 132
Guatemala, City.
Guatemala, Central America

香港東華醫院主任先生鑒：

逕啟者茲隨函付上滙洋柒拾夭元正係由上滙廣東銀行滙呈到日收妥請

即支撥入旅瓜地馬拉國華僑總會本年

十月六日撥交國輪船運回先友灝清三十具之已蕆搬運費並為善與費之慮

凡此保存之費凡費合慮

台祺

旅瓜華僑總會會長何全華

中華民國二十二年十二月二十日

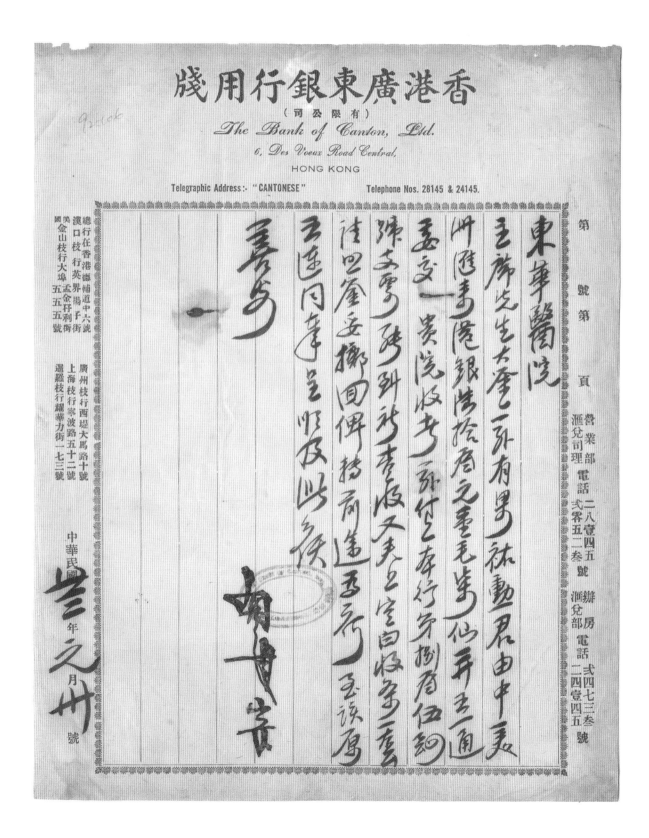

香港廣東銀行用牋
（有限公司）

The Bank of Canton, Ltd.

6, Des Voeux Road Central,

HONG KONG

Telegraphic Address:- "CANTONESE"　　　　Telephone Nos. 28145 & 24145.

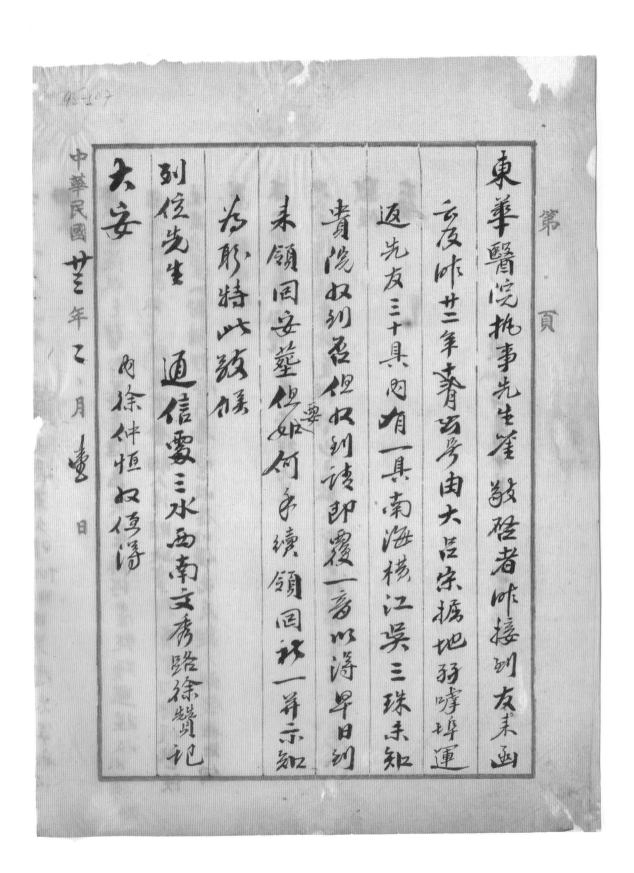

第一頁

東華醫院值事先生鑒 敬啓者咋接到友來函

云及咋廿三年春函号由大昌宗據地孖嘮埠運

返先友三十具因有一具南海橫江吳三珠未知

貴院収列否但収列請即覆一音以得早日到

未領回安葬但如何手續領回祈一芼示知

為耶特此敬候

列位先生 通信處三水西南文秀路徐贊記

大安

中華民國廿三年乙月 日

　内徐仲恒奴傳浮

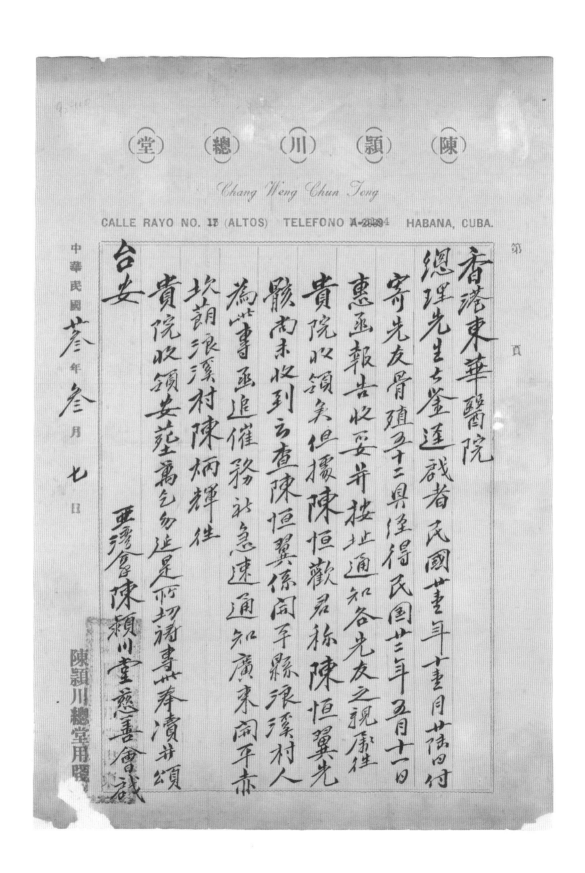

堂　總　川　穎　陳

Chang Weng Chun Tong

CALLE RAYO NO. 15 (ALTOS)　TELEFONO A-2094　HABANA, CUBA.

第　頁

香港東華醫院

總理先生大鑒迳啟者　民國廿三年舊曆正月廿六日付

寄先友骨殖五十三具逕得民國廿三年五月十一日

惠函報告收妥并按址通知各先友之親屬往

貴院收領矣但攄陳恒歡君稱陳恒翼先

骸尚未收到云查陳恒翼係開平縣浪溪村人

為此專函追催務祈急速通知廣東開平亦

坎頭浪溪村陳炳輝往

貴院收領妥速萬勿多延是所切禱專此奉瀆并頌

台安

中華民國廿三年　叁月　七　日

亞灣會陳穎川堂慈善會啟

陳穎川總堂用箋

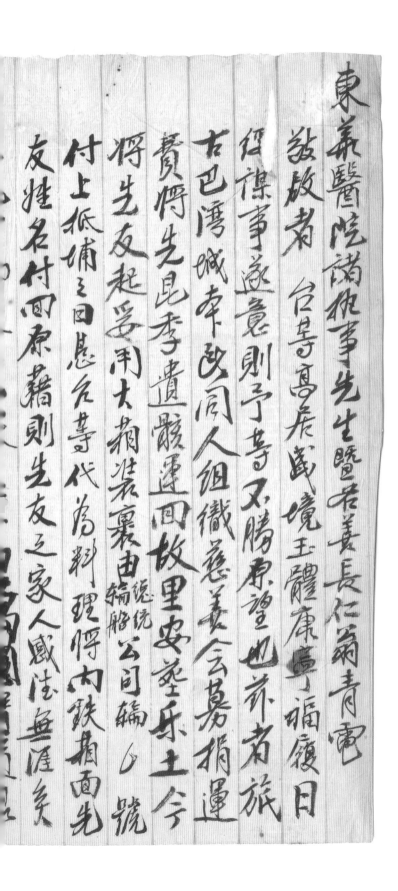

東華醫院諸執事先生曁若姜長仁翁青電

敬啟者　台壽高厪武境玉體康寧福履日

綏祺事遂意則予壽又不勝原望也茲者旅

古巴灣城本邑同人組織慈善會募捐運

費將先昆季遺骸運回故里安堂樂土今

將先友起妥用大箱裝裹由輪船

德統公司輪6號

付上抵埔之日懇乞壽代為料理將內鉄相面先

友姓名付回原籍則生友之家人感法無涯美

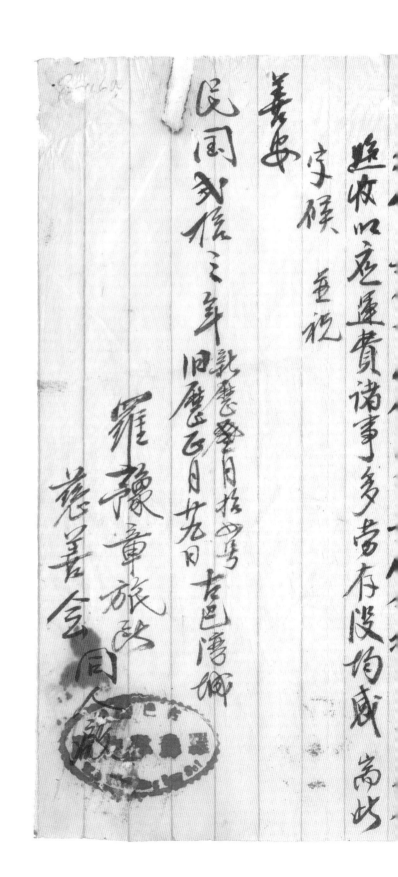

羅義穩字傳說先友　乃廣東開平縣月山堡羅村鄉

羅宗耀先友　乃廣東台山縣郡衙　金居村人氏

羅蕃翔先友　乃廣東開平縣南塘里人氏　吉安村人氏

羅沛軒先友　乃廣東開平縣月山堡羅村鄉　南塘里人氏

羅齊盛先友　乃廣東開平縣平岡村人氏　羅村鄉南塘里人氏

羅連協先友　乃廣東開平縣月山堡羅村鄉

羅文篤先友　乃廣東開平縣單水口月山堡羅村鄉

羅烈儀先支　乃廣東開平縣單水口月山堡羅村鄉　南塘里人氏

羅社真先友　廣東開平縣單水口月山堡羅村鄉　南塘里人氏

羅祺光先友　乃廣東開平縣單水口　鶴州里人氏

譚美閏先友　乃廣東新會坊人氏

伍連登先友　乃廣東台山何冲堡巷裡村人氏

伍洪喬先友　乃廣東台山端被朗堡　端棠村人氏

麥阿卓先友　乃廣東鶴山豪村木佳頭村人氏

以上先友共捐勸名印將付美之數　　長根之每

名先友黃給壹貴祖伍元尚有報付元作

為選賣股銀暫由之用

蒙先友名下有單水口散情向單水口

覺善堂還回以便若人領取壙丸

多勞

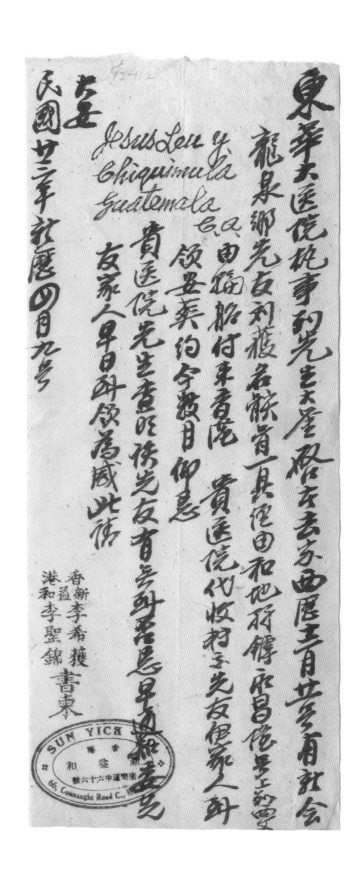

東華大醫院執事列先生大鑒敝李去家西曆五月廿三日於本会

龍泉鄉先友利獲名骸肯一具煩由和砲行轉來昌隆長工前曾

由搭船付來貴港 貴醫院代收轉交先友便家人到

領安葬約今数目仰惠

貴醫院先生查照俟先友有人到若是早頂轉交

友家人早日到領為感此托

Jesus Leu y
Chiquimula
Guatemala
C.A.

香新李希獲
港益
和李聖錦 書寄
東

民國廿三年新歷四月九号

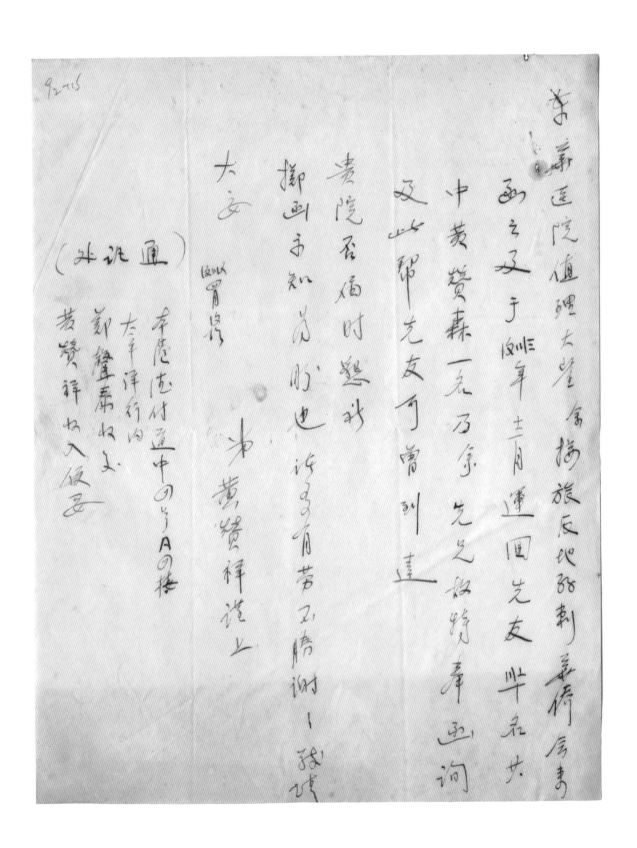

貴院值理大鑒 今據旅居他邦割棄僑居事

函之吾叔于昨年十月運回先友骸骨

中黃贊森一名而余先先故骸骨亦询

及此郑先友可曾到達

撷函示知花附遂許多有苦不勝謝一謝謝

貴院吾儕时懇求

大安

黄贊祥謹上

（通訊处）

本港港仔道中の号A の楼

郑鐙森故友

黄贊祥收入便是

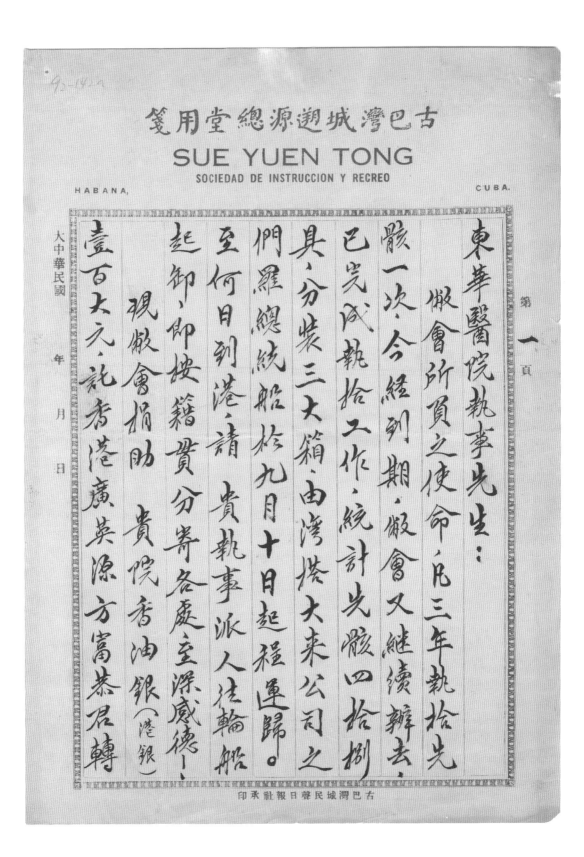

古巴灣城遡源總堂用箋
SUE YUEN TONG
SOCIEDAD DE INSTRUCCION Y RECREO
HABANA,　　　　　　　　　　　　CUBA.

第 一 頁

東華醫院執事先生：

敝會所員之使命，民三年執拾先
骸一次，今經到期，敝會又繼續辦去，
已完成執拾工作，統計先骸四拾捌
具，分裝三大箱，由灣搭大來公司之
門羅總統船於九月十日起程運歸。
至何日到港，請貴執事派人往輪船
起卸，即按籍貫分寄各處，至深感德，
現敝會捐助 貴院香油銀（港銀）
壹百大元，託香港廣英源方富恭 君轉

大中華民國　　年　　月　　日

古巴灣城民聲日報社承印

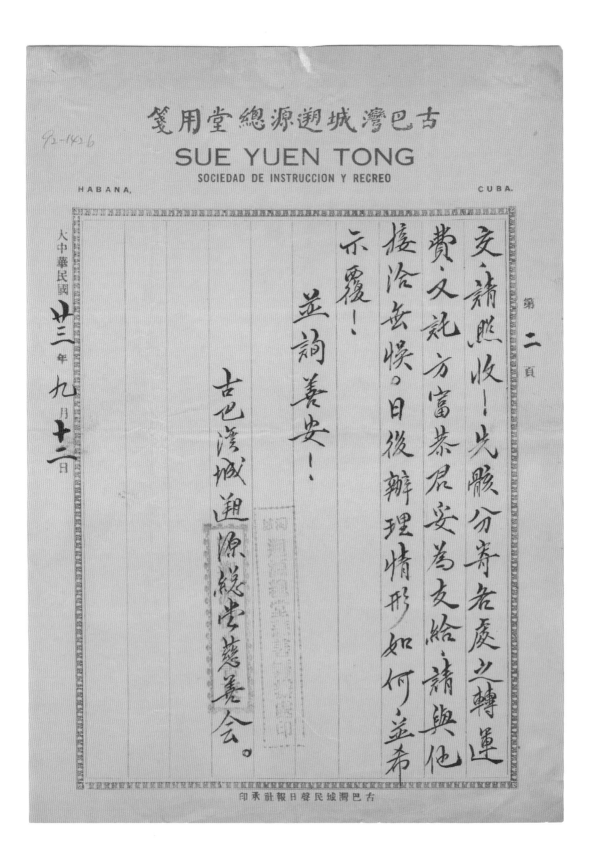

篁用堂總源邅城灣巴古
SUE YUEN TONG
SOCIEDAD DE INSTRUCCION Y RECREO
HABANA,　　　　　　　　　　　　　　CUBA.

第二頁

交、請照收！共骸分寄各處之轉運
費、文託方富恭君妥為支給、請與他
接洽、匰候。日後辦理情形如何、並希
示覆！

　　　益韵善安！

　　古巴灣城邅源總堂慈善会。

大中華民國卅三年九月十二日

古巴灣城民聲日報社承印

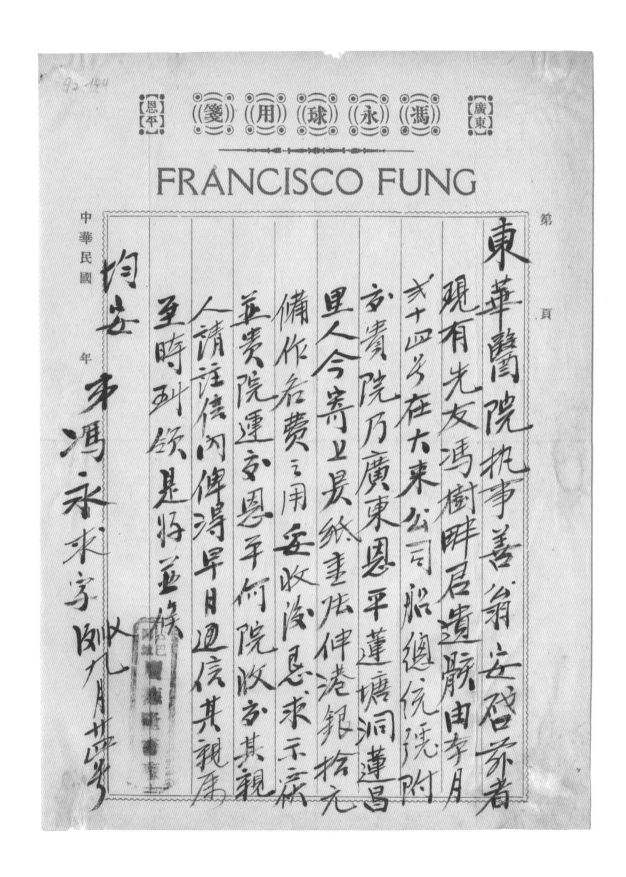

【恩平】【廣東】
【箋】【用】【球】【永】【馮】

FRANCISCO FUNG

東華醫院執事善翁安啓亦者

現有先友馮樹畔君遺骸由本月

廿四號在大來公司船總候院附

交貴院乃廣東恩平蓮塘洞蓮昌

里人令寄之長紙連佐俾港銀拾元

備作各費言用至收後恩求示幾

華貴院運之恩平俾院收方其親

人請注信內俾得早月迴信其親屬

至時到領是將蓋族

均安

中華民國　　年

事　馮永球來字　即九月廿四号

東華醫院總理先生公鑒 運柩費現蒙付

上香油伸港銀拾大元到日查收區〻微物

是扅不誠事係蒙因遠境耳請求見諒

弟蒙覩在西人長生三店亦理先友回國內家

俱係蒙親屬畫俱林立維先友通平蜆崗

堡水皆村人畫俱林舉旋先友台山城東南安

村人在古巴搭大來公司值頭船西歷九月廿日

啟程到時蒿請貴 總理依照該先友箱

面縣節村君分茂代蒙寄家人領收按葬祖國

以慰死者在天之靈生者亦殊深感謝此請

　　　董頌

　羣安

　　　　　　　開平人 林立惇
　　　　　旅吉　台山人 林德濃仝叩

大中華民國廿三集 九月廿四日

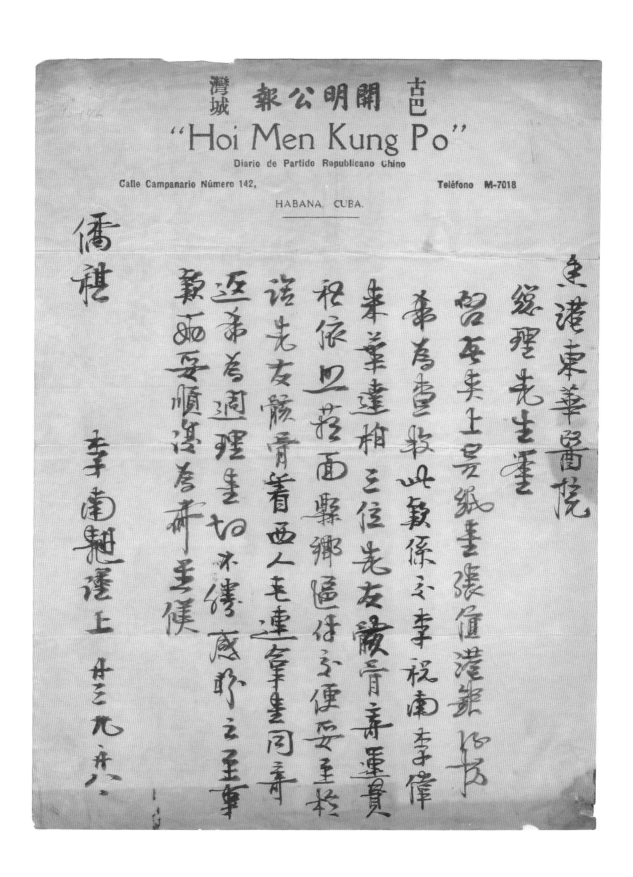

灣城　報公明開　古巴
"Hoi Men Kung Po"
Diario de Partido Republicano Chino

Calle Campanario Número 142,　　　　Teléfono　M-7018

HABANA, CUBA.

東港東華醫院

總理先生鈞鑒

啟者茲上是紙壹張值港銀比方

弟為曹牧此剪係承李祝南李偉

來華達相三位先友嚴骨壽運費

祀依四莊面縣鄉區任承便安壹移

諸先友嚴骨著西人毛運拿壹壹同壽

逐弟為週理壹切未儀感於之壹事

覆而安順淺者耑壹僕

僑祺

李南翹運上　廿三九 · 廿八

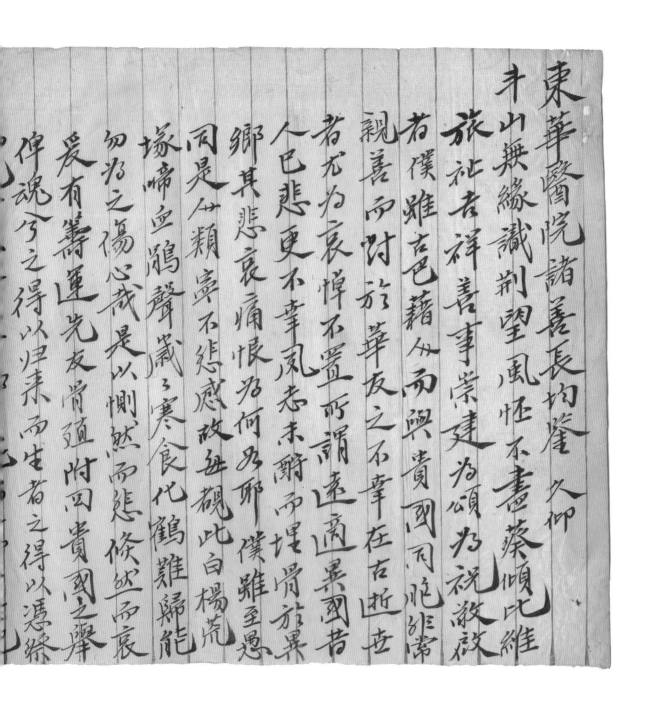

東華醫院諸善長均鑒　久仰
斗山無緣識荊望風怀不盡蔡頃此維
旅祉者祥善事業建為頌為祝敬啟
者僕雖古巴藉人而與貴國同胞比常
親善而付於華友之不幸在古逝世
者尤為哀悼不置所謂遠通異國昔
人巴悲更不幸凡志未酬而埋骨於異
鄉其悲哀痛恨為何乃耶僕雖至愚
同是仙類寧不怵感故母觀此白楊荒
塚啼血鵑聲歲歲寒食代鶴難歸能
勿為之傷心哉是以惻然而哀
爰有籌運先友骨頣附回貴國之舉
停魂兮之得以旧秉而生者之得以憑祭

貴院完竣茲將儀紙一張附呈

貴院僕棄知　貴院專辦理慈善事務為

宗旨如抵埗之日請即起運先友之骨殖

暫時存貯於　貴院計南各先友之骨殖

頭共弍拾具如費用幾何請向各先

友之戚屬收回便妥僕業已去函通知

各先友之親人到港領收矣臨風佈憶

不盡欲言倘逢郵便望惠德音肅此

並候

善祺

一九三四、十、三

古巴國僑弟磨連金手謹上

中國黃植鴻致東華醫院信件

1934年10月22日

東華醫院善長執事先生大鑒敬啓者茲接灣城遡源堂慈
善會通告謂九月十日將灣城先骸付船歸國未悉現在
抵步否如抵步後未悉貴院代轉（先友原籍）與各縣慈善機關候親
屬領回或要親到貴院領取因弟先父遺骸亦由該帮
運回係書（黃文禧順德第七區龍山海口埠忠興社）弟今
不在順德居住遷往南海九江落籍故先父遺骸亦欲運回
九江安葬如貴院代運各先友回原籍者請將該殘骨殖
運回（南海）九江可也切勿運往順德深盼貴院賜函示知俾得明
白領取手續不勝感銘之至矣專此敬候
台安
弟黃植鴻謹上 廿三年十月廿二日
通訊處南海九江大正坊怡昌押交弟收可也

秘魯旅秘中山會館致東華醫院信件

1934年10月24日

旅秘中山會館用箋

SOCIEDAD CHUNG SANG HUY CUN

LIMA - Calle San Cristobal N. 804 - Apartado N. 1455 - PERU

92153

東華醫院
諸位執事先生大鑒 敬啟者 茲有先友孫公耀生遺
骸一具 由弟經手 於安文是期日本輪船墨洋丸号
運返
貴院 於該日輪抵步時 請即派人將該骸起上 代為
存下 候孫耀生之子孫培居秉是期美輪隨後到
時 當來
貴院領取 帶返家鄉安葬 倘另遲延孫培居收抵
此孫培到院時 請照該原票收領為荷 專此奉瀆
並候
公安
附載紙一張 請查照收入
弟歐陽安上
廿三年十月廿四日

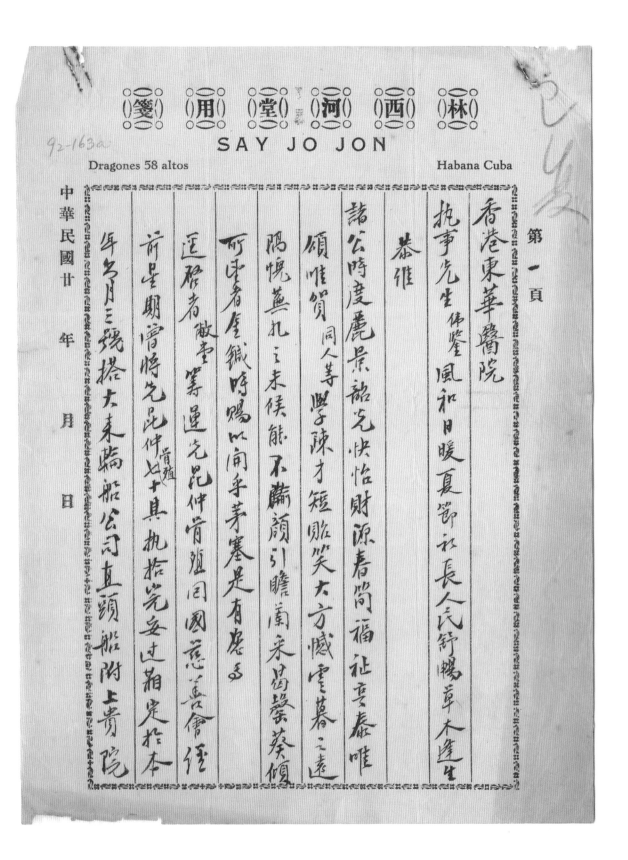

（箋）（用）（堂）（河）（西）（林）

SAY JO JON

Dragones 58 altos　　　　　　　　　Habana Cuba

第一頁

香港東華醫院

執事先生偉鑒 風和日暖夏節社長人民舒暢草木逢生

恭維

諸公時度麗景韶光快怡財源春筍福祉重泰唯

頌唯賀 同人等 學陳才短貽笑大方憾雲暮之遠

隔愧蕪札之未候能不覥顏引瞻南采菌縈葵傾

阿乎者金鍼時賜以南乎茅塞是有磨子

逕啟者 敬查籌運先昆仲骨殖回國慈善會經

前星期曾將先昆仲七十具执拾完妥过箱定拾本

年八月三號搭大來輪船公司直頭船附上貴院

中華民國廿 年 月 日

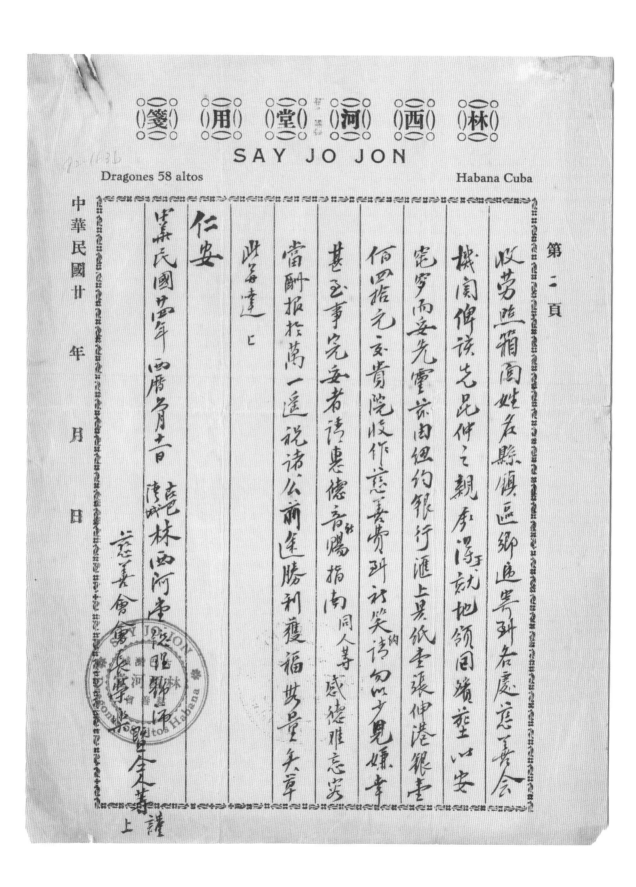

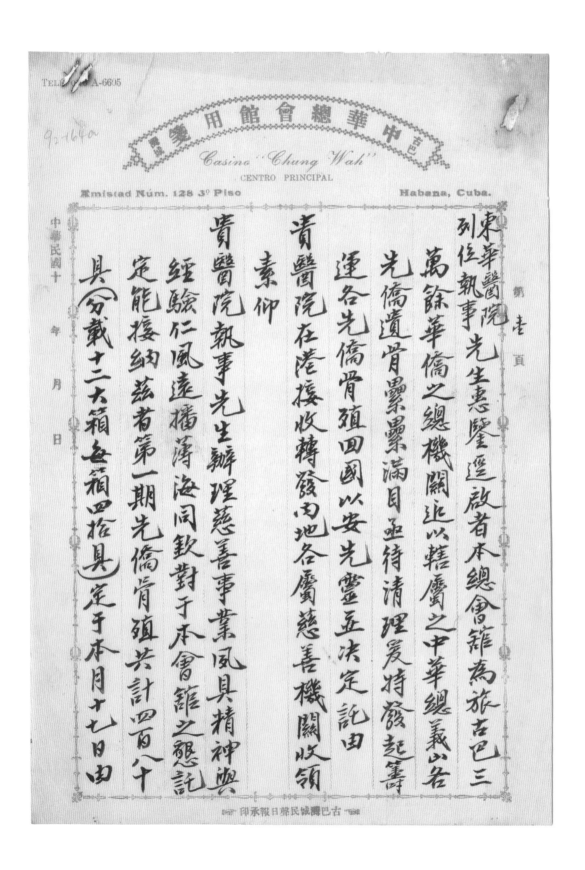

TEL. A-6605

中華總會館用箋
Casino "Chung Wah"
CENTRO PRINCIPAL

Amistad Núm. 128 3º Piso　　　　　Habana, Cuba.

第壹頁

東華醫院
列位執事先生惠鑒逕啟者本總會籌為旅古巴三
萬餘華僑之總機關近以轄屬之中華總義山各
先僑遺骨纍纍滿目亟待清理爰特發起籌
運各先僑骨殖回國以安先靈並決定託由
貴醫院在港接收轉發內地各屬慈善機關收領
素仰
貴醫院執事先生辦理慈善事業風具精神與
經驗仁風遠播薄海同欽對于本會館之懇託
定能接納茲者第一期先僑骨殖共計四百八十
具(分載十二大箱每箱四拾具)定于本月十七日由

中華民國十　年　月　日

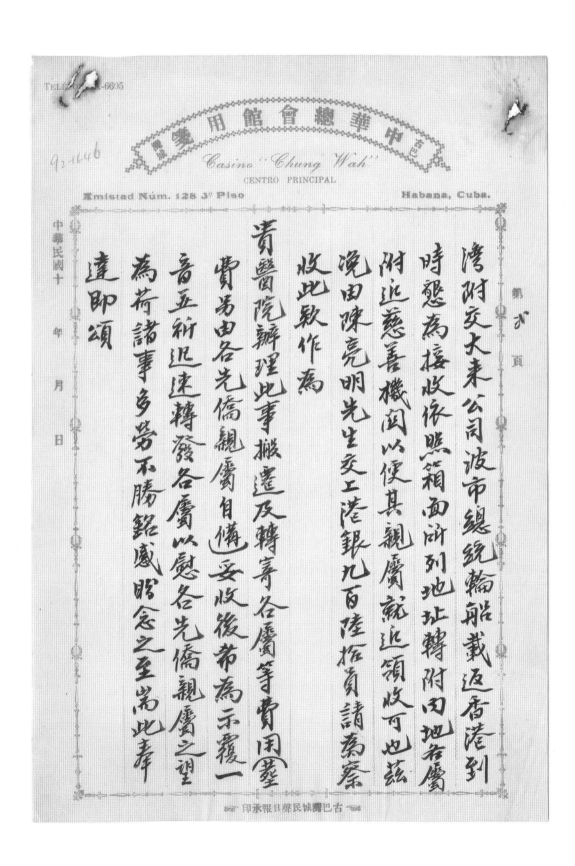

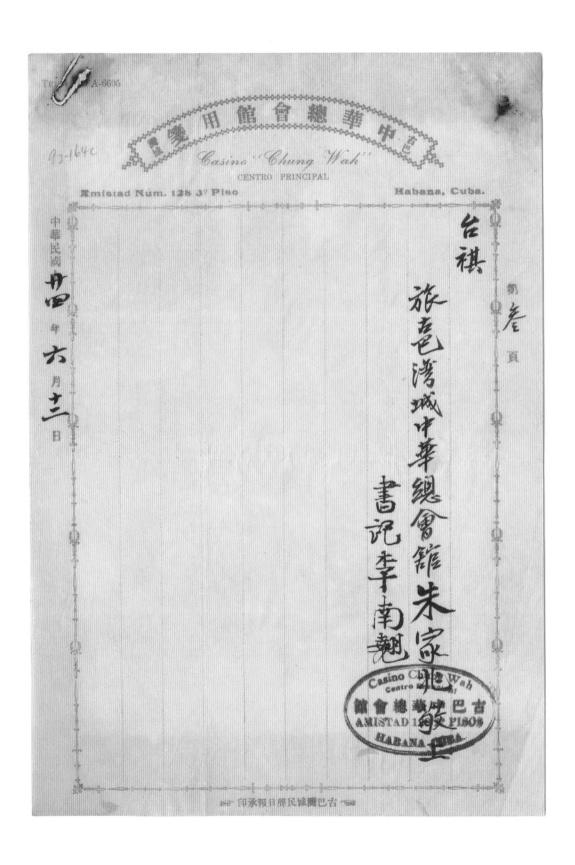

中華總會館用箋

Casino "Chung Wah"

CENTRO PRINCIPAL

Amistad Núm. 128 3º Piso　　　　　　　　Habana, Cuba.

台祺

旅吉邑灣城中華總會舘朱家駝

書記李南翹

中華民國廿四年六月十二日

第參頁

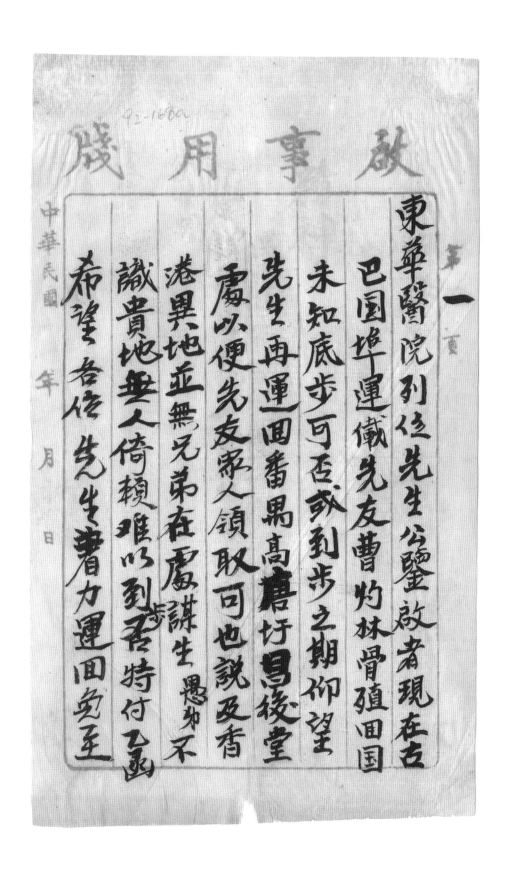

箋用事啟

東華醫院列位先生公鑒 啟者現在古
巴圓埠運僝先友曹灼林骨殖回國
未知底步可否 或到步之期仰望
先生再運回番禺高塘圩昌後堂
屬以便先友家人領取可也 說及香
港異地並無兄弟在屬謀生 愚弟不
識貴地無人倚賴難以到君特付乙函
希望吾信 先生費力運回覓至

中華民國　年　月　日

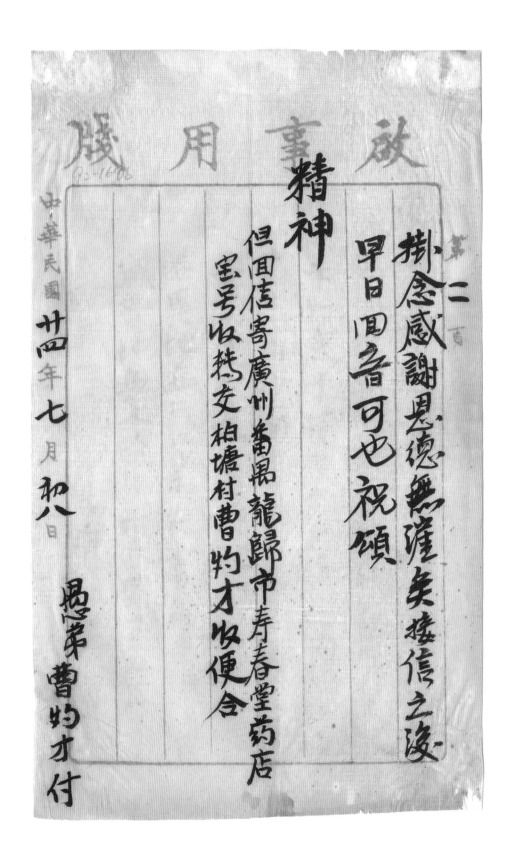

啟用牋

精神

掛念感謝恩德無涯矣接信之後

早日回音可也祝頌

但因信寄廣州番禺龍歸市壽春堂藥店

寶號收轉交柏塘村曹灼才收便合

中華民國廿四年七月卅八日

愚弟曹灼才付

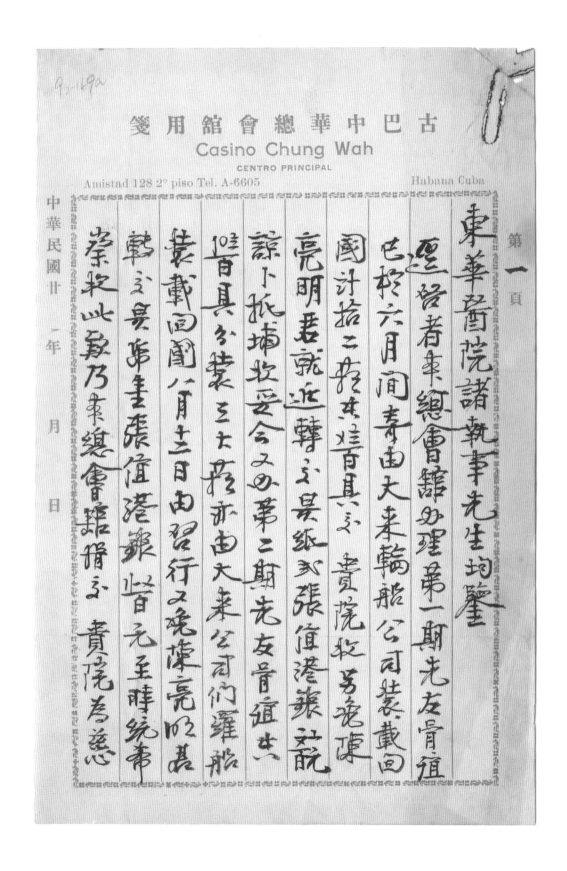

笺用舘會總華中巴古

Casino Chung Wah

CENTRO PRINCIPAL

Amistad 128 2° piso Tel. A-6605 　　　　Habana Cuba

第一頁

東華醫院諸執事先生均鑒

逕啟者東總會舘辦理第一期先友骨殖

已於六月間壽由大來輪船公司裝載回

國計拾二抬來裝骨具云　貴院投另冤陳

亮明君就近轉交吳紙武張値港銀琥

諒卜抵埗收受合乃第二期先友骨殖共

晉具分裝三大箱亦由大來公司們羅船

裝載回國八月十二日由啟行又冤陳亮明甚

乾之景車查張値港銀晉元至時統希

榮啟此冤乃東總會舘晉示 貴院為慈

中華民國廿一年　月　日

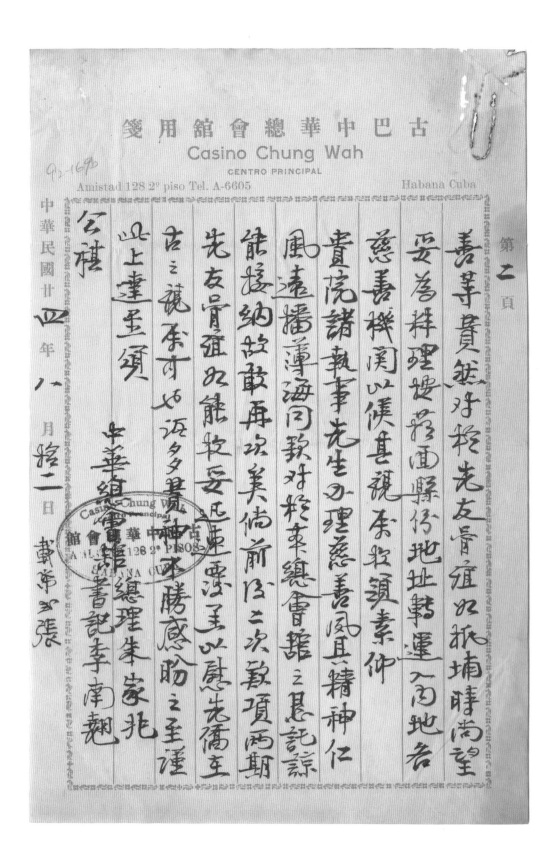

第二頁

善耆貴懿好稱先友骨殖如抵埔時尚望

妥為辦理轉回縣份地址轉運入兩地舍

慈善機關以候甚視奉寄領素仲

貴院諸執事先生為理慈善風氣精神仁

風遠播薄海同致好稱東總會諸之懸記諒

能接納故敢再次美僑前陰之次致項兩期

先友骨殖如能敉妥民運要陔玉以慰先僑主

古之視奉寸也海外其神本勝感盼之至謹

此上達玉頌

公祺

　　　　中華總會館

　　　　　　總理朱家兆

　　　　　　　書記李南翹

中華民國廿四年八月拾二日　載葫乃張

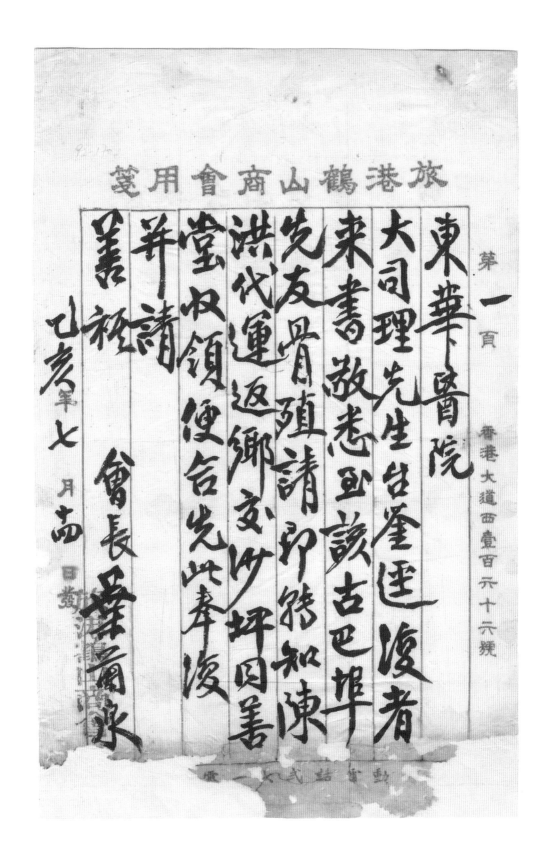

旅港鶴山商會用箋

第一頁

香港大道西壹百六十六號

東華醫院
大司理先生台鑒 逕復者
來書敬悉 茲查古巴埠
先友骨殖請即轉知陳
洪代運返鄉亥沙坪因善
堂收領 便合先此奉復
並請
善祉

會長 呂譜眉泉

乙亥年七月 日發

香港台山商會致東華醫院信件

1935年8月12日

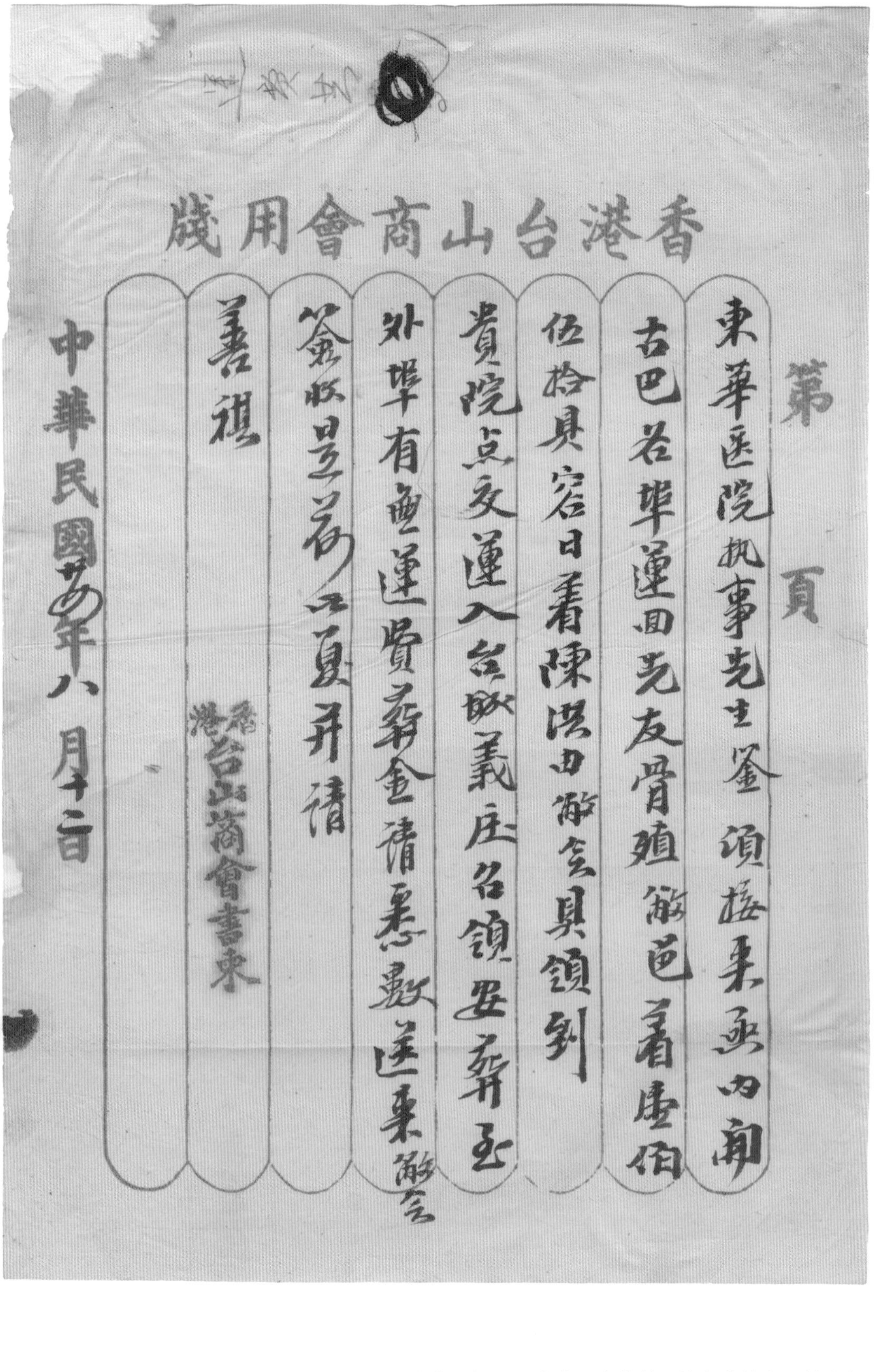

香港台山商會用牋

第　頁

東華医院執事先生鑒　頃接來函內開

古巴若華運回先友骨殖敝邑著歷伯

伍拾具容日着陳洪由敝会具領到

貴院點交運入台城義庄各領安葬至

外埠有無運遞費每金請悉數送來敝会

簽收是荷　此覆并請

善祺

香港台山商會書柬

中華民國廿四年八月十二日

香港駐港中山僑商會所致東華醫院信件

1935 年 8 月 14 日

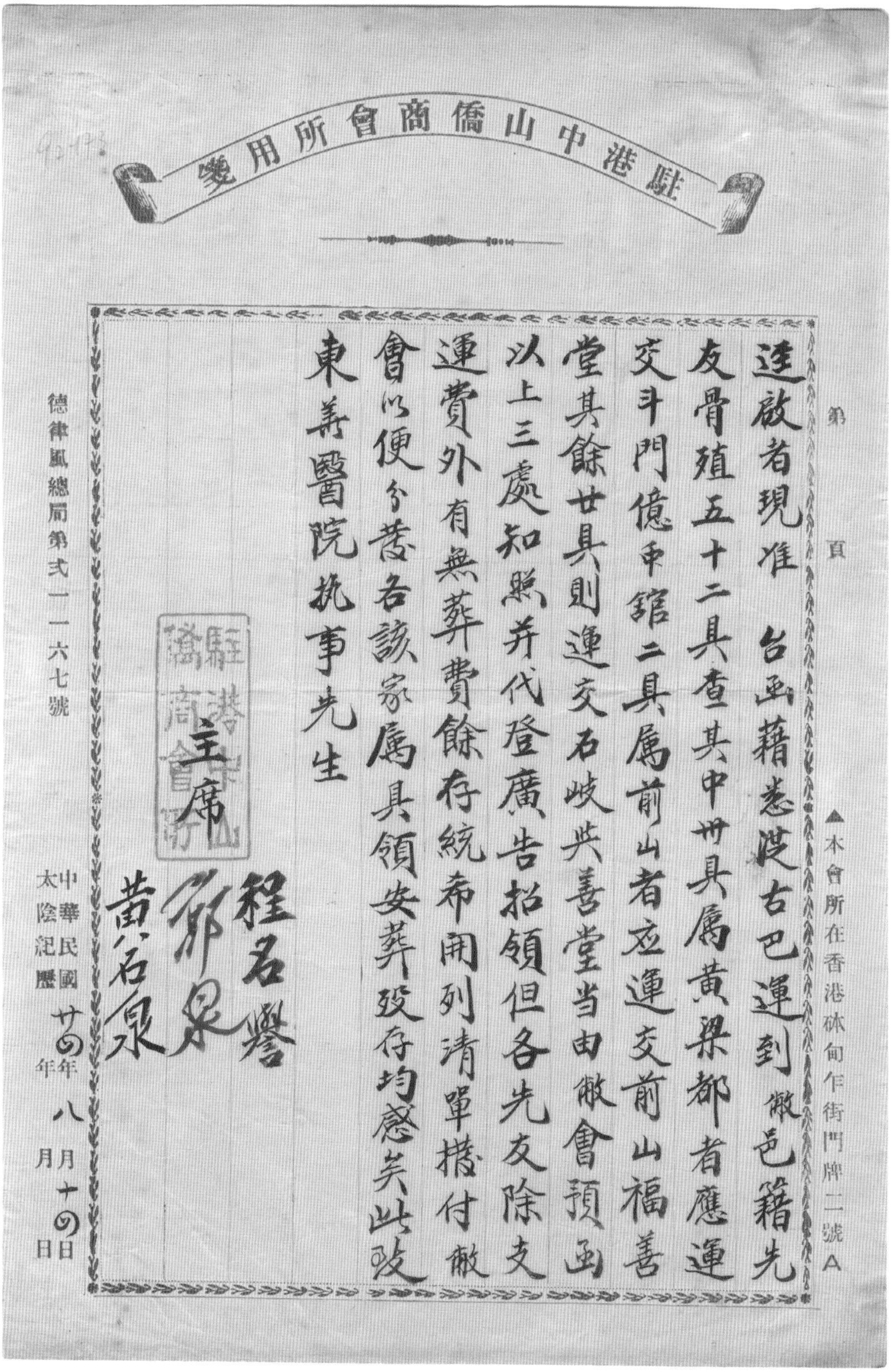

駐港中山僑商會所用箋

第　頁

逕啟者現准　台函藉悉從古巴運到敝邑籍先友骨殖五十二具查其中卅具屬黃梁都者應運交斗門億平館二具屬前山者應運交前山福善堂其餘廿具則運交石岐共善堂当由敝會預函以上三處知照并代登廣告招領但各先友除支運費外有無葬費餘存統希開列清單撥付敝會以便分登各該家屬具領安葬歿存均感矣此致

東華醫院執事先生

駐港中山僑商會所
主席　程君譽
鄧泉
黃石泉

中華民國廿四年八月十四日
太陰紀歷　年　月　日

德律風總局第弍一一六七號

▲本會所在香港砵甸乍街門牌二號A

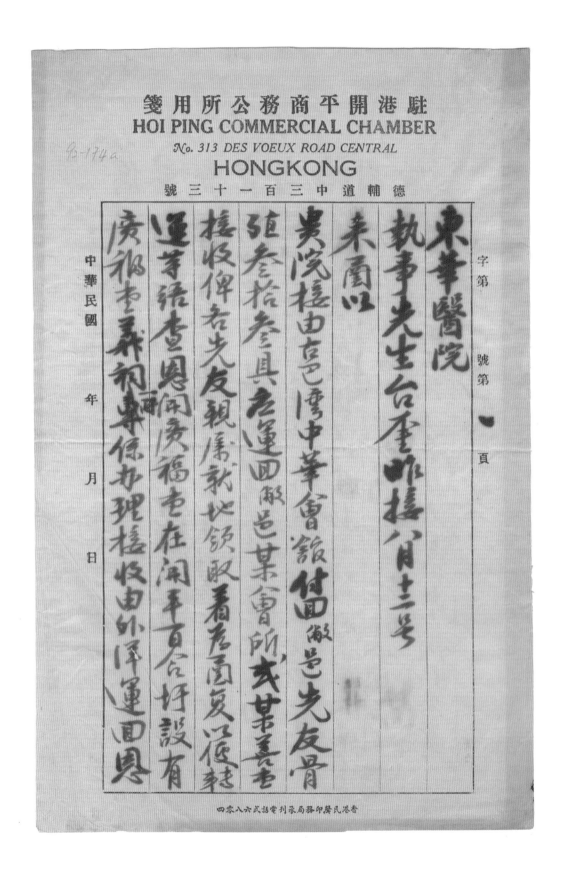

箋用所公務商平開港駐
HOI PING COMMERCIAL CHAMBER
No. 313 DES VOEUX ROAD CENTRAL
HONGKONG
號三十一百三中道輔德

東華醫院

執事先生台鑒昨接八月十二號

來函以

貴院擬由古巴運回中華會館付回敝邑先友骨

殖叁拾叁具交運回敝邑某會所戈某善舉

接收俾各先友親屬就地領取看骨囊以便轉

運各縣查恩囑僑福專在閘平百合好設有

廣福壽莊祝安保辦現接收由外洋運回恩

中華民國　年　月　日

149　中南美洲西歸先友

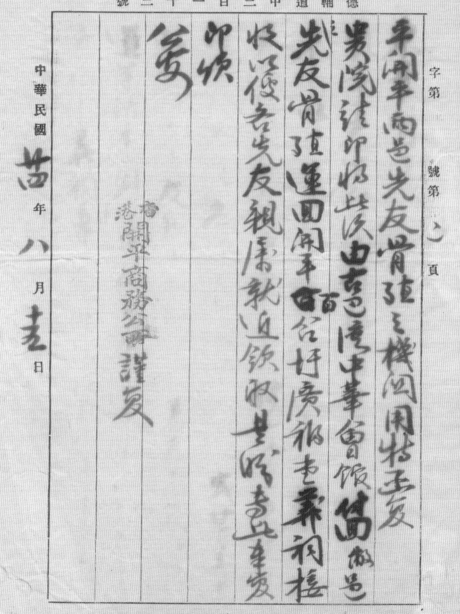

駐港開平商務公所用箋
HOI PING COMMERCIAL CHAMBER
No. 313 DES VOEUX ROAD CENTRAL
HONGKONG
德輔道中三百一十三號

字第　　　頁
號第（二）頁

中華民國　茂年 八 月　圭日

港開平商務公所　謹复

香港民聲印務局承印電話式六八零四

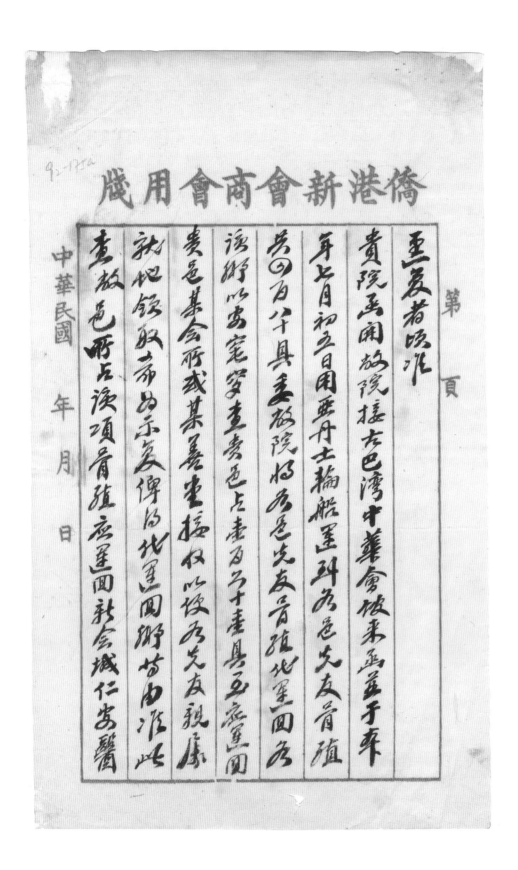

僑港新會商會用牋

第　頁

逕覆者頃准

貴院函開　敬覆接查巴灣中華會館來函藍于本

年七月初五日用亞丹士輪船運到敝邑先友骨殖

共四百廿具蒙敝院招為敝邑先友骨殖地運回各

該鄉以安窀穸查敝邑先友骨殖四十畫具五疱運回

貴邑基會亦某善畫接枚以後為先友親屬

就地領致一帝易示衷傳為北運回鄉茍由准此

查故邑爾占該項骨殖運回新會城仁安醫

中華民國　年　月　日

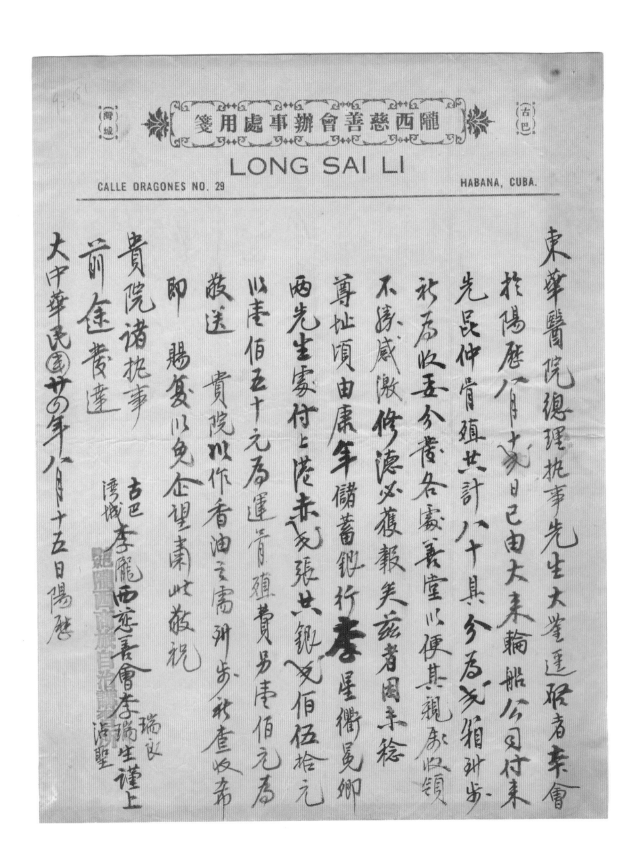

隴西慈善會辦事處用箋

LONG SAI LI

CALLE DRAGONES NO. 29　　　　　　　HABANA, CUBA.

東華醫院總理執事先生大鑒逕啓者本會
於陽歷八月十一日已由大來輪船公司付來
先昆仲骨殖共計八十具分爲兩箱計廿步
祈爲收䎹分䎹各寄囊堂以便其親來收領
不勝感激修德必獲報美茲者圅來稔
尊址項由康年儲蓄銀行李星衢覓卿
西先生寄付上港赤尅張共銀壹佰伍拾元
以壹佰五十元爲運費殖費易壹佰元爲
敬送 貴院以作香油之需卅步祈查收斋
即 賜復以兔企望肅此敬祝
貴院諸執事
前途䎹達
　　　　　古巴
　　　　　灣城李隴西慈善會李瑞生謹上
即　　　　　　　　　　　瑞良
大中華民國廿四年八月十五日陽歷

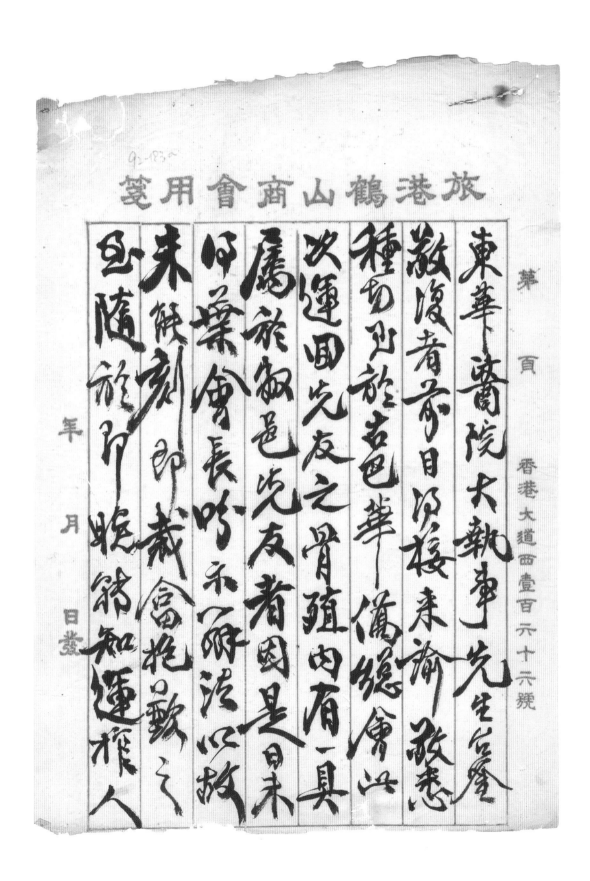

旅港鶴山商會用箋

東華醫院大執事先生台鑒

敬復者本日准接來諭敬悉

種回敝邑華僑總會此

次運回先友之骨殖內有一具

屬於敝邑先友者因是日未

回藥會長吩示佢法以故

未能刻即裁奪抱歉之

至隨於眈翁細知運棺人

年　月　日發

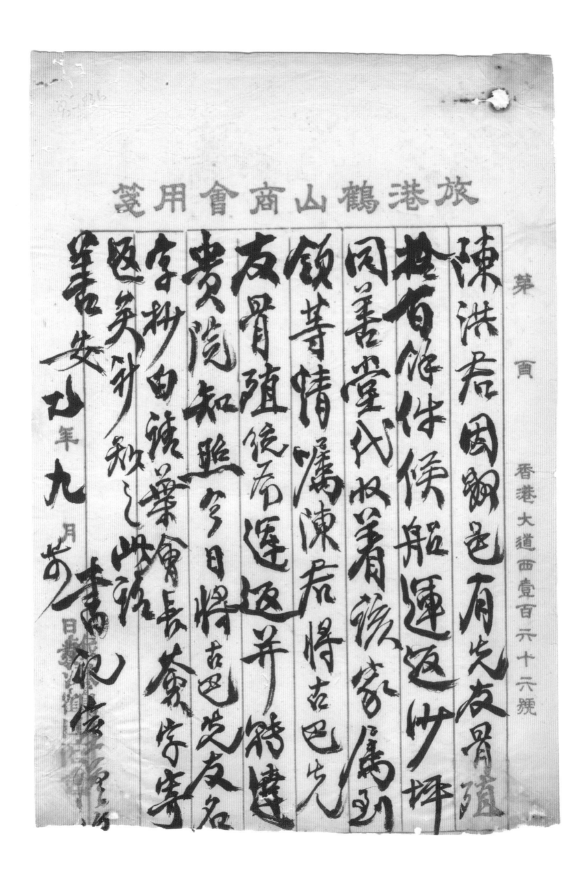

旅港鶴山商會用箋

華頁　香港大道西壹百六十六號

陳洪若因鋼邑有先友骨殖

港百餘件侯船運返沙坪

同善堂代收著孩家屬到

領等情屬陳若情古巴先

友骨殖後居還返並特遣

貴院知照今日將古巴先友名

字抄由諒藥會長奏寄

區英分敘之此流

善安山年九月荀

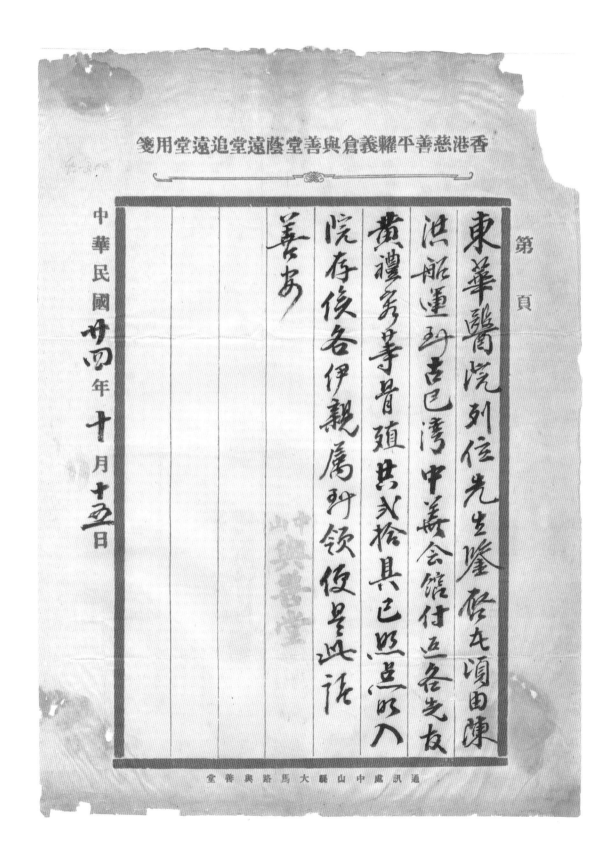

香港慈善平耀義倉與善堂蔭遠堂追遠堂用箋

第　頁

東華醫院列位先生鑒 啟者頃由陳
洪船運到吉巴灣中華會館付上各先友
黃禮等骨殖共貳拾具已照品明入
院存俟各伊親屬到領便是此託
善安

　　　　　中山與善堂

中華民國廿四年十月十五日

通訊處中山縣大馬路與善堂

東華醫院

執事先生台鑒昨連有士者

大函拜悉種切查悉敝處向來接到外埠恵善

機關付來失友骨殖各名單及安葬費印金係付印

失友名單傳遞問葬費付回開單百合好做查義

祠分別給領同時將失友名單寧開恩西射

吾持市貴眾妥方檀賑以便各失友親屬周知

到欲凡外埠恵善機閒並兼葬費付回此辦查

二每具獲給葬費貳元以安窀穸杴

合好做去舞初清時呈曾以姓名別闹

刻付去便做去現當手接到先友名單並煌付印

開將五號

貴院即將及歷月普匯備芭席之先友骨殖

上字其姓名籍貫查核示意下俾得付印事四

備芭席叩臨八佈以便去先友親屬週知到領去所

書此奉懇並祈

台安

愚 廣福堂書束 伍志芸

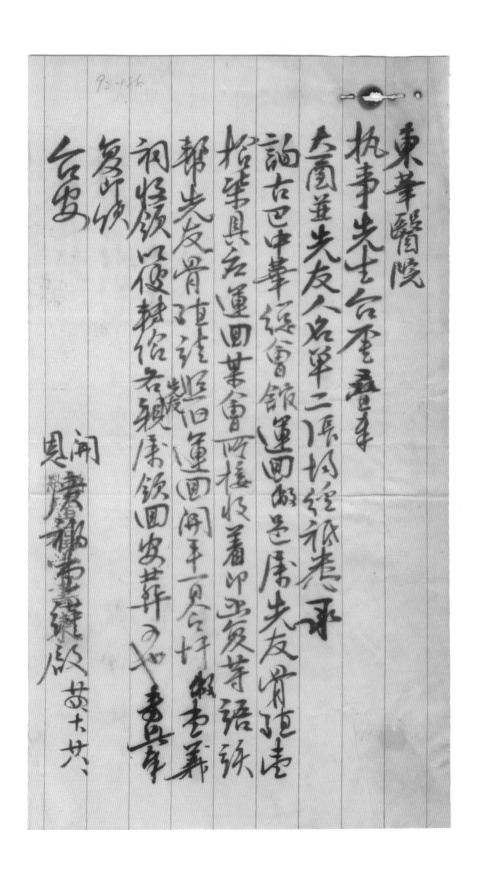

東華醫院

執事先生台電台鑒

大團善失友人名單二張均經敝巷承

詢古巴中華經會館運囬骸邑屬失友骨殖

拾柴具台運囬葉會兩接收着即亟發葬語孫

郡失友骨殖連辛運囬畢一頁祭计敝書義

祠怦領以便耕俗各親屬領囬安葬之如嘉

复所領

台安

開恩廣福堂謹啟 黄大共

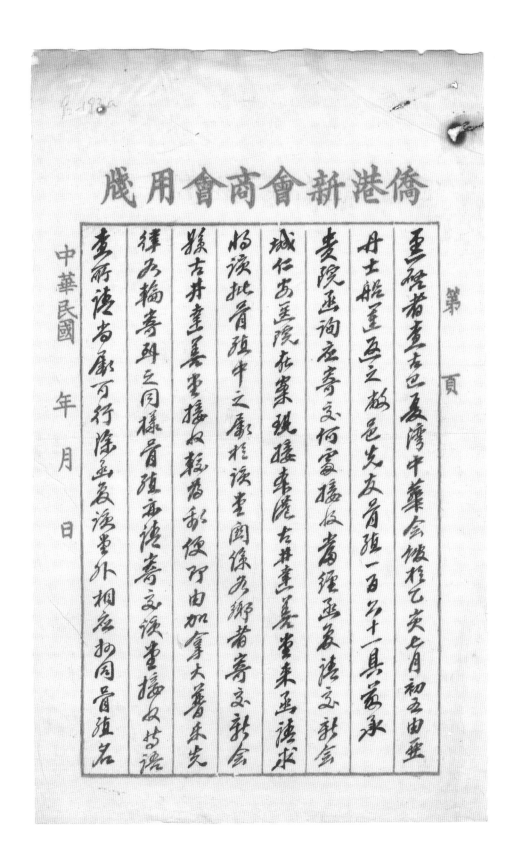

僑港新會商會會用牋

第頁

逕啟者查古巴夏灣中華會館撥於乙亥六月初五由亞
丹士船運至之敝邑先友骨殖一百六十一具蒙承
貴院函詢在寄交何寓撥收嵩經函覆語之新會
城仁安醫院在案現據本港古井達善堂來函語求
將該批骨殖中之屬於該堂團係屬於鄉者寄交新會
擬古井達善堂擬收報為永便刃由加拿大普佛先
將所輪壽殖之同樣骨殖並語壽交領堂撥收哲語
查所語壽者尚可行隨函套議當外相應抄同骨殖芳名

中華民國　年　月　日

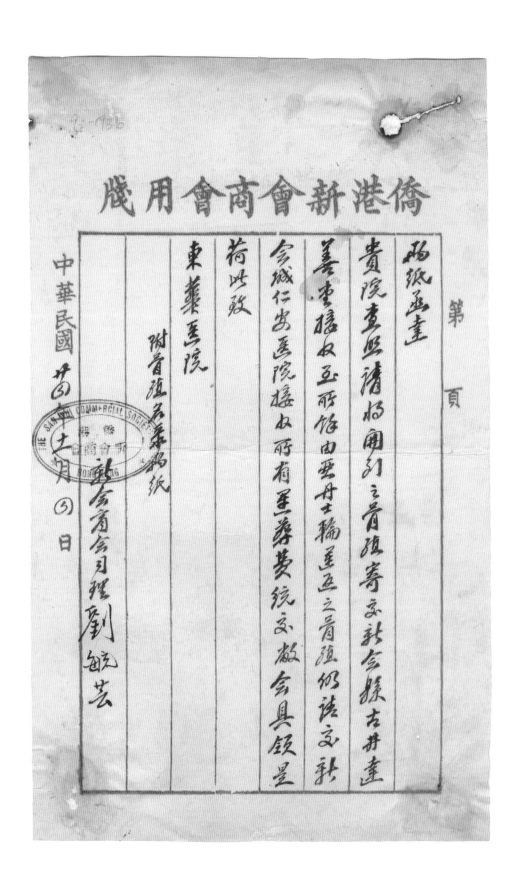

僑港新會商會會用牋

第　頁

逕啟者

　　貴院素照請將用引之骨殖壽衣敬心移交古井達

　　善堂接收並所餘由西丹士輪運返之骨殖仍請交新

　　會城仁安醫院接收所有運費統由敝會具領呈

　　荷此致

東華醫院

附骨殖名單一紙

中華民國廿四年十二月初三日
　　　　　　敝會首會司理劉鑑芸

中國南海佛山救濟院方便所致東華醫院信件

1935 年 11 月 7 日

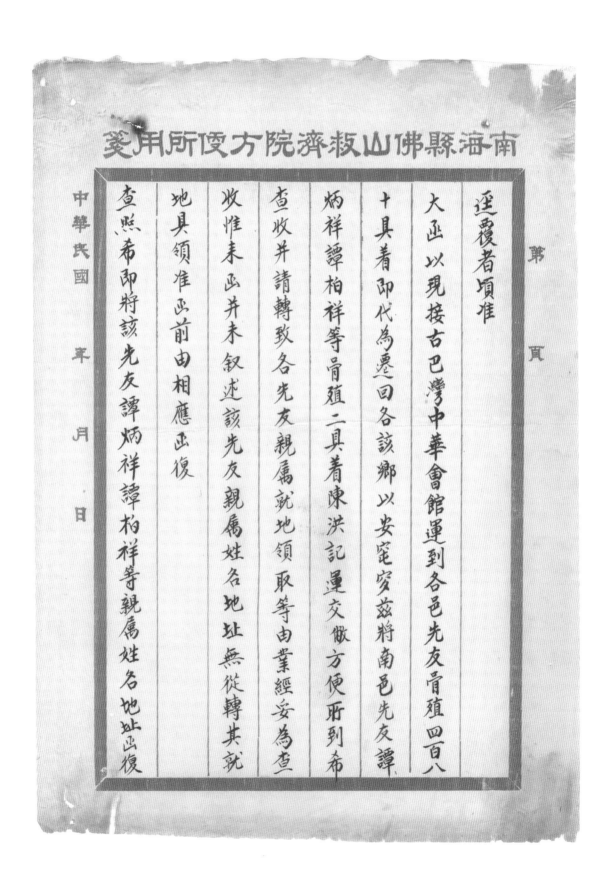

南海縣佛山救濟院方便所用箋

第　頁

逕覆者頃准

大函以現接古巴灣中華會館運到各邑先友骨殖四百八

十具着即代為轉回各該鄉以安窀穸茲將南邑先友譚

炳祥譚柏祥等骨殖二具着陳洪記運交徹方便所到希

查收并請轉致各先友親屬就地領取等由業經妥為查

收惟未函并未叙述該先友親屬姓名地址無從轉其就

地具領准函前由相應函復

查照希即將該先友譚炳祥譚柏祥等親屬姓名地址函復

中華民國　　年　　月　　日

南海縣佛山救濟院方便所用箋

第　頁

過所以凴分別轉知就近領回安葬爲荷此致

東華醫院

列位執事

南海縣佛山救濟院方便所
（即原日佛山方便醫院）

啟

中華民國　卅　年十一月　七　日

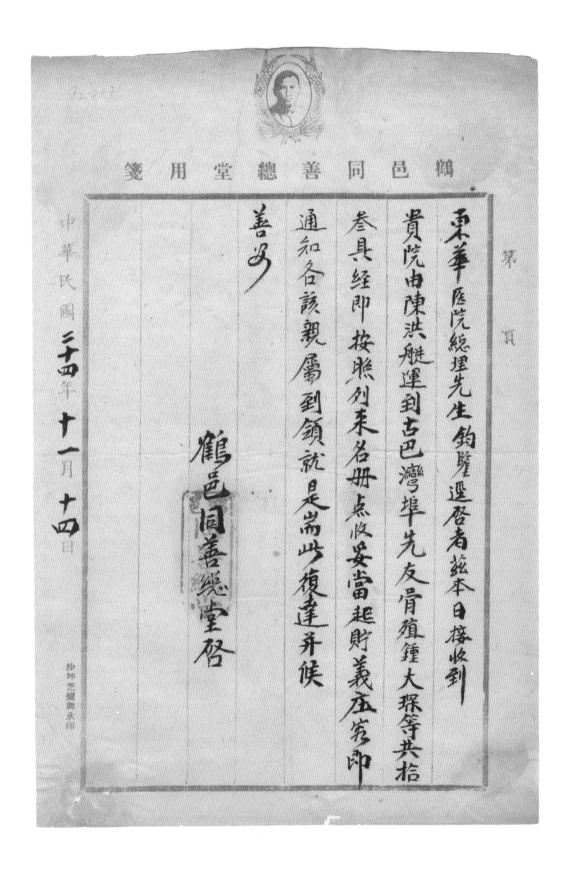

箋用堂總善同邑鶴

第　頁

東華醫院總理先生鈞鑒逕啓者茲本日接收到
貴院由陳洪艇運到古巴灣埠先友骨殖鍾大琛等共拾
叁具經即按照列來名冊點收妥當起貯義庄安即
通知各該親屬到領就是耑此復達並候
善安

鶴邑同善總堂啓

中華民國二十四年十一月十四日

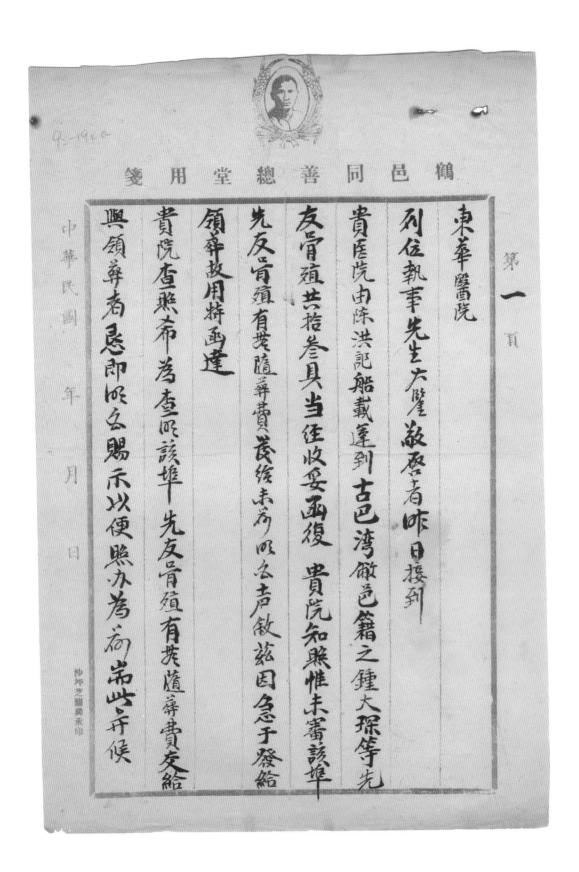

箋用堂總善同邑鶴

東華醫院

列位執事先生大鑒　敬啟者昨日接到

貴醫院由陳洪記船載運到古巴灣僑邑籍之鍾大探等先

友骨殖共拾叁具當即收妥函復　貴院知照惟未審該埠

先友骨殖有否隨葬貴養給來前以免去聲敘茲因急于發給

領葬故用特函達

貴院查照希為查明該埠先友骨殖有否遺葬貴交給

興領葬者懇即見賜示以便照辦為荷　專此奉候

中華民國　年　月　日

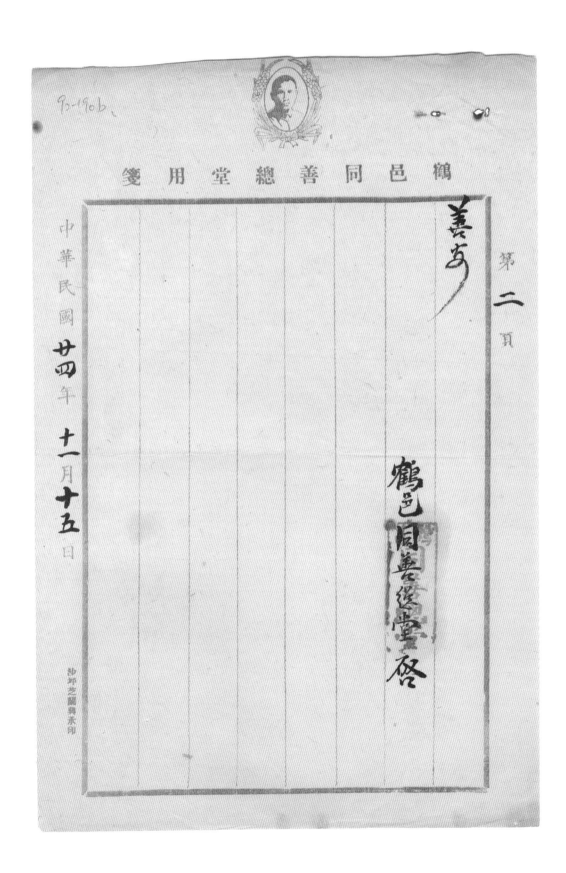

9-190b.

鶴邑同善總堂用箋

善安

第二頁

鶴邑同善堂啟

沙邊老蘭堂承印

中華民國廿四年十一月十五日

鶴邑同善總堂用箋

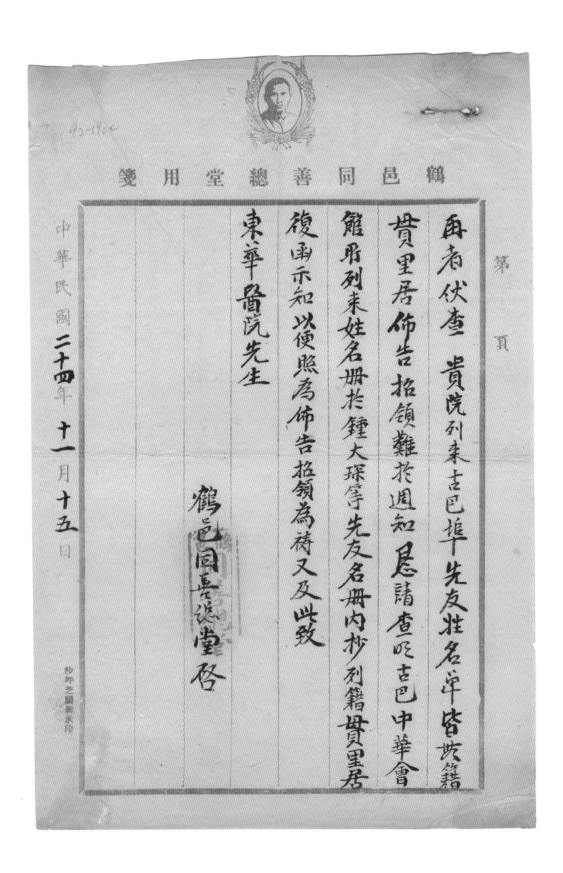

第　頁

再者伏查 貴院列來古巴埠先友姓名单皆缺籍

貫里居佈告招領難於週知 懇請查呢古巴中華會

館即列來姓名册於鍾大琛等先友名册內抄列籍貫里居

復函示知以便照為佈告招領為禱又及此致

東華醫院先生

中華民國二十四年十一月十五日

鶴邑同善總堂啟

抄邨芝蘭與承印

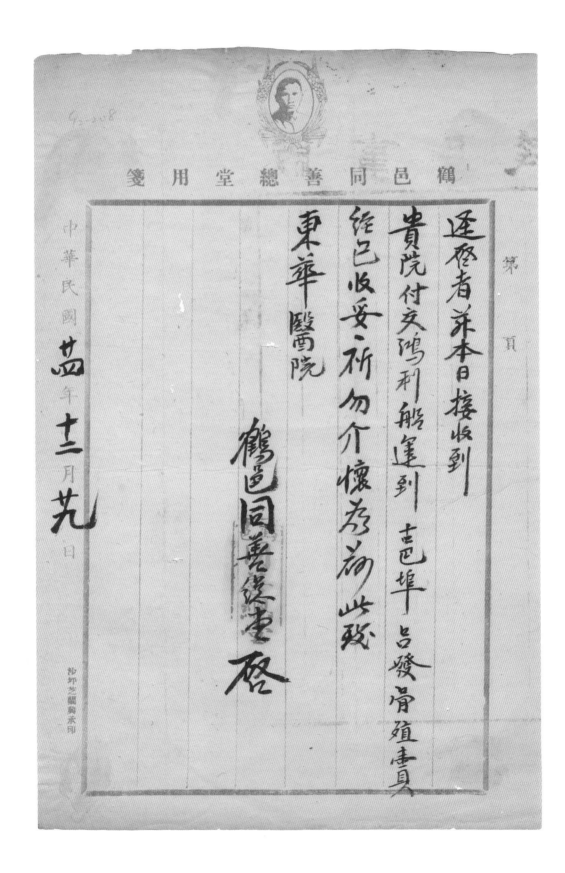

鶴邑同善總堂用箋

第　頁

逕啟者并本日接收到
貴院付交鴻利船運到 邑埠 吕發骨殖書責
經已收妥 祈勿介懷為荷 此致

東華醫院

鶴邑同善總堂　啟

中華民國廿四年十二月廿九日

沙坪芝蘭閣承印

北美洲西歸先友

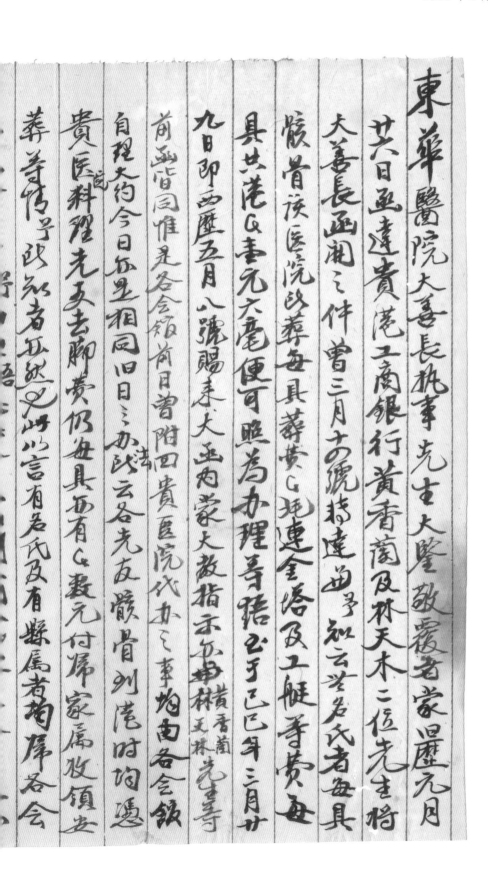

東華醫院大善長執事先生大鑒 敬覆者蒙復歷元月

廿二日函達 貴港工商銀行黃香蘭及林天木二位先生將

大善長函開之件曾三月十四號持達並承知云若氏者每具

骸骨按醫院改葬每具蔣黃G坭連金塔及工艇等費每

具共港G壹元六毫便可興為辦理等語公于己巳年三月廿

九日即西歷五月八號賜來大函內蒙大教指示辦事均兩念領

前函皆同惟是各會領前日曾附四 貴醫院代辦之事均兩念領

自現大約今日並是相同日三辦政云各先友骸骨列港時均應

貴醫料理先友去脚費仍每具西有G壹元付歸家屬收領並

葬等情早政知者並欲及此以言有若氏及有縣屬者相舉各會

遺骸橫佈荒野牛羊踐踏閗潤者見者莫不慘然惻惜是以吾就地

左右相近之廣籌些數項挑捨遺骸改塟者有各有縣各有姓名將云魂

有歸乘亨家人之祭祀但各有姓名各縣各會銀在廣自行領回

自辦支理安葬芸若乎二人擔負惟指定芸若名氏者芸人承領者方敢

直意求清辦法而已仍其着人列各廣符尋其有遺骸之姓名

者仍求各人列來報名及各縣屬由此立廣收領或报有止址者尚有空村

四家人之波領交勝過義地之安葬也此事將實情报工仍當

一人擔負火船載脚及医院代方安葬之費二筹受时何月何日何船到

回尾自當早日付上先友三為册及芸若氏每當列明何處箱及其具數之

复寄芸及箱头滬之芸寄此时故工恐气以为康法不忘端此呈

上並請

公安　氏國六年五月初六日即西歷卅六月十三滬　弟　梅雄文鞠躬

美國向田金山三藩市　奉

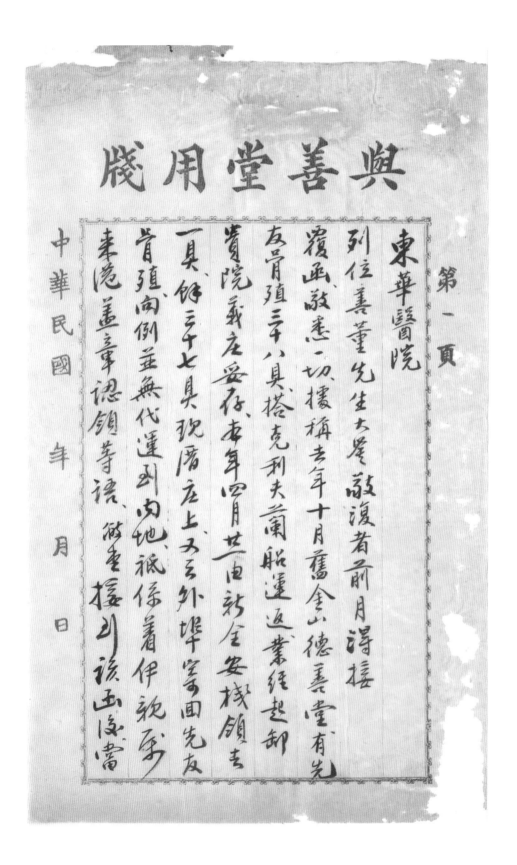

興善堂用牋

第一頁

東華醫院

列位善董先生大鑒敬復者前月得接
覆函敬悉一切據稱去年十月舊金山德善堂有先
友骨殖三十八具搭克利夫蘭船運返業經起卸
貴院義庄妥存本年四月共由新金安棧領去
一具餘三十七具現屠左上云云外埠等函先友
骨殖向例並無代運到內地祇係着伊親屬
來港蓋章認領等語俟重接到該函後當

中華民國　年　月　日

興善堂用牋

第二頁

即將興意轉達各先友親屬部之以便磋商茲
接該款辱又素微電漢及查各埠先友首頒
多有付返　貴院轉運辦電代存多數在候
伊親屬到鎖安葬　今法各善電絕無運費
交革　貴院轉運內地勢必無法代送今
將　貴院付返原玉轉佈諸各先友親
辱速候舨和法善電無運費付回
貴院文并非微電有三意當難泒沛不

中華民國　年　月　日

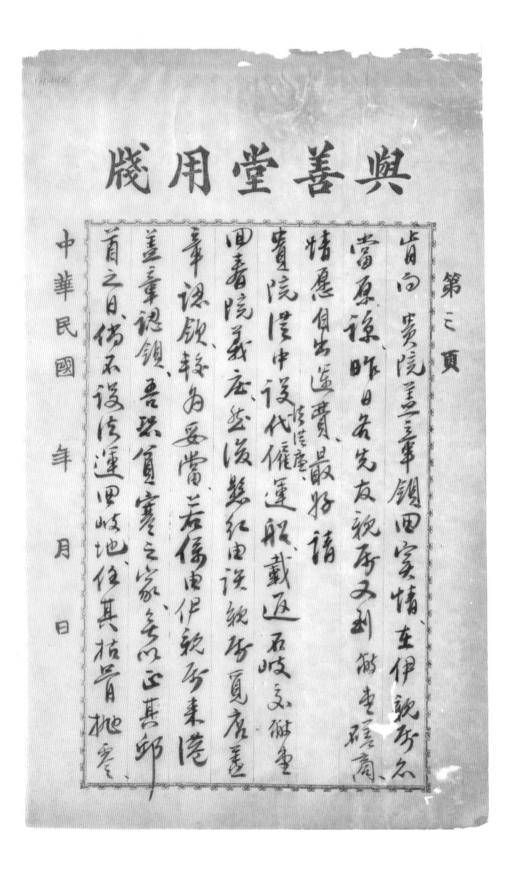

興善堂用牋

第三頁

肯向 貴院善三華鋪四家情在伊認為允

當原諒、昨日為先友親辱又到 術事磋商、

情願負出運費、最好請

貴院還中設代僱運船戴返石岐之術事

田春院載在登後些紅由誤認辱頁店運

事課領、較為妥當、若僑東伊認辱來港

蓋章認領、吾珠頁寒之家各向正其鄉

首之日、俾不設法運回岐地住其枯骨拋棄、

中華民國　年　月　日

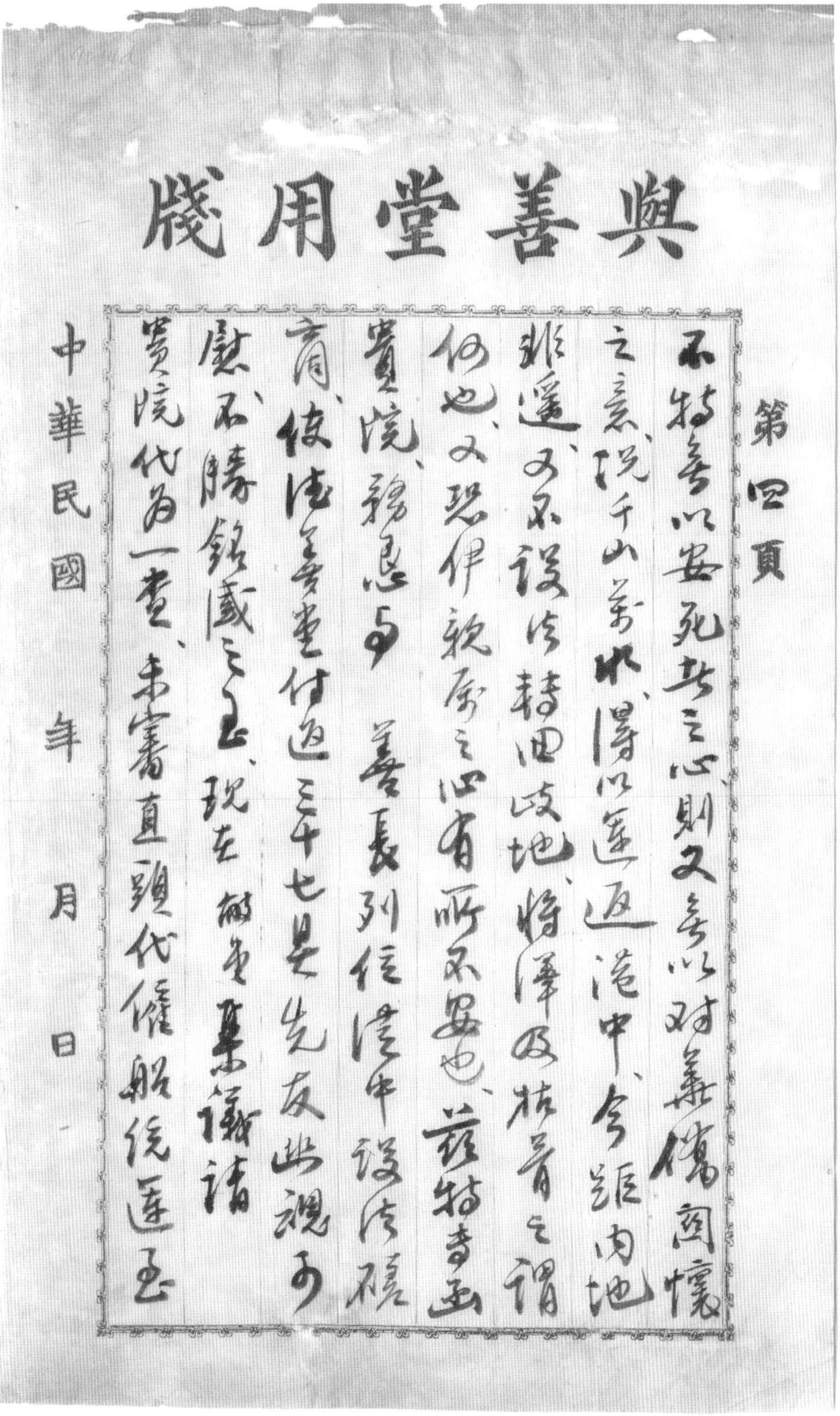

興善堂用牋

第四頁

不特善以安死者之心則又善以對善僑商懷
之意，況千山萬水得以運返港中，今詎內地
非遙，又不設法轉回政地，將澤及枯骨之謂
何也，又恐伊執原之心有所不安也，茲特專函
貴院，務思與　善長列位僉摉諄設法穩
商，使速爲舉行返三千七五先友此視可
慰不勝銘感之至，現在儹辦集議諸
貴院代為一盡，未審直頭代僑骸線運返

中華民國　年　月　日

興善堂用箋

第三頁

峽後價若平抑或由　貴處直港僱船搭至峽渡
尾拖運到微薪留書院名上註價若平、並請兩
（代為一晝、）
掟亦沒耘以管查憂行先即迅
賜覆音、以便持遙各先友轂为知之、事
闇另邑諸費
精神安吉西綏、此上即請
善安六府為
朗照不宣、

中華民國十六年七月十日　即旧六月初四

中山……善堂同人謹禀

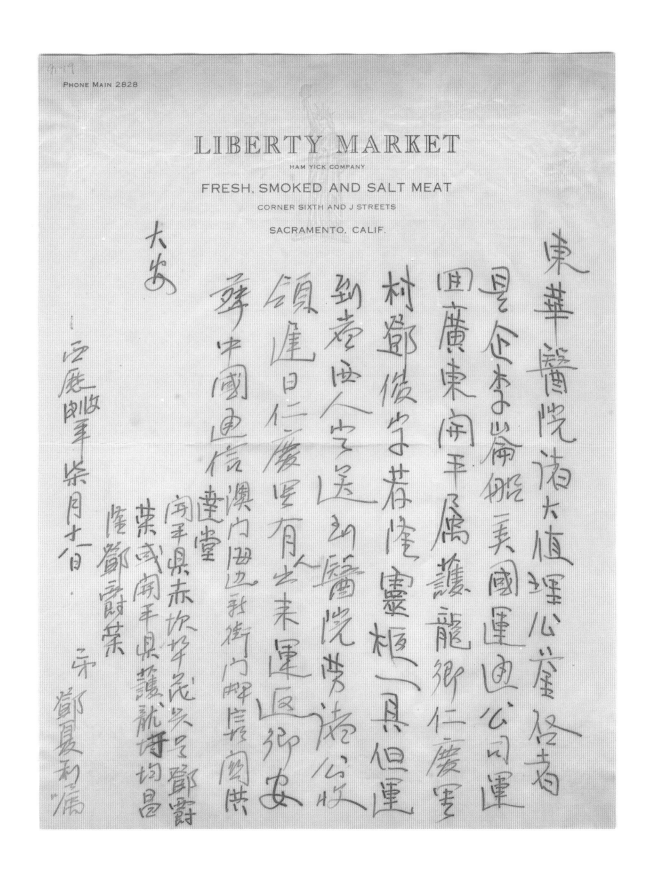

PHONE MAIN 2828

LIBERTY MARKET

HAM YICK COMPANY

FRESH, SMOKED AND SALT MEAT

CORNER SIXTH AND J STREETS

SACRAMENTO, CALIF.

東華醫院諸大值理公壼啓者

具企本台崙船美國運通公司運

囘廣東南平屬護龍鄉仁慶雲

村鄧俊少荇陸靈柩一具但運

到省城人字送到醫院勞港公收

領進日仁慶運匪有出來運返鄉安

舜中國通信達堂

濠門迎边新街内群信堂囘供

南平縣赤坎坪花笑至鄧爵

榮或南平縣護就埗均昌

隆鄧蔚榮

大安

　　西歷二十八年柒月十八日

　　　　　　　　　　示　鄧夏利緘

信箱壹肆壹叁號　　　篆　用　泰　茂　同　　　電話總局肆零壹壹號

Cable Address:
"UNDERB'O HONGKONG"
P. O. Box No. 1413.

TONG MOW TAI
Importer Exporter
and Commission Agents
9, LI SING STREET,
HONGKONG.

TEL. C. 4011

（號　九　街　升　李　港　香）

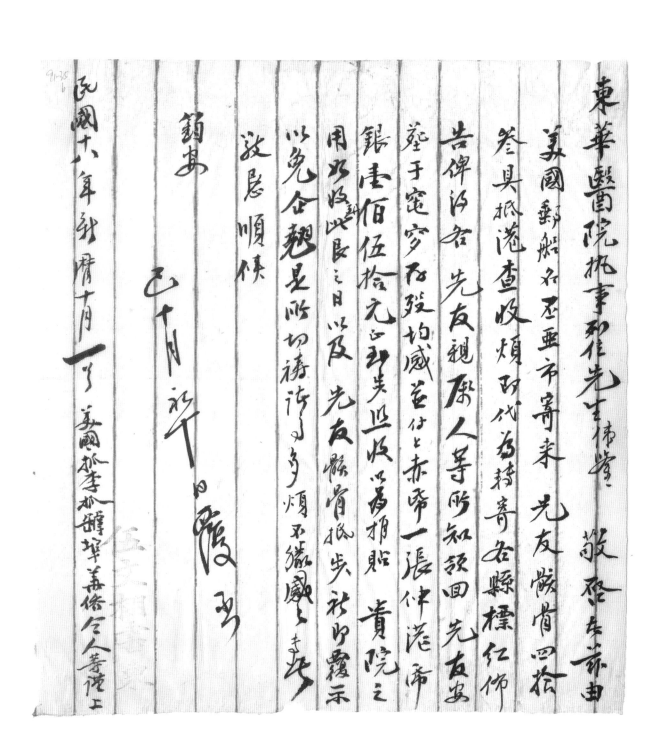

茲將各先友姓名縣鄉列明于後

傅訓賢　台山深井龍田里人氏　黃廷普　台山工南浮月村人氏

伍先忠　台山下坪村人氏　黃廷純　台山潮境下村人氏

黃章任　台山潮境西村人氏　廖烈錦　會邑砂堆人氏

黃溢章　台山潮境西村人氏　朱英叢　會城潮溪里內泗冲朱村人氏

何大　開邑龍塘白龍里人氏　蟹雕隆　台山醬屋村人氏

朱子林　台山西先冲村人氏　黃百合　開邑水口人氏

黃學攜　會邑坑山頂里人氏　胡振和　儒良里龍舉里人氏

李宏英　台山窗冲文冲村人氏　許佐　台山水步榮安村人氏

吳三才　恩邑平安僑廣塘村人氏　鍾孔　會邑古井人氏

許炳桂　台山斗洞鳳鸞村一氏　蔡就　台山沙冲人氏　馬元

鍾欽 会邑古井烟管咀村仝　　　李杰衍 台山南村山背里人仝

區洪優 台山廣海橫祉村人仝　　薛喬箋 会邑長沙鄉人仝

黃啟胤 台山潮墟西村人仝　　　高振瀼 会邑那伏人仝

李玉 台山容冲玉枕村人仝　　　李積 台山容冲玉枕村人仝

李河 台山寮冲瀝潮村仝　　　　李則 台山寮冲瀝潮村仝

劉社星 台山白石村人仝　　　　劉周易 台山白石村人仝

朱昌華 会城潮溪村人仝　　　　朱昌合 会城潮溪村人仝

朱箕源 会城潮溪村人仝　　　　張荀女 台山薑溪村人仝

張旺相 台山薑溪村人仝　　　　張成效 台山薑溪村人仝

劉尊輝 台山白石村仝

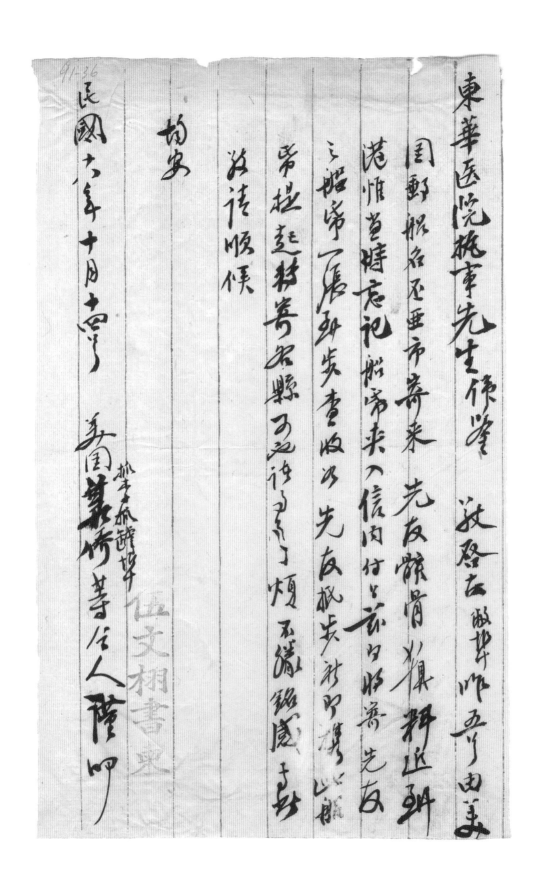

東華醫院執事先生偉鑒 敬啟者 昨此五月由美

國郵船各匯亞市壽來 先友嬪骨一據連飛

港惟其特意記船帶來入信內付上芸由貼濟先友

三船帶回展盈發書收妥 先友枢夫新內穩以服

弟接速耕等客縣不遠許可煩五港鈔銘感 妻姓

敬諸順候

均安

91-36

民國六年十月十四號

美國華僑等仝人 陸叩
抓李抓罅埠

伍文棚書票

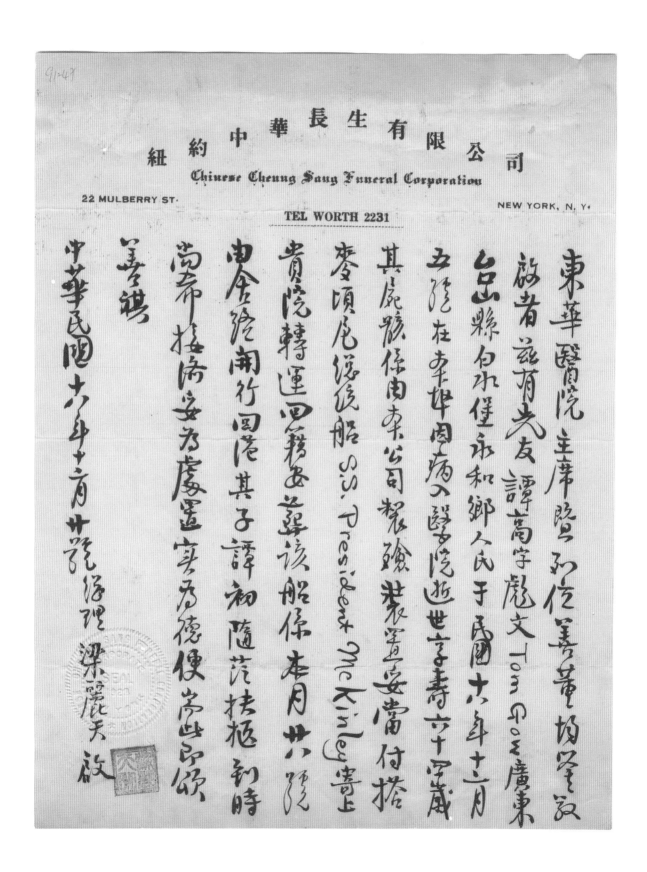

中華長生有限公司

紐約 中華長生有限公司
Chinese Cheung Saug Funeral Corporation

22 MULBERRY ST·

NEW YORK, N. Y·

TEL WORTH 2231

東華醫院主席暨列位善董均隆之鑒

啟者茲有先友譚高字麗文 Tom Gow 廣東

台山縣白水堡永和鄉人氏于民國六年十二月

五號在本埠因病入醫院逝世享壽六十二歲

其屍骸保由本公司殮驗裝殮妥當付搭

麥順尾輪渡船 S.S. President Mckinley 壽山

貴院轉運回籍安葬該船保本月廿六號

由金沙開行回港其子譚初隨柩扶柩到時

尚希接濟安為慶還實為德便崇此即頌

善祺

中華民國十六年十二月廿六號經理 梁麗天 啟

TELEPHONE WORTH 6984

所公華中約紐國美

Chinese Consolidated Benevolent Association

16 MOTT STREET
NEW YORK CITY, N.Y.

香港東華醫院院長先生大鑒

逕啟者茲有先友譚高字彪文西字

TOM GOW 廣東台山縣白水堡永和鄉人氏于

民國十八年十二月五日在本埠醫院逝世

享壽六十四歲其屍嚴由本埠長生公司

付搭麥乾尼總統船 S.S.President Mckinley

寄回香港 貴院特運回原籍安葬

該船係本月廿六号由會臨埠南行該先

友抵港時請求

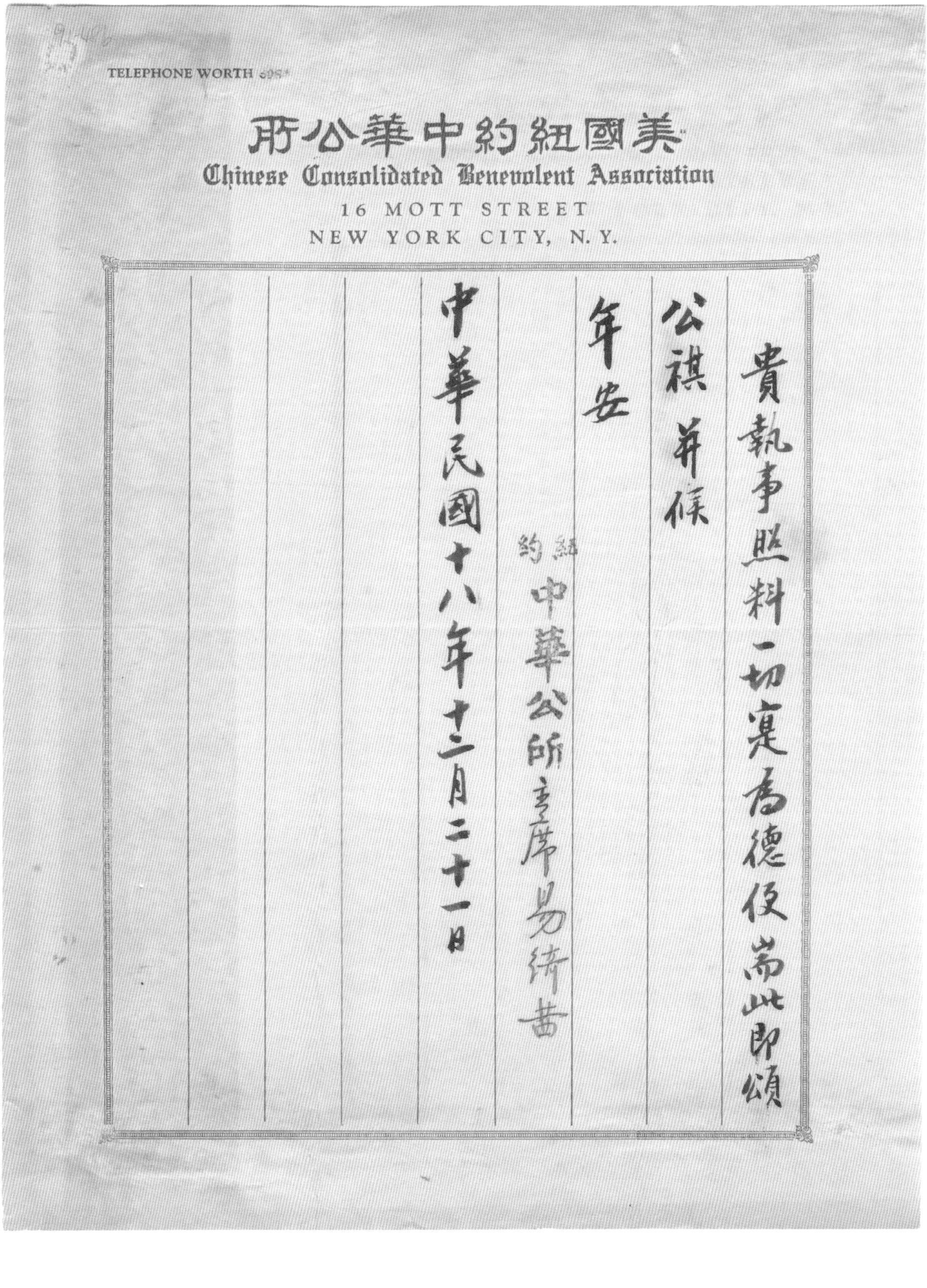

TELEPHONE WORTH 6984

美國紐約中華公所
Chinese Consolidated Benevolent Association
16 MOTT STREET
NEW YORK CITY, N. Y.

貴執事照料一切寔爲德便耑此即頌
公祺 并候
年安
紐約 中華公所主席易綺番
中華民國十八年十二月二十一日

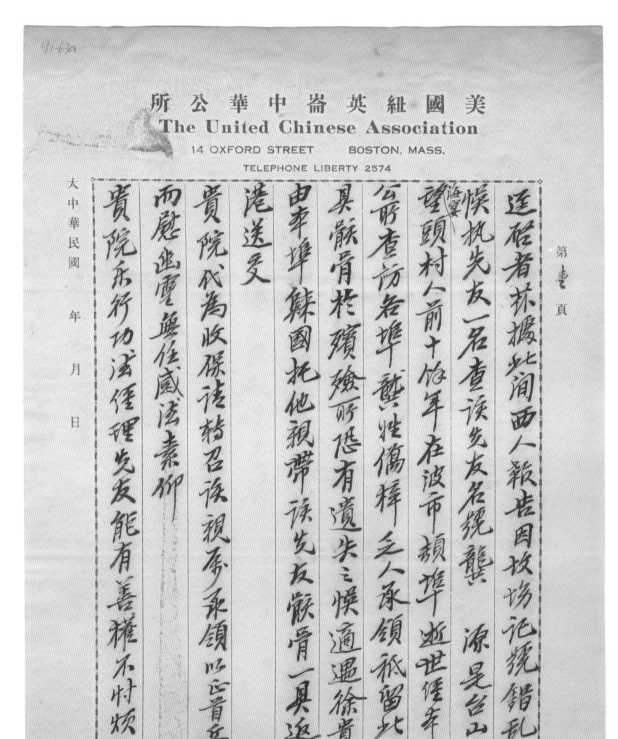

所公華中崙英紐國美
The United Chinese Association
14 OXFORD STREET　　　BOSTON, MASS.
TELEPHONE LIBERTY 2574

第壹頁

逕啓者茲據北間西人報告因故場記號錯亂

慎抗先友一名查誤先友名竟襲　源是台山

望頭村人前十餘年在波市頭埠遊世運年

公前查訪各埠熟知姓僑拜之人承領祇留北

具骸骨於殯儀所懇有遺失之慎適遇徐貴

由幸埠蘇國托他親帶誤先友骸骨一具連

港送交

貴院代為收儲请耑召誤親参承領以正首丘

而慰逝靈無任感法素仰

貴院所行功法使理先友能有善權不忖煩

大中華民國　年　月　日

91-636

所公華中崙英紐國美
The United Chinese Association
14 OXFORD STREET　　BOSTON, MASS.
TELEPHONE LIBERTY 2574

第八頁

續勞為收發藉思之施存發廳忘此發

香港東華醫院諸善長先生

紐莫崙中華公所啟
紐英崙中華公所

計開

龥　源先友骸骨壹具

台山縣海宴望頭村人係西歷壹千玖百壹

拾捌年八月間在美國波市歿準掛號

大中華民國十九年元月廿九日

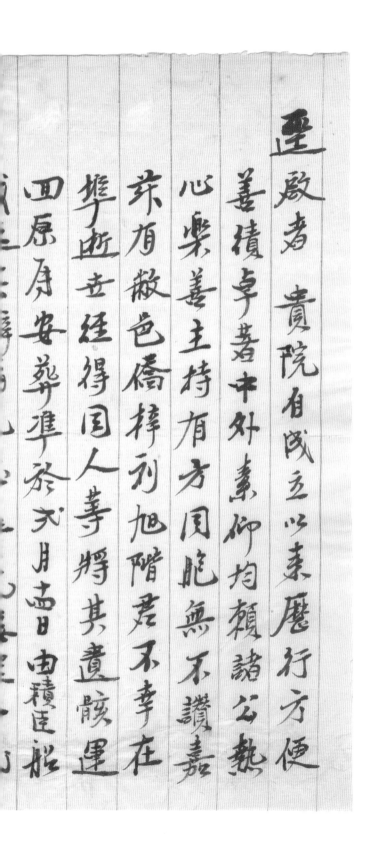

逕啟者　貴院自成立以來歷行方便

善積卓著中外素仰均賴諸公熱

心樂善主持有方固脆無不讚嘉

茲有敝邑僑梓利旭階君不幸在

埠病逝迄得同人等將其遺骸運

回原處安葬準於天月壹日由積臣船

囙死者家鄉安葬用特函知屬時葬

望幫忙玉成善舉同人等感激靡似

美此致

駐港東華醫院主席暨

列位執事先生均鑒

大埠康讚安堂

主席 林□□

書記 譚□日

民十九年四月二十日

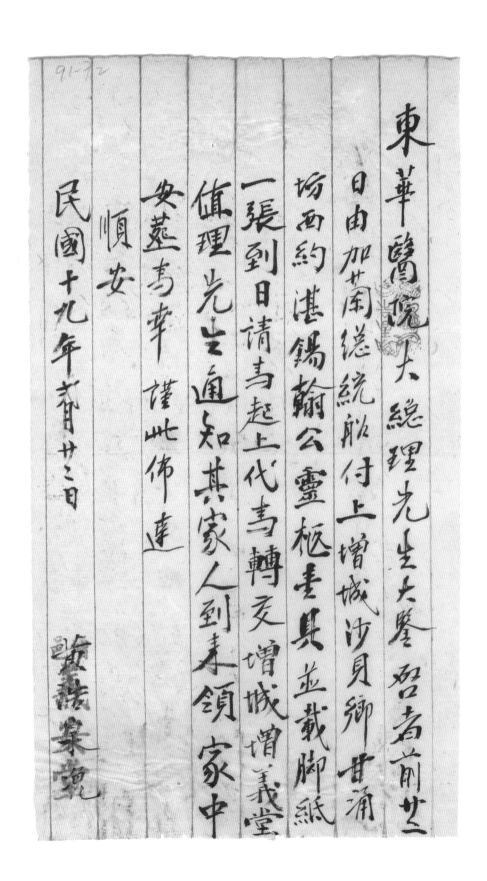

東華醫院大總理先生大鑒 啟者前廿

日由加拿兩總統船付上增城沙貝鄉甘涌

坊西約湛錫翰公靈柩壹具並戴腳紙

一張到日請查起上代為轉交增城增義堂

值理先生通知其家人到來領家中

安葬為幸 謹此佈達

順安

民國十九年貳月廿二日

中國黃焯致東華醫院信件

1930 年 3 月 2 日

東華醫院執事列位先生均鑒敬啟者弟南先
十年前在美國咸水埠所故身之華
僑名骸骨經前年寄回貴院轉
發名家未知是否收妥先生代
弟查看新会古井大朗坡鄉黃植華
之名有無誤骨付回仰祈示知
諸事有勞順此祗
台安
庚三月十四覆
弟 黃焯安
三月二號

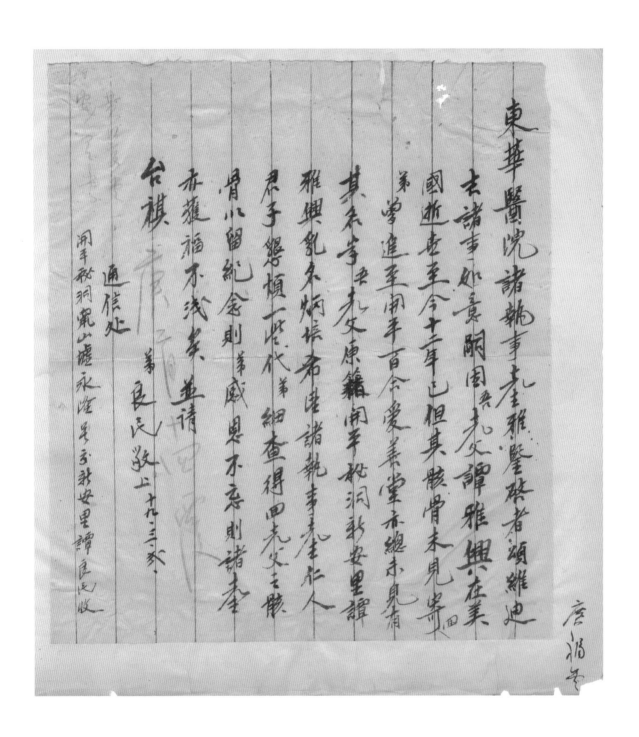

東華醫院諸執事先生雅鑒敬者頌維迪

吉諸事如意闔固燕爾先父譚雅興在美

國逝遠至今十二年正但其骸骨未見寄來

第掌進至開年百余愛慕堂亦總未見有回

其先字是父康籍開年秘洞新安里譚

雅興乳名炳辰希進諸執事先生各人

君手懇煩一些代第細查得回先父之骸

骨小留紀念則第感恩不忘則諸奉

亦獲福不淺美至請

台祺

　　通信处
　　　　　第良民敬上十九三二

闰年秋羽霓山塘永淀　　　　　新安里譚良民足收

唐福弟

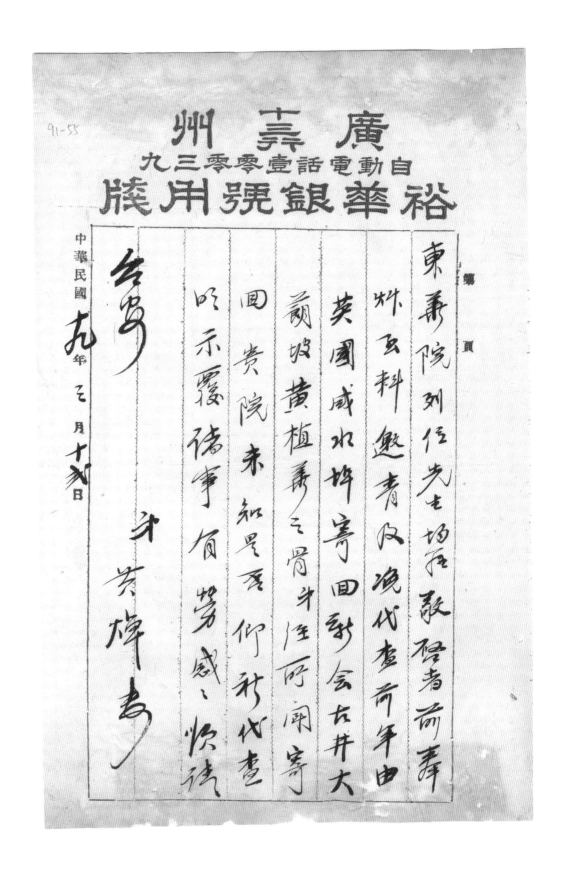

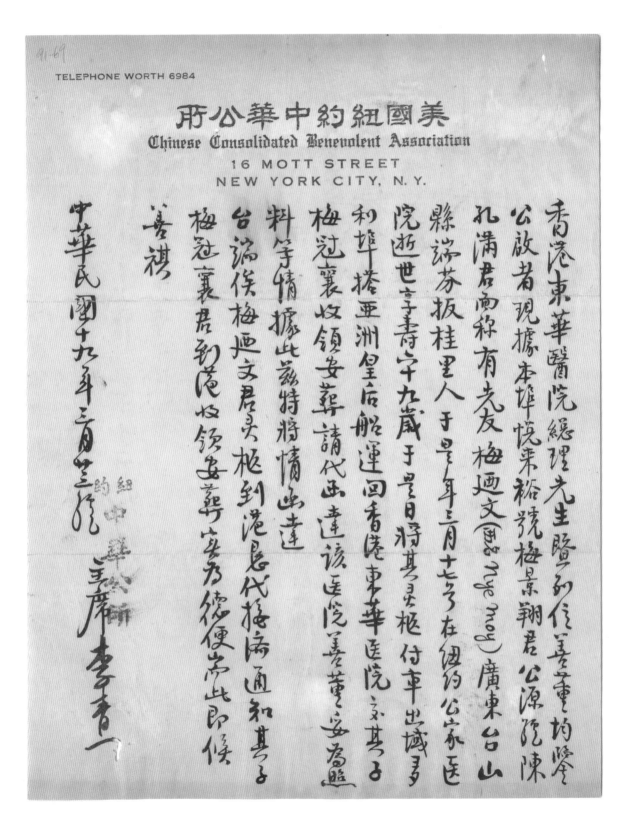

TELEPHONE WORTH 6984

府公華中約紐國美

Chinese Consolidated Benevolent Association

16 MOTT STREET
NEW YORK CITY, N.Y.

香港東華醫院總理先生暨列位善董台鑒

敬啟者現據本埠悅來裕號梅景翔君公源陀陳

孔滿君而稱有老友梅迺文（即 Nye moy）廣東台山

縣端芬扳桂里人于是年三月十七号在紐約公家醫

院逝世享壽五十九歲于是月將其靈柩付車出城乘

和埠搭亞洲皇后船運回香港東華醫院交其子

梅冠裹收領安葬請代函達該醫院暨善董安葬

料等情據此兹特將情函達

台端俟梅迺文君臾柩到港慰代搬搞通知其子

梅冠裹君到港收領安葬實為德便耑此即候

善祺

　　　　　　紐約中華公所

中華民國十九年三月廿三號　　主席　李省一

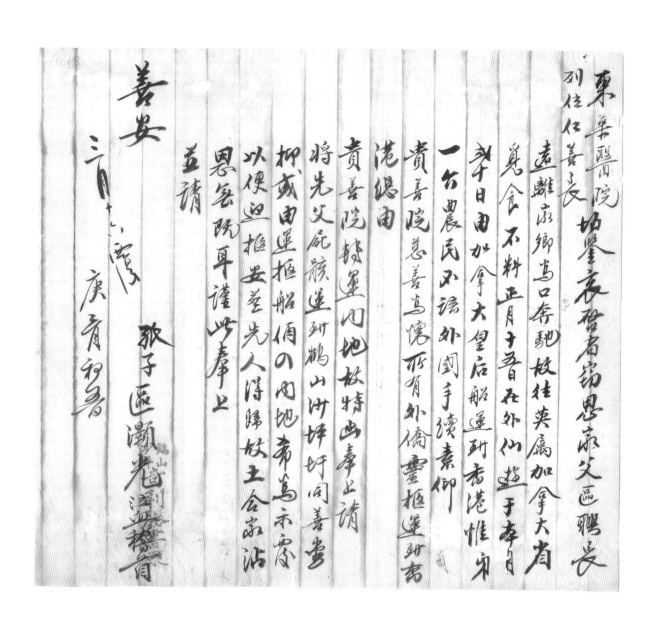

善安

三月初六日

庚午初六日

張子區灝光頓首

益請

恩荃院耳謹此奉上

以便迎接安葬先人浮歸故土合眾沾

柳城由運梓船伯の內地壽焉示審

將先父屍骸運到鶴山沙坪坪同善堂

貴善院解運心地敬特函奉上請

港總由

貴善院慈善為懷乃有外僑靈柩運到

一台農民不諳外國手續素仰

辛巳由加拿大皇后船運到香港惟求

覓食不料正月于晉在外仙遊于辛月

遠離家鄉為口奔馳故往柬屬加拿大省

列位仁善長

東華醫院坤鑒茲啟者竊思嚴父區聘長

美國必珠卜中華會館致東華醫院信件

1930 年 4 月 4 日

港〻東華醫院執事先生鈞鑒　久仰
貴院利濟實宏
名譽昭著　甚佩甚佩　敝會館本屆檢起先友
遺骸柒拾捌具　分裝拾叁大箱　蓋面書明各先
友姓名籍貫　於三月初六日由敝埠上車輸運回
國　特將載紙呈上　請
貴院接理起卸　並請按其名籍分送各邑善
堂　以便各先友之家眷收領　現付上庚帝一紙
伴港幣玖佰叁拾陸元　內除交每位先友泉骸葬
費伍元外　餘存伍佰肆拾陸元　統交
貴院為轉運之需　逢日寄上各先友名冊一本
及証根柒拾捌條　此等証根懇同時轉寄各善
堂　為對照領者收條之用　手續雖繁　惟較慎
重　依據辦理　至為感荷　專此　敬頌
公祺

美國珠必中華會館　主席余錫中　書記余毅禮　余寶三　謹達

民國十九年三月初五日寄

115〈頁一〉加拿大域多利同福支堂致東華醫院信件

1930 年 4 月 19 日

加拿大域多利恩平同福支堂用牋
HONG FOOK TONG SOCIETY
525½ FISGUARD STREET, VICTORIA, B. C.

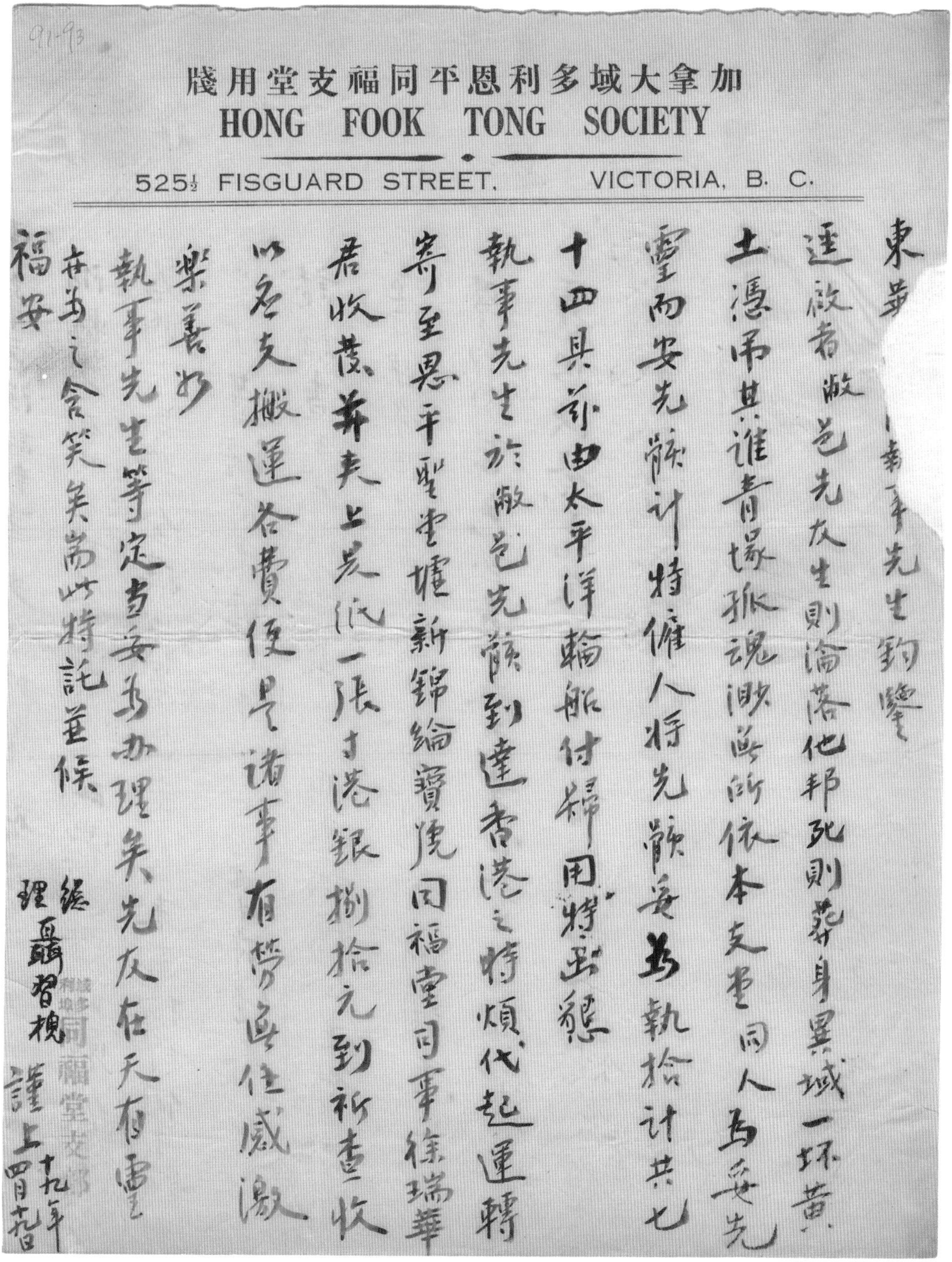

東華……事先生鈞鑒

逕啟者敝邑先友生則淪落他邦死則葬身異域一坏黃土憑吊其誰青燐飛魂渺無所依本支堂同人爲無先靈而安先骸計特僱人將先骸無爲執拾計共七十四具前由太平洋輪船付歸用特函懇

執事先生於敝邑先骸到達香港之時煩代起運轉寄至恩平墨壁墟新錦綸寶號同福堂司事徐瑞華君收葬并夫上落代一張寸港銀捌拾元到祈查收以爲支撥運各費便是諸事有勞無任感激

樂善好

執事先生等定當安爲辦理矣先友在天有靈亦當之含笑矣耑此特託並候

福安

總理聶習槐謹上
十九年四月十九日

域多利同福堂支部

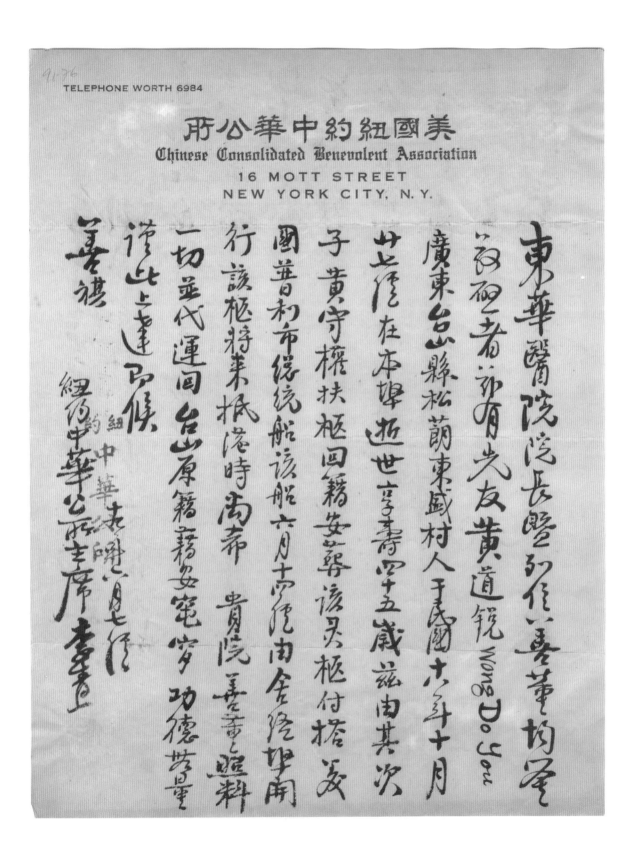

東華醫院院長醫印作善華均鑒

敬啟者茲有先友黃道銳 Wong Do you

廣東台山縣松蓢東邊村人民國十六年十月

此症在本埠逝世享壽四十五歲茲由其次

子黃守權扶柩回籍安葬該靈柩付搭

國昌和市總統船該船六月廿一號由金灣駛開

行該柩將來抵港時為荷 貴院善為照料

一切並代運回台山原籍俾妥窀穸功德莫量

謹此並達耑此候

善祺

紐約中華公所主席 書

紐約中華公所謹啟六月七日

東華醫院並值列位先生大鑒

敬啟者茲由去秦公司總統輪船運

圓貴院代收馮良先友柩重

具並夾信內俸紙三張到步榮為

照料馮良先友乃保南海九江鄉人

民具村名拜石里具子馮煊到領

該輪船大約七月十三日到港矣故特

舉方通知諸廢神馳感德英忘

謹此奉達

中華民國十玖年肖日

南海九江馮登拜況

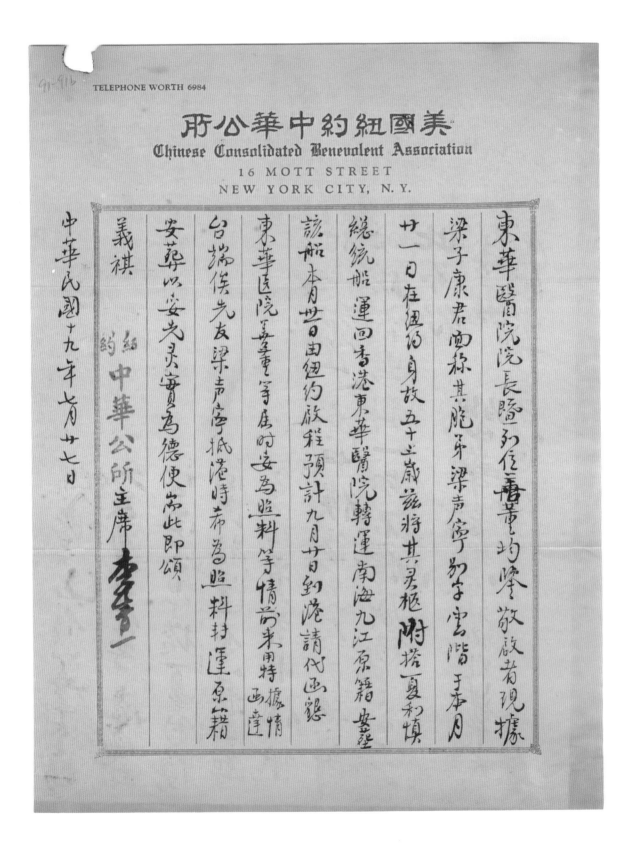

TELEPHONE WORTH 6984

所公華中約紐國美
Chinese Consolidated Benevolent Association
16 MOTT STREET
NEW YORK CITY, N.Y.

東華醫院院長暨列位董事均鑒　敬啟者現據

梁子康君面稱其胞弟梁聲寧別字雲階于本月

廿一日在過沽身故五十五歲茲將其靈柩 附搭夏和煩

總統船運回香港東華醫院轉運南海九江原籍安葬

該船本月廿日由紐約啟程預計九月廿日到港請代函懇

東華醫院善董等屆時安為照料等情前來用特據情函達

台端俟先友梁聲寧寄抵港時希為照料封運原籍

安葬以安先灵實為德便耑此即頌

　　義祺

　　　紐約中華公所主席　李〿〿一

中華民國十九年七月廿七日

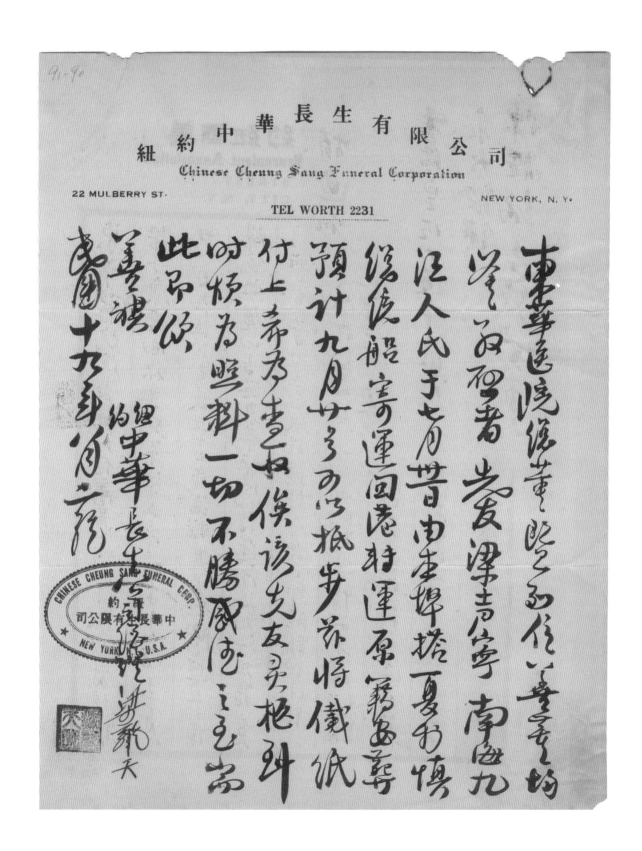

長生有限公司
紐約 中華
Chinese Cheung Sang Funeral Corporation

22 MULBERRY ST·
TEL WORTH 2231
NEW YORK, N. Y·

東華醫院僉董鈞鑒敬啟者 茲發運吉位 南海九
澤二邑 回港 先友華民 于七月廿晉由金邊搭 夏 印慎
緩 後 船 寄 運 回 港 特 運 原 籍 安 葬
預計九月廿六日抵步 茲將儀紙
付上 希為查 收 俟 該先友靈柩到
時煩為照料一切 不勝感荷 耑 此 並請
此 佈 頌
善福
貴 團 十 九 年 八 月 二 號

紐 中華長生有限公司 梁 敬 天

中國黃偉致東華醫院信件

1930 年 8 月 7 日

東華醫院列位仁翁先生均鑒敬啓者弟之叔
母黄羅氏（即中山長洲雲閑之媳婦）因家窮困在美國自
屍其柩由梓友義捐於二月初四運到香
港寄入　貴院処置然先人以息土為
安弟恐其暴露但其家貧欲回運原籍
安厝而乏經濟費無所出待今年積存一
幫貴善堂出資代理載回原籍未悉
然否如是者何日可以運回哉不然以
何手續可以運回請示其詳想
到位先生以善為懷諒不我却也賜函請
交中山石岐大馬路誠信號收入可也
並頌
時祉
庚午七月十三日　弟　黄偉上言

篾用堂慶餘陽寧利多域大拿加

Ning Young Yee Hing Tong

P. O. BOX 1512

538 Cormorant St.　　　　Victoria, B.C.　　　　Canada.

逕啟者本餘慶堂專各邑善堂枱行疏理令

屬此間加拿大厲 我僑先友事宜自十五年

年頒布首以至于今方行依束本屆手續現

計連年檢起箱裝先友遺骸共有千八百

具向之數屬于廣村人民居多公立延願

整筑附返

鈞醫院起收如前蒞迴相庬先行呈報

鈞醫院查知預為照料妥速乘機宜

遵行為荷此致

香港東華醫院大董事

中華民國十九年十月十六日

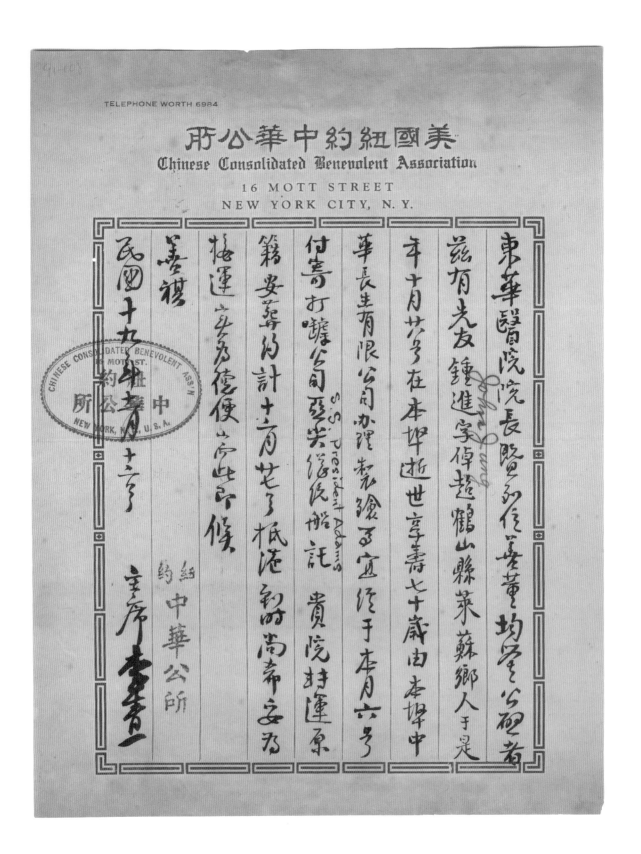

TELEPHONE WORTH 6984

所公華中約紐國美
Chinese Consolidated Benevolent Association
16 MOTT STREET
NEW YORK CITY, N. Y.

東華醫院長醫生列位善董均鑒逕啟者

茲有先友鍾進家偉趙鶴山縣萊蘇鄉人于是

年十月艹六号在本坤逝世享壽七十歲由本坤中

華長生有限公司辦理裝殮至宜行于本月六号

付壽打嚹公司亞哥輪船運原　貴院持運原

S.S. President Adams

籍安葬約計十有艹号抵港鈞此尚希妥為

接運立安為德便佇此佈候

台禮

民國十九年十月十二号

紐約中華公所

主席李壽宣

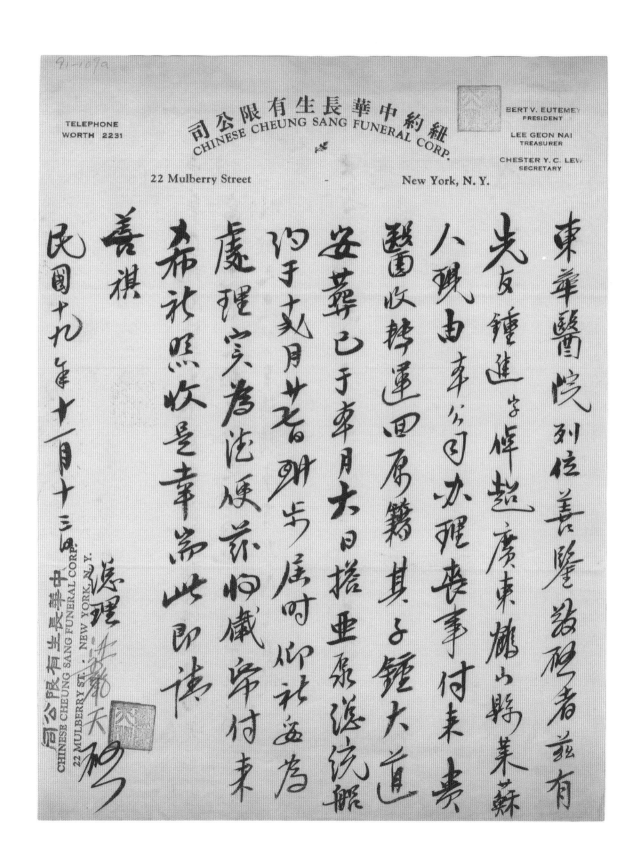

東華醫院值理暨諸執事先生偉鑒、

敬啟者月前運為之先友遠骸、請未

貴院接收辦理未見不復、誅承已安

為轉運各邑以暨各善堂按班去續分

詒安不至有政錯漏也、惟應各報近接

各先友家屬報知各善堂已聲先友遠骸

華費銀式元怡那各先友寄着報告書

預告之礼葉費相差大半矊為驚異、

昨承不敢以深信也、至昨閱樓岡月刊

第七年第廿九卷之族閱欄政載該處之

失友遠骸葬費確是式元致令各僑

脆向敝會館毋事人執問原委以以

以激之甚話復對然其中惰形想

貴院執事先生定能明白、今特將

正誘詢希為早日詳復以釋群

疑是華順候

公安

　　　　　　　　必珠卜
　　　　　　　　中華會館謹上

民國十九年十一月十香

TELEPHONE
WORTH 2231
WOrth 2-2231

司公限有生長華中約紐
CHINESE CHEUNG SANG FUNERAL CORP.

22 Mulberry Street — New York, N. Y.

BERT V. EUTEMEY
PRESIDENT

LEE GEON NAI
TREASURER

CHESTER Y. C. LEW
SECRETARY

東華醫院執事先生大鑒 敬啟者茲有先友

余國慶 Yee On 廣東台山縣荻海慶和里

人于民國十九年十一月十七号在紐約布崙街醫

院因病逝世享壽年四十九歲是日其親屬扶柩

由本埠搭車出金路趕乘昊晨慎德綸船該船

定本月廿五號由金陵動輪運回香港請

貴院代收妥為轉運原籍埋葬藉安窀穸

而安先靈實多德便耑此即候

台祺

中華民國十九年十二月

紐約中華長生有限公司謹啟 梁耀天

CHINESE CHEUNG SANG FUNERAL CORP.
22 MULBERRY ST. - NEW YORK, N.Y.

東華醫院列位總理先生大鑒本月初二日由泗益棧交來

大函內開美國必珠卜中華會館是屆運回之先友骨殖開平籍吳亦楨

等十二具查係由霑號代領轉運回內地當時敝院經照每具給以葬費五

元共六十元一統送上寶歸並章收妥茲敝院接到必珠卜中華會館來函

云敝舘近接各先友親屬來報知各善堂祇發先友遺骸葬費銀式元恰

與各先友家眷報告書禎告之五元葬費相差大半殊為驚異始而不以

為深信也至昨閱樓同月刊第七年第九卷之族開欄所載該處之先友

遺骸葬費雖是式元致令各僑胞向敝會舘辦事人抗問原委無以明澈各

復等語特此函達請為代查示復以便轉後前途等因奉此查敝堂向例對

於外洋各埠運回之先友骨殖凡由敝堂辦運費呂每具發給葬費式

少均將該欵先行撥歸敝堂然後由敝堂交辦運費呂毎具發給葬費式

元以歸劃一此次美國必珠卜中華會館運回開平先友吳亦楨等骨殖十二

具由

貴院代該會舘交泗益棧轉交敝堂收銀六十九經敝堂司理吳竪潤告

如數收妥進入敝堂數內交辦此係依照向例辦理以免紛歧用特函達

台端尚希 轉覆前途以釋羣疑實級公誼耑此即頌

善祺

中華民國十九年十二月 廿三 日

開恩廣福堂書東

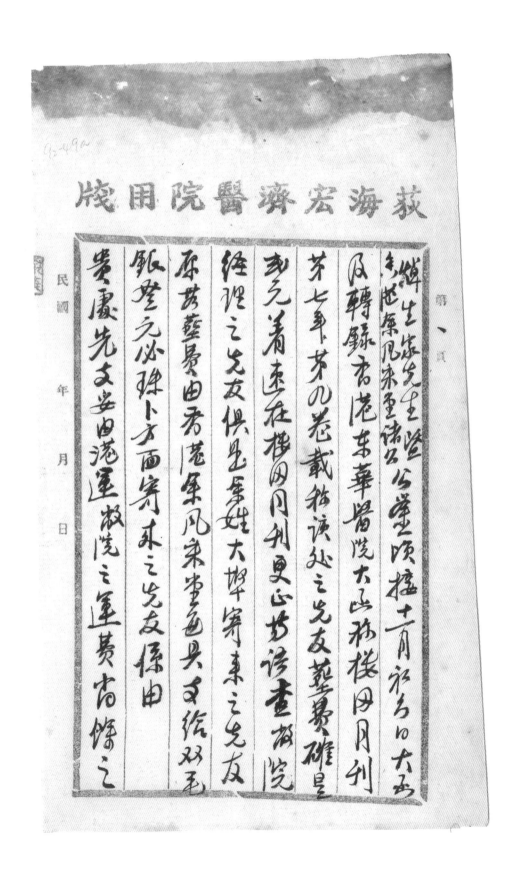

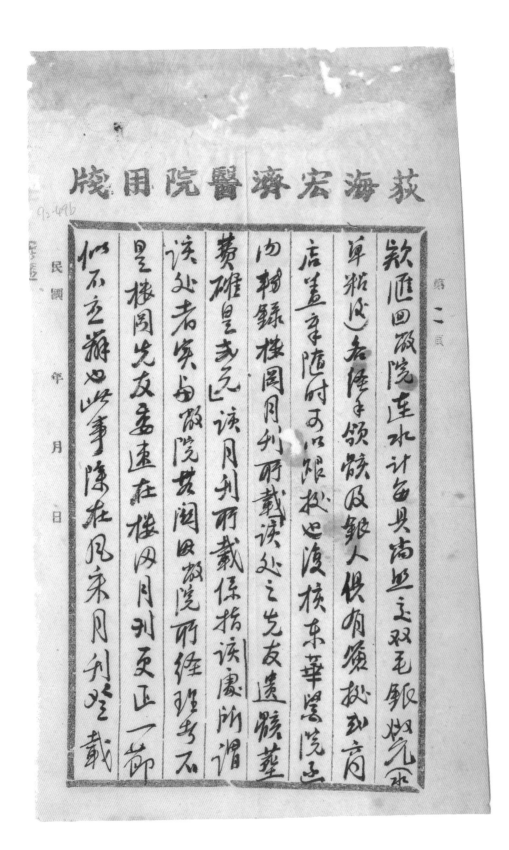

荻海宏濟醫院用牋

第二段

敬匯回敝院連水計叁具滿壺之双毛銀燉光（水

草粘帋）各隆平領骸及銀人俱有領抷到有

店盡事隨時可跟柲巴渡梹東華醫院正

仍輯錄樓閩月刊所載誤處之先友遺骸塋

費雄皇去之）該月刊所載保指誤處所謂

誤处者實與敝院茸閩及敝院所經理亭不

皇樓閩先友孟遠在樓內月刊更正一節

似不立辨四此事陳在風來月刊燈載

民國　年　月　日

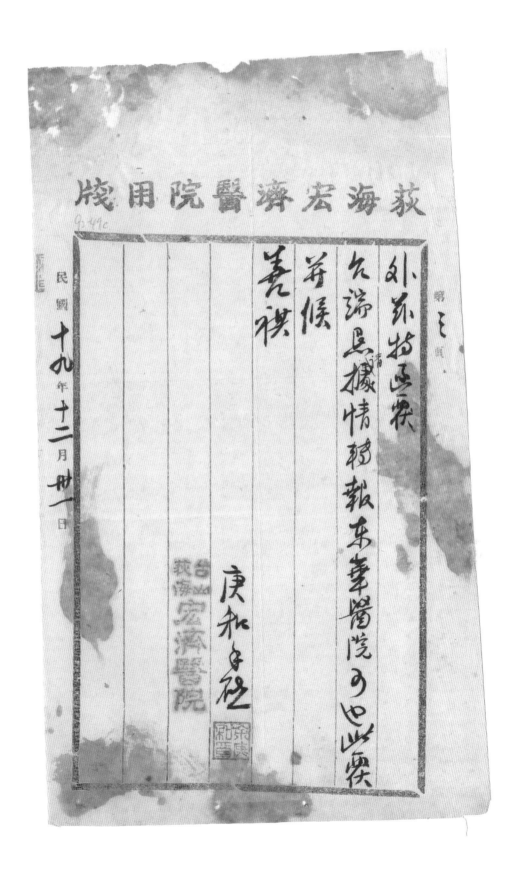

萩海宏濟醫院用牋

民國十九年十二月卅一日

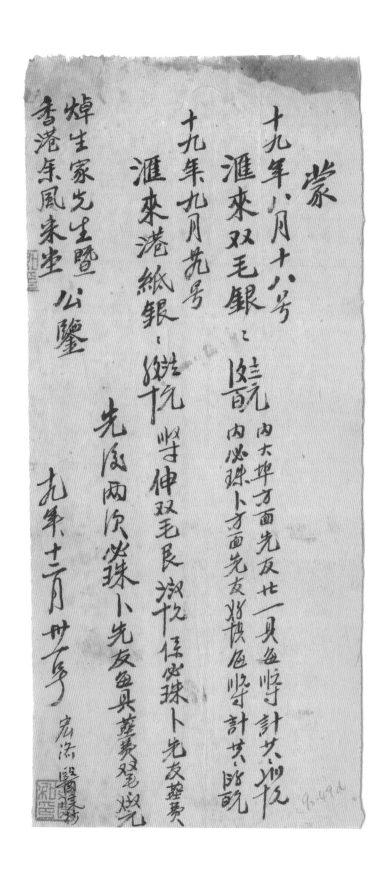

篆用堂慶餘陽寧利多域大拿加

NING YOUNG YEE HING TONG

P. O. BOX 1512

538 CORMORANT ST.　　　　　VICTORIA, B. C., CAN.

東華醫院總理先生大鑒 逕啟者 本堂自成立以來

向以辦理僑界慈善事業為主旨即執先友遺骸

駐加各邑善堂麻屆均推舉 本堂辦理亦荷蒙

貴院鼎力助勸 湛恩汪濊沒存均感現屆經去年

年執拾完竣共計有一千八百餘具亟待運回故

土俾正首丘前年十月十六日曾具蕪函正報

貴院請 示機宜祇遵辦理乃望眼將穿未蒙

示覆 想前函定為洪喬所誤茲特庚修寸楮奉

呈

貴總理等可否依照前屆辦法將先友遺骸附回

貴院查收再勞分發各縣慈善機關查收分領是

否可行仍懇迅賜

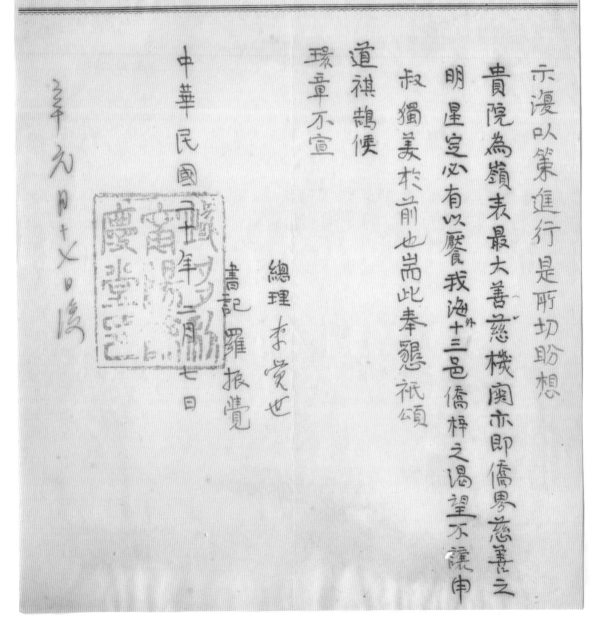

加拿大域多利寧陽餘慶堂用箋
NING YOUNG YEE HING TONG

P. O. BOX 1512

538 CORMORANT ST.　　　　VICTORIA, B. C., CAN.

示復以策進行是所切盼想

貴院為嶺表最大善慈機關亦即僑界慈善之

明星定必有以饜我海外十三邑僑梓之渴望不讓申

叔獨美於前也耑此奉懇祇頌

道祺鵠候

璈章不宣

中華民國三十一年三月七日

　　　　總理李覺世

　　　　書記羅振覺

三年九月十七日復

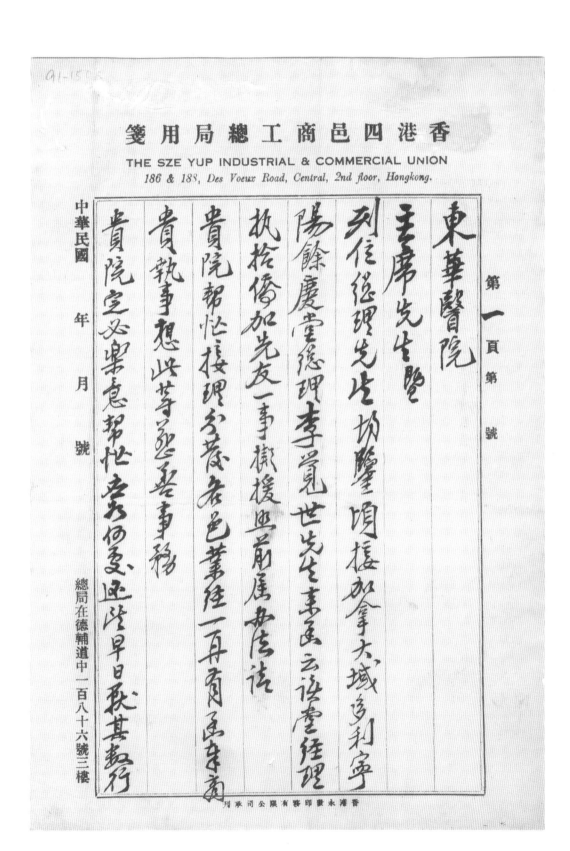

篆用局總工商邑四港香

THE SZE YUP INDUSTRIAL & COMMERCIAL UNION

186 & 188, Des Voeux Road, Central, 2nd floor, Hongkong.

第一頁第　號

東華醫院

主席先生鑒

列位總理先生均鑒　頃接加拿大域多利寧

陽餘慶堂總理李覺世先生來函畧經理

執拾僑加先友一事轉援與前屬各信語

貴院帮忙接理分蒙各邑葦徑一再有函來商

貴執事想此葦並善善事務

貴院定必樂意帮忙矣仍冀延此早日我其執行

中華民國　年　月　號

總局在德輔道中一百八十六號三樓

香港永興印務有限公司承印

香港四邑商工總局用箋
THE SZE YUP INDUSTRIAL & COMMERCIAL UNION
186 & 188, Des Voeux Road, Central, 2nd floor, Hongkong.

第二頁第號

指示一切俾得從容籌慶堂李經理等妥心寄運以妥者

先友之幽魂安為德便專此敬頌

善祺萬福

當年主席 譚焕書

辛酉九月十七日

中華民國辛酉年三月弍號

總局在德輔道中一百八十六號三樓

香港永發印務有限公司承辦

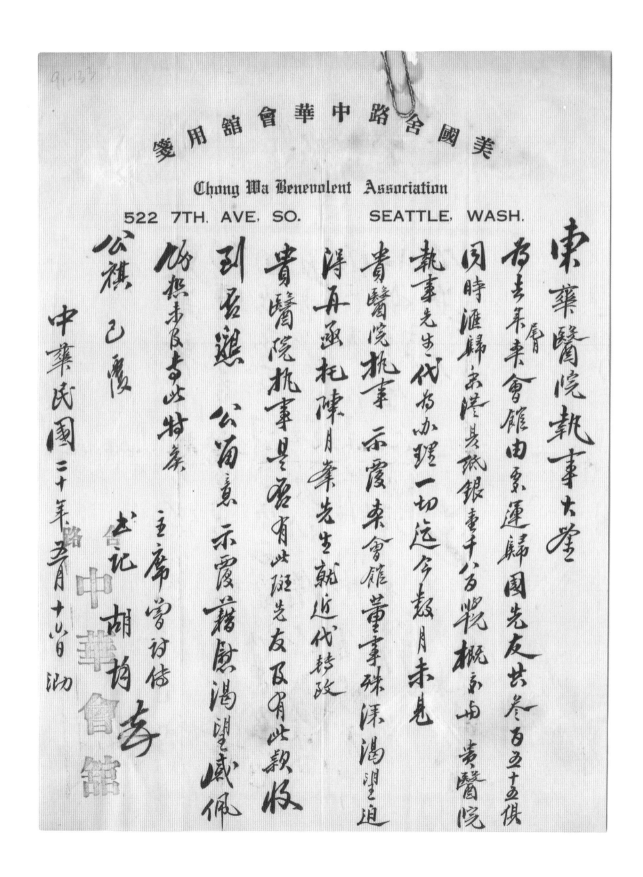

美國舍路中華會舘用箋

Chong Wa Benevolent Association

522 7TH. AVE. SO.　　SEATTLE, WASH.

東藥醫院執事大鑒

為本屆西歸來會舘由京運歸國先友共叁百五十五俱

同時滙歸香港共拢銀壹千八百餅概交由貴醫院

執事先生代為辦理一切�今截月未先

貴醫院執事示霞來會舘董事殊深渴望追

得再函托陳月棠先生就近代轉政

貴醫院執事甚感有此諸先友及有此穎收

到晉邀　公有意示霞藉慰渴望感佩

仍照本良去此特荣

公祺己覆

中華民國二十年五月十六日泐

主席曾詠佐

舍記胡柏安

中華會舘

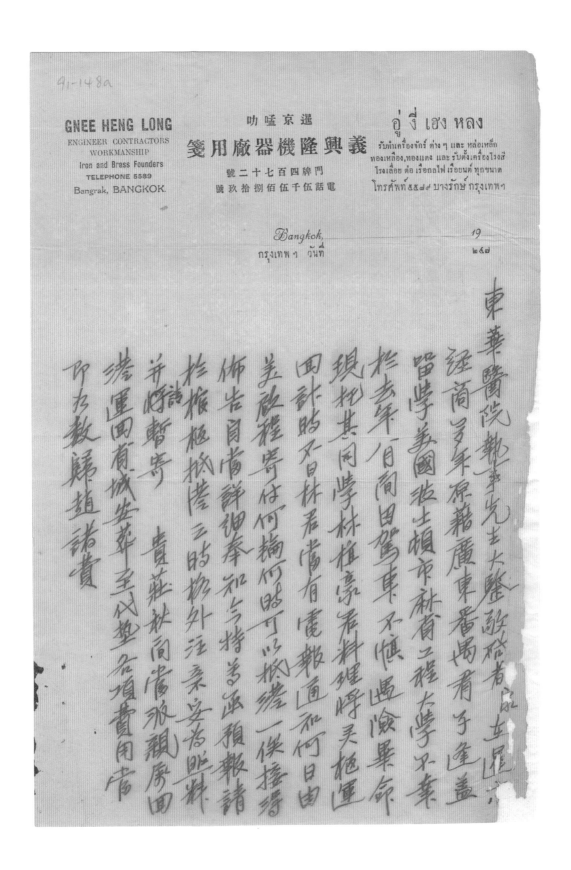

GNEE HENG LONG
ENGINEER CONTRACTORS
WORKMANSHIP
Iron and Brass Founders
TELEPHONE 5589
Bangrak, BANGKOK.

暹京嗌叻
義興隆機器廠用箋
門牌四百七十二號
電話五千伍佰捌拾玖號

อู๋ งี่ เฮง หลง
รับทำเครื่องจักร์ ต่าง ๆ และ หล่อเหล็ก
ทองเหลือง,ทองแดง และ รับตั้งเครื่องโรงสี
โรงเลื่อย ต่อ เรือกลไฟ เรือยนต์ ทุกขนาด
โทรศัพท์ ๕๕๘๙ บางรัก กรุงเทพฯ

Bangkok, 19

กรุงเทพฯ วันที่ ๒๔๗

東華醫院執事先生大鑒敬啓者茲有暹羅

經商呂宅年原籍廣東番禺省于逢蓋

留學美國波士頓市林省工程大學卒業

於去年一月間因駕車不慎遇險喪命

現將其同學林植豪君料理美柩運

回訃貼習林君尚有噩報通知何日由

美啓程寄往何輪何時可以抵埠一俟接得

佈告自當詳細奉知今持另派預報諸

於柩抵港之時務外注意妥為照料

並可暫寄 貴莊秋間當派親屬來

港運回省城安葬主代墊各項費用當

即為數歸趙諸費

GNEE HENG LONG
ENGINEER CONTRACTORS
WORKMANSHIP
Iron and Brass Founders
TELEPHONE 5589
Bangrak, BANGKOK.

暹京嗎叻

義興隆機器廠用箋

門牌四百七十二號

電話伍仟伍佰捌拾玖號

อู๋ งี่ เฮง หลง

รับทำเครื่องจักร์ ต่าง ๆ และ หล่อเหล็ก
ทองเหลือง,ทองแดง และ รับตั้งเครื่องโรงสี
โรงเลื่อย ต่อ เรือกลไฟ เรือยนต์ ทุกขนาด
โทรศัพท์ ๕๕๘๙ บางรัก กรุงเทพฯ

Bangkok,
กรุงเทพฯ วันที่

19
๒๗

公安

清禪石學均感盍啟請

國華肖怡

周鏡崇書寄

箋用館會總陽寧山台利多域大拿加

HOY SUN NING YUNG
BENEVOLENT ASS'N
HEAD OFFICE

P. O. BOX 1512　　538 CORMORANT ST.
VICTORIA, B. C. CANADA.

香港東華醫院

顏戒坤董事先生曁列位執事先生鑒一

逕啓者現拿大域多利埠台山寧陽總會館是

屆執拾各邑先友骸骨統計合共一櫬現由

詩亞公司俄國皇后輪船裝載四港頌

貴善院僱工起收並將邑先友轉運回各該邑

善堂安置以候先友家屬領收妥葬以慰靈爽

功德無量矣茲付四港瓦喬壹張值銀伍百大元

請查照收此應支需惟是本總會館戰員連年

更換懇對于辦理難免人生路不熟之處或有未

能的當之處尚希賜以指教是所感盼

此致

　　總理李黨世

民國二十年

七月廿八日

　　書記黃世錄

篆用館會總陽寧山台利多域大拿加

HOY SUN NING YUNG

BENEVOLENT ASS'N
HEAD OFFICE

P. O. BOX 1512　　　538 CORMORANT ST.
VICTORIA, B. C. CANADA.

東華醫院

顏成坤先生暨各董事先生鑒

逕啓者早月呈函曾經商量運寄先友

法拿蒙亦復照准辦理現查執拾骸骨統

計合共叨祺准期于八月一日由詩巫亞公司俄

國皇后輪船載運回港俱應亟達

貴院屆時僱工起收代為分送各邑善堂俾

骸親收領安葬是則壹惟此魂各得其所

貴院為善之熱誠富亦積德無量矣此致

崇安

　　　　　　　　總理李覺也
　　　　　　　　書記黃世錦

中華民國二十年七月廿八日

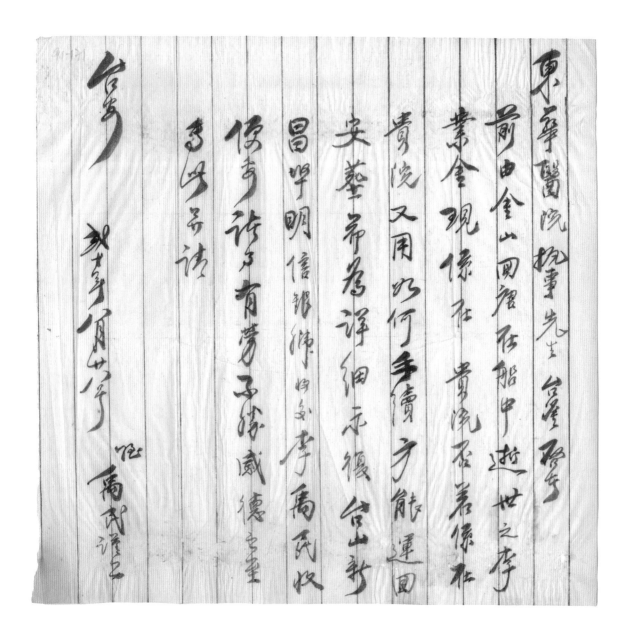

東華醫院執事先生台鑒敬啟者

前由金山囘唐居於船中逝世之李

業金現係在貴院存葬係在

貴院又用以何手續方能運囘

安藝帝為詳細示復金山新

昌埠明信報師好名李禹民收

倘幸諸子孫威德重重

專此奉達

統此 卅年八月廿八号

李禹民謹啟

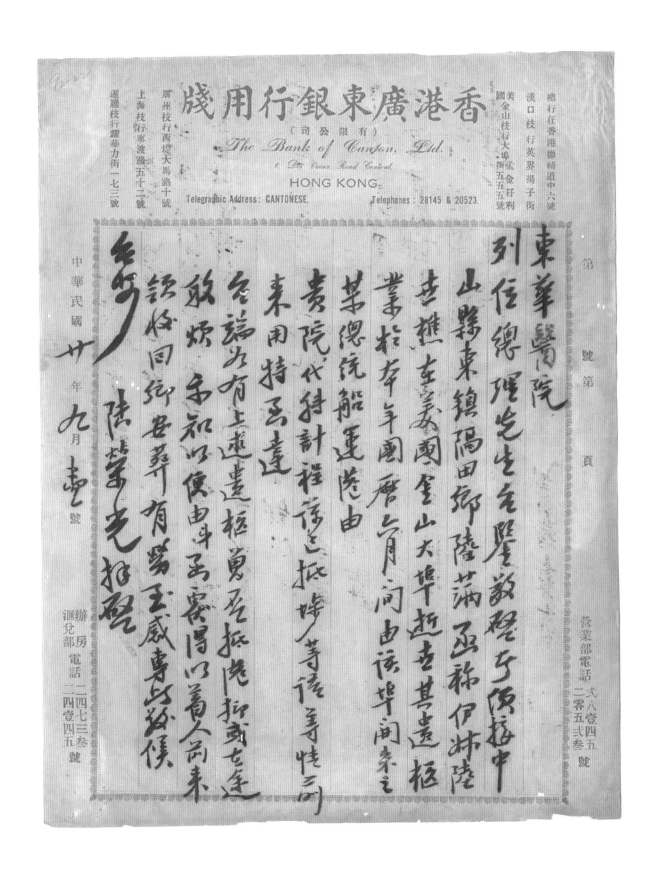

香港廣東銀行用牋
（有限公司）
The Bank of Canton, Ltd.
6 Des Voeux Road Central
HONG KONG.

Telegraphic Address: CANTONESE.　　Telephones: 28145 & 20523.

總行在香港德輔道中六號
漢口枝行英界揚子街
美國金山枝行大埠孟金孖利國街五五五號
廣州枝行西堤大馬路十號
上海枝行寧波路五十二號
暹羅枝行耀華力街一七三號

第　號第　頁

營業部電話　弍八壹四五號
營業部電話　二零五弍叁號

辦房　　電話　二四七三叁號
滙兌部　電話　二四壹四五號

東華醫院

列位總理先生毛鑒敬啟者頃接中
山縣東鎮隅田鄉陸蒲函稱伊妹陸
去攜去美國金山大埠逝去其遺柩
業於本年團曆貳月間由該埠運柩之
敝總院船運陸由
貴院代代計程諒已抵埠等情等特三同
來用特函達
色端為有上述遺柩甚君君抵院折或去金
敢煩予祖以便由斗弄弄賽得以善人向來
鍚給同鄉並希荷蒙玉感專此敬候
　　　　陸榮光拜啟

中華民國廿年九月壹號

敬啓者東華醫院大德理顏成坤善長

先生鑒：逕啓者于勝華陸輩當春爲

祝立廠設招爲業父在花縣仙遊去歲由

西正月初旬自由美國據悉父先運返去歲

東華醫院轉交仍濁東邦佳邑查喪

查問辦事人員言及有收經民寄中山

回春醫萬功专去中山查問與善堂經

理言及新舊

年之久未有交料但保理溽接此

信生先生寫明運費洗用銀多事

由宋查山善長爲農俱濟回查中山君

岐南基派慶信海味店収糖寄等便任

即鄭賞容昌鴻靈柩五懷子此件快報發

即請

勛安

　　　　顏先生鈞安

辛省八月日緣　鄭鏡祥邱禀

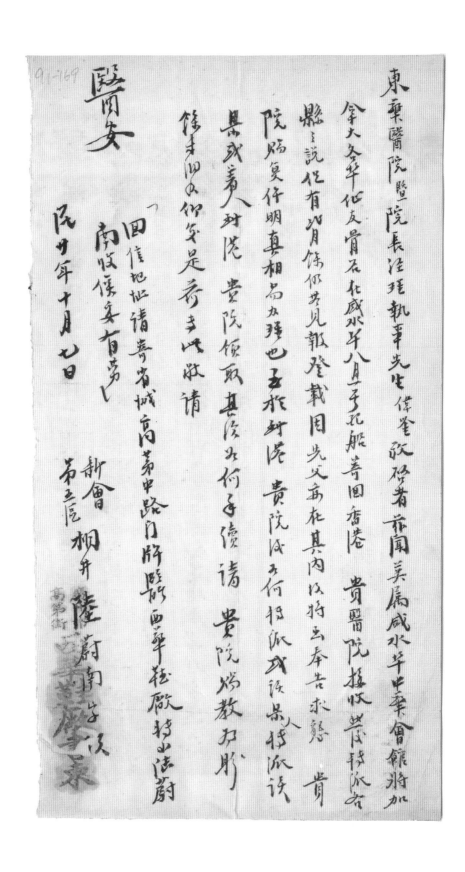

91-169

東華醫院暨院長注理執事先生偉鑒 敬啟者 前聞美屬咸水埠中藥會館將加

金大弍平 仆友骨右在咸水埠八月乘花船荡回香港 貴醫院接收弍後特派弍

縣主說從有與餘弍 仆弍見報登載因先父弍在其內以弍弍奉告求懇 貴

院燭窺詳明真相為要 弍 至於弍港 貴院汲弍何招派或誤弍弍特派誤

甚咸弍 對院 貴院領取甚院弍何子續請 貴院燭教弍弍

餘弍弍仰望是荷弍弍敬請

醫院安

南收候弍百芳弍

新會

弟三区 楊并

陸蔚南弍弍弍

院廿年十月七日

「回信地址請弍省城高弍中路門牌弍西華莊啟」特此注弍

9l-167a

箋用館會總陽寧山台利多域大拿加
HOY SUN NING YUNG
BENEVOLENT ASS'N
HEAD OFFICE

P. O. BOX 1512　　　　538 CORMORANT ST.
VICTORIA, B. C. CANADA.

東華醫院列位善董先生鑒

逕啟者本總會館前八月一日由俄國皇后船付囘

各先友費銀伍佰大元諒已妥收並各邑先友臺

仟捌佰餘具想承妥為安置惟轉駁運返各邑

善臺一切費用各邑善臺自行料理但經西兩個月餘

末得 貴院囘音賜教本總會館董事等殊

為焦應注 貴院善董從速賜函指示俾得

領教而免縈懷是所切盼此致

並候

文祺

總理李覺世
書記黃世銓

民國二十年十月十日

加拿大域多利台山寧陽總會館用箋
HOY SUN NING YUNG
BENEVOLENT ASS'N
HEAD OFFICE

P. O. BOX 1512　　　　538 CORMORANT ST.
VICTORIA, B. C. CANADA.

荔崎各邑先友角列

台山鋒慶臺　　　　付交台城東寧外義庄祠起收

中山福善臺　　　　箱壹　吊鐵箱一个

同卅福慶臺收　　　付交會城新威街仁安醫院起收

開平廣福臺

增城仁安臺

恩平同福臺

番禺昌后臺

東莞保安臺

南海縣臺

順德行安臺

鶴山縣臺

新安縣臺

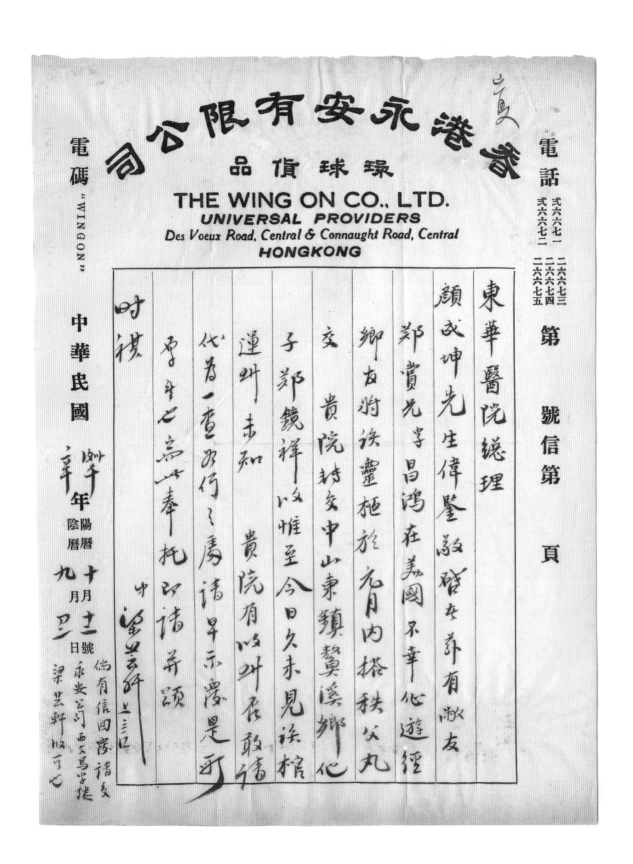

香港永安有限公司

環球貨品

THE WING ON CO., LTD.
UNIVERSAL PROVIDERS
Des Voeux Road, Central & Connaught Road, Central
HONGKONG

電話

弍六六七一
弍六六七二
二六六七三
二六六七四
二六六七五

第 號信第 頁

電碼 "WINGON"

中華民國 辛未年 陰曆 九月
陽曆 十月 十二 日

東華醫院總理

顏武坤先生偉鑒敬啟者弟友
鄭賞先亭昌鴻在美國不幸仙遊經
鄉友將該靈柩於有內搭秩父丸
交貴院轉交中山東鎮麓溪鄉化
子鄭鏡祥收惟至今日久未見誤槓
運料未知 貴院有以辦理否敢請
代為一查究竟以免請早示當是所
感專此奉托即請荓頌
時祺
中 梁芸軒之三口

永安公司西文寫字樓
僑有信回煩諸交
梁芸軒收可也

紐港東華醫局

列位執事先生大鑒　謹啓者敝善堂是屆議

決奉辦檢運先骸事務目下經已着手檢集妥

茲大小合共弍十具擇準於本月十一日由此間附搭

胡佛德統 S.S. Pres. Hoover 轉運東扛直寄交

貴局暫為收存故用特預函告達屆時如該先骸等

運抵貴埠時希即代為妥存諸請發函下列地

址俾得前往提領為盼附夾上載紙乙揆仰祈查

照是荷諸費清神謝々尚此預達并頌

公安

民國廿一年三月十一日　中山都恭上　集善堂謹啓

侯領人通信地址以下

（中山縣下柵圩茂昌號

轉交卓篤先收

梁厚晃收）

Peng Sin Tong Assn
814 Grant Ave
San Francisco Calif USA

周鏡輝及周鏡如致東華醫院信件

1932 年 3 月 19 日

特字

東華醫院主席執事　鑒

啟者茲今廿一

年新曆三月十九号昭行太平洋公司

復統搬旋國運來尸棺一具乃係

廣東省番禺縣慕德里司南村宏

仁里人周義和名由美屬域多利埠

儎回有常先生親手到步請查收領

代為駁運番邑城北高塘墟候他鄉

親屬領回安葬就惟可是匯運駁費

用若干請來函港匯安公司匯返店內

轉干諾道西如祥社為交安號事芳

請代備覆音

順請

善安

廿一年三月十九号　周鏡輝如　拜托

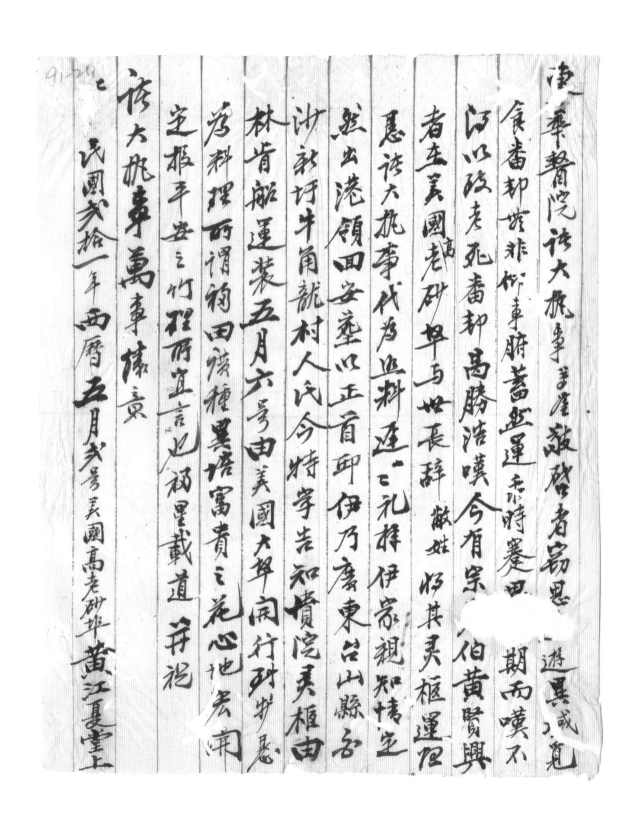

東華醫院諸大執事善長鈞鑒敬啟者竊思人遊異或覽

食睿却地非鄉事俯蓄並運以時蹇困期而嘆不

沿以致老死壽却為勝浩嘆今有宗一伯黃賢興

者在美國老砂埠為與世長辭敬姑以其靈柩運回

懇諸大執事代為並料連二礼拜伊蒙視知情定

然出港領田安藿以正首卹伊乃廣東台山縣各

沙新讨牛角就村人氏今特字告知貴院靈柩由

林肯航運裝五月六号由美國大埠囚行政步懇

為科理西謂禍田墳種異培富貴之花心地宏南

定報平安之代理所宜言也初星載道并祝

諸大執事萬事樣意

民國弍拾一年西曆五月弍号美國高老砂埠黃江夏堂上

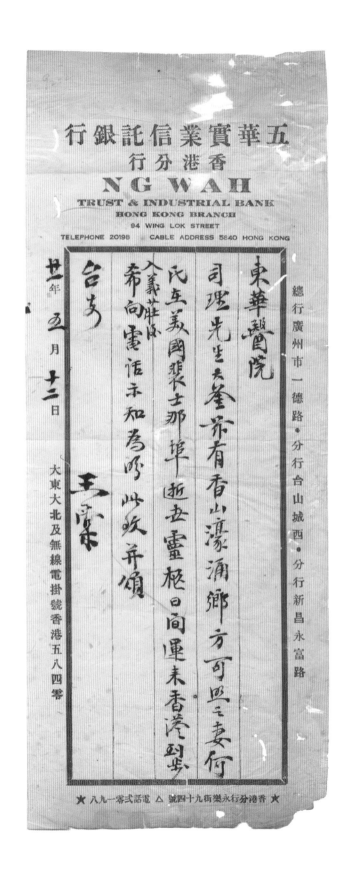

行銀託信業實華五
行分港香
NG WAH
TRUST & INDUSTRIAL BANK
HONG KONG BRANCH
94 WING LOK STREET
TELEPHONE 20198　CABLE ADDRESS 5840 HONG KONG

總行廣州市一德路．分行台山城西．分行新昌永富路

東華醫院
司理先生大鑒：茲有香山濠涌鄉方可興之妻何
氏在美國羅士那埠逝世靈柩日間運来香港到步
入義莊內
希向電話未知為叨　此致并頌
台安

廿一年　五月　十三日
　　　　　　　王棠

大東大北及無線電掛號香港五八四零

★八九一號式話電△號四十九街樂永行分港香★

東華醫院諸執事先生暨眾位執事素荷諸執事慈善為怀惻憶者

心久有感 名如雷貫耳獨惜事寄幽他邦緣墮乎瞻韓飄逢異

域而鮮於識荊悵何如之惟有仰天遙祝諸執事 先生百歲延

釐千羊緝慶繁庶孟集嘉祉咸臻而已耳茲有哀懇其事有胞

弟名劉錫廣乃順德縣騰冲鄉人氏因事屋羨美洲碎喪華時遭不

幸痛於本年正月下旬身故令將其靈柩運回祖國以正首坵准于

五月拾日由他輪總統航運回計時下月約　茅日可以抵港但抵港之

後定必淅停厝於東華醫院候親人茅剩來領收帶回家鄉安

葬茅名有作寄為嘱託劉錫建劉源湘兩人剩　貴院申諸執事

先生商量領收帶為安窀以慰幽魂　伏乞　貴院諸執事　先生驗

明俾他兩人早日帶為安窀沒存均感玉於柩内并夾帶違禁

物品為有不妥之處隨時可以迴訊查究事為完全員責之人素

仰　貴院諸執事　先生嚴明慈善常為各地僑胞所乐道事不揣

冒昧故敢特字一函告藉助一臂諸事有劳容申拜謝

辰年五月廿六号晚　　弟劉錫堅拜上

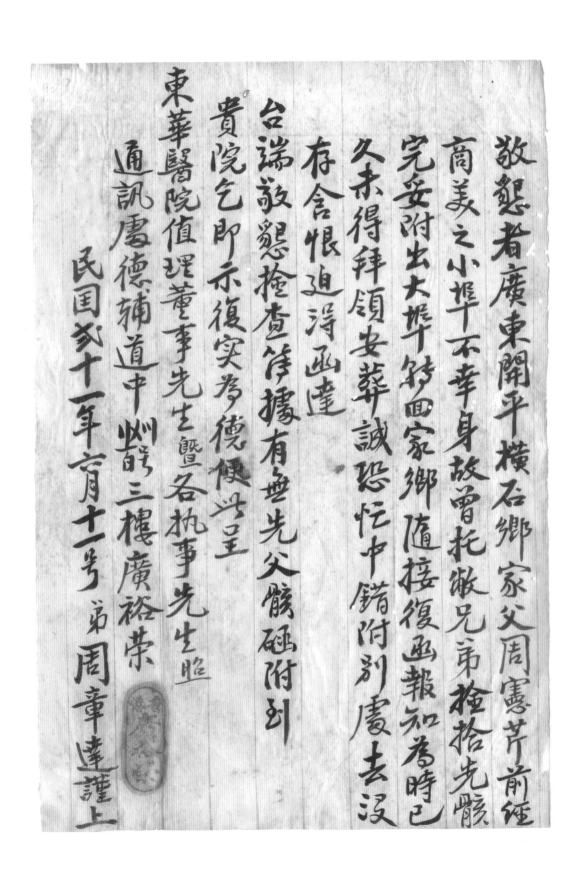

敬懇者廣東開平橫石鄉家父周憲芹前經

商美之小埠不幸身故曾托徽兄弟檢拾先骸

完妥附出大埠筹回家鄉隨接復函報知着時已

久未得拜領安葬誠恐忙中錯附別廬去沒

存合恨追得函達

台端敬懇撿查等據有無先父骸砠附到

貴院乞即示復寔考德便為呈

東華醫院值理董事先生暨各执事先生照

　　通訊盧德輔道中州號三樓廣裕榮

　　民國甘十一年肎十二号　弟周章達謹上

東華醫院諸報事先生鑒 逕啟者茲有先中蔡贈英像

台山縣公益區大江沙浦中美村人昨六月初旬在雲哥華埠

逝世茲將其遺骸雲貞由亞洲皇后船六月十八号船姐運回

运港另死者有夾碼箱雲貞内有四衣物亦是同船壽未用呈函

達 貴院查收懇為料理運其框四原籍妥葬至

抵夾碼箱萬通知重港上環西街學德栈油舖饮四件

变其妻子收领足荷素仰 貴醫院慈善為懷永理好

華長當今蒙妥理此事存殳均感崇此佈達印詢

羊義安

旅雲哥華埠沙浦房同人 蔡傑夫
蔡英錦仝啟

民國廿一年六月十五号 沙

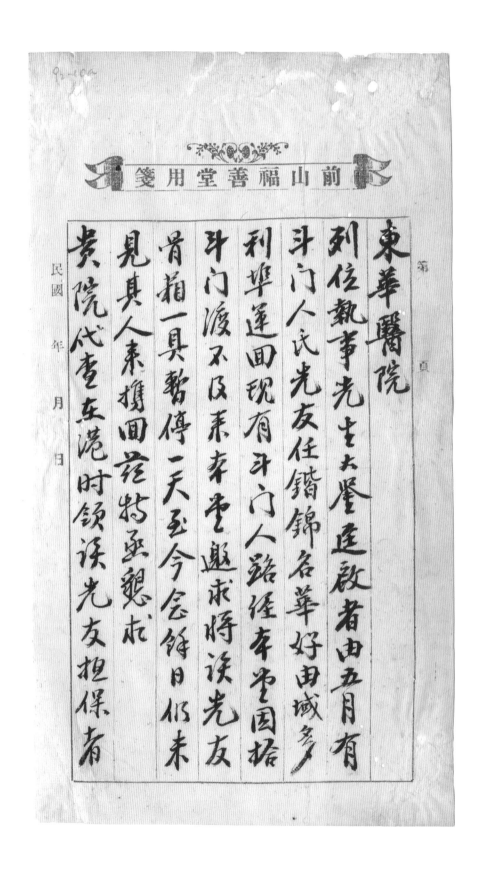

前山福善堂用箋

第　　頁

東華醫院

列位執事先生大鑒逕啟者由五月有

斗門人氏光友任鍇錦名華好由域多

利埠運回現有斗門人路經本堂因搭

斗門渡不及乘來暫邀求將該光友

骨殖一具暫停二天至今會餘日仍未

見其人來攜回差特丞懇求

貴院代查東港時領該光友担保者

民國　年　月　日

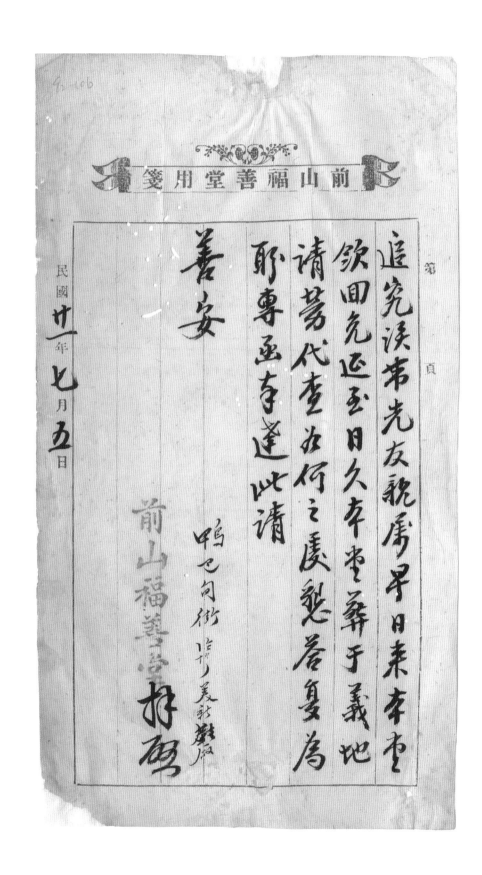

前山福善堂用箋

第頁

追究溪帶先友親屬早日來本市
欽回免延玉日久未安葬于義地
請勞代查法何之處懇善復為
耶專函奉達此請

善安

民國廿一年七月五日

前山福善堂林砥

鴨巴甸街正街美新機版

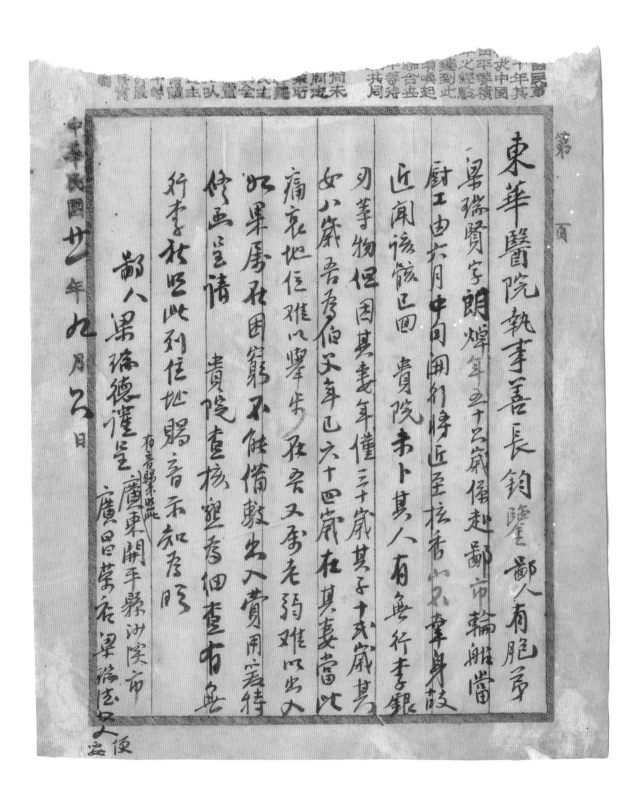

第一頁

東華醫院執事善長鈞鑒 敝人有胞弟

梁瑞賢字朗燁年五十六歲僱起鄉而輪船當

廚工由六月中旬開行停近至本省小衣章身故

近聞該骸已回 貴院未卜其人有無行李銀

刃筆物但因其妻年僅三十歲其子十或歲其

女八歲吾為伯父年已六十四歲在其妻當此

痛哀地任難以舉失 在吾又季老弱難以出入

如果屬私困窮不能償敷出入費用等待

修函呈請 貴院查核 塑者細查有無

行李在此列信地賜音示知為盼

　　　　　敝人梁瑞德謹呈

　　　　　　　廣東開平縣沙溪市

　　　　　　　廣昌榮店梁瑞德

中華民國廿一年九月六日

91-197a

DOLLAR STEAMSHIP LINES
AND
AMERICAN MAIL LINE

ROUND THE WORLD   TRANS-PACIFIC
NEW YORK-CALIFORNIA   NEW YORK-ORIENT
CALIFORNIA-NEW YORK   ORIENT-NEW YORK

PO 352 JWM

Hongkong,
October 19,1932

File: C-3-C

Tung Wah Hospital,
Hongkong

Gentlemen: -

On the arrival of our ss "President Monroe" V-27, on
May 14th,1932, the remains of one of our steerage passengers,
Francisco Lee Soon, age 33, was delivered to you.

Francisco Lee Soon died on board our "President Monroe"
on May 6th, while that steamer was enroute to Hongkong. The
cause of death was tuberculosis. Francisco Lee Soon was a
passenger on board the "President Monroe" from Havana and
was destined to Hongkong, and the body was embalmed and
delivered to the Tung Wah Hospital on arrival of the "President
Monroe" at this port.

Will you please be good enough to address to me a
letter confirming that the remains of Francisco Lee Soon
was turned over to you and also advising us as to what
disposition was made of the remains?

Very truly yours,

J.W. MORRIS
Passenger Agent

JWM:MC

91-1976

本年二月十四曰曾總統船搭客李宣書年三十三歲

當下多物注已交付貴院

李宣椿身有百圓肺癆僑死於船中而當時本

船未在連次回港之時也

李宣書是由夏灣拿李港者他的户籍已於船

挽時交付貴院矣

請貴院示發証明李宣之遺物確已交付

貴院及另所處置此事遺物

孤清好青
內宣

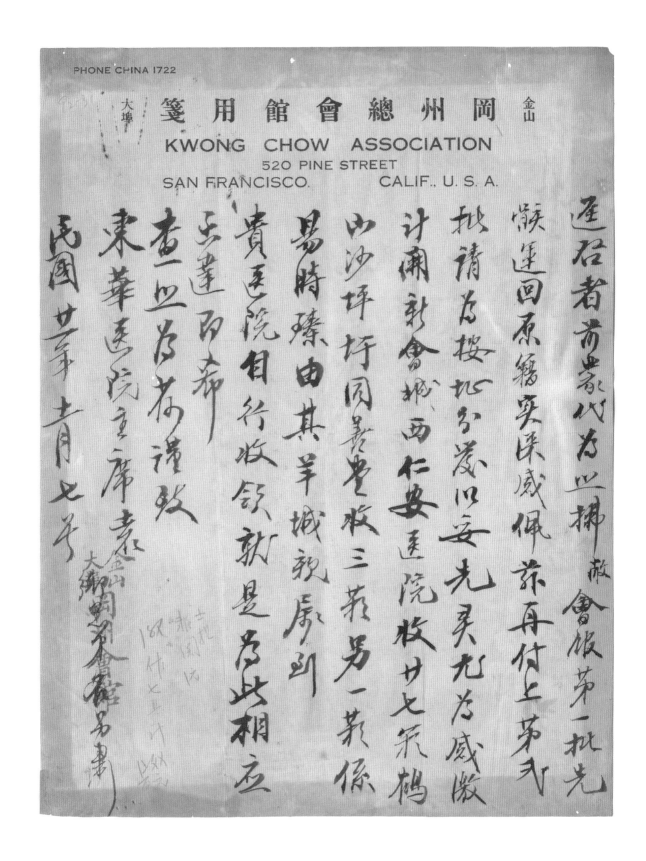

PHONE CHINA 1722

金山 岡州總會館用箋 大埠

KWONG CHOW ASSOCIATION
520 PINE STREET
SAN FRANCISCO.   CALIF., U. S. A.

逕啟者前此蒙代為此辦敬會服第一批先

僥運回原籍實深感佩茲再付上第貳

批請為按批分發以安先叟先叔為感激

計開新會城、西仁安醫院收廿七莊鵝

山沙坪圩同善堂老收三莊另一莊係

易時瑔由其羊城親屬到

貴醫院自行收領就是另此相立

玉蓮阿嬸

查一一為荷謹致

東華醫院主席惠表

民國廿一年十一月七号
金山
大埠岡州總會館謹書

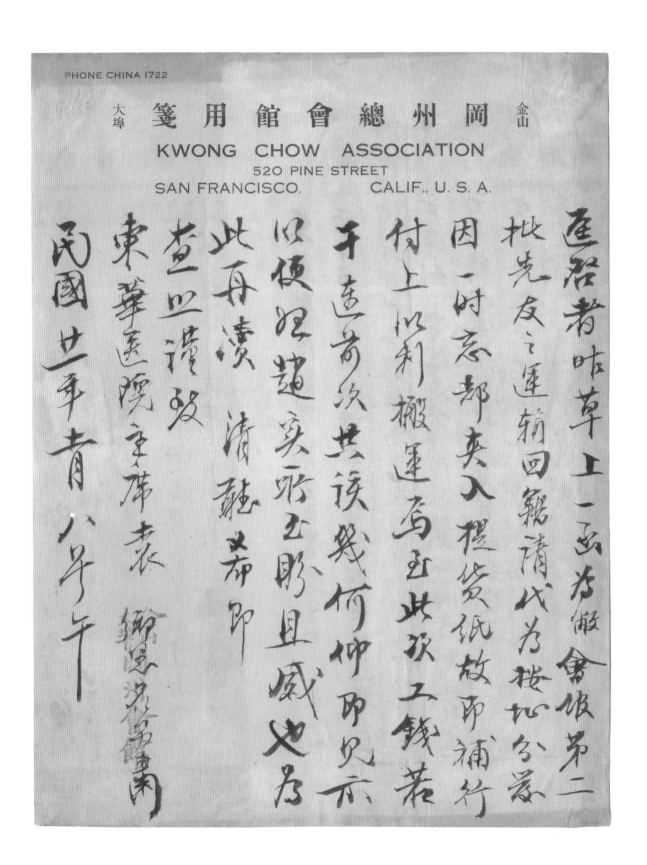

PHONE CHINA 1722

大埠　箋用館會總州岡　金山
KWONG CHOW ASSOCIATION
520 PINE STREET
SAN FRANCISCO.　　CALIF., U. S. A.

逕啟者昨草上一函諒荷
會垣第二
批先友之運輸回籍請代為接地分察
因一時忘郵夾入棺貨紙故而補行
付上批利搬運為玆此次工錢若
干連前次共該幾何仰即見示
以便趕趕實亦為明且感也為
此再瀆
清聽幾希亮即
查照瀆敬
東華醫院主席表
　　　　　　　　翁運汝鞠南
民國廿年青八号午

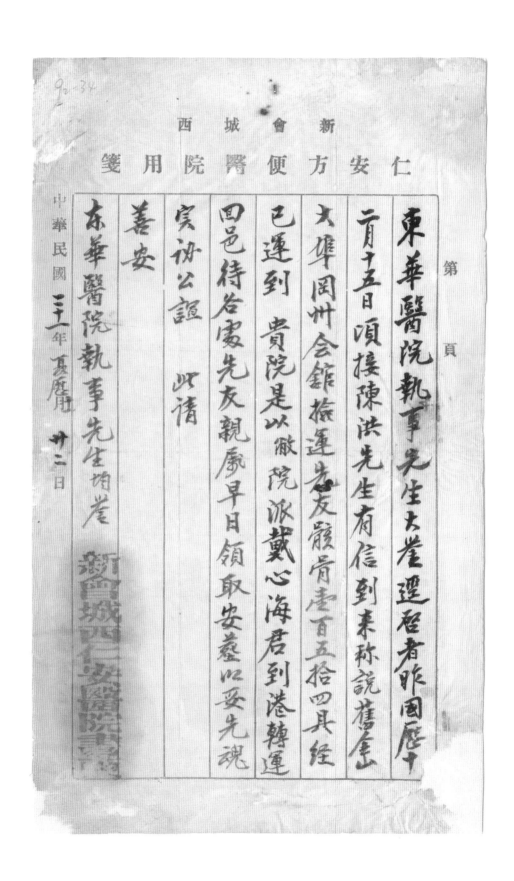

新會城西仁安便方醫院用箋

第頁

東華醫院執事先生大鑒逕啓者昨因歷十

二月十五日頃接陳洪先生有信到來稱說舊金山

大埠岡州会館撥運先友骸骨壹百五拾四具経

已運到貴院是以敝院派戴心海君到港轉運

四邑待各處先友親屬早日領取安葬以妥先魂

實紉公誼 此請

善安

東華醫院執事先生均鑒

中華民國三十一年真歷用 廿二日

〔新會城西仁安醫院門〕印

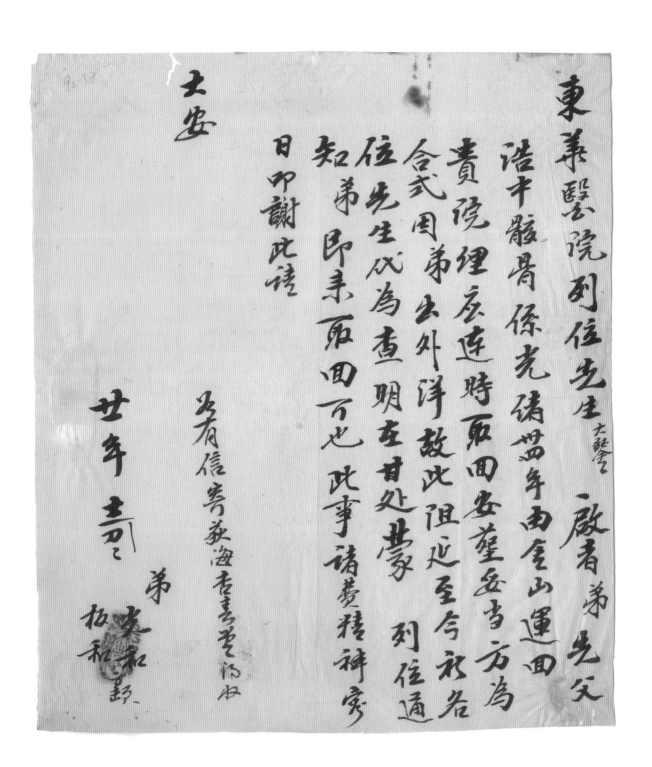

東華醫院列位先生大醫會 啟者弟先父

浩中骸骨係先緒當年西金山運回

貴院理應連時頂囘安葬妥當方為

合式因弟出外洋故此阻延至今祈各

位先生代為查明主甘此處並蒙 列位通

知弟即來頂囘可也此事請費精神幸

甚 日叩謝此請

士安

另有信寄荻海杏春堂另內由

廿年十二月〔廿〕〔日〕

弟 長和謹

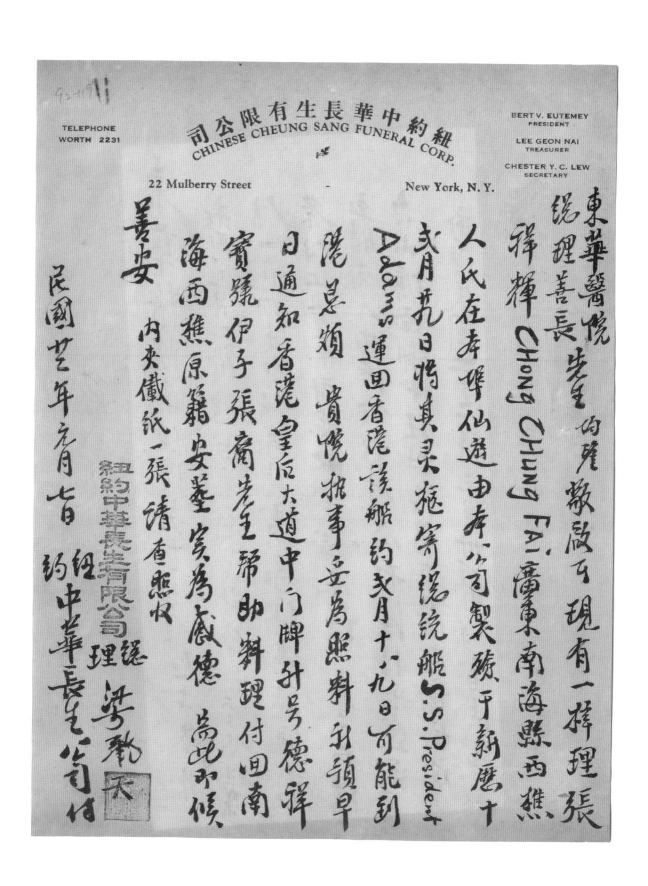

TELEPHONE
WORTH 2231

紐約中華長生有限公司
CHINESE CHEUNG SANG FUNERAL CORP.

22 Mulberry Street — New York, N.Y.

BERT V. EUTEMEY
PRESIDENT

LEE GEON NAI
TREASURER

CHESTER Y. C. LEW
SECRETARY

東華醫院

銳理善長先生 均鑒 敬啟者 現有一樣理張

祥輝 Chong Chung Fai 廣東南海縣西樵

人氏 在本埠仙遊 由本公司製殮 于新曆十

文月九日將其靈柩寄銳銳銳船 S.S. President

Adams 運回香港該船約文月十九日可能到

港慕類 貴院批事妥為照料 先領早

日通知香港皇后大道中门牌升号德祥

寶號 伊子張商先生稀助料理付回南

海西樵原籍安墓安為感德 肅此如候

善安

内夾儀纸一張 请查照收

紐約中華長生有限公司 銳

理 梁勒 〔印〕

民國廿二年元月旬 紐中華長先公付

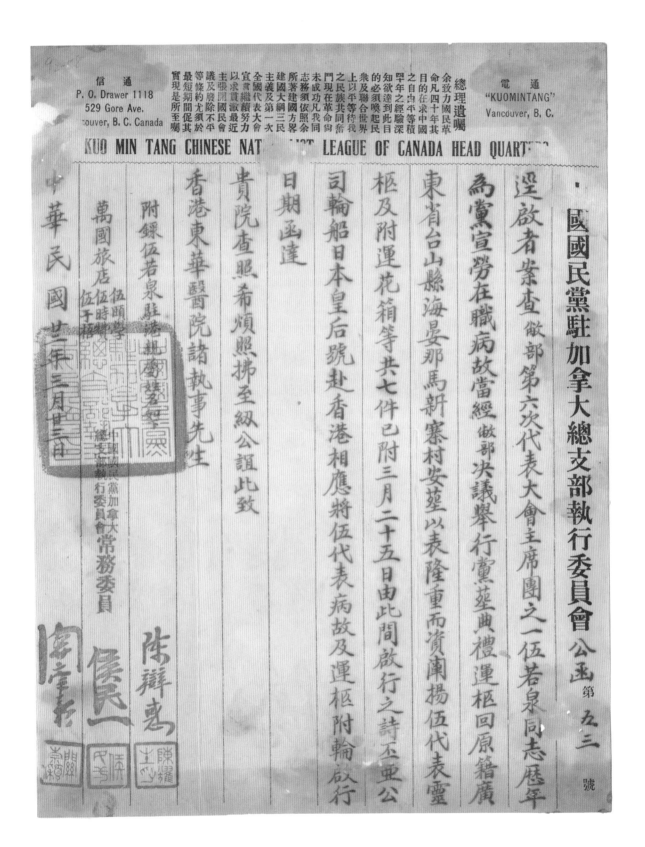

信通
P. O. Drawer 1118
529 Gore Ave.
...couver, B. C. Canada

電通
"KUOMINTANG"
Vancouver, B. C.

KUO MIN TANG CHINESE NAT... LEAGUE OF CANADA HEAD QUARTERS

國國民黨駐加拿大總支部執行委員會公函　第五三號

逕啟者業查　敞部第六次代表大會主席團之一伍若泉同志歷年

為黨宣勞在職病故當經敞部決議舉行黨葬典禮運柩回原籍廣

東省台山縣海晏那馬新寨村安葬以表隆重而資闡揚伍代表靈

柩及附運花箱等共七件已附三月二十五日由此間啟行之詩丕亞公

司輪船日本皇后號赴香港相應將伍代表病故及運柩附輪啟行

日期函達

貴院查照希煩照拂至級公誼此致

香港東華醫院諸執事先生

附錄伍若泉駐港批圖致名…

萬國旅店　伍于禧　伍時學　伍頭學

中華民國廿二年三月廿三日

陳辟惠　侯民一　關…

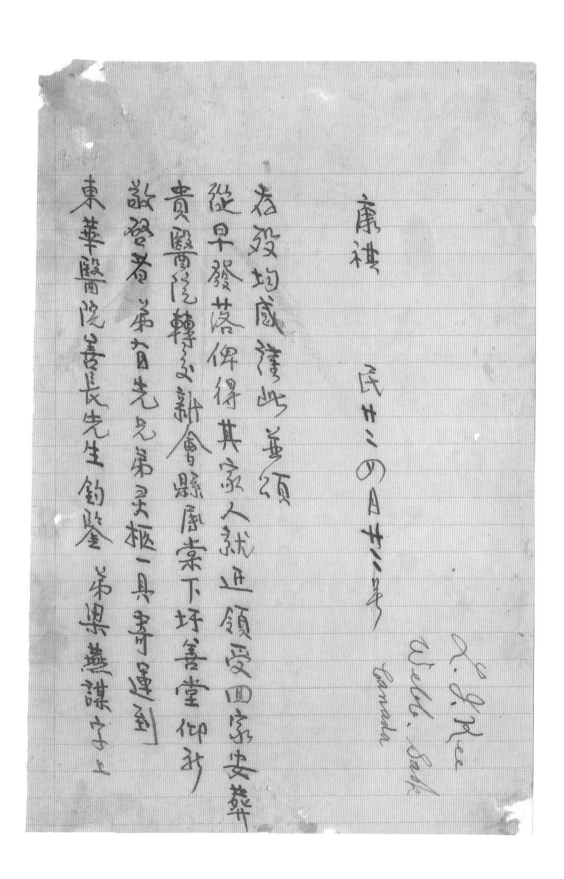

康祺

民廿二〇四廿二號

L. Y. Kee
Wells, Sask.
Canada

敬啟者弟日前弟美權一具專運到
貴醫院轉交新會縣屏棠下圩善堂仰新
從早發落俾得其家人就近領受回家安葬
去歿均感肅此並須

東華醫院善長先生鈞鑒 弟梁燕謀上

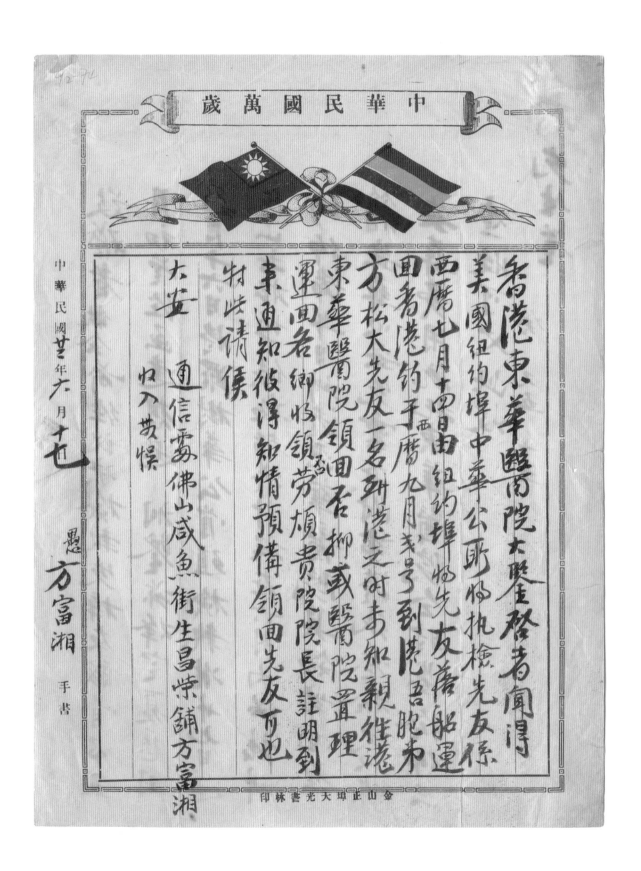

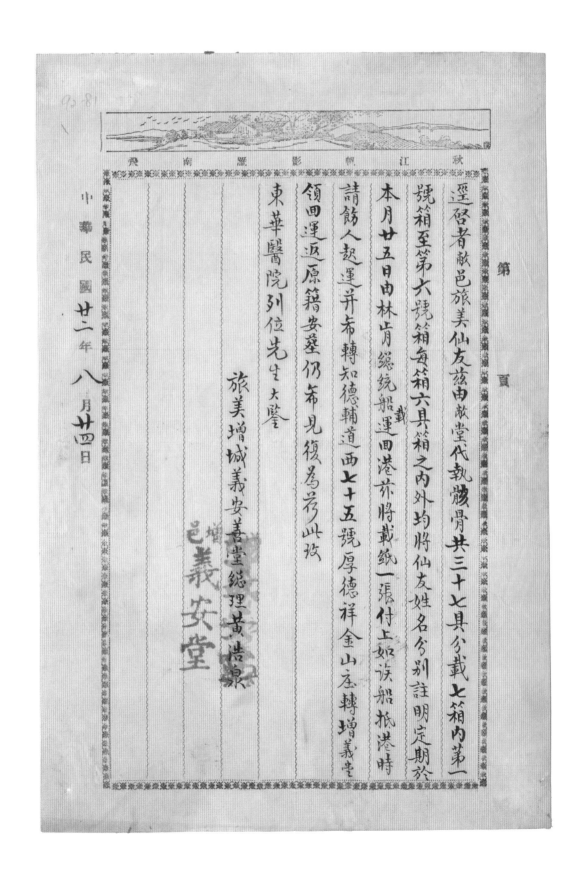

秋江帆影雁南飛

第頁

逕啟者敝邑旅美仙友茲由敝堂代執骸骨共三十七具分載七箱內第一

號箱至第六號箱每箱六具箱之內外均將仙友姓名分別註明定期於

本月廿五日由林肯總統船運回港亦將載紙一張付上如誤船抵港時

請飭人趕運并希轉知德輔道西七十五號厚德祥金山庄轉增義堂

領回運返原籍安葬仍希見復為荷此致

東華醫院列位先生大鑒

旅美增城義安善堂總理黃湛泉

中華民國廿二年八月廿四日

邑義安堂

增義安堂

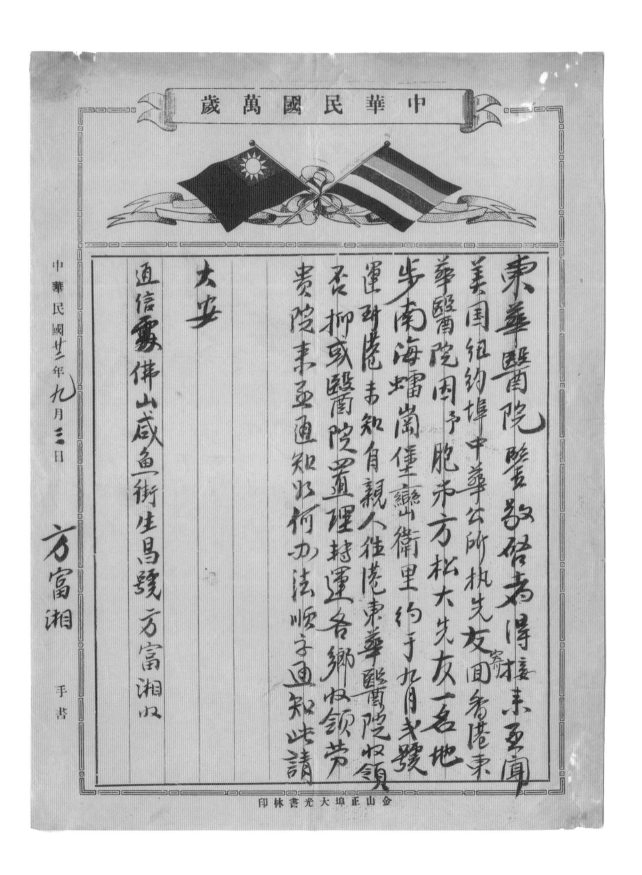

中華民國萬歲

東華醫院醫務啓者得接來函囑
美国紐約埠中華公所机先友囘香港東
華醫院囘予胞弟方松大先友一名地
步南海蟬崗堡戀衛里約于九月戈號
運新港未知有親人往港東華醫院收領
否柳或醫院置理持運各鄉收領勞
貴院素至通知以何办法順子通知此請

太安

中華民國廿二年九月三日
方富湘 手書

通信霧佛山咸魚一街生昌號方富湘收

金山正埠大光書林印

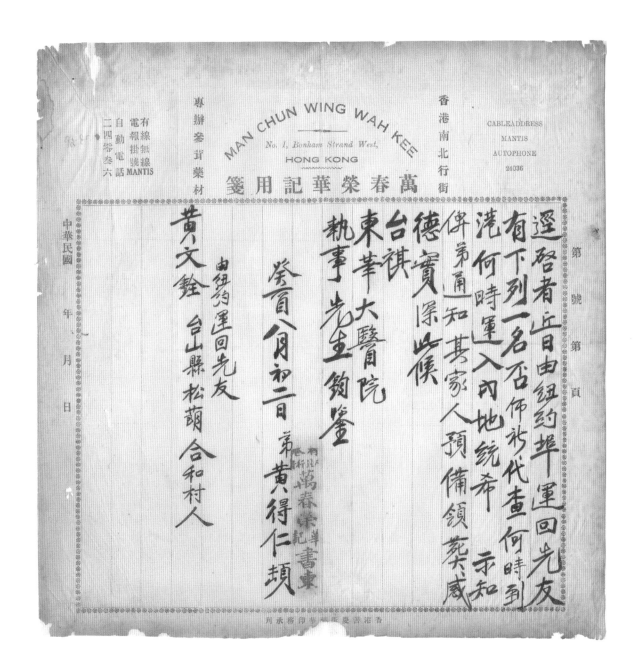

逕啟者 近日由紐約埠運回先友
有下列一名 否師衿代查何時到
港 何時運入内地統希
俾弟通知 其家人預備領葬威 示知
德寶深候
台祺
東華大醫院
執事先生鈞鑒
癸酉八月初二日 弟黃得仁頓
黃文銓 台山縣松蔭 合和村人
由伊約運回先友

(Copy of Letter from Hong Kong, China)

October 15, 1933

Hong Kong, China

Zane Fook

Dear Cousin:

　　　　I received a letter from Shin You saying that my
son Wong Ah You is coming to Hong Kong on the S.S. Coolidge.
When she arrived I didn't find him, but later I received a
letter from you saying he did come on that ship, so I went in
more details.　Next I find him dead on ship and was taken care
of at Dung Wai Yee Yan, undertaker.　I am taking his belongings
and trunk.　Do you know how much cash he took along, so I can
claim it here and take his body back to the village to bury.

　　　　　　　　　　　　　Wong Fook Sui

　　　　　　　　　　　　　　Sin Kai

Hong Kong　　　　　　　　　Sar Tan

曾福兄鑒前接 辛有來信云

小兒黃亞有乘哥列治總統航

來港但係接船不見蹤跡及

後再得接兄出云他實搭該

船來港經詳細調查始悉

他在船上身故遺柩由東華醫

院辦理其遺下行李等件已

由弟收領但未悉他有另現款

遺下如 兄知其詳請示

弟以便在此會將收妥然後將

其遺柩運回鄉間安葬

弟 十月五手 黃德瑞

（新曆沈田）

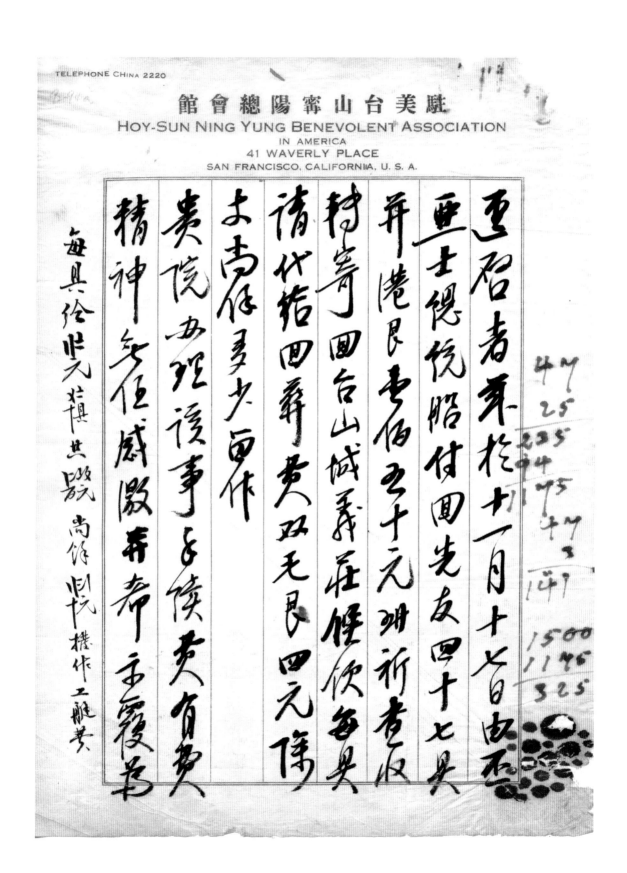

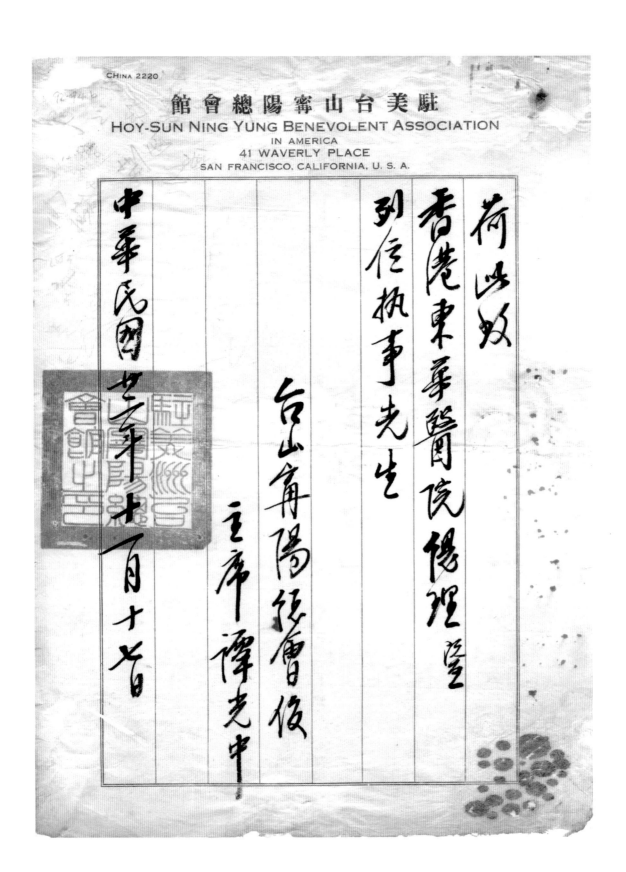

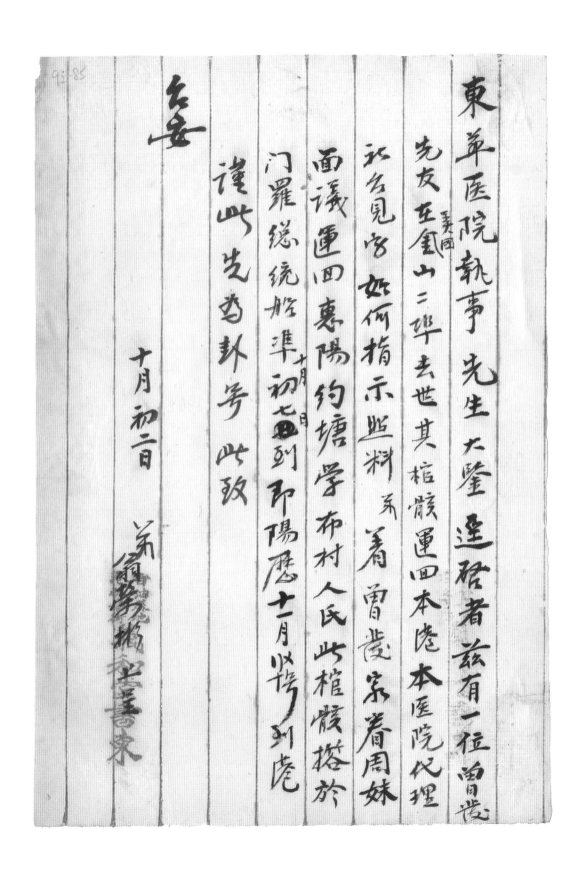

東華医院執事 先生大鑒 逕啟者茲有一位曾愛

先友在金山三埠去世其棺骸運回本港本醫院代理

註名見字如何指示照料系 蕭曾愛宗眷周妹

面議運回惠陽約塘學布村人民此棺骸搭於

门罗總統舩準初七日到即陽歷十一月十九到港

謹此先為扑號等此致

姜

　　十月初二日　　弟翁榮彬　書東

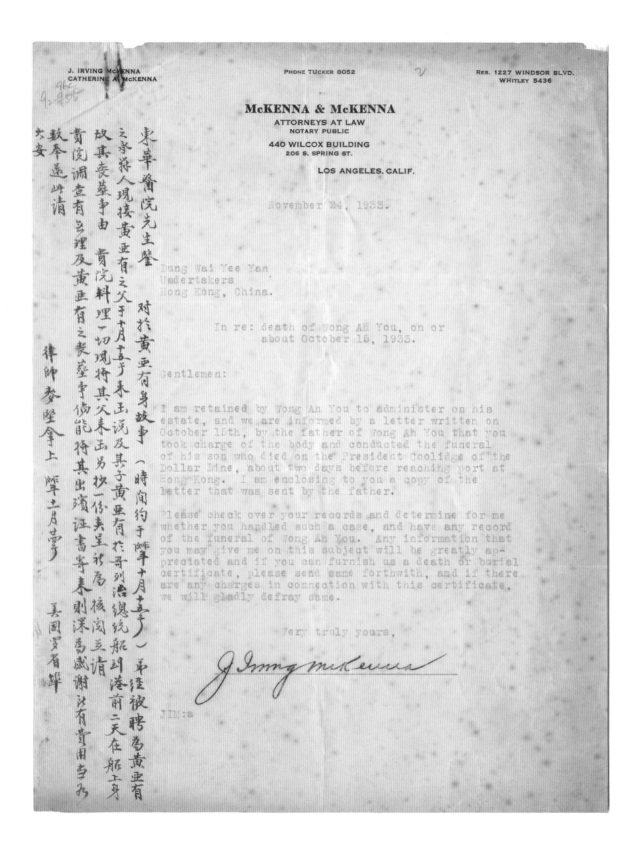

McKENNA & McKENNA
ATTORNEYS AT LAW
NOTARY PUBLIC
440 WILCOX BUILDING
206 S. SPRING ST.

LOS ANGELES, CALIF.

J. IRVING McKENNA
CATHERINE A. McKENNA

PHONE TUcker 8052

RES. 1227 WINDSOR BLVD.
WHitley 5436

November 24, 1933.

Dung Wai Yee Yan
Undertakers
Hong Kong, China.

In re: death of Wong Ah You, on or
about October 15, 1933.

Gentlemen:

I am retained by Wong Ah You to administer on his
estate, and we are informed by a letter written on
October 15th, by the father of Wong Ah You that you
took charge of the body and conducted the funeral
of his son who died on the President Coolidge of the
Dollar Line, about two days before reaching port at
Hong Kong. I am enclosing to you a copy of the
letter that was sent by the father.

Please check over your records and determine for me
whether you handled such a case, and have any record
of the funeral of Wong Ah You. Any information that
you may give me on this subject will be greatly appreciated and if you can furnish us a death or burial
certificate, please send same forthwith, and if there
are any charges in connection with this certificate,
we will gladly defray same.

Very truly yours,

J Irving McKenna

JIM:a

東華醫院先生鑒　對於黃亞有身故事（時間約于昨年十月十五干）弟經被聘為黃亞有

之弟孫人現接黃亞有之父于十月十五于未玉誠及其子黃亞有於哥列濟總統船斗港前二天在船上身

故其喪葬事由　貴院料理一切現將其父未玉另抄一份夾呈祈屬　核閱立請

貴院調查有無理及黃亞有之喪葬事倘能將其出殯証書等寄來則深為感謝並有貴用等亦

數奉遠此請

大安

律師　麥堅拿上　昨年十一月廿三

美國罗省埠

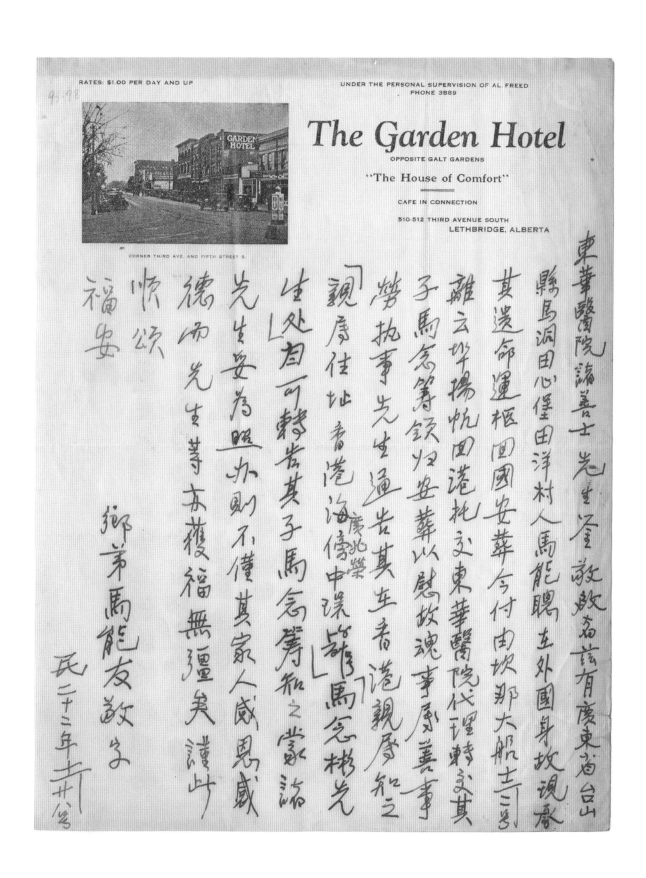

RATES: $1.00 PER DAY AND UP

4.98

UNDER THE PERSONAL SUPERVISION OF AL. FREED
PHONE 3889

The Garden Hotel

OPPOSITE GALT GARDENS

"The House of Comfort"

CAFE IN CONNECTION

510-512 THIRD AVENUE SOUTH
LETHBRIDGE, ALBERTA

CORNER THIRD AVE. AND FIFTH STREET S.

東華醫院諸善士先生鈞鑒 敬啟者茲有廣東省台山

縣馬洞田心堡田洋村人馬能聘 左外國身故現暫

其遺命運柩回國安華今付由坎那大船士二引

離云埠揚帆回港托交東華醫院代理轉交其

子馬念籌領歸安葬以慰故魂事屬善事

勞執事先生通告其在香港親屬知之

「親屬住址 香港海僑中議彰馬念彬先

生處為可轉告其子馬念籌知之 尚語 廣兆榮

先生妥為照 亦即不僅其家人感恩感

德而先生等亦獲福無疆美讚此

順頌

福安

鄉弟馬能友敬亭

民二十二年十一月廿八號

賤用堂善從都隆山香檀

Lung Do Chung Sin Tong

P. O. Box 1873

HONOLULU, HAWAII

東華醫院

列位善長鄉先生均鑒

伏處海嶠雲霄迴隔瞻言

台曜驤音為勞辰維

勛祺光昭

聲華卓越綜持公孟辟畫精深大力回旋美

無不舉宜乎中外閧風群相引重善堂中

嵩僂一指矣茲跂檀嶠徒滋塵累自維才

短莫展一籌乃蒙桿僑不棄公舉主持從善堂

事務緩短汲深時虞叢脞倘身等之與諸公地

雖作李郭之同舟而志芘切良平之倚箸

中華民國　年　月　日

地址檀香山正埠

信箱壹捌柒叁號

檀香山隆都從善堂用箋
Lung Do Chung Sin Tong
P. O. Box 1873
HONOLULU, HAWAII

第二頁

諸公閱才卓識其將何以教之也茲有懇者是

年敝堂檢執先友數凡九拾六名準於十二月十

五日附乘朴總統輪邉返歸葬宗邦以免飄泊異

域查素未至港主其事全仗

貴院諸公獨力勇為庶畢乃事固已頌聲載道

有口皆碑且

諸公對於此舉尤屬駕輕就熟一措一施自當

有條不紊加以茲事體大斷不能驟易生手致

有舛岐用特肅函句諸左右務望代援一臂力

成此舉屆時旅骨剞㔉萬請妥為買舟付返

石岐與善堂權為安放並請代篆一書力託該

中華民國　年　月　日

地址檀香山正埠

信箱壹捌柒叁號

檀香山隆都從善堂用牋
Lung Do Chung Sin Tong
P. O. Box 1873
HONOLULU, HAWAII

第三頁

堂董事諸公出紅登報招人到領俾得先友得

正首丘則雲天高誼不獨身受者感戴已也茲

付返港銀壹佰大員以資代辦之用敬乞照信檢

收除支各用之外其餘盡送

貴院以作善費倘蒙妥辦之後尚祈賜楮

示知有濟

清神歡及莫可舉似統希

鑒恕臨穎禱馳亦伸謝臆專此敬頌

崇安

隆都從善堂

總理黃寶信

秘書林仲池　〔池仲林印〕

中華民國二十二年十一月三十日

地址檀香山正埠

信箱壹捌柒叁號

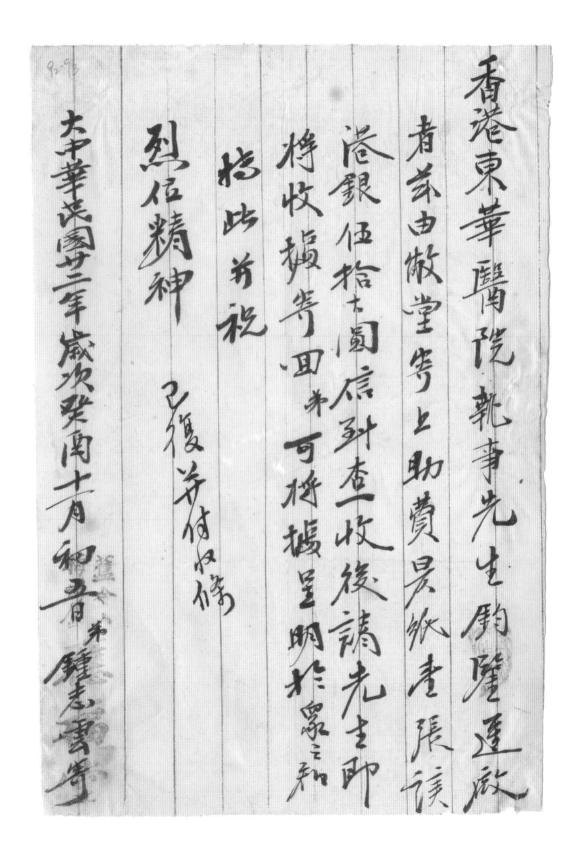

香港東華醫院執事先生鈞鑒逕啟

者茲由敝堂寄上助賞吳紙李張議

港銀伍拾大圓信到祈查一收後請先生即

將收據等四并可攜呈明於衆之知

特此芳祝

烈位精神

已復芳付收條

大中華民國廿二年歲次癸酉十月初吉 弟 鍾志雲等

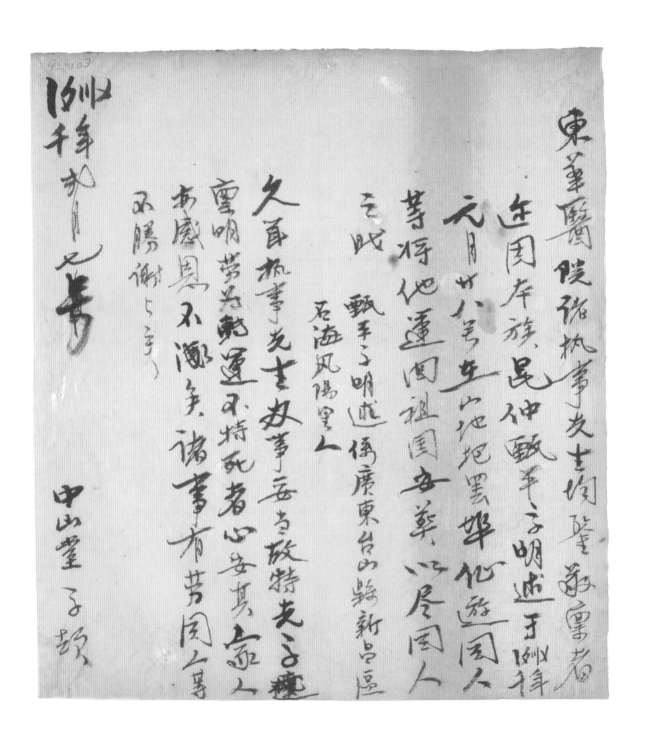

東華醫院諸执事先生均鑒 敬啟者

逕因本族 昆仲 甄羊子明述于卅祥

元月廿八号 先生地托寄華仏游返国人

茅得 他運回祖国安葬 以盡国人

之此 甄羊子明述 係廣東台山縣新昌區

石海风陽里人

久百枫事先士均事岳为故特夫子返

雲明劳苦勤運不特死者心安其 亟人

而感恩不涯矣 諸事有劳国人等

不勝謝之至一

中山堂子頌

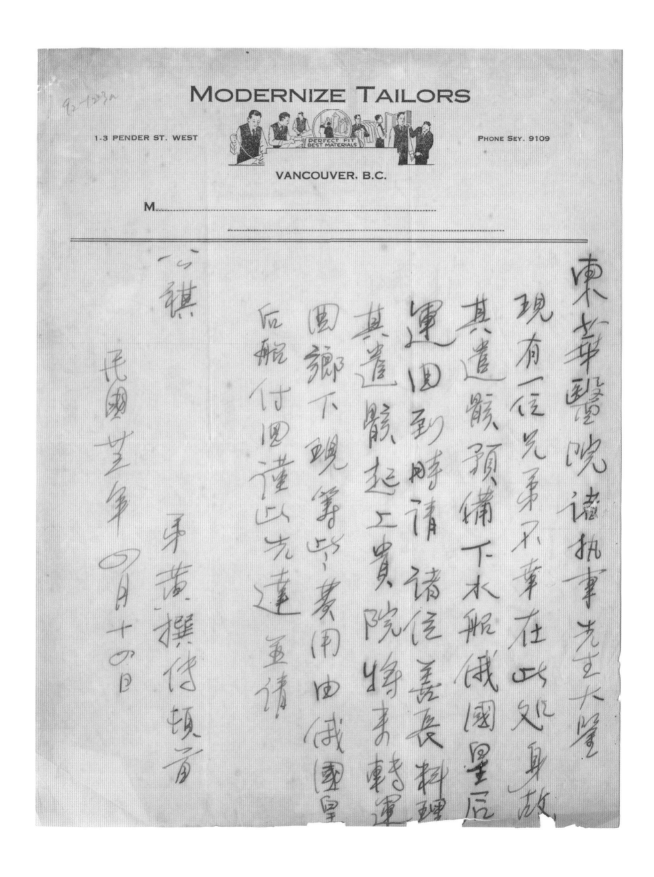

MODERNIZE TAILORS

1-3 PENDER ST. WEST

PHONE SEY. 9109

VANCOUVER, B.C.

M

東華醫院諸執事先生大鑒

現有一位先弟不幸在此處身故

其遺骸預備下水船俄國皇后

運回到時請諸位善長料理

其遺骸起工貴院特寄來轉運

回鄉下現筆些費用由俄團皇

后船付回謹此先達並請

公祺

民國廿三年四月十四日

弟黃撰傳頓首

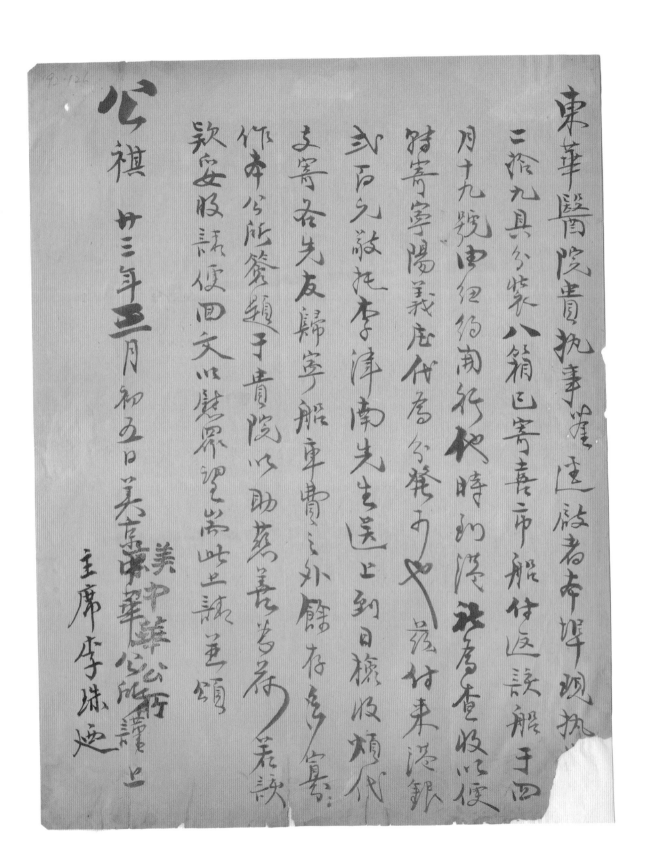

東華醫院貴執事董達啟者本埠現執

二拾九具分裝八箱已寄喜市船付返談船于四

月十九號由紐約開行代時扺港北魚查收以便

特寄寧陽義庄代為分發可也最付東港銀

或百元敬把李津南先生送上到日檢收煩代

文寄吞先友歸寧船車費之外餘存之喜

作本公所簽題于貴院以助慈善善為荷餘款

款安股諒便回文以慰眾望崇此上頌至頌

心祺 廿三年三月初五日美京中華公所謹上

美中華公所謹上

主席李珠烟

MODERNIZE TAILORS

9-1336 1-3, PENDER ST. WEST

PERFECT FIT
BEST MATERIALS

PHONE SEY. 9109

VANCOUVER. B.C.

M

東華醫院諸執事先主大鑒

茲付四港員抗請新畫收為運

吾兄接傳遺骸返入內地之用黃

棺木現由俄國皇后船運回到

時請公等料理將棺木起回

貴院何日運回鄉下新由弟等

定之先木船弟會有函報告料

已知之謹此並請

公祺

　　　　　弟黃撰傳上

民國廿三年四月廿日

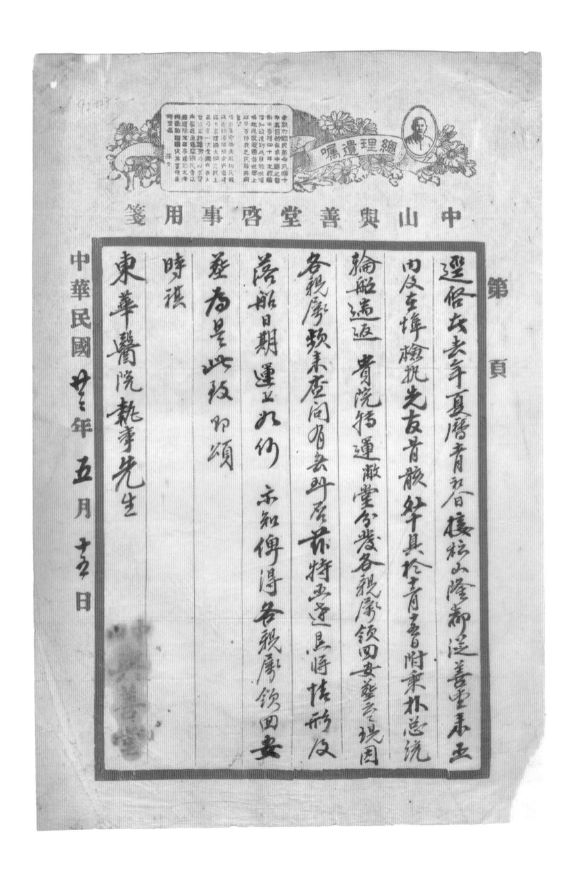

總理遺囑

中山與善堂啟事用箋

第　頁

遂俗去去年夏曆青弟各檀粒山隆御送善童承亞
囘及去埠檢視光友青骸外其於青書附東林總統
輪船遄返　貴院特運澈堂分發各親屬領囘安葬意現因
各親屬頻來盛問有去對屍葬特函達且將情形及
落船日期運上九竹　示知傳得各親屬領囘安
藝為是此致卬頌
　時祺
東華醫院執事先生

中華民國廿三年五月十五日

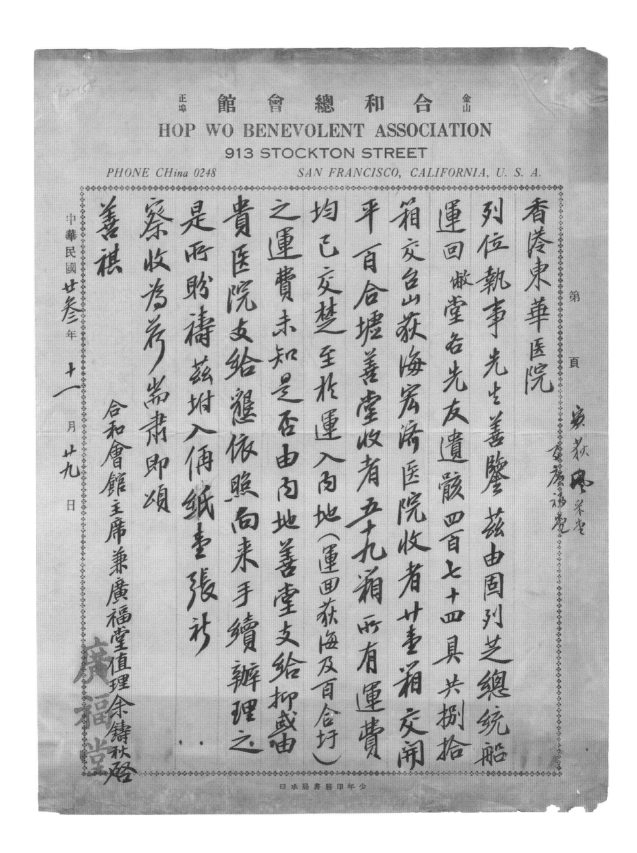

正埠　館　會　總　和　合　金山

HOP WO BENEVOLENT ASSOCIATION

913 STOCKTON STREET

PHONE CHina 0248　　　　SAN FRANCISCO, CALIFORNIA, U. S. A.

香港東華医院

列位執事先生善鑒 茲由固列芝總統船

運回敝堂各先友遺骸四百七十四具共捌拾

箱交台山荻海客濟医院收者廿壹箱交開

平百合塘善堂收者五十九箱而有運費

均已交楚 至水運入內地（運囬荻海及百合圩）

之運費未知是否由內地善堂支給抑或由

貴医院支給 遲依照向來手續辦理之

是所盼禱 茲坿入俾紙壹張祈

察收為荷 耑肅即頌

善祺

　合和會館主席兼廣福堂值理余鑄秋啓

中華民國廿叁年 十一月 廿九 日

第　頁

荻海

廣福堂

中國雷述周致東華醫院信件
1935 年 8 月 15 日

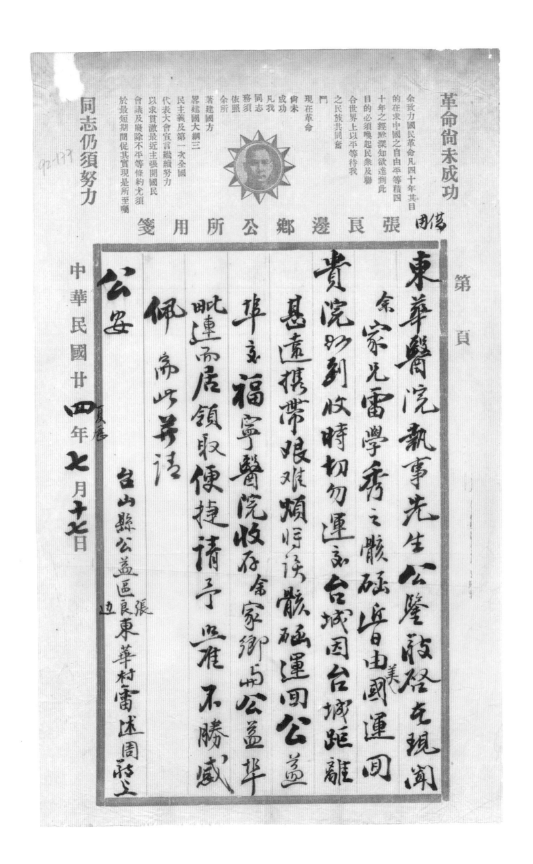

革命尚未成功

余致力國民革命凡四十年其目
的在求中國之自由平等積四
十年之經驗深知欲達到此
目的必須喚起民眾及聯
合世界上以平等待我
之民族共同奮
鬥
現在革命
尚未
成功
凡我
同志
務須
依照
余所
著建國方
略建國大綱三
民主義及第一次全國
代表大會宣言繼續努力
以求貫澈最近主張開國民
會議及廢除不平等條約尤須
於最短期間促其實現是所至囑

同志仍須努力

偉團
張良邊鄉公所用箋

第　頁

東華醫院執事先生公鑒敬啟者現閱
余家兄雷學秀之骸砥近日由國運回
貴院即到收時切勿運高台城因台城距離
甚遠攜帶娘娘頗煩恳候骸砥運回公益
毗連而居領取便捷請于　惟不勝感
華立福寧醫院收存余家鄉之公益华
佩　為此专语

中華民國廿四年七月十七日

公安

台山縣公益區良東華村雷述周谨上

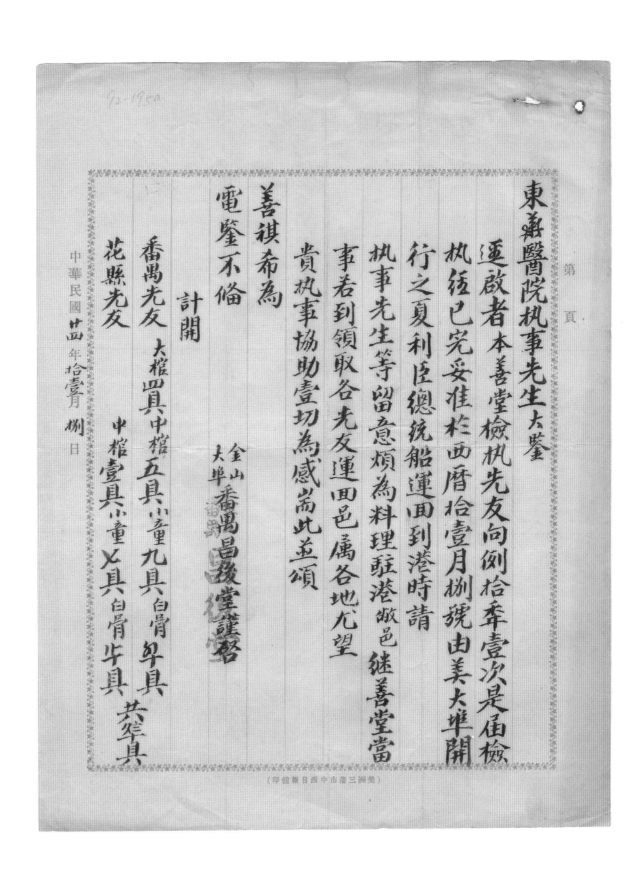

東華醫院执事先生大鑒

　第　頁

逕啟者本善堂檢枞先友向例捨秊壹次是屆檢

枞徑已完妥准柂西曆拾壹月捌號由美大埠開

行之夏利臣總統船運囘到港時請

执事先生等留意煩為料理駐港敞邑繼善堂當

事若到領取各先友運囘邑屬各地尤望

貴执事協助壹切為感耑此益頌

善祺希為

電鑒不偹

　　計開

　　　　　　　　　金山
　　　　　　　大埠番禺昌後堂謹啟

花縣先友　　　中棺壹具小童乂具白骨毕具其羣具

番禺先友　大棺肆具中棺五具小童九具白骨㚄具

中華民國廿四年拾壹月　捌日

（美三洲藩市中市西日報省會印）

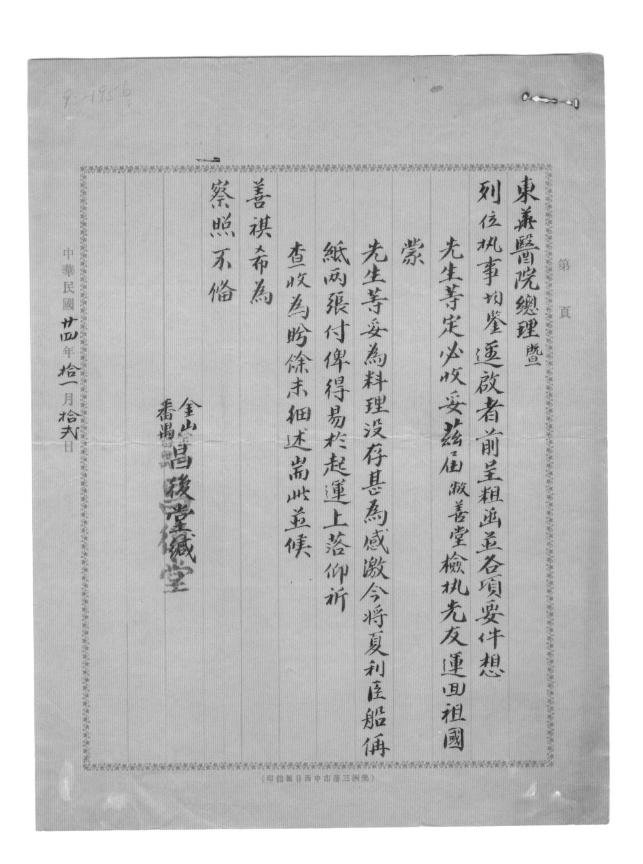

東華醫院總理暨

第　頁

列位执事均鑒遙啓者前呈粗函並各項要件想

先生等定必收妥兹屆溦善堂檢执先友運回祖國

蒙

先生等委為料理沒存甚為感激令將夏利匹船倆

紙兩張付俾得易於起運上落仰祈

查收為盼餘未細述耑此並候

善祺希為

察照不備

金山
番禺昌後堂緘堂

中華民國廿四年拾壹月拾六日

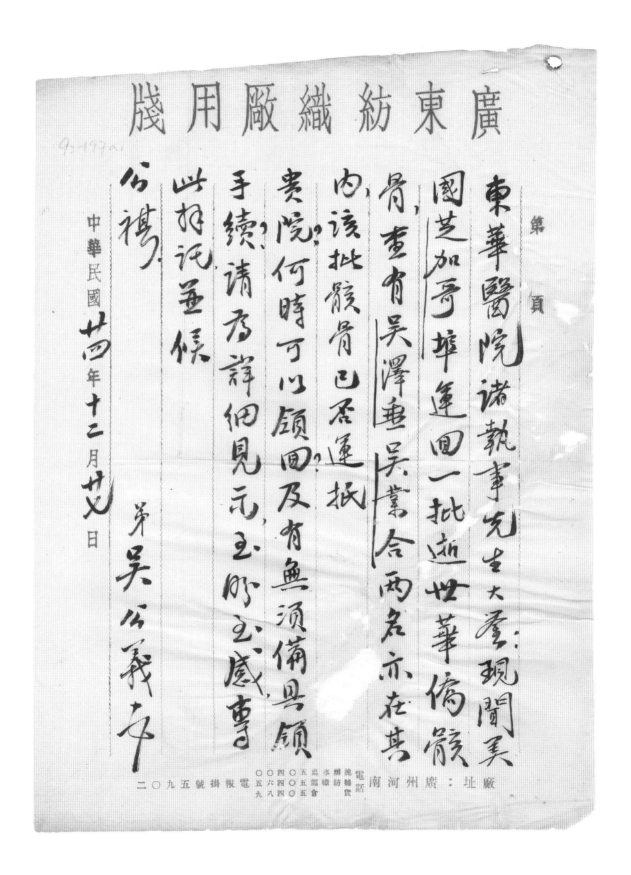

廣 東 紡 織 廠 用 牋

廠址：廣州河南
電話
總紡棉貨〇五五四〇
本部織〇五四四〇
總部會〇五六八九
電報掛號五九〇二

第 頁

東華醫院諸執事先生大鑒：現聞美

國芝加哥埠運回一批逝世華僑骸

骨，查有吳澤垂吳業合兩名亦在其

內，該批骸骨已否運抵

貴院？何時可以領回及有無須備具領

手續，請為詳細見示，玉所玉感事

此報訊並候

公祺，

中華民國廿四年十二月廿又日

弟吳公義啟

廣東紡織廠用箋

第頁

東華醫院諸執事先生惠鑒：前接到

美國芝加哥埠 Chicago 通訊，謂該埠省身

故僑脆骸骨數百具，內有新會縣人吳澤垂

吳業含兩人骸骨同時寄返，轉知屬時前赴

領回等語；弟即於去年十二月底函詢

貴院，對於上列骸骨，何時運抵

貴院，及具領手續如何，請予查明詳細

見示，迄未奉復，茲特再為函詢，務請

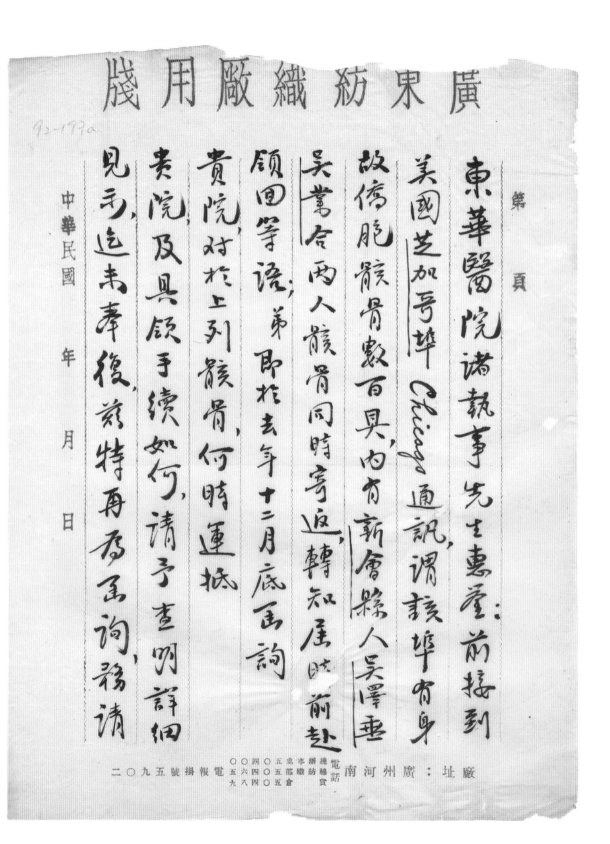

中華民國　　年　　月　　日

廠址：廣州河南　電話　總紡織辦事處：○五五○四　市郡總會：○五四六八　掛號電報五九○二

廣東紡織廠用牋

92-1970

第　頁

壹明芳復，以便赴港具領，想慈祥如

執事等，定需予指示必要。此相託並候

喬祺。

弟吳以乂義 敬

廠址：廣州河南

電話
總務棧貨　〇四五〇
本織部倉　五四六八
　　　　　〇五四九

電報掛號五九二〇

中華民國卅二年 一月 六日

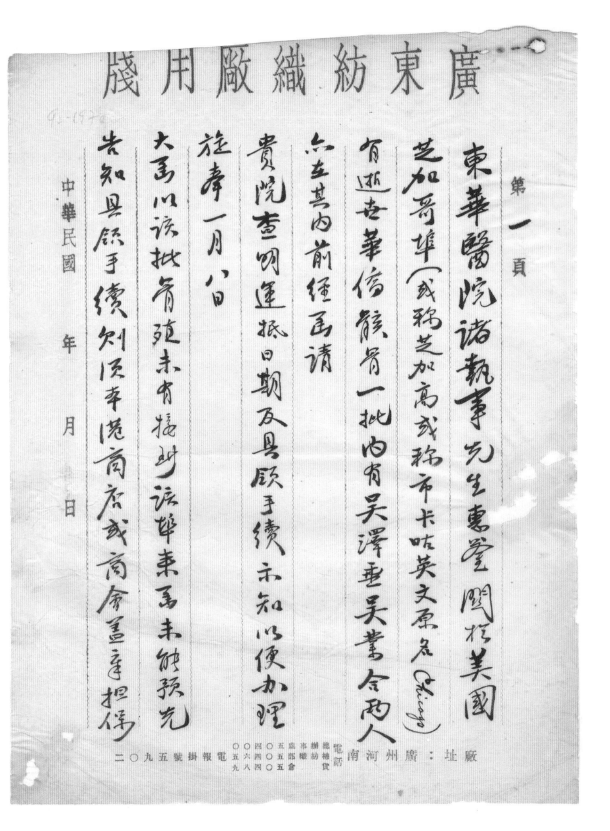

廣東紡織廠用牋

第一頁

東華醫院諸執事先生惠鑒 閣下美國
芝加哥埠（或稱芝加高或稱市卡哦英文原名 Chicago）
有逝世華僑骸骨一批內有吳澤垂吳業令西人
尚未查明前經函請
貴院查明運抵日期及是頒手續未知以便加理
旋奉一月八日
大函以誤批骨殖未有撿妙誤華東籌未能預先
告知具領手續刻須事港商店或商會蓋章擔保

電話 總經售
辦織 ○五五○
事織 ○四四○
廠部 ○四六九
電報掛號五二○九

廠址：廣州河南

中華民國　　年　　月　　日

廣東紡織廠用牋

第二頁

方針領四等誤查上述吳澤垂係本人脆兄

吳業念係老兄蘇為避免去港覓商為商

會担保蔴欺起見擬請

貴院准予通融辦理由本人派余徑賣兩赴

港直接領四吳澤垂吳芝合骨殖兩具運

返新會縣原籍安葬以歸簡便想

貴院慈善為懷當予人以便利之再該批

骨殖歸扇芝於予逝安華僑修帳出口時必經

中華民國　年　月　日

廠址：廣州河南
電話
總棉貸
本紡部
會計
○五○四
○五○四
九八五六
電報掛號五九一○

廣東紡織廠用牋

金山大埠或金路埠 誠恐用該兩埠中

華會館名義運返亦未可料仍請

詳為查明倘確未運到俟運抵時

乞為見示為荷並此奉候

台祺

廣東紡織廠會計課 譯玉吳仁義

中華民國廿二年 一月廿一日

廠址：廣州河南

電話

總綿貨 〇五〇四
辦紡織 〇四四五
市部會 五六八九
電報掛號五九〇二

亞洲西歸先友

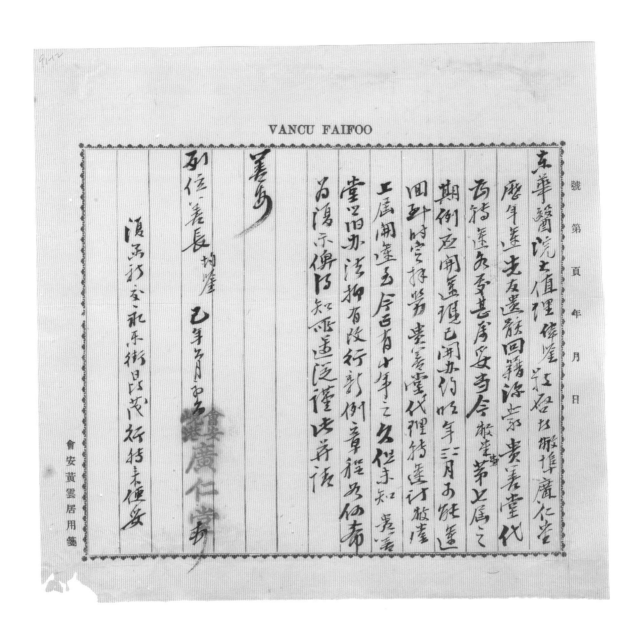

VANCU FAIFOO

號　第　頁　年　月　日

東華醫院主值理偉鑒　茲啟者敝埠廣仁堂
歷年遇先友遺骸回籍源崇　貴善堂代
為轉運及奉善厚安當蒙　敝堂第此屬之
期例亞開運已閱多年昨年三月承難運
回到時堂批勞遺骨蒙堂代理特運討敝堂
工屆開運云今昏有十年之久倘未知敝善
堂四办法抑有改行新例章程及何希
為簡示俾阰知祇遵泛謹此耑覆

善安

敬復善長均鑒
　　乙年 月 日
會安廣仁堂

訊為轉交永東街昆昌茂行持未便安

會安黃雲居用箋

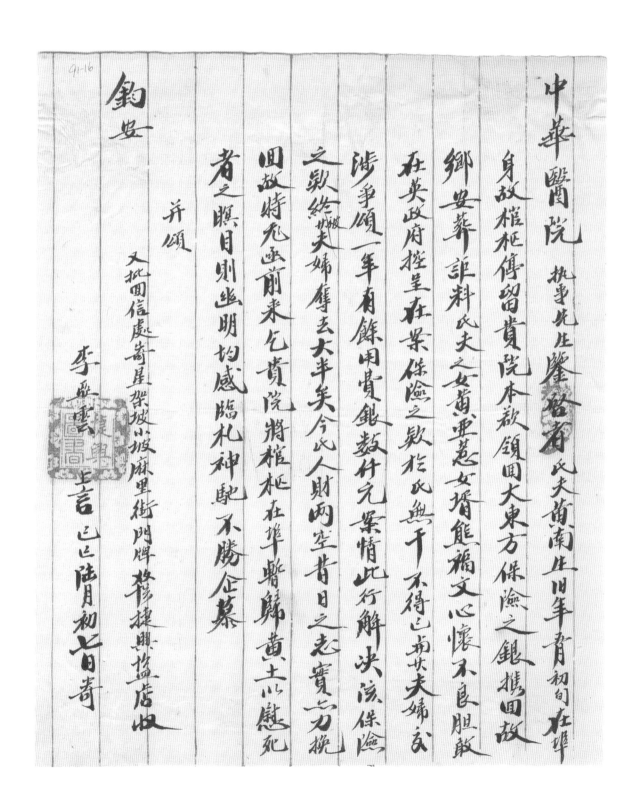

91-16

中華醫院 執事先生鑒啓者 氏夫蔺南生卅年育初旬在埠

身故棺柩傳留貴院本欲領回大東方保險之銀攜回故

鄉安葬詎料氏夫之女黃亞慈女婿能福文心懷不良胆敢

在英政府控呈在案保險之欵恐氏無千不得已尚妷夫婦成

涉爭頌一年有餘用貴銀數什元案情此行解決該保險

之欵絲妷夫婦奪去大半矣今氏人財兩空昔日之志實方挽

回故特无函前來乞貴院將棺柩在埠瞥歸黃土以慰死

者之瞑目則幽明均感臨札神馳不勝企慕

　并頌

釣安

又批回信處寄星架坡小坡麻里街門牌駁移捷興監店收

李亞雲上言己巳陸月初七日寄

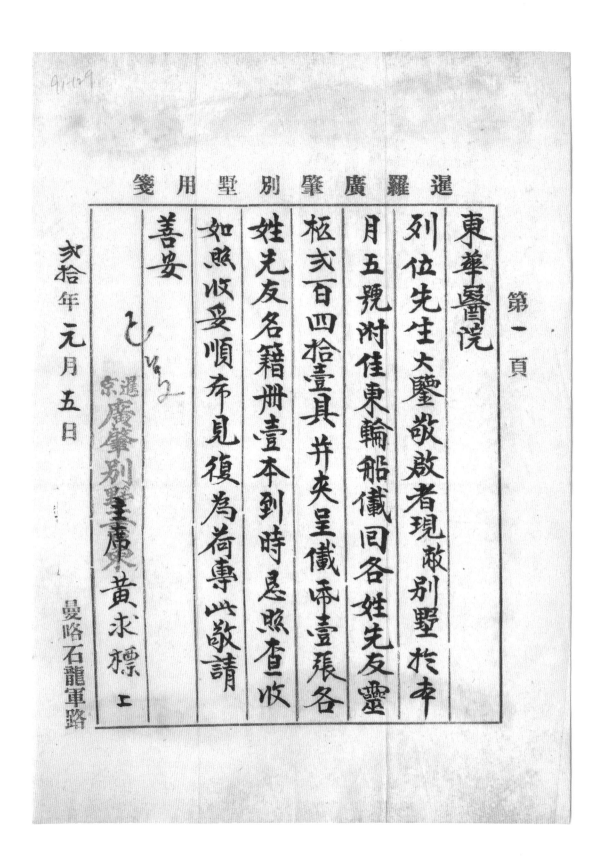

暹羅廣肇別墅用箋

第一頁

東華醫院

列位先生大鑒敬啟者現敝別墅於本

月五號附佳東輪船儎回各姓先友靈

柩弍百四拾壹具并夾呈儀冊壹張各

姓先友名籍冊壹本到時恳照查收

如照收妥順布見復為荷專此敬請

善安

　　　暹京廣肇別墅主席 黃求標 上

弍拾年元月五日　　　曼咯石龍軍路

9,-130a

暹羅廣肇別墅用箋

第一頁

東華醫院

列位先生大鑒敬啟者現敝別墅於本月五號

附佳東輪船懺回各姓先友靈柩貳百四拾壹

具除遺輪呈上懺冊壹張各姓先友名籍冊

壹本外茲由郵局寄上振盛行匯票壹張計

港幣柒佰叄拾員到時思照查收所有領

取手續徐照舊例每名發給葬費銀貳員

外尚存之欵作為費用支銷便是諸費

年　月　日　　曼咯石龍軍路

9/-1306

暹羅廣肇別墅用箋

精神順希見復為盼專此敬請

善安

第二頁

暹京廣肇別墅主席 黃求標上

叁年 元月 五日

曼咯石龍軍路

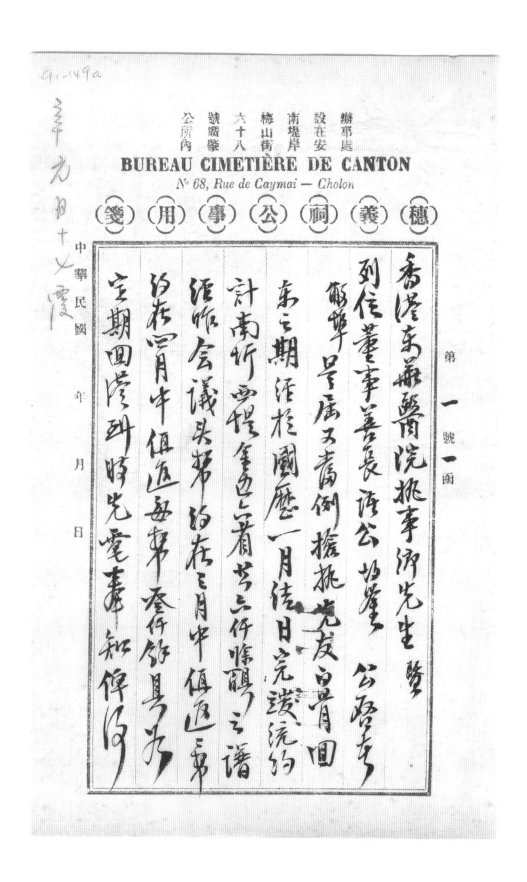

辦事處
設在安
南堤岸
梅山街
六十八
號鋪壁
公所內

BUREAU CIMETIÈRE DE CANTON
Nº 68, Rue de Caymai — Cholon

（穗）（義）（祠）（公）（事）（用）（箋）

中華民國 廿年 乙 月 十三 日

公安

第　一　號 二 函

敬復駁船俾埋義冢春炉五柩搬運
工費每付淡昌君干詢敝社　至知以候匯
上經辦涂詳此諗

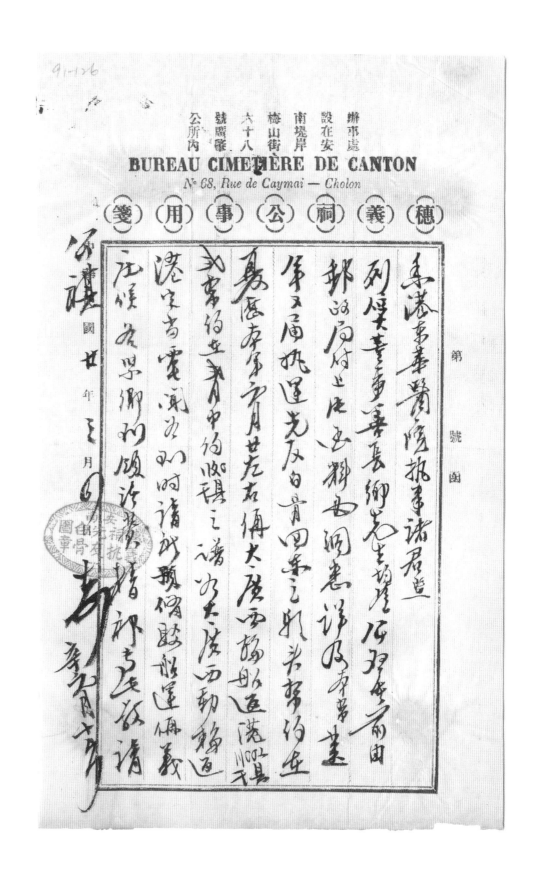

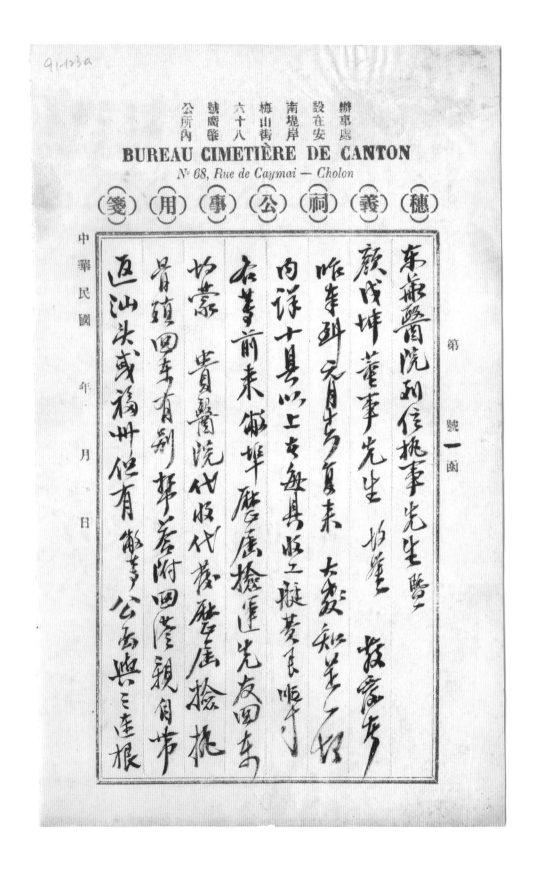

辦事處
設在安
南堤岸
梅山街
六十八
號麗譙
公所內

BUREAU CIMETIÈRE DE CANTON

Nº 68, Rue de Caymai — Cholon

（箋）（用）（事）（公）（祠）（義）（穗）

第 一函 號

東華醫院列位執事先生曁

顏戊坤董事先生 均鑒 敬啟者

唯日元月廿七日寄來 大函 敬悉 並承

內詳十具以上如有收工竣費用臨時以

衣等前來礕岸歷廣撥運先友回唐

均蒙 貴醫院代收代費歷廣撿挑

骨殖回車有別 華葬附回港預自節

返汕头或為卅位有 敝等公啟與三達根

中華民國　年　月　日

辦事處
設在安
南堤岸
梅山街
六十八
號閣鄰
公所內

BUREAU CIMETIÈRE DE CANTON
No. 68, Rue de Caymai — Cholon

（穗）（義）（祠）（公）（事）（用）（箋）

第　號　乙函

樹勳李詩祉仰諗晋莊云來車攜
云芸室無甚華費倒良武兄弟甫由
陳朱歷行大廈西孤俪回啞埠諗孤约
在本月廿七動孤迴滄水主期啓行
宫衙電華宛五拾工艇費候彼來亊
歷程沿往工艇費及津勵華費一亊
滙上當因正期公司孤迴滄三候特為覆
先諗之華神不孫歲兄壽此敬覆

中華民國　年　月　日

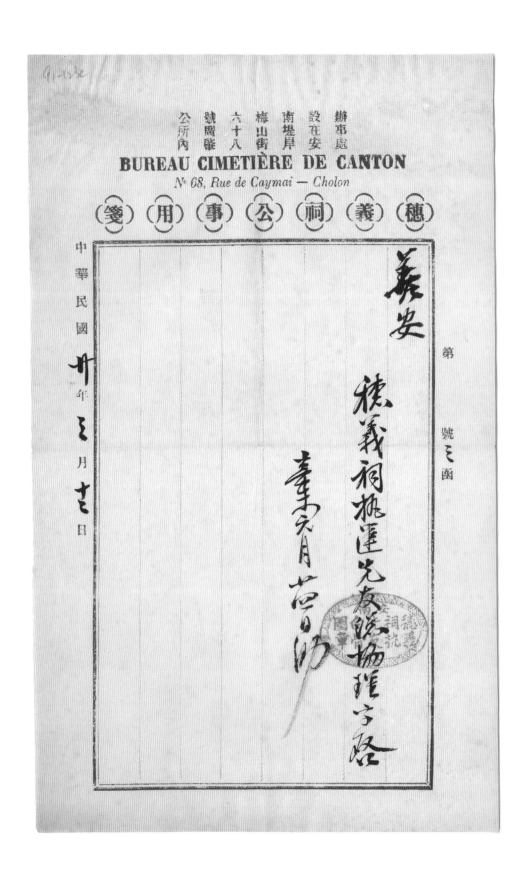

辦事處
設在安
南堤岸
梅山街
六十八
號膠籐
公所內

BUREAU CIMETIÈRE DE CANTON

Nº 68, Rue de Caymai — Cholon

（穗）（義）（祠）（公）（事）（用）（箋）

中華民國 廿年 三月 吉日

第　號三函

養安

積義祠搬運先友骸塴瑤字路

臺安月□□

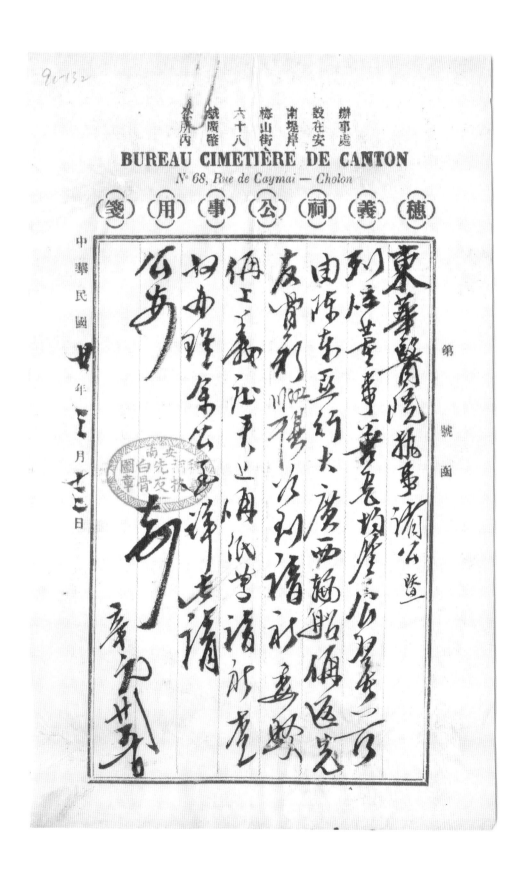

辦事處
設在安
南堤岸
梅山街
六十八
號廣肇
茶所內

BUREAU CIMETIÈRE DE CANTON
Nº 68, Rue de Caymai — Cholon

（穗）（義）（祠）（公）（事）（用）（箋）

第　　號函

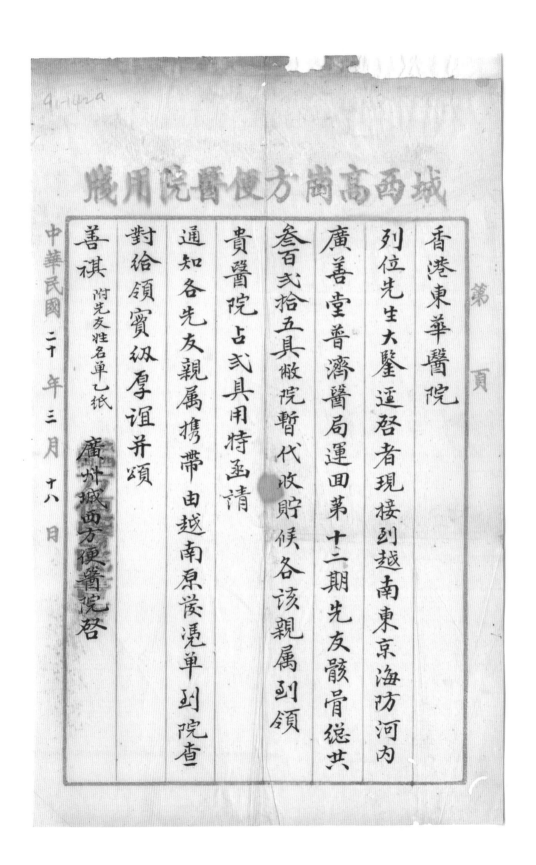

城西高崗方便醫院用箋

第　頁

香港東華醫院

列位先生大鑒逕啟者現接到越南東京海防河內

廣善堂普濟醫局運回第十二期先友骸骨總共

叁百弍拾五具敝院暫代收貯候各該親屬到領

貴醫院占弍具用特函請

通知各先友親屬攜帶由越南原歲凴單到院查

對給領賓級厚誼并頌

善祺　附先友姓名單乙紙　廣州城西方便醫院啟

中華民國二十年三月十八日

越南東京海防廣善堂普濟醫局運回第十二

期先友骸骨

計開

陳周氏 番禺人　海防北埠

鄧黃氏　河字咈埗

以上弍具情

東華醫院查傳各親屬攜同原葬憑單来省到院

查對給領寫荷

民國二十年　三月　十八日

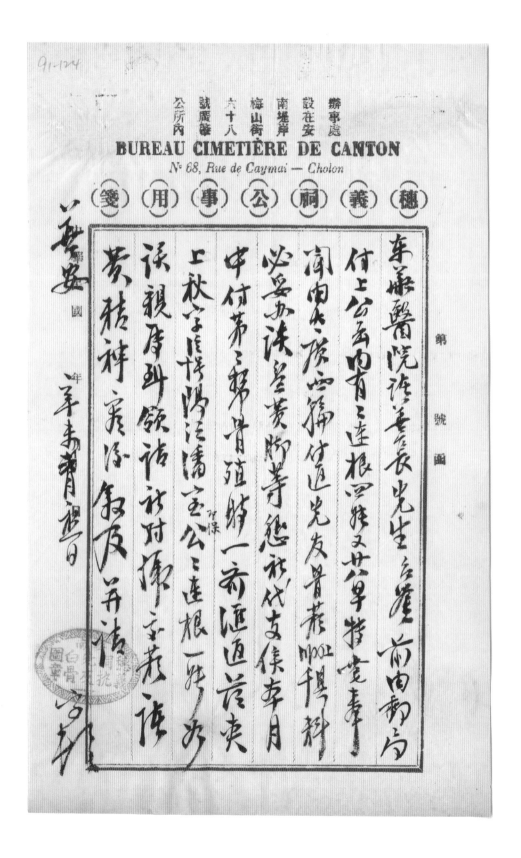

逕啓者遠涉瀛天涯騰壤如工人之情已我儕居先友覊旅

孤魂十年飄泊不有善後岁以慰先靈而变友道同人善

固妥抄將義地之塋壘加整理緣訂能遂遷去約尤下

庶一律由族有掰國曆正月底附北野丸裝回

籍抄權厝　貴院报為縣料一切素仰

貴院见義勇為首仁不讓言敬巻秦梓善与人

同似辦理程序如何未法　貴院章程用敢就

友伏祈詳示俾俟遵行附呈通知先友関係人

尚自一命話為代登省港报名二份在登一星期

寄浩將登載在由寄一份得洵祈柬為幸

所支款項家意望遠波畧省勞毋任感謝

此致

東華醫院大總理

中華民國二十年三月廿七日

日本長崎
廣東會所謹稟

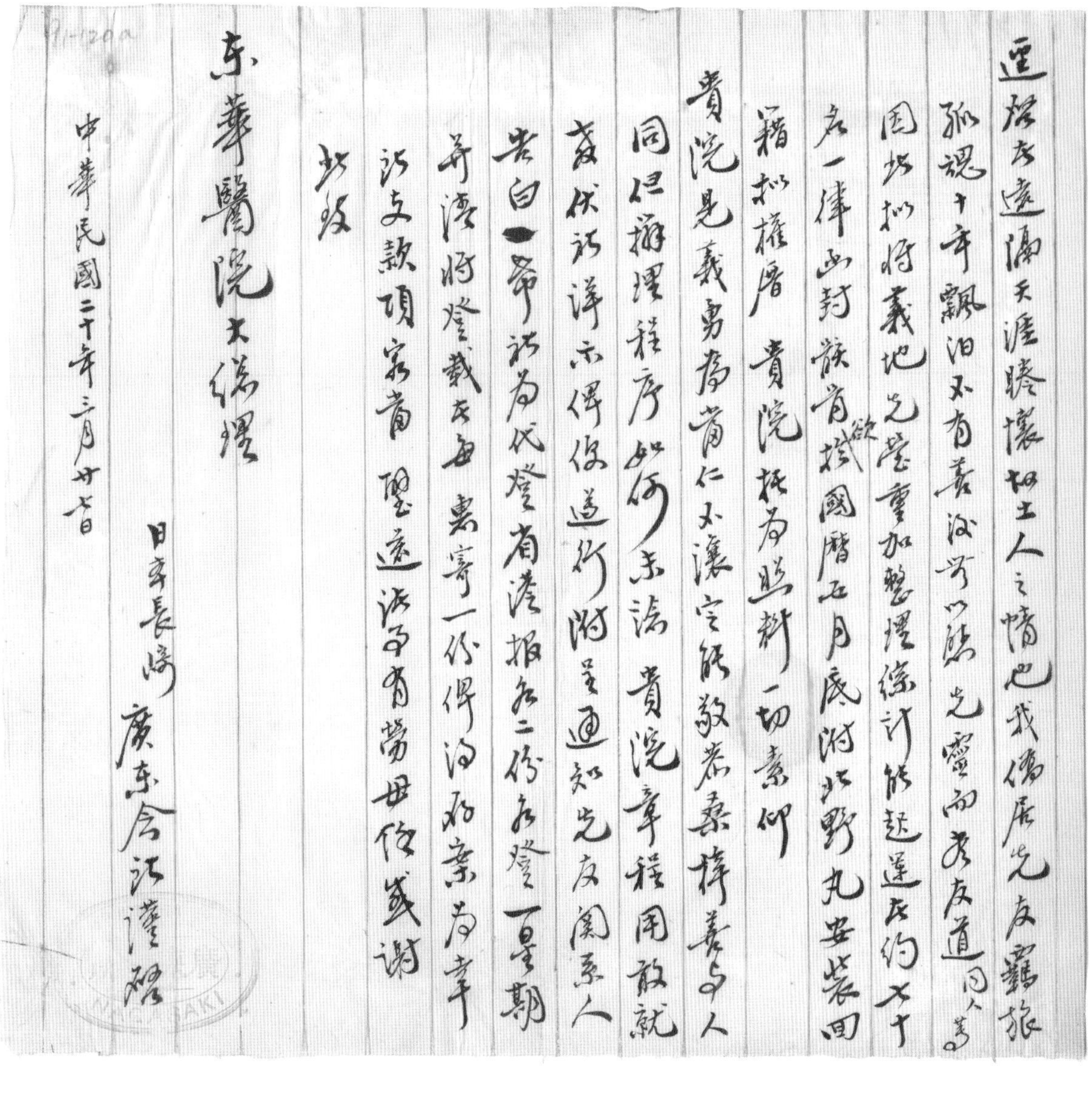

日本長崎廣東義地起遷先友

本會所自置之廣東義地原為便利本幫僑民暫時寄
葬之需向例凡葬後滿十年者即須起遷回籍俾得騰
出餘地以供後來者之須要茲經本會同人議決定於本年
月底興工起遷先友約於本年五月底裝運回粵托由香港
東華医院按置仰各先友親屬屆時到港查明領葬特此
通告

日本長崎廣東会所啓

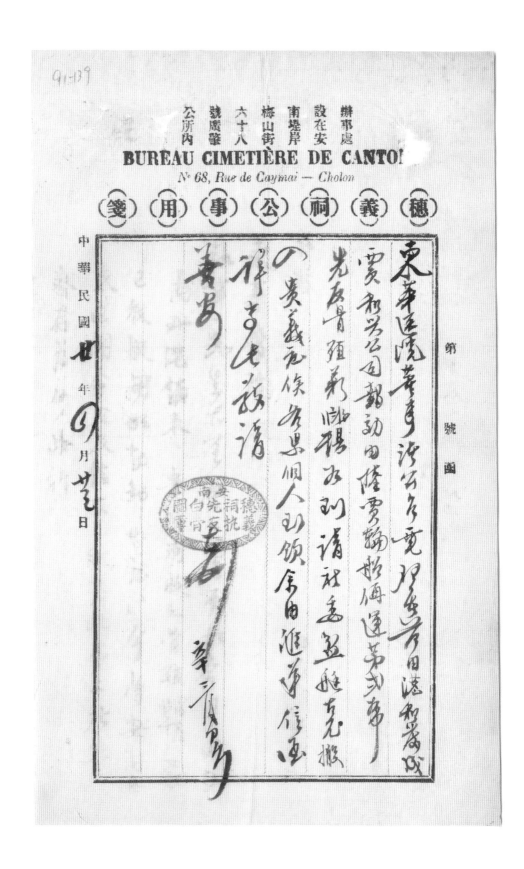

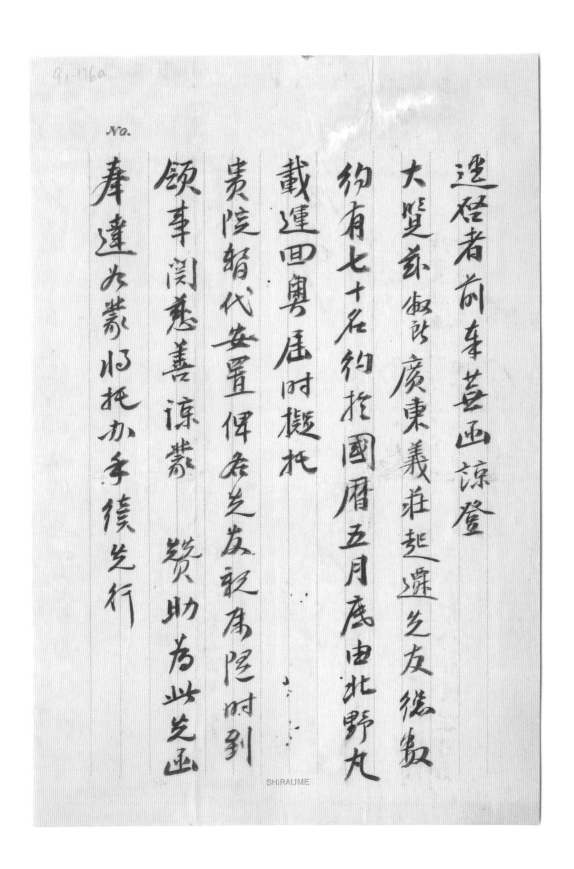

敬啟者前車蓋函諒登

大覽茲敝所廣東義莊起遷之友骸數

約有七十名約於國曆五月底由北野丸

載運回粤屆時擬托

貴院協代安置俾彼先友親屬隨時到

領事周慈善諒荷

贊助為此先函

専達以叢仰托辦李續先行

91-1166

承知花為感禱此收

東華醫院大總理分鑒

中華民國二十年四月廿四日

日本長崎廣東会所簡肯黍啟

安南堤岸穗義祠致東華醫院信件

1931 年 4 月 26 日

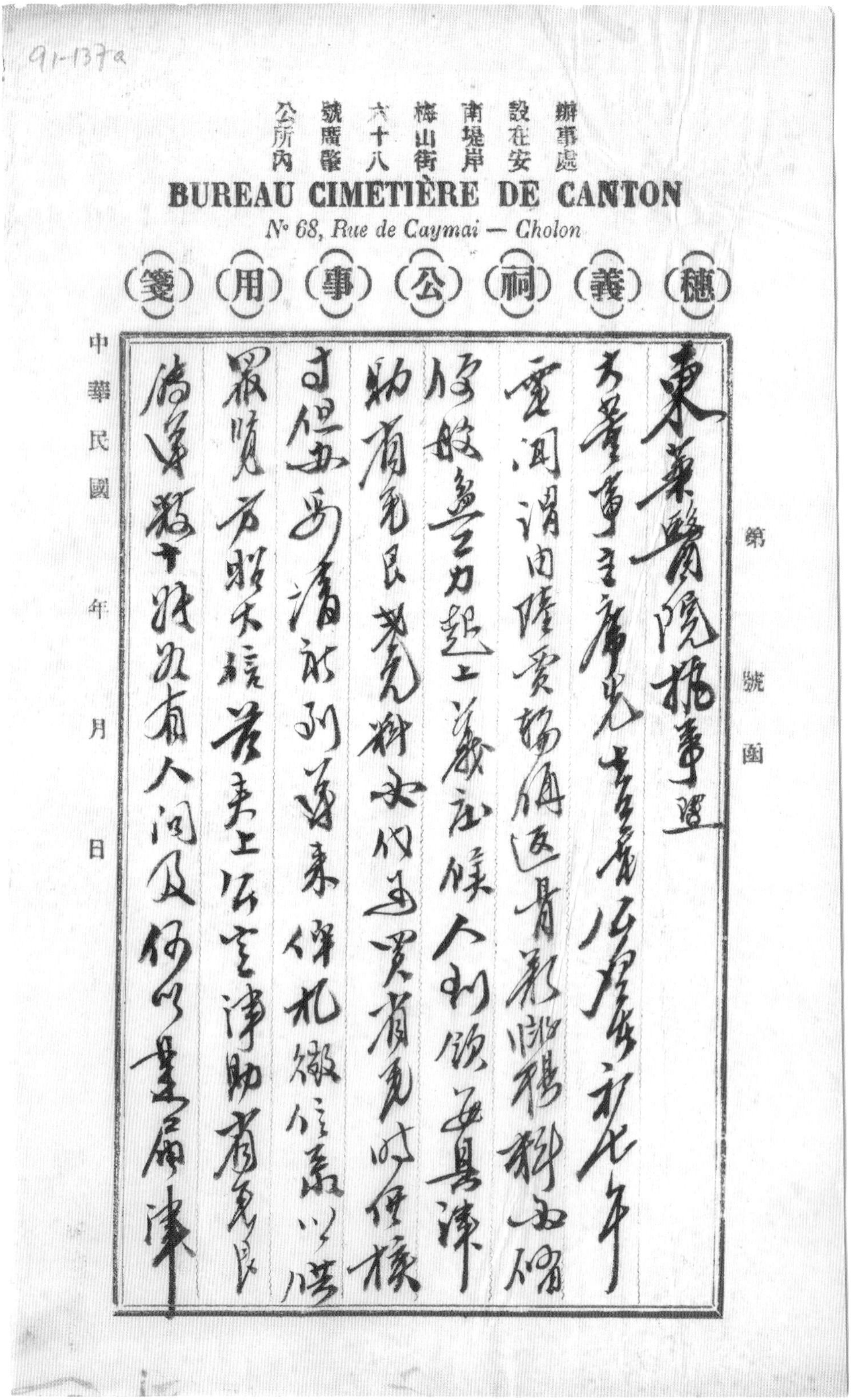

91-137a

辦事處設在安南堤岸梅山街六十八號廣肇公所內

BUREAU CIMETIÈRE DE CANTON

N° 68, Rue de Caymai — Cholon

穗義祠公事用箋

第　　號函

東華醫院總理暨
大董事主席先生台鑒 啟者前年
覆函謂由堤貴埠備返骨殖總辦西僑
修竣無力起上茲議俟人到領無異議
物前免民發先料代為買前免收價
寸保安妥清訖到後來俾執繳信款以昭
衆覽方能不悞前來上佛堂津助前免良
僑單務十餘名有人問及何以甚屬津

中華民國　年　月　日

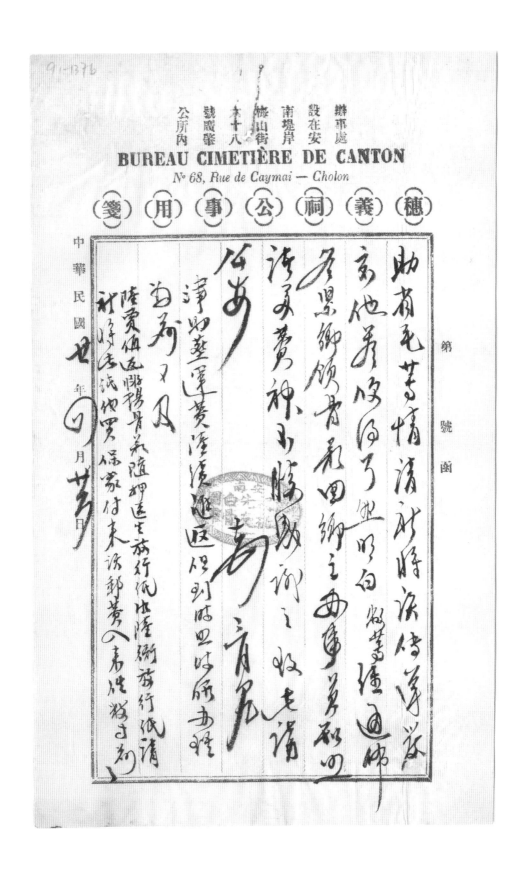

辦事處
設在安
南堤岸
梅山街
六十八
號肇慶
公所內

BUREAU CIMETIÈRE DE CANTON

N° 68, Rue de Caymai — Cholon

（穗）（義）（祠）（公）（事）（用）（箋）

第　號函

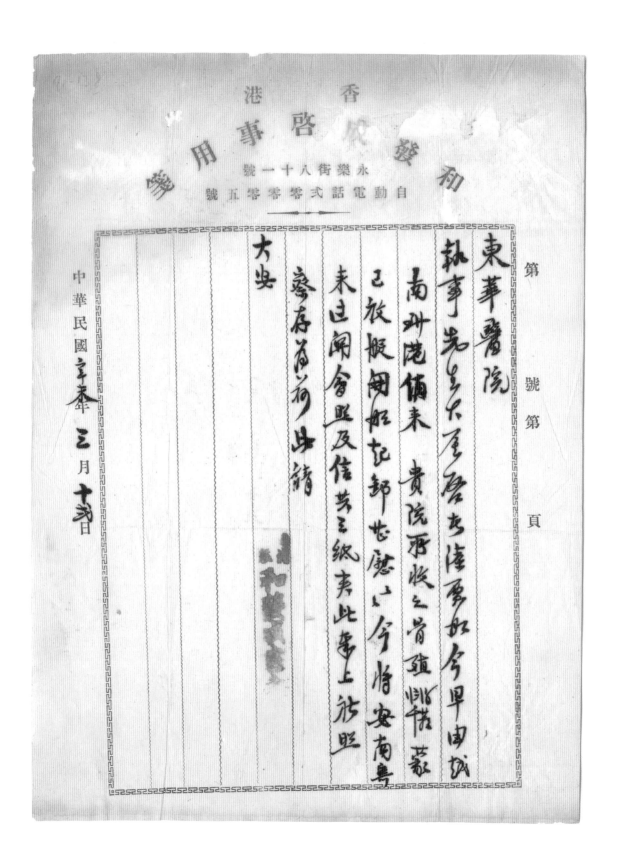

香港
和發成啟事用箋
永樂街八十一號
自動電話弍零零零五號

第　號第　頁

東華醫院

執事先生大鑒逕啟者頃今早由城

南卅港僑來　貴院所收之骨殖提蒙

已妥領勿照起卸此愿之令將安南粵

來逕開會縣及僑芳紙寄此奉上祈照

隆存荷此　請

　大安

中華民國辛未年三月十弍日

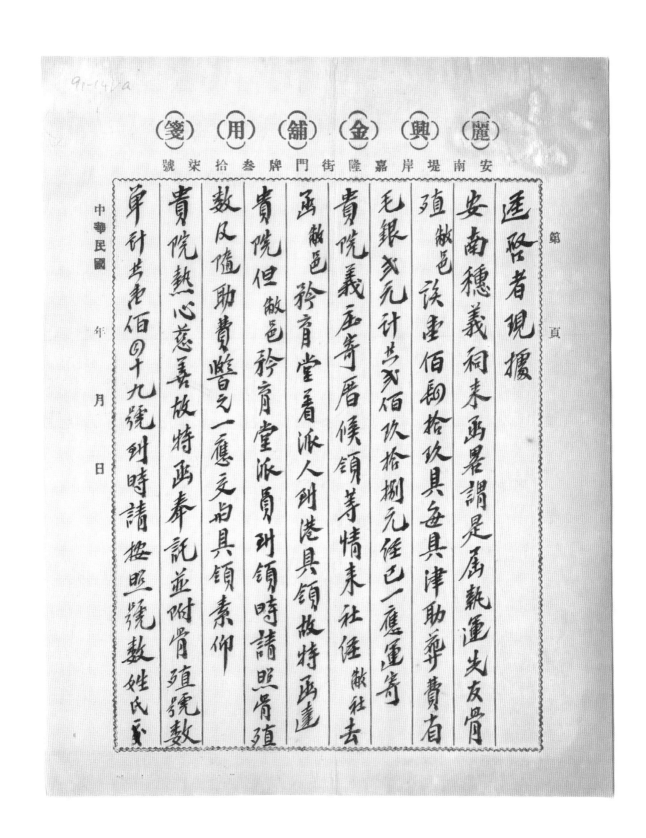

（麗）（興）（金）（舖）（用）（箋）

安南堤岸嘉隆街門牌叁拾柒號

第頁

逕啓者現據

安南穗義祠來函畧謂是屬執運先友骨

殖敝邑誤重佰嗣拾玖具每具津助葯費者

毛銀式元計共式佰玖拾捌元任已一應運寄

貴院義生等屆候領等情來社任敝社去

函敝邑矜育堂看派人到港具領故特函達

貴院但敝邑矜育堂派員到領時請照骨殖

数及随助費醫之一應支的具領素仰

貴院熱心慈善故特函奉託並附骨殖號數

草計共壹佰〇十九號到時請按照號數姓氏麥

中華民國　年　月　日

（笺）（用）（舖）（金）（興）（麗）

號柒拾叁牌門街隆嘉岸堤南安

第二頁

案對支領專此奉懇祇請

善安

東華大醫院列位扡事先生台鑒

旅越四會公益社啟

中華民國廿年

五月五日

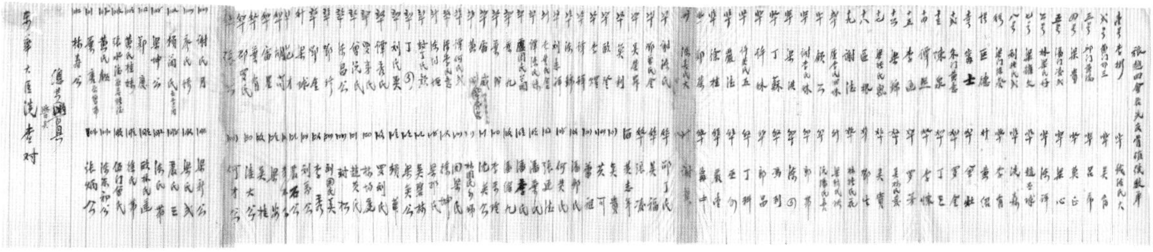

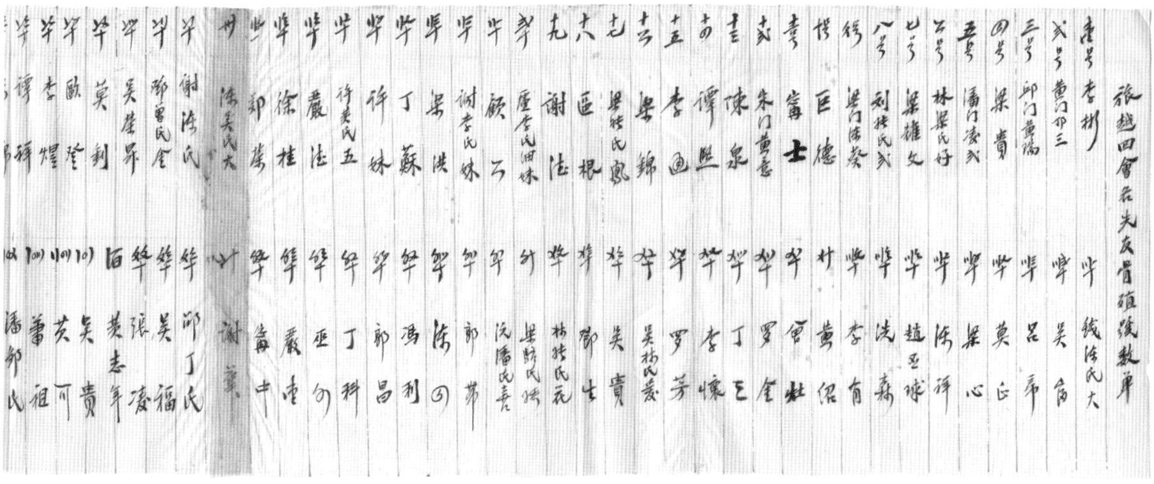

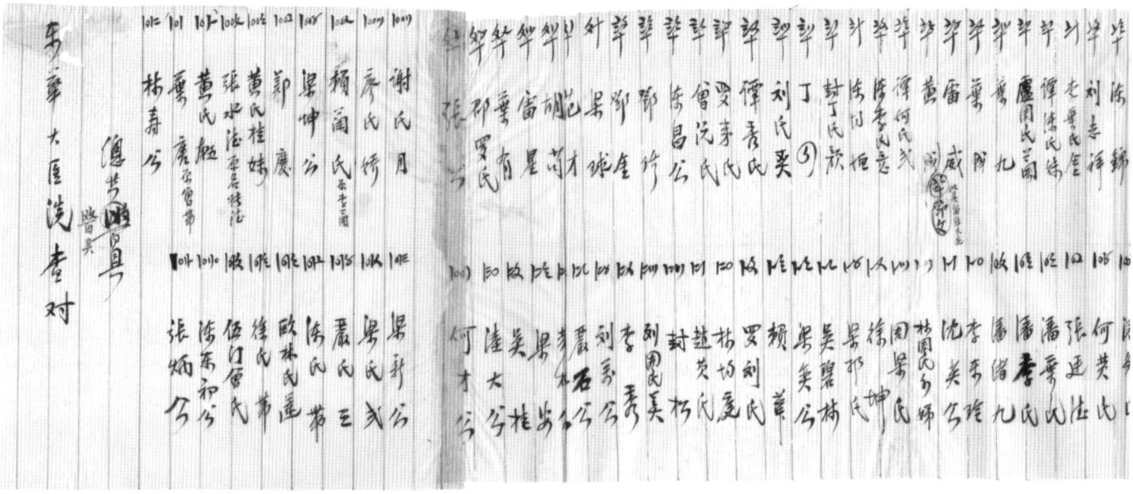

日本長崎廣東會所致東華醫院信件

1931 年 5 月 10 日

東華医院大總理鑒 逕啟者昨奉 大函敬悉
現敝所義莊起遷先友業已竣事定於本年五
月十八日（即舊曆四月初一日）將先友骸函附北野丸輪
船運港到達时務懇代為安置以便各先友親屬隨
時到領各先友親屬早經發函通知似可不用登
報茲寄上先友名冊一紙（詳細名冊容再奉上）煩
將致各屬公共團体以便將達各处鄉村週知十八
日隨船滙上港幣五百元以应
貴院代办一切之需如有殘餘請撥之
貴院慈善之用至先友親屬領葬補助費每名發
給港幣五元俟查明實数亦於同日滙上為此奉托
祇請
公安

日本長崎廣東会所簡肖蔡啟

中華民國二十年五月 十 日

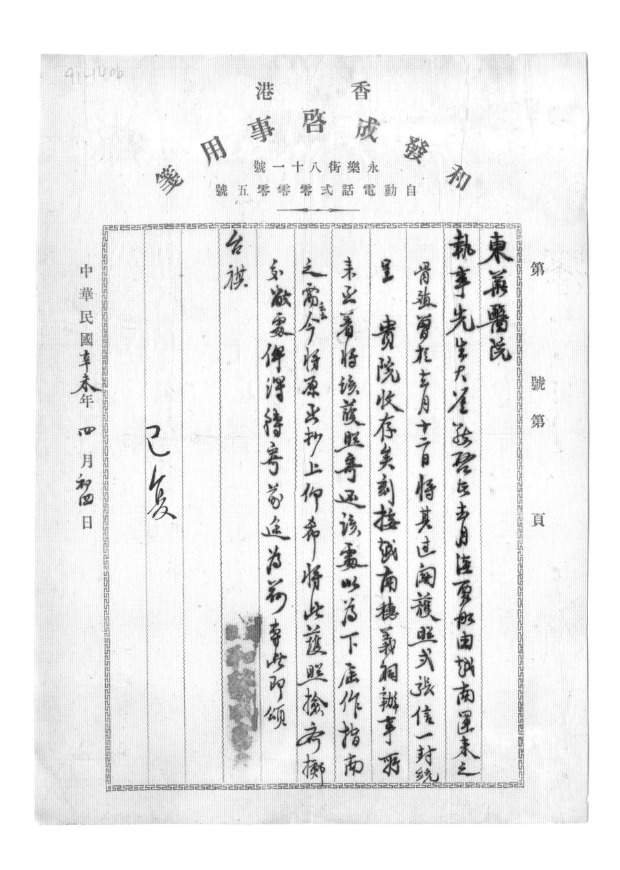

香港
和發成啓事用箋
永樂街八十一號
自動電話弍零零零五號

第　號　第　頁

東華醫院

執事先生大鑒 茲啟者本月連夏船由城南運來之

骨殖貨九壹百拾貳具連護照弍張信一封統

呈 貴院收存共刻接收南穗義祠辦事處

來丞著將該護照寄還 該處以為下屆作指南

之需今將原函抄上仰希將此護照撿齊擲

交徽委俾得寄回途為荷 專此即頌

台祺

己發

中華民國辛未年 四月弍十四日

敬啟者越南穗義祠函事現奉函條

私呈大啟曰執事諸鄉先生大厦公啟者荷報効由陸夢和

俱送院之骨殖其衛生紙與兩貴祠陸醫廳放行紙由

貴祠押保返院此紙呈君交東華醫院神戚交院和貴公

祈收前二子幸達 貴執事祈通知返港情該放行醫生紙

倘附返來僑存橋下屋西堤幫長依樣葫蘆園五年一屆

後任幫長全不知頭緒恐取問存貯以便著手俟西提各衛簽

字是君有煩請於留意直至陸輩求為付來諸費神不懍

感納之玲也條後詳此請

台安

穗義祠函事啟 三月廿首
設提岸廣肇公所內

198〈頁一〉中國陳進光致東華醫院信件

1931 年 6 月 13 日

9143

東華醫院義庄

列位執事先生大鑒敬啓者茲聞日本長崎埠有大幫先人骨石運回原籍亦貴院義庄分派弟有先母於光緒拾七年在日本長崎埠逝世至今骸石尚未運回但此次未知有先母骨石在内否倘有陳盛祥或用開富或開記等字樣之妻黃氏骸石在内伏乞通知南海平洲鄉村頭龍光坊四拾叁号陳進光俾得前來領取是為德便草此拜懇敬請

均安

弟陳進光叩 四月廿四日

辛未四月廿八復

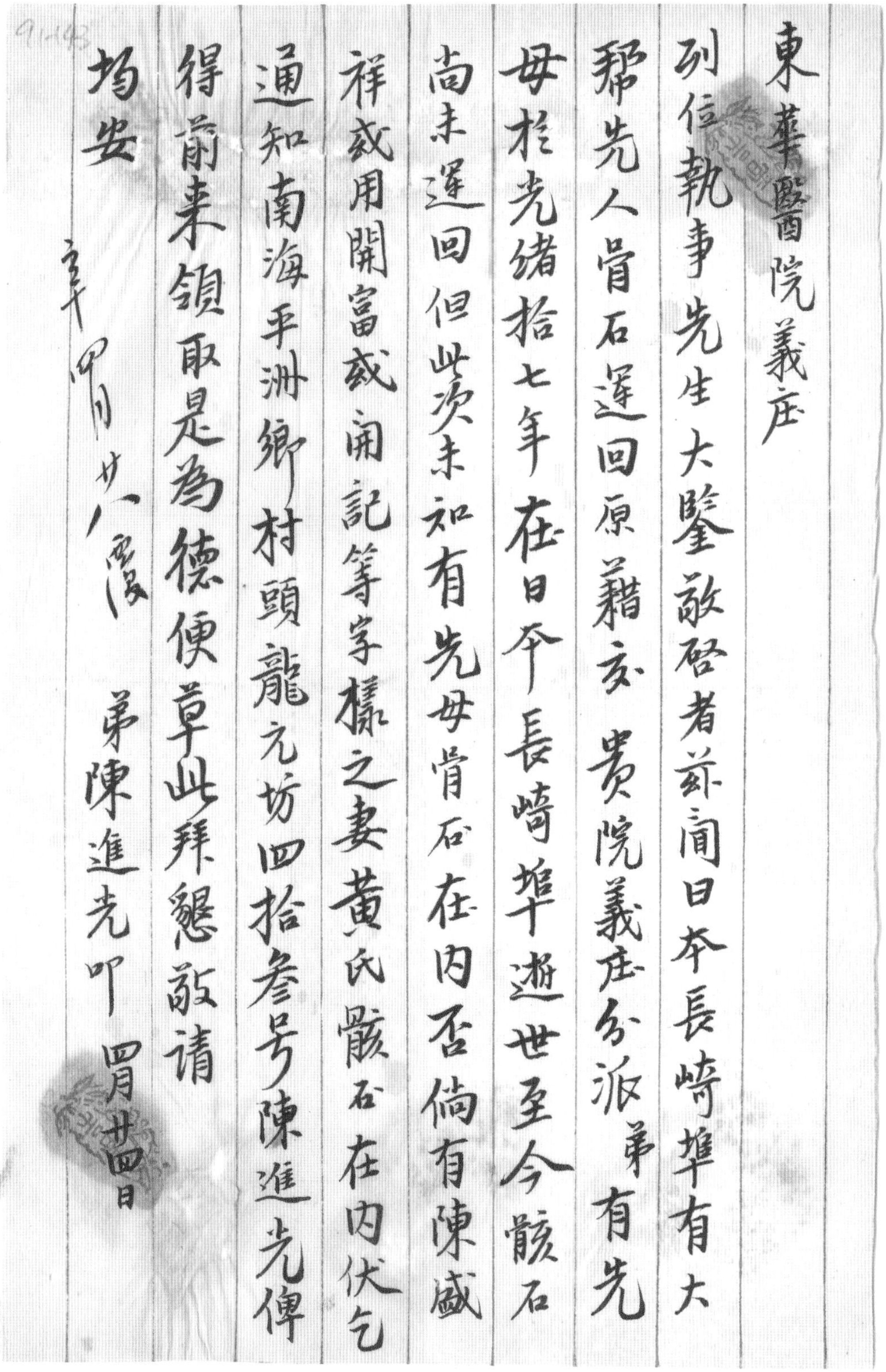

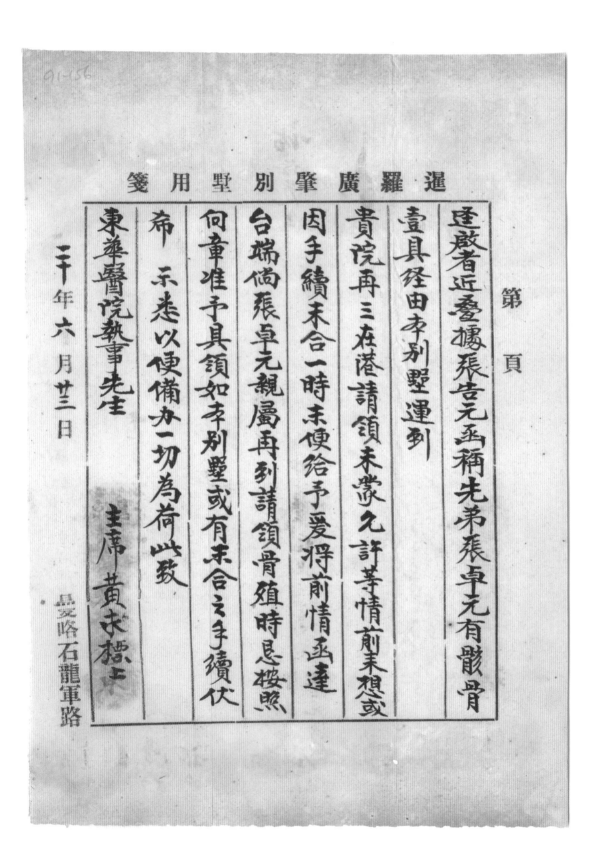

暹羅廣肇別墅用箋

第　頁

逕啟者近疊據張吉元孟稱先弟張卓元有骸骨

壹具經由孝別墅運到

貴院再三在港請領未蒙允許莘情前末想或

因手續未合一時末便給予爰將前情函達

台端倘張卓元親屬再到請領骨殖時悉按照

向章准予具領如孝別墅或有末合之手續伏

帝　示悉以便備辦一切為荷此致

東華醫院執事先生

　　　　　　　　主席黃求攄上

三十年六月廿三日　　　　　蔴峪石龍軍路

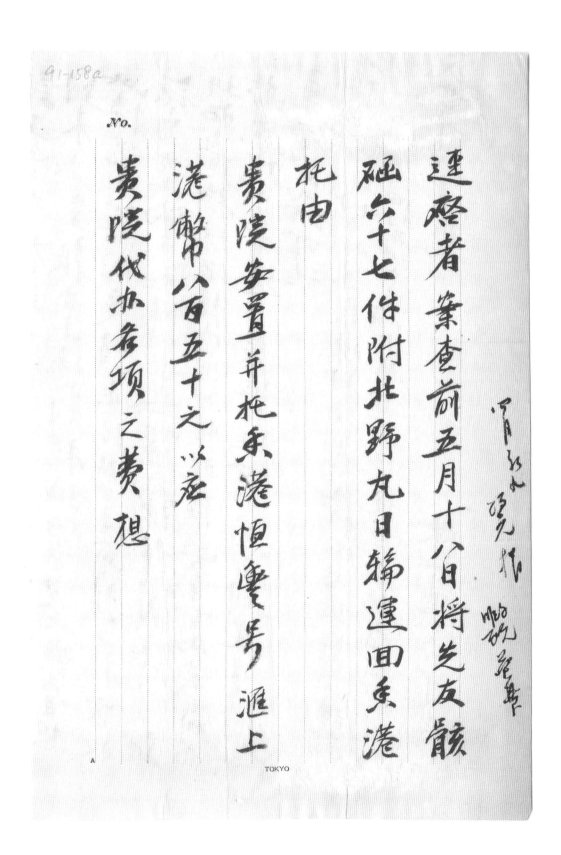

逕啟者筆查前五月十八日將先友骸

硯六十七件附北野丸日輪運回来港

托由

貴院安置并托乘港恒豐号滙上

港幣八百五十元以応

貴院代办各項之費想

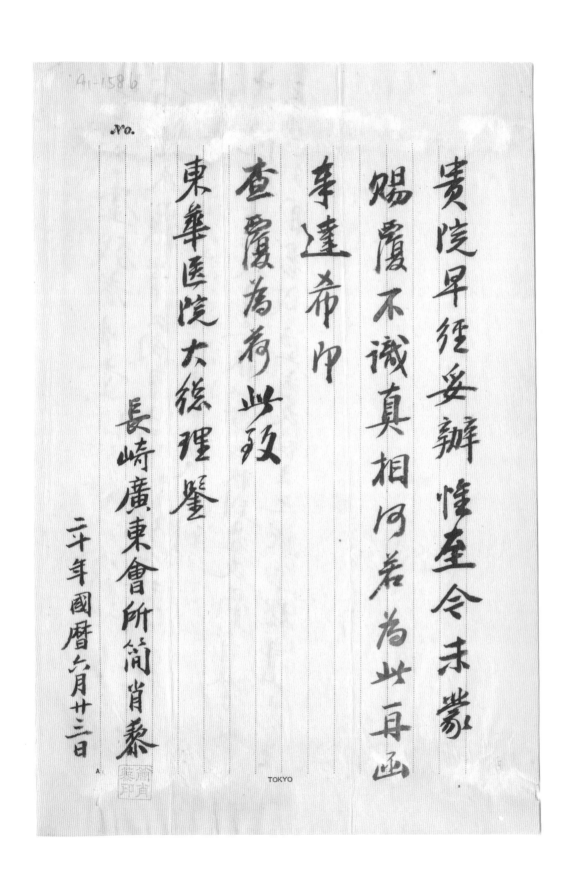

貴院早經妥辦惟查令未蒙

賜覆不識真相何若為此再函

奉達希即

查覆為荷此致

東華醫院大總理鑒

　　　長崎廣東會所簡肖泰

二十年國曆六月廿三日

孫總理遺囑

余致力國民革命凡
四十年其目的在求
中國之自由平等積
四十年之經驗深知
欲達到此目的必須
喚起民眾及聯合世
界以平等待我之民
族共同奮鬥

現在革命尚未成功
凡我同志務須依照
余所著建國方略建
國大綱三民主義及
第一次全國代表大
會宣言繼續努力以
求貫徹最近主張開
平等條約尤須於最
短期間促其實現是
所至囑

虎門太平溥善堂用牋

第　頁

東華醫院

執事諸公大鑒

敬啟者前閱報紙得悉安南各先友金
骸經已裝運到　貴院已有月餘惟今
日久未蒙分發寄運　敝堂虎門鄰鄉一
帶茲今各鄉先友親屬攜領金骸紙到　敝堂
問及茲故專函奉達請祈示覆為禱此頌

善祺

中華民國　貳拾年　七月　拾日

巳嫠

（太平溥善堂承發印）

安南堤岸廣肇公所致東華醫院信件

1931年8月14日

堤岸廣肇公所用牋

第　頁

逕啟者于夏曆五月廿六日匯港怡興隆交
貴院收港幣叁千元是次首由法郵船交匯港怡興隆交
貴院收港幣五千元連二月廿六日匯交銀五千元三共交銀〡〣〇〇〇萬元
頭帮付先僑骸骨〣〇〇〥十具二帮付先僑骸骨〣〦十具二共付骸骨〥〨十具
應支每具上落艇脚費〦〥十該銀〤〥〣元每具助港幣〦〥十該銀〤〣萬元
二共支港銀〤〣〤〧萬元除匯交之外尚欠銀〤〤〧〥仟元此有別項應支過從
共欠若干未為示知俾得此數照匯交足但求早日分送各
縣之骸骨與慈善机関收以得各親屬領葬回各縣之

中華民國　年　月　日

堤岸廣肇公所用牋

第　頁

親屬早已由越旋鄉候領日久且各縣慈善机關屢之東

信追向之故請祈見諒多費精神不勝深感耑此盂頌

善祺

東華醫院

主席先生

列位善長

代理堤岸廣肇郡長馮燦

中華民國廿年八月十四日

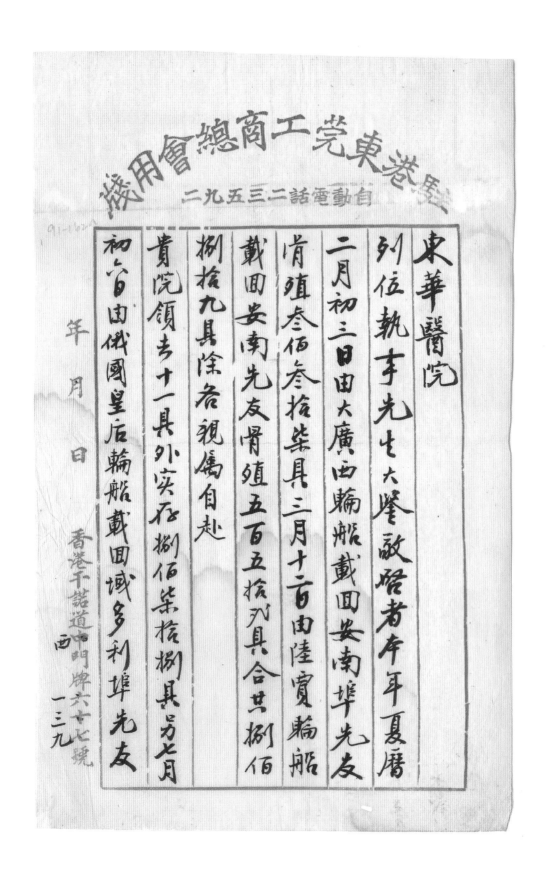

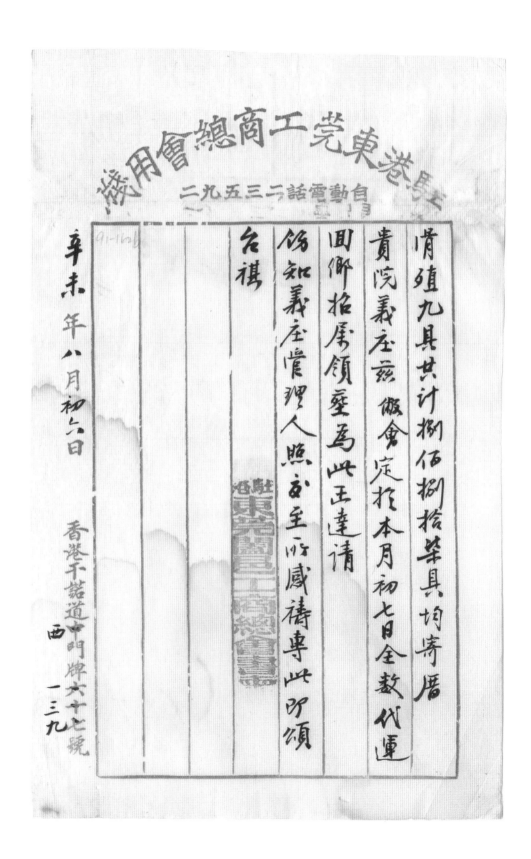

駐港東莞工商總會用箋

自動電話二三五九二

骨殖九具其計捌佰捌拾萃具均寄厝

貴院義庄茲俶會定於本月初七日全數代運

囫僻招屬領毫為此正達請

飭知義庄管理人照方至肞感禱專此所頌

名祺

辛未年八月初六日

香港干諾道中門牌六十七號

西

一三九

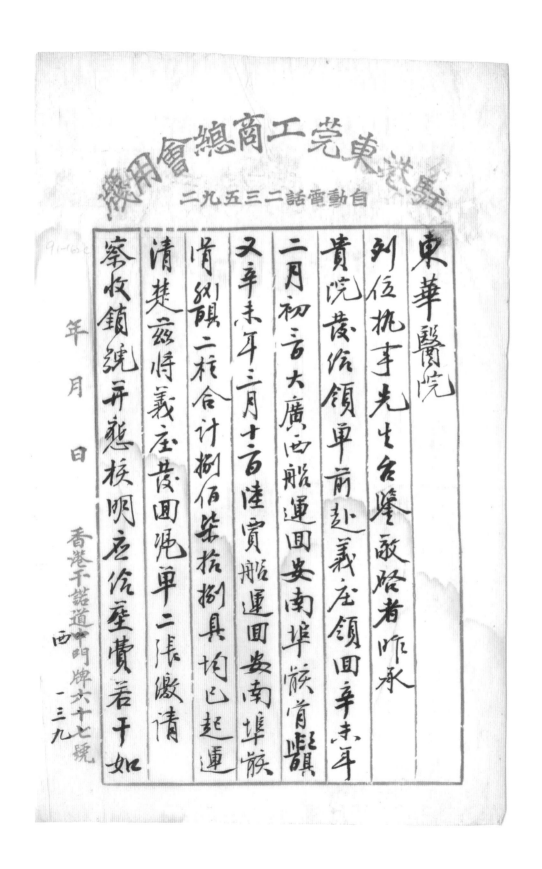

東莞工商總會用牋

自動電話二三五九二

東華醫院

列位執事先生台鑒 敬啟者昨承

貴院義伯領單前赴義庄領回辛未年

二月初三日大廣西船運回安南埠骸骨壹

又辛未年三月十二日達實船運回安南埠骸

骨剋韻二柩合計捌佰柒拾具均已起運

清楚茲將義庄骸回凭單二張繳情

寄收鎮魏開慈核明庶免遺費若干如

年　月　日　　香港干諾道中門牌六十七號
西一三九

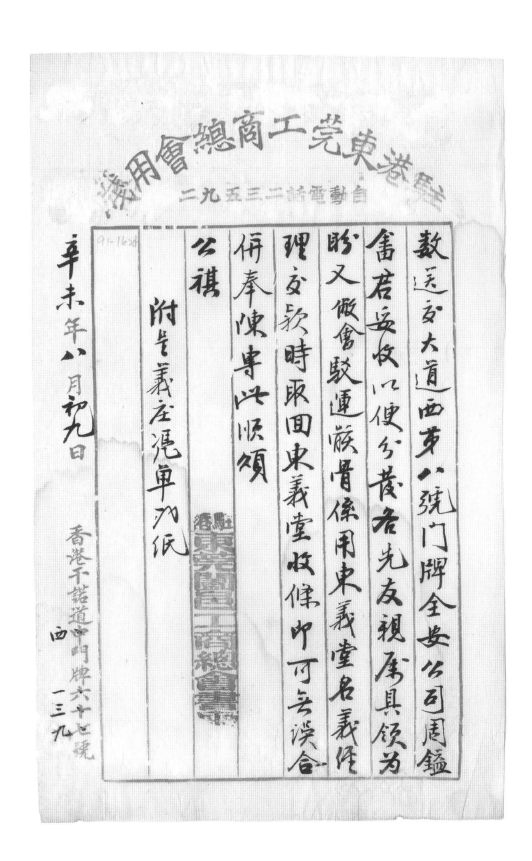

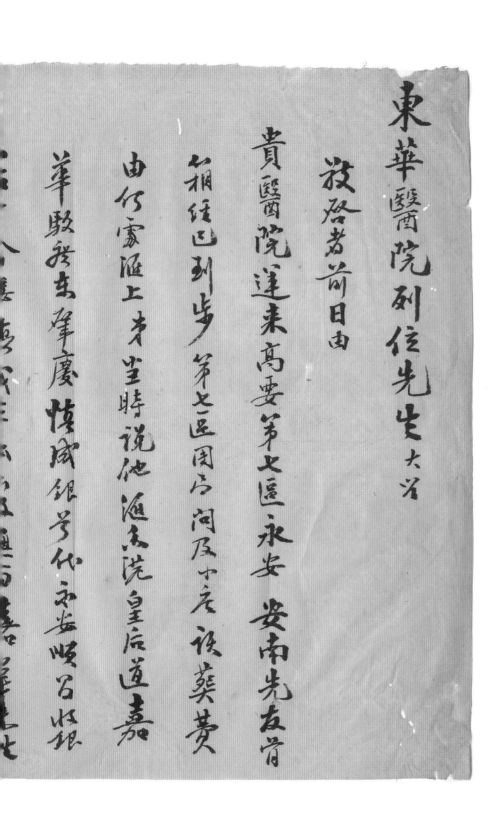

東華醫院列位先生大名

敬啟者前日由

貴醫院送來高要第七區、永安、安南先友骨
相繼已到步、弟七區因有問及中彥該葬費
由伍家滙上、弟當時說他滙交洗皇后道嘉
華駁發去肇慶惜威銀號代兩安順呈收銀

貴醫兩院直送到肇慶慎成代收居收西諸到

收拿并交吉為諸多有勞

清神不勝銘感寔畫啲謝等語

台安

廿年六月七号

　安本

　羅幹生稟

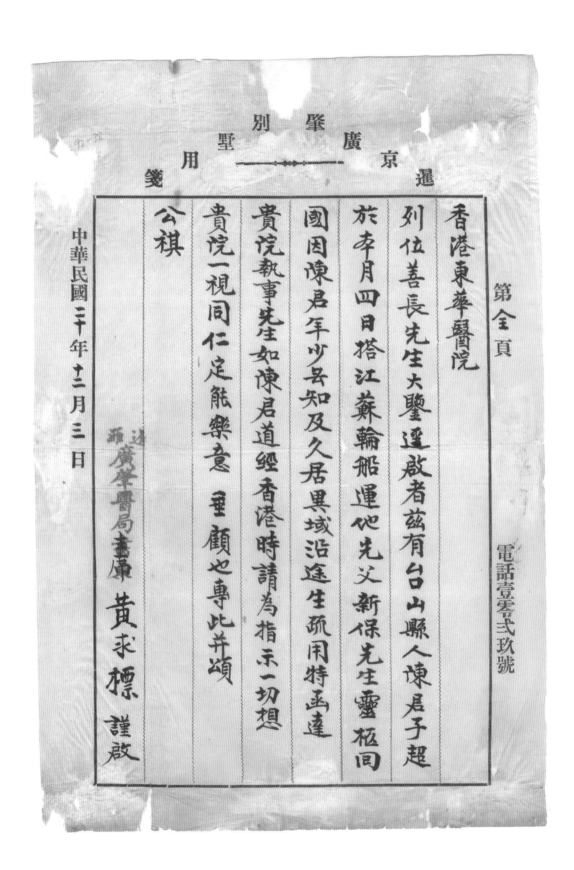

第全頁

電話壹零弍玖號

暹　京　廣　肇　別

用　墅

箋

香港東華醫院

列位善長先生大鑒逕啟者茲有台山縣人陳君子超

於本月四日搭江蘇輪船運他先父新保先生靈柩囘

國因陳君年少弈知及久居異域沿途生疏用特函達

貴院執事先生如陳君道經香港時請為指示一切想

貴院一視同仁定能樂意　重顧也專此并頌

公祺

中華民國二十年十二月三日

暹廣肇醫局書廉　黃求標　謹啟

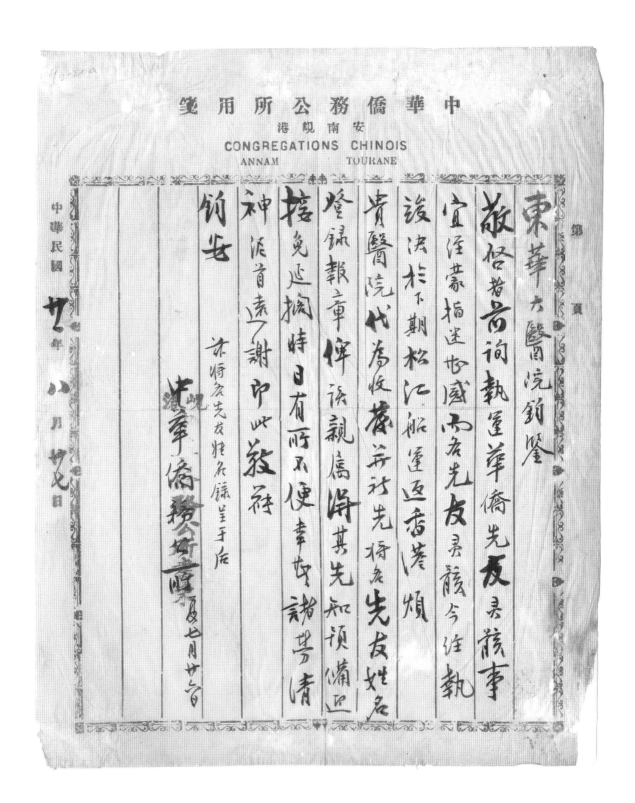

中華僑務所公用箋
安南峴港
CONGREGATIONS CHINOIS
ANNAM   TOURANE

第　頁

東華大醫院釣鑒

敬啟者　詢執篋華僑先友長骸事

宜涇蒙指送世盛兩名先友長骸今住執

後決於下期松江船運返香港煩

貴醫院代為收葬並祈先將各先友姓名

燈錄報章俾該親屬得其先知預備迎

接免延擱時日有所不便幸望諸事清

神泥首遠了謝印此敬祥

銷安

　　　　　亦將各先友姓名錄呈于后

　　　峴

港　華僑務所謹启 夏七月廿七日

中華民國 廿　年 八月 廿七日

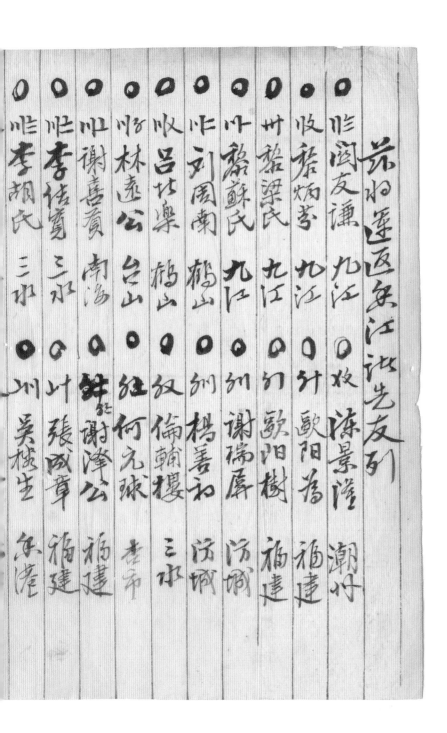

茲將運返各江祖先友列

○形　閏友謙　九江　○收　陳景溏　潮州

○收　蔡炳芳　九江　○升　歐陽為　福建

○卅　譚梁氏　九江　○升　歐陽樹　福建

○卅　蔡蘇氏　九江　○列　謝瑞屏　防城

○作　劉周南　鶴山　○列　楊善和　防城

○收　呂拈樂　鶴山　○叔　倫輔樓　三水

○彤　林遠公　台山　○紅　何元球　香市

○卅　謝喜貫　南海　○針　謝漢公　福建

○作　李佶寬　三水　○葉　張成章　福建

○作　李胡氏　三水　○州　吳棧生　香港

○廿 鳳祥 出 中山
廿一 吳卓華 澳門

○卅 鄭立楷 出 中山
廿二 劉硯汪 中山

○奴 涞有芳 出 中山
涟 劉奈民 中山

○姓 張泰安 出 中山
改 劉伍氏 中山

○姓 吳通初 出 中山
汁 吳寶鑾 南海

○姓 涞宗詠 出 中山
汉 黃牵氏 中山

○炸 涞鄭氏 出
扮 黃朝韓 中山

合共卅具 昨十具

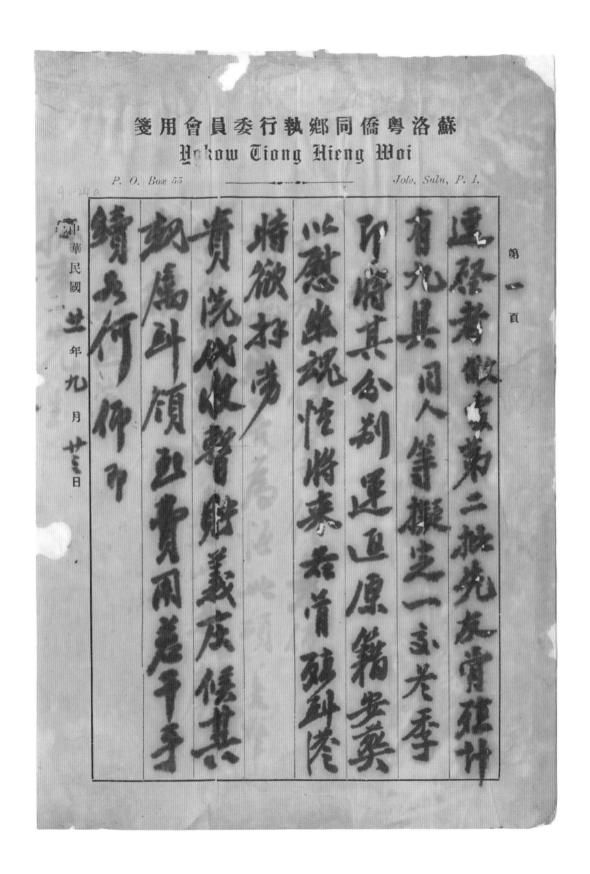

蘇洛粤僑同鄉執行委員會用箋

Yokow Tiong Hieng Woi

P. O. Box 55 ——— Jolo, Sulu, P. I.

第二頁

承知以便籌備兼仰

貴院采著為恆此項美舉

必不見却此事此并廣

免禮

朱蒜匯院

執事先生

中華民國　艺年　九月　廿三日

少年務

梁維熙

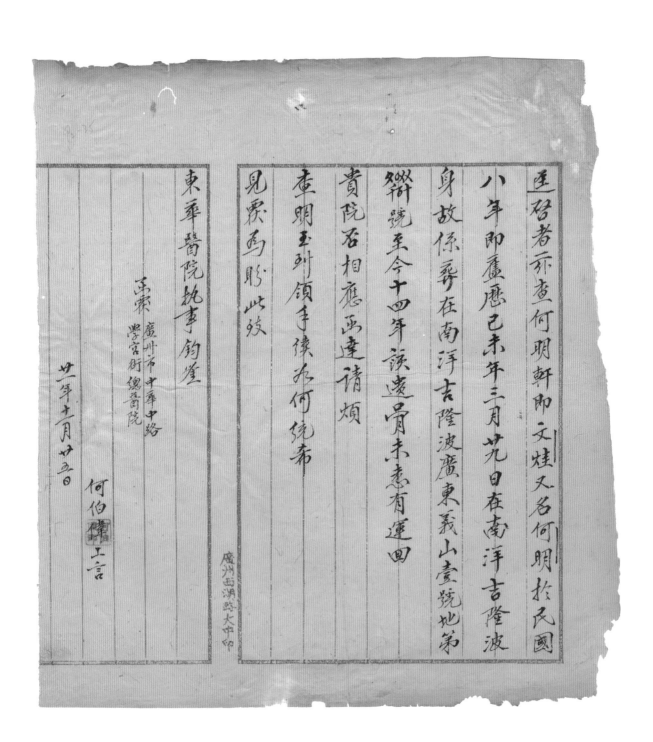

逕啟者茲查何明軒即文娃又名何明於民國

八年即廬應己未年三月廿九日在南洋吉隆波

身故係葬在南洋吉隆波廣東義山壹號地第

號號至今十四年誄遺骨未悉有運回

貴院否相應函達請煩

查明並列領手續希何統希

見示為荷此致

東華醫院執事鈞鑒

　　　　　　　　　　　廣州市十甫中路
　　　　　　　玉函　　學宮街總善院

廿一年十一月廿五日

何伯偉（印）上言

廣肇醫院
KWONG SIU HOSPITAL
391, New Road

Telephone 1029

Bangkok,

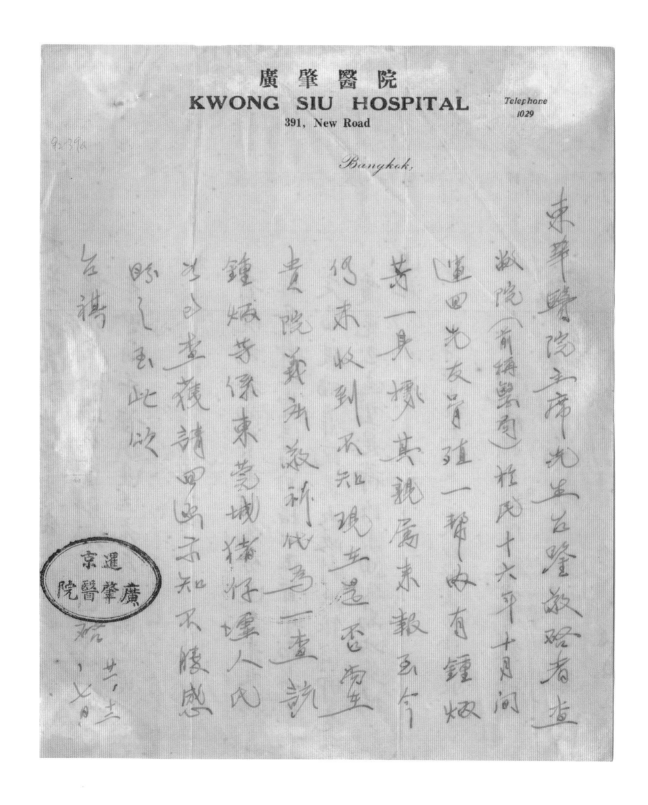

東華醫院主席先生左右鑒敬啟者查

敝院（前稱粵局）於民十六年十月間

據四光友華僑一幫收有鍾炳

芳一具燒其親屬來報云今

得來收到不知現在送否查

貴院義成敬祈代為一查訊

鍾炳芳係東莞城豬仔壞人民

為此查復請即函示知不勝感

盼此致

台祺

暹京廣肇醫院 謹

廿一、十二

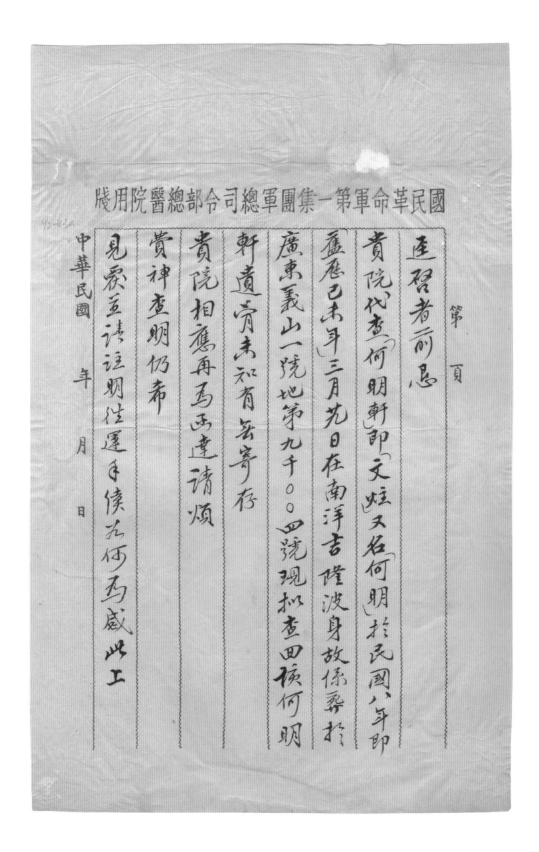

國民革命軍第一集團軍總司令部總醫院用牋

第　頁

逕啟者前患

貴院代查（何明軒）即（文娃）又名（何明）於民國八年即

蘆曆己未年三月先日在南洋吉隆波身故係葬於

廣東義山一號地第九千〇〇四號現擬查四嫂何明

軒遺骨未知有否寄存

貴院相應再為函達請煩

貴神查明仍希

賞神查明往運手續由何為感此上

見覆並請証明往運手續由何為感此上

中華民國　年　月　日

落葉歸根——東華三院華僑原籍安葬檔案選編（上冊）

國民革命軍第一集團軍總司令部總醫院用牋

香港東華醫院執事台鑒

第一頁

何伯偉謹啟

中華民國 廿二年 一月 八日

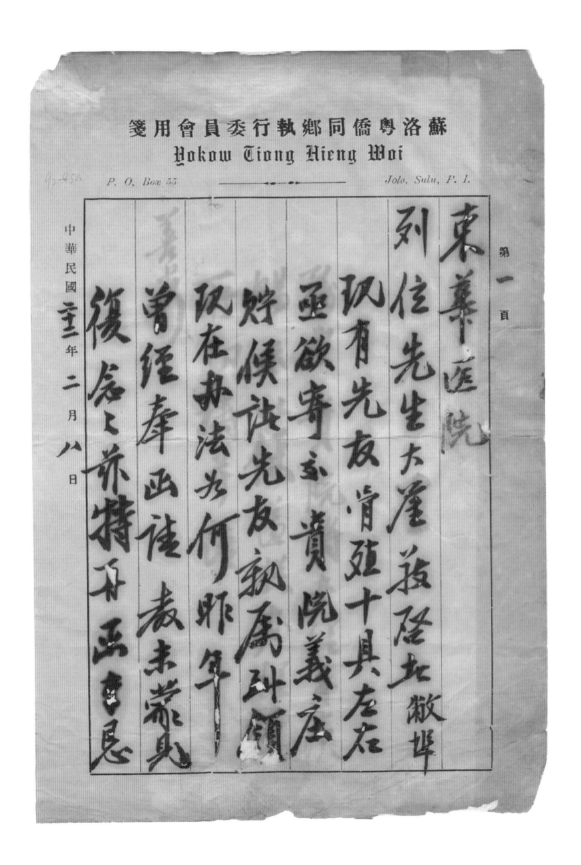

蘇洛粵僑同鄉執行委員會用箋
Yokow Tiong Hieng Woi

P. O. Box 55 　　　　　 Jolo, Sulu, P. 1.

第一頁

東華醫院

列位先生大鑒敬啓者

現有先友骨殖十具左右

亟欲寄交貴院義莊

好候諸先友執屬科領

現在辦法為何那年

曾經庫函註表來蒙貴

復爲之聲明不勝感恩

中華民國廿二年二月八日

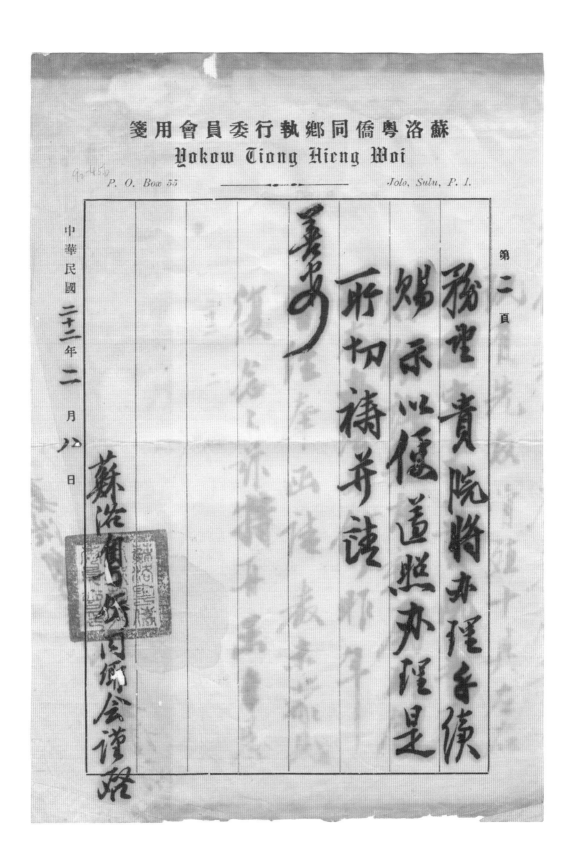

蘇洛粵僑同鄉執行委員會用箋
Yokow Tiong Hieng Woi

P. O. Box 55　　　　　　　　Jolo, Sulu, P. I.

第二頁

務望 貴院將亦理手續
賜承以優道照亦理是
所切禱並頌

中華民國二十三年二月八日

蘇洛粵僑同鄉會謹啓

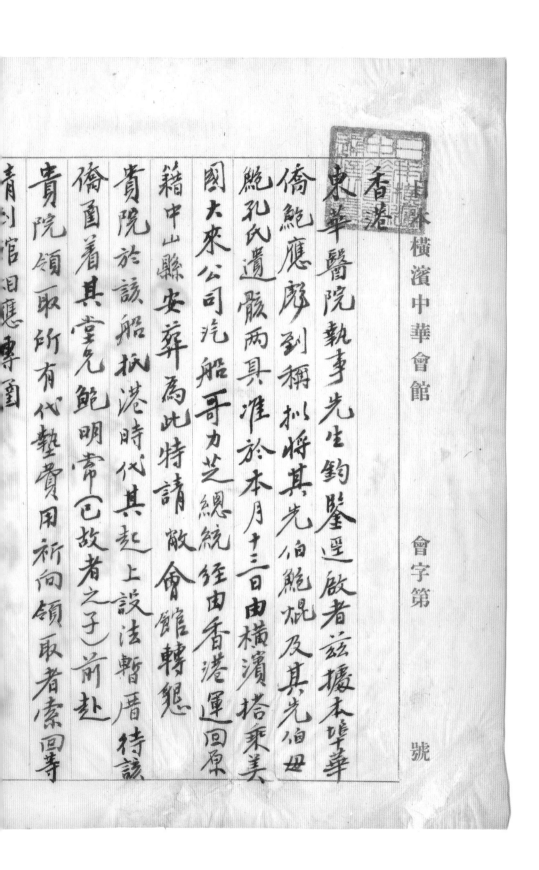

日本橫濱中華會館

會字第　　　　號

東華醫院執事先生鈞鑒逕啟者茲擾本埠華

僑鮑應廖到稱擬將其先伯鮑焜及其先伯母

鮑孔氏遺骸兩具准於本月十三日由橫濱搭乘美

國大來公司汽船哥力芝總統經由香港運回原

籍中山縣安葬為此特請敬會館轉懇

貴院於該船抵港時代其起上設法暫厝待該

僑圖著其堂兄鮑明壽（已故者之子）前赴

貴院領取所有代墊費用祈向領取者索回等

情刊官相應專函

9-46

中華民國二十二年二月十日

代理慈務理事黃碑民

善安

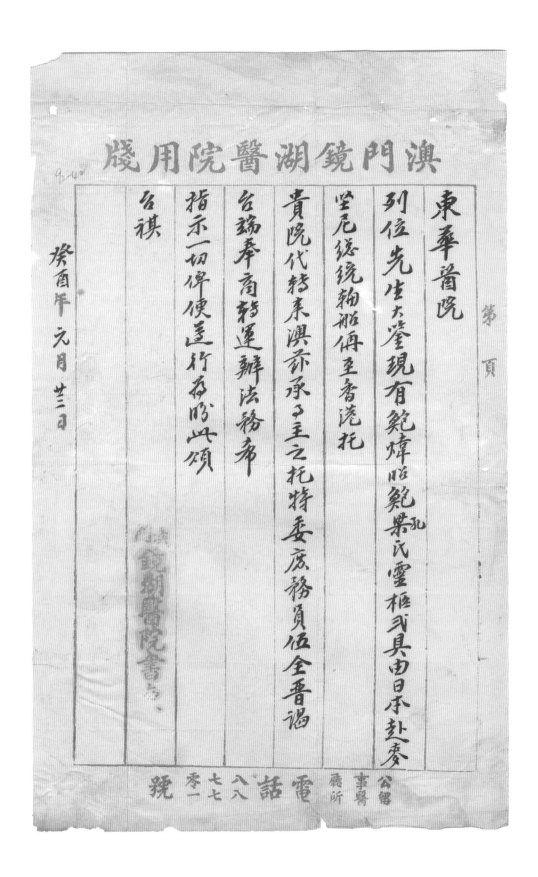

澳門鏡湖醫院用牋

東華醫院

第　頁

　列位先生大鑒現有敝埠旅敝棧氏靈柩弍具由日本赴麥

堂尼總統輪船傴至香港託

貴院代特束澳祈承□主之託特委庶務員伍全晉謁

台端奉商轉運辦法務希

指示一切俾便運行為盼此頌

台祺

癸酉年元月廿三日

鏡湖醫院書

公曆
畫醫
震所

電
話
八八
七七
零一
號

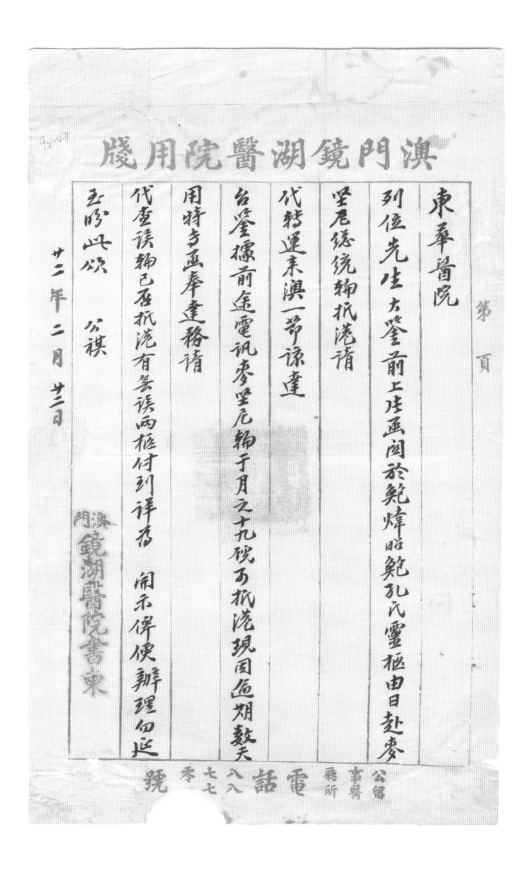

澳門鏡湖醫院用牋

第　頁

東華醫院

列位先生大鑒前上壺函閱於麥煒昭麥孔氏靈柩由日赴麥

望見綏統綢抵港諸

代轉運來澳一節諒達

台鑒據前途電訊麥望尼輪于月之十九號可抵港現固逾期數天

用特寺孟奉達務諸

代查誤輪已居抵港有兾誤兩柩付到詳查　開示俾便辦理勾延

玉照此欵　公祺

廿二年二月廿二日

澳門鏡湖醫院書東

電話　八七七零

號

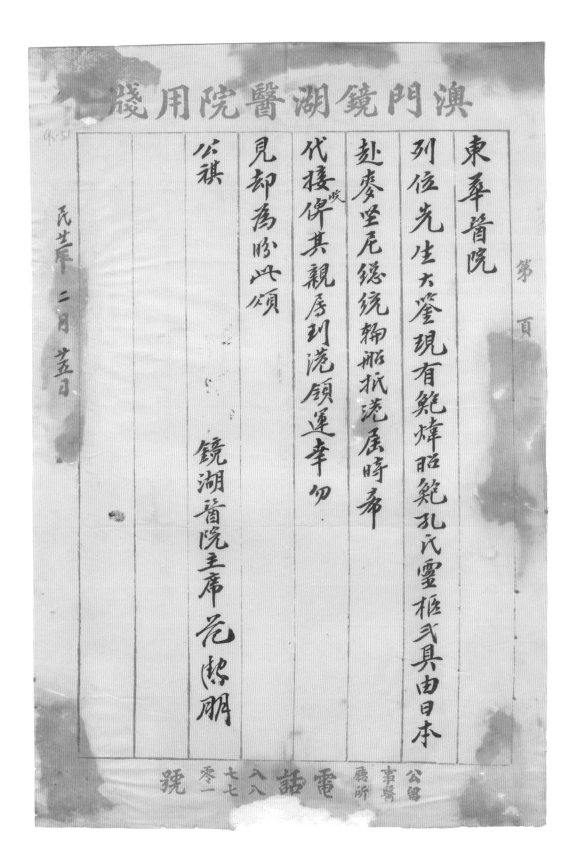

澳門鏡湖醫院用箋

第頁

東華醫院

列位先生大鑒現有鮑煒昭鮑孔氏靈框弍具由日本

赴麥堅尼總統輪船抵港屆時希

代接俾其親屬到港領運幸勿

見却為盼此頌

公祺

鏡湖醫院主席花瀊朋

民廿弍年二月廿五日

公館
書醫
寓所
電話
八八
七七
零一
鐵

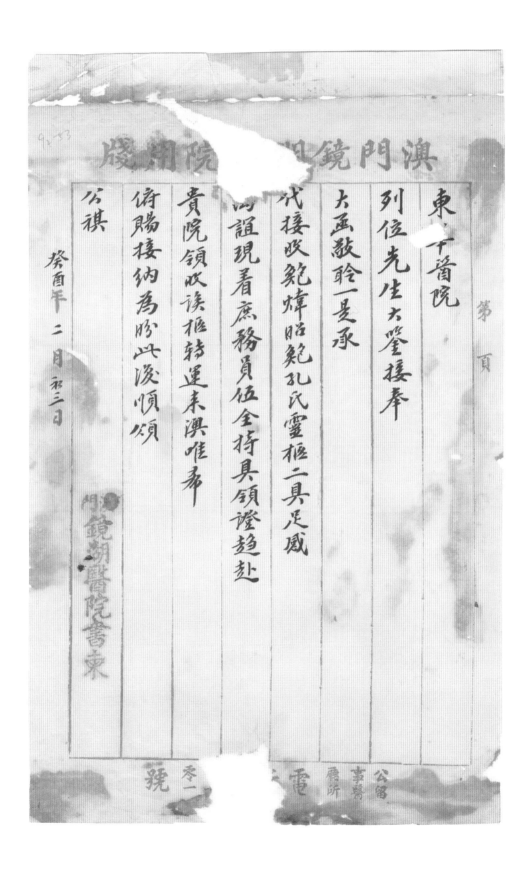

澳門鏡湖醫院致東華醫院收據

1933年2月26日

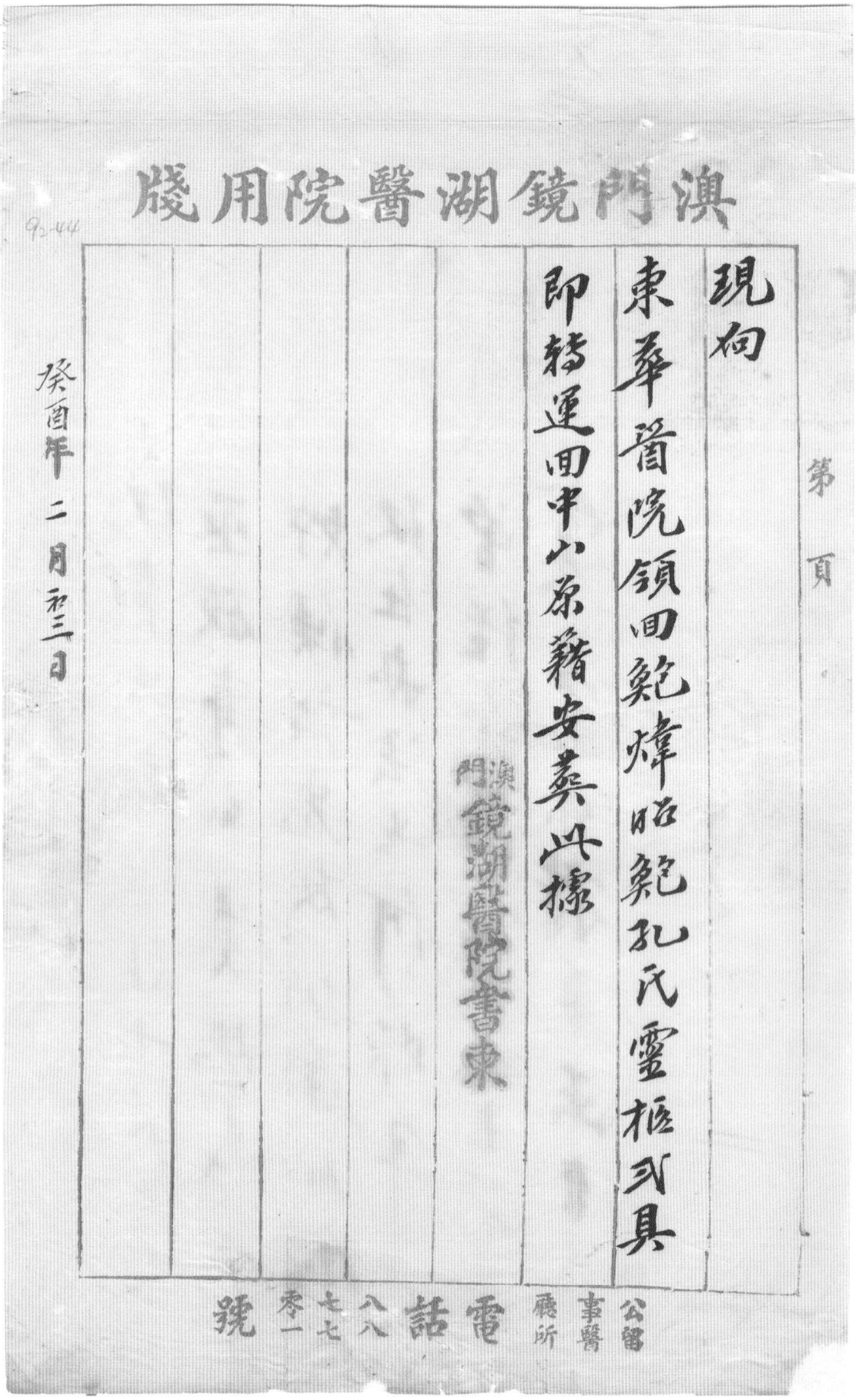

澳門鏡湖醫院用箋

92-44

第　頁

現向

東華醫院領回鄭煒昭、鄭孔氏靈柩弍具

即轉運回中山原籍安葬此據

澳門鏡湖醫院書柬

癸酉年二月初三日

公事廳　電話八七零號
留醫所　電話八七一號

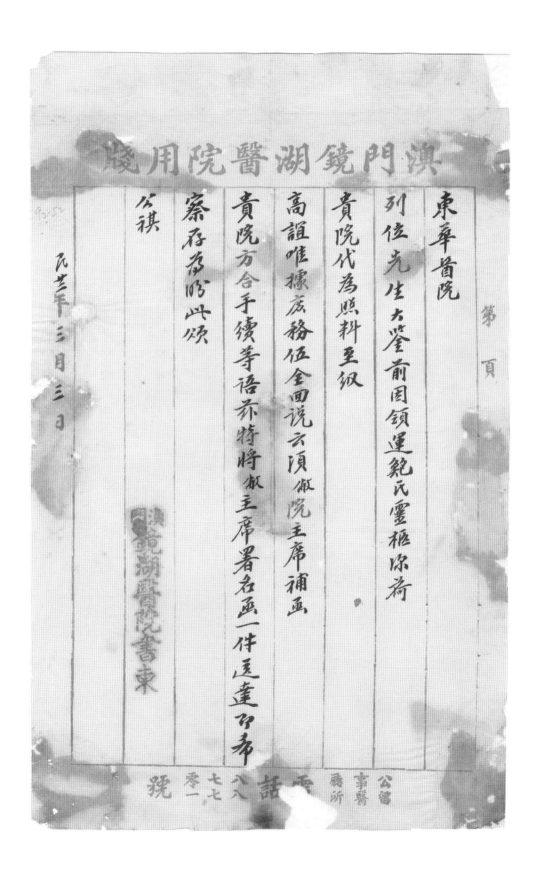

澳門鏡湖醫院用箋

第　頁

東華醫院

列位先生大鑒前因領運范氏靈柩承荷

貴院代為照料至級

高誼唯據庶務伍金回說云頂敝院主席補回

貴院方合手續等語茲特將敝主席署名函一件送達即希

察存為盼此頌

公祺

民廿二年三月三日

澳門鏡湖醫院書柬

電話

西

公醫事務所

八七

七零一

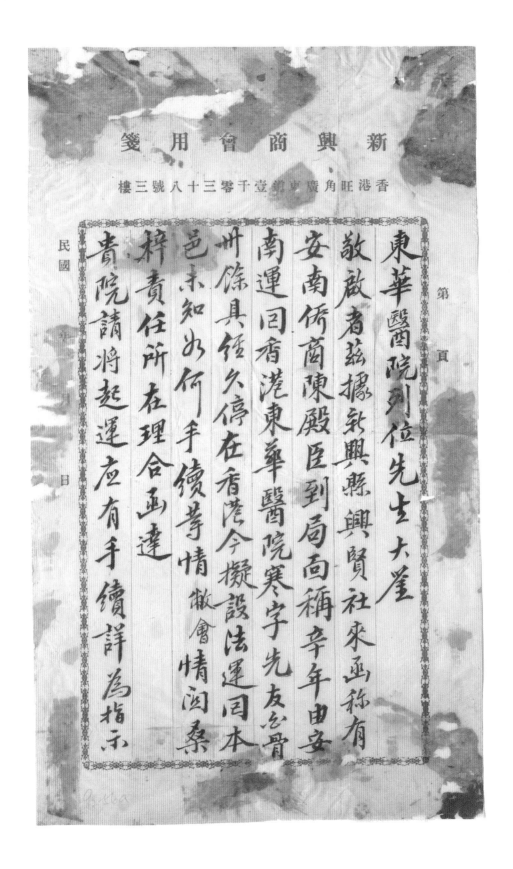

新興商會用箋

香港旺角廣東道壹千零三十八號三樓

第　頁

東華醫院列位先生大鑒

敬啟者茲據敝興縣興賢社來函稱有安南僑商陳殿臣到局面稱辛年由安南運回香港東華醫院寒字先友忞骨冊條具經久停在香港今擬設法運回本邑未知以何手續等情徹會情殷桑梓責任所在理合函達

貴院請將起運應有手續詳為指示

民國　　　年　　　月　　　日

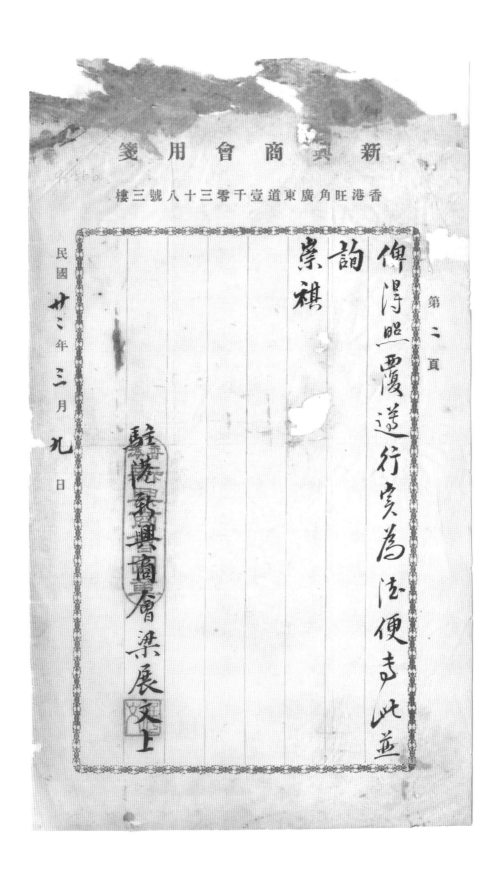

新興商會用箋

香港旺角廣東道壹千零三十八號三樓

第二頁

俾得照覆遞行實為法便專此並

詢

崇祺

民國廿三年三月九日

駐港新興商會梁展文上

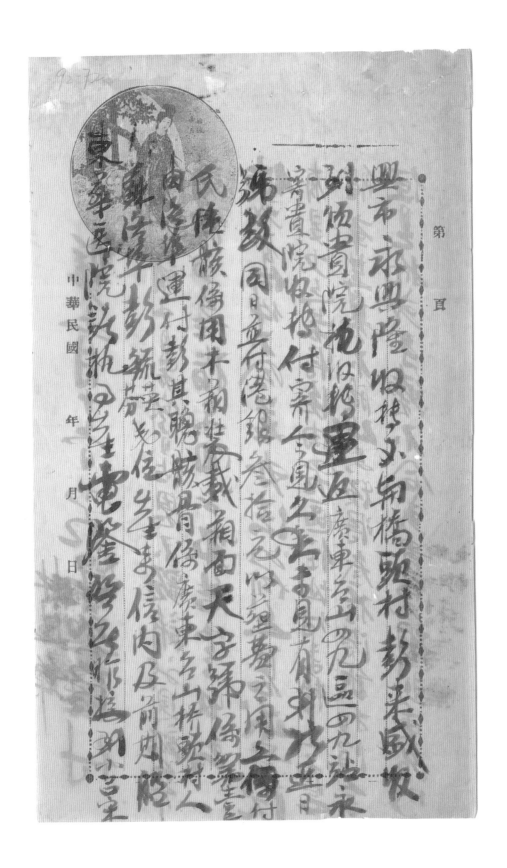

第　頁

興布永興隆收棺永生橋頭村彭來盛收

列煩貴院抛埋於廣東台山㐱區四九站永

啓貴院收棺付寄人字圓名共正日期料並正

謹啓同日並付港銀叁拾元㐱經費之用又得付

民陸骸僑用木箱裝載相面天字歸僑營壹

運付彭其聰骸骨僑廣東台山橋頭村人

故運付彭毓菱先生去信交事信內及前期略

東華醫院敬執照此生電鑑察此永興隆謹启

中華民國　　年　　月　　日

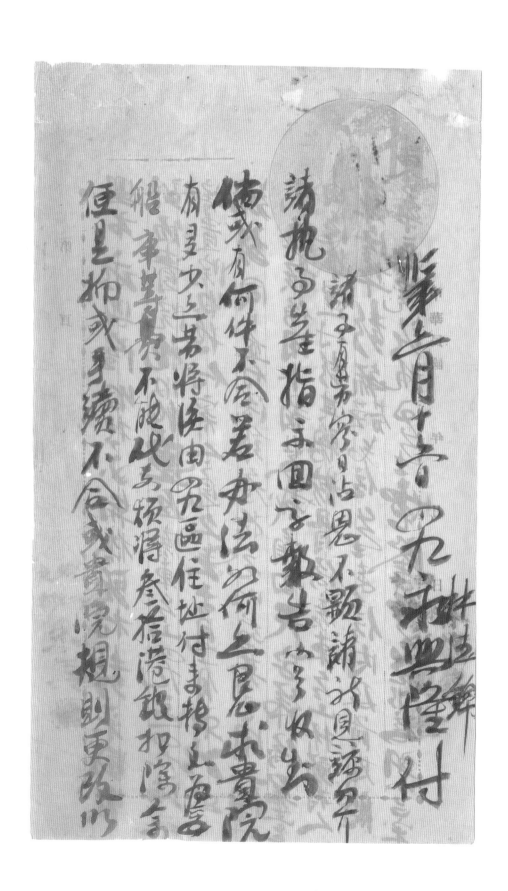

筆前二月十六日兄和興隆付

諸子年四萬多日店思不顕諸光見訪見一

諸兄弟差指示圓二寄告以多收出

倘或有何件不合若辦法以何之思未畫院

有是兄弟將往由四九迴任址付去揚上有事

船事畧頂不能此之頻得參看港飲杠隨金

恆三將或手續不合或費院想則更孩以

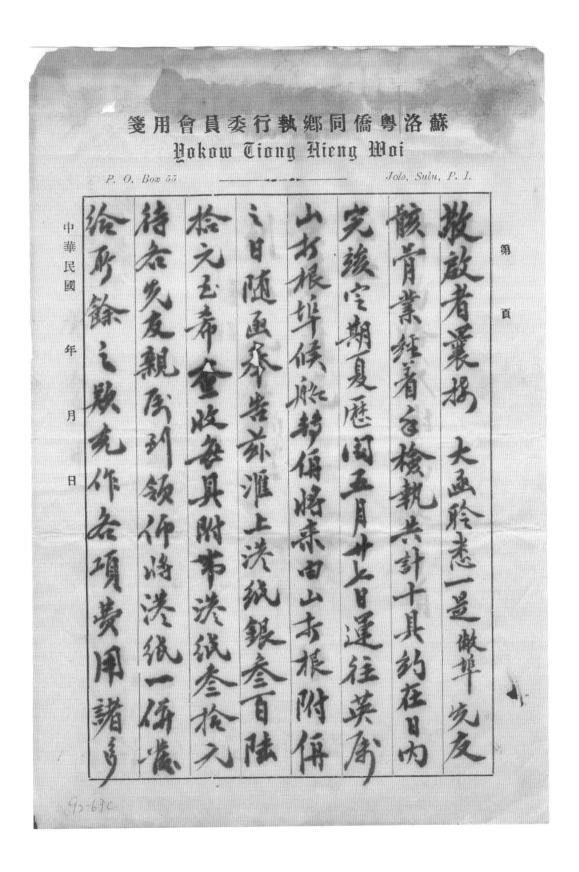

蘇洛粵僑同鄉執行委員會用箋
Yokow Tiong Hieng Woi

P. O. Box 55　　　　　　　　　　Jolo, Sulu, P. I.

第　頁

敬啟者　叢塚　大函敬悉一是　敝埠先友

骸骨業經着令檢執共計十具約在日內

完竣定期夏歷閏五月廿七日運往英属

山方根埠候艦轉僑將來田山方根附僑

三日隨函奉告茲滙上港紙銀叁百陸

拾元玉希金收各具附帶港紙叁拾元

待念先友親戚到領仰將港紙一併發

給所餘之歉充作各項費用諸

中華民國　年　月　日

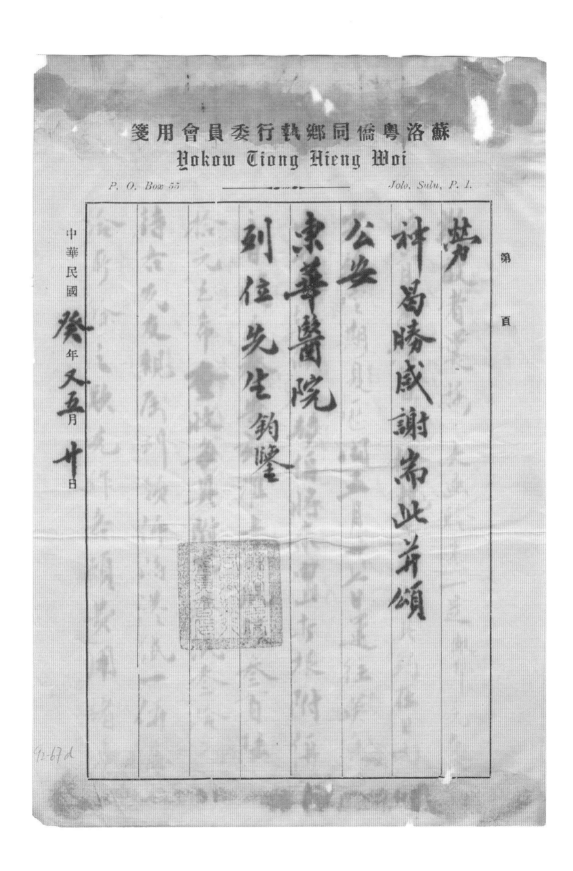

蘇洛粵僑同鄉執行委員會用箋
Yokow Tiong Hieng Woi
P. O. Box 55　　　　　　　　　Jolo, Sulu, P. I.

第　頁

勞神昌勝感謝耑此并頌

公安

崇華醫院

到位先生鈞鑒

中華民國 癸年又五月 十日

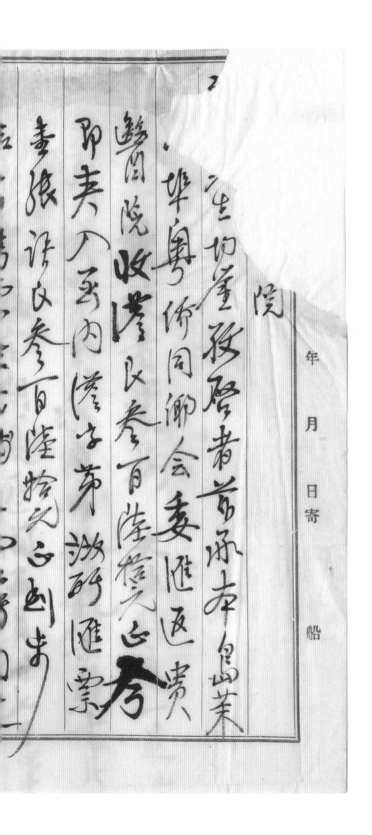

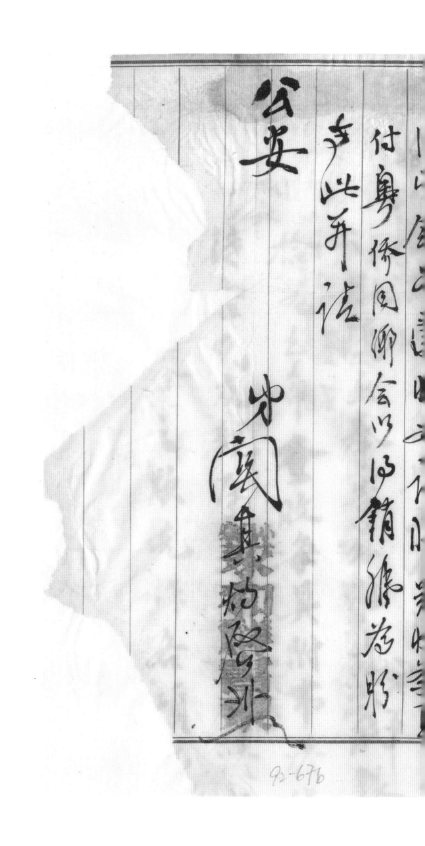

一、□金□議此二十日止此章

付粵僑同鄉會以便銷源為附

聲此辨法

公安

中國東約改乡州

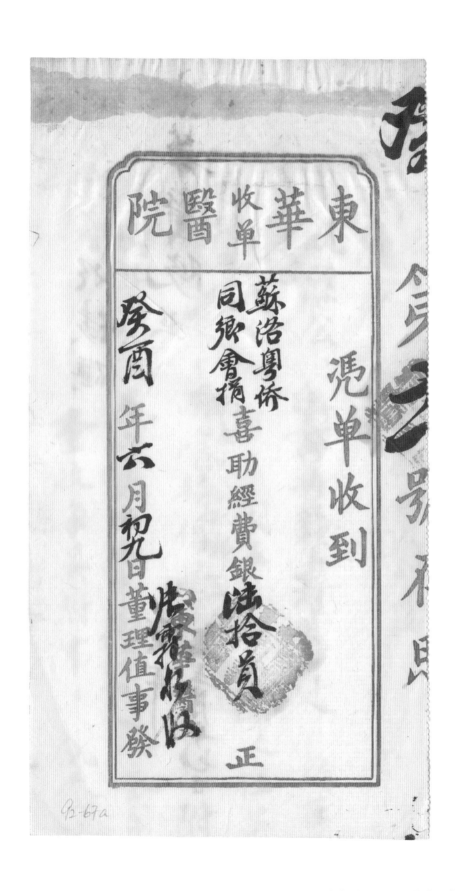

東華
醫院
收單

憑單收到

蘇浴粵僑
同殮會捐喜助經費銀伍拾員
正

癸酉年六月初九日董理值事發

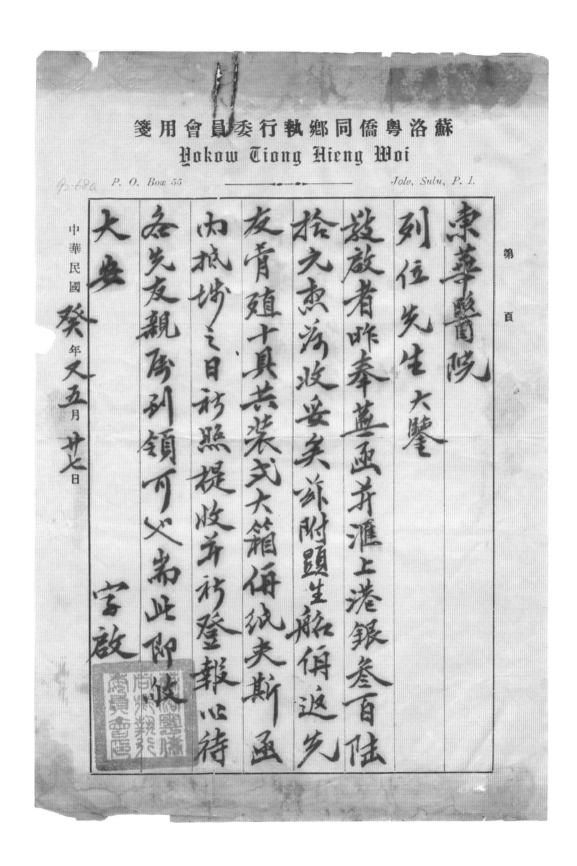

蘇洛粵僑同鄉執行委員會用箋
Yokow Tiong Hieng Woi

P. O. Box 55　　　　　　　　　　　Jolo, Sulu, P. I.

東華醫院

列位先生大鑒

敬啟者昨奉蕙函幷滙上港銀叁百陸

拾元惠為收妥笑莞附題生痲佰返矢

友膏殖十貝共裝弍大箱佰紙夾斯函

內抵埗之日祈照提收幷祈登報心待

各先友親屬列領可父弟此即致

大安

宮啟

中華民國癸年又五月廿芒日

蘇將各先友庄氏籍貫開列後

第一號箱　封毓傑公　新寧瓖庇台林夫村人

第二號箱　溫壁公　南海橫檻鄉三甲人

第三號箱　羅樹華公　九山荻游大井僑村人

第四號箱　余聯康公　台山荻游新边村人

第五號箱　關津民公　平海九江玉西村順和社人

第六號箱　陳沆元氏　新會陳沖人

第七號箱

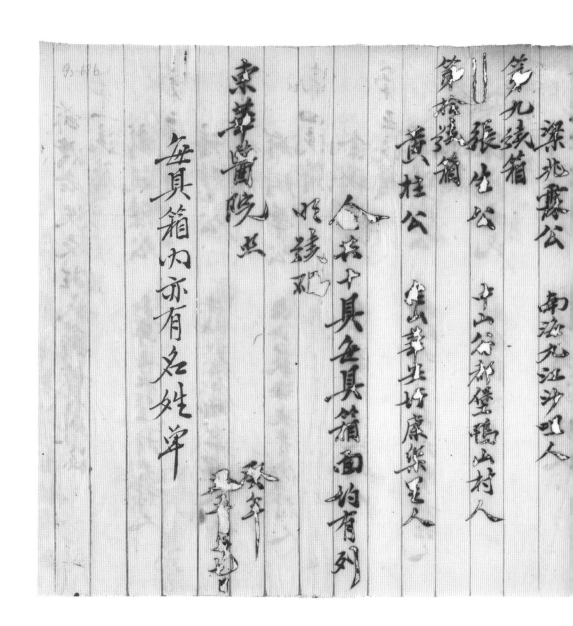

第九號箱　梁兆霖公　南海九江沙咀人

張生公　中山公叙堡鴨山村人

第拾號箱

黃桂公　□武□生坊廣樂區人

□號碼

令共十具金具箱面均有列

東華醫院此

□□張立□

每具箱內亦有名姓單

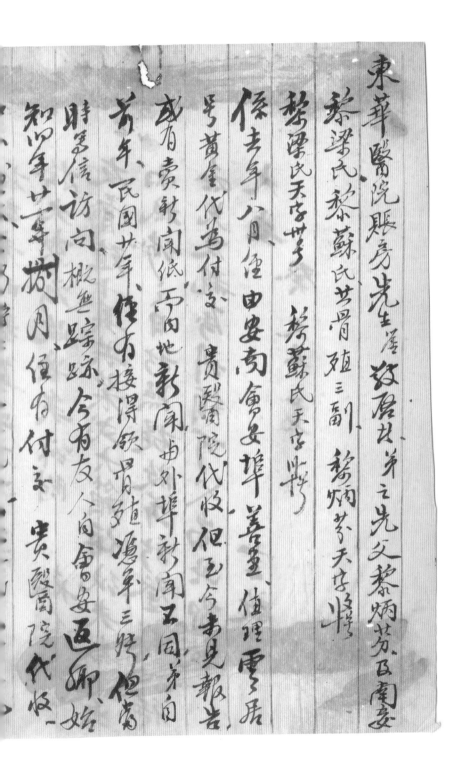

東華醫院賬房先生尊鑒　敬啟者　弟之先父黎炳芳及先妣

黎梁氏黎蘇氏其骨殖三副、黎炳芳天字扙

黎梁氏天字扙　　黎蘇氏天字扙

係去年八月經由安南會安埠善堂代理運居

號黃金代為付交　貴醫院代收但至今未見報告

或有賣新聞低雲內地新聞由外埠新南五同芽自

若年、民國廿年、僅有接得領骨殖馮卓三號個號

時無信訪問概無踪跡、今有友人自會安運卿姑

知四年廿華拊月僅有付交　貴醫院代收

首飾店將弟收領玉骨雖三兩暫留敝院存弟到
敝可以或貴院不用代付先要弟親到港領或托親友
攜憑証到取方合手續先衫衫而親送單雖有
寫明有贈送返家安葬副統但誤埠有缺付到
貴院一定要出亦無別件羅瑞衫為
查且亦覆荷、要平亦九江亓去年新中秋已了
轉交弟收可也專此敬頌

善安

廿一年七月廿日

弟黎妁居謹啓

中國林德錦致東華醫院信件

1933 年 8 月 30 日

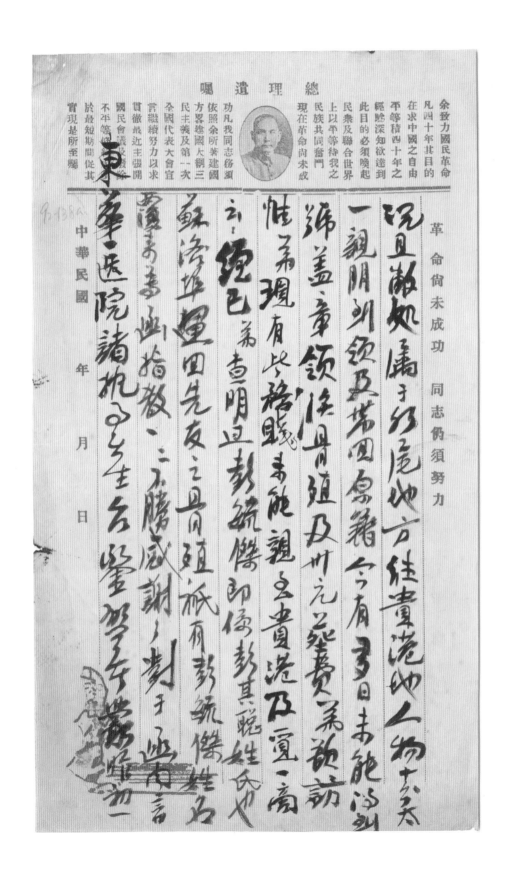

總理遺囑

余致力國民革命凡四十年其目的在求中國之自由平等積四十年之經驗深知欲達到此目的必須喚起民衆及聯合世界上以平等待我之民族共同奮鬥現在革命尚未成功凡我同志務須依照余所著建國方略建國大綱三民主義及第一次全國代表大會宣言繼續努力以求貫徹最近主張開國民會議及廢除不平等條約尤須於最短期間促其實現是所至囑

革命尚未成功　同志仍須努力

東華醫院諸執事先生台鑒[illegible]

蒙貴善堂函指教，不勝感謝，對于函內言

蘇洛華運回先友之骨殖祇有彭毓傑姓名

云云，經已弟查明過彭毓傑即係彭其晚姓氏也

惟弟現有些路職，未能親至貴港及覓一處

綿蓋、章領係骨殖及卅元之經費，弟欲訪

一親朋到領及帶回原籍，今有多日未能詳細

況且敝處屬于偏僻地方，往貴港地人物十分太

中華民國　年　月　日

9-1386

革命尚未成功　同志仍須努力

總理遺囑

余致力國民革命
凡四十年其目的
在求中國之自由
平等積四十年之
經驗深知欲達到
此目的必須喚起
民眾及聯合世界
上以平等待我之
民族共同奮鬥
現在革命尚未成

功凡我同志務須
依照余所著建國
方略建國大綱三
民主義及第一次
全國代表大會宣
言繼續努力以求
貫徹最近主張開
國民會議及廢除
不平等條約尤須
於最短期間促其
實現是所至囑

中華民國　年　月　日

新枕事先生代做些的善事係陰積福功德

收埋尼橋頭村政府收回五之型　新興市　新興陸

比街时火車望的参山四九區的九啟　此住址由

会樓四之整費　他带回做境或此住址由

楸此方光樣戈領回政流傻之卅連及先发

一趬寅知已我可以进于我故地帝寄人妳

新枕子先生而以做利代為办逼上弟在处代覧

太州及七小子福州乎十分為難最好有林書院

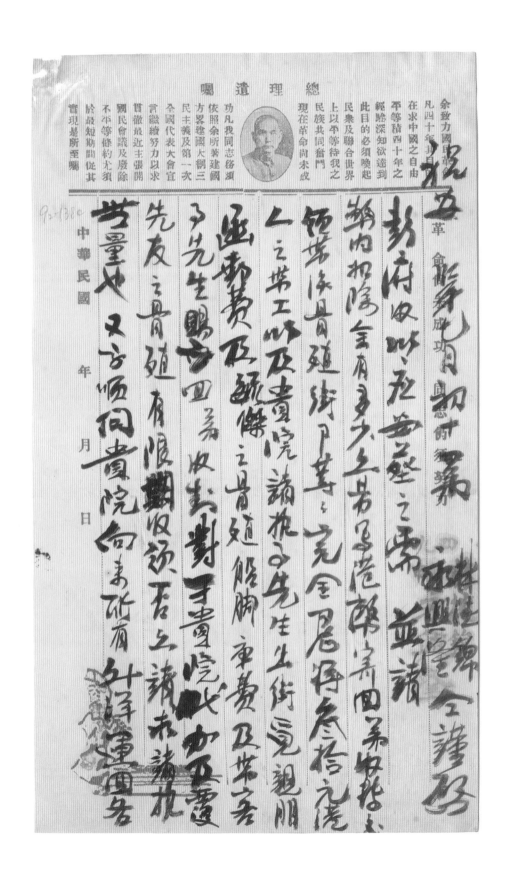

總理遺囑

余致力國民革命凡四十年，其目的在求中國之自由平等。積四十年之經驗，深知欲達到此目的，必須喚起民眾及聯合世界上以平等待我之民族共同奮鬥。現在革命尚未成功，凡我同志，務須依照余所著建國方略、建國大綱、三民主義及第一次全國代表大會宣言，繼續努力，以求貫徹。最近主張開國民會議及廢除不平等條約，尤須於最短期間促其實現。是所至囑。

中華民國　　年　　月　　日

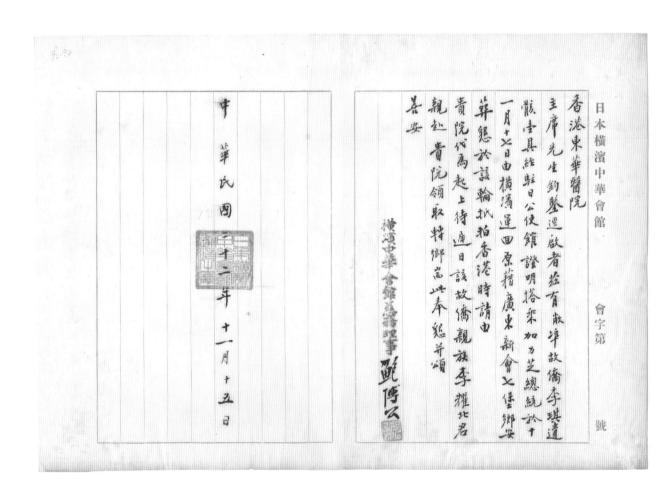

日本橫濱中華會館　　　會字第　　　號

香港東華醫院
主席先生鈞鑒逕啟者茲有敝埠故僑李琪遺
骸業具經駐日公使館證明搭乘加力芝總統於十
一月十七日由橫濱運囬原籍廣東新會之坮鄉安
葬懇於該輪抵拍香港時請由
貴院代為起上待進日該故僑親族李耀北君
親赴　貴院領取特卽耑此奉懇並頌
善安

橫濱中華會館董兼理事　甄傳公

中

華

民

國

二

十

二

年

十

一

月

十

五

日

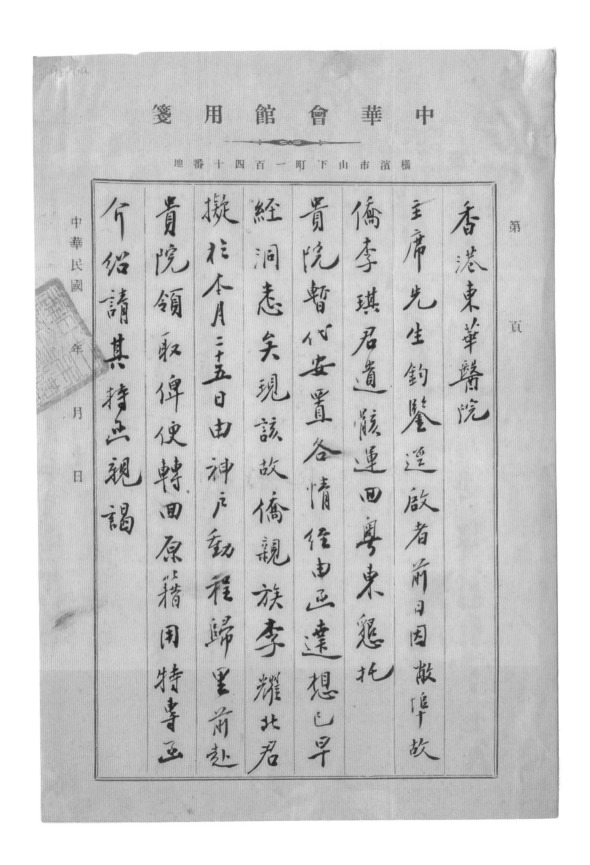

中華會館用箋

横濱市山下町一百四十番地

第　頁

香港東華醫院

主席先生鈞鑒逕啟者前日因敝阜故

僑李琪君遺骸運回粵東懇托

貴院暫代安置各情經由區達想已早

經洞悉矣現該故僑親族李耀北君

擬於本月二十五日由神戶勁程歸里前赴

貴院領取俾使轉回原籍用特專函

介紹請其持函覿謁

中華民國　年　月　日

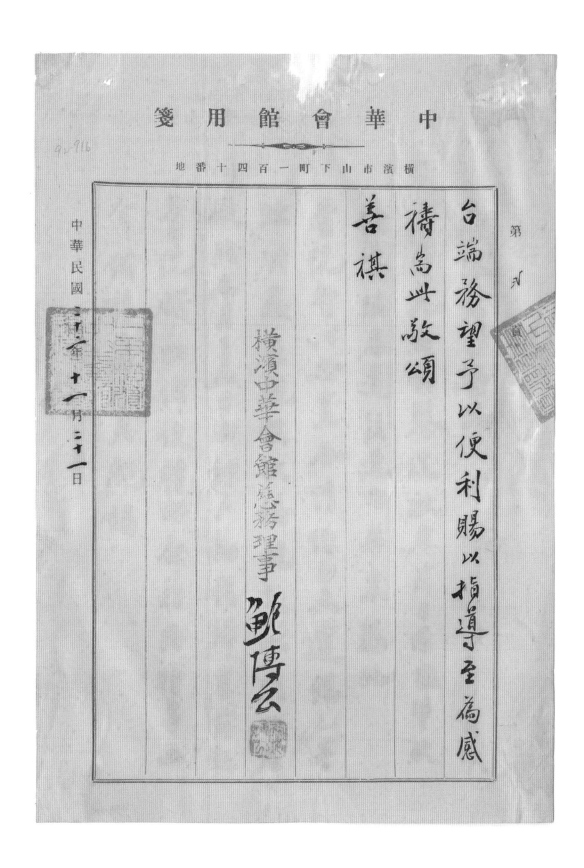

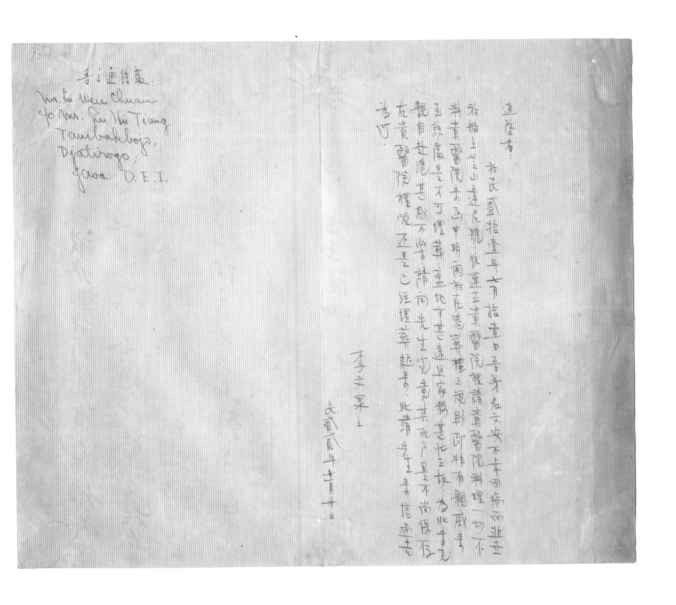

逕啟者：

於民貳拾壹年七月拾壹日吾弟名文安不幸因病而逝去

於船上名山達尼號後達本埠醫院裡請貴醫院料理一切不

料貴醫院來函中明言在港無權之規則而非有親戚來

致該家是不可埋葬並此了甚遠且家務悉忙之故為此弟不克

親自赴港甚感不安請向先生究其死亡是不尚保存

在貴醫院裡呢還是已經理葬起事此請先生幸信通達

告知

李文泉上

民貳貳年十月十日。

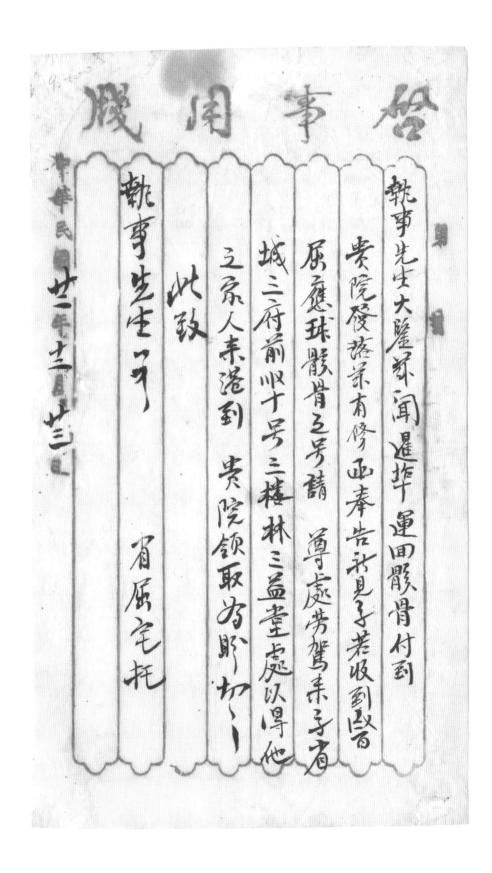

啟者

執事先生大鑒茲聞運回骸骨付到

貴院發落茲荣有修函奉告祈見子若收到啟者

屈應珠骸骨之号請　尊處勞駕柬子若者

城三府前順十号三楼林三益堂處以得他

之京人来港到　貴院領取為那切～

此致

執事先生台前

省屈宅托

中華民國廿二年十二月廿三日

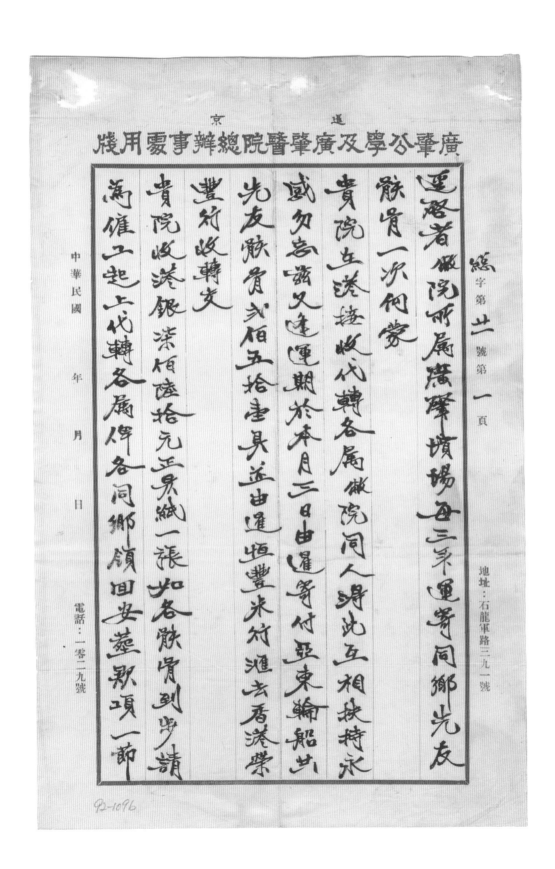

暹京

廣肇公學及廣肇醫院總辦事處用牋

總字第 卅 號第 一 頁

地址：石龍軍路三九一號

逕啟者敝院所屬廣肇墳場每三年運寄同鄉先友

骸骨一次何蒙

貴院立港接收代轉各屬敝院同人得此互相扶持永

感勿忘茲又運期於本月二日由暹寄付亞東輪船此

先友骸骨貳佰五拾壹具益由暹恆豐米行滙去香港榮

豐行收轉交

貴院收港銀柒佰陸拾元正另紙一張如各骸骨到步請

為催工起上代轉各屬俾各同鄉領回安葬費項一節

中華民國　年　月　日

電話：一零二九號

P2-1096

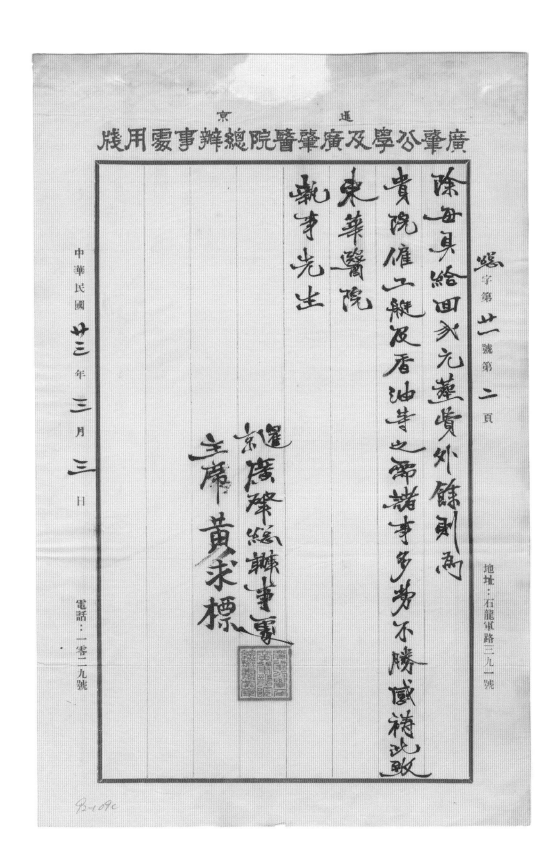

京 進

廣肇公學及廣肇醫院總辦事處用牋

總字第卅一號第二頁

地址：石龍軍路三九一號

除每具給回及元邊貴外餽則爾

貴院催工縱及香油等之需諸事多勞不勝感禱此敬

東華醫院

執事先生

邏京廣肇總辦事處
主席 黃求標

中華民國廿三年三月三日

電話：一零二九號

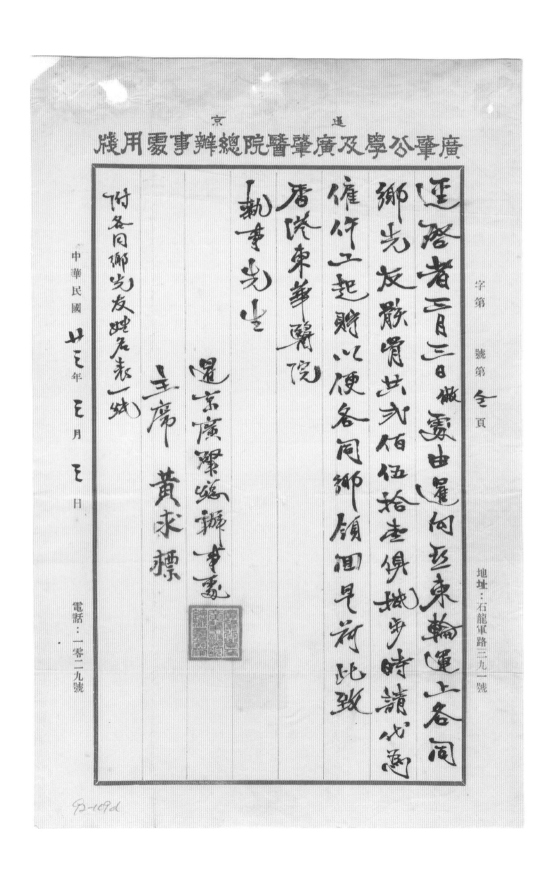

廣肇公學及廣肇醫院總辦事處用牋

京　　暹

字第　　號第　令頁

地址：石龍軍路三九一號

逕啟者三月三日微霧由暹向亞東輪運上各同鄉先友骸骨共弍佰伍拾壹俱搬妥時請代邀催行工起附以便各同鄉領迴是荷此致

唐僑東華醫院

執事先生

暹京廣肇總辦事處

主席　黃求標

附各日鄉先友牌名表一紙

中華民國廿三年三月三日

電話：一零二九號

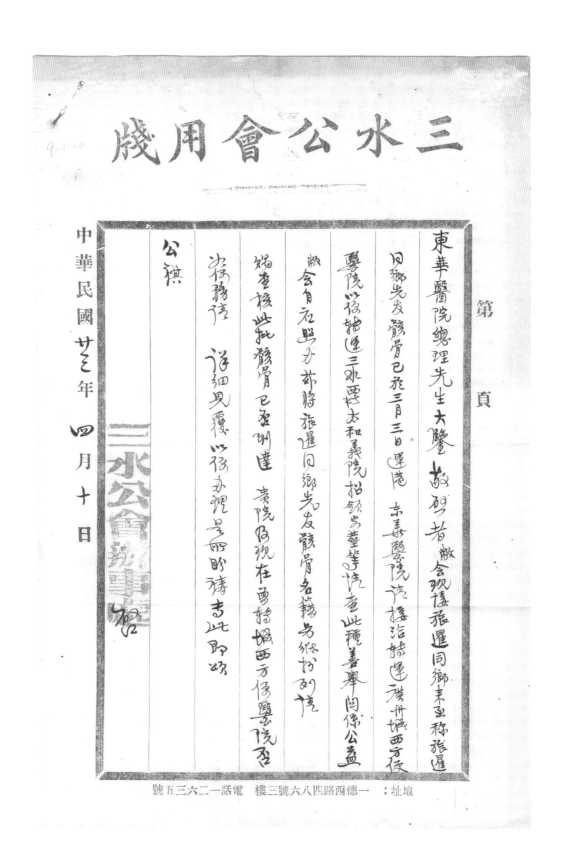

三水公會用牋

地址：一德西路四八六號三樓　電話一二六三五號

第　頁

三水旅滬同鄉先友骸骨姓名籍貫一覽

梁乃讓	三水	崗頭	鄧雲禧	三水	伏戶塘口坊
梁方氏	三水	崗頭	潘耀輝	三水	周杜
麥永	三水	蘆苞麥街	陳楊氏	三水	西南東閘
麥盧氏	三水	蘆苞麥街			

以上所列之骸骨巳于青吉運港

東華大醫院收

中華民國廿三年四月十日

三水公會

233
〈頁一〉

越南東京廣善堂運先友辦事所致東華醫院信件

1934年8月15日

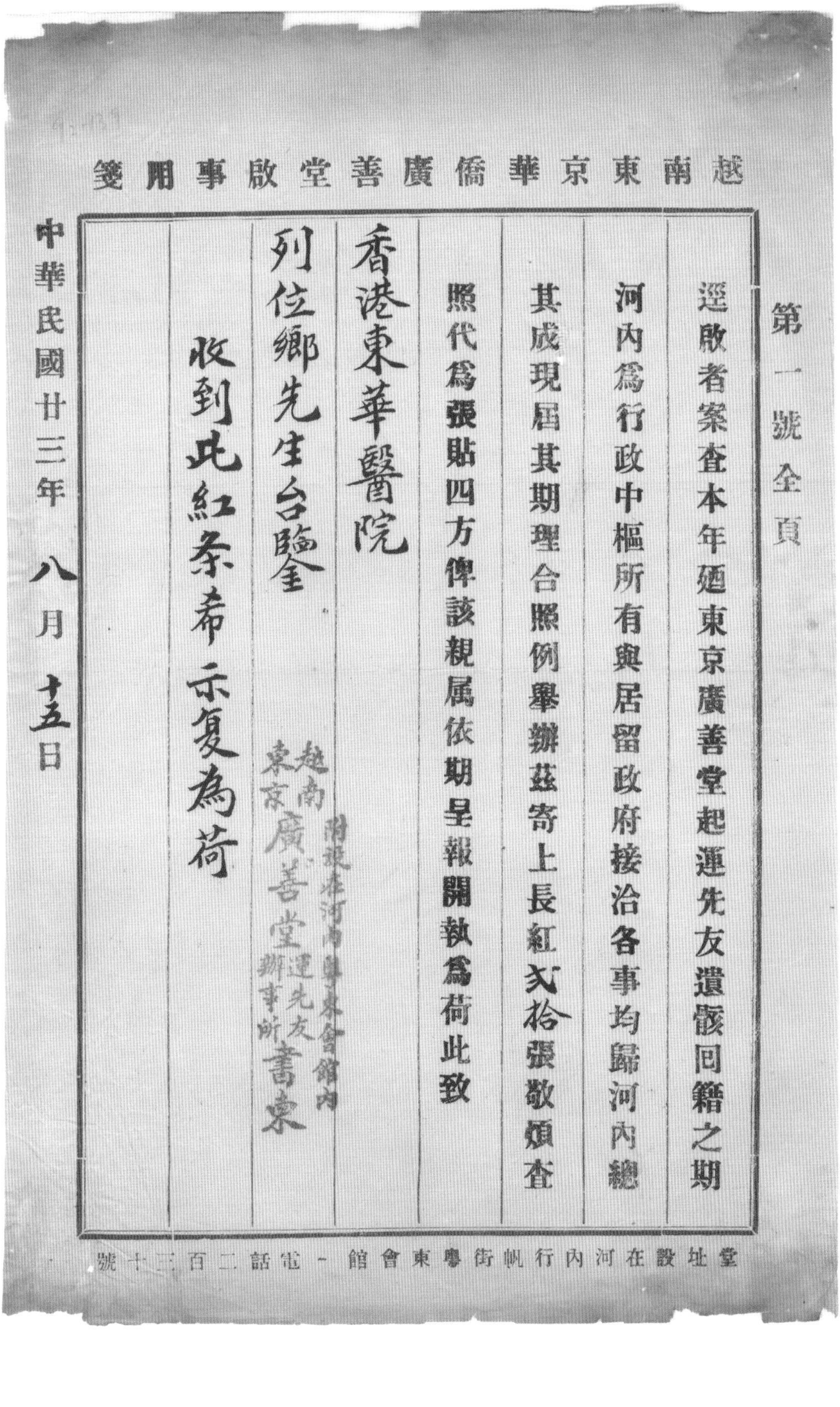

越南東京華僑廣善堂啟事用箋

第一號全頁

逕啟者案查本年廼東京廣善堂起運先友遺骸回籍之期河內爲行政中樞所有與居留政府接洽各事均歸河內總其成現屆其期理合照例舉辦茲寄上長紅文拾張敬煩查照代爲張貼四方俾該親屬依期呈報開執爲荷此致

香港東華醫院

列位鄉先生台鑒

越南東京廣善堂運先友辦事所書柬

附設在河內粵東會館內

收到此紅祈希示复為荷

中華民國廿三年八月十五日

堂址設在河內行帆街粵東會館 - 電話二百三十號

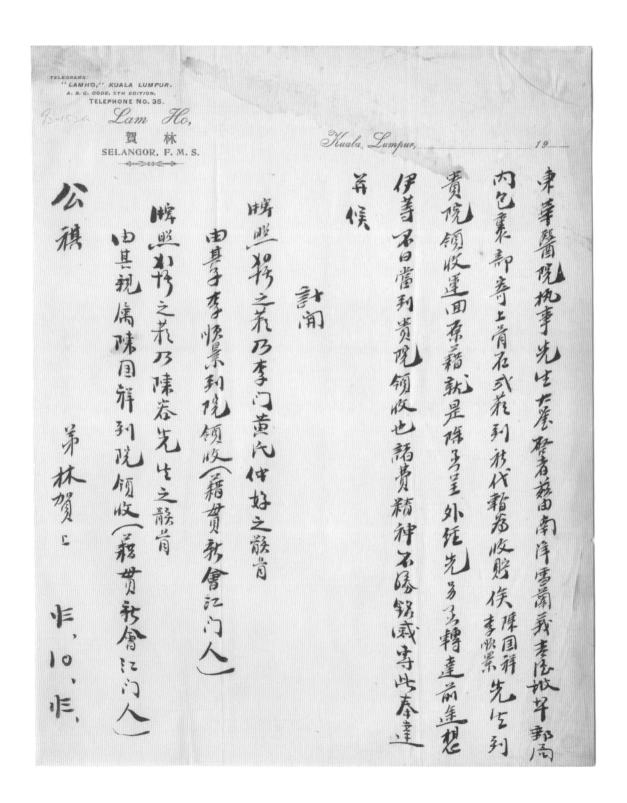

TELEGRAMS:
"LAMHO," KUALA LUMPUR.
A. B. C. CODE, 5TH EDITION.
TELEPHONE NO. 35.

Lam Ho,
賀林
SELANGOR, F. M. S.

Kuala Lumpur, _____ 19___

東華醫院执事先生大鑒 啟者兹由南洋雪蘭莪寄歷坺幷郵局
內包裹部寄上骨石或莪到敝代籍荼收賠候 陳国祥先生到
貴院領收運回原籍 就是 降马呈外孫先另為轉達前途想
伊等召到 貴院領收也 請貴精神石勝銘感寺此奉達

荓候

計開

晓照 羊之荼乃李門黄氏仲好之骸骨
由其子李顺景到院領收（籍貫新會江門人）

晓照 之荼乃陳春先生之骸骨
由其親屬陳国祥到院領收（籍貫新會江門人）

公祺

弟 林賀 上

昨, 10, 昨,

TELEGRAMS:
"LAMHO," KUALA LUMPUR.
A. B. C. CODE, 5TH EDITION.
TELEPHONE NO. 35.
Lam Ho,
賀林
SELANGOR, F. M. S.
92-1526
Kuala Lumpur, _____ 19____

（関于領收先人骨不事）

秉華醫院执事先生均鑒 啟者兹有 陳國祥 李悅景 兩君乃新

會江門人到貴院領收前由南洋雪蘭莪僑寄檀板到郵

局內包裹部寄回先人骨石及莊牌照 如彩 如彩 見字煩

祈 伊等接洽為作感 專此奉達等候

公祺

弟林賀上

作、10、作、

啟事用牋

第　　頁

東華大善院列位先生鈞鑒　逕啟者茲有
邑人梁文軒昨日到敝堂調查事因伊父
梁窝松往年間往往嗎嘩埠經營不
幸在該埠身故源由該埠華僑善
堂將外亡僑胞遺骸合幫寄返台送
各原籍招領查梁窝字燦垣廣東
中山石岐張溪鄉人停於民十一年三月間

中華民國　　年　月　日

石岐南基兆全店監製

啓事用牋

第弍頁

90-1626

許幫忙由嗎嗲寧返當時因其家人
完全不知其事時至今茲有由誤
嗲回唐梓里但其查向招發覺諳
死在係於上述年間寧運回洗由
貴院句送各該籍招領安塟昨日該課
某到畫毛由瀨畫　理事人將歷年各
嗲寧運回邑之亡骸各姓清查偏查

中華民國　年　月　日

石岐南基兆全店監製

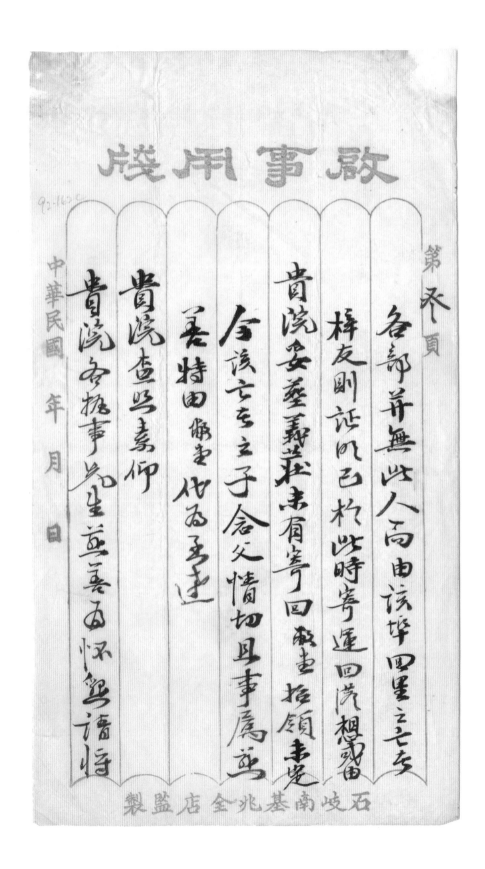

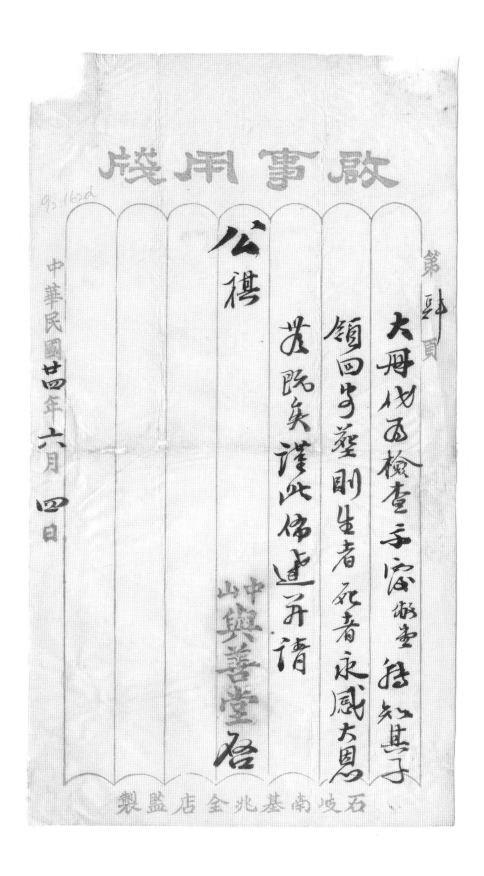

啟事用牋

第　頁

大冊代西檢查予容辦理　俾知其子

領回生塟則生者死者永感大恩

芳院矣謹此佈達并請

公祺

興善堂啟

中華民國廿四年六月四日

石岐南基北全店監製

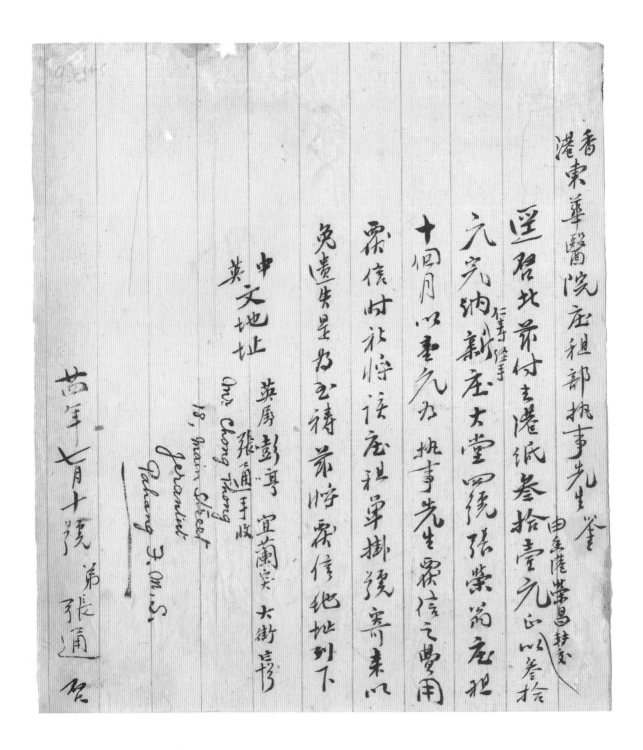

香

港東華醫院庄祖部辦事先生鈞鑒

逕啟北弟付去港紙叁拾壹元　由金慶隆昌轉交　以叁拾

六元完納新庄大堂四便陸號義冢庄祖　仁壽堂手

十個月以雪九九辦事先生眾信之費用

眾信時祈將該庄祖單掛號寄來以

免遺失星為玄待弟將眾信地址列下

中文地址　　　英屬彭亨宜蘭實大街言號

英文地址　　　張通手收

Chr. Chong Thong

18, main Street

Jerantint

Pahang F.M.S.

黃年七月十號　弟張通　啟

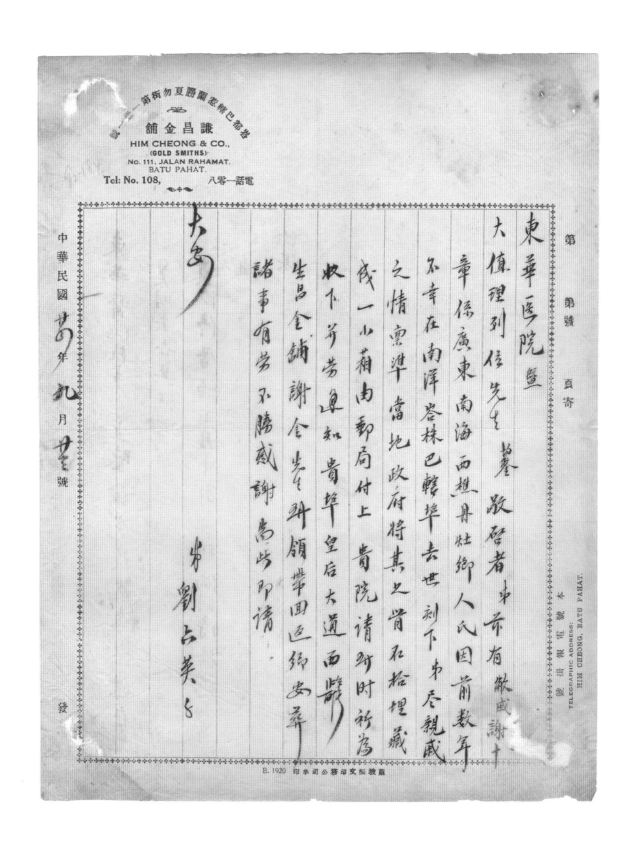

街衖勿夏勝羅峇都峇

舖金昌謙

HIM CHEONG & CO.,
(GOLD SMITHS)
No. 111, JALAN RAHAMAT.
BATU PAHAT.
Tel: No. 108, 八零一話電

第　號　頁寄

掛號掛電報本

TELEGRAPHIC ADDRESS:
HIM CHEONG, BATU PAHAT.

B. 1920　印承司公務印文振發蘇

東華醫院鑒

大值理列位先生　台鑒　敬啟者中茲有欲感謝十

章係廣東南海西樵舟牡鄉人氏因前數年

不幸在南洋峇株巴轄華去世剎下中盡親戚

之情稟準當地政府將其之骨不捨埋藏

戌一小蒲南郵局付上　貴院请新时祈為

收下芳劳更知貴埠皇后大道西醫

生昌金舖謝余斗領帶回返鄉安葬

諸事有劳不勝感謝為此即请

大安

中華民國廿四年九月廿三號

弟劉六英　敬

發

大洋洲西歸先友

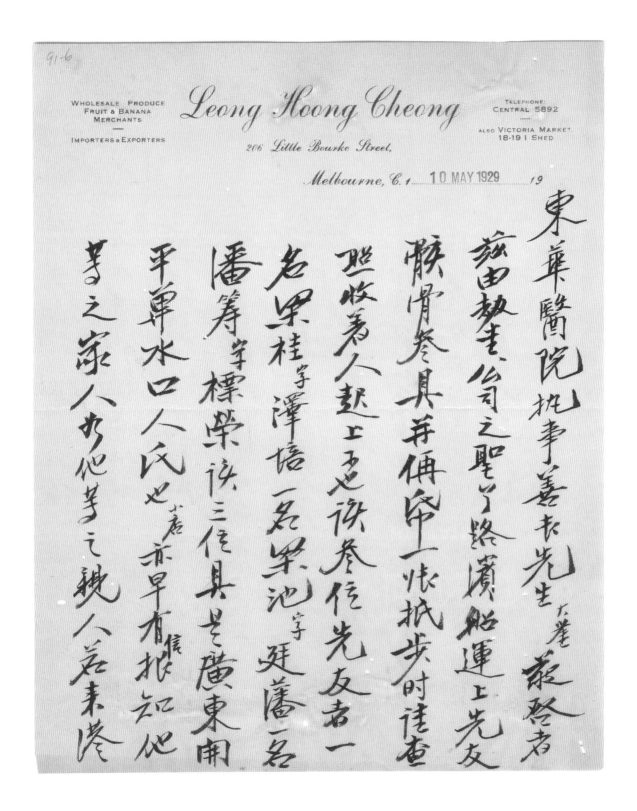

WHOLESALE PRODUCE
FRUIT & BANANA
MERCHANTS
—
IMPORTERS & EXPORTERS

Leong Hoong Cheong

206 Little Bourke Street,

Melbourne, C.1 10 MAY 1929 19

TELEPHONE:
CENTRAL 5892

ALSO VICTORIA MARKET,
18-19 I SHED

東華醫院執事善長先生大鑒 敬啓者

敬由敝 公司之聖約路濱船運上先友

骸骨叁具并佩印一張抵埠时諸查

照收為人趨上忌誌叁信先友吉一

名梁桂字澤培一名梁池字廷蕃一名

潘籌字標榮谈三信具是廣東開

平單水口人氏也大者亦早有根知他

事之家人如他事之魏人皆来港

WHOLESALE PRODUCE
FRUIT & BANANA
MERCHANTS

IMPORTERS & EXPORTERS

Leong Hoong Cheong

206 Little Bourke Street,

Melbourne, C.1　10 MAY 1929　19

TELEPHONE:
CENTRAL 5892

ALSO VICTORIA MARKET,
18-19 I SHED

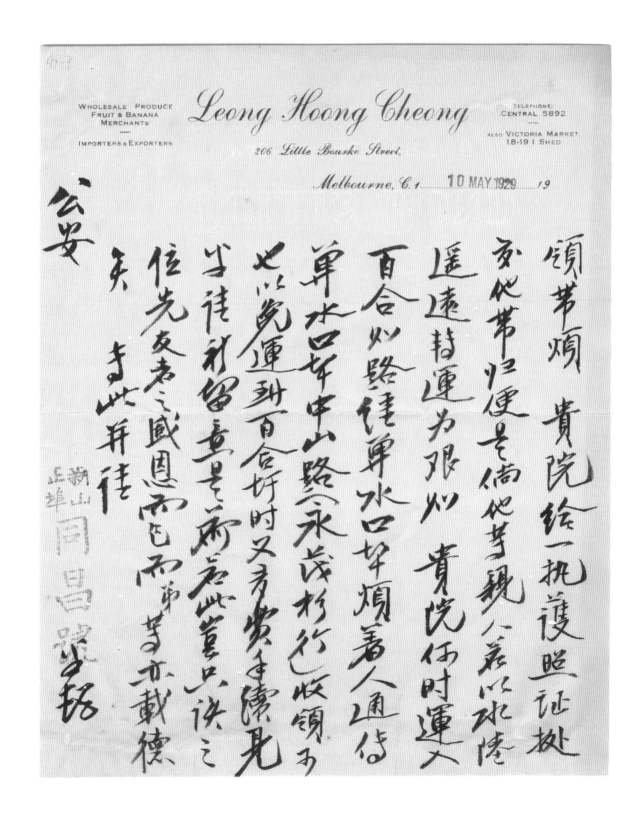

領茆煩　貴院給一執護照証挑

交他茆歸便老倘他芽親公盖以水陸

遥遠特運为艱以　貴院伺时運入

百合以路佳單水口芋煩善人通传

單水口芋中山路（永茂杉行）收領可

此以免運到百合圻时又为貴手讀見

半佳补留盖畫前老此萱呈诀之

位先交来之感恩而已而弟芽亦載德

矣　专此並佳

公安

橫山
正埠
同昌號　缄

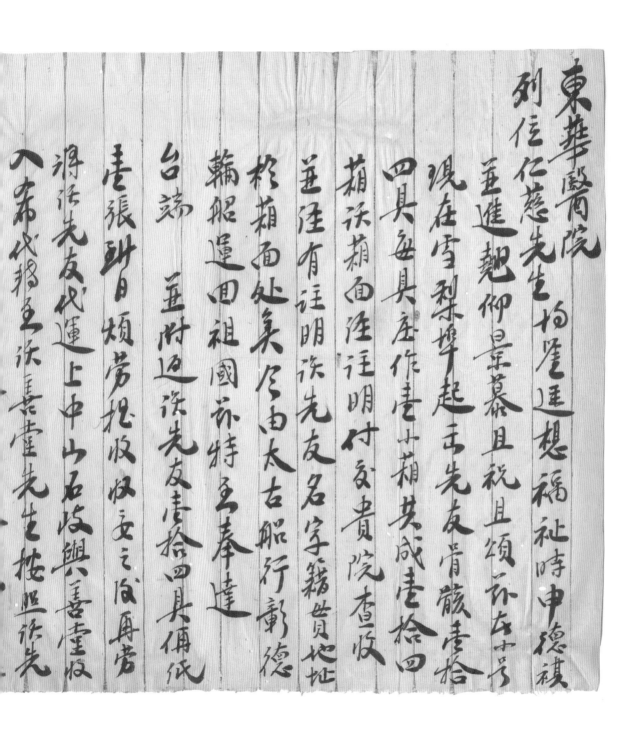

東華醫院

列位仁慈先生台鑒　逕想福祉時申德祺

茲進懇仰景慕且祝且頌茲有本號

現在雪梨堆起本先友骨骸壹拾

四具每具座作本先友骸其咸壹拾四

荷誤本面逐逐註明付交貴院查收

茲逐有註明逐先友名字籍貫地址

於本面处集尽由太古船行彰德

輪船運回祖國蘇特本奉達

台端　茲附迴逐先友壹拾四具侭低

本張阴日煩勞接收交之成再啓

將逐先友代運上中山石收與善堂收

八密代報至浼善堂先生祈照浼先

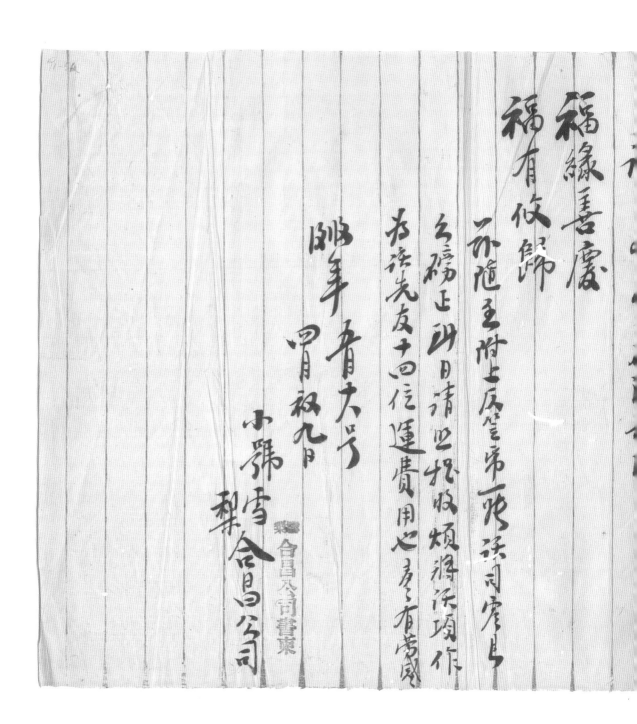

福緣善慶

福有收歸

示隨並附上庶管第一班溪司雲島

么碼正班日清廿班收煩将溪項作

為碼先友十四信運費用以專者有帶感

編羊普大号

四月初九日

小弟雪

梨合昌公司

合昌公司書柬

落葉歸根——東華三院華僑原籍安葬檔案選編（上冊）

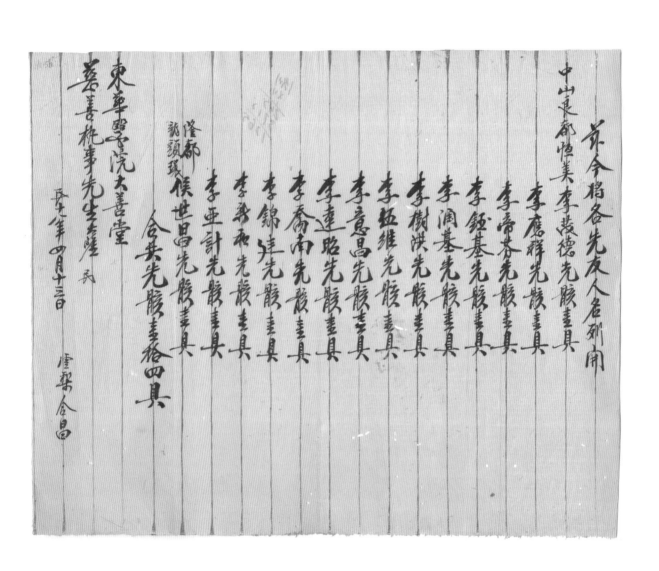

茲令將各先友人名列開

中山遠都恒美李蔭德先骸壹具

李應祥先骸壹具

李帝芬先骸壹具

李鉅基先骸壹具

李潤基先骸壹具

李樹洪先骸壹具

李鉅維先骸壹具

李意昌先骸壹具

李連昭先骸壹具

李喬南先骸壹具

李錦建先骸壹具

李鑫兩先骸壹具

李亞計先骸壹具

隆都

窩頭環候世昌先骸壹具

合共先骸壹拾四具

東華雲醫院大善堂

慈善枱事先生台鑒　民

戊午年四月十三日　倉琢金昌

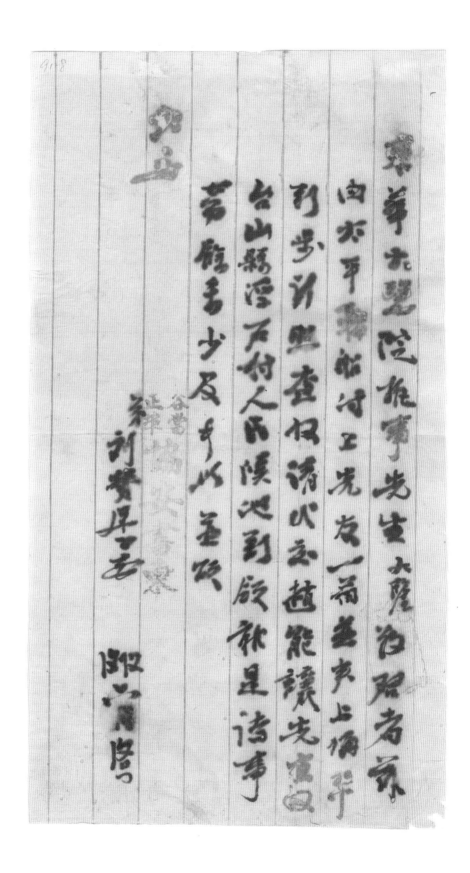

東華醫院 大善長暨

列位先生均鑒

敬啟者，茲華向在澳冊昆省加剌弥剌埠經營
西人生意，宇各埠將生意賣去，惟思華
友壽梓于本年正月十有餘名，華梓去世洛梁
盧先友骸骨永當外域不若遷應，故逐一
靴柩而搭呈陵彰法船壽返貴院
代肢但礦琵，先友龍人去和，故今由郵付呈
滙票銀達拾伍磅新此，提收敢晨先生
用持登報俾，先友等屬頷回盍座
惰代登報費之外，餘頃所作運先友回唐
主用諸費清神印此粘頌

云安　筷滙票收條

　　　　加剌弥剌埠
旅澳洲昆時梮省
　　差厘贊記袁法梅
　　　鄭維壽全泐
陳贊

北帶宗寬永遠接
連和香港金生泰之厘山庄
門解陳輔道西辦某日平安亦搭下渡
返院

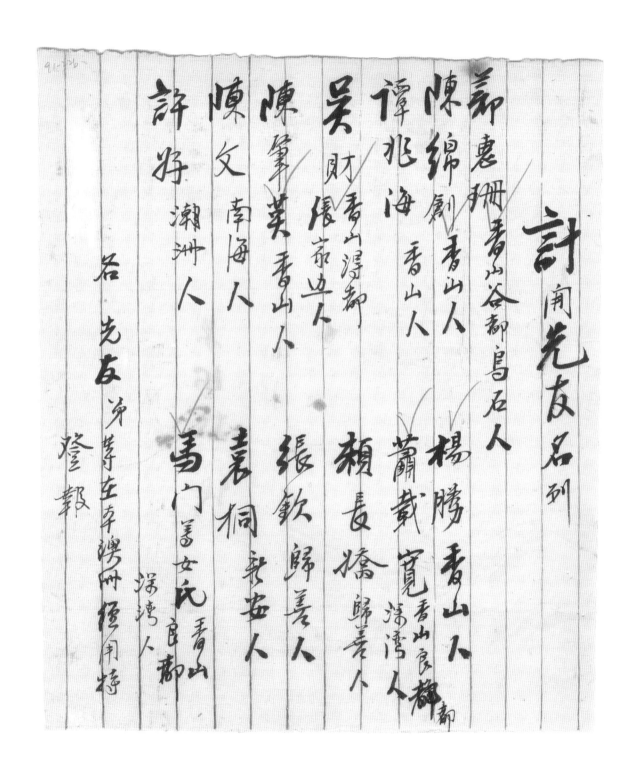

計 開先友名列

節惠珊　香山谷都鳥石人
陳綿創　香山人　　　　　楊勝　香山良都欄都
譚兆海　香山人　　　　　蕭戴寬　潘灣人
吳財　香山得都　　　　　賴長橋　歸善人
陳筆葉　香山人　　　　　張欽　歸善人
陳文　南海人　　　　　　裏桐　新安人
許好　潮洲人　　　　　　馬門□女氏　香山都　深灣人

右　先友　並等左卓灣冊經交持
各　先友　　　詧報

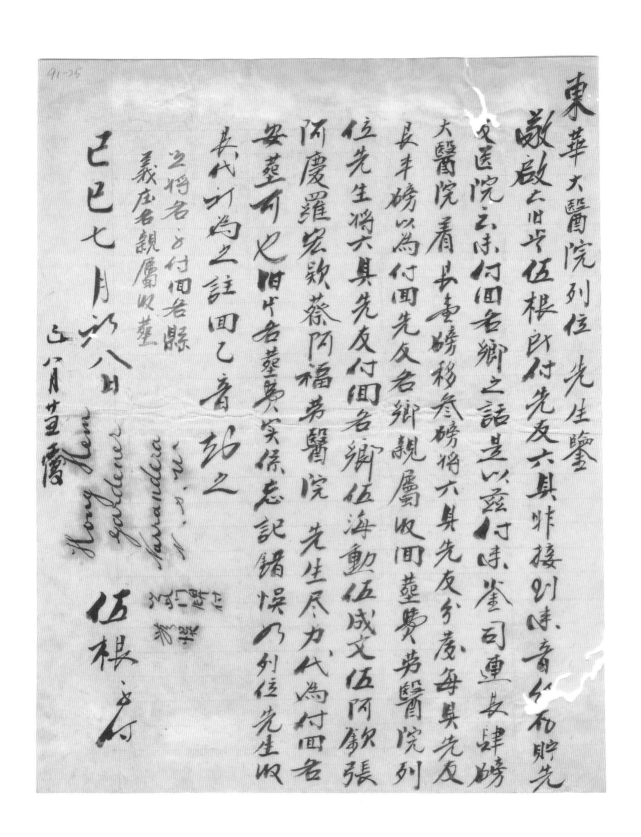

東華大醫院列位　先生鑒

敬啟者旧代伍根即付先友六具非接到味音竝和貯先

友送醫院云味付個名鄉之話是以盛付味鑒司連長肆磅

大醫院看長壽磅移參磅將六具先友分慶每具先友

長丰磅以為付個先友名鄉親屬收回塟費勞醫院列

位先生將六具先友付個名鄉伍海勛伍咸文伍阿欽張

阿慶羅宏欵蔡阿福勞醫院　先生尽力代為付個名

安塟可也旧代名塟費实係志記錯悮乃列位先生收

長代刊為之註回乙音竝之

　立得名之付個名縣

　義庄君親屬收塟

己巳七月初八日

之八月廿二日董喬

Hong Liam

gouldence

Narrandera

伍根卜啟

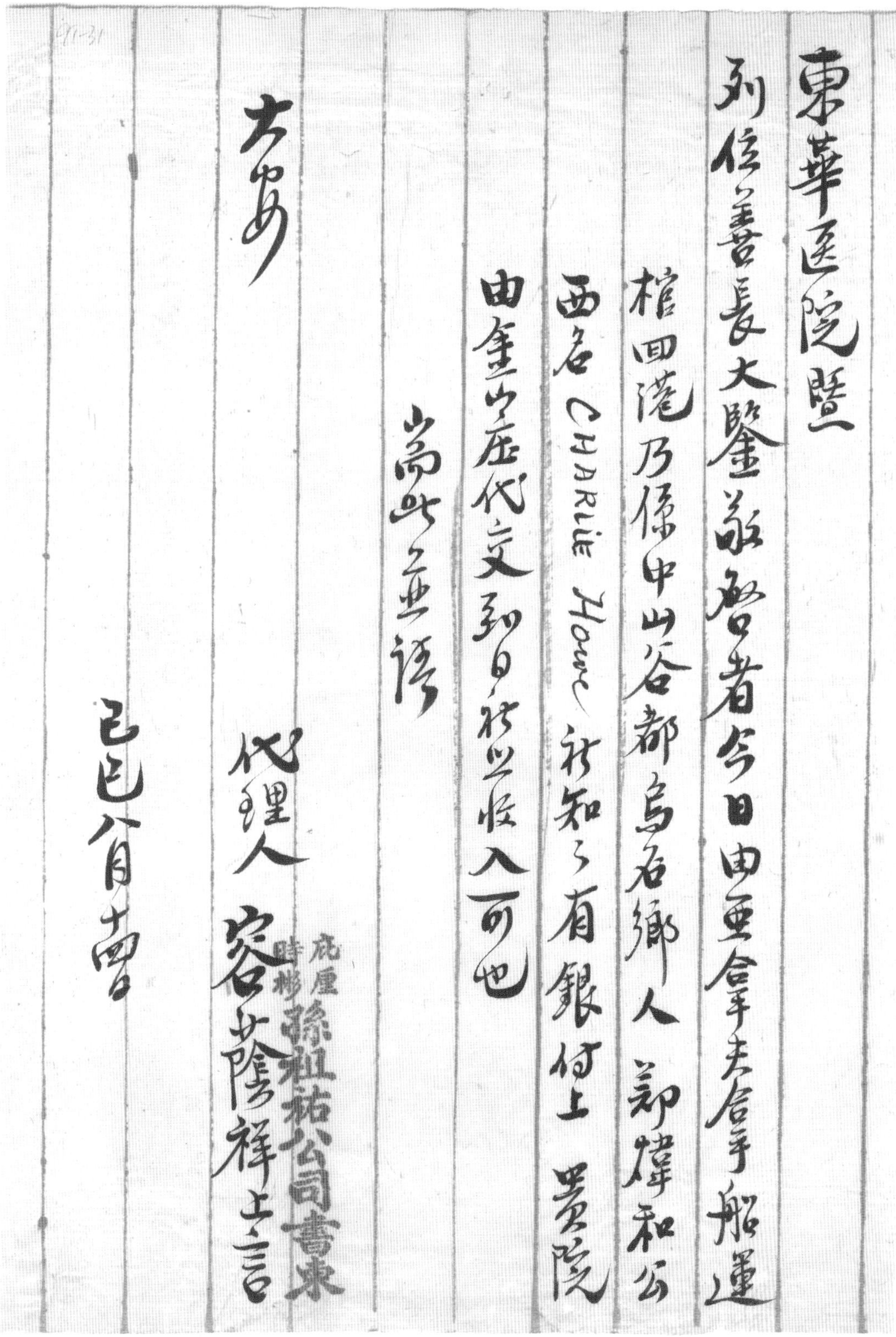

澳洲容蔭祥致東華醫院信件

1929年9月16日

東華醫院暨
列位善長大鑒　敬啓者　今日由亞拿夫拿船運
棺回港　乃係中山谷都烏石鄉人　鄭偉和公
西名 CHARLIE HOWE　祈知　有銀付上　貴院
由金山庄代交　到日祈照收入可也
嵩此並請
大安
代理人　容蔭祥上言
庇厘時彬孫祖祐公司書柬
己巳八月十四日

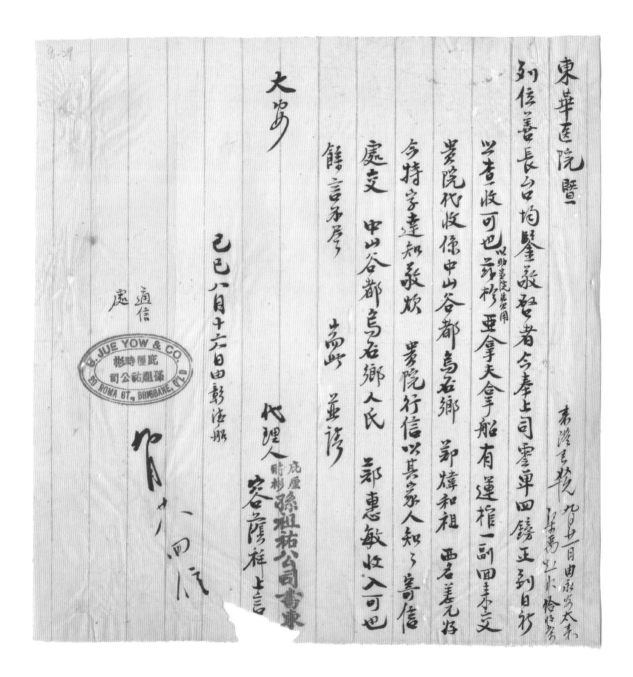

東華醫院暨

列位善長台均鑒敬啓者今奉上司雲車四鑄正到日前

香港言銳九月廿一日由原寄去太平

南馬士水恰恰寄

興查收可也蒸彬亞拿夫合手船有運棺一副回手本二文

以助醫院先支用

貴院代收傷中山谷都烏石鄉郭煒和祖西名善元將

今特字達知張欽　貴院行信以其家人知之寄信

處交　中山谷都烏石鄉人民　郭惠敏收入可也

餘言承層　　壽　亞諺

大安

代理人庇厘時彬孫祖祐公司書來

容兆隆祥上言

己巳八月十六日由彰德船

東華醫院司理先生偉鑒 敬啟者

現十月初一日由鐵行公司丹域船

付回伍文惶先生之骸骨共壹

樘字段告煩 先生代為照收

暫存醫院延不其莫人或其

親屬鈔來收領可也兩言本

尚有信通知其蒙人矣諸事

多勞銘感之而高此即頌

籌祺

中華民國十八年十月一日由雪梨伍俊之上言

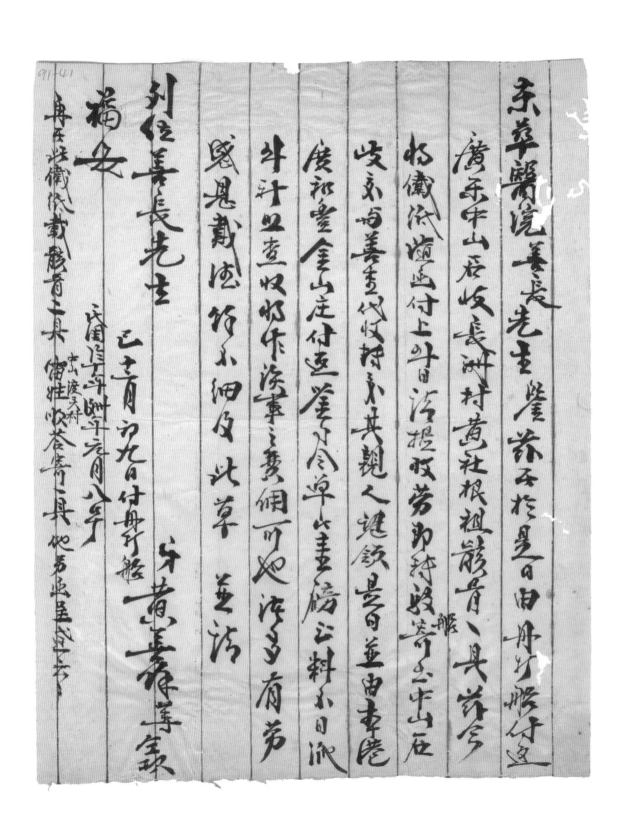

東華醫院善長先生鑒 茲者於是日由舟行船付運

廣平中山君收長洲村萬社根祖骸骨入具苦參

收儀照慎函付上叼日活提收勞助珠殷寄丁丁中山庄

收亲與善翁代收拾示其親人連領是日並由車港

廣郵壹金山庄付运崖人丞草此盍廓云料不目沭

斗計四查收收作沭事三費銅叼叼泽多有勞

感見戴德佇示細及此草 並活

列位善長先生

福安

弟黃善餘等全球

己丂首廿九日付舟行船

天國十年四月元首八年

舟于此儀俗戴骸骨二具 留姓收荅寄一具他另亚呈戊丁木

東華醫院貴善長先生大鑒 敬料下安 諸事遂事

以意為頓矣 茲者移玉日由丹打輪船付返處

東中山縣長洲村黃社根祖骸骨一具 茲議係

另由郵政寄上一炙 請查收 鑒同含單長臺榜上

斗月查收双貴善長 即着人往船查收所持

骸骨付返中山莊受母善善代收着其親人認

領便是 諸事有勞功德云云 望善善代收善緒感激

諸未細及 此為 此候

福安

列位貴善長仝前

庚午壹月壹号

澳洲 黃善餘筆緘

己巳閏係將十一月十二日

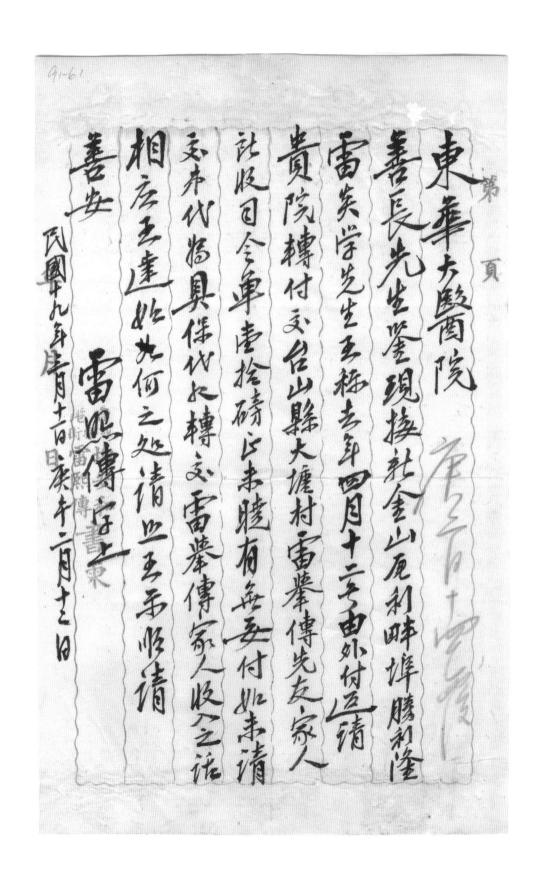

東華大醫院

第　　頁

善長先生鑒現換新金山厘利畔埠勝利隆

雷笑学先生玉稱去年四月十二壬曲外付五清

貴院轉付交台山縣大壙村雷舉傳先友家人

社收日今車電拾磅正未瞭有無交付如未清

交亦代為具保代之轉交雷舉傳家人收之話

相应玉達如此何之处请以玉乎修清

善安

雷熙傳字上

民國十九年庚午二月十二日

249
〈頁一〉

澳洲鳥修威祖密埠四邑會館致東華醫院信件

1930 年 4 月 16 日

東華醫院先生大鑒 敬啓者本會館經已檢
拾先友五具仙骸用鉄箱分裝外共裝一木箱即買
保險由太古輪船之太平輪船付回貴醫院收
入以便付回各縣也至船抵港時請照起卸以便
按名分發回縣 先友親屬領收安葬成斯善
舉功德無涯矣至於 貴醫院經費已
由香港陸怡興先生處付回也 嵩此順請
大安
澳洲四邑館 澳洲鳥修威祖密埠四邑會館 頓

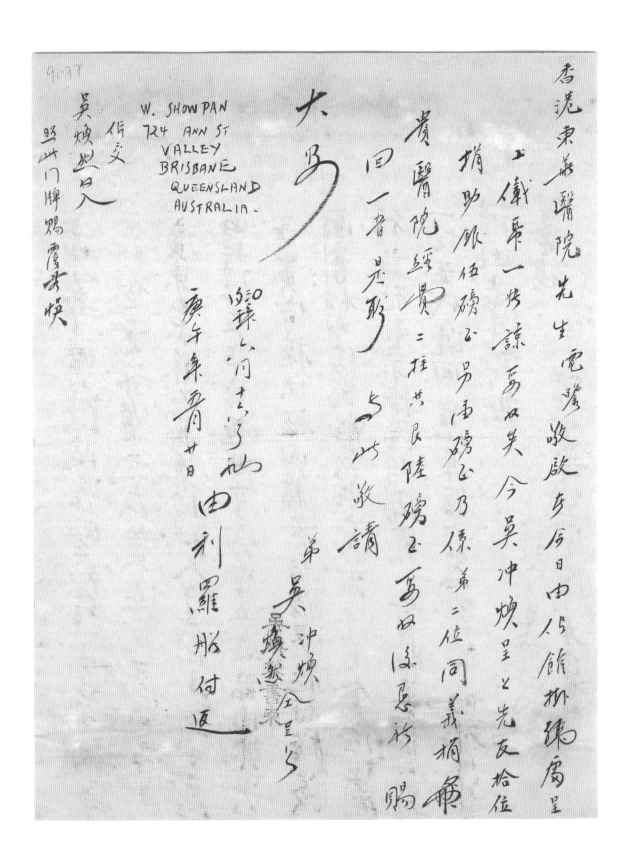

香港東華醫院先生電鑒 敬啟者昨日由小館抽瑞為呈

上儀票一份諒為收矣 今吳沖煥呈之先友拾位

捐助銀伍磅乞另備磅乞乃係弟二位同義捐叅

貴醫院經費三柱共民陸磅乞寄乜後恩祈賜

回一音吳形与此敬請

大安

弟 吳沖煥仝呈

吳煥樂書東

知弟六月十六号仙

庚午年肩廿日

由利羅州付返

W. SHOW PAN
724 ANN ST
VALLEY
BRISBANE
QUEENSLAND
AUSTRALIA.

佈交
吳煥然兄入

照此門牌鴻還為悅

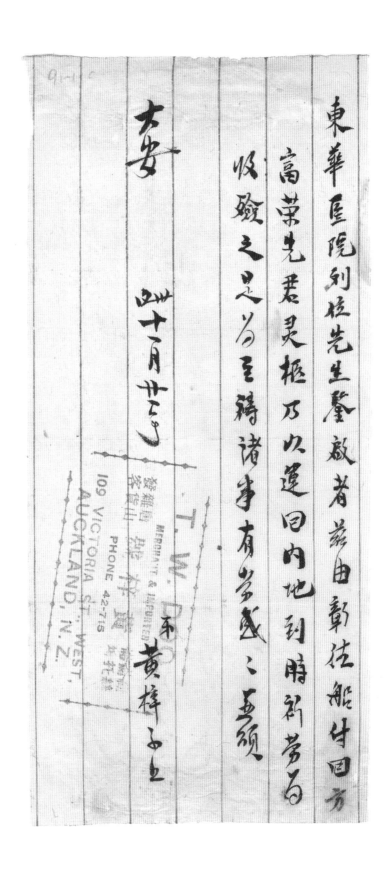

東華醫院列位先生鑒啟者兹由鄰往船付回方

富榮先君靈柩乃以運回內地到膊衪勞者

收驗之足為主禱諸事有勞威心專頌

大安

卅十月廿二

T. W. DOO
MERCHANT & IMPORTED
發雜貨
客籍山　陽存興

109 VICTORIA ST., WEST,
PHONE 42-715
AUCKLAND, N.Z.

黃梓手上

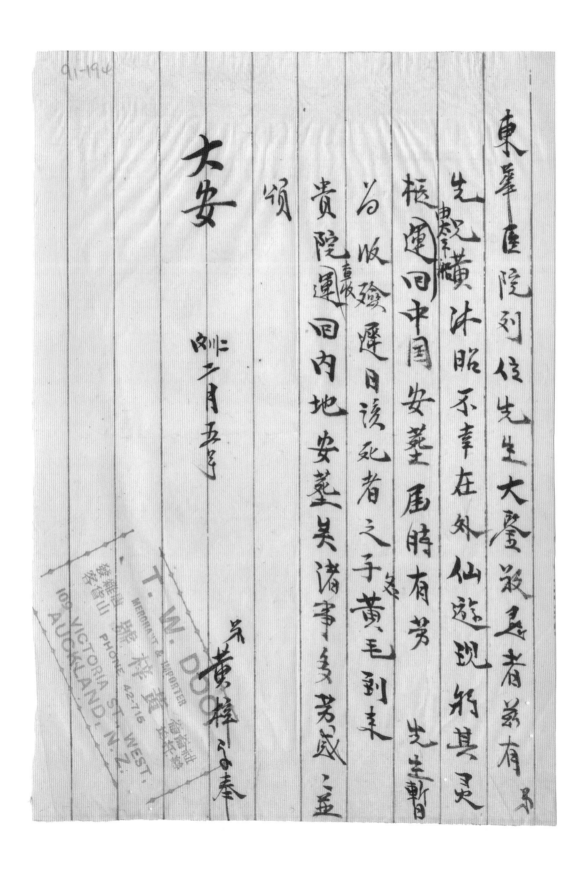

東華醫院列位先生大鑒敬啟者茲有

先兄黃沐昭不幸在外仙遊現將其靈

柩由本院交銀運回中國安葬屬時有勞

貴院運回內地安葬吳諸事多勞威盟

為收殮歷日後死者之手黃毛到來

先生暫

大安

頌

二月五日

黃梓敬奉

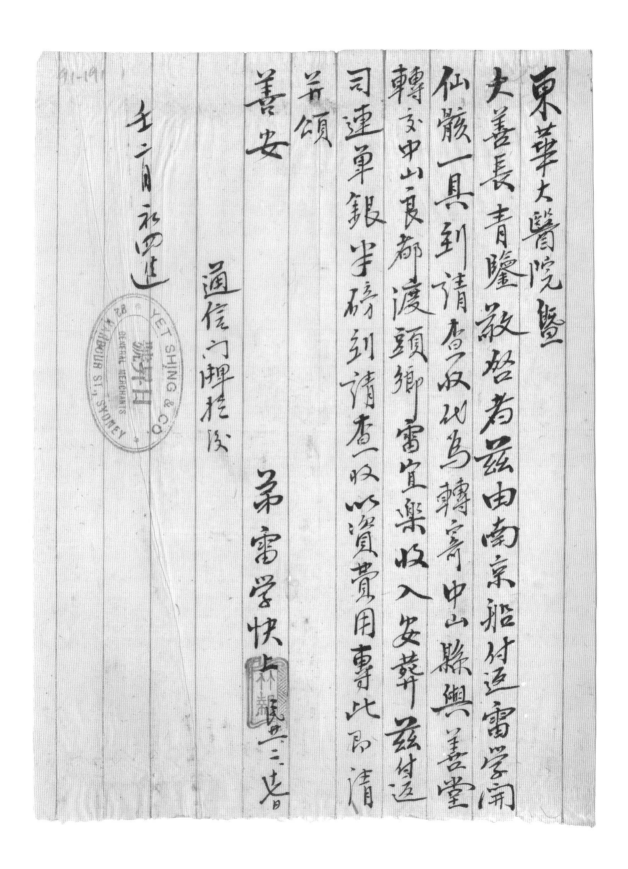

東華大醫院曁

大善長青鑒　敬啟為茲由南京船付返雷學開

仙嚴一具到請查收以爲轉寄中山縣與善堂

轉交中山長郡渡頭鄉雷宜樂收入安葬茲付返

司運單銀半磅到請查一收以資費用專此耑請

荓頌

善安

　　　　通信門押揆侯

　　　　　弟雷學快上

壬二月初四到

東華醫院列位值理大羹磬奏蘇由彰庄船付返僑邑先生

遺骸玖具至日北為查收全僑邑駐港商會力理梛

址代為運返原籍俾囘歸塟故郷即殯在内感功

庄無量矣滙上英上船行僊幣之拾工司連票乙拾

茲長伍鎊正礼為譽收以作置用寺攺口鎮順頌

善安

　　庄二月廿六日
　　姚青廿四号 庇厘時浜東邑公義堂

全程

茲將先友姓名郷籍列左

Kong Gee Tong
To Lee Chew of West St
Brisbane Q old
Aust

葉安　東莞道滘村　　　任佛全美村　東莞峽内東坑

謝睿　東莞峽内東坑　井美村　　　袁藉縣 東莞員山目村　東莞峽内東坑

袁观諾員山目村　東莞峽内東坑　黄观林漏嶺村　東莞峽内東坑

陳連錫郎目村 東莞峽内東坑手撫滙　　陳泰郎目村 東莞峽内東坑

吳日光 氷屮村 東莞峽内東坑手撫滙

香港三盛昌致東華醫院信件

1932年12月6日

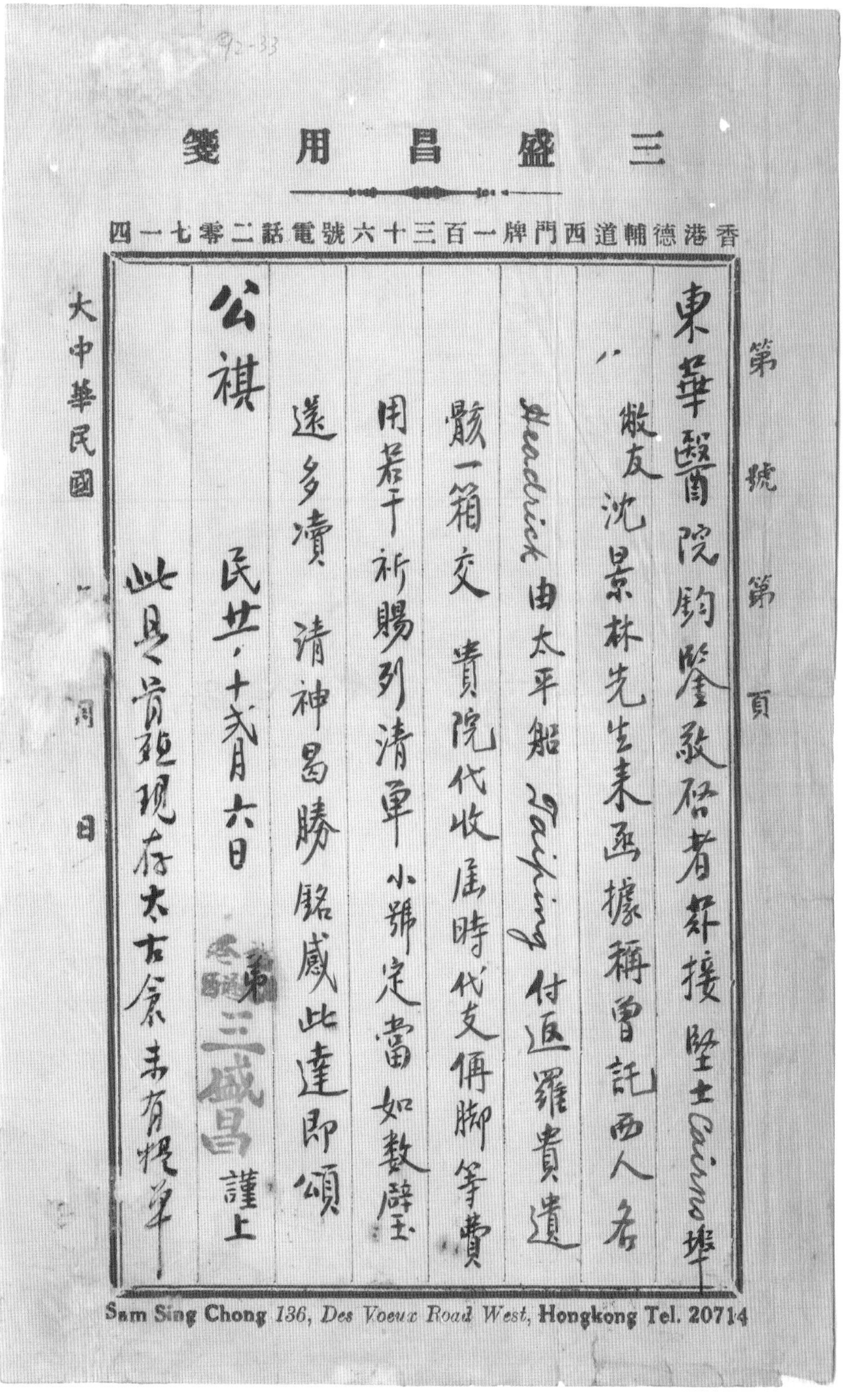

三盛昌用箋

香港德輔道西門牌一百三十六號電話二零七一四

第　號第　頁

東華醫院鈞鑒敬啓者茲接　堅士Cairns埠
敝友沈景林先生來函據稱曾託西人名
Hendrick由太平船Taiping付返羅貴遺
骸一箱交　貴院代收屆時代支佣脚等費
用若干祈賜列清單小號定當如數璧
還多瀆　清神曷勝銘感此達即頌
公祺
民廿一，十弍月六日　三盛昌謹上
此是貴院現存太古倉未有提單

大中華民國　年　月　日

Sam Sing Chong 136, Des Voeux Road West, Hongkong Tel. 20714

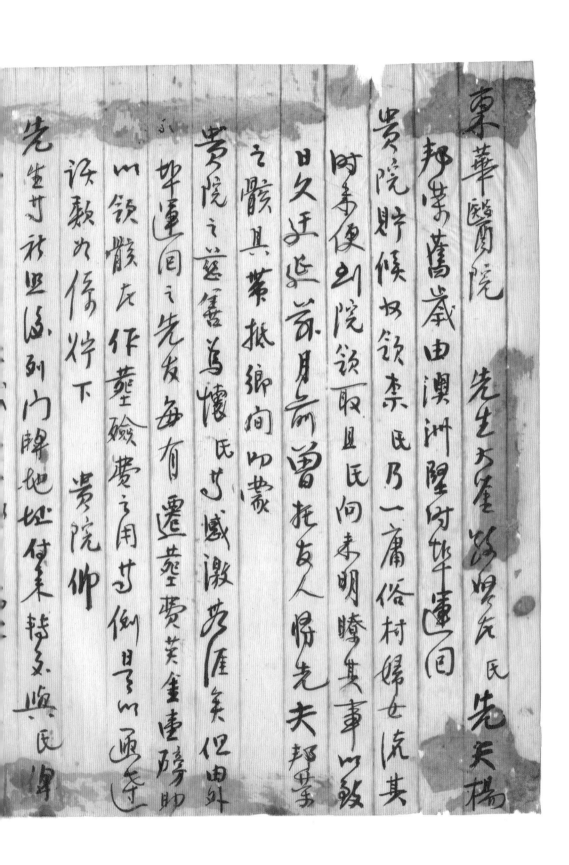

東華醫院　先生大鑒　敝埠舊金山氏先矢楊

貴院貯候好領柬氏乃一庸俗村婦女院其

時來便到院領取且氏向來明瞭其事以敢

日久廷延荏月前曾托友人帶先夫邦某

之骸具業抵鄉間收葬

貴院之慈善為懷氏亦感激勞勞匯美但由外

埠運回之先夫每有遷塵費美金運殯助

以領骸左作塵殮費之用甘倒是以函達

誤勞九儔埠下　貴院仰

先生寸衷祈望源列內韓地址俾某轉交阮氏傳

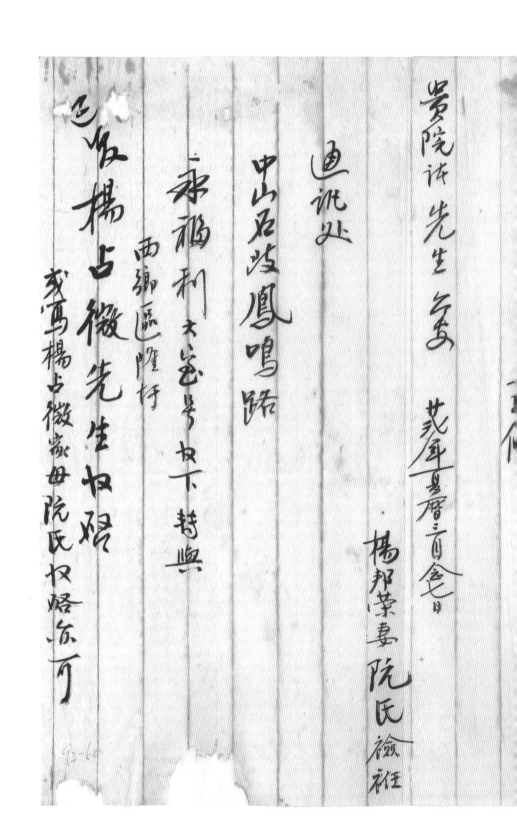

貴院諸先生 公安 茲屆舊曆三月念七日

楊邦榮妻 阮氏檢祖

通訊处

中山召岐鳳鳴路

永福利大窑号女下齊興

西爾區隆行

已故楊占微先生收啟

或寫楊占微家母阮氏收烙你可

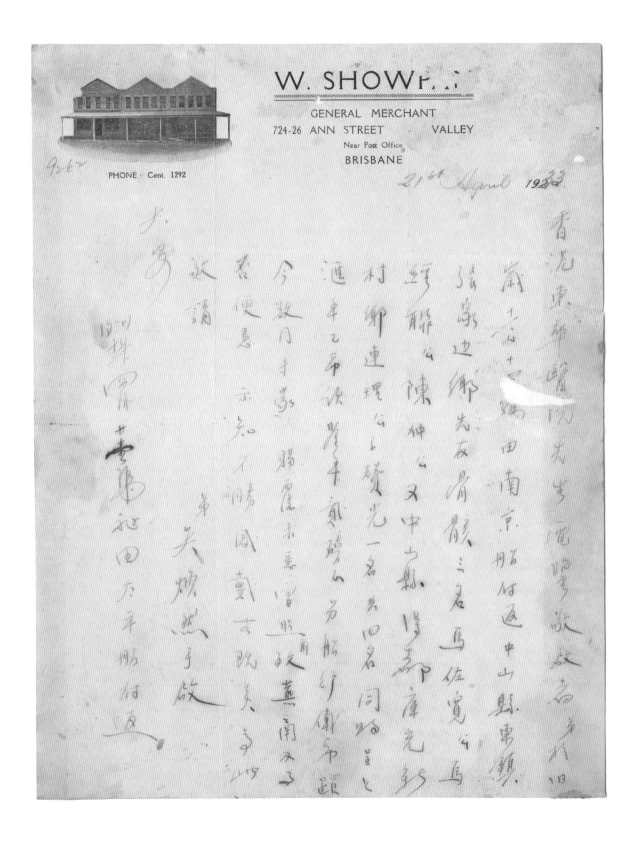

W. SHOWN...

GENERAL MERCHANT
724-26 ANN STREET　　VALLEY
Near Post Office
BRISBANE

PHONE : Cent. 1292

21st April 1933

香港東華醫院先生鑒惠啟者茲啟舊

茲者十四號田南京船先返中山縣專類

張家邊鄉先友骨骸三名馬佐寬名馬

鍟聯名陳仲公又中山蘇郡康元勤

村鄉連理公贊光一名共四名同路呈之

匯单乙部諒蒙年肆贐品為暫行候收乃頓

今啟月丰幙贐壓未善曾此致蕪南不

着便息示知不勝威激可附美矣附

敬請

大安

此斟羅十壽喬廼田五平帖付呈

　　　　弟吳煥然手啟

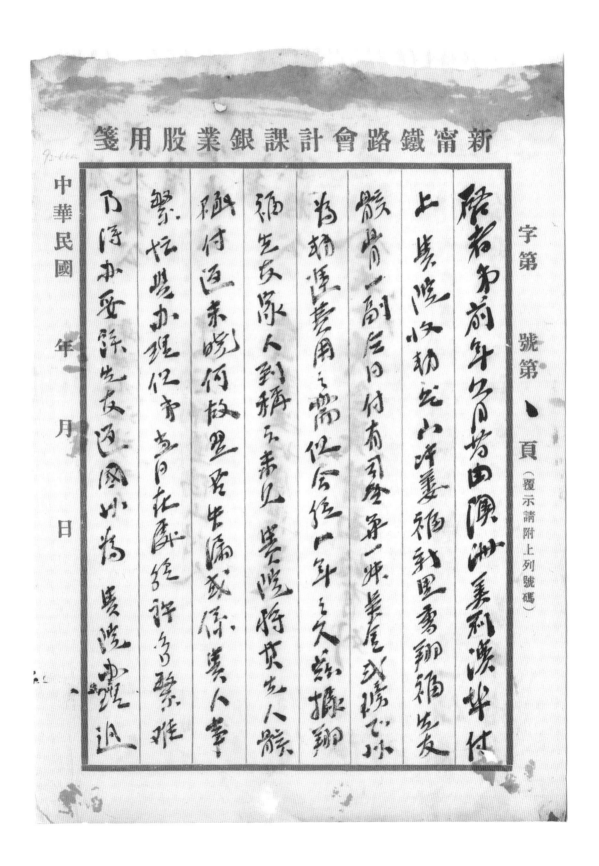

新甯鐵路會計課銀業股用箋

字第　　號第　二　頁（覆示請附上列號碼）

逕諗事宣佈遂蒙臺料蒙院收到該款
承先嚴一稔內匯回來字回發行欣年久仰素
代為運返康鄉辦年是只致有卻情請
恢養俟理歸發盡以族先嚴下葬恍快函
至書翔稝萬人領致敦筵遵付返以保恨
家人得早日安葬生人此是公德兩使請留
心亦裡是耐好坒

中華民國廿二年　x　月　六　日

森喬醫院　執理生先兄

潘伯恒上

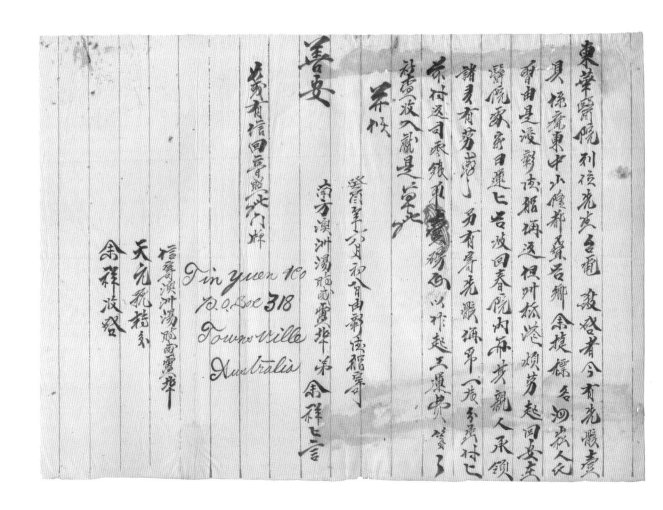

東華醫院列位先友台電　敬啟者今有先骸壹

具係廣東中山隆都蒼岩鄉　余捷標名洞歲人氏

曾由是後彰唇稻埔送俱州松港煩芳起回安去

醫院承辦寄日運七告汝回春院内庥其親人承領

諸集有芳歲卽　另有尊先骸俯卽一廣分親付已

茶村送司承鏡費收費務而以作起天壤貴等了

被費收入嚴是草也

荣候

　　　　癸酉年六月初八日由鄭讀稻寄

善交

　　　　南方澳洲湯顺喊賓華弟　余祥上言

此家有信回章船代交門牌

信寄澳洲湯顺喊賓華

　　　　天元飛稿象

　　　余祥波啟

Tin yuen Wo
P. O. Box 318
Townsville
Australia

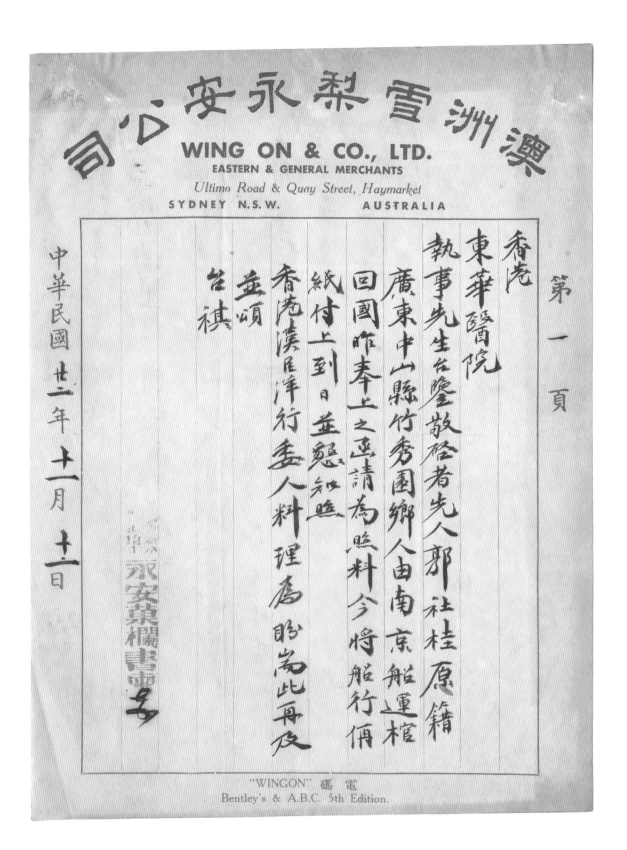

WING ON & CO., LTD.
EASTERN & GENERAL MERCHANTS
Ultimo Road & Quay Street, Haymarket
SYDNEY N.S.W.　　　AUSTRALIA

第
一
頁

香
港

東
華
醫
院

執
事
先
生
台
鑒
敬
啟
者
先
人
郭
社
桂
原
籍

廣
東
中
山
縣
竹
秀
園
鄉
人
由
南
京
船
運
棺

回
國
昨
奉
上
之
函
請
為
照
料
今
將
船
行
佣

紙
付
上
到
日
祈
懇
知
照

香
港
漢
民
洋
行
委
人
料
理
為
盼
尚
此
再
及

益
頌

台
祺

中
華
民
國
廿
二
年
十
一
月
十
一
日

永
安
菓
欄
書

"WINGON" 碼電
Bentley's & A.B.C. 5th Edition.

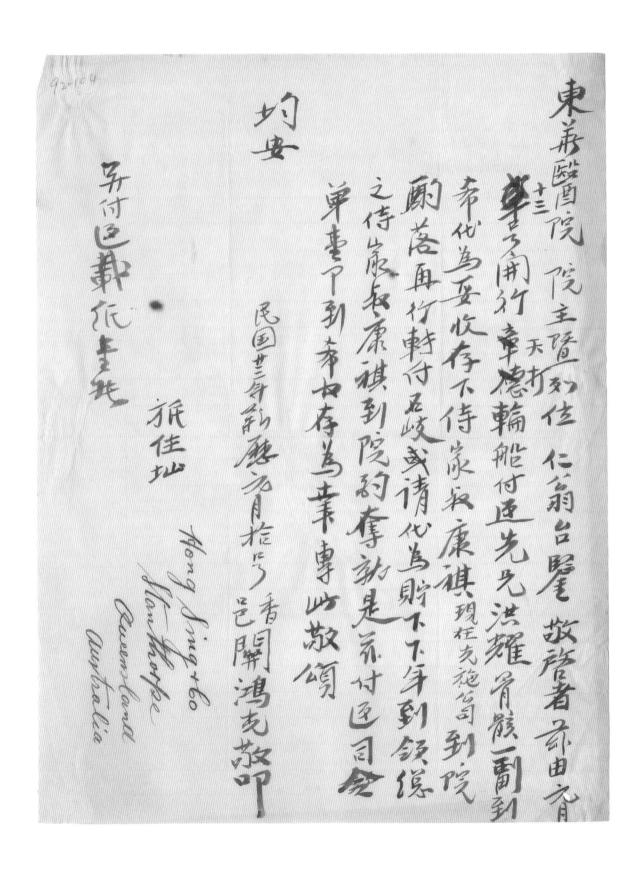

東華醫院　院主暨列位　仁翁台鑒　敬啓者茲由本月
十三號　華昌開行章德輪船付逓先先洪耀骨骸一劏到
天拆
希代為妥收存下俟歲底康祺現在克施公司到院
爾落再行轉付石岐或請代為賸下下年到領煩
之侍歲底康祺到院約奪就是荒付逓同念
單專平到希台存為業專此敬頌
均安

　　　　　　　　　民國廿三年新歷方月拾叨香　邑關鴻光敬叩

　　　　另付逓載派去花

寄住址
　　Hong Sing+60
　　Stonthorpe
　　Queensland
　　Australia

澳洲雪梨增城聯福堂致東華醫院信件

1934 年 2 月 10 日

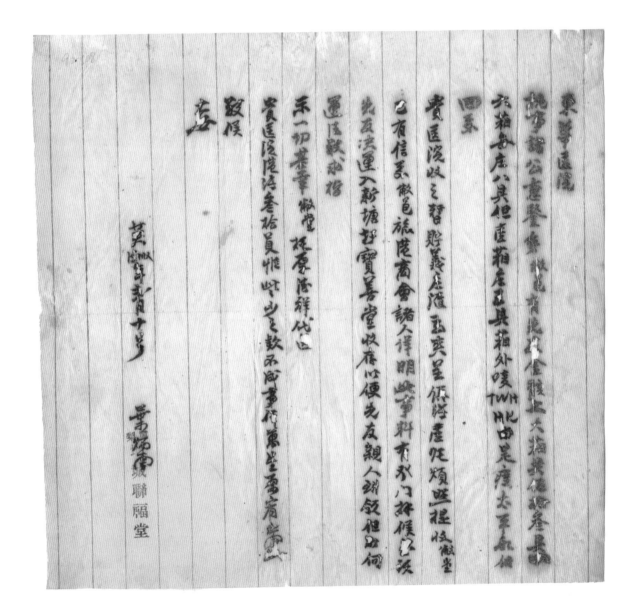

東華醫院

執事諸公台鑒敬啟者茲有值上大梅洪儂翁長男

六福母舅八具柩厝箱已具箱外嘜TWH此田是廣太平机個

四柱

貴處滾收之替辦義庄滙玉英呈係將厝厝煩照程收骸堂

已有信來微邑旅港商會諸人譯明喚章料有來門撥候示後

敬友洪運入新塘村寶善堂收存以便先友親人認領如何

運屆歉船認指

未一切蓋章微室　援麎僑祥代心

貴醫院陰陽諸參拾員怖此少之歉不啻事代慮堂裔府端心

敬候

台安

　　澳洲雪梨增城聯福堂

　　　　民國廿三年二月十号

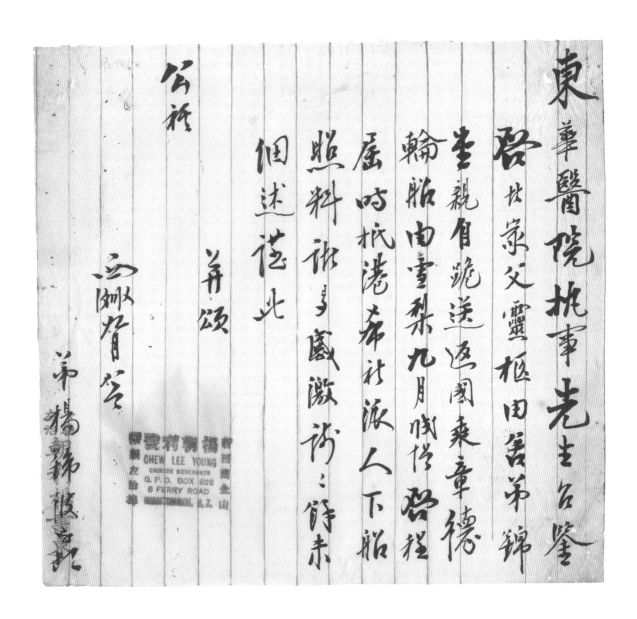

東華醫院執事先生台鑒

啟者 共蒙父靈柩由善弟錦

生親自跪送返國乘章德

輪船由雪梨九月啟行啟程

屆時抵港希祈社派人下船

照料諸多感激諸君餘未

個述謹此

公祈

並頌

西澳賀咨

弟楊朝錦複謹此

號利朝楊
CHEW LEE YOUNG
CHINESE MERCHANTS
G. P. O. BOX 822
6 FERRY ROAD
CHRISTCHURCH, N.Z.

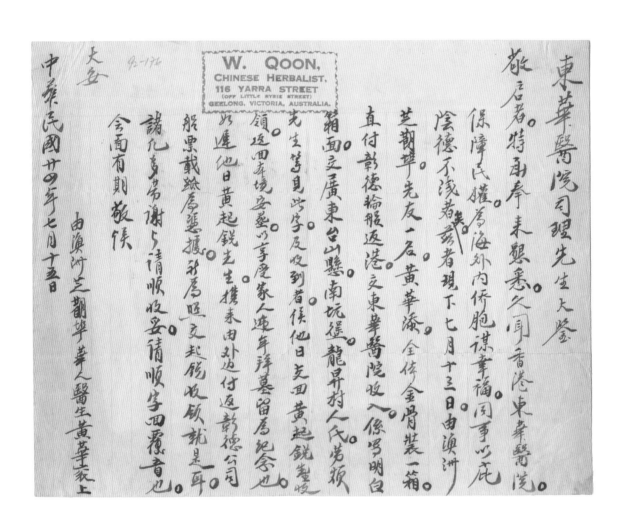

東華醫院司理先生大鑒

敬啟者特再奉來懇懇久聞香港東華醫院。

保障氏權為海外內僑胞謀幸福同事以庇

陰德不淺者現下七月十三日由澳洲

芝窩畢先友一名黃華添全係金骨裝一箱。

直付彰德輪船返港交東華醫院收入係唔明白

箱面之廣東台山縣南坑逕龍昇村人氏芳額

先生等見此字及收到著候他日先由黃起銳鑒收

領返回本境安藝以享慶家人遽年拜基留屬紀念也。

此匯他日黃起銳先生攜來由外迆付返彰德公司

船票載蝦厚運攜弟屬照交起銳收領就是一耳。

諸兄身勞謝另請順收並請順字四覆者也。

會面有期敬候

中華民國廿四年七月十五日

由澳洲芝窩畢華人醫生黃華衮上

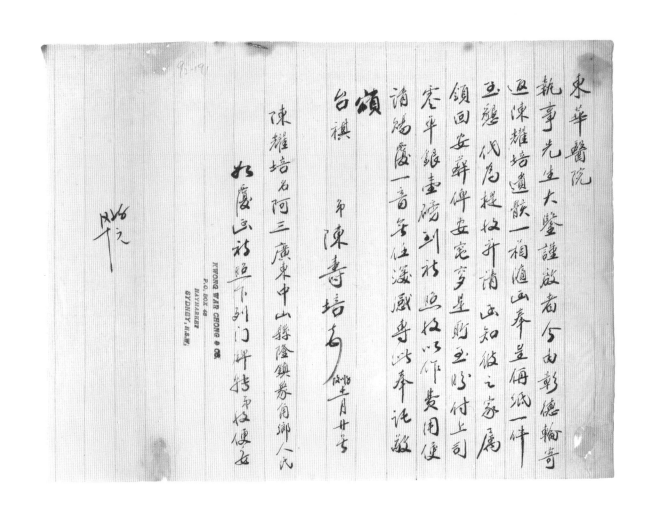

東華醫院

執事先生大鑒謹啟者今由彰德輪寄

返陳耀培遺骸一相連函奉呈每紙一件

並懇代為提攷並請函知彼之家屬

領回安葬俾安窀穸是所至盼付上司

寒平銀壹磅到祈照攷以作費用便

請賜覆一音等住深感專此奉託敬

頌

台祺

即 陳壽培書 十一月廿号

陳耀培名阿三廣東中山縣隆鎮券甬鄉人氏

KWONG WAR CHONG & CO.
P.O. BOX 48
HAYMARKET
SYDNEY, N.S.W.

如慶正祈照下列门牌持即攷便女

内地及香港西歸先友

中國旅鄂中山會館致東華醫院信件

1930年3月14日

中山會館籌備檢運先友委員會用箋

東華醫院
列位紳董先生惠鑒逕啓者日前奉蕪函
倫詳敝邑旅鄂同鄉運送先友回籍道經
盛埠敢請代為照料轉運回鄉等情諒邀
台閱到時必
允為所請也今有先友骸棺兩副一副運往中
山下柵墟金山學堂收一副運往石岐興善堂
收另有骸骨拾壹大箱另柒箱運往下柵墟金
山學堂收另四箱運往前山福善堂收另一箱
運往石岐興善堂收可也敝處業經派有譚益

中華民國　年　月　日

中山會館籌備檢運先友委員會用箋

照君隨船押送該先友來港到時請與該押儀人

接洽便知其詳細此今由國民銀行匯上香港通用

紙銀叁百陸拾元請照

察收以偹代為催艇轉運各鄉接收之寓此次先

偹送之欵乃按照去年（獻此）四大兩都運送先友經

過約略之數而已查去年（獻此）四大兩都運送先友亦由

貴醫院代為轉運云〃然四年月變遷搬運手續

或有出入固不能一概而論將來辦理完竣所需

費用或超過昕按之額數或有餘剩統請问

貴埠泰安棧程名譽君接洽可此今將副

中華民國　年　月　日

中山會館籌備檢運先友委員會用箋

籤紙各壹張請照

查收煩飭人照料一切專此拜托以有貴

清神昌勝鷗感之至臨風佈意不盡區之順頌

公安

三

中華民國十九年三月　日

蕭鏡心先生

旅漢

中山會館籌備檢運先友委員會　印鑒

鞠躬

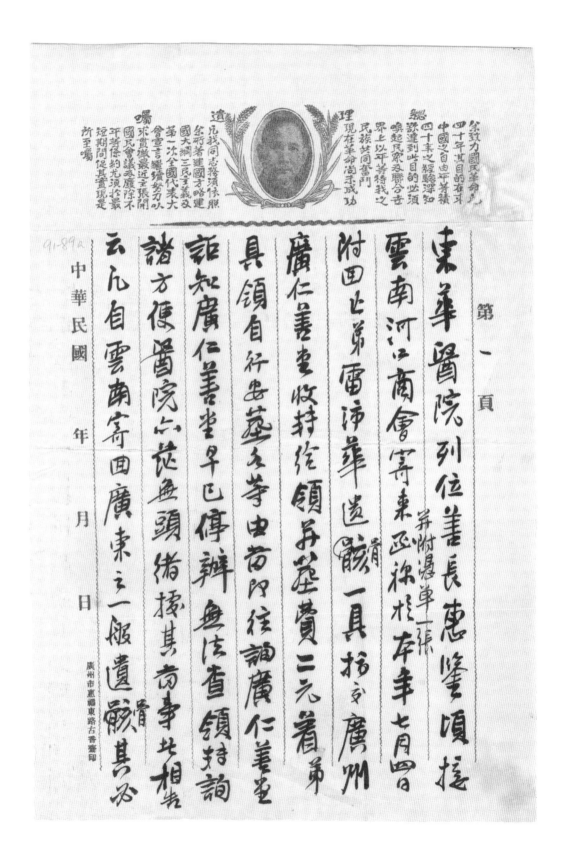

第一頁

東華醫院列位善長惠鑒頃接
雲南河江商會寄來函稱 並附淒單一張 本年七月曾
附田此弟雷沛華遺骸一具 捨寄廣州
廣仁善堂收持給領其遺骸貳元着弟
具領自行妥蓖交茅由苗即往調廣仁善堂
茲知廣仁善堂早已停辦無法查領持詢
諸方便醫院六慈無頭緒接其來事此相告
云凡自雲南寄回廣東之一假遺骸其必

中華民國　年　月　日

廣州市惠福東路右吾齋印

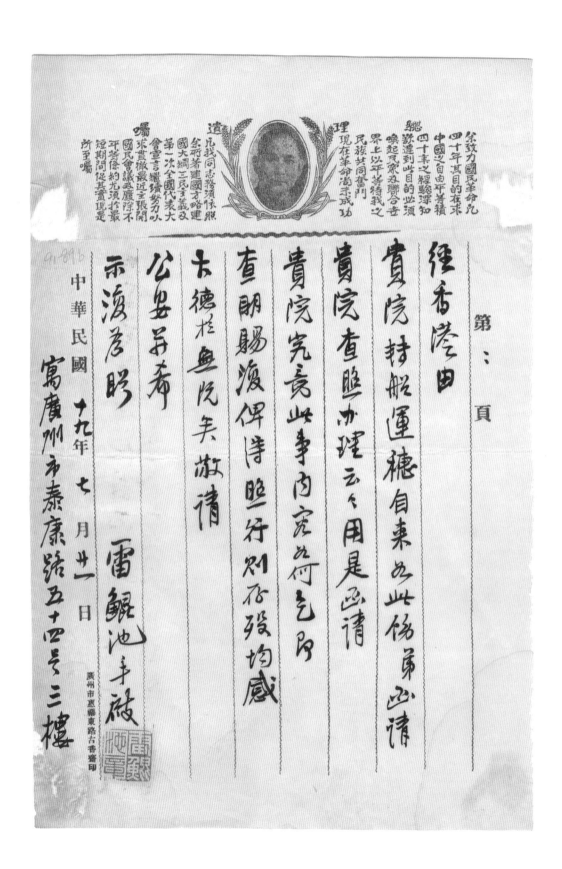

第二頁

經香港由

貴院特船運穗自東於此偽第函請

貴院查照辦理云々用是函請

貴院完竟此事內容如何乞見

查明賜覆俾待照行別有殘均感

卡德柆無院美敬請

公安祈希

示覆彥照

中華民國 十九年 七月 廿一日

寫廣州市泰康路五十四号三樓

雷鯤池手啟

廣州市惠愛東路六香審印

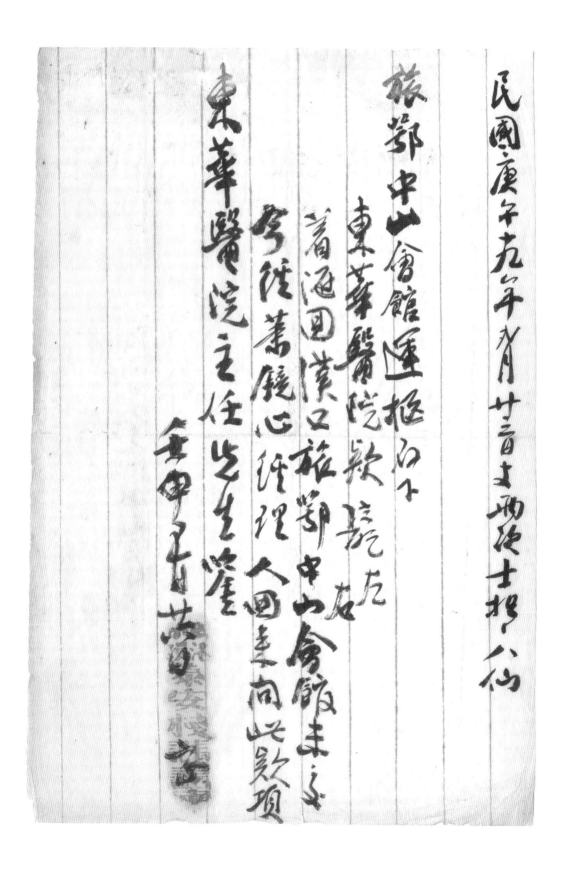

民國庚午九年五月廿三日西歷十拆八仙

旅鄂中山會館匯抵白不

東華醫院欵銀左右

着涵回漢口旅鄂中山會館去之

密陸萋鏡心經理人回去向此欵項

東華醫院主任先生鑒

壬申千荔月

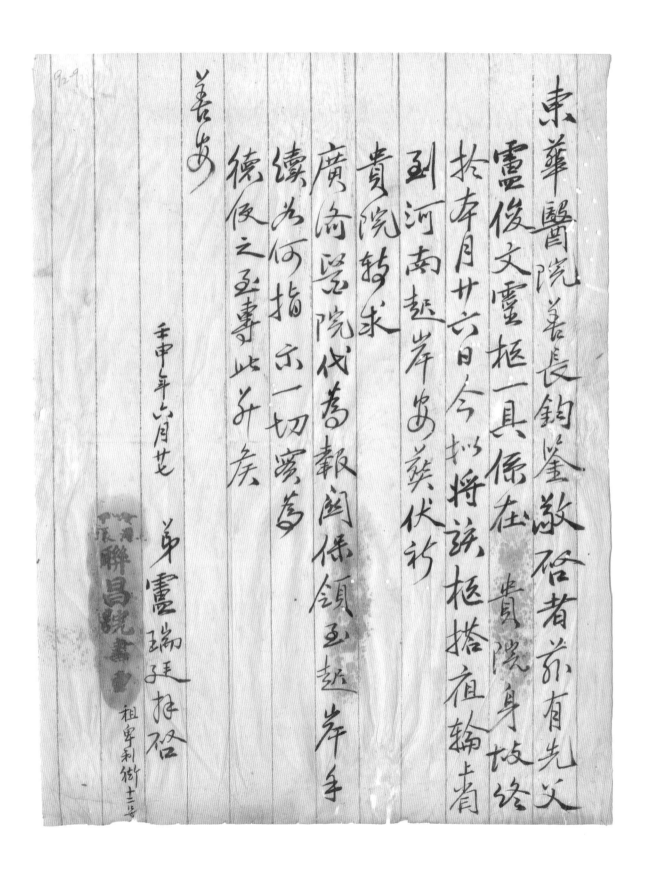

東華醫院善長鈞鑒敬啟者茲有先父

靈柩文靈柩一具保在

於本月廿六日今拟將該柩搭□貴院身坡輪回

到河南越岸安葬伏祈

貴院轉求

廣僑醫院代為報關保領並越岸手

續為何指示一切實為

德便之至專此并頌

善安

壬申年六月廿□

先靈瑞廷拜啟

祖家利街十□號

香港福壽殯儀致東華醫院信件

1932年9月10日

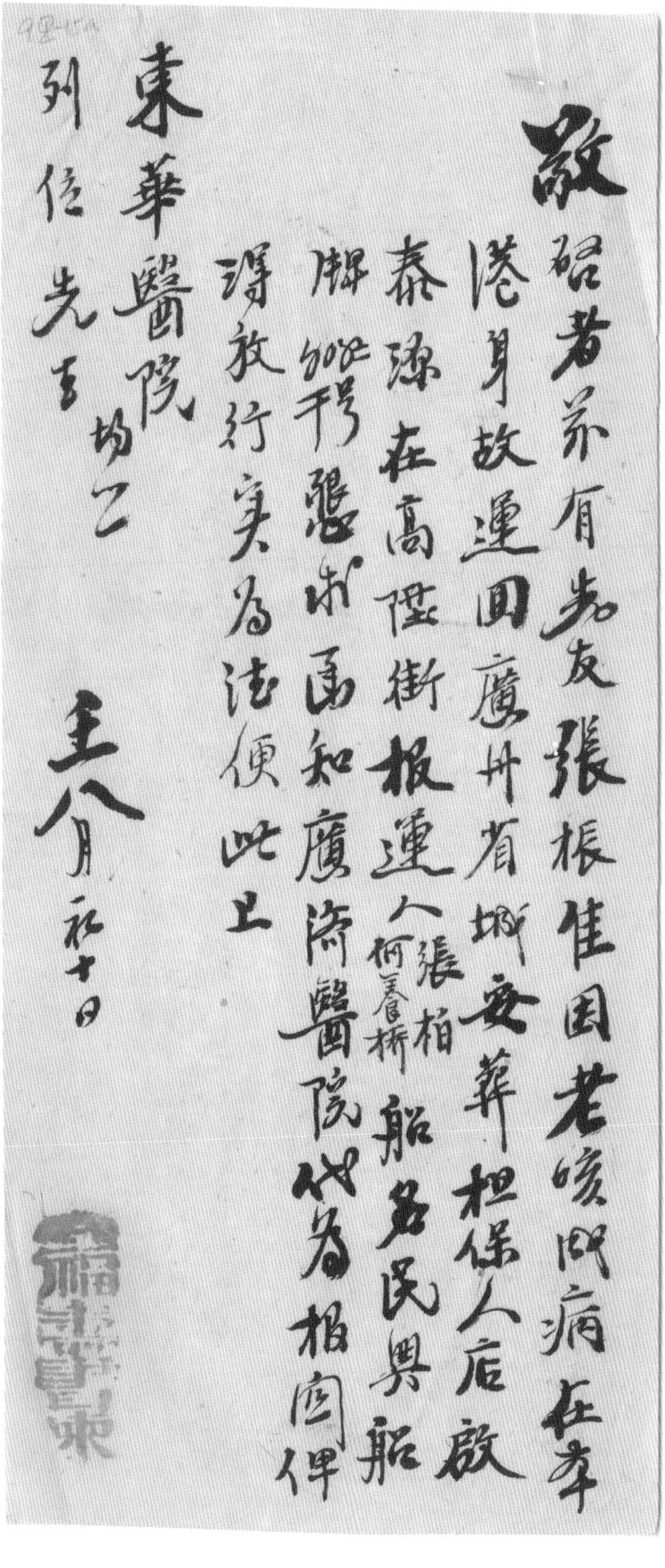

敬啟者茲有先友張振佳因老咳嗽病在本港身故運回廣州省城安葬担保人店啟泰號在高陞街根運人張柏（何景倉梯）船名民興船請船政署函知廣濟醫院代為招呼俾得放行實為德便此上

東華醫院
列位先生 均鑒

壬八月初十日

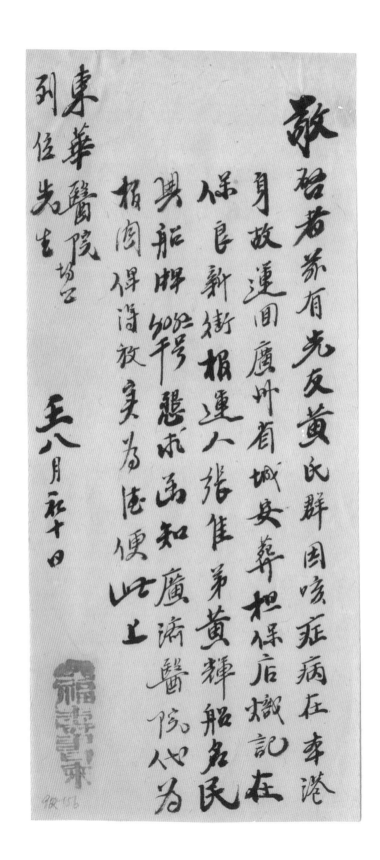

敬啟者茲有先友黃氏群因喘症病在本港
身故運回廣州省城安葬把保店燜記在
保良新街相連人張崔弟黃輝船名民
興船牌5002號懇求為知廣濟醫院代為
相關俾得敉實為德便此上

東華醫院執事
列位先生

三二八月二十日

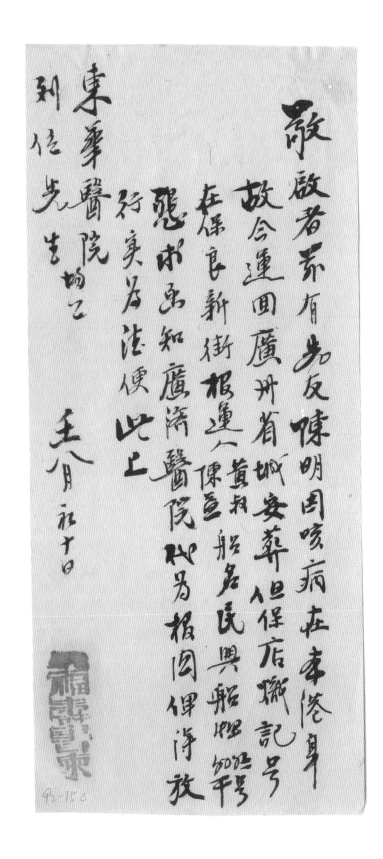

敬啟者茲有先友陳明周咳病在本港身
故今連回廣州省城安葬但係店職記號
在保良新街根運人黃根船名民興船鈕如平號
惻求示知廣濟醫院地另根回俾得浮葬
行實為德便　此上
東華醫院均可
到信先生均一

壬申八月初十日

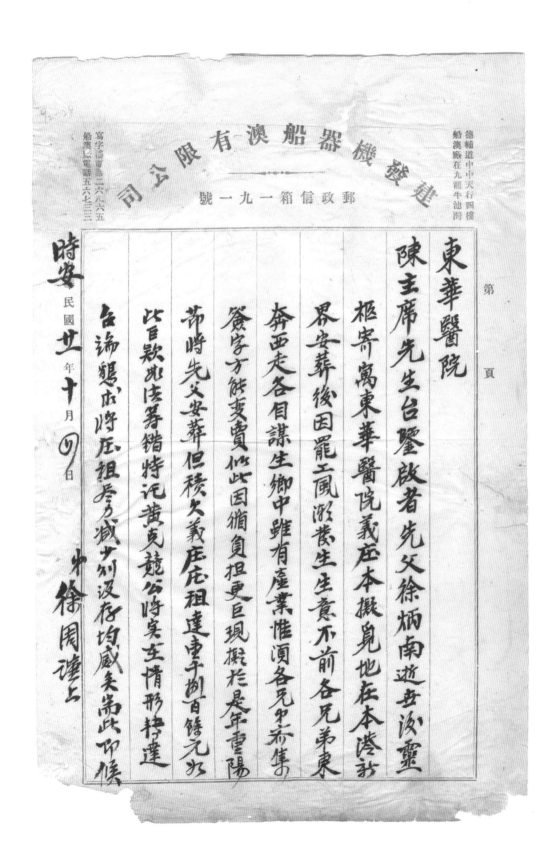

東華醫院

陳主席先生台鑒啟者先父徐炳南遊嶽逝靈

柩寄寓東華醫院義庄本擬覓地在本港領

界安葬後因罷工風潮養生生意不前各兄弟東

奔西走各目謀生鄉中雖有產業惟須各兄弟齊集

簽字方能變賣似此因循負擔更巨現擬於是年重陽

節將先父安葬但積欠義庄庄租達壹千捌百餘元此

此巨歎地法籌錯特託黃亮竸公將實左情形轉達

台端懇求將庄祖峕為減少列沒存均感美高此叩候

時安

民國廿年十月四日

徐周謹上

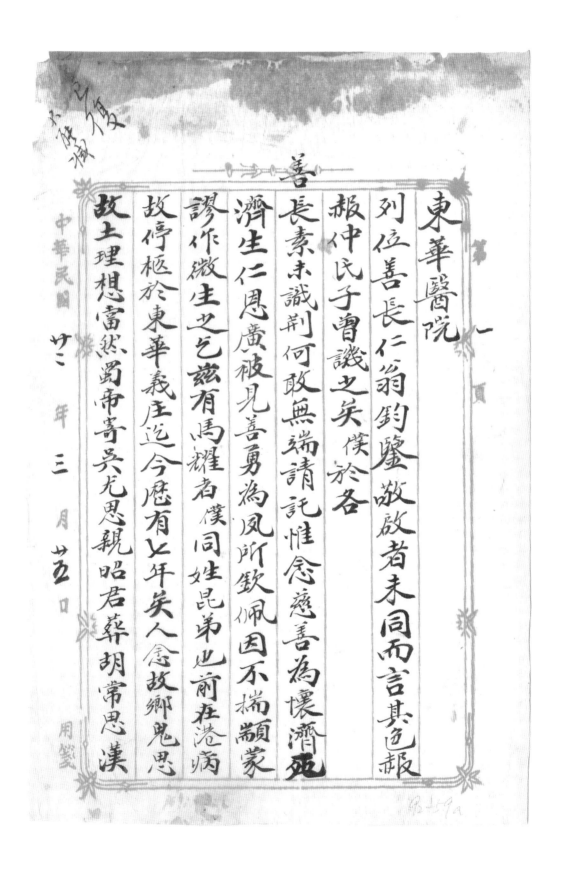

善

東華醫院

列位善長仁翁鈞鑒敬啟者未同而言其通報

報中氏子曾識之矣僕於各

長素未識荊何敢無端請託惟念慈善為懷濟貧

濟生仁恩廣被見善勇為凡所欽佩因不揣顓蒙

謬作微生之乞茲有馬耀者僕同姓昆弟也前在港病

故停柩於東華義莊迄今歷有七年矣人念故鄉鬼思

故上理想當然蜀帝寄吳尤思親昭君葬胡常思漢

中華民國 廿二 年 三 月 廿五 日

用箋

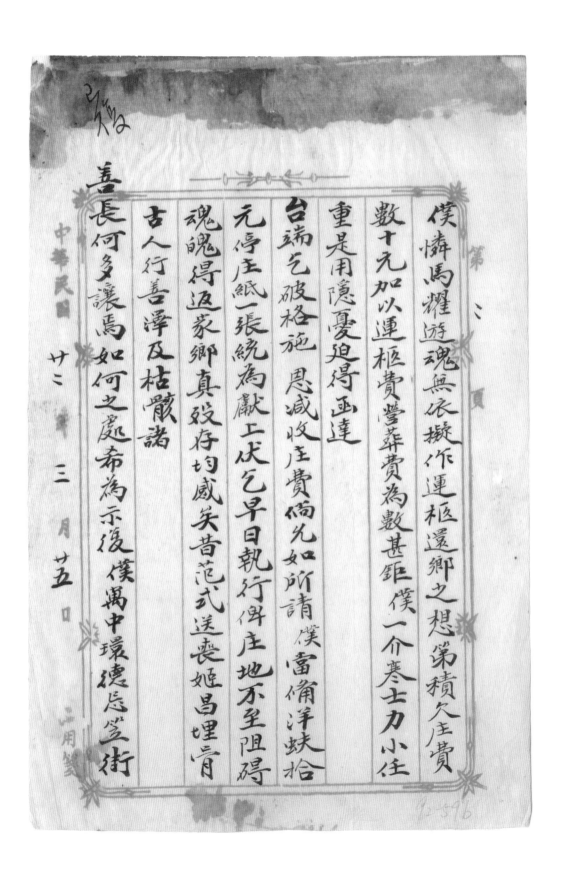

僕憐馬耀遊魂無依擬作運柩還鄉之想第積欠住費

數十元加以運柩費營葬費為數甚鉅僕一介寒士力小任

重是用隱憂迫得函達

台端乞破格施恩減收住費倘先如所請 僕當備洋蚨拾

元停庄紙一張統為獻工伏乞早日執行俾庄地不至阻碍

魂魄得返蒙鄉真骸存均感矢昔范式送喪姬昌埋骨

古人行善澤及枯骸諸

善長何多讓焉如何之處希為示復僕寓中環德忌笠街

中華民國 廿二年 三月 廿五日

第二頁

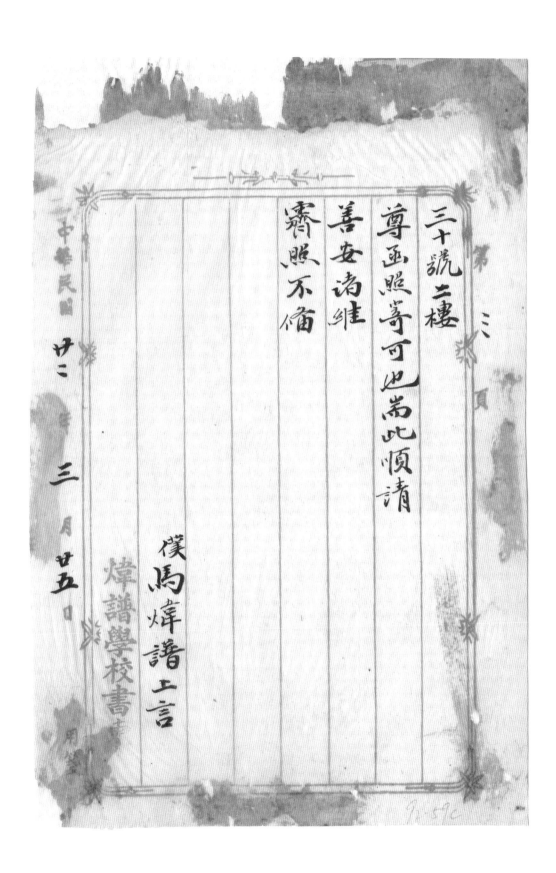

三十號二樓

尊函照荅可也耑此順請

善安諸維

鑒照不備

僕馮煒譜上言

煒譜學校書

中華民國廿二三月廿五日

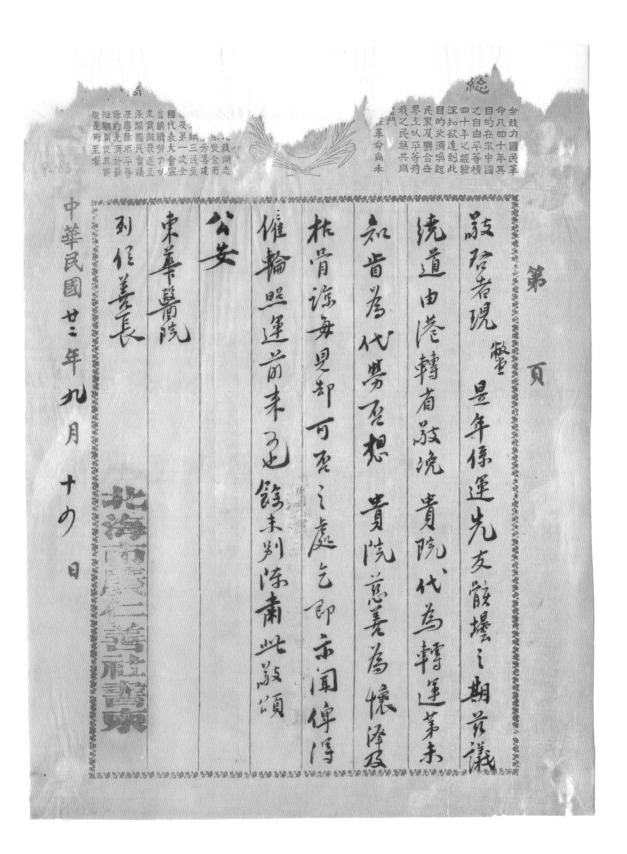

第一頁

敬啓者現 是年保運先友骸壜之期景議

繞道由港轉省敬浼 貴院代為轉運莫未

知肯為代勞否想 貴院慈善為懷隆及

桔骨諒每見卻可否之處乞即示聞俾得

催輪照運前來乃諸未別陳肅此敬頌

公安

東華醫院

列位善長

中華民國廿三年九月十四日

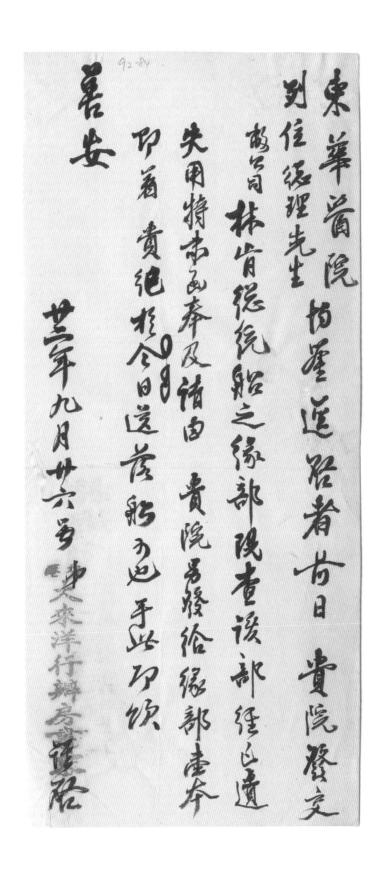

東華醫院
列位經理先生均鑒 逕啟者本日 貴院發文

敝公司 林肯總統船之緣由 閱查後 部經照遺

失用特專函奉及 諸由 貴院另發給緣部壹奉

即著 貴絕於今日送彥船以迎于此可頌

善安

卅二年九月廿六多事　大來洋行辦房謹啟

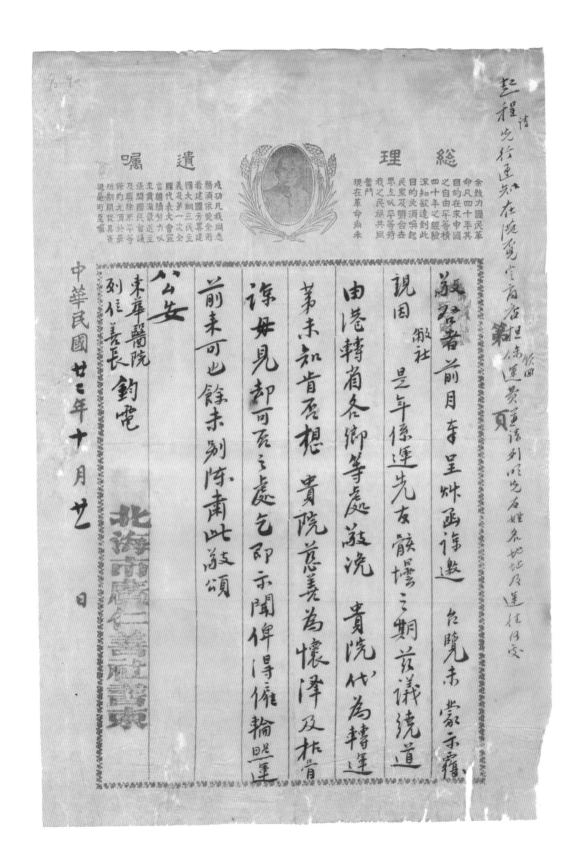

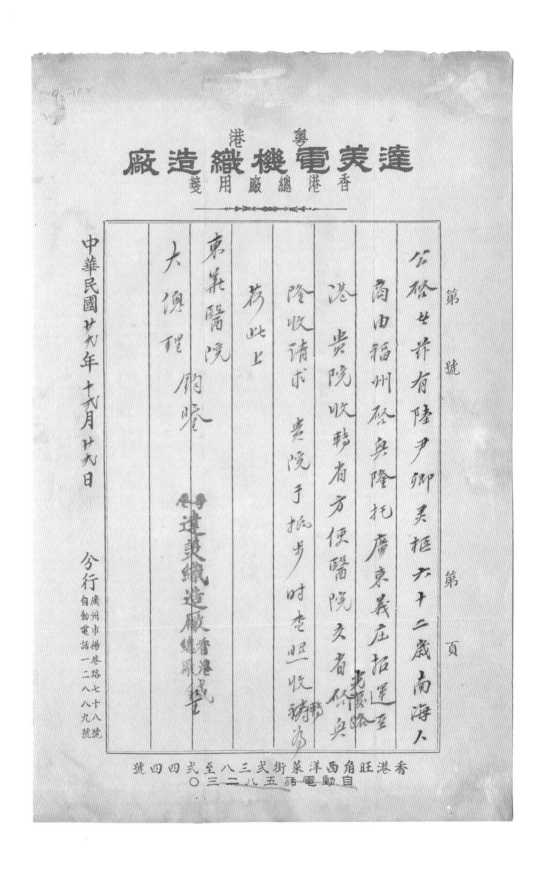

粵港

達美電機織造廠

香港總廠用箋

廠造織機電美達

第　號　　第　頁

公啟者茲有陸尹鄉吳框六十二歲南海人

商由福州啟與隆托廣東義莊扛運至

港貴院收轉有方便醫院交者

隆收請求貴院手振步時查照收轉

荷此上

東華醫院

大總理均鑒

達美織造廠香港總廠啟

中華民國廿九年十弍月廿六日

分行

廣州市楊巷路七十八號
自動電話一二八八九號

香港旺角西洋菜街弍三八至弍四四號
自動電話五八二三〇

香港潤安祥猪油莊致東華醫院信件

1934年3月9日

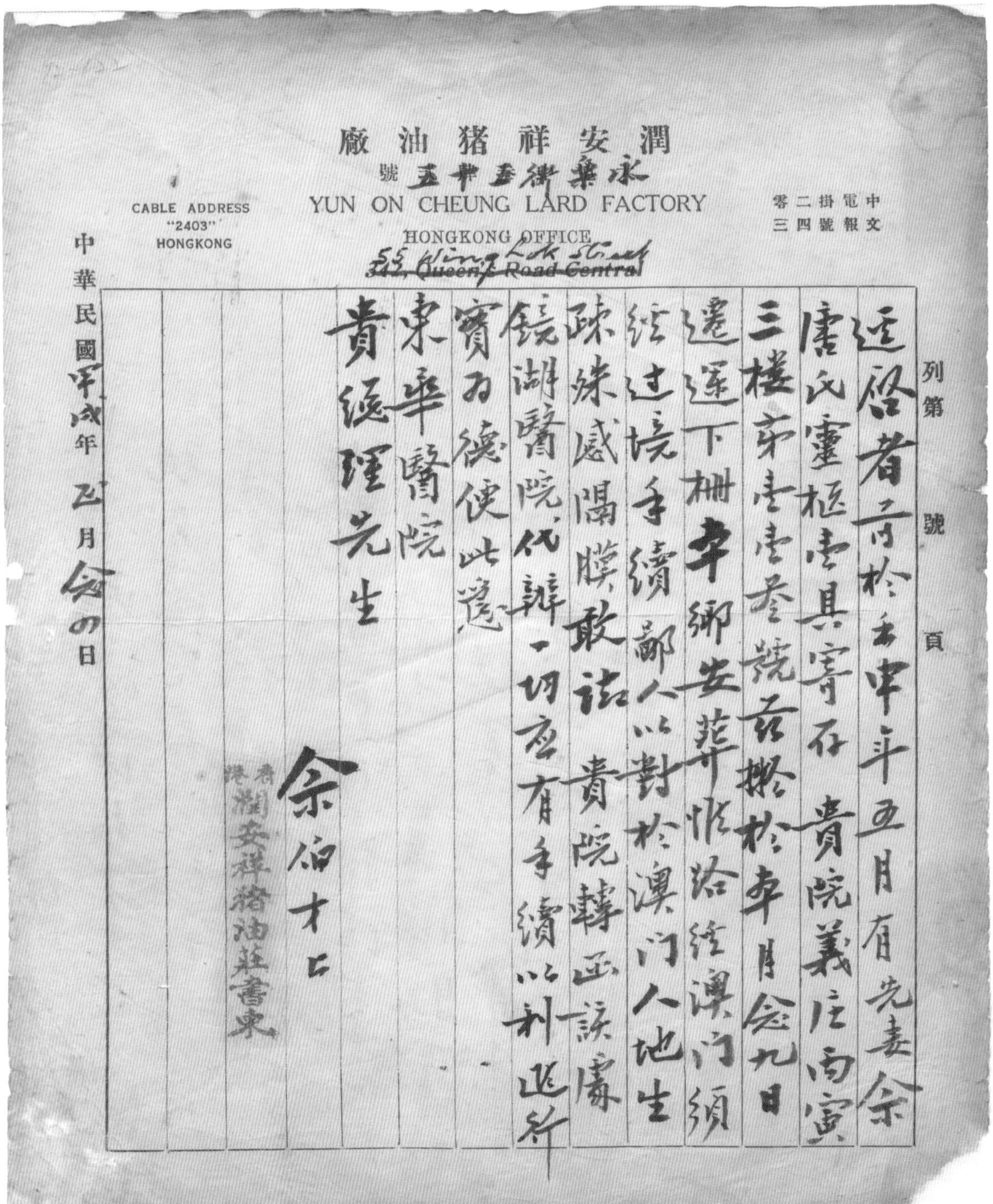

潤安祥猪油廠
永樂街五十五號
YUN ON CHEUNG LARD FACTORY
CABLE ADDRESS "2403" HONGKONG
中文電報掛號二四零三
HONGKONG OFFICE
55 Wing Lok Street
~~342, Queen's Road Central~~

列第　號　頁

逕啓者　前於壬申年五月有先妻余唐氏靈柩壹具寄存　貴院義莊丙寅三樓第壹壹叁號　茲擬於本月念九日遷運下柵本鄉安葬　惟路經澳門須經過境手續　鄙人以對於澳門人地生疏　殊感隔膜　敢請　貴院轉函該處鏡湖醫院代辦一切應有手續　以利進行　實為德便　此達

東華醫院

貴總理先生

余伯才上

香港潤安祥猪油莊書柬

中華民國甲戌年正月念四日

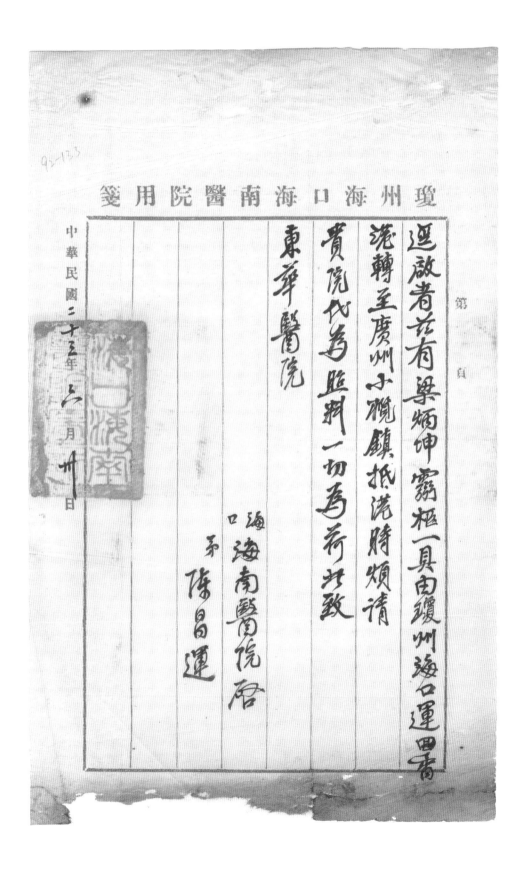

逕啟者茲有梁炳坤靈柩一具由瓊州海口運囘香

港轉至廣州小欖鎮抵港時煩請

貴院代為監料一切為荷此致

東華醫院

海南醫院啟

子陳昌運

中華民國二十三年六月卅日

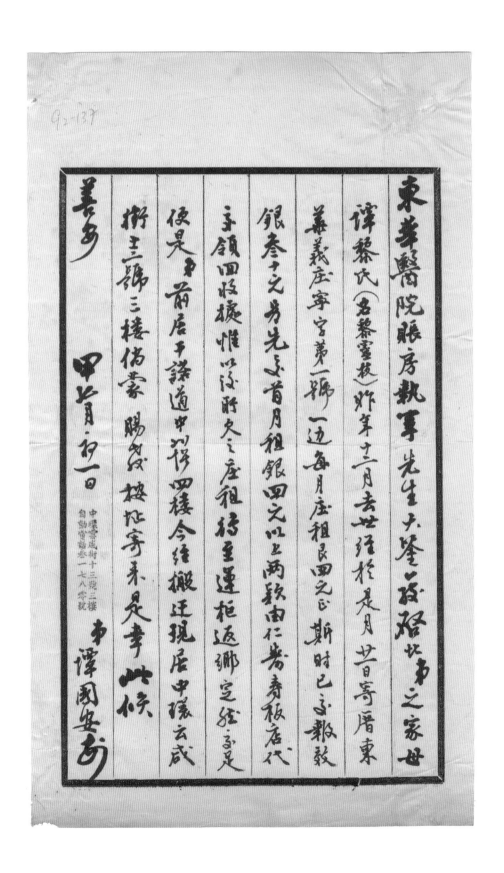

香港譚國安致東華醫院信件

1934年8月10日

92-137

東華醫院賬房執事先生大鑒 敬啟者 弟之家母
譚黎氏（名黎靈枝）昨年十二月去世 經於是月廿日寄厝東
華義庄寄字萬一號一邊 每月庄租銀四元正 斯時已交數
銀叁十元為先交首月租銀四元 以上兩款由仁壽壽板店代
交領回收據 惟以後所欠之庄租待至運柩返鄉完結之交足
便是 弟前居干諾道中卅捌四樓 今經搬遷現居中環云咸
街十三號三樓 倘蒙 賜覆 按址寄來是幸 此候
善安

甲戌七月初一日

中環雲咸街十三號三樓
自動電話叁一七八零號

弟譚國安頓

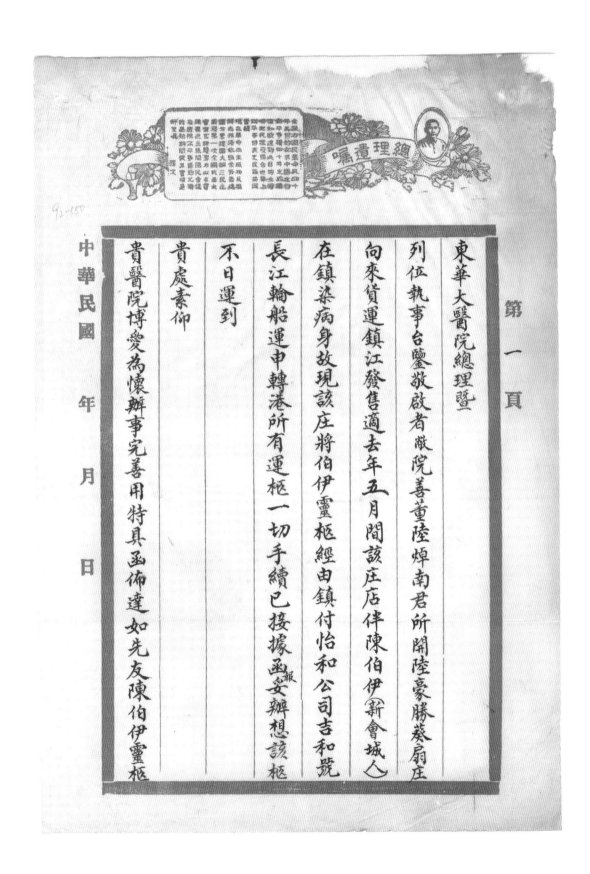

第一頁

東華大醫院總理暨

列位執事台鑒敬啟者敝院善董陸焯南君所開陸豪勝蔡扇庄

向來貨運鎮江發售適去年五月間該庄店伴陳伯伊（新會城人）

在鎮染病身故現該庄將伯伊靈柩經由鎮付怡和公司吉和號

長江輪船運申轉港所有運柩一切手續已接據函妥辦想該柩

不日運到

貴處素仰

貴醫院博愛為懷辦事完善用特具函佈達如先友陳伯伊靈柩

中華民國　　年　　月　　日

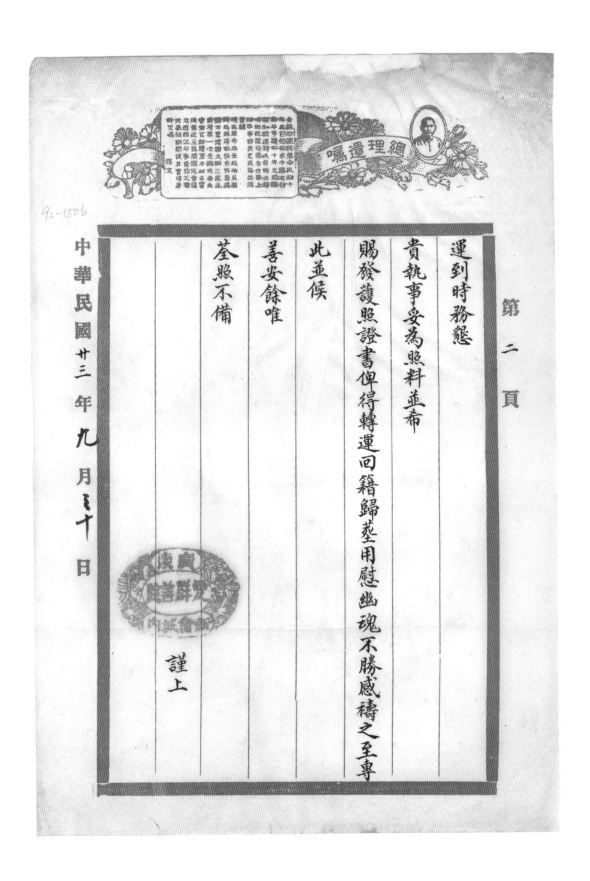

總理遺囑

第二頁

運到時務懇

貴執事妥為照料並希

賜發護照證書俾得轉運回籍歸塋用慰幽魂不勝感禱之至專

此並候

善安餘唯

荃照不備

中華民國廿三年九月三十日

謹上

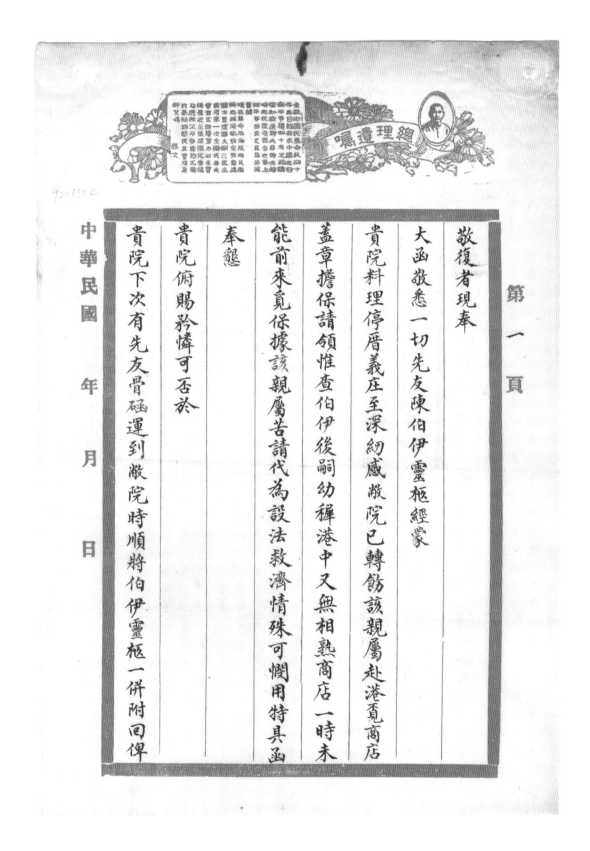

第一頁

敬復者現奉

大函敬悉一切先友陳伯伊靈柩經蒙

貴院料理停厝義庄至深紉感敝院已轉飭該親屬赴港覓商店

蓋章擔保請領惟查伯伊後嗣幼稺港中又無相熟商店一時未

能前來覓保據該親屬苦請代為設法救濟情殊可憫用特具函

奉懇

貴院俯賜矜憐可否於

貴院下次有先友骨砠運到敝院時順將伯伊靈柩一併附回俾

中華民國　　　年　　月　　日

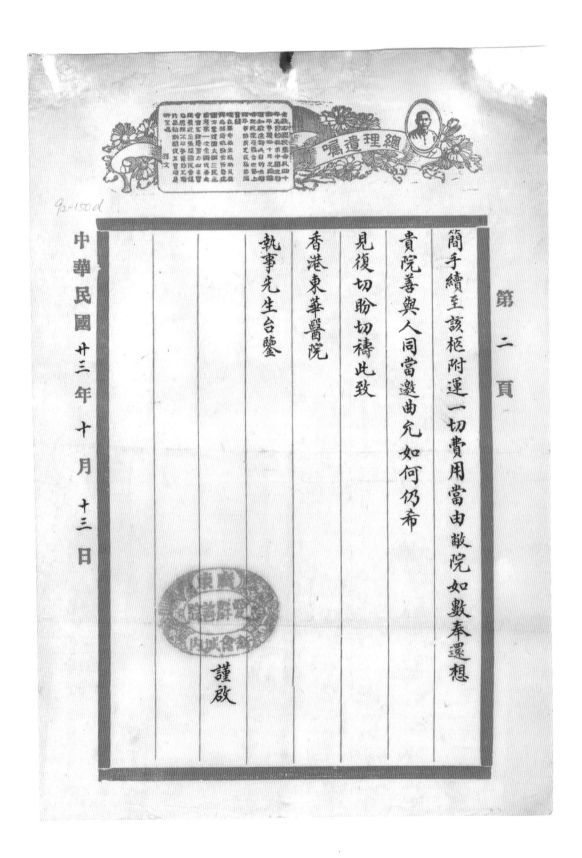

第 二 頁

簡手續至該柩附運一切費用當由敝院如數奉還想

貴院善與人同當邀曲允如何仍希

見復切盼切禱此致

香港東華醫院

執事先生台鑒

謹啟

中華民國廿三年十月十三日

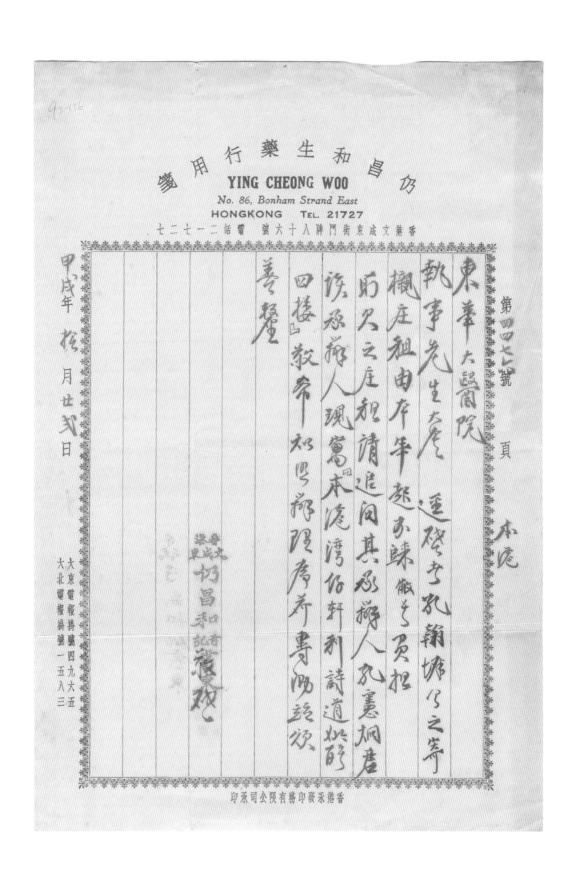

行藥生和昌仍
YING CHEONG WOO
No. 86, Bonham Strand East
HONGKONG　TEL. 21727
七二七一二話電　號六十八牌門街東成文港香

第四四七八號　　頁　　本店

東華大醫院
執事先生台鑒 逕啓者孔翰堂乃之等
攬庄祖由本年趣赤臻徹之負招
而凡之庄祖清追向其承辦人孔憲炯君
茲承辦人現寫寄本港澤仔軒刮詩道桃醇
四樓教希㝷四辦限廣存專函詢詢
善鑒

甲戌年 拾 月 廿 弐 日

大東電報掛號四九六五
大北電報掛號一五八三

仍昌和記謹啓

印承司公限有務印發承號港香

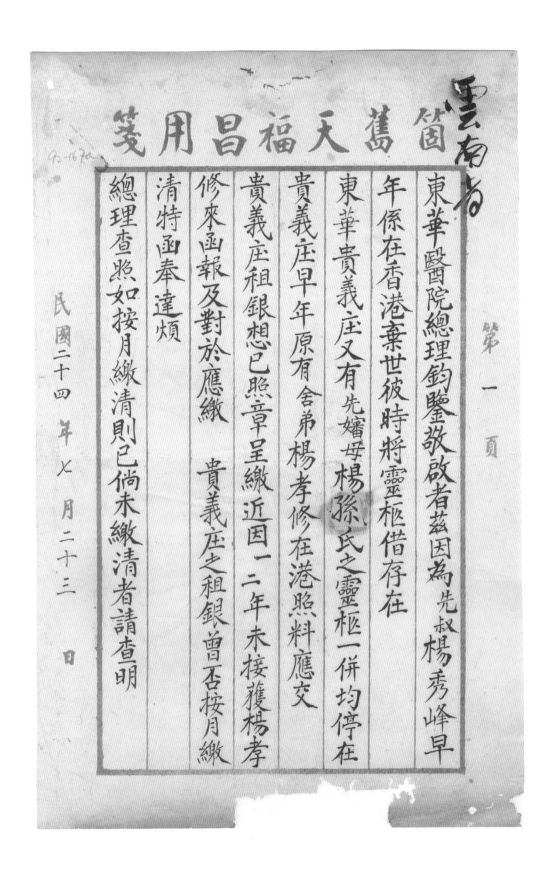

雲南箇舊天福昌用箋

第一頁

東華醫院總理鈞鑒敬啟者茲因為先叔楊秀峰早

年係在香港棄世彼時將靈柩借存在

東華貴義庄又有先嬸母楊孫氏之靈柩一併均停在

貴義庄早年原有舍弟楊孝修在港照料應交

貴義庄租銀想已照章呈繳近因一二年未接獲楊孝

修來函報及對於應繳　貴義庄之租銀曾否按月繳

清特函奉達煩

總理查照如按月繳清則已倘未繳清者請查明

民國二十四年七月二十三　日

箋用昌福天舊箇

第二頁

示知自當照數呈繳至於先叔父楊秀峯先嬸母楊孫氏

兩付靈柩敬懇

總理轉飭東華義庄管理人妥為保存若有欠少租金

縈廾一律負擔甘認滙來繳清決不能欠少分亳諸事

叩

光容當後報餘事未詳專肅敬請

鈞安并請

東華醫院諸公 台安

民國二十四年七月二十三　日

箇舊天福昌用箋

第三頁

外批回示祈帶至雲南箇舊縣綠沖花街天福昌

錫號交楊榮升收

楊榮升翰轉

民國二十四年七月二十三日

不知先友西歸地

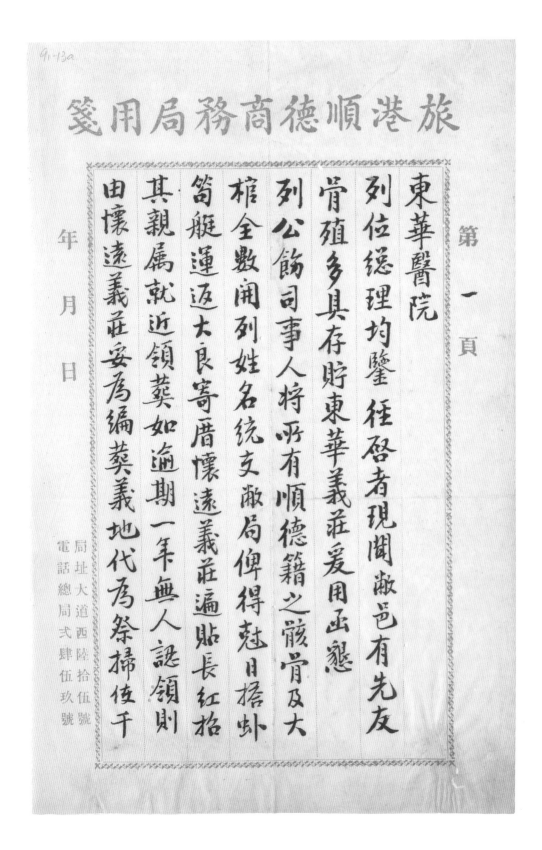

旅港順德商務局用箋

第一頁

年　月　日

東華醫院
列位總理均鑒　徑啟者現聞敝邑有先友
骨殖多具存貯東華義莊爰用函懇
列公飭司事人將所有順德籍之骸骨及大
棺全數開列姓名統支敝局俾得趕日搬妥
筍艇運返大良寄厝懷遠義莊遍貼長紅招
其親屬就近領葬如逾期一年無人認領則
由懷遠義莊妥為編葬義地代為祭掃俟干

局址大道西陸拾伍號
電話總局弍肆伍玖號

旅港順德商務局用箋

第 二 頁

里遺骸得歸故土魂兮有知定感

大德於靡既矣專此並敀

善安唯

照不宣　　旅港順德商務局主席辛聖三上

乙巳年五月十一日

局址大道西陸拾伍號
電話總局式肆伍玖號

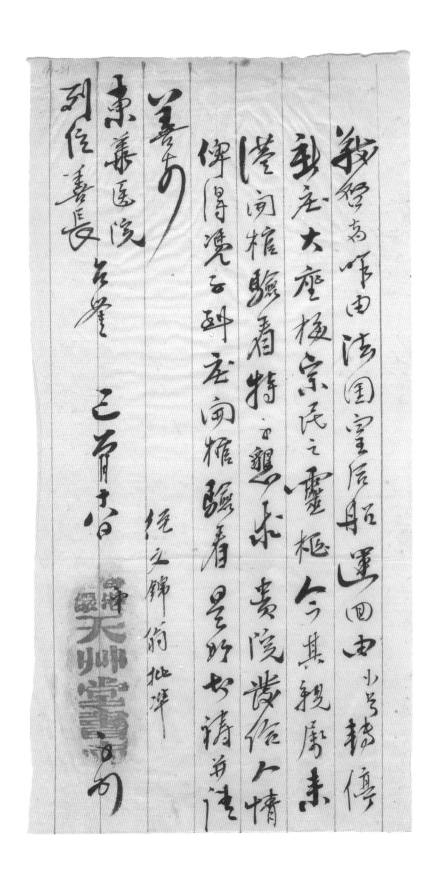

敬啟者昨由法國寔厘船運回由小呂轉僑港係大應極宗民之靈柩今其親屬來港詢棺驗看特懇求貴院發俗人情俾得憑之斜產詢棺驗看是所切禱耑請

善為

貴東華醫院

列位善長台鑒

憑之錦約批準

東華醫院

善長台鑒

香港天草堂書局

三萬十台

中國黃焯致東華醫院信件

1930 年 2 月 16 日

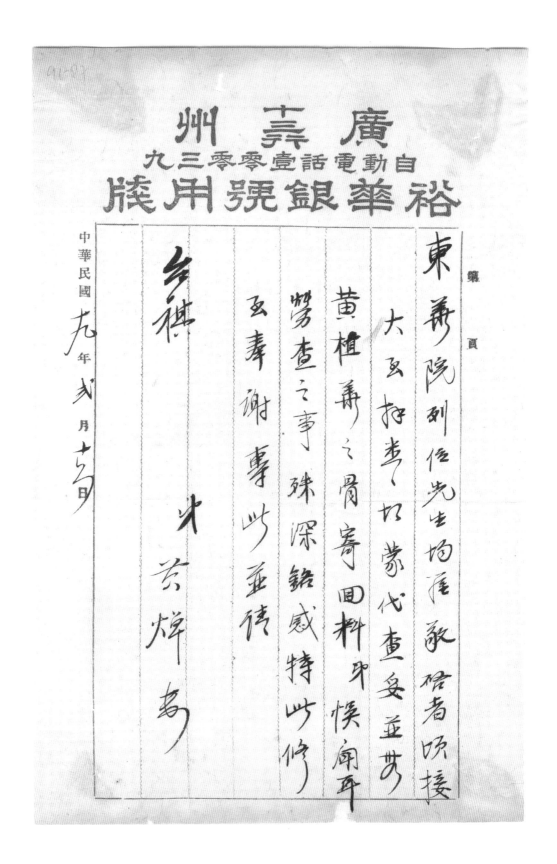

廣嵩州

自動電話壹零零三九

裕華銀號用牋

東華院列位先生均鑒敬啟者頃接

大函拜悉祇蒙代查要並蒙

黃植蕃之骨寄回料必慎庾耳

勞查之事殊深銘感特此修

玉壽謝事此並請

台祺

弟黃焯啟

中華民國九年貳月吉日

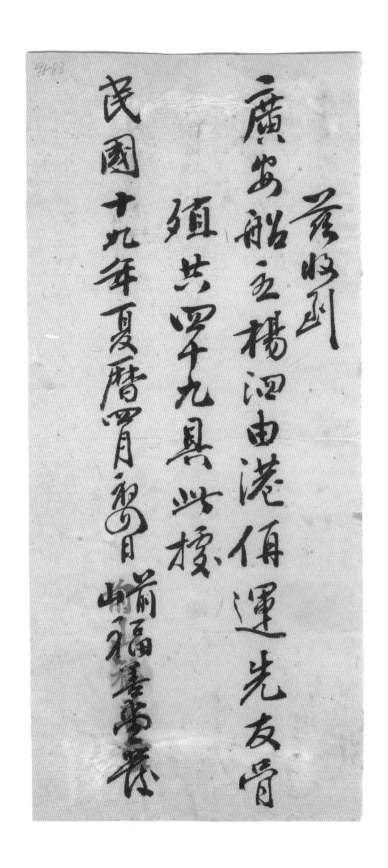

茲收到

廣安船主楊泗由港俱運先友骨
殖共四十九具此據

民國十九年夏曆四月初一日 前山福善堂收

東華醫院諸執事先生鈞鑒敬啟者　弟為先父多身故

越見所封手遠歇尚未運回家鄉安葬　弟甚為惆悵之至再

思吾父既終于異國者吾人所共悲以此如論之弟豈無憾焉因此

已決意循例將先父之遺歇運回貴院轉交中山縣得都大

牛溪朗鄉鄭品八位見長樓收俾他覓吉地安葬以慰先父

在天之美惟弟素知貴執事之仗義施恩樂善奉怀故敢

以下情上達伏祈貴代勞毋見郤則先人身甚弟銘感無

忘此題者弟已□□□□見送回費用銀壹傳□伏祈照收

為禱尚此奉達致謝　再者先父名鄭美容

卅年元月念八日　　弟鄭望源叩肩

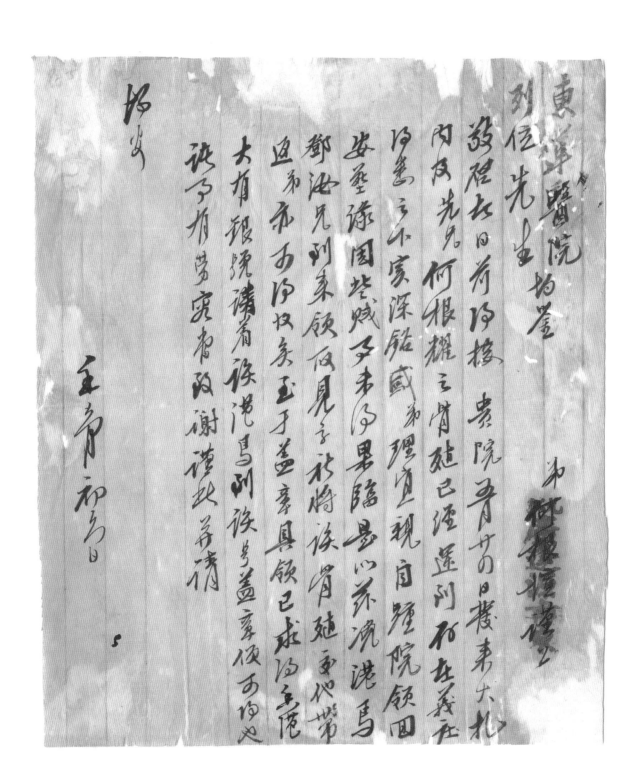

東華醫院

列位先生均鑒

敬啟者日前接 貴院來函

內及先先 何根耀二骨殖已經運到

弟謹三不勝深銘感激 理當親自赴院領回

安塟謹因垫賤不果 特着舍親 弟

鄧泗兄到来領回 見即将諒骨殖重代帶

迶 弟亦可放故矣 至蓋塟事具領已求

大有銀號請看 候港罵到疑当盡量候可

諸予有勞 實有望玉政謝謹此奉復

順安

壬申初九日

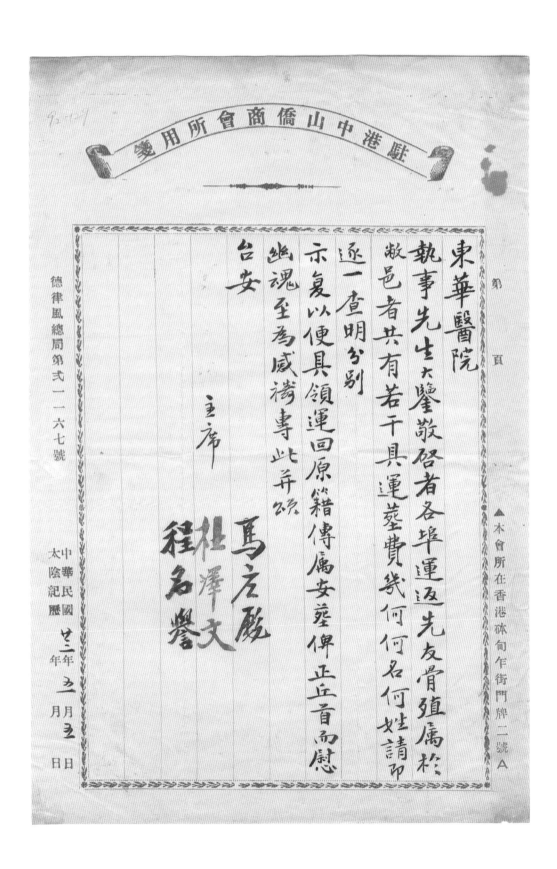

第　頁

▲本會所在香港砵甸乍街門牌二號 A

東華醫院

執事先生大鑒敬啟者各埠運返先友骨殖屬於
敝邑者共有若干具運蓬費幾何何名何姓祈

逐一查明分別

示復以便具領運回原籍傳屬安葬俾正首邱慰

幽魂至為感禱專此并頌

台安

　　　　主席　馬文厝
　　　　　　　杜澤文
　　　　　　　程名譽

德律風總局第弍一一六七號

中華民國廿三年三月五日
太陰紀歷

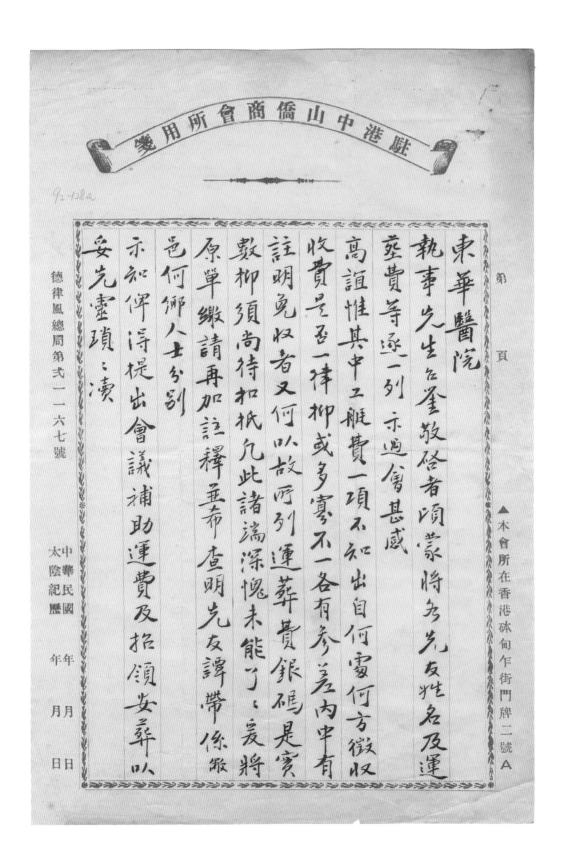

第　頁

東華醫院

執事先生台鑒敬啟者頃蒙將各先友姓名及運
葬費等逐一列示過會甚感
高誼惟其中工艇費一項不知出自何處何方徵收
收費是否一律柳或多寡不一各有參差內中有
註明免收者又何以故所列運葬費銀碼是實
數柳須尚待扣抵凡此諸端深愧未能了然將
原單繳請再加註釋並希查明先友譚帶係徵
邑何鄉人士分別
示知俾得提出會議補助運費及招領安葬以
妥先靈瑣瑣瀆

德律風總局第弍一一六七號

中華民國　　年　月　日

太陰紀曆　　年　月　日

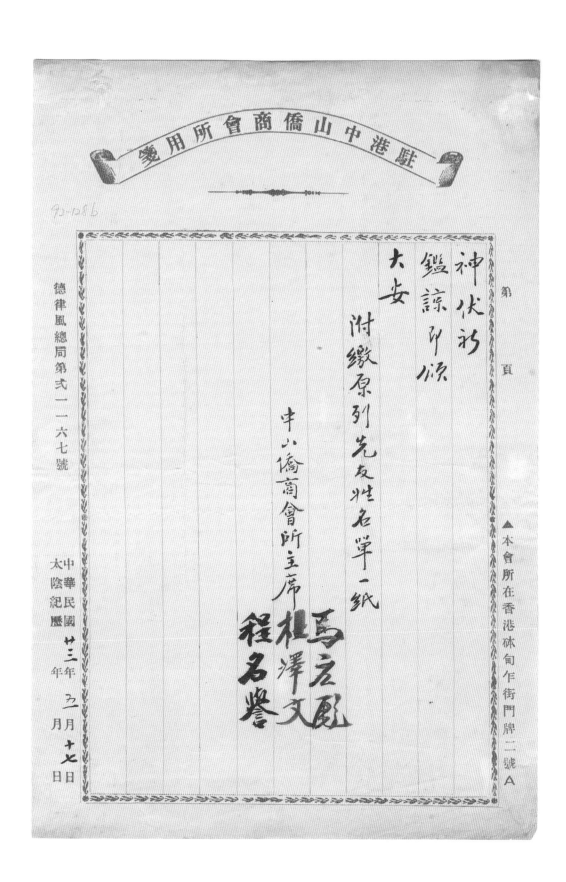

駐港中山僑商會所用箋

第 頁

▲本會所在香港砵甸乍街門牌二號A

德律風總局第弍一六七號

神伏祈

鑑諒印頌

大安

附繳原列先友姓名單一紙

中山僑商會所主席

馬亦風
祖澤文
程名譽

中華民國廿三年 三月 十七 日

太陰紀曆

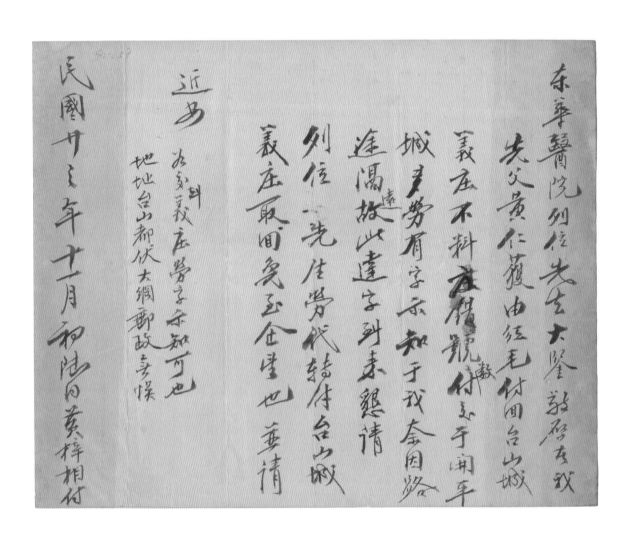

東華醫院列位先生大鑒 敬啓者我

失父黃仁覆由經毛付回台山城

義庄不料在省親付起于開車

城之勞有字示知于我奔回路

進隔故此達字到來懇請

列位先佳勞代轉存台山城

義庄取間免至全生也 耑請

近安

　　茲欲義庄勞字余知可也

　　地址台山都伏太網郵政寄候

民國廿三年十一月初陸日黃梓相付

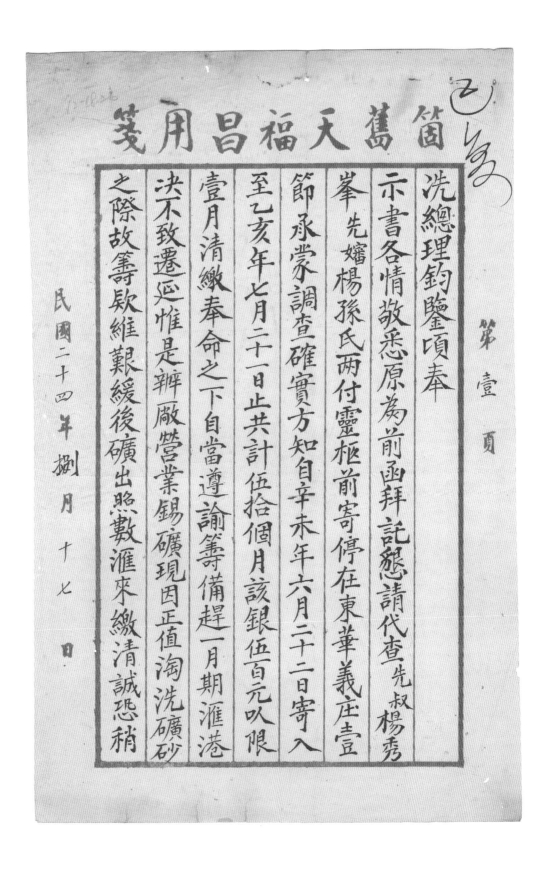

箋用昌福天舊簡

第壹頁

冼總理鈞鑒頃奉

示書各情敬悉原為前函拜託懇請代查先叔楊秀

峯先嬸楊孫氏兩付靈柩前寄停在東華義庄壹

節承蒙調查確實方知自辛未年六月二十二日寄入

至乙亥年七月二十一日止共計伍拾個月該銀伍百元以限

壹月清繳奉命之下自當遵諭籌備趕一月期滙港

決不致遷延惟是辦廠營業錫礦現因正值淘洗礦砂

之際故籌欵維艱緩後礦出照數滙來繳清誠恐稍

民國二十四年捌月十七日

舊箇天福昌用箋

第貳頁

有眈延尚祈

總理通融寬限數月萬不致效前番舍弟之拖延耳想

總理鴻度海量寬仁厚德諒能俯賜從寬發存均感

實叨恩便餘事未詳專肅敬請

鈞安并請

東華醫院執事諸公台安

民國二十四年八月十七日

楊榮潲昌書覆

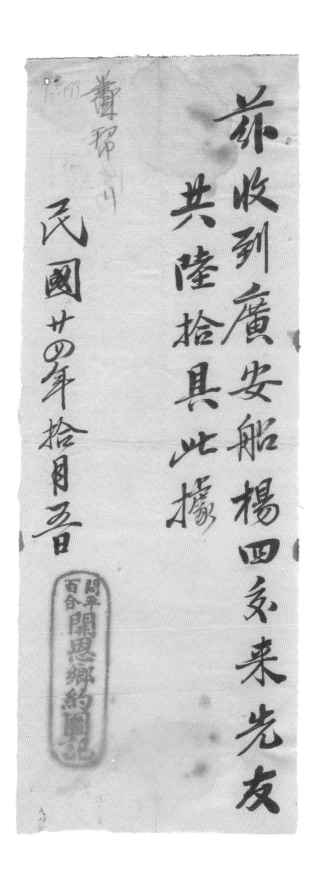

茲收到廣安船楊四永來先友
共陸拾具此據

民國廿四年拾月五日

開平百合開恩鄉約圖記

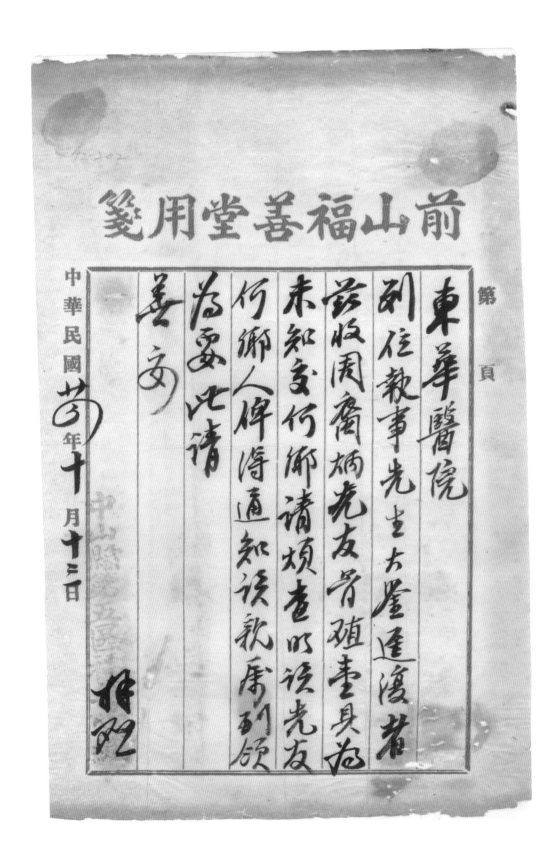

前山福善堂用箋

第　頁

東華醫院

列位董事先生大鑒 運漢番

誤收園喬炳光友骨殖壹具為

未知委何鄉請煩查明該光友

何鄉人俾得通知欸屬到領

為要此請

善安

中華民國廿四年十月十三日

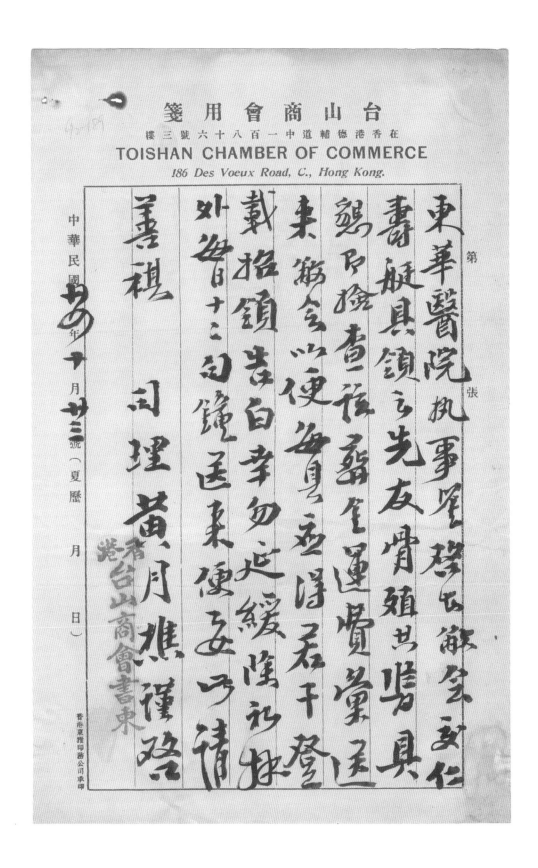

台山商會用箋

在香港德輔道中一百八十六號三樓

TOISHAN CHAMBER OF COMMERCE

186 Des Voeux Road, C., Hong Kong.

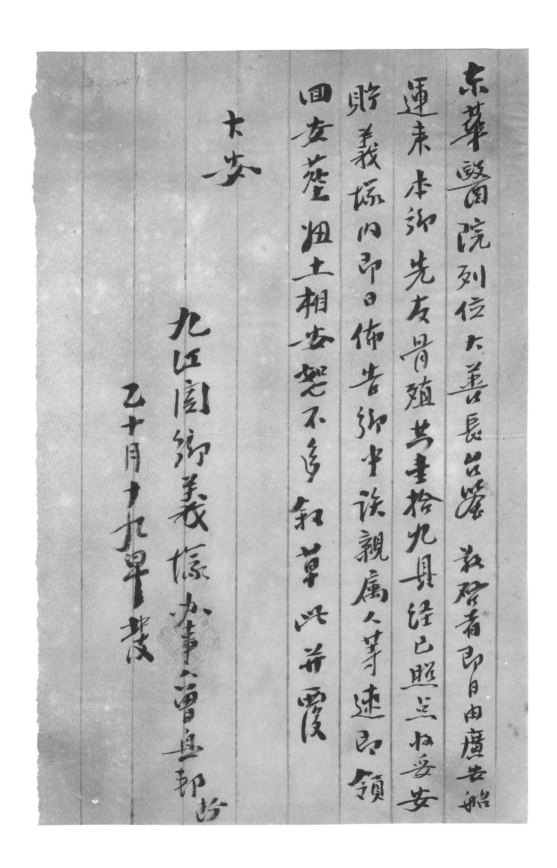

東華醫院列位大善長台鑒　敬啟者即日由廣安號

運來本邦先友骨殖共壹拾九具經已照達妥委

貯義塚內即日佈告俾中誤親屬人等速即領

回安葬俾土相安耑不多敘草此并覆

　　　大安

九江鄉義塚辦事曾興邦鈞

乙十月十九早發

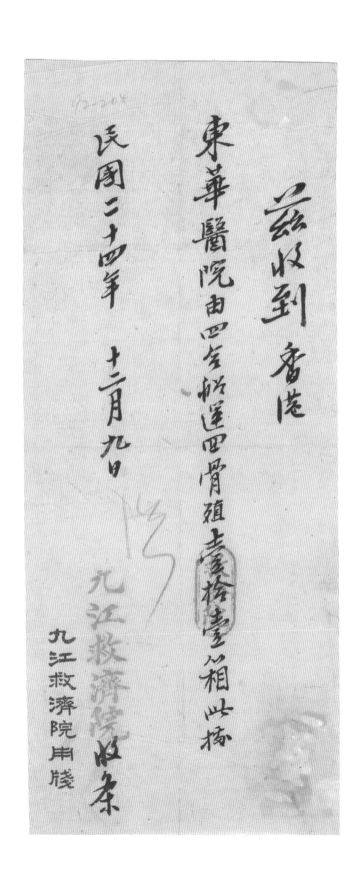

附錄

```
親屬領取骨殖          →   原籍安葬
Bones claimed by          Burial in
relatives                 hometown

無人認領骨殖          →   安葬義山
Unclaimed bones           Burial in
                          Communal free
                          cemetery
```

安葬家鄉
Burial in hometown

善堂代葬義山
Burial in communal free cemetery by
charitable association

（羅湖沙嶺墳場）
(Sandy Ridge Cemetery at Lo Wu)

（新會金牛山華僑義塚）
Jinniushan Free Cemetery for overseas Chinese
at Xinhui

1874

《循環日報》刊載由日本運回 30 餘具
粵人遺骸寄存東華醫院待領
News published on *Tsun Wan Yat Pao* regarding the repatriotion
of more than 30 dead bodies of people of Guangdong from Japan
awaiting people to claim in Tung Wah Hospital

1875

文武廟將其牛房義莊
交由東華醫院辦理
Man Mo Temple handed over
its coffin home in Slaughter
House to Tung Wah Hospital

1899

建立東華義莊
Tung Wah Coffin H
was established

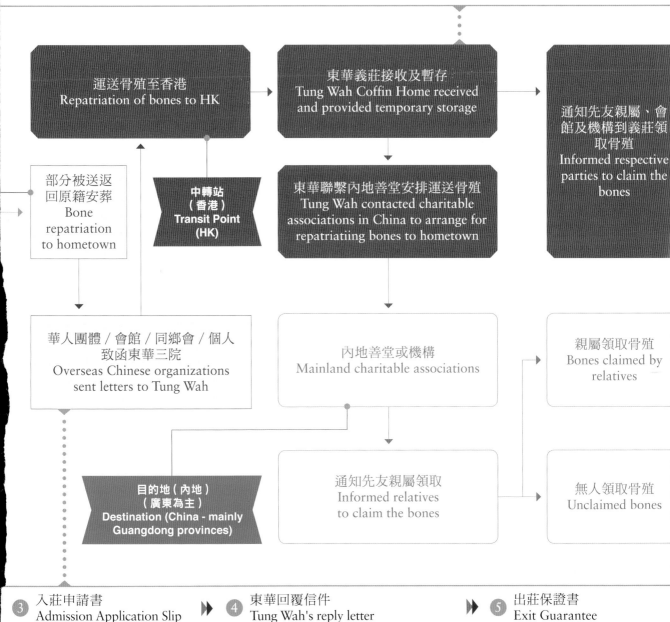

運送骨殖至香港
Repatriation of bones to HK

東華義莊接收及暫存
Tung Wah Coffin Home received
and provided temporary storage

通知先友親屬、會
館及機構到義莊領
取骨殖
Informed respective
parties to claim the
bones

部分被送返
回原籍安葬
Bone
repatriation
to hometown

中轉站
（香港）
Transit Point
(HK)

東華聯繫內地善堂安排運送骨殖
Tung Wah contacted charitable
associations in China to arrange for
repatriatiing bones to hometown

華人團體／會館／同鄉會／個人
致函東華三院
Overseas Chinese organizations
sent letters to Tung Wah

內地善堂或機構
Mainland charitable associations

親屬領取骨殖
Bones claimed by
relatives

目的地（內地）
（廣東為主）
Destination (China - mainly
Guangdong provinces)

通知先友親屬領取
Informed relatives
to claim the bones

無人領取骨殖
Unclaimed bones

3 入莊申請書
Admission Application Slip

4 東華回覆信件
Tung Wah's reply letter

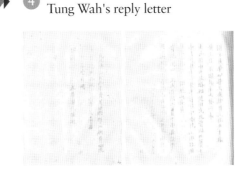

5 出莊保證書
Exit Guarantee

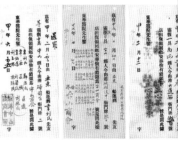

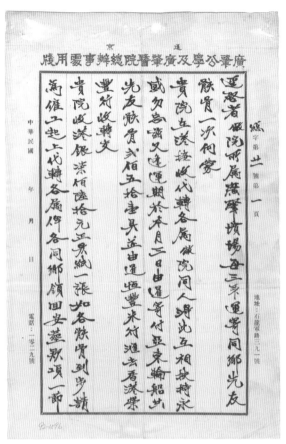

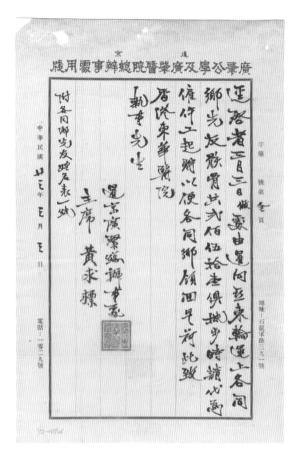

1934 年 3 月 3 日（3 March 1934）
檔案：暹京廣肇會館致東華三院書信及電報一則
Archive: Correspondence from Kwong Siew Association, Siam to Tung Wah Group of Hospitals

暹京廣肇會館致函東華三院，謂251副先友骸骨將乘亞東船至香港，請東華代起上，並通知各同鄉領回安葬，同日附上相關電報一則。
A letter from Kwong Siew Association in Siam to Tung Wah Group of Hospitals stated that 251 sets of deceased Chinese's bones would take the *SS President Adams* to Hong Kong. Tung Wah was asked to take care of the bones and inform the deceased's native people to claim the bones for burial in their hometown. A telegram was enclosed.

東華三院與海外華人落葉歸根之旅（東華檔案實例）

Tung Wah Group of Hospitals and the journey of overseas Chinese returning to their roots (A case study from Tung Wah archives)

東華三院由 19 世紀末至 20 世紀中協助於海外去世的華人返回家鄉安葬，保存於東華三院文物館數以萬頁計的檔案反映華人重視落葉歸根的傳統及各地慈善機構通力合作完成先僑的心願。以下是一個檔案實例。

From the late 19th to mid-20th centuries, the Tung Wah Group of Hospitals assisted in the deceased overseas Chinese returning to their hometown for burial. There are tens of thousands of relevant pieces of archives preserved by Tung Wah Museum which reflect the strong Chinese tradition of fallen leaves returning to their roots as well as the spirit of mutual assistance of native societies and charitable associations in different places working together to fulfil the hope of the deceased Chinese. Here is a case study from Tung Wah archives.

年份 Year	1934 年 1934
發信機構 Sending organization	暹京廣肇會館 Kwong Siew Association of Siam
收信機構 Receiving organization	香港東華三院 Tung Wah Group of Hospitals of Hong Kong
骨殖目的地 Destination of bones	中國廣東各邑 Guangdong provinces, China
個案 Case	二百五十一名先僑的骸骨經香港被運返家鄉下葬 251 sets of deceased Chinese' bones to be sent to their hometown via Hong Kong

1870 ▸ 1873

東華醫院成立
Tung Wah Hospital
was founded

《東華醫院徵信錄》
載有義莊規條
Regulations of coffin home
in *Zhengxinlu of Tung Wah
Hospital*

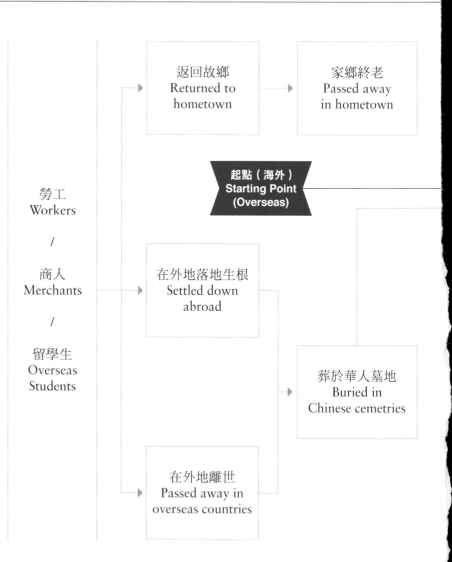

十九至二十世紀
華人出洋
Chinese went
abroad
from 19th to 20th
centuries

勞工
Workers
/
商人
Merchants
/
留學生
Overseas
Students

返回故鄉
Returned to
hometown

家鄉終老
Passed away
in hometown

起點（海外）
Starting Point
(Overseas)

在外地落地生根
Settled down
abroad

葬於華人墓地
Buried in
Chinese cemetries

在外地離世
Passed away in
overseas countries

1 海外致東華書信及電報
Correspondence to Tung Wah

2 柯打簿
Order Registry

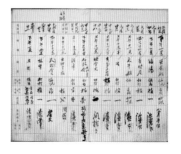

1934 年 3 月 16 日（16 March 1934）
檔案：外埠棺木骨殖提單及柯打登記簿（1932-1957）
Archive: Order Registry of overseas coffins (1932-1957)

骸骨乘搭亞東船到達香港日期為二月初三（即 3 月 16 日），由公壽長生店起上。
Carrying the deceased's bones, the *SS President Adams* arrived in Hong Kong on the 3rd day of the 2nd lunar month (16 March). The Kung Sau Funeral Service unloaded the bones.

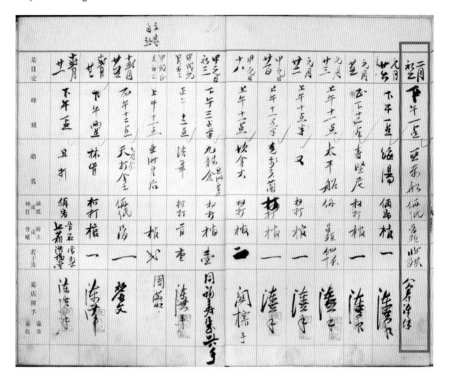

③ **中轉站——香港東華三院**
Transit point –Tung Wah Group of Hospitals of Hong Kong

1934 年 3 月 16 日（16 March 1934）
檔案：外埠棺骨入莊申請書
Archive: Admission Application Slip of overseas coffins and bones

公壽長生店向東華義莊遞上申請書，申請 251 具骸骨入莊紙。
Kung Sau Funeral Service submitted an application slip to apply for an admission permit for the bones to enter the coffin home.

4 中轉站——香港東華三院
Transit point –Tung Wah Group of Hospitals of Hong Kong

1934 年 3 月 21 日（21 March 1934）
檔案：東華致外界函件
Archive: Tung Wah's reply letter to sender

東華三院回覆暹京廣肇會館，確認骸骨已暫存義莊及收到葬費，並會通知商會領取。
Tung Wah Group of Hospitals replied to Kwong Siew Association confirming that the bones were temporarily stored in the coffin home and burial fees were received. Respective commercial associations would be informed to collect the bones.

（檔案原件模糊不清，附上文字版）
(The ink of the Chinese archive is fading, transcribed text is for reference)

公祺

廿三

三

廿一

　　　　東華醫院謹啟

暹京廣肇公學及廣肇醫院總辦事處

黃主席求標先生大鑒頃奉

大函稱由亞東船運囬先友骨殖二百五十

壹具及由香港榮豐行轉交敝院收港銀陸

百柒拾元一節經照收妥查

貴院運囬之先友骨殖二百五十壹具經于三

月十六號抵達香港已由敝院在亞東船起上

義莊停厝即通知各邑商會到來領取承委

每先友發給式元葬費其餘撥作工艇費敝院

自當遵照辦理特此函復希為

查照是荷此頌

5 中轉站——香港東華三院
Transit point –Tung Wah Group of Hospitals of Hong Kong

1934 年 3 月 26 日、5 月 19 日及 7 月 16 日
(26 March, 19 May and 16 July 1934)
檔案：外埠棺骨出莊保證書
Archives: Exit Guarantees of overseas coffins and bones

正心茶樓、香港台山商會及駐港中山僑商會分別擔保部分同鄉的骸骨回鄉安葬。最終在香港及家鄉未被認領的骸骨，東華及內地慈善團體分別把它們葬於當地義山，好讓先僑入土為安。
Ching Sum Restaurant, Hong Kong Toi Shan Association and Chung Shan Commercial Association of Hong Kong claimed the bones from Tung Wah. For those bones which were eventually unclaimed in Hong Kong and the deceased's hometown, Tung Wah and the deceased's respective charitable associations in mainland buried them in the free cemeteries in Hong Kong and China respectively so that the deceased could be laid to rest in peace.

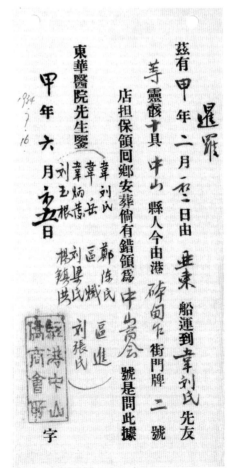

離鄉別井──海外
Leaving home - Overseas

美國加州昔日的華人小鎮
Former Chinese towns in California, USA

圖片集
Photo Album

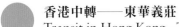

二十世紀中期的東華義莊
Tung Wah Coffin Home in the mid-20th century

東華義莊近貌
Recent view of Tung Wah Coffin Home

羅湖沙嶺的東華義塚
Tung Wah's free cemetery at Sandy Ridge Cemetery in Lowu

廣東新會金牛山義塚
Jinniushan Free Cemetery at Xinhui, Guangdong

落葉歸根，魂歸故里
—— 海外華僑骸骨的原籍安葬
（一八五○——一九四九）

譚金花博士
五邑大學廣東僑鄉文化研究中心副教授

簡介

五邑地區位於廣東省西南部，古屬百越地，秦漢時屬南海郡，南北朝設新會郡，隸屬封州，唐朝改封州為岡州，州治在今會城鎮，故新會又名岡州。新會郡轄下十二縣，其中包括現今五邑地區的新會、台山全境及開平、恩平、鶴山的部分地域，後台山、開平、恩平和鶴山相繼立縣。在北美和大洋洲的早期中國移民裏，以廣東人為主，而且大多是來自台山、開平、新會、恩平四縣的失業鄉民，因文化語言相通而自稱「四邑人」，成立「四邑會館」或「四邑公所」等團體，互相抱團取暖。十九世紀中「土客械鬥」的起始地鶴山始終未被列入四邑範疇（《新寧縣志》一八九三年版、《赤溪縣志》一九二○年版、《開平縣志》一九三三年版）。二十世紀八十年代開放改革之後，政府改編行政管轄地域，才把鶴山納入江門地區，連同新會、台山、開平、恩平四縣合稱「五邑」，始有今日五邑之行政分區。

鴉片戰爭後，清朝國力贏弱，割讓香港島給英國，廣州自此再不是中國唯一的對外通商口岸，不少原在廣州工作的五邑勞工失去謀生機會，位於丘陵地帶的五邑屬地人多地少，又逢天災，農業歉收；另一方面，以台山、開平、鶴山、佛山等地為主戰場的珠三角西南地區爆發了支援太平天國的「紅巾起義」，後逐漸發展為本地人與客家人之間的矛盾，發生了持續十多年的「土客械鬥」（一八五四—一八六七年），使本來就欠發達的四邑地區雪上加霜，民不聊生。而此時的中國，中英《南京條約》（一八四二年）和中美《望廈條約》（一八四四年）簽訂後，適逢殖民者開發東南亞和中中南美洲諸國，加上西方奴隸制度沒落，部分商人及種植園主遂轉向中國招募勞工；同時，北美（美國加州，一八四八年；加拿大卑詩省，一八五八年）和大洋洲（墨爾本，一八五一年；紐西蘭，一八六八年）發現金礦並迅速形成淘金熱，再逢美國、加拿大連貫東西大鐵路的修築。毗鄰香港、澳門縣份的破產鄉民遂出洋尋找機會，先後赴東南亞、中南美洲、北美洲、大洋洲等地謀生。繼各地的淘金潮之後，華僑勞工參加了中央太平洋鐵路（一八六三—一八六九年）、南太平洋鐵路（一八七三—一八八三年）、北太平洋鐵路（一八七〇—一八八三年）、加拿大太平洋鐵路（一八八一—一八八五年）等鐵路的建築。可以說，從十九世紀六十至九十年代，華工們成為了這些鐵路建設和運作的中堅力量（芭芭拉・沃斯，二〇一九）。

除了早期的淘金和鐵路建築，華僑在海外還開墾農田、種植蔬菜、從事漁業、洗衣業、雜貨業、或者當工廠工人、廚工、住家工人，以及經營唐人街的各種商業等。

對於五邑地區華僑出洋謀生的原因，一八九三年的台山《新寧縣志》有清楚的記載：「自紅匪客匪構亂後，適洋務大興，壯者輒走外國四野，為積小家，府畜維艱。」（清光緒九年《新寧縣志》卷八〈輿地略〉）

然而，因當時清朝政府贏弱，缺乏國際地位，華僑的文化習慣與居住國文化多有不同，加上華僑勤勞和負責任的特點贏得當地僱主的青睞，故華工的存在對當地的勞工市場產生威脅。十九世紀後期起，五邑華僑主要的旅居地——美國、加拿大、澳洲和紐西蘭等國相繼爆發排華暴動並最終形成排華法案；一八八二年美國頒發了排華法案（一八八二—一九四三年），是歷史上通過的第一部針對特定族群的歧視性移民法；加拿大於一八八五年鐵路完工之後，即以徵收「人頭稅」為由限制中國人入境，後於一九二四年再頒佈限制華工入境的移民條例（一九二四—

一九四七年）；十九世紀末澳洲和紐西蘭地區都以「語言測試」為由限制亞裔人群入境——要求凡是入境該國者，必須通過以任何一種歐洲語言讀一段話的測試，澳洲更於一九〇一年頒佈「白澳政策」（一九〇一—一九七二年），認為澳洲的土地是屬於白色人種居住的，從而限制有色人種入境。華僑面對的不但是在遠離家鄉的陌生文化環境裏受歧視，更重要的是，以其華工的身份，難以在居住國建立家庭，安心生活。

很多無法在當地落地生根的華僑都選擇回鄉下建立家庭，鄉下的父母妻子兒女，呼喚海外華僑把僑匯寄回家鄉；而在排華情緒高漲的外國，那種「無家」的感覺促使華僑們把積蓄帶回鄉建設家園，投資商業。在十九世紀末至二十世紀初的幾十年間，因僑匯的增多和海外華僑的建設熱情，五邑僑鄉社會發生巨變，逐漸形成富有地域色彩的「僑鄉」景觀——碉樓、洋樓、騎樓林立，新式學校和圖書館如雨後春筍般出現在鄉村之間，民智開啟；商業貿易興旺，水陸交通發達，來自國外省外的物資豐富，民居裏面更增添了抽水泵、馬桶、壁爐、浴缸、電話、汽車等進口設備（譚金花，二〇一三）。僑鄉社會也逐漸轉型，由原來極其依賴土地生活的農村封建社會，變成為以工商業為主、農業為輔的半封建社會。

在外國謀生的華僑們，失卻家庭照顧，生活孤單，唐人街的會館、公所、宗親會成為他們的家，他們互相照顧，鄰里關係密切。幸運者賺足盤纏可以返回中國享受家庭之樂，不幸者則客死異域。故唐人街的會館紛紛成立善堂，負責購買墳地，安排死者下葬，超度亡靈，待遺體化成骨殖後經特定的儀式再把骨殖送回原籍安葬，助其達成落葉歸根之夙願（葉漢明，二〇〇九；冼玉儀、劉潤和，二〇〇六）。百多年來，海外華僑都秉承把靈柩或者骸骨送回原籍安葬的傳統。自一八七〇年代始，香港東華醫院（於一八七〇年依法例成立，其後增加兩間醫院，至一九三一年三間醫院統一辦理，改稱「東華三院」）承擔接收海外骨殖的善舉。早期因為忌諱談論骨殖運送原籍歸葬的事情，海內外學者對於這個課題的研究較少，但近二十年來發生較大的改變，先是新會史家歐濟霖和美國舊金山州立大學譚雅倫教授等人對新會華僑義塚的研究，再是香港東華三院開放相關檔案，使香港及外國學者得以展開研究東華醫院及其義莊與華僑骨殖運歸原籍安葬這一聯動全球網絡的善舉。

一九九二年，新會縣在新會城郊建設圭峰高科技工業村的時候發現位於黃坑海槐的華僑義塚三百八十七穴，新會本地史家歐濟霖遂據此展開調查，在附近共發現六處華僑義塚，三千八百穴，始揭開華僑義塚的面紗（歐濟霖，一九九五、二〇〇一）。譚雅倫教授根據華僑在美國的生活經歷，對黃坑海槐的金山華僑義塚的資料展開研究，分析海外華僑骨殖回歸家鄉安葬的內因與外因（譚雅倫，二〇〇一）。

香港史專家高添強在〈喪葬服務與原籍安葬〉（載《益善行道——東華三院 135 周年紀念專題文集》）介紹了東華醫院的喪葬服務及東華義莊在接收、暫存和運送海外骨殖，助其回原籍安葬等方面的服務（高添強，二〇〇六）；歷史學家丁新豹博士在他的《善與人同——與香港同步成長的東華三院（一八七〇一九九七）》一書介紹了香港東華義莊的建立和在幫助海外華人骨殖原籍歸葬方面的服務（丁新豹，二〇一〇）；香港中文大學歷史系葉漢明教授在《東華義莊與寰球慈善網絡——檔案文獻資料的印證與啟示》一書中，以東華三院文物館館藏的歷史檔案和實地考察分析了這一善舉的全球網絡（葉漢明，二〇〇九）；香港大學香港人文社會研究所名譽教授冼玉儀在她的《穿梭太平洋：金山夢、華人出洋與香港的形成》（*Pacific Crossing: California Gold, Chinese Migration, and the Making of Hong Kong*）（Sinn, 2013）中，從南北行和金山莊商業網絡的角度，闡述香港在全球華僑貿易當中的地位及其國際物流網絡，從中帶出香港在全球骨殖運送過程中至關重要的地位（Sinn, 2013）；美國學者 Sue Fawn Chung 在她的《大洋兩岸：美籍華僑的隔離喪葬》（*An Ocean Apart: Chinese American Segregated Burials*）詳細記錄了早期美國的華僑社會如何對待在異域他鄉離世的華僑，以及如何處理骨殖和喪葬服務（Chung, 2019）。

上述的研究，讓我們看到了太平洋彼岸的喪葬服務，也看到了在根深蒂固的傳統文化影響之下骨殖運送回原籍安葬的全球網絡，以及香港東華醫院及東華義莊在幫助運送海外華僑骨殖回原籍歸葬的操辦，卻鮮有研究涉及骨殖從東華義莊運送回原籍安葬的過程，尤其骨殖運送至原籍保存、安葬的風俗習慣等。本文將聚焦於海外靈柩和骨殖在運送回鄉後安葬的情況，着力還原從海外臨時葬地撿骨，到香港東華義莊，再運送到鄉下安葬的整個過程。

傳統喪葬

一、喪葬觀念

對於喪葬傳統，古有土葬、水葬、天葬、火葬等，都是一種信仰，是寄託對死者的哀悼的方式，是一種社會文化現象，唯中國的傳統喪葬以土葬居多。

殷商時期，逐漸形成靈魂不滅之觀念，始有埋葬死者，並有儀式安撫靈魂，乃成土葬喪禮。

及至春秋時期，有了規範的喪禮禮儀——周禮之喪制，是帝王將相喪葬之禮。《周禮》、《儀禮》

及《禮記》記載的喪葬制度和禮儀規範為後世所沿襲。後世流行的葬前禮儀、五服制度、居喪守

孝、祭祀亡靈等喪禮，基本程式都出於「三禮」（《福建省志・民族志》，二〇一三）。

對於死，道家認為生老病死乃自然規律，是傳統生活的重要組成部分，須對死者致以極大的

尊重。儒家《論語》有「生，事之以禮；死，葬之以禮，祭之以禮」的教導。中國的土葬傳統一

向認為「人死為大，入土為安」，人死後埋入土中，死者方得安息，生者方覺心安。土葬成為了

中國最為普遍的殯葬傳統，源於根深蒂固的傳統文化思想。

首先，土葬與華夏民族的崇土文化息息相關。幾千年的農耕文化已經成為生命之本，將土地

深深烙印在人們的靈魂深處。女媧捏土造人的傳說也從另一個側面昭示了生命輪迴的軌跡——從

泥土中來，死後又回到泥土中去。這也符合萬物生死輪迴的自然之道。《禮記・祭義》子曰：「眾

生必死，死必歸土，此謂之鬼。骨肉斃於下，陰為野土。」漢韓嬰《韓詩外傳》曰：「人死曰鬼，

鬼者歸也。」精氣歸於天，肉歸於土。」

其次，土葬與傳統風水信仰有關。郭璞的風水經典《葬經》曰：「葬者，藏也，乘生氣也。」

夫陰陽之氣，噫而為風，升而為雲，降而為雨，行乎地中則為生氣。」《葬經》中的這些理論對

後世影響頗深。傳統風水認為，屍骨不入土，就不能接收大地中的生氣，因此入土才能完成輪迴。

再者，土葬與隆喪厚葬，香火永繼的觀念有關。古人相信靈魂不滅，土葬不但強調保護死者

遺體，更要保證逝者（包括遺體和靈魂）進入陰間後的生活舒適。於是便有一套約定俗成的禮儀程式去送喪、下葬和造墓等。

此外，土葬與傳統孝道有關。儒家孝道觀把送喪看成是盡孝的主要標誌之一，認為不入土，不厚葬就是不孝順，所謂「三綱五常，百善孝為先」。擇吉地埋葬遺體，既令靈魂得以安息，又可保佑子孫繁榮昌盛；若不擇風水而隨便埋葬，便被認為是罔顧禮法，視為不孝。勸善書《明心寶鑒》曰：「事死如生、事亡如存，孝之至也。」《論語》中曾子曰：「慎終追遠，民德歸厚矣。唯有入土，先人的骨血才能融入地脈，保佑子孫繁榮昌盛。」（陳淑君、陳華文，二○○八；王計生等，二○○二）

為了表達對逝者的哀傷之情及盡孝，居喪（或稱守孝、丁憂）是生者必須遵循的禮制。守孝三年的主張成為奠定中國倫理社會秩序的重要基礎之一。自先秦至清代的兩千多年間，居喪制度一直存在，官員為父母守孝而不能履職的事情常有發生。孝子須在墓旁搭茅廬守墓以表達久哀之意，近代以來，於墓廬居喪之舉已從簡，一些地方（如廣東潮汕地區）至今仍然保留在墓地旁邊建一小屋的風俗，象徵墓廬，以表孝意（高添強，二○一二）。

對於僑鄉或者海外華僑來說，「入土」有更深一層的含義，那就是為了安置回歸的靈魂。從陽界去到陰界的入口，視為「土」，它既是連接此岸與彼岸的中介，也是逝者靈魂的安居之所。如果不能把死者及早安葬，對死者未免殘忍，對生者也是一種折磨。因故百多年來，海外華人皆秉承傳統，竭力運送先友骸骨回原籍安葬。

二、二次葬俗

從已有的考古證據來看，關中地區的西安半坡文化遺址、中原地區鄭洛仰韶文化遺址、山東半島大汶口文化早期遺址和荊楚、百越等地區均有二次葬習俗，又稱「拾骨葬」（《新華網》，二○○七年五月九日、二○○七年十一月十日；丁蘭蘭，二○○八；王文艷，二○一○；廣東省博物館，一九七八）。

根據著名的民族學學者凌純聲的研究，二次葬並不是漢族所固有，而是環太平洋原始民族中普遍存在的一種文化特質，廣及中國大陸的中原及東南沿海（包括台灣）各省的漢人、壯族、藏族等少數民族、東南和東北亞洲、南太平洋諸島、以及南北美洲，最遠可達到非洲東部的馬達加斯加。他認為，整個洗骨文化圈裏諸民族所採行的洗骨文化，基本上來自相同起源的一個文化習俗，而這個習俗最早的起源地是古百越族所分佈的華南地區（凌純聲，一九七九）。

最早有相關文字記載是戰國時期的《墨子》卷六〈節葬下〉：「楚之南有炎人國，其親戚死，朽其肉而棄之，然後理其骨，乃成為孝子。」此外，《隋書》卷三十一〈地理志下〉，也曾記載過荊州地區土人的二次葬習俗，「始死，即出屍於中庭，不留室內。斂畢，送至山中，以十三年為限。先擇吉日，改入小棺，謂之拾骨。」明末清初學者顧炎武在其《天下郡國利病書》卷一百〈廣東四〉一書中，記錄了明代粵北人「死三日則權厝之中土，三年後取遺骸為墳葬之」；清代興梅客家地區亦如是「俗父母葬十年皆議改葬。改葬者以罌易棺，撿骨而置之」。

對於二次葬俗形成的歷史與流行的原因及其原始意義，法國人類學家列維．布留爾從原始思維的角度出發，認為是原始人的二次死亡觀，是一種生命的過渡儀式。他認為二次葬儀式的目的在於徹底斷絕死者與社會集體生活的互滲與聯繫。這個終結儀式（二次葬）使死完成，成為完全意義上的死，也就是說，當這一終結儀式結束喪期時，死者與他生前所屬的社會集體的關係就徹底斷絕了，從而成為完全的死（列維·布留爾，一九八五）。

上海著名民族學家仲富蘭教授從風俗文化與信仰的角度進行分析，他認為有的是因死者客死他鄉，遂就地瘞之，待適當時機遷回故里重新安葬，所謂「葉落歸根」；有的是人亡既葬之後，其子孫中有發跡者，遂再行厚葬，所謂「光宗耀祖」；有的是夫妻一方先亡，後需移骨合葬，所謂「生則同衾，死則同穴」；有的是受風水迷信的影響，擇風水寶地重葬祖先，可佑子孫發達（仲富蘭，二○一二）。

二次葬俗在嶺南各地甚為常見，至今依然盛行。與古代相比，嶺南地區現存的二次葬風俗沒有太大變化。在親人死後，將其屍體連同棺木埋入土中，三、五、七年（甚至十數年）之後，待其屍體腐朽，再拾骨（廣東珠三角稱「撿骨」、「執骨」或「撿金」、「執金」）重葬。

拾骨由死者親屬和有經驗的村中老人共同完成。搭棚遮光，先把骨頭按從頭到腳的順序從棺木中取出，用白酒、草紙、碎布等物將屍骨擦洗乾淨，焚香烘乾。再按從腳到頭的順序放入陶甕（廣東人叫「金甕」、「金埕」或「金塔」）中立式貯存，按人體骨格結構自下而上將骸骨放置於陶甕中，整副骨架形如蹲坐狀。陶甕內除骸骨外，沒有其它隨葬品，甕蓋內蓋用毛筆寫上死者姓名和生卒年月，封蓋之前有「睇金」儀式——死者的後代一同到場瞻仰骸骨——意謂與死者見最後一面。密封後擇吉時拿到預先擇好的風水地點下葬，搬遷陶甕下葬的過程皆用黑傘遮蓋。這一過程在廣東珠三角風俗中稱為「望風水」（根據開平風水師譚卓勇的採訪，二○一八年十一月二十日）。

此後，每年清明掃墓拜祭。

關於「墳」與「墓」的稱謂，古時稱築土為墳，穴地為墓；又說墓之封土成丘者為墳，平者為墓，通稱「墳墓」（《辭海》，一九七八：五二九、六○四）。然而，傳統上廣東珠三角地區認為第一次葬之簡易土堆為「墳」，無碑；第二次葬的永久風水穴地視為「墓」，立碑。

清明掃墓，是對祖先的「思時之敬」。其習俗由來已久，五邑地區習慣於清明當日去拜祭簡易無碑盛行（張醜平，二○○六）。廣東各地掃墓習慣不一，秦朝之後逐漸形成習慣，至唐朝始的土堆（第一次葬）──「墳」，而於清明節前的一個月根據各家時間去拜祭立了碑的永久風水穴地（第二次葬）──「墓」。

一、移民情況

歷史上唐宋時期，中國南方諸省屬地皆有華僑出洋短期經商，惟鴉片戰爭後，適逢西方殖民者在東南亞和中南美洲開發，始有大量勞工往海外謀生。根據大清律例，擅自出國謀生視為違法。

但是西方殖民者開發東南亞和中南美洲需要大量勞動力，當時適逢奴隸制度末落，華僑勞工被捲入勞工移民的大潮。鴉片戰爭後中英簽訂的《南京條約》就有條款准許英國公司到中國招募勞工，使中國勞工出洋成為合法，當時東南亞諸島、英屬哥倫比亞（加拿大卑詩省）、澳洲維多利亞、紐西蘭等地都是大英帝國的殖民地，英國的條例也適用於這些地方。一八六八年清政府與美國政府簽訂的《蒲安臣條約》使兩國公民有權自由移民，中國勞工移民美國的大門比之前更加敞開。

早期赴外洋謀生的華僑，基於對祖籍文化及自我身份的認同，自稱「唐人」，稱其寓居之地為「唐人街」，稱其家鄉祖籍地為「唐山」，稱回國為「旋唐」，稱他們所說之鄉音為「唐話」。早期赴外募工的華僑，以男性為主，缺乏家庭支持，為求自保和互助，皆聚集而居，形成大小不一的「唐人街」。唐人事務，大至對政治排華的駁斥及權益討訴，小至日常生活中的柴米油鹽，皆以唐人街為中心尋求解決。唐人街的公所與會館成為了華僑們名副其實的「家」。

二、東南亞

移居東南亞的華僑大多來自閩南、粵北與梅客家地區、潮州、廣府和海南等地，華僑在此地的居住歷史長，自唐宋以來即有華僑至南洋經商，有些華僑甚至在十六世紀西方殖民者開發東南亞的時候就參與其中，華僑從事採礦、橡膠種植、商業等不同行業，至一九二○年代，在東南亞英屬海峽殖民地和馬來半島的華僑人口超過一百萬，達到一百五十五萬三千一百三十七人（陳達，二○一一：六五）。東南亞地區以閩南人、客家人和潮汕人為主，華僑在東南亞的歷史長，他們的出海港為廈門和汕頭，相對來說，受西方文化的影響較少，更重要的是，他們文化影響大，們在土著和西方殖民者之間處於中間人的地位，當地未形成法律上的大規模排華現象，故不少華僑可以在當地成家立室，更可擁有自己的產業和開辦生意，在家鄉和海外保持兩頭家的現象較為普遍（李恩涵，二〇一五）。

三、古巴及秘魯

華僑赴中南美洲當勞工肇始於鴉片戰爭前後西方殖民者對於中南美洲的開發，古巴和秘魯勞動力短缺，奴隸買賣暗中進行。華僑於一八三九年開始踏足古巴，一八四七年第一批來自廈門的契約勞工（俗稱「豬仔華工」）二百一十二名到達夏灣拿，一八四九年第一批來自澳門的七十五名契約勞工到達秘魯。隨着奴隸制度的終結，華工直到十九世紀末成為了中南美洲甘蔗園和鳥糞礦開採的主要勞動力，此外，他們還參與咖啡業、工廠業、建造業和礦業、鐵路修築等工作。此後三十年，超過十四萬華僑到達古巴，十萬人到秘魯，大約百分之九十五是來自廣東地區，並且幾乎全是男性。

經歷過奴隸待遇的古巴華工，從一八六八年起後的三十年，積極參與古巴獨立戰爭當中。有兩三千名華僑義勇軍參加過戰鬥和將近五千人參加後方的後勤工作。對於華僑參戰的歷史，古巴獨立紀念功碑座銅牌如此銘記：「沒有一個古巴華僑逃兵，沒有一個叛變的古巴華僑。」（龐炳庵，二〇一三；楊安堯，二〇〇〇：四七—五三；Narvaez, 2010: 52,78）

四、美國

普遍認為華僑「移民」美國最早在一七八五年，美國人奧多奈爾（John O'Donnell）招募了三十二名印度以及四名中國水手，搭乘美國商船「帕拉斯號」（Pallas）抵達馬利蘭州的巴爾的摩，首次將亞洲貨品輸送到美國（Chin, 2015）。較大的移民潮始於十九世紀五十年代，一八四八年美國加利福尼亞州（以下簡稱加州）發現金礦的消息傳到珠三角，大量華僑湧加入淘金熱潮，此為第一波移民潮；一八六三至一八六九年美國修築中央太平洋鐵路需要大量勞工，掀起第二波移民潮，約有一萬二千至一萬五千華工參與了鐵路的建築；一八六八年《蒲安臣條約》簽訂之後，大量華僑移民湧入美國，從事鐵路建築、採礦、開墾農田、種植果蔬、漁業、洗衣、餐飲等行業，至一八七〇年代，在美華僑約十五萬（唐人街會館的統計數字為十五萬一千三百人，美國政府的人口統計是十萬七千四百八十八人）。一八八二年通過的排華法案對華工諸多限制——不能與美國籍民結婚，不能擁有財產等等，不少唐人街甚至產生排華暴動，兩萬多名在回美國路上的華工被拒絕入境。一九〇六年三藩市地震大火燒毀移民局檔案後，很多華僑虛報自己為籍民，從而獲得申請籍民兒子赴美的資格，更有一些華僑把虛報的出生證明（當地人稱「出生紙」）賣予其他家庭，以「紙兒子」（當地人稱「紙生仔」）的身份移民。惟此舉受到美國政府懷疑，自一九一〇年開始設天使島移民拘留所審查入境的移民，十七萬五千名華僑在此經歷過難堪的審訊。到一九三〇年，華人人口保持在十萬人左右（美國人口普查資料為十萬二千一百五十九人）。男女比例差距極大，唐人街一度被認為是「寡佬社會」（劉伯驥，據墨爾本澳華博物館資料，華僑移民澳洲的歷史可追溯至一八一〇年代，廣州木匠馬世英於一八一八年抵達悉尼，成為第一個到達澳洲的華僑。此後，第一批移民是契約勞工，廣東來的三千名契約華工（一八四八——一八五三年），因牧羊業發達，新南威爾士殖民政府僱用了從福建和廣東來的三千名契約華工；第二批是淘金工人（一八五一——一八七七年），一八五一年維多利亞發現金礦，福建和廣東的華僑聞訊蜂擁而至，尤以廣東四邑（台山、開平、新會、恩平）、中山、三邑（南海、番禺、順德）人居多，一八五七年墨爾本地區淘金的華僑達到二萬四千零六十二人，一八九〇年在澳華僑大約四萬九千人，九成來自台山、開平、新會、恩平四個縣，大多從事礦業、種植業、漁業和木工傢俬製造等職業。一八八〇年代殖民地時期至一九〇一年澳洲聯邦時期排華較為嚴重，為了限制華僑入境，一九〇一年澳洲第一屆聯邦議會通過立法，頒佈排華法例「白澳政策」，要求所有移民必須通過任何一種歐洲語言五十個詞的聽寫測試後才能入境。此政策很成功，沒有任何一個中國勞工可以通過語言測試而入境。澳洲的華僑人口自此減少，當年約為二萬九千人（亨利‧簡斯頓，二〇一〇；Price, 1987: 176）。

五、澳洲

一九七六；Chinn, 1969: 20; U.S. Census Data, 1840-2010, Amanik and Fletcher, 2019: 7-10）。

六、加拿大

一七八八年澳門來的一群中國木工跟隨一名叫詹姆斯·梅爾斯的英國海軍船長在英屬哥倫比亞西岸登陸，此為華人首次踏足加拿大的土地（Ma and Cartier, 2003）。一八五八年，在英屬哥倫比亞湯普遜河（Thompson River）發現金礦的第二年，時在加州淘金的華僑聽到消息就跨過邊界到菲沙河谷一帶淘金，在加里布山谷的巴克維爾淘金區有一半的淘金者為華僑，周邊的淘金小鎮也有規模不小的唐人街，包括里奇菲爾德、史坦萊、范溫克爾、奎內爾、安特勒、奎內爾·佛斯等小鎮，此為第一批華僑移民潮（Skelton, 1980）。

一八八一至一八八五年的加拿大太平洋鐵路的建築工程招募了大約一萬五千至一萬七千名華僑勞工，此為第二批華僑移民潮。與美國中央太平洋鐵路的情況一樣，華僑負責加拿大太平洋鐵路中最艱巨的一段，在建設艱險的洛磯山脈路段時，約共四千名華僑失去生命。淘金熱和鐵路建設之後，華僑基本上從事種植業、漁業、洗衣、餐飲等行業。鐵路於一八八五年建設完工。同年，加拿大政府開始限制華僑入境，向華僑徵收入境「人頭稅」五十加幣、一九〇〇年增至一百加幣、一九〇三年增至五百加幣。一九二三年更通過「中國移民法案」，禁止華僑勞工入境（學生、外交人員和特許人員除外）（Chow, 2014；黎全恩，二〇一三）。在工作上也排斥華人，一八九〇年溫哥華市政府在批准提供資金給予卑詩煉糖廠時列明，資金和土地是市長連同市議會協助設立該糖廠的優惠方式，條件是該公司於任何時間不得僱用任何華裔勞工在上述糖廠工作或從事糖廠相關的工作（Yu, 2018: 43）。

綜上所述，大部分近代海外華工隻身出外謀生，在異域生活缺乏家庭溫暖，不但工作艱苦，更重要的是文化差異，語言障礙，所在國的排華情緒高漲，國內親人的苦等與呼喚，使他們的思鄉之情倍增，落葉歸根的思想尤為明顯。因此，若華僑客死異鄉，皆希望自己的骸骨可以回歸原籍安葬，讓靈魂得以安息，而生者也盡力助其達成夙願。根據故鄉二次葬的風俗，早期在外域去世的華工，一般由其鄉親進行簡單的埋葬，待到一定的年限再起骨並送回原籍永久安葬。否則，他們擔心會淪為無人拜祭的孤魂野鬼。

　　自先僑開始執骨運回原籍安葬至一九四九年中華人民共和國成立禁止了這一傳統，無法統計共有多少副骨頭被運回中國，當年幾乎凡是有華僑居住的地方，都有這一習俗。有報道稱僅一九一三那一年，便有超過一萬箱骸骨運離美國（Sinn, 2013: 268）。

　　百年後旅居加拿大維多利亞的番禺籍楊鏡初先生曾寫詩緬懷那些客死他鄉的築路華工，依然擔心那些無法返鄉的孤魂：

應聘華工遠道來，
築修鐵路貫東西。
維亞修成秋後扇，
妒疑異己盡排擠。
累年受食寒林下，
遠寄孤魂怎返鄉。

清明重九無祭掃，

異地無親倍悲傷。

（楊鏡初，一九九七：六〇）

七、執骨背景

在西方文化圈，墳場通常指死者遺體、遺物、骸骨或者骨灰埋葬的地方，多為管理處規劃好的穴位，按照固定排位下葬。一九四九年以前的中國民間，傳統禮俗是民間生活的重要部分，二次葬俗依然盛行，所有的墓地都是風水先生經過翻山越嶺多方尋找所得，以其風水點為墓穴位置，有時上下左右稍微偏離都有可能偏離風水位，最多是包含家庭成員在內的家族墓園，並未出現大規模群葬的現代墳場的概念。

八、會館及善堂

華僑以勞工身份大量赴外洋謀生，始到東南亞，再到其他地區。這些勞工大部分是單身寡佬，缺乏家庭溫暖，於是他們很快就用中國鄉村社會的傳統禮教和宗族制度建立起海外華僑社會的秩序網絡——採用明清時期都市盛行的以同鄉或者同業為基礎組成不同的團體。他們以原籍地為基礎設立同鄉性質的「會館」，以同姓家族為基礎設立宗親性質的「公所」，以行業為基礎而設立互助性質的「堂」。在會館內或者一些較大的公所，設立善堂專門處理原籍先友的骸骨撿運和安撫家屬等，這些組織管理嚴密，互相交錯，管理唐人街的社會秩序。廣東台山籍曹亞志（又名曹亞珠），曾在澳門當木匠，後到馬來半島謀生，於一八一九年在新加坡創建他的家族組織——公所，是海外華僑最早建立的以血緣為紐帶的組織。一八二二年他又建立新加坡甯陽會館，是海外華僑最早建立的以地緣為基礎的會館組織。對於公所和會館的功能，其紀錄稱「曹家自東而西由南而北，足跡所經不止美利堅屬之地。遠至英屬島多里，無墓不查，有報皆執。凡番邑先梓，岡使或遺焉。若遇未化之屍，內用鉛箱罐、外用木箱妥裝封固。至於因溺水葬身魚腹，或被害而埋沒其屍，及瘞於僻靜之處，屍經番人盜去用為藥餌，或暨有墳而失去墓簽，追尋未獲者，皆歸招魂箱，用銀牌書其名，一同運返。」（余定邦，一九八七：八）

關於「番人盜墓」的報道，在美國的報紙裏也時有報道，一九〇八年的《西雅圖之星》警告買假髮的人，稱假髮可能是從華人墓地裏盜用他們的長辮製作的（*The Seattle Star*, July 27, 1908）。因此，華人對於死後墓地安全的擔憂更能直接體現會館和公所成立善堂撿運骸骨的迫切性。

廣東人在一八四〇至一八五〇年代開始大批赴北美和大洋洲謀生，此後幾年間，便形成了以會館、公所、堂為基本社會秩序網絡的三藩市唐人街，稍後形成的其他唐人街的社會管理秩序也相類似。

各大會館視喪葬管理為重要之事，大多專門成立「善堂」，負責幫助老而窮者回鄉終老、管理喪葬事務、安撫家屬、執骨送歸原籍安葬、墳場墓地等事務。一八八二至一八八六年駐三藩市總領事黃遵憲呈送給中國駐美公使鄭藻如的一份稟文對此曾有描述：

（黃遵憲，二〇〇三：五二〇）

善堂以慈善為懷，以幫助僑居海外的梓里葉落歸根為其主要目的。故其功能有二；一是撿運先人骸骨，二是盡可能幫助貧窮的華僑會員，根據會員部的紀錄，審查屬實後，資助船費，助其回鄉終老的夙願。

九、海外墳場

華僑身故後的喪禮和多年後執骨運回原籍安葬等事務，皆由會館和善堂處理。華僑向來重視死後「下輩子」的造化，重視死後的埋葬地，重視死後的骸骨和靈魂是否可以葉落歸根回到自己的家鄉，他們最大的希望是以後每年清明皆有後子孫後代前來敬奉，而不至於成為無人拜祭的孤魂野鬼。墳場是死後的埋葬地，哪怕是短暫的第一次葬，也是極為重要的臨時安息地。如果能夠，海外墳場多選擇建在海邊或可以仰望大海的地方，其祭壇和香爐面向大海的方向——那是太平洋對岸的家鄉。

一些早期華僑墳場建有「敬如在」或者「伯公」神位拜祭亡靈和供奉土地神，而由會館善堂購買的墳場則有由善堂設立的拜壇和焚香爐，每年春秋二祭，必有善堂組織會員到場拜祭先友。在排華情緒高漲的年代，找一塊地做墳場並不容易，歧視華僑的行徑十分明顯，更有地方法例的限制。白人不相信另一個世界的精神和活着的人之間有很強的聯繫。他們的墳場往往是以宗教信仰為藉口與華僑墓地隔離，也有些兄弟團體拒絕將埋葬空間分配給「異教徒中國人」。即使有些華僑成功地購進了某個當地人的墳場，但也常會被降級，他們習慣把當地白人和華僑的墓地隔開為不同的部分。大多數白人墓地不埋葬華僑，唯一的例外就算那些忠心耿耿的中國僕人可能與白人家人一起葬在他們的私人公墓裏。一般的華僑都支付不起用藥水處理屍體再連同棺材運送回鄉的費用，故他們必須選擇在隔離墳場或華僑墳場進行臨時埋葬，然後數年後撿運回中國作永久埋葬。

靠近華僑聚居城市的華僑墳場，常常出現因為人多而墳場空間不夠的情況，以三藩市台山寗陽餘慶堂公墓和其他地方聯合購置的六山墳場為例，他們就在入口處設置一塊空地作為臨時埋葬用地，常常需要在三、五年的時間進行起骨，以騰出空間給後來者。挖出的骸骨用箱處理好，存放在墳場內專門用於存儲骸骨的小屋中，等待運送回國。

雖然回家鄉安葬是當時公認的習俗，但也有小部分美國化的、有家庭後代在美國的人，希望被安葬在美國，這是因為他們覺得美國是他們的家，因為他們的後代和親人生活在美國。

一八九六年，The San Francisco Call 報道了一則另類的新聞：一名叫「余阿太」的華僑願意長眠在美國這片土地（"His Bones to Lie in This Land." *The San Francisco Call*, June 14, 1896）。

在一些沒有那麼歧視華僑的小埠地區，華僑及其他少數族裔都可以在當地的公墓裏埋葬，因為當地的公墓是所有居民的最後安息地。十九世紀七十年代的貝克斯菲爾德（Bakersfield）便是其中之一（Amanik and Fletcher, 2019: 28）。

執骨歸葬耗費巨大，工作繁重，向以美國三藩市和加拿大卑詩省的域多利（維多利亞）為主要的骸骨集中地，統一組織運送。筆者以三藩市唐人街喪葬的管理架構為例，簡單梳理會館與善堂之間的關係如下：

甯陽會館人數眾多，財力雄厚，故他們有能力購買地塊建成甯陽會館「餘慶堂墳場」，專門服務台山梓里，其餘六大會館的華僑共同購買地塊，建成「六山墳場」，安葬除台山甯陽會館之外的六大會館的梓里，這些墳場的運作都有專人負責，而善堂主要負責與執骨、運送原籍相關的事務。對於那些不屬於任何地區會館或姓氏公所的人、或是位於郊區小埠，當地沒有地緣會館和血緣公所可以加入的人，不在此列（他們一般會加入到當地的洪門堂或協勝堂、合勝堂、致公堂、萃勝堂、安良堂等堂口，這些堂口也有為會員撿運骸骨的服務）。

以上會館善堂及其墳場分配的關係列表如下：

三藩市華僑主要會館及善堂列表（一八四九──一九四九年）

成立時間	會館名稱	組成地區	善堂名稱	墳場名稱
一八四九	四邑會館	台山、新會、開平、恩平（一八五四年後更名為新會鶴山為主的岡州會館）		
一八五〇	三邑會館	南海、番禺、順德	南海福陰堂、順德行（恒）安堂、番禺昌後堂	六山墳場
一八五〇	人和會館	寶安、惠陽、梅縣、赤溪的客家人	不設專門處理喪葬事務的善堂	六山墳場
一八五二	陽和會館	香山（中山）、東莞、增城、博羅	同善堂、積善堂、喜善堂、敦善堂、集善堂、歸善堂、德善堂、良善堂、樂善堂、博善堂、義安堂、東莞寶安堂、增城仁安堂	六山墳場
一八五四	甯陽會館	台山	甯陽餘慶堂	餘慶堂墳場
一八五四	岡州會館	新會，鶴山	新會福慶堂、同德堂、鶴山德厚堂	六山墳場
一八六二	合和會館	台山余姓與開平的鄧、謝、胡、朱、潘、利、區及恩平的鄭姓	廣福堂	六山墳場
一八七六	肇慶會館	開平、恩平	廣福堂	六山墳場

十、撿運過程

一八四八年美國加州發現金礦，淘金熱吸引大批華人到北美謀生。一八五三年開始，四邑會館開始為故去的同鄉好友執骨並運送回原籍安葬（劉伯驥，一九七六：一六五）。一八五五年七月二十二日香港《德臣西報》（*The China Mail*）的一則小新聞報道了從美國三藩市運來的一批特別貨物——九十四箱華人骸骨（高添強，二〇〇六：一〇二；葉漢明，二〇〇九：二三）。

加州關於華人骸骨撿運的早期新聞見報於一八五八年一月六日的《加利福尼亞阿爾塔日報》（*Daily Alta California*），稱「華人掘坑把裏面的骸骨挖出並運送回中國」。三藩市三邑會館下轄的善堂——番禺昌後堂也於咸豐八年（一八五八年）開始組織人力，籌措資金，啟動撿運工作。約七至十年左右撿運一次，現存歷屆《金山昌後堂徵信錄》，詳細記載撿運的過程，如資金籌措，執骨過程的複雜與困難等。該邑僑梓在香港成立繼善堂，負責從香港運送骸骨回番禺原籍安葬（加州軒佛三邑會館檔案）。

（一）資費籌措

善堂的款項，主要依賴邑人的捐助和自籌置業以幫補。費用的主要支出在三方面：到各處執骨的費用，骨箱運回香港的運費，給家屬的安葬費。當時一個骨箱的運費大約為五美元，外加十美元的衞生費，給家屬的安葬費從五至十美元不等（譚雅倫，二〇〇一：V3-2）。到了一八六〇至一八七〇年代，骸骨的「船票」升至二十美元一副（Sinn, 2013: 268）。會館和善堂的運作費用皆來源於會員的會費或者特別因執骨撿運而發起的針對性捐助。捐資者都能拿到一張收費票據——俗稱「出港票」（還有其他形式的捐款也可以充當出港票），意謂華僑出港乘坐輪船回中國的時候，用於上船的通行憑據。各個會館為了保障能夠有足夠的費用來妥善處理骸骨原籍安葬，以及贊助老而窮的同鄉回國的船費，故有點強制性地要求會員繳交會費或者捐助執骨費用。會館有人在上船處設卡檢查，持有「出港票」方能通行，若無繳費票據，則日後不幸身故，也不予執骨回鄉。

撿運費用異常昂貴，以番禺昌後堂為例，一八六三年的徵信錄記載第一次撿運總經費為二萬五百元，撿運靈柩二百五十八副，另招魂湮沒者五十九名，每柩附派葬金七元，特委四人隨船護送；一八七六年的第二次的撿運費用為四萬多，運靈柩八百五十八具，另招魂箱二十四個，每給葬金銀十美元（《金山昌後堂徵信錄》，一八六三年、一八七六年）。如此昂貴的運作經費，若非有強大而妥善的組織，以及普遍認同的文化觀和價值觀，絕非容易之事。

撿運過程中，一般都公推有負責任而有誠信的本邑人擔任「撿」與「運」的專員進行催收督撿。這些專人需長途跋涉赴各埠催收捐款，登記發票予捐助者。能否順利完成執骨，有賴於當時的捐助，時多時少。故一般都有嚴格的記帳部，並發給捐助者票據，對於不捐資者，則其死後不予撿運，此舉可以保證有足夠的籌款撿運——生者捐資是為了幫助他人，也為自己死後有人幫忙撿運。

除卻每屆執骨都派專人赴各埠向梓里催收捐資外，值理執事者也考慮投資物業來幫補支敷。不少善堂都在唐人街或者香港、中國鄉下等地置業，所得利息用以幫補將來執骨之需。

（二）執骨過程

善堂公選催收督撿運的專人，僱仵工執骨。凡從各埠上報至善堂者，皆盡力赴該處尋找骸骨。在加拿大還沒有開始撿運業務之前，他們的足跡甚至到達後來才納入加拿大版圖的英屬哥倫比亞域多利地區。因為執骨是極為嚴肅的事情，故在僱人執骨之前，會館從一開始就草擬了執骨的要求讓仵工去執行。按照人體從頭到腳的順序進行撿拾，並描述各骨的特點和要求，悉數收回。

一八六七年五月二十三日墨爾本的《阿德雷德畫報》報道了一個名為坎德爾的白人講述他跟四個中國人朋友在本迪戈外面的白山公墓一起執骨的過程：

先拿頭骨，然後是椎骨，肋骨，最後是手骨，腳骨。聚集墳墓周圍的十幾個華僑非常認真地細數着那些骨頭，很高興地看到骨頭一塊都沒丟——即使是一顆牙齒也不能遺漏，每一顆牙齒都要牢固地固定在頜上。然後腿和腳被取出來。在移骨架的整個過程中，有一對華僑夫婦在忙碌地擦拭骨頭，把它們擺放在適當的位置，然後在陽光下攤開，那些手、腳等骨頭一曬乾就放進不同的包裹裏捆紮起來，並貼上標籤。整個骨架被放在一個大約一點二米長的小長方形箱子裏。

事實上，並不是所有死者都有下葬的墳墓寄存屍體；並不是所有的墳頭墓碑都保存完好，清

（艾瑞克‧羅斯，二〇〇九：二六五—二六六）

晰辨認；若能覓得墓碑確認骸骨者，則裝箱並清晰記錄死者姓名地址；因種種原由未能尋得骸骨而知其底細者，則全部招其魂魄進箱，一同送回原籍。

為了處理好撿運工作和杜絕貪污，善堂對執骨工有種種要求。因嚴格賬務管理而謝絕本邑人充擔。昌後堂光緒四年歲次戊寅善後章程第八條規定「凡遇興工檢〔撿〕運之時，本邑人不能承接檢〔撿〕運工頭，如有外邑接辦人而暗入本邑人份子者，倘有確據查出，外內每罰銀一千元，例在必行，決不寬恕」（光緒四年歲次戊寅善後章程：一八七八）。

（三）運回原籍

在北美，美國的三藩市和加拿大的域多利（維多利亞）兩個唐人街的會館負責把骸骨收集並組織運送回香港。約每隔七至十年左右運送一次。人口眾多的會館善堂（如甯陽會館餘慶堂）可以自行組織撿運，一些小眾的會館只能付費托鄰近縣份的善堂幫忙，以客家人為主的三藩市人和會館便沒有設善堂。也有一些華僑不是很多的地方，則多個善堂聯合撿運。在搬運骸骨箱下船之前的工作也非常細緻，記錄好所有死者的名單和骨箱，絕不馬虎。一八六四年八月二十日馬克·吐溫在他供職的報紙《三藩市早報》（*San Francisco Daily Morning Call*）報道了他在甯陽會館所看到的處理骨殖運送的情況：

在太平洋沿岸的中國人都屬於一個或多個公司或者組織，這些公司有會員的資料，他們的花名冊，並且負責在他們死後運送回國。四邑公司是其中最大者，甯陽公司緊跟其後，擁有會員一萬八千名。甯陽的總部設在三藩市，有一個不錯的廟宇，數位管理人，幾位神職人員（仵工）。在那裏我看到了會員花名冊，有死者的名單和運送回國日期等資訊。

（《三藩市早報》，筆者譯）

華僑於一八六三年至一八六九年參與建築的中央太平洋鐵路段位於加州沙加緬度與內華達州鹽湖城之間，是美國橫貫大陸鐵路建築當中最艱險的路段，死傷甚眾。鐵路建設過程中死去的華工的骸骨的運送情況也時有報道：

一八七〇年一月五日內華達州埃爾科的地方報紙 Elko Independent 報道有六卡車的華僑骸骨運往三藩市；同年三月，內華達州溫尼馬卡的《銀州報》（Silver State）報道說兩輛華僑殯葬車在橋街過境點附近，為死者回歸家鄉做準備。他們把骸骨裝箱，並標上死者的名字、死亡日期及其所屬的會館，然後通過三藩市運往香港；同年六月三十日，加州沙加緬度的當地報紙 Sacramento Reporter 報道了約有二萬磅骸骨（估計為一千二百名華僑死者或者十分之一華工）正在運往中國。

（Amanik and Fletcher, 2019: 8-9，筆者譯）

對於運送骸骨到香港的旅程，番禺昌後堂一般都派專人全程護送到埠並負責聯繫香港負責人，接洽轉運回鄉，其中旅費，均由善堂支付。另外，根據當年善堂所收捐款情況而酌情撥付每副骸骨約五至十元葬費。護送專人還負責骸骨到達家鄉後的安葬事宜——請法師（喃嘸佬）到場進行超度亡靈的法事。然後把骸骨放在當地的義莊或者善堂、方便醫院等地方，等候家屬前來領取回鄉下葬，讓亡靈安息。對於未有家屬前來領取的骸骨，則由海外的善堂組織建設義塚（或稱義山、義墳等）統一安葬，每年拜祭（光緒四年昌後堂檢〔撿〕運章程）。

如果撇開華人的喪葬信仰而從商業的角度來看待原籍安葬，華人屍骨運送至香港也是一項不錯的生意。美國的衛生局和船運公司都從自己的角度去把握這個賺錢的商機。一九○○年三藩市的 *The San Francisco Call* 報紙稱將「魚骨」運往中國成為當地一個重要的產業，當地衛生局向運送骸骨至香港的華人徵收每具骸骨十美元的稅金，但華人為了逃稅，與船務經理合謀串通，謊稱運往香港的骸骨為「魚骨」而免稅（*The San Francisco Call*, April 20, 1900）。一九一一年美國檀香山的《太平洋商業廣告》報紙刊登了一則以優惠價格運送華人屍骨回香港的廣告，稱運送「白人屍體需要二百三十美元一具，而故去一年內的華人屍體為五十五美元一具，一年以上的為三十五美元一具」（Makes A Low Rate For Chinese Corpses, The Pacific Commercial Advertiser, May 27, 1911）。

香港中轉

一、香港角色

第一次鴉片戰爭後，香港於一八四一年開埠成為英國的殖民地，同年實行自由港政策，港英政府以其便利的航運優勢，致力於建立一個貿易自由、投資便利、金融開放、人員進出自由的自由港。

一八四八年美國發現金礦的消息經香港傳到珠三角，失業農民開始湧去淘金，當年香港船政廳即開通香港至美洲的海上航線，第二年便有二十三艘輪船開往三藩市；一八五二年的政府報告稱該年經香港往三藩市的華僑不下三萬人，而其時的香港總人口只有三萬九千人（高添強，二〇〇六：一〇二），與此同時，還有不少華僑經香港前往東南亞諸島，以及一八五一年發現金礦的澳洲墨爾本本地區；一八六〇年，進出香港的輪船達到二千八百八十八艘（丁新豹，二〇一〇：一八），增長速度極其驚人。一八七七年，由香港開往以珠三角為主的廣東各地的註冊民船達到一百二十一艘（高添強，二〇〇六：一一三）。因為毗鄰廣東的地理優勢和航運發達的交通優勢，香港逐漸成為了珠三角尤其是五邑地區華僑出洋謀生及從海外回歸家鄉的中轉站，同時建立起香港與珠三角內陸河道的交通網絡、以香港為中轉地的南北行和金山莊等商業網絡（Sinn, 2013: 297-304）。

東華醫院成為海外華僑信任的、可以託付接收骸骨的慈善機構，除了有香港發達的航運交通

和毗鄰珠三角的地理位置的便利的優勢之外，東華總理的人緣關係也不容忽視。東華醫院的十三

位創院總理之中，有十二位是洋行、南北行、金山莊的著名買辦和商人（高添強，二〇〇六：一

〇三），這些人或本身是同鄉會的總理，與海外不同國家的同鄉會組織相熟悉，又或是通過商業

網絡而與海外有各種聯繫，早已建立起彼此間的信任；再者，得益於香港的自由港政策、連接北

美與南洋、靠近廣東的地理優勢，金融開放等特點，不少海外同鄉會組織的聯絡總部設在香港，

尤其負責收集海外捐輸回鄉建設的慈善捐款；香港金融發達，銀行林立，易於處理來自外國銀行

的匯票，香港銀號在港處理匯票後可以通過其鄉下的聯號店鋪送達華僑的家屬，香港因此成為海

外僑匯的中轉站。熟人社會的網絡在起着至關重要的作用。

至此，龐大的全球華僑慈善網絡以香港為中心而建立起來。

二、東華醫院創立

香港開埠初期，人口只有五千人，因各方面的建設都需要勞力，到香港募工的廣東省各縣的

民眾逐漸增多。加上太平天國之亂，五邑地區土客械鬥（一八五四—一八六七）波及整個五邑地

區及旁邊的佛山、高明一帶，十多年的打鬥，兩敗俱傷，民不聊生，不少人因此逃離到香港，至

一八六〇年，香港人口增至九萬二千四百四十二人（丁新豹，二〇一〇：一八）。一八五六年爆

發第二次鴉片戰爭後，廣州民眾縱火燒毀廣州外貿大本營的商館區，外國洋行紛紛把總部遷到香

港，隨之而來的還有洋行的買辦和更多來自珠三角的募工者，香港華人人口不斷增長。然而，華

人的生活、生老病死等問題並沒有成為主流社會考慮的問題，香港的華人社會精英因此而組織起來，幫助處理華人的慈善事務。一八五一年，以原籍開平的譚才為首的十四名香港行業代表和商人請求港府撥地，華人籌資於上環太平山街建立「廣福義祠」，以放置客死香港而無親無故的華人的神主牌位，故又稱「百姓廟」（丁新豹，二〇一〇：一七—二五）。

根據香港本地史專家高添強先生的多方考證，一八七〇年前未有上層華人安葬於香港的痕跡，極有可能是香港的上層華人身故後被運回原籍下葬。一九一五年香港仔華人永遠墳場正式設立之前，香港也沒有專門為中上層非基督徒華人而設的墳場，因此家境稍微殷實，能足夠支付靈柩運回原籍下葬的，都不願意去世後在香港下葬（高添強，二〇〇六：九九）。

隨着洋行的興起和華人買辦的增多，在香港的華商階層開始崛起，他們出面與政府交涉華人事務，早於一八六六年華人精英已經向政府倡建華人醫院事宜，遭拒。一八六九年《香港孖剌西報》（*The Hong Kong Daily Press*）報道廣福義祠因管理不善，不少生命垂危的病人被送至此地等死，屍體與臨危病人共處一屋，衛生環境異常惡劣。當時的港督麥當勞（Richard Graves MacDonnell）迫於壓力，遂於一八六九年批地撥款建設東華醫院，作為服務華人的中醫院及慈善機構（何佩然，二〇〇九：一八；丁新豹，二〇一〇：一七—二五）。

一八七二年二月十四日，東華醫院舉行開幕典禮。據《德臣西報》（*The China Mail*）報道，當天上午舉行祭祀中國古代傳說中的藥王神農氏的儀式，場面盛大。據說神農氏嘗百草，最終創立了中國醫學和藥物學的系統理論和知識，被公認為中醫藥的始祖，故東華醫院也設立供奉神農氏的神位。

三、東華義莊

關於義莊的歷史，始於《宋史・范仲淹傳》記載范仲淹「……而好施予，置義莊里中，以贍族人」；清馮桂芬的《復宗法議》：「惟宋范文正創為義莊，今世踵行，列於旄典。」范氏義莊包含學堂、田地、祠堂，設立良好的管理機制，從扶幼、養老、婚嫁、喪葬、濟貧、救災、助學等方面幫助貧困族人（唐力行，一九九七：一九〇—一九九）。范氏義莊在清代，尤其是江南地區產生深遠的影響，富有大族效法設義莊，救助同族貧困者，清代蘇州府的義莊總數達到一百七十九個之多（王衛平，一九九八：八四—九七）。惟規模較小的義莊，其功能減縮為安放無親無故的亡靈牌位的義祠和暫時停放棺柩之所。早期香港華人集資建設的廣福義祠，即為此種觀念的延伸。

在東華醫院建院期間，把建設所在地（原華人墓地）發現的華人墳墓遷葬至「牛房義山」，開啟東華醫院參與喪葬服務的歷史。東華醫院建成後，大量入院的貧民在院內去世，施棺代葬遂逐漸成為施醫贈藥之外的重要服務。另有資料顯示，一八七五年文武廟在位於堅尼地城山邊的「牛房義山」旁設立一座義莊，後由東華接管。又從東華三院現存最早的《一八七三年東華醫院徵信錄》中看到「莊房規條」，次年改為「義莊規條」，由此知道東華醫院在創院初期已設義莊安置屍骨（丁新豹，二〇一〇：二五；高添強，二〇〇六：八〇—九九）。

關於東華醫院何時開始接收海外骸骨，未找到確切的紀錄。但從一八七四年四月八日香港

《循環日報》刊登的一則小新聞「火船名日本，美國公司之郵船也」，從日本神戶載來棺木三十餘具，皆粵人之旅於日本而身死者也。抵港寄停東華醫院，不日書明籍貫、居址，招人運回。其盤柩之費，例有資助，近者十五元，遠者二十元。此誠盛德事也」（高添強，二〇〇六：一〇三）。

證明至少那個時候東華醫院就已經與海外接洽接收和短暫寄存海外棺柩的服務。

光緒八年（一八八二年）三藩市廣福堂的《勸捐倡建義塚義莊安葬故友小引》提到「廣福堂向邑內工商按名科收銀兩專辦檢（撿）裝故友遺骸運回香港暫寄東華醫院義莊，助以葬費，招其親屬領回」（一九〇二年三藩市廣福堂徵信錄）。由此可以肯定於一八八〇年代，海外骸骨由東華醫院接收並寄存於義莊已經成為海外負責撿運的善堂的恆常工作概念了。彼時東華醫院向港英政府提交建設新義莊的申請獲批，這所位於香港西大口環的新義莊正式命名為「東華義莊」，建立起東華醫院以香港為基點服務世界各地華僑的慈善網絡。這張慈善網絡往外伸至南北美洲、亞洲、大洋洲、歐洲、甚至非洲；北達美國、南至古巴、秘魯、智利；西至英國，法國，挪威，荷蘭；東南亞至越南、泰國、馬來亞、印尼、新加坡，再到澳洲和紐西蘭等地；還有遠在非洲的桑給巴爾島；往內通過河道網交通伸至廣東省各地的四十三個接收點，以及山東、浙江、福建、雲南等省、上海和天津等城市（葉漢明，二〇〇九：一七五、一八五—一八七）。目前東華三院文物館保存數千封來自各地機構或個人關於原籍安葬的信件。

落葉歸根

原籍安葬過程的最後一站——回到家鄉，是整個過程中最令人心慰的一集：海外靈魂終得安息，不再漂泊——落葉歸根，魂歸故里。對於海外骨殖運回家鄉後的善後之事，一般由駐香港的慈善機構與家鄉的慈善機構共同完成原籍安葬。

一、家鄉善堂／醫院

在僑鄉各地，一般都是由當地的慈善機構，如慈善性質的醫院、義莊、義祠或者善堂來對接處理海外運回的骸骨。香港的對接慈善機構是東華醫院。

在番禺、華縣、從化等縣，以紐西蘭華僑徐肇開為首於一八八二年建設的昌善堂為接骨總堂，設於禺北高唐墟，置有產業以幫補資費。昌善堂專為「起拾番（番禺）、花（花縣）、從（從化）的先友骸骨運回家鄉安葬。當先友骸骨運抵總堂時，就派人尋訪先友骸骨之所屬親人，通知其領回安葬，並給以奠儀葬費，俾能達入土為安之義」（周耀星，一九九五：一七）。

在新會，海外華僑捐資建置新會城西仁安醫院、仁育堂、積德社等處理骸骨，目前，新會發現的幾處義塚主要由該三個慈善機構分別進行安葬，另有義莊臨時安放運回等候認領的骸骨。根據新會本地史專家林震宇對當地慈善醫院和義莊的考究；仁安醫院前身為創辦於清光緒二十四年（一八九八年）的方便醫所。當年，新會爆發鼠疫，一些鄉紳倡議效仿香港東華醫院的做法在城西設立方便醫所，施醫贈藥及處理死後無人收殮的屍體。清光緒二十八年（一九〇二年），易名新會城西仁安醫院，資金來源靠發出緣簿，向國內外人士勸捐。在越南、美國、加拿大、古巴、澳洲等國的一些華僑聚居地都設有勸捐員。仁安醫院曾負責建設黃沖坑鶴嘴（又稱「金牛山」）及黃坑大槐兩處華僑義塚。建於雍正三年（一七二五年）的新會義祠，專門用以安放貧死者及無後者的神主牌位，但用以臨時存放骸骨的新會義莊的建設年代，並未有記載（倫海濱，一九八六：六；歐濟霖，二〇〇五：二五；林震宇，二〇一六年一月一日）。

在台山，光緒七年（一八八一年）海外華僑捐資建設義莊寄存海外骸骨，香港台山商會負責運送骸骨回鄉、處理認領和建設義塚安葬無人認領者。光緒十七年（一八九〇年），得美國華僑捐助一萬三千多美元，在台山青雲路設明善社，更以武廟為堂設贈醫所，次年建明善社方便醫院，收留老病者。中間供奉象徵廣施恩惠的民間神——呂祖像（光緒十九年《新寧縣志》，一九六八：三六六）。

具有類似施醫贈藥、收留老病者、收殮無主死屍等功能的還有一八九八年建成的荻海同濟醫院及新昌寧濟醫院、廣海樂善堂（清光緒年間）、公益福寧醫院（一九二一年）、四九區五十壚普濟醫院（一九二七年）等。一九二五年，海外華僑捐資在荻海興建宏濟醫院，院後設一百八十平方米的方便所。以贈醫贈藥、收容危病人、放置海外華僑骸骨等為主要業務（《台山縣衛生志》，一九八八：八二—八五）。

在開平，光緒二十年（一八九四年），開平和恩平的華僑在開平縣百合壚建立「恩開鄉約」，負責聯絡接收海外運歸的骸骨、以及建設義塚埋葬無人認領者，附近的金花廟和三靈宮作為臨時骸骨停放處。運到開平的骸骨可以在荻海碼頭上岸，一般由當地的愛善堂統一接收並安排認領。各地善堂負責把無人認領者埋葬在當地的義塚／義墳。自一八八五年第一所愛善堂——馬岡愛善堂建成以後，陸續有赤坎愛善堂、水口愛善堂、百合愛善堂、秘洞愛善堂、長沙愛善堂、茅岡愛善堂、蜆岡愛善堂、赤水沖口愛善堂、許族愛善堂、義興愛善堂、小海愛善堂等共有十七所愛善堂相繼成立。部分善堂設有方便所、慈善醫院，設施醫贈藥、接收病危鄉民、施棺代葬、接收骸骨、建設義塚安葬死者等服務，有些善堂不設施醫贈藥服務，而僅是施棺代葬、收殮無主死屍、接收海外骸骨等（《開平縣衞生志》，一九八八：三—五；《廣東歷代方志集成——民國開平縣志》，二○一四：一四○—一四一）。

二、招魂及超度

海外的靈柩或骸骨回鄉後首先請法師做法事超度亡靈，然後才讓家屬認領或者建設義塚下葬。咸豐八年（一八五八年）昌後堂第一次檢〔撿〕運章程明確提出操作指南：「租船載先友靈柩回鄉至省城左右登岸，營齋超度。」然後「遍貼長紅，預聞各鄉，以便親屬到廠領回，或孤貧無靠者，即就地立義塚安葬，以盡歸土為安」。

三、招魂

中國的傳統喪葬思想認為，客死他鄉的魂魄迷途難歸，異鄉漂泊，成為餓鬼，失卻投胎轉生的機會，亦不能享受香火的奉祀、食物的供養和經文的超度，淒苦不堪。故其家人必須替他舉行「招魂」儀式，使他聽到期盼他的聲音，讓他循着聲音回家。招魂儀式起源很早，遠在周代的文獻便有記載，死者親屬要從前方屋頂去招魂，手拿死者的衣服面北呼叫其名，死者的魂魄乃可循着聲音返回衣服，然後家屬從屋的後面下來，把衣服敷在死者身上，這件衣服又叫做「腹衣服」。據說這件「衣服」有「肉體」和「氣息」的雙重聯繫，魂魄會被它所吸引，依着熟悉的味道或形狀而歸附回來。此外，對於在外身故之人，則又有「招魂葬」俗。

對於旅居外洋的華僑而言，他們死後，其屍體埋葬在海外，靈魂停留在太平洋的彼岸，需要等待多年才能撿骨歸葬。很顯然，僑鄉的招魂風俗來源於古代的「招魂葬」。在僑居國執骨之時，找不到屍首骸骨者，即設「招魂箱」，沿途作招魂之舉，帶其回鄉。此舉即為華僑對於古代傳統風俗的遵循，他們或根據當時的環境局限而在形式上作了改變，然而，招魂葬的傳統觀念並未變。

家鄉的親人在接到骸骨後舉行招魂儀式把其靈魂召回。由於身在外洋的靈魂需要「坐船」才能回歸。因此，擅長水性的鴨子被賦予「舟」的功能。招魂當日，法師準備旌旗一條，上書死者名字和地址，繫於竹尾，鴨子一隻，腳上繫一根長細繩，帶領家屬親人到附近河道碼頭，以三牲祭奠，家屬親戚哭喊，以示哀悼；然後法師把鴨子用力扔到河面上，手拿繩子，讓鴨子在河面上遨遊。法師再以酒祭奠，口中念咒，呼死者姓名，喚其「乘舟」歸家，同時搖動寫有死者名字的竹尾，以提醒靈魂「乘船」的方向和地點。爾後，法師慢慢收回繩子，把鴨子收回。招魂禮畢，法師手抱鴨子，走在前面，其後回村進屋，在家中設靈位拜祭，俗稱「安座」。

至此，華僑的靈魂經歷半個地球終於回家，達成落葉歸根之夙願，從此可以享受自己親人及後代的拜祭。此風俗在僑鄉地區盛行了一個多世紀，至今仍然時有發生，此為筆者親歷兩次招魂儀式的紀錄。

四、超度

超度乃道教和佛教用語，是指家屬親人以虔誠之心，邀請法師為亡者開示、誦經，做法事，令亡靈得以往生淨土，此乃善後超度。以佛教而言，凡界眾生共分為天、人、神、鬼、傍生（牛馬乃至蚊蟻等動物）、地獄六大類，在此六類之中生來死去，又死去生來，稱為六道輪迴。佛教使人超出並度脫了這六道輪迴的生死之外，稱為超度。

佛教認為，超度亡靈的最佳時間是死後七天內在陰間尋求投胎的生緣，以七日為一期，若七日過後，仍未尋到生緣，則可以再續七日，到第七個七日終。七七四十九日內這段時間的誠心超度，可使亡者投生更好的去處，四十九天之後，其靈魂已經投生，再難改變。

然而，對於未能在七七四十九日內為親人超度者，《盂蘭盆經》認為亦可在每年的七月十五設壇作佛事進行補救，「其功德能超薦七世父母離苦得樂」（密宗：二〇〇二）。是故，縱使華僑骸骨在去世十數年後才被運回故里，主事者仍然秉承傳統，虔誠辦理超度儀式之後，方通知家屬前來領取骸骨。

五、華僑義塚

根據記載，各地僑鄉負責接洽處理海外運歸骸骨的慈善機構，都建設義塚安葬無人認領之骸骨，讓其「安葬義地俾享祭於千秋」（摘自光緒四年（一八七八年）昌後堂的檢〔撿〕運章程）。

由於年代久遠，且各地經濟發展迅速，很多義塚墓地已經被毀，現今能夠找到義塚墓地最多的為廣東新會，共有六處，約三千八百穴，分佈於：黃坑海槐「旅美華僑義塚」，葬於一八八○年，約二百穴；黃坑大槐的「華僑共三百八十六穴；黃坑木山「安南華僑義塚」，葬於一八九三年，先友義塚」，葬於一九三六年，有「仁安醫院立」字樣，共四百四十一穴；黃沖坑鶴嘴華僑義塚，有「仁安醫院立」字樣，約一千五百穴；黃坑坑下華僑義塚，約八百穴，已毀；大雲山，約四、五百穴，已毀（歐濟霖，二○○五：四—六）。

以台山華僑最多的三藩市四邑會館於一八五三年開始組織撿運骸骨回原籍安葬，但是台山的華僑義塚都消失在社會發展的洪流中，其義莊所在地目前已經是台城市中心，僅留一面牆壁。

開平的情況與新會、台山的處理方法有所區別，運歸新會的骸骨多由城西仁安醫院、仁育堂、積德社等處理，並設有義莊安放骸骨；台山也由華僑捐資建設義莊和明善社方便醫院負責接收骸骨，香港台山商會作為負責喪葬的慈善機構，直接參與骨殖的運送和義塚的建設。

開平與恩平兩縣於光緒九年（一八八三年）在開平百合墟成立「恩開鄉約」——恩開兩邑旅

外同鄉捐資撿運已故華僑歸葬統一由鄉約料理。同時，開平各地的善堂建設較為活躍，全縣華僑還捐資購買田地作為公管之善產，來支持施醫贈藥和處理骸骨的諸事。因此，開平的義塚多由當地善堂建設，負責善後安葬。共有二十一處由善堂組織建設的義塚，安葬無人認領的骸骨及無後貧病死者。二十一處義塚的分佈分別是：

四九洞、長沙塘、縣城南、秘洞、樓崗後竹笏坑、東河灣曲水村後、波羅長崗尾、龍塘鯉魚山（光緒七年建）、沙岡、矮嶺頭、峽巷口、狗山、橫橋墟（百足山赤坎善堂建）、牛淹水（民國三年司徒教倫堂建）、水口市螺山（民國七年水口善堂建）、四九洞馬山（民國九年楊藹如等倡建）、泮村（大岡底宣統二年建）、舊墟地（民國四年建）、旱葫廊前（民國十年建）、縣城西崗尾墟（民國二十年捕屬車路公司建）（《開平縣志》卷十〈建置上〉，一九三三）。

六、台山華僑義墳

一九四八年，台山海外鄉親最後一次運骸骨回家鄉，也是台山慈善機構最後一次建設華僑義塚，當時台山的報章為此事頗有宣傳。除了面向全縣鄉民的《新寧雜誌》外，其他各個家族月刊相繼報道，周知各鄉，讓相關的家屬到義莊認領骸骨。一九四八年十一月初出版的台山《至孝篤親月刊》刊登名為「邑僑遺骨千具由美運港，陳芝璿返台主理營葬」的新聞，即使沒有他們家族的先人骸骨，還是把這件大事給族人公佈：

香港台山商會主辦之餘慶堂，即「白骨會」，專司辦理各埠華僑遺骸，轉運安葬事項，戰前接由美洲運回白骨二百六十餘具，內有靈柩雷維略、雷炎學、劉一維、馬振元、黃傳燕等五具，仍在香港東華醫院，其遺族及地址不詳，該院作函白骨會妥置，本月二日美琦號船抵港，又運到白骨會一千零六十三具，香港台山商會理事長雷蔭蓀，經召開理事會議，決定運葬辦法多項，並派海生祥司理陳芝璿赴台，以台城中和路天信金舖辦理其事。查陳氏經於前十三日抵步，分向縣府參議會黨部洽商後，前十四日會同參議會催件工赴本邑義莊，勘踏戰前運回之白骨六百餘具，每具安葬費發給港幣五元，惟當時主持人將數移作別用，至使白骨仍未妥葬，此次已將十年來所有骸骨編列號數，調查其遺族及地址，定日間通知各鄉公所，專知各遺族，兩個月內到領，自行安葬，否則即在縣義莊妥為安葬。以後運返白骨，亦分別公佈於板端云。

（《至孝篤親月刊》，一九四八年十一月十五日，頁四四）

對於有本族先人骸骨在列的，則把先人的名字公佈，讓族人看到並可以互相通知。一九四八年《溫邊月刊》刊登的「美國先友骨殖招領，屬本族者有李百如等四具」的新聞，寫明認領骸骨的時間地點和可以領取十五元葬費等資訊：

香港台山商會，日前派該會理事陳芝璿，運回本縣美國先友及該會代運歷年寄存東華醫院義莊骨殖一批，計共一千二百九十餘具抵縣，其中屬於本族者，有溫邊村百如、李長華、溫邊舊村李維清、松梅村李來安等四具，現寄存於台城東門義莊，業於上月杪函知鄉公所分別通知各親屬到領，並每具發給安葬費金圓券一十五元，認領者可到台城正市街均盛號李權應處掛號認領，茲探錄認領辦法刊佈如下：（一）認領者須係先友之直系嫡親（如無直系嫡親可由旁系至親認領之）。（二）認領者須具有鄉公所之證明，或台城區殷實商號之保證。（三）認領者須填具本會印定之收條三張，一存義莊，一存本會，一匯寄所屬之外埠會館，以昭縝密。（四）認領期限，由本年十月十五日起至卅八年四月十五日止，六個月內來義莊領妥，如逾期不領，即由本會義莊安葬，無得異言云。

《新寧雜誌》是面向海內外台山人的最熱門的通訊，海外華僑通過該刊物瞭解國內和家鄉所發生的事情，同時也是海外華僑向家鄉傳遞外國資訊、交流思想的媒介，國內、省內、縣內的大事，香港、澳門的與四邑人相關的新聞，以及海外華僑所僑居國家的移民政策等統統包含。

一九四九年一月份連續兩期報道餘慶堂墳場事宜，第一期以「餘慶堂新闢石花山墳場，安葬南北洋僑骸千餘具」為題，洋洋灑灑千餘言，詳細報道骸骨運送、葬費安排、義莊認領、建設義塚安葬無人認領者等情況，同時可見台山香港商會是從香港至鄉下這段路程的操辦者，也是原籍安葬最後一站的資金保障機構。

《新寧雜誌》民國三十七年第一期報道了墳場的奠基場面，除了縣長外，很多政府要員都參加奠基儀式，可想而知當時的「華僑義墳」工程可謂縣內大事，得海內外邑人關注。

《新寧雜誌》的第二期以「石花山劃地八百井，餘慶堂墳場動工，紀念亭八座向海外捐建」為題向台山海內外鄉親公佈墳場的規劃、西方墳場的規劃理念、建設紀念亭，以及關於資金的籌措等情況。

輻射全台山的報刊，除《新寧雜誌》連續兩期刊登墳場下葬和工程營建的工作外，台山《大同日報》也於民國三十七年十二月十四日和十五日，連續兩天刊登相關新聞，詳細報道墳場奠基的盛況和墳場建築工程的情況。然而，筆者查找此後多年的僑刊，現存數百冊，但再沒有看到關於義墳建造的新聞，對於義墳建成之後如何，及其運作情況等，甚少報道。惟在一九五七年第一期的《新寧雜誌》看到了譚庭標寫的一篇關於清明節祭掃華僑義墳的散文，題為「溪山景物最堪憐——清明節祭掃石花山華僑先友墳墓記」，記錄了華僑義墳建成後的情況：

吃過早飯後，參加清明節祭掃台山華僑先友墳墓（台山闔邑餘慶堂公墳）的歸僑和僑眷手持鮮花，從四面八方湧到台城西安路台山歸國華僑聯合會的門前來。接着各機關團體的首長和社會各界人士也陸續趕到。……僑眷也攜男帶女形成了一支兩百餘人的掃墓隊伍。台山歸國華僑聯合會早已具備豐富的祭品：如黃糖糍、白糖糍、燒豬、白肉、白蛋、甘蔗、酒、香燭等。

掃墓儀式開始了，由歸僑陳厚父主祭，大家都到前行禮，獻上鮮花，表示對繁榮桑梓經濟，離鄉別井，客死海外的華僑先友致無限的崇敬。祭禮完畢，共同拍照，以留紀念。

（《新寧雜誌》，一九五七年一月十五日，頁八九—九一）

結語

一、慈善精神

華人有生俱來的濃厚鄉土觀念，所謂「落葉歸根」，對於遠在外洋的華工，更是如此。假若生前不能回鄉終老，死後歸葬原籍便是他們最後的願望。同時，「人死為大、入土為安」等觀念根深蒂固，成為在文明古國禮制薰陶下的華人矢志不渝地遵循的傳統，加上國外並不如意的生活經歷，才形成持續大半個世紀、工程如此浩大的原籍安葬習俗。

至此，可以總結出原籍安葬的總路線：海外會館或善堂——香港東華醫院（東華義莊暫時寄存）——香港東華醫院、駐港善堂或會館（運送回鄉）——家鄉善堂（處理骨殖認領和建設義塚），從外國回到家鄉的各段路程都與「善堂」對接。支撐如此浩大工程背後所反映的，不僅僅是骸骨回歸原籍安葬這件事情本身，更重要的是其背後所蘊含的文化與傳統，是中華傳統文化信仰中對鬼神的敬畏，是儒家禮教文化的社會道德觀念，是海內外華人社會的誠信與精誠合力，是中華文化傳統中的慈善精神，才建立起一張如此嚴密的慈善社會網絡。這種慈善思想在特定的歷史時期、特定的生活環境裏、特定的文化信仰裏被催化至極致——「慷慨樂助，大發慈心，可免先骸之暴露。善舉亦是我輩之仔肩也。古人有言，作善降祥，又曰福祿善慶，是助黃金以取白骨，未始非種福之基也」（一九一六年五月十六日「開邑廣福堂廣告」，金山西北角華裔研究中心網站）。

這樣的精神，在撿運徵信錄的章程裏每有體現，要求值事們秉承「同心協力，勿分黨、勿偷安，公爾忘私；勿畏口、勿徇情，克勤克儉；勿苟簡、勿濫用，表裏如一，始終不懈。刻刻以質神明為心，時時以廣善為念，由是德修獲報，定卜克昌厥後矣，是所厚望焉」（光緒廿三年歲祀丁酉公議昌後堂善後章程列第一條）。

為了警醒值事之人時刻謹記傳統道德與倫理觀念，以慈善為懷，更在徵信錄裏刊登「值事具焚誓章格式」（昌後堂多屆徵信錄刊登），周知值事在任期間，需按照格式填上姓名，在靈前祭祀，焚燒誓言，恭請神明監督。原文格式，頗為虔誠，摘錄如下：

番禺昌後堂值事 ＸＸＸ 等，謬膺眾願，辦理檢（撿）運先梓里靈柩旋粵事務，撫心自問，有忝厥職，惟是數目銀兩並無糊塗，如有私心匿數，吞騙肥己等情，伏乞神明鑒察，私則降殃，公則降祥，不勝俟命之至。

年　月　日　的筆

二、原因略探

若追究海外骸骨原籍安葬的風俗，從東華三院的原籍安葬檔案來看，來自北美及中南美洲的骸骨遠遠多於人口眾多的東南亞地區，執骨運回原籍安葬未能如北美般成為約定俗成的「風俗」盛行其中。究其原因，筆者以為至少有三：

首先，東南亞地區的政治氣候較北美和澳洲等地區輕鬆，沒有法律上的排斥，不少華人擁有家庭，當地有華文學校傳承中華文化，也不甚擔心死後沒有後代祭掃墓地。然而，在北美和澳洲等排華的國家，大部分華人難以在當地建立家庭，贍養父母和照顧家鄉的妻子兒女成為了他們工作上的精神支撐和動力，居住國被看作是短暫的賺錢養家的寓居之地。加拿大溫哥華的中文報紙《大漢公報》一九一六年五月十六日的「開邑廣福堂廣告」道出了撿運先友骸骨寄運回鄉的原因——「運回故國，毋任長埋異域，飲恨胡泉」（金山西北角——華裔研究中心網站）。

其次，東南亞諸如馬來亞和新加坡等國有專門法例限制骸骨運輸。一九三四年東華醫院回覆新加坡廣惠肇方便留醫院函「藉悉 貴埠政府對於撿運骨殖條例已有解放之意，惟聲明要照香港現行辦法辦理，故着敝院將香港撿執骨殖現行規例華英文各一份寄奉，以便呈請政府依照辦理，事關公益，自應效勞。」一九三五年吉隆坡廣東義山義務司理給香港東華醫院的來函提及「海外華僑常有將先人骸骨運返祖國安葬之舉。惟政府因衛生起見，取締頗嚴，辦理手續非人之易明，費用由此增加，故欲執骨者每有心力相違之感」（葉漢明，二○○九：二五○—二五一）。事實上，美國也有限制屍骨運送的法例，申請手續也頗為繁瑣。

同樣的限制運送屍骨，同樣需要辦理繁瑣的手續才能寄送，然而，在不同的政治環境裏，所產生的心理效果不一。

第三，香港東華醫院建立義莊、船上施棺、接收骸骨的善舉以及香港作為國際自由貿易港在航運業務上的全球網絡所帶來的便利，是其他華人出海港所不能比擬的。旅居北美、中南美洲、澳洲和紐西蘭等國家的華人以廣東人為最，他們的海外會館與香港的同類機構有緊密的聯繫，確保骸骨回到香港後有機構接洽和負責運送回原籍下葬。香港的南北行、金山莊等商業貿易以香港為中心，聯繫全球建立原籍安葬的慈善網絡，既是商機，亦為善舉（Sinn, 2013；葉漢明：二〇〇九）。

三、原籍安葬之外

若從近代僑鄉社會發展史的角度，這些骸骨背後的家庭與社會，值得深思。華僑出洋謀生，往往背負家庭重擔。他們為家庭、為家鄉的發展可謂鞠躬盡瘁。然而，一旦身故，其背後的家庭隨之改變，其身後女人的一生，也因此而改變。縣志裏被標榜為「烈女、節婦」的長長名單裏記載的，大多有其夫「客死外洋」字眼：

陳氏許字李北斗，未婚，而北斗客死外洋，陳聞訃痛哭，奔喪守節，事姑以孝聞，撫繼子十餘年，鄉裏共賢之。迨子年長，又為之冠娶。乃曰：吾事已畢，可以見夫於地下矣！遂浮海而死。黃氏許字陳純平，未婚，而夫客僑鄉大地矗立的華麗碉樓與洋樓別墅裏，常常居住着用一輩子等夫歸的女人。丈夫海外身故後，她們或撫養遺子，或撫養繼子（俗稱「螟蛉子」），已成俗。

回顧大半個世紀的原籍安葬過程，頗為感慨：無論功成名就，抑或一無所成，最後都是一個棺柩、一副骸骨歸鄉。一九〇二年，紐西蘭華人富商徐肇開的遺體與昌善堂其他五百具華工遺骸一起，隨着文特諾號（SS Ventnor）沉歸海底（周耀星，一九九五：一七）。又正如譚雅倫教授所言，原籍安葬服務是「公平的葉落歸根安排」（Marlon Hom, 2002:38，轉引自葉漢明，二〇〇九：二四）。

葉落歸根的文化傳統在華僑之間盛行一百多年後的今日，世界發生逆向發展。隨着排華法案的廢除和當代移民政策的改變，海外華人可以在居住國入籍結婚生子，落地生根，安居樂業。安家於海外的華人開始擔心父輩的墳墓留在故鄉太孤獨，無後人拜祭。因而有不少移民海外的華人回家鄉把父輩的骨灰帶到海外安葬，便於照料和拜祭。實際上，這同樣還是出於傳統文化思維的考慮——落地生根，福蔭子孫。

本書所選編的東華義莊檔案的信件，不但反映了海外華人葉落歸根的渴望，更證明華人之間在海外、香港和中國大陸的本土社會和慈善團體在原籍安葬事件上通力合作的互助精神。因此，香港東華三院致力於保存東華義莊及其歷史檔案，作為這段海外華人歷史的見證。

Fallen Leaves Returning to Their Roots
– Repatriating the Bones of Overseas Chinese (1850-1949)

Dr. TAN Jinhua

Associate Professor, Guangdong Qiaoxiang Cultural Research Center,
Wuyi University

Introduction

The Wuyi area, or Five Counties, is located in the south western part of Guangdong province. In ancient times, it was part of the kingdom of Baiyue; in the Qin and Han dynasties, it belonged to Nanhai prefecture; during the Northern and Southern dynasties, Xinhui prefecture was established under the jurisdiction of Fengzhou; in the Tang dynasty, Fengzhou was renamed Gangzhou and the district government was set up in present-day Huicheng – Xinhui was thus also named Gangzhou. There were 12 counties under the jurisdiction of Xinhui prefecture, including today's Xinhui, all of Taishan, Kaiping, Enping and part of Heshan in the Wuyi area, whereas Taishan, Kaiping, Enping and Heshan were later established as independent counties. Meanwhile, the majority of early Chinese emigrants to North America and Oceania were natives of Guangdong province, and most of them were unemployed villagers from the four counties of Taishan, Kaiping, Xinhui and Enping. Since they shared the same culture and spoke similar dialects, they called themselves "Siyi (Sze Yap) people" (people from the Four Counties) and set up native associations to support one another when they were overseas. All along, Heshan, where the Punti-Hakka Clan Wars originated, was not included in the Sze Yap area (County Records of Xinning, 1893; County Records of Chixi, 1920; County Records of Kaiping, 1933). It was only in the 1980s, when the government re-divided the districts for administrative jurisdiction as China underwent reform and opening-up, that Heshan was incorporated into Jiangmen. Heshan, along with the other four counties Xinhui, Taishan, Kaiping and Enping, were known as Wuyi (Five Counties). This was how the present-day administrative division of Wuyi came into being.

The First Opium War, which left China weak and vulnerable, ended with the cession of Hong Kong to Britain. As Guangzhou was no longer China's only trading port, many Wuyi laborers in the city found themselves out of work. Back on the hilly terrain of Wuyi, there was insufficient land for farming and harvest was particularly poor when natural calamities struck. Meanwhile, an uprising with most of the fighting taking place in Taishan, Kaiping, Heshan and Foshan broke out in the south western part of the Pearl River Delta, as the Red Turban Rebellion supporting the Taiping Rebellion. Subsequently, local people clashed with Hakka people, and the confrontations sparked the decade-long Punti-Hakka Clan Wars (1854-1867), making life in the underdeveloped Wuyi area even more difficult than before. By this time, China had signed the Treaty of Nanking (1842) with Britain and the Treaty of Wanghia (1844) with the United States, while European settlers and colonizers opened up countries in Southeast Asia, Central America and South America. Due to the decline of slavery in the west, some merchants and plantation owners turned to China to recruit laborers. At the same time, the discovery of gold in North America (1848 in California, USA; 1858 in British Columbia, Canada) and Oceania (1851 in Melbourne, Australia; 1868 in New Zealand) led to the gold rush, whereas large-scale railroads linking the east and west coasts of the United States and Canada were being constructed. Against this backdrop, penniless villagers from mainland Chinese counties near Hong Kong and Macau left their hometown in search of opportunities. They travelled to Southeast Asia, Central and South America, North America and Oceania to earn a living. After the gold rush in various cities, Chinese laborers were hired to build the Central Pacific Railroad (1863-1869), the Southern Pacific Railroad (1873-1883), the Northern Pacific Railway (1870-1883) and the Canadian Pacific Railway. Between the 1860s and 1890s, the Chinese laborers played a vital role in the construction and operation of these railroads (Voss, 2019). In addition to gold mining and railway construction in the early days, overseas Chinese were engaged in cultivation, vegetable farming, fishing, laundry services, restaurants and the grocery industry. They also worked as factory workers, chefs and domestic helpers, as well as ran various kinds of businesses in Chinatown.

The 1893 county records of Taishan (Xinning) clearly states why Chinese from the Wuyi area travelled abroad to earn a living, "After the chaos created by the Taiping Rebellion and Punti-Hakka Clan Wars, and in the meantime western culture became very popular, those in their prime went overseas to earn a living and support their families. Life for the weak and poor become very difficult here." (Volume 6, About the Land, *County Records of Xinning*, 9th year of Qing Emperor Guangxu's reign)

In a time when the vulnerable Qing government was yet to be accepted into the international arena, the culture of Chinese people was different from that of the countries they lived in. While employers were impressed by their diligence and sense of responsibility, the existence of the Chinese laborers posed a threat to local labor markets. In the late 19th century, anti-Chinese riots broke out in the United States, Canada, Australia and New Zealand – countries where most Chinese from Wuyi lived in. The riots ended with the enactment of anti-Chinese laws; in 1882, the United States promulgated the Chinese Exclusion Act, the first ever discriminating immigration law targeting a particular ethic group; in 1885, following the completion of the railroads, Canada restricted Chinese immigration through imposing a poll tax on Chinese persons; subsequently in 1924, Canada enacted the Chinese Immigration Act to restrict Chinese laborers from entering the country (1924-1947); in the late 19th century, Australia and New Zealand restricted Asian people from entry through implementing a "language test" – any person seeking to enter the country had to pass the test by reading a passage out loud in a European language; in 1901, Australia even enacted the White Australia Policy (1901-1972) in which Australia was seen as a country for white people, thereby restricting entry of non-white persons. The Chinese overseas were not only discriminated in an alien culture and environment far away from home, but also, being Chinese laborers, it was hard for them to start a family and have peace of mind in a foreign country.

Many Chinese who could not take root in foreign countries chose to return to their hometown to start a family. Their families at home asked them to send money to them, while the feeling of "homelessness" they had amidst strong anti-Chinese sentiments prompted them to send their savings back to China to develop their hometown and invest in business. In the late 19th and early 20th centuries, the hometown of overseas Chinese in Wuyi underwent dramatic changes as a result of increased overseas remittances and the overseas Chinese's desire to develop their hometown. Gradually, the hometown of overseas Chinese developed unique landscapes – made up of *diaolou* (fortified multi-storey watchtower), western style buildings and shop-houses in market towns – with a strong local accent. Modern schools and libraries were established in the villages to enlighten people; commerce and trade flourished while land and water transportation was well developed. Goods and materials from all over the country and the rest of the world were widely available, and people acquired water pumps, flush toilets, fireplaces, bathtubs, telephone sets, cars and other imported goods (Tan, Jinhua: 2013). Meanwhile, the hometown of the overseas Chinese evolved from rural feudal communities dependent on farming to half-feudal societies emphasising industry and commerce more than agriculture.

Far from their families, Chinese overseas earning a living abroad led lonely lives. The Chinese native societies, communal halls and clan associations in Chinatown became their home, and members watched out for one another as they developed a close bond. The lucky ones earned enough money to return to their families in China, while those who were less fortunate died abroad. Against this backdrop, the Chinese associations established charitable / benevolent associations to help them, acquiring land to build burial grounds. The deceased were buried while their spirits were appeased; after their bodies turned into bones, special ceremonies were performed and the bones were exhumed and repatriated to the deceased's hometown, as it was their final wish to return to their roots (Yip, 2009; Sinn, & Lau, 2006). In over a century, overseas Chinese perpetuated the tradition of sending the deceased's coffins or bones to their hometown for permanent burial. Meanwhile, Tung Wah Hospital in Hong Kong took the repatriated bones into its care from the 1870s. (The Tung Wah Hospital was founded in 1870, two more hospitals were later added, and in 1931, the three hospitals were amalgamated as the Tung Wah Group of Hospitals.) Since discussing bone repatriation was a taboo in the early days, not many scholars – at home and abroad – conducted research on this topic. In the past 20 years, however, big changes have taken place, Xinhui historian Ou Jilin and Professor Hom, Marlon K. of San Francisco State University, among others, conducted research on the communal burial grounds of overseas Chinese in Xinhui, while the Tung Wah Group of Hospitals allowed access to its archives, so that scholars in Hong Kong and abroad can start research on the charitable deeds of Tung Wah Hospital, its coffin home and the global bone repatriation network.

In 1992, when building Guifeng Hi-Tech Village in the outskirts of Xinhui, the local county authority discovered 387 graves belonging to overseas Chinese in a burial ground in Haihuai, Huangkeng. Xinhui historian Ou Jilin started an investigation and discovered a total of 3,800 graves in six burial grounds in the vicinity for overseas Chinese. This lifted the veil on this kind of burial grounds (Ou, 1995, 2001). At the same time, Professor Marlon K. Hom drew on the experience of Chinese living in the United States and conducted research on the burial ground in Haihuai, Huangkeng, analysing the internal and external factors for the return of the bones of overseas Chinese to their hometown for burial (Hom: 2001).

In his essay "Funeral services and bone repatriation", published in *Publication of Research Project on the History of Tung Wah–A Collection of Commemorative works of Tung Wah in celebration of its 135th Anniversary*, expert on Hong Kong history Ko Tim-keung introduces the funeral services of Tung Wah Hospital as well as the bone repatriation service offered by Tung Wah Coffin Home, which included taking the bones sent to Hong Kong from abroad into its care, storing them and transporting them to the deceased's hometown for burial (Ko, 2006); historian Professor Joseph Ting documents the establishment of Tung Wah Coffin Home as well as its bone repatriation service in his book *Tung Wah Group of Hospitals and the Chinese Community in Hong Kong (1870-1997)* (Ting, 2010); in *The Tung Wah Coffin Home and Global Charity Network: Evidence and Findings from Archival Materials*, Professor of History of The Chinese University of Hong Kong, Yip Hon-ming, analyses the global charitable network through studying the archives of Tung Wah Museum and conducting field research (Yip, 2009); Elizabeth Sinn, Honorary Professor of the Institute for the Humanities and Social Sciences of the University of Hong Kong, illustrates Hong Kong's status in the global overseas Chinese trade and its international logistics network from the perspective of the trading company network while highlighting Hong Kong's indispensable role in the global bone transportation in her book *Pacific Crossing: California Gold, Chinese Migration, and the Making of Hong Kong* (Sinn, 2013); American scholar Sue Fawn Chung in "An Ocean Apart: Chinese American Segregated Burials" meticulously documents how early Chinese communities in the United States treated fellow Chinese who passed away abroad as well as how bone repatriation and funeral services were handled (Chung, 2019).

The aforementioned research sheds light on burial and funeral arrangements on the other side of the Pacific Ocean, the global bone repatriation network influenced by deeply rooted traditional culture, as well as how Tung Wah Hospital and Tung Wah Coffin Home helped repatriate the bones of overseas Chinese to their hometown for burial. However, little has been said about the actual process of repatriation from Tung Wah Coffin Home to the destination. In particular, there is yet to be in-depth research on the transportation of bones to the deceased's hometown for storage and burial customs among other topics. This essay investigates the burial arrangements for coffins and bones repatriated to the deceased's hometown from abroad, with a focus on revealing the entire process of repatriation, from the exhumation of bones abroad to the bones' arrival in Tung Wah Coffin Home and the eventual burial in the deceased's hometown.

Traditional Funeral and Burial Customs

1) Funeral and Burial Beliefs

Traditional burial practices, which include interment, water burial, sky burial and cremation, are forms of beliefs. They are ways to mourn the deceased, as well as socio-cultural phenomena. In traditional Chinese society, interment was the prevalent burial practice.

In the Shang dynasty, people began to believe that the human spirit was immortal. They started to bury the deceased and perform ceremonies to soothe their spirits. Such was the beginning of interment. By the Spring and Autumn time, there were norms of funeral rites – the *Rites of Zhou* specifies rites for the funerals of emperors, kings, generals and government officials. The funeral system and rites recorded in the *Rites of Zhou*, the *Book of Etiquette and Ceremony* and the *Book of Rites* were adopted by later generations. In fact, the funeral rites practised by later generations, such as pre-burial rituals, mourning clothing, mourning observation and sacrificial offerings to the deceased, all originated from the three ritual books (Ethnography, County Records of Fujian, 2013).

In Taoism, birth, ageing, sickness and death make up the circle of life and death is an important part of life according to tradition. The utmost respect should thus be given to the deceased. In the *Analects*, Confucius teaches his disciples, "To serve our father and mother with courtesy whilst they live; to bury them and pay respect to them with courtesy when they die." According to the Chinese interment tradition, "death is very important and the deceased should be buried in the earth." It is only through burying the deceased in the earth that they can be laid to rest and the living can be at peace. Thus interment, which originated from deeply rooted traditional culture, became the most prevalent burial practice in China.

First of all, interment was intricately related to Chinese people's veneration of the earth. China's millennia-old farming culture became the essence of life, etching the earth on the deepest part of our soul. Meanwhile the myth of Nüwa creating mankind with clay reflects the circle of life–mankind originates from clay and returns to the earth after death. This also tallies with the law of reincarnation in the natural world. According to the *Book of Rites: Meaning of Sacrifices*, "All the living must die, and, return to the earth; this is called *kwei* [ghost]. The bones and flesh, moulder below, and, hidden away, become the earth of the fields." In *Illustrations of the Didactic Application of the Classic of Songs (Hanshi Waizhuan)*, Han Ying from the Eastern Han dynasty writes that, "When humans die, they are called ghosts; in Cantonese, the sound of the character "ghost" is similar to that of "return". The spirit returns to the heaven, while the flesh returns to the earth".

Secondly, interment was linked to fengshui. In the classic work of fengshui, the *Book of Burial*, Guo Pu writes that, "The Chinese character of "bury" means to "preserve". Burial is contingent upon shengqi – vital energy. The "qi" of "yin" and "yang" breathes out as wind, rises up as clouds, descends as rain, and runs underground as vital energy." The theories in the *Book of Burial* had a profound influence on later generations. According to traditional fengshui belief, if the deceased's body is not buried in the earth, it cannot receive the vital energy there. In other words, humans must be buried in the earth in order to complete their reincarnation.

Interment was also linked with elaborate funerals and perpetual offerings. Ancient people believed the human spirit was immortal. Interment does not only protect the deceased's body, but also ensures that the deceased (body and spirit) will have a comfortable life in the underworld. In this light, burial rites, covering funeral arrangements, interment and tomb building, were established through common practice.

In addition, interment was linked with traditional filial piety. In Confucianism, taking part in funerals is considered a key indicator of filial piety. If the deceased is not buried in the earth and given an elaborate funeral, their descendants are thought to have neglected their filial duties. While emphasising the "Three Principles and Five Virtues", filial piety is upheld as the most important good deed in Confucianism. If the deceased is laid to rest in a plot with auspicious forces, their spirit can find eternal peace, while their descendants will thrive and prosper; if the deceased is randomly buried without considering the fengshui of the burial plot, their descendants are thought to have ignored ceremonial rites and neglected their filial duties. The *Mind-enlightening Classics (Mingxin Baojian)*, a collection of aphorisms and quotations from the Chinese classics reads, "Respecting the dead as if he is alive and respecting the deceased as if he is around - this is filial piety at its finest." In the *Analects (Lunyu)*, Zengzi says, "Heed the dead, follow the past, and the soul of the people will again grow great." Only through interment can the deceased fuse with the earth and bring prosperity to their descendants (Chen & Chen, 2008; Wang et el, 2001).

Funeral rites require the living to observe mourning in order to express their grief over the deceased and carry out their filial duties, and the three-year mourning period became an important cornerstone for Chinese ethics and social order. Over two millennia, from the pre-Qin period to the Qing dynasty, the mourning system had been kept in place. Filial sons were required to build a hut next to their parent's tomb and stay there in order to show their grief. More than often, some government officials could not carry out their duties as they stayed home to conduct the mourning for three years in the hut next to their parent's tomb. In recent years, very rarely that mourning is observed in a hut by the tomb – in some places (such as the Chaoshan area in Guangdong province), people still build a small structure next to the tomb to symbolise the mourning hut and show their respect for the deceased (Ko, 2012).

For overseas Chinese and their families in China, "interment" carried even deeper meaning as it provided a final resting place for their returning spirit. The gate between the living world and the underworld is known as the "earth". It is a medium between the two worlds, as well as the resting place for the deceased's spirit. If interment is delayed, it is not only a cruelty to the deceased but also a form of torture for the living. Thus, over the past century, overseas Chinese have upheld traditions and repatriated the bones of their deceased friends to their hometown for burial.

2) Second Burial

Existing archaeological research has yielded evidence of second burial, also known as "bone collecting", in the Banpo heritage site in Xi'an, the Yangshao cultural site in Zhengzhou and Luoyang of the Central Plain, the early Dawenkou cultural site in the Shandong peninsula, the Chu kingdom (present-day Hubei province) as well as the Baiyue area (Xinhua Net, 10 November 2007, 9 May 2007; Ding, 2008; Wang, 2010; Guangdong Provincial Museum, 1978).

The research of renowned ethnology scholar Ling Chunsheng points out that second burial was not only practised by the Han people. Instead, it was a cultural feature of primitive tribes in the Pacific Rim. Second burial was practised in Han, Zhuang, Tibetan and other ethnic minority communities in the Central Plain and along the south eastern coast (including Taiwan) of China, Southeast and Northeast Asia, the South Pacific Islands, the Americas and as far as Madagascar in East Africa. He contends that the "bone washing / collecting" practice of the various ethnic groups all stemmed from the same custom, and this custom originated in South China, where the ancient Baiyue tribes were located (Ling, 1979).

The earliest written record can be found in *Mozi: Simplicity in Funerals II (Jiezang Xia), Volume 6,* from the Warring States period, "In the South of Chu Kingdom there was a cannibal tribe. Upon the death of the relatives the flesh was scraped off and thrown away, while the bones were buried. And by following this custom one became a filial son." Meanwhile, *Geography II, Volume 31 of the Book of Sui (Shuishu)* also documents second burial practised by the indigenous people of the Jingzhou area, "After death, the body of the deceased is placed in the courtyard and not kept indoors. After the funeral, it is buried in the mountain for no more than 13 years. An auspicious date is then picked to move the bones of the deceased into a small coffin. The process is known as 'bone collecting'". The late Ming and early Qing dynasty scholar Gu Yanwu wrote in Chapter 100, *Volume 4, On the natural advantages and vulnerabilities of provinces and prefectures of the Chinese empire (Tianxia Junguo Libing Shu)* that people in northern Guangdong province "buried the deceased in a temporary grave within three days after they died. After three years, the remains were collected and buried in a tomb." It was the same in the Xingmei Hakka area during the Qing dynasty, "According to local customs, the deceased were re-buried after 10 years. Their bones were collected from the coffin and placed in a pottery/earthen jar to rebury."

French anthropologist Lucien Levy-Bruhl illustrates the history of second burial, the reason for its popularity as well as its primitive significance from the perspective of primitive mentality. He claims that primitive man saw the second death as a transition ceremony in life, while second burial was practised to completely sever the interaction and link between the deceased and the collective activities of society. Completion of the second burial ceremony symbolised total death; in other words, when the mourning period ended along with the ceremony, the deceased's connection with the society he once belonged to was completely severed and they were considered completely dead (Levy-Bruhl, 1985).

Professor Zhong Fulan, a renowned ethnologist from Shanghai, discussed second burial from the perspective of customs, culture and belief. He claims that in some cases, Chinese who passed away abroad were buried in the foreign countries until their remains could be repatriated to their hometown for second burial at an opportune time, as in the saying, "fallen leaves returning to their roots". In other cases, the deceased were buried after their death, but their descendants subsequently made fortune and arranged an elaborate second burial for them, in order to "bring glory to the family". There were also instances when the remains of one person were exhumed to be buried together with the other half who passed away later, so that the married couple "shared a bed when they were living and a tomb after they died". Sometimes, driven by fengshui or superstitious beliefs, ancestors were reburied in plots with auspicious forces to bring wealth and prosperity to their descendants (Zhong, 2012).

Even today, the practice of second burial remains common in the Lingnan area, and the customs are similar to the past. The deceased are buried in a coffin for three, five or seven years (or even more than 10 years). After the body has decomposed, the bones are exhumed (known as "jiangu" and "zhigu" [collecting bones], or "jianjin" and "zhijin" (collecting gold) in the Pearl River Delta) and reburied.

The bones are exhumed by the deceased's relatives and elders in the village who are experienced in the matter. A canopy is erected over the grave to shelter it from the sun before the bones are exhumed from the coffin from head to toe. Next, the bones are cleaned with rice wine, rough straw paper and rags. Incense sticks are burnt and the bones are dried over heat. Then, the bones are vertically placed inside an earthen/pottery jar (known as "jintan", "jincheng" or "jinta" [golden jar] in Guangdong) from toe to head according to the structure of the human skeletal system, such that the skeleton seems to be in a squatting position. The earthen / pottery jar only contains the bones – there are no burial objects – and the deceased's name along with the dates of birth and death are written in ink on the inside of the lid. Before the jar is sealed, the descendants pay their last respects to the bones - hence the deceased. An auspicious time is selected for the sealed jar to be buried in a plot with auspicious forces. During removal and burial, a black umbrella shields the earthen jar. This process is known in Guangdong province of the Pearl River Delta as "wang fengshui" (observing fengshui) (extracted from the interview of Tan, Zhuoyong, fengshui master at Kaiping, 2018.11.20).

Descendants pay their respects at the tomb every year on Ching Ming Festival after the "wang fengshui" process.

As to the terms "fen" (grave) and "mu" (tomb), in ancient times graves were dug into the ground, while tombs were built in caves. Some say that tumuli were raised over graves, whereas tombs had flat tops, thus the generic term, "fenmu". (*Cihai* 1979: 529, 604) Yet in Guangdong province of the Pearl River Delta, a first burial grave casually covered with a mound of earth and without a headstone was traditionally known as grave; a tomb, with a headstone, was built in a permanent burial plot with auspicious forces for the second burial.

"Grave sweeping" on Ching Ming Festival is a display of respect and remembrance for the ancestors. The practice had a long history, but it became customary in the Qin dynasty and gained popularity in the Tang dynasty (Zhang, 2006). Throughout Guangdong province, different grave sweeping customs are practised. In the Wuyi area, people visit the simple graves without headstones (for first burial) – *fen* – on Ching Ming Festival, whereas in the month before Ching Ming, families visit the permanent *fengshui* tombs with headstones (for second burial) – mu – according to their own schedules.

Bone Exhumation and Repatriation

1) The Chinese Migration

In the Tang and Song dynasties, people in the southern provinces left China for short periods of time to trade with merchants in other countries. It was not until after the First Opium War in the mid-19th century, when western colonizers began to open new frontiers in Southeast Asia as well as Central and South America that large numbers of Chinese laborers travelled overseas to make a living. According to the law of the Qing dynasty, it was illegal to leave the country to earn a livelihood. Yet the western colonizers who were setting up colonies in Southeast Asia and Central and South America required extensive laborers, and as slavery declined in the west, Chinese were caught up in the wave of emigration. The Treaty of Nanking, signed after the First Opium War, contained clauses permitting British companies to recruit workers in China, making it legal for Chinese workers to earn a living abroad. The clauses were also applicable to British colonies, such as Victoria (British Colombia, Canada), Australia and New Zealand. In 1868, the Qing government and the United States signed the Burlingame Treaty, giving citizens of the two countries the right to emigrate freely from one to the other. This led to more Chinese workers emigrating to the United States.

Chinese who earned a livelihood abroad in the early days called themselves "tangren" (meaning Chinese people from the Tang Dynasty) and where they lived "tangren jie" (Chinatown; literally Tang Chinese people street) due to their self-identity as well as identification with their homeland and culture. In addition, they called their home country "Tangshan" (literally Tang mountain, meaning China), returning to China "xuantang" (literally returning to Tang mountain, meaning returning to China) and the dialect they spoke "tanghua" (literally Tang language, meaning their home language). The early Chinese workers were mostly men without support of their families. In order to protect themselves and help one another, they lived close together and formed Chinatowns of different sizes. Matters big and small – from resisting the anti-Chinese campaigns and fighting for the rights of Chinese people to the simple necessities of everyday life – were all resolved in Chinatown. As such, the clan associations and native societies in Chinatowns became the "home" of overseas Chinese.

2) Southeast Asia

Chinese immigrants in Southeast Asia largely originated from southern Fujian province, the Hakka area in Xingmei of northern Guangdong province, Chaozhou, Guangdong and Hainan among others, and they had a long history of living in the region. Chinese had traded in Nanyang (Southeast Asia) as early as the Tang and Song dynasties, whereas others emigrated to Southeast Asia in the 16th century when western colonizers opened new frontiers there, working in various industries including mining, natural rubber and commerce. By the 1920s, there were 1,553,137 Chinese persons in the British Straits Settlements and the Malay Peninsula in Southeast Asia (Chen, 2011). Most Chinese people in Southeast Asia were natives of southern Fujian province, Hakka people and people from Chaozhou and Shantou. They had a long history in Southeast Asia and exerted great influence on the culture of the region. Since they left China from the ports of Xiamen and Shantou, they were less influenced by western culture. More importantly, they were middleman minorities between the indigenous population and the western colonizers. There were yet to be anti-Chinese laws in these colonies, so many Chinese started families, acquired properties and opened businesses there. It was common for them to have one family at home and one abroad. (Li, 2015)

3) Cuba and Peru

Chinese went to Central and South America to earn a living when western colonizers started to develop new frontiers there before the First Opium War. At that time, there was a severe laborer shortage in Cuba and Peru, and slavery trade was carried out in the dark. In 1839, Chinese began to set foot in Cuba; in 1846, the first group of 212 indentured Chinese workers from Xiamen arrived in Havana; in 1849 the first group of 75 indentured Chinese workers from Macau arrived in Peru. Following the end of slavery, Chinese workers made up most of the workforce at the sugar cane plantations and guano mines in Central and South America during the late 19th century. They were also employed by the coffee manufacturing, construction as well as mining industries, and as railroad builders. In the three decades that followed, more than 140,000 Chinese arrived in Cuba and 100,000 went to Peru. 95% of them originated from Guangdong province, while nearly all of them were men.

Having come out of slavery, Chinese workers in Cuba played an active role in the Cuban War of Independence in the thirty years after 1868. 2,000 to 3,000 Chinese volunteer soldiers took part in fighting whereas close to 5,000 people joined the work in the rear. The inscription on a commemorative stele that pays tribute to their unfaltering contribution towards the independence of the Cuba reads, "*(Spanish) No hubo un chino Cubano desertor, no hubo un chino cubano traidor* (There was not one Chinese Cuban that deserted, not one Chinese Cuban that betrayed [the cause])". (Pang, 2013; Naravaez, 2010; Yang, 2000)

4) United States

It is generally believed that the first Chinese migrated to the United States in 1785, when US national John O'Donnell hired 32 sailors from India and 4 from China to transport the first Asian products to Baltimore, Maryland on the US merchant vessel *Pallas* (Chin, 2015). Emigration on a larger scale took place in the 1850s: in 1848, news about the discovery of gold in California spread to the Pearl River Delta, resulting in the first wave of emigration when large numbers of Chinese joined the gold rush; between 1863 and 1869, the United States needed a lot of workers to build the transcontinental railroad and some 12,000 to 15,000 Chinese laborers were hired to build the railroad in the second wave of emigration; after the Burlingame Treaty was signed in 1868, large numbers of Chinese flocked to the United States to work in a number of industries, including railroad construction, mining, cultivation, vegetable farming, fishing, laundry services, as well as restaurants. By the 1870s, there were approximately 150,000 Chinese in the United States (151,300 according to the statistics of the Chinese associations in Chinatowns across the country; 107,488 according to the US census). The Chinese Exclusion Act passed in 1882 imposed many restrictions on Chinese workers – they were forbidden to marry US nationals and own properties, whereas anti-Chinese riots broke out in Chinatowns in different parts of the country. More than 20,000 Chinese workers returning on the way to the United States were refused entry, leading to a decline in the Chinese population. In 1906, immigration records were destroyed in a fire that broke out after the San Francisco earthquake. Many Chinese falsely claimed they were US nationals and were thus able to sponsor their children born in China to emigrate to the United States. Some Chinese even sold their improperly obtained birth registration records to other people, so that they could emigrate to the United States as "paper sons". The US government suspected fraudulence, and in 1910 Angel Island Immigration Station was set up to detain and interrogate immigrants entering the United States. As many as 175,000 Chinese were subject to humiliating interrogation there. By 1930, there were some 100,000 Chinese persons in the United States (102,159 according to the US census). There was a serious gender imbalance, to such an extent that Chinatown was once called a "bachelor society" (Liu, 1976; Chinn, 1969; US Census Data 1840-2010; Amanik & Fletcher, 2019).

5) Australia

According to records in the Melbourne-Chinese Museum, the history of Chinese emigrating to Australia can be dated to the 1810s. Ma Shiying, a carpenter from Guangzhou, arrived in Sydney in 1818 – he was the first Chinese person to arrive in Australia. After Ma, the first group of Chinese immigrants in Australia were 3,000 indentured workers (1848-1853) from Fujian and Guangdong, hired by the colonial government of New South Wales to work in sheep farming. The second group of Chinese immigrants were gold diggers (1851-1877) who flocked to Australia from Fujian and Guangdong following the discovery of gold in Victoria in 1851, and most of them were from Siyi (Taishan, Kaiping, Xinhui and Enping), Zhongshan and Sanyi (Nanhai, Panyu and Shunde) in Guangdong province. In 1857, there were 24,062 Chinese mining gold in Melbourne; in 1890, there were some 49,000 Chinese in Australia, 90% of whom came from the four counties of Taishan, Kaiping, Xinhui and Enping. The majority of Chinese immigrants worked in the mining industry, plantations, the fishing industry and carpentry. Anti-Chinese sentiments were particularly strong from the colonial period in the 1880s to the federation of the colonies in 1901. To limit Chinese immigration to Australia, the first Federal Parliament passed the Immigration Restriction Act. The law formed the basis of the White Australia policy, requiring all immigrants to pass a 50-word dictation and listening test in any European language. The policy was successful, as no Chinese laborer could pass the language test and enter Australia. At that time, the Chinese population in the country was about 29,000, but the figure had since declined. (Gunstone, 2010: 2; Price, 1987:176)

6) Canada

In 1788, a group of Chinese carpenters from Macau landed in British Columbia with British naval captain John Meares. They were the first Chinese persons to set foot in Canada (Ma & Cartier, 2003). In 1858, one year after gold was discovered along the Thompson River in British Columbia, Chinese who were mining gold in California got wind of the discovery and crossed the border to look for gold in the Fraser Valley area. Half of the gold diggers in the Barkerville gold mines in Cariboo Valley were Chinese, while Chinatowns had been set up in the gold rush towns nearby, including Richfield, Stanley, Van Winkle, Quesnellemouthe (present-day Quesnel), Antler and Quesnelle Forks. These were the first Chinese immigrants in Canada (Skelton, 1980).

Between 1881 and 1885, approximately 15,000 to 17,000 Chinese laborers were hired for the construction of the Canadian Pacific Railway, sparking the second wave of Chinese emigration. Like their counterparts who worked on the Central Pacific Railroad in the United States, the Chinese laborers were made to build the most treacherous section of the Canadian Pacific Railway. During the construction of the section through the Canadian Rocky Mountains, some 4,000 Chinese lost their lives. After the gold rush and railway construction, Chinese mostly worked in plantations, the fishing industry, laundry services as well as restaurants. Construction of the railway was completed in 1885. In the same year, the Canadian government began to limit Chinese immigration. A poll tax of 50 Canadian dollars was imposed upon Chinese persons wanting to enter the country. In 1900, the tax was increased to 100 Canadian dollars; in 1903, it was further increased to 500 Canadian dollars. In 1923, the Chinese Immigration Act was enacted, banning Chinese immigrants (with the exception of students, diplomats and persons being granted special permission). (Chow, 2014; Li, 2013) Chinese people were also discriminated against in the labour market. When granting financial subsidy and land to the British Columbia Sugar Refining Company in 1890, the municipal government of Vancouver stipulated that "...offer the grant and land by way of bonus, in aid of the establishment of the said sugar refining business, is enacted by the Major and Council thereof on the condition that the said Company shall not at any time employ Chinese laborers in and about the said works." (Aug.4.1890) (Yu, 2018: 43)

All in all, most Chinese laborers in modern times left their home on their own to earn a living abroad. Away from their families, they did strenuous work in an unfamiliar environment. There were cultural differences, language barriers and strong anti-Chinese sentiments. They missed their homeland deeply and longed to return to their awaiting families, if not during their lifetime then at least after death. Therefore, Chinese who died overseas all wished that their bones could be repatriated to their hometown for burial, so that their spirits could have eternal peace. Meanwhile, those living tried their utmost to fulfil these last wishes: according to second burial customs, Chinese laborers who died abroad in the early days were given simple burials by fellow clansmen and after a certain period of time their bones were exhumed and repatriated to their hometown for permanent burial. In this way, they would not become desolate spirits with no one paying respects to them.

From the beginning of bone repatriation to the ban on the tradition following the founding of the People's Republic of China in 1949, uncountable sets of bones had been sent back to China. In those days, bone repatriation was practised wherever there was a Chinese population. In 1913, over 10,000 boxes had reportedly been repatriated from the United States (Sinn, 2013).

Mr Yang Jingchu, who lived in Victoria, Canada in his senior years, wrote a poem about the Chinese railway workers who died abroad, expressing his concern for the lonely spirits who did not have the chance to return home:

> *The Chinese workers came from afar*
> *To build the railway from coast to coast.*
> *Unwanted they became when the work was complete –*
> *Marginalised they were, and discriminated against.*
> *They were tormented by cold and hunger till they died.*
> *How could their desolate spirits return home?*
> *Who would sweep their graves on Ching Ming and Chung Yeung?*
> *With no family, on foreign land – they were doubly sad.*

(Yang, 1997:60)

7) Background for Exhumation

In western cultures, "cemetery" and "graveyard" refer to the places where deceased persons and their belongings, bones or ashes are buried. The deceased are usually buried in plots designated by the management office. In Chinese society before 1949, traditional customs and rituals were an important part of people's lives. The practice of second burial was widely popular: all burial grounds were meticulously selected by *fengshui* masters, whereas the tomb itself was located at the *fengshui* point with the strongest auspicious forces – the location of the tomb had to be precise, since a slight deviation could mean departure from the umbrella point. The largest burial grounds were family graveyards, where members of the same extended family were buried. The concept of modern cemeteries, which provide a final resting place to a large number of deceased persons, was yet to take shape.

8) Native Societies and Charitable/Benevolent Associations

Chinese laborers first travelled to Southeast Asia on a large scale, and then to other regions, to earn a living. Most of the workers were bachelors without family support who quickly established social networks in overseas Chinese communities using the traditional rites and clan systems of Chinese rural societies – organizations were formed based on the native or industry associations that were popular in the Ming and Qing dynasties. There were native societies called "huiguan", clan associations known as "gongsuo" and industry associations with a special purpose known as "tang". In the native societies and larger clan associations, charitable or benevolent associations were set up to oversee the bone repatriation process and offer support to the deceased's families. The well managed and intricately connected organizations maintained order in the Chinatowns. Cao Yazhi, also known as Cao Yazhu, was a native of Taishan, Guangdong province. He worked as a carpenter in Macau before travelling to the Malay Peninsula to earn a living. In 1819, he established a clan association, known as "*gongsuo*", in Singapore. It was the first clan association established by overseas Chinese based on blood connections. In 1822, Cao founded the Ning Yeung Wui Kuan in Singapore, the first native society founded by overseas Chinese based on geographical connections. The purpose of the Cao's clan association and native society are clearly recorded, "Members of the Cao clan left their footprints all over the world, in America and even British Victoria. All graves were checked, whereas bones were exhumed from every grave upon receiving report to the association. No deceased friend from our native county was missed out. If the body had not yet fully decomposed, the remains were first placed in a lead can and then sealed in a wooden box. Sometimes, the deceased was drowned and his body was consumed by fish, or the deceased was murdered and buried in a secluded place, and his body was later stolen by foreigners, or the marker of the grave went missing and the identity of the deceased could not be traced. In such cases, the name of the deceased, if known, was written on a small silver plaque, attached to a 'spirit summoning' box, and repatriated [to China]." (Yu, 1987: 8)

The story of "graves were stolen by foreigners" was sometimes reported in American newspapers. The *Seattle Star* once warned that the wigs might be made from long braids stolen from Chinese graves (*The Seattle Star*, July 27, 1908). Therefore, Chinese people's concern about the safety of cemeteries gradually became one of the key reasons to the establishment of *shangtang* (charitable association) in clan and native associations to collect bones and return them to their places of original for burial.

People from Guangdong began to leave their hometown in large numbers to earn a living in North America and Oceania in the 1840s to 1850s. In the few years that followed, Chinatown in San Francisco, with its network of native societies, clan associations and industry associations, was established. The

Chinatowns that emerged later in other places were managed in similar manners.

The native societies took funeral and burial matters seriously. Most of them established charitable/benevolent associations to help old and poor Chinese return to their hometown, manage funerals and burials, offer support to the deceased's families, repatriate the bones of deceased Chinese to their hometown for burial as well as manage graveyards. In a letter to Zheng Zaoru, the Chinese Minister to the Unites States, Huang Zunxian, the Chinese Consul-General in San Francisco between 1882 and 1886, wrote that:

> *Every time a ship arrives, the district associations look after the newcomers, taking their belongings and helping them rent accommodation. In the case of incidents, the directors sort out matters for the members. When someone without a family dies of illness, the association exhumes their bones and repatriate them to the deceased's hometown for burial. (In some cases, this matter is not handled by the district association but by the charity tang established by the counties.)*

> (Huang, 2003: 520)

The charitable associations set out to help fellow clansmen abroad return to their roots. They served two functions: firstly, exhume and repatriate the bones of deceased Chinese; secondly, provide assistance to impoverished members in the best way they could. After verifying membership records, the associations offered subsidies to the members to pay for the ship tickets so that they could spend their last years in their hometown.

9) Overseas Cemeteries

The funeral as well as the subsequent bone exhumation and repatriation of deceased Chinese were undertaken by the native societies and charitable associations. Chinese attached great importance to the fortune of their "next life", where they were buried after they died and whether their bones and spirit could return to their hometown. Their greatest wish was: every year on Ching Ming Festival their descendants would visit their graves, so that they would not become desolate spirits. The cemetery was where deceased people were buried. Even for transient first burials, it was an important temporary resting place. If possible, overseas cemeteries were built by the sea or where there was a view of the sea, while the altar and incense burner faced the direction of the sea – home on the other side of the Pacific Ocean.

At some early overseas Chinese cemeteries, spirits and the Earth God were revered, whereas altars and incense burners were set up in the cemeteries purchased by native societies and charitable associations. Every year on Ching Ming and Chung Yeung, their representatives would visit the cemeteries and pay respect to the deceased.

During the time when anti-Chinese sentiments were strong, finding a piece of land to build a cemetery was not easy. Chinese were blatantly discriminated against, and there were restrictions due to local laws. White people did not believe that spirits in another world had strong connections with the living. Their cemeteries were usually separated from the graveyards of Chinese in the name of religion, whereas some religious groups refused to allocate burial space to the "heathen Chinese". Even though some Chinese managed to purchase land in a local cemetery, the burial space was often downgraded – the usual practice was to separate the graves of white people and those of Chinese. Most graveyards of white people did not allow Chinese persons to be buried there, with the exception of loyal Chinese servants, who might be buried with the white families they served in the families' private burial grounds. Meanwhile, since most Chinese could not afford to have their remains embalmed and repatriated to their hometown in a coffin after they died, they could only have their remains buried temporarily in a segregated cemetery or overseas Chinese cemetery. After a few years, their remains would be exhumed and repatriated to China for permanent burial.

The Chinese cemeteries near the cities with a significant Chinese population often ran out of space. For example, at the entrance of Hoy Sun Ning Yung Cemetery and the Chinese Cemetery in San Francisco, a piece of land was designated as temporary burial ground. The bones were exhumed once every three to five years to make room for other deceased Chinese. After exhumation, the bones were put in boxes and then placed in a small shed used for storing bones in the cemetery until they were repatriated to China.

Even though burial in the deceased's hometown in China was the common practice in those days, some Americanised Chinese people who had families and descendants in the United States chose to be buried there. This was because they regarded the United States as their home – their descendants, relatives and families all lived in the US. In 1896, *The San Francisco Call* ran an unusual story, entitled "His Bones to Lie in This Land", about a Chinese named Yee Ah-tai who would like to be laid to rest in the United States. (*The San Francisco Call*, 14 June 1896)

In some small towns where anti-Chinese sentiments were less strong, Chinese and other ethnic minorities could be buried in public cemeteries, the final resting place of deceased local residents. Bakersfield was one of these towns in the 1870s (Amanik & Fletcher, 2019: 28).

Exhumation and repatriation were costly and laborious. The bones were usually transported to San Francisco of the United States and Victoria, British Columbia of Canada, and then repatriated to China. Based on the funeral and burial management framework of the San Francisco Chinatown, the author has briefly figured out the relationship between the native societies and charitable associations:

Ning Yung Benevolent Association had a large membership and ample financial resources, and could afford to purchase land and build Hoy Sun Ning Yung Cemetery for people from Taishan. Meanwhile, Chinese of the other six large native societies jointly purchased a plot of land and established the Chinese Cemetery, where deceased members of the six native societies were buried. These cemeteries were run by dedicated personnel, whereas the charitable associations were responsible for matters related to bone exhumation and repatriation. These arrangements did not apply to those Chinese not belonging to any native society or clan association, or those who lived in rural towns with no native society or clan association for them to join. (They would usually join their local Chinese Freemasons, Hip Sing Tong Association, Hop Sing Tong Association, Chee Kung Tong Association, Suey Sing Tong Association and On Leong Tong Association, which also offered bone exhumation and repatriation service for their members.) The link between the native societies, charitable associations and the cemeteries are illustrated in the table below:

Major Native Societies and Charitable Associations in San Francisco (1849-1949)

Year of Establishment	Name of Native Society	Corresponding Counties in China	Name of Charitable/ Benevolent Association (Tong)	Name of Cemetery
1849	Sze Yup Benevolent Association	Taishan (Hoy Sun), Xinhui (Sun Wei), Kaiping (Hoi Ping), Enping (Yan Ping) (Renamed Kong Chow Benevolent Association led by Xinhui and Heshan in 1854)		
1850	Sam Yup Benevolent Association	Nanhai (Nam Hoy), Panyu (Poon Yu), Shunde (Shun Duck)	Nam Hoy Fook Yum Benevolent Society Hung On Tong Pon Yup Chong How Benevolent Association	Chinese Cemetery
1850	Yan Wo Benevolent Association	Hakka communities from Bao'an, Huiyang, Meixian and Chixi	No designated charitable associations to undertake funerals or burials matters	Chinese Cemetery
1852	Yeong Wo Benevolent Association	Xiangshan (Zhongshan), Dongguan, Zengcheng, Boluo	Tung Sen Association, Jack Sen Benevolent Association, Hee Sen Association Tun Shen Association, Jup Shin Tong, Gway Sen Association, Duck Sen Association, Leong Sen Association, Lock Sen Association, Bok Sen Association, Yee On Association Tung Goon Bo On Association, Yan On Tong	Chinese Cemetery
1854	Ning Yung Benevolent Association	Taishan (Hoy Sun)	Yee Hing Tong	Hoy Sun Ning Yung Cemetery

Year of Establishment	Name of Native Society	Corresponding Counties in China	Name of Charitable/ Benevolent Association (Tong)	Name of Cemetery
1854	Kong Chow Benevolent Association	Xinhui (Sun Wei), Heshan (Hok Shan)	Sun Wei Fook Hing Tong, Tung Duck Tong, Hok Shan Duck How Tong	Chinese Cemetery
1862	Hop Wo Benevolent Association	Yu (Yee) clan from Taishan; Deng, Xie, Hu, Zhu, Pan, Li and , Ou clans from Kaiping; Zheng clan from Enping	Quong Fook Tong Benevolent Association	Chinese Cemetery
1876	Sue Hing Benevolent Association	Kaiping (Hoi Ping), Enping (Yan Ping)	Quong Fook Tong Benevolent Association	Chinese Cemetery

10) Exhumation and Repatriation

In 1848, gold was discovered in California of the United States, and many Chinese were drawn to North America by the gold rush. As early as 1853, the Sze Yup Benevolent Association began to exhume the bones of deceased friends and repatriate them to their hometown for burial (Liu, 1976:165). On 22 July 1855, *The China Mail* of Hong Kong reported briefly on a special cargo shipment from San Francisco, USA – 94 boxes containing the bones of Chinese (Ko, 2006: 102; Yip, 2009: 23). Meanwhile, the 6 January 1858 issue of *Daily Alta California* contained one of the earliest newspaper reports about bone repatriation for Chinese in California that Chinese dug holes in the ground, exhumed the bones and sent them back to China. The Pon Yup Chong How Benevolent Association under Sam Yup Benevolent Association of San Francisco began to gather manpower and raise funds for bone repatriation in the 8th year of Qing Emperor Xianfeng's reign (1858). The bones were exhumed and repatriated once every seven to ten years, and the entire process – including fund-raising and difficulties encountered during exhumation–was documented in detail in all the accounting journals of Chong How Benevolent Association in San Francisco preserved till today. Their clansmen founded Kai Sin Tong in Hong Kong to undertake repatriation of the bones from Hong Kong to Panyu for burial (Archives of Sam Yup Benevolent Association, Hanford, California).

1. Fund Raising

The charitable associations were largely funded by donations from fellow clansmen and income generated by properties they owned. In terms of expenses, money was spent on exhuming the bones, sending the bones to Hong Kong in boxes and burial fees paid to the deceased's families. At that time, it cost approximately 5 US dollars to transport a box of bones to Hong Kong. There was a sanitary charge of 10 US dollars, and burial fees of 5-10 US dollars were offered to the family of each deceased friend (Hom, 2001: V3-2). By the 1860s to 1870s, the cost of sending one set of bones to Hong Kong by sea had risen to 20 US dollars (Sinn, 2013: 268). The operations of the native societies and charitable associations were supported by membership fees collected from the members or money donated especially for bone repatriation. Every donor received a receipt called "exit permit" that functioned as a "boarding pass" for Chinese travelling to China by sea (there are other forms of donations that can also serve as an "exit permit"). Meanwhile, to ensure adequate funds to cover the costs of bone repatriation and to provide ship ticket subsidies for old and impoverished clansmen, the native societies somewhat forced members to pay membership fees or donate money for bone exhumation. There were inspection points being set up on the vessels. Chinese must present an exit permit in order to board the vessel; for those who failed to present an exit permit, the association would not be responsible for exhuming and repatriating their bones if they happened to pass away in the United States.

The costs of exhumation and repatriation were very high. According to the accounting journal of Chong How Benevolent Association in 1863, the total costs for the association's first repatriation was 20,500 dollars. 258 sets of remains and 59 "spirit summoning" boxes were repatriated. Burial fees of 7 US dollars were offered for each set of remains, whereas four persons were appointed to escort the remains to Hong Kong. In 1876, the total costs of the second repatriation had risen to more than 40,000 dollars. 858 sets of remains and 24 "spirit summoning" boxes were repatriated. Burial fees of 10 US dollars were offered for each set of remains (*Accounting Journal of Chong How Benevolent Association of San Francisco 1863 & 1876*). Considering the high operational costs, the repatriation of bones would not be possible if not for well-established organizations as well as shared cultural views and values.

Responsible and trustworthy clansmen were appointed to oversee the exhumation and repatriation process. These dedicated persons would travel from city to city to collect donations and issue receipts to the donors. The association relied heavily on donations, which might vary from time to time, to support bone exhumation work. A donation record was kept and receipts were issued to the donor. Those who did not make a donation would not have their bones exhumed and repatriated after their passing. This measure helped guarantee adequate funding for bone exhumation and repatriation – the living donated money not only to help others, but also to ensure that their own remains would be exhumed and repatriated after their death.

Apart from collecting donations from fellow clansmen during bone exhumation, the general committee members of the associations also considered investing in real estate so as to generate income. Many benevolent associations acquired properties in Chinatowns, Hong Kong or the villages in mainland China, and the interest collected would be used to cover bone exhumation expenses.

2. Process of Exhumation

The persons designated by a charitable association to oversee the exhumation process would hire workers to exhume the bones, and they travelled from city to city, trying their utmost to look for bones while cases were reported to the association. Before bone exhumation and repatriation were officially carried out in Canada, these people even travelled from the United States to Victoria of British Columbia – which was yet to be incorporated into Canada at the time – searching for the graves of deceased Chinese. Since bone exhumation was a serious matter, the native societies would spell out the requirements of exhumation before hiring workers. The workers should exhume the bones, in order, from head to toe, and the article also described the feature of each piece of bone.

On 23 May 1867, *The Illustrated Adelaide Post* of Melbourne published an account by a white person named Kandell describing how he and four Chinese friends exhumed bones in White Hills Cemetery in Bendigo, Victoria, Australia (Ross, 2009: 265-266)

First the skull was removed, followed by the backbone, ribs, arm and leg bones. A dozen of Chinese people gathered around the grave, counting the bones meticulously. They were happy to see that no bone was missing – not even a tooth could be left out. Every tooth had to be secured to the jaws. Then, the bones in the legs and foot were set aside. During the exhumation process, a Chinese couple were busy cleaning the bones and placing them in the appropriate place. The bones were laid out under the sun. After the arms bones, leg bones and other bones became dry, they were placed in different bags, tied and labelled. The whole skeleton was placed in a small rectangular box about 1.2 metres long.

As a matter of fact, not all deceased persons were buried in graves and not all headstones were well preserved with clear information about the deceased. If the bones could be identified, they would be placed in a box marked with the deceased's name and address; if, for whatever reason, the bones could not be located, the deceased's spirit would be summoned into a box and repatriated.

In order to manage the exhumation and repatriation well and also prevent corruption, there were strict requirements that the exhumation foreman had to meet. Due to stringent financial management, the native society would not hire a person from their own county as exhumation foreman. The 8th clause of the rules and regulations of Chong How Benevolent Association in the 4th year of Qing Emperor Guangxu's reign stipulated that, "Persons from our county would not be hired as exhumation foreman. If it is proved that a foreman from another county secretly hired men from our own county, both parties would be fined 1,000 dollars. No exemption would be made with regard to this rule" (Rules and regulations for bone repatriation in 1878).

3. Transporting to Hong Kong

In North America, the native societies in the Chinatown of San Francisco, USA, and Victoria, Canada, collected the bones of the deceased and repatriated them to Hong Kong. Repatriation was carried out once every 7 to 10 years. While native societies and charitable associations with a large membership (such as Yee Hing Tong of Ning Yung Benevolent Association) could organize their own repatriation, smaller native societies could only pay the charitable associations of neighbouring counties to help them. For instance, Yan Wo Benevolent Association, a Hakka organization in San Francisco, did not have their own charitable association to take care of bones. As to places with a small Chinese population, several charitable associations would carry out joint exhumation and repatriation. A great deal of care and attention was paid to loading the boxes containing the bones of deceased persons onto the ships. The deceased's names and the boxes carrying their bones were meticulously recorded. On 20 August 1864, Mark Twain published an article in the *San Francisco Daily Morning Call* about the bone repatriation he had witnessed in Ning Yung Benevolent Association:

> *On the Pacific coast the Chinamen all belong to one or another of several great companies or organizations, and these companies keep track of their members, register their names, and ship their bodies home when they die. The See Yup Company (Sze Yup Benevolent Association) is held to be the largest of these. The Ning Yeong Company (Ning Yung Benevolent Association) is next, and numbers eighteen thousand members on the coast. Its headquarters are at San Francisco, where it has a costly temple, several great officers..., and a numerous priesthood. In it I was shown a register of its members, with the dead and the date of their shipment to China duly marked.*

The section of the Central Pacific Railroad built by Chinese between 1865 and 1869 was located between Sacramento, California, and Salt Lake City, Nevada. It was the most treacherous section in the construction of the US transcontinental railroad: many workers were killed or injured. There were newspaper reports about repatriation of the bones of Chinese laborers who died while building the railroad:

> *On January 5, 1870 the Elko Independent reported six carloads of deceased Chinese destined for San Francisco and then probably to China. According to the Silver State (Winnemucca, Nevada) in March 1870, two designated Chinese funeral cars were on a siding near the present-day Bridge Street grade crossing preparing the deceased for their final trip home. The bones were boxed, labelled with the name of the individual, and listed the date of death and association (tang) name, which were then shipped to Hong Kong via San Francisco. On June 30, 1870 the Sacramento Reporter (Sacramento, California) stated that 20,000 pounds of bones (an estimated 1,200 deceased Chinese or 1 in 10 Chinese workers) were enroute to China.*
>
> (Amanik & Fletcher, 2019:8-9)

Generally speaking, the charitable associations would appoint representatives to escort the bones to Hong Kong and liaise with persons-in-charge in Hong Kong with regard to the final leg of the journey from Hong Kong to the deceased's hometown. The delivery charges were paid by the charitable associations. Meanwhile, depending on the amount of donations collected in that year, the charitable associations would offer burial fees of 5-10 dollars for each set of remains. The representatives of the charitable associations would also oversee the burial of the remains in the deceased's hometown. Pray masters were hired to perform rituals to pacify the deceased's spirits. Afterwards, the bones were placed in the local coffin home, charitable association or shelter/clinic, so that the deceased's families could collect the bones and bury them in their hometown. Any unclaimed bones would be buried in the communal graveyards built by the overseas charitable associations, whereas sacrifices would be offered to the deceased every year (Rules and regulations for bone exhumation and repatriation of Chong How Benevolent Association, 1878).

If the burial of Chinese people was viewed from a commercial perspective apart from their funeral beliefs, the shipment of Chinese bones to Hong Kong was also a good business. Health authorities and shipping companies in the United States took this lucrative opportunity on their own terms. In 1900, The *San Francisco Call* in San Francisco reported that shipping "fish bones" to China had become an important local industry. The local health bureau imposed a tax of 10 dollars per set of bones on the Chinese who transported the bones to Hong Kong. But the Chinese, in order to evade taxes, colluded with the shipping manager to falsely claim that the bones shipped to Hong Kong were "fish bones" (*The San Francisco Call*, April. 20, 1900) In 1911, The *Pacific Commercial Advertiser* in Honolulu published an advertisement "Makes A Low Rate For Chinese Corpses", reporting that "corpse of white person, $230; corpse of Chinese, dead less than one year, $55; corpse of Chinese, dead over one year, $35." (The Pacific Commercial Advertiser, May 27, 1911)

Transit in Hong Kong

1) Hong Kong's Role

After the First Opium War, Hong Kong became a British colony in 1841. In the same year, it was declared a free trading port – the British Hong Kong government made use of Hong Kong's advantage in shipping to build a trading port which supported free trade, convenient investment, an open financial system and free flow of people.

In 1848, news of the discovery of gold in the United States spread to the Pearl River Delta via Hong Kong, and farmers who were out of work began to flock to the United States. In the same year, Hong Kong's Harbour Master Office opened the sea route between Hong Kong and the Americas; in the following year, 23 vessels sailed from Hong Kong to San Francisco; according to a government report in 1852, as many as 30,000 Chinese travelled to San Francisco via Hong Kong in that year, while the total population Hong Kong was only 39,000 (Ko, 2006: 102). At the same time, many Chinese travelled to the islands in Southeast Asia by way of Hong Kong, and also to Australia after gold was discovered in Melbourne in 1851. By 1860, the number of vessels sailing in and out of Hong Kong had soared to 2,888 (Ting, 2010: 18). In 1877, civilian boats that sailed from Hong Kong to destinations in Guangdong province – mostly in the Pearl River Delta – totalled 111 (Ko, 2006: 113). Due to its proximity to Guangdong province along with its well-developed shipping industry, Hong Kong gradually became a transit point for Chinese from the Pearl River Delta, especially the Wuyi area, travelling abroad to earn a living or returning home from overseas. Meanwhile, a transportation network connecting

Hong Kong and the inland water channels in the Pearl River Delta, as well as a commercial network for gold mountain trade with mainland China and North America was established. (Sinn, 2013:297-304).

During this time, Tung Wah Hospital emerged as a charitable organization entrusted by overseas Chinese to handle the bones repatriated from abroad. In addition to Hong Kong's well-developed shipping industry and its proximity to the Pearl River Delta, the interpersonal network of the Directors of Tung Wah Hospital was also an important factor. Of the 13 founding Directors of Tung Wah Hospital, 12 were prominent compradors in foreign trading companies or merchants specialising in trade with North and South China, South-east Asia and North America (Ko, 2006:103). These individuals were often directors of native societies who maintained close relationship with the native societies in different countries, or they had already established a stable, trusting relationship with overseas parties through their commercial network. Meanwhile, taking advantage of Hong Kong's free trade policy, the connections with North America and Southeast Asia, the proximity to Guangdong as well as the city's open financial system, many overseas native societies set up liaison offices in Hong Kong to – for the most part – collect overseas donations for the development of their hometown. Hong Kong had a prosperous financial industry. The city's many banks could easily handle funds remitted from overseas counterparts, whereas native banks in Hong Kong could send the funds to the families of overseas Chinese compatriot affiliated shops in their hometown. Against this backdrop, Hong Kong developed into a transit point for the remittance from overseas Chinese. Interpersonal network played a crucial role here.

A large global charitable network centred on Hong Kong had since been established.

2) Founding of Tung Wah Hospital

When Hong Kong first opened its port to foreign trade, it only had a population of 5,000. As the city developed, there was a labour shortage and people from various counties in Guangdong province came to Hong Kong to earn a living. Meanwhile, during the Taiping Rebellion and the Punti-Hakka Clan Wars, which lasted more than 10 years from 1854 to 1867 and affected the entire Wuyi area as well as Foshan and Gaoming nearby, life was extremely difficult for the people. Many of them came to Hong Kong to escape the turmoil. By 1860, the population of Hong Kong had surged to 92,442 (Ting, 2010: 18). Meanwhile, after the Second Opium War broke out in 1856, the people of Guangzhou burned down the Thirteen Factories, where most foreign trading companies were based, prompting the foreign trading companies to move their headquarters from Guangzhou to Hong Kong. Subsequently, compradors of the foreign trading companies moved to Hong Kong while more and more people from the Pearl River Delta came to the city looking for work. Hong Kong's Chinese population continued to grow. Nevertheless, mainstream society cared little about the livelihood, healthcare and burial arrangements of Chinese people. Hong Kong's Chinese elite thus got together to work for the welfare of Chinese. In 1851, 14 Hong Kong industry representatives and merchants, led by Kaiping native Tam Ah choy, applied to the Hong Kong government for land allocation while they raised funds to build Kwong Fook I-Tsz, a communal ancestral hall for the spirit tablets of Chinese who passed away in Hong Kong and had no family. The ancestral hall was thus also called "Temple of One Hundred Family Names" (Ting, 2010: 17-25).

According to the research by Ko Tim-keung, an expert on local Hong Kong history, there is no trace of upper-class Chinese persons buried in Hong

Kong before 1870, presumably because their remains were repatriated to their hometown for burial. Before the Chinese Permanent Cemetery at Aberdeen was established in 1915, there was no cemetery for non-Christian upper-class Chinese in Hong Kong. Those who could afford the costs of transporting their coffins to their hometown for burial would, therefore, not choose to be laid to rest in Hong Kong after death (Ko, 2006: 99).

Along with the rise of the foreign trading companies and the increase in the number of Chinese compradors, Hong Kong's Chinese merchants began to gain influence and dealt with the government on matters regarding the Chinese community. Hong Kong's Chinese elite first sought the government's approval for a Chinese hospital to be built in 1866, but their request was turned down. Subsequently in 1869, the *Hong Kong Daily Press* published a report about the poor management of Kwong Fook I-Tsz. Many critically ill patients were left to die in this communal ancestral hall, which also housed the remains of deceased persons. Naturally, hygiene conditions were very appalling. In 1869, then Hong Kong governor Richard Graves MacDonnell gave in to public pressure and granted land for the building of Tung Wah Hospital – a Chinese medicine hospital and charitable organization for the Chinese community. On 30 March 1870, the Legislative Council of Hong Kong passed "The Chinese Hospital Incorporation Ordinance, 1870" and Tung Wah Hospital was established (Ho, 2009:18; Ting, 2010: 17-25).

On 14 February 1872, Tung Wah Hospital was inaugurated. According to *The China Mail*, an elaborate sacrificial ceremony for Shennong, the God of Medicine in Chinese legend, was held in the morning. It is believed that Shennong tested medicinal herbs on his own body and compiled theories on Chinese medicine. He was thus hailed as the creator of Chinese medicine. The spirit tablet of Shennong was revered in Tung Wah Hospital.

3) Tung Wah Coffin Home

The origin of coffin homes can be traced to *History of Song: Biography of Fan Zhongyan*. According to the historical text, Fan Zhongyan "...was very kind-hearted and generous who established the Fan charitable estate to provide various relief services for the underprivileged members of the clan". In the Qing dynasty, Feng Guifen wrote in *Discussion on the Patriarchal Clan System* that, "the charitable estate founded by Fan Wenzheng [Fan Zhongyan] of the Song dynasty has set an example for future generations." Comprising schools, farmland and an ancestral hall, the charitable estate of Fan established a sound management system to help needy members of the clan in the areas of child and elderly care, weddings and funerals, poverty and disaster relief, and education (Tang, 1997: 190-199). The charitable estate of the Fan clan exerted a profound influence in the Qing dynasty, especially in the region south of the Yangtze River. Wealthy clans followed suit and established their own charitable estates to help poor members of the clan; in the Qing dynasty, there were as many as 179 charitable estates in Suzhou (Wang, 1998: 84-97). Meanwhile, some smaller scale estates served as communal ancestral halls for the spirit tablets of deceased persons with no family, or coffin homes providing temporary refuge for coffins. Kwong Fook I-Tsz, built with funds raised by Chinese in Hong Kong, was an exemplification of this concept.

While Tung Wah Hospital was under construction, the graves of Chinese persons discovered on the site (originally a graveyard for Chinese people) were moved to Slaughter House Cemetery. This marked the start of the funeral services of Tung Wah Hospital. After the hospital opened, many poor people died there, and offering free coffins and burials became an important service of Tung Wah in addition to free medical services. Meanwhile, historical records reveal that Man Mo Temple built a coffin home adjacent to Slaughter House Cemetery, which was located on a slope in Kennedy Town; in 1875, management of the coffin home was subsequently handed over to Tung Wah. The section "Room Regulations" in the *Zhengxinlu of Tung Wah Hospital in 1873* – the earliest accounting journal of Tung Wah in existence today – was changed to "Coffin Home Regulations" in the following year, suggesting that Tung Wah Hospital already operated a coffin home in its early years (Ting, 2010: 25).

There is no evidence to determine when Tung Wah Hospital began to take bones repatriated from overseas into its care. Yet a short article in the 8 April 1874 issue of Hong Kong's *Tsun Wan Yat Po* recorded that "a steamship operated by American Shipping Company transported some 30 coffins from Kobe, Japan, to Hong Kong, which belonged to Guangdong natives who died in Japan. Upon arrival in Hong Kong, the coffins were temporarily placed in Tung Wah Hospital, and would be repatriated to the deceased's hometown in due course. Subsidies for transportation were offered, 15 dollars for destinations close to Hong Kong and 20 dollars for destinations farther away. This was indeed a great act of benevolence" (Ko, 2006: 103). According to this news, Tung Wah Hospital was already taking coffins repatriated from abroad into its care temporarily at that time.

In the 8th year of Qing Emperor Guangxu's reign (1883), the *"Guidelines for the Communal Graveyard Fundraising Campaign"* of Quong Fook Tong Benevolent Association in San Francisco mentioned that "Quong Fook Tong collected donations from shops run by fellow clansmen in order to exhume the bones of deceased friends and repatriate them to Hong Kong, where they would be placed temporarily in the coffin home of Tung Wah Hospital. The families of the deceased were asked to collect the remains, while burial fees were offered to them" (From the Accounting Journal of Quong Fook Tong Benevolent Association, San Francisco, 1902). This confirms that in the 1880s, overseas benevolent associations were already placing bones repatriated from abroad in the care of Tung Wah Hospital. As more and more bones were sent to Hong Kong, space ran out in the small coffin home managed by Tung Wah Hospital. In 1899, Tung Wah Hospital obtained approval from the government to build a new coffin home. Located in Sandy Bay on the western part of Hong Kong Island, Tung Wah Coffin Home greatly expanded Tung Wah's charity network where services were offered to Chinese all over the world from Hong Kong. The network extended to the Americas, Asia, Oceania, Europe and Africa, covering the United States and Canada in the north; Cuba, Peru and Chile in the south; Britain, France, Norway and the Netherlands in the west; Vietnam, Thailand, Malaysia, Indonesia, Singapore in Southeast Asia; Australia and New Zealand; and even the Zanzibar Archipelago in Africa. In China, the network reached 43 destinations in Guangdong province, in addition to provinces like Shandong, Zhejiang, Fujian and Yunnan as well as the cities of Shanghai, Tianjin and more through inland water channels (Yip, 2009: 175, 185-187).

Returning to the Roots

The last stop of the repatriation process was the deceased's hometown. Finally, the deceased returned to their roots and could have eternal peace. Generally speaking, funeral and burial arrangements in the deceased's hometown were undertaken by the charitable organizations in Hong Kong in cooperation with their counterparts in the deceased's hometown.

1) Charitable Associations and Charitable Hospitals in the Deceased's Hometown

In the hometown of overseas Chinese, the bones repatriated from abroad were usually handled by charitable hospitals, coffin homes and communal ancestral halls or benevolent associations. Their main connecting charitable organization in Hong Kong was Tung Wah Hospital.

In Panyu, Huaxian and Conghua counties, the charitable association, Cheong Shing Tong, founded in 1882 by Choie Sew Hoy, a Chinese compatriot in New Zealand, took delivery of all bones repatriated from abroad. Based in Gaotang Xu in northern Panyu, the headquarters of the association acquired properties to generate income to support its operations. Cheong Shing Tong was founded to "help repatriate the bones of deceased friends from Panyu, Huaxian and Conghua to their hometown for burial. When the bones arrived in the headquarters, they would try to locate the families of the deceased friends and inform them to collect the remains for burial. Burial fees were also offered to the families. The deceased could be laid to rest in peace" (Zhou, 1995: 17).

In Xinhui, overseas Chinese raised funds to establish the charitable hospitals and associations namely, Xinhui Chengxi Ren'an Yiyuan, Renyu Tang and Jideshe to handle the bones. Burials in the communal graveyards discovered in Xinhui to date were undertaken by these three charitable associations, whereas bones awaiting collection by the deceased's families were placed in coffin homes. According to the research of Lin Zhenyu, an expert in Xinhui local history, on the charitable shelters and clinics as well as coffin homes in the county, the predecessor of Ren'an Yiyuan was a Fangbian Yisuo (charitable shelter and clinic) founded in the 24th year of Qing Emperor Guangxu's reign (1898). In that year, bubonic plague broke out in Xinhui. Members of the local gentry proposed the founding of a shelter and clinic in the western part of the county, like Tung Wah Hospital in Hong Kong, to offer free medical services and handle unclaimed bodies. In the 28th year of Emperor Guangxu's reign (1902), the shelter and clinic were renamed Xinhui Chengxi Ren'an Yiyuan and appealed to Chinese at home and abroad for donations to support its operations, and appointed fundraising officers in Chinese communities in Vietnam, the United States, Canada, Cuba and Australia. Ren'an Yiyuan built the communal free graveyards in Hezui (also known as Jinniushan), and Dahuai, and Huangkeng. The Xinhui Yici (communal ancestral hall), built in the 3rd year of Qing Emperor Yongzheng's reign (1725), housed the spirit tablets of the deceased who were poor and had no descendants; yet it is not known when Xinhui Coffin Home, used to store the bones of Chinese temporarily, was built (Lun, June 1986; Ou, 2005: 25; Lin, January 1, 2016).

In Taishan, a coffin home for storing bones repatriated from abroad, was built with funds donated by overseas Chinese in the 7th year of Qing Emperor Guangxu's reign (1881). Meanwhile, Toi Shan Association in Hong Kong was responsible for transporting the bones to the deceased's hometown, contacting the deceased's families to claim the remains as well as building communal free graveyards for unclaimed remains. In the 17th year of Emperor Guangxu's reign (1890), Chinese donated some 13,000 US dollars for the establishment of a charitable association known as Mingshan She in Qingyun Road, Taishan, and a free clinic in the Wu Temple. In following year, Mingshanshe Fangbian Yiyuan was founded to look after the sick and elderly. The deity Luzu, an embodiment of benevolence, was revered at the clinic for worshipping (County Records of *Xinning*, 19th year of Qing Emperor Guangxu's Reign, 1968: 368).

Similar charitable establishments which offered free medical services, looked after the sick and elderly and buried unclaimed remains of the deceased were found in various towns and market towns. They were Tongji Yiyuan in Dihai and Ningji Yiyuan in Xinchang built in 1898, Le Shan Tang in Guanghai built in the reign of Emperor Guangxu, Funing Yiyuan in Gongyi Town (1921), Puji Yiyuan in Sijiu Xu Wushi Xu (1947) and more. In 1925, Hongji Yiyuan, which had a 180-square-metre shelter, was built in Dihai with funds donated by overseas Chinese. The hospital offered free medical services, took in critically ill patients and stored bones of Chinese repatriated from abroad (*Taishan Weishengzhi* 1988: 82-85).

In the 20th year of Qing Emperor Guangxu's reign (1894), Chinese from Kaiping and Enping established the "Enkai Xiangyue"(Rural Alliance) in Baihe Xu, Kaiping to coordinate bone repatriation from abroad, built communal free graveyards for unclaimed remains, as well as set up temporary bone storage facilities in Jinhua Temple and Sanling Temple nearby. The bones repatriated to Kaiping could be unloaded at the piers in Dihai or Baihe Xu, and were generally received by the local charitable Ai Shan Tang established by different clans, which would make arrangements for the deceased's families to collect the bones. Unclaimed bones were buried in the local communal free graveyards. After the first Ai Shan Tang – Magong Ai Shan Tang – was founded in 1885, 17 more Ai Shan Tangs were successively set up, including Chikan Ai Shan Tang, Shuikou Ai Shan Tang, Baihe Ai Shan Tang, Midong Ai Shan Tang, Changsha Ai Shan Tang, Maogang Ai Shan Tang, Xiangang Ai Shan Tang, Chishui Chongkou Ai Shan Tang, Xu-clan Ai Shan Tang, Yixing Ai Shan Tang and Xiaohai Ai Shan Tang. Most of these charitable "tang" offered medical services and took in critically ill villagers through the shelters, clinics and hospitals they operated; they also offered free burial services and assistance with bone repatriation, as well as built communal free graveyards. Meanwhile, some charitable associations did not offer free medical services, but only provided free burial services, buried unclaimed remains and took bones repatriated from abroad into their care (*Kaiping Weishengzhi*, 1988: 3-5; *Guangdong Lidai Fanzhi Jicheng – Miguo Kaiping Xianzhi*, 2014: 140-141).

2) Spirit Summoning and Releasing the Deceased's Spirit from Purgatory

When coffins or bones repatriated from abroad arrived in the deceased's hometown, rituals would be performed to release their spirits from purgatory. The remains were then claimed by the deceased's families or buried in communal free graveyards. In the 8th year of Qing Emperor Xianfeng's reign (1858), the rules and regulations for the 1st bone repatriation of Pon Yup Chong How Benevolent Association stipulated that, "A boat would be hired to transport the coffins of our deceased friends to the county capital, and rituals would be performed to release their spirits from purgatory." Subsequently, "notices would be put up in the villages urging the deceased's families to claim the remains, whereas those deceased friends who have no families would be laid to rest in the communal free graveyard."

3) Spirit Summoning

According to traditional funeral beliefs, the spirits of those who die in foreign land become hungry and desolate ghosts who lose the opportunity to be reincarnated. They cannot receive offerings or incense sticks or food, and their spirits cannot be released from purgatory either. Therefore, the deceased's families must perform a "spirit summoning" ritual for them, in the hope that the spirits will hear the voices of summoning and go home. The spirit summoning ritual originated a long time ago, as described in historical records from the Zhou Dynasty (1056-256 B.C.), the family of the deceased should call the spirit from the roof at the front. Facing north, they should hold the deceased's clothing and call out his name, so that the deceased's spirit would follow the sound and return to the clothing. The family of the deceased should descend at the back of the house and put the clothing on the deceased's body. This piece of clothing was also called "fuyifu (literally abdominal clothing)". It was believed that the clothing had links with the deceased's "body" and "breath", and the deceased's spirit would be attracted to it and return following a familiar scent or form. Meanwhile, for those who died away from their hometown, a custom called "spirit burial" was practised.

For Chinese sojourning in foreign countries, their bodies were buried overseas after they died, and their spirits stayed on the other side of the Pacific Ocean for many years until their bones were repatriated. Obviously, the spirit summoning customs of the hometown of overseas Chinese originated from the ancient practice of "spirit burial". While bone exhumation was carried out in foreign countries, the spirits of those deceased Chinese whose remains could not be found were summoned into boxes and repatriated to their hometown. Overseas Chinese practised spirit summoning according to ancient customs. Adaptations might have been made to suit the circumstances at the time, yet the traditional concept of spirit burial remained unchanged.

After collecting the bones, the deceased's family in his hometown performed a ritual to summon his spirit. Since the spirit needed to "take a boat" to return to his hometown from abroad, a duck served the function of the boat in the ritual. On the day of spirit summoning, the ritual master would prepare a banner with the deceased's name and address, tying on top of a bamboo tail; he would also prepare a piece of long, thin string to the foot of a duck and take the family of the deceased to a nearby pier along the river. Three animal sacrifices were offered to the deceased, while the deceased's family cried and mourned. Next, the ritual master threw the duck with force into the river and held the string as the duck swam. The ritual master then offered wine and food to the deceased, chanted spells and called the deceased's name, asking him to "take the boat" home. At the same time, he waved the bamboo tail with the deceased's name and address written on it, in order to remind the spirit of the "boat's" direction and location. Subsequently, the ritual master slowly retrieved the string. After the spirit summoning ritual was over, the ritual master carried the duck and led the deceased's family back to the village and into the deceased's home. A spirit tablet could now be set up for the deceased. The spirit of the deceased could eventually return home from the other side of the globe. Fallen leaves returned to the roots, and the deceased could be revered by their loved ones and descendants. This custom has been widely practised in the hometown of overseas Chinese for more than a century; until today, it is still occasionally practised. The account represented above is of two spirit summoning rituals the author experienced in person.

4) Releasing the Deceased's Spirit from Purgatory

In Taoism and Buddhism, the family of deceased persons commission ritual masters to enlighten the deceased, chant prayers and perform rituals, so that the deceased could go to pure land and their spirits could be relieved from suffering. In Buddhism, human beings exist in one of the six realms: Deva (heavenly), Manusya (human), Asura (demigod), Preta (ghost), Tiryak (animal like ox, horse or even mosquito and ant) and Naraka (residents of hell). The actions of a person lead to a new existence of the realms after death in an endless cycle, whereas Buddhism helps the deceased break free from the cycle and release him from purgatory.

Buddhism believes that the best time to perform rituals to release the deceased's spirit from purgatory is within seven days after death, when the spirit can take a new form to reincarnate. It is believed that seven days is a period. If the new form is not yet determined after seven days, the search can be continued for another seven days until the seventh period ends. During these 49 days, if rituals are sincerely performed, the spirit can find a better form. After 49 days, the deceased would have been reincarnated, and it would be impossible to change anything.

Nevertheless, for those deceased persons whose spirits are not released from purgatory within 49 days of death, the *Ullambana Sutra* states that rituals can still be performed on the 15th day of the 7th lunar month every year to relieve their spirits from suffering. "The merits can release seven generations of ancestors from purgatory." (Mi, 2002)

Therefore, even though the bones of overseas Chinese were repatriated to their hometown more than a decade after their passing, the responsible charitable organization could still perform the traditional rituals to release the deceased's spirits from purgatory before informing their families to collect the bones.

5) Communal Free Graveyards for Overseas Chinese

Records reveal that charitable associations in the hometown of overseas Chinese, which were responsible for handling bones repatriated from abroad, have all built communal free graveyards for unclaimed bones, so that the deceased could be "laid to rest and receive sacrificial offerings" (From the rules and regulations for bone repatriation of Pon Yup Chong How Benevolent Association in the 4th year of Qing Emperor Guangxu's reign, 1878).

As local economies develop, many communal free graveyards, which were built a long time ago, have been destroyed. Today, Xinhui in Guangdong has the largest number of communal free graveyards. There are some 3,800 tombs in six graveyards: 386 tombs in the communal free graveyard for overseas Chinese from the United States in Haihuai of Huangkeng, built in 1893; about 200 tombs in the communal free graveyard for overseas Chinese from Vietnam in Mushan of Huangkeng, built in 1880; 441 tombs in the communal free graveyard for overseas Chinese in Dahuai, Hengkeng, built in 1936 by Ren'an Yiyuan ; some 1,500 tombs in the communal free graveyard for overseas Chinese in Hezuishan of Huangchongkeng, built by Ren'an Yiyuan; about 800 tombs (already damaged) in the communal free graveyard for overseas Chinese in Kengxia, Huangkeng ; and about 400 to 500 tombs (already damaged) in Dayun Shan. (Ou, Jilin 2005: 4-6)

In 1853, Sze Yup Benevolent Association in San Francisco, with Chinese from Taishan making up most of its membership, began to exhume and repatriate the bones of deceased Chinese to their hometown. However, the communal free graveyards for overseas Chinese in Taishan have all disappeared during the process of urbanization, while the original site of the coffin home, located in present-day Taicheng city centre, stands only the remains of the wall.

In Kaiping, the situation is a bit different from that of Xinhui and Taishan. The bones repatriated to Xinhui were mostly received by the charitable Ren'an Yiyuan, Ren Yu Tang and Ji De She, and coffin homes were set up to store the bones. In Taishan, the bones were handled by the coffin home built with funds donated by overseas Chinese as well as Ming Shan She. Meanwhile, Toi Shan Association of Hong Kong was a charitable organization which oversaw funerals and burials. It directly participated in bone repatriation and establishment of communal free graveyards.

In the 9th year of Qing Emperor Guangxu's reign (1883), the counties of Kaiping and Enping established the "Enkai Rural Alliance" in Baihe Xu, Kaiping (not far from Enping) to handle the bones of deceased overseas Chinese repatriated with funds raised by native societies abroad. At the same time, many charitable associations were built across Kaiping; Chinese from the county even donated money for the purchase of farmland as communal property to generate income to fund free medical services as well as bone repatriation and burial. Therefore, most of the communal free graveyards in Kaiping were built by local charitable associations, which also oversaw burial affairs. There were a total of 21 communal free graveyards built by the charitable associations for unclaimed bones or deceased and destitute sick people without descendants. They are located in: Sijiudong ; Changshatang ; Xianchengnan ; Midong ; Louganghou Zhugoukeng ; Donghewan Qushui Cun ; Boluo Changgangwei ; Longtang Liyu Shan built in the 7th year of Qing Emperor Guangxu's reign; Shagang ; Ailingtou ; Yuanshanzai ; Xiaxiangkou ; Goushan ; Hengqiaoda, built by Chikan Shantang in Baizusha, Niuyanshui, built by Situ Jiaolun Tang in the 3rd year of the Republic of China; Shuikoushi Luoshan, built by Shuikou Shantang in the 7th year of the Republic of China; Mashan, Sijiudong, built by Yang Airu and others in the 9th year of the Republic of China; Dagangdi, Pancun, built in the 2nd year of Qing Emperor Xuantong's reign; Jiuxudi, built in the 4th year of the Republic of China; Hanlang Langqian, built in the 10th year of the Republic of China; Gangweida, Xianchengxi, built in the 20th year of the Republic of China; next to Bushu Bus Company. (Book 10, Jianzhi Shang, County Records of Kaiping, 1933).

6) Communal Free Cemetery for Overseas Chinese in Taishan

In 1948, the last batch of bones of overseas Chinese from Taishan were returned to their hometown. This was also the last time that charitable organizations in Taishan built a communal free graveyard for overseas Chinese, and the initiative was widely publicized in Taishan newspapers. In addition to the coverage in *Xinning Magazine*, which targeted all residents of the county, the monthly magazines of different clans also reported on the repatriation, so that the deceased's families could claim the bones from the coffin home. In Taishan, *Zhixiao Duqin Monthly*, published in early November 1948, ran a story entitled "Chen Zhixuan returns to Taishan to oversee repatriation of 1,000 sets of bones from US". Even though the bones repatriated did not belong to any member of their clan, they still reported on the repatriation:

> *Yu Qing Tang (Yee Hing Tong), also known as "White Bones Society" and run by Toi Shan Association in Hong Kong, was responsible for the repatriation of bones for deceased overseas Chinese from different cities. It repatriated some 260 sets of bones from the United States before the war. The bones of Lei Weiluo, Lei Yanxue, Liu Yiwei, Ma Zhenyuan and Huang Chuanyan are still placed in Tung Wah Hospital in Hong Kong as the families and addresses of the deceased are not known. The hospital wrote in a letter and asked the White Bones Society to handle the matters properly. On the 2nd day of this month, another 1,063 sets of bones arrived in Hong Kong by ship. Lei Yinsun, the Chairman of Toi Shan Association, called a general committee meeting and decided on several ways to repatriate and bury the bones. Chen Zhixuan, the manager of Hai Sheng Xiang Store, would come to Taishan and set up an office to oversee the matter in Tianxin Gold Store on Zhonghe Road,*

Taicheng. We understand that Chen has arrived in Taicheng on the 13th day of this month. After discussing with the county assembly, he went to the coffin home in our county with funeral workers hired by the county assembly on the 14th day of this month. With regard to the 600 or so sets of bones repatriated before the war, burial fees of 5 Hong Kong dollars should have been offered for each deceased person. Yet the manager at the time used the funds for other purposes, such that the bones are still not buried. This time, all the bones repatriated in the past decade have been numbered, and efforts have been made to locate the families of the deceased. The respective village offices would be informed in due course, and the deceased's families would be asked to collect the remains for burial in two months. Otherwise, the county coffin home would bury the bones. Meanwhile, bone repatriation thereafter would be announced on the notice board.

(*Zhixiao Duqin Yuekan*, November 15, 1948: 44)

If members of the clan were included in the repatriation, the names of the deceased would be announced so that clan members could inform one another. In 1948, *Wenbian Monthly* published the article "Bones of four deceased clan members including Li Bairu repatriated from US are to be claimed", informing the deceased's families of the time and place to collect the bones, and that burial fees of 15 dollars would be provided,

Toi Shan Association of Hong Kong has sent a general committee member Chen Zhixuan to repatriate some 1,290 sets of bones of overseas Chinese of our county and those which were temporarily stored in the coffin home of Tung Wah Hospital over the years. The bones of four members of our clan, Li Bairu and Li Changhua of Wenbian Village, Li Weiqing of old Wenbian

Village, Li Lai'an of Songmei Village, are now deposited in the Dongmen Coffin Home at Taicheng. Last month, the respective village offices have been asked to inform the deceased's families to collect the bones, and that burial fees of 15 dollars would be offered for each deceased friend. Families of the deceased may claim the bones from Li Quanying of Junsheng Hao on Zhengshi Street, Taicheng. The following should be noted with regard to collecting the bones: (1) The claimant should be a member of the deceased's immediate family (if the deceased has no immediate family, a member of his extended family can claim the bones); (2) The claimant must present a certificate issued by the village office, or a note of guarantee from an honest business in Taicheng; (3) The claimant must fill in three receipts prepared by our society, one to be kept by the coffin home, one by our association, and one to be sent to the respective overseas charitable association; (4) The bones should be claimed in the six months from 15 October of this year to 15 April of the 38th year of the Republic of China (1949); remains not claimed after that would be buried by the coffin home of our association and no disagreement would be entertained.

(*Wenbian Yuekan*, November 15, 1948: 9-10)

Xinning Magazine is the most popular newsletter for Taishan people at home and abroad. While learning about what was happening in China and their hometown through the magazine, overseas Chinese used the magazine as a medium to pass information about foreign countries to their hometown and exchange ideas with fellow clansmen. The magazine covered major events in the country, province and county, news related to Siyi people in Hong Kong and Macau, as well as immigration policies of foreign countries where overseas Chinese reside. In January 1949, two consecutive issues of the magazine reported on matters regarding Yu Qing Tang Cemetery). The first issue contains an article entitled "The Yu Qing Tang Cemetery newly established a cemetery in Shihuashan to bury some 1,000 overseas Chinese". It provides a detailed account of the bone repatriation process, burial fees arrangement, collection of bones from the coffin home and the construction of a communal free graveyard to bury unclaimed remains. It also reveals that Toi Shan Association in Hong Kong was responsible for transporting the bones from Hong Kong to Taishan, and guaranteed funds for the last part of the bone repatriation process." (*Xinning Magazine*, January 1, 1949: 28-29)

The first issue of *Xinning Magazine* in the 37th year of the Republic of China reported on the foundation laying ceremony for the cemetery in Shihuashan, which was attended by the county magistrate as well as prominent government officials. This shows that the construction of a communal free graveyard for overseas Chinese was a major event in the county concerning people both at home and abroad. (*Xinning Magazine*, January 1, 1949: 28)

The second issue of *Xinning Magazine* contains an article entitled "Construction work for the new 80000 square feet Yu Qing Tang Cemetery in Shihuashan begins, with 8 memorial pavilions built with funds to be raised abroad", illustrating to Taishan people in China and overseas the planning of the cemetery, the concept of western cemetery construction as well as the construction of the memorial pavilions. The article also gave an update on the fundraising campaign (*Xinning Magazine*, January 15, 1949: 51-52).

In addition to reports on the construction of the cemetery published in two consecutive issues of *Xinning Magazine*, *Datong Daily* of Taishan, which was also circulated across the county, published detailed reports on the foundation laying ceremony and the construction work on 14 and 15 December in the 37th year of the Republic of China. The author looked through hundreds of overseas Chinese magazines published in the following few years, but did not find any news about the construction of the cemetery. There was little coverage on the completion and subsequent operation of the cemetery. Nevertheless, the first issue of *Xinning Magazine* in 1957 contains an essay by Tan Tingbiao on visiting the cemetery on Qing Ming Festival. The essay, entitled "Scenery arousing deep thoughts – paying homage to deceased in Shihuashan on Qing Ming Festival", depicts the communal free graveyard for overseas Chinese after completion,

> *After breakfast, returnees and relatives of overseas Chinese who gathered on the Qing Ming Festival to sweep the tombs of ancestors and friends of overseas Chinese in Taishan (the Yu Qing Tang Cemetery for the county of Taishan) came to the door of the Returned Overseas Chinese Federation on Xi'an Road of Taicheng, from all sides, carrying flowers. Then the heads of various organizations and people from local community also arrived one after another. ...Families of overseas Chinese men and women relatives; they brought a team of more than 200 people to visit the cemetery. The Taishan Returned Overseas Chinese Federation has already prepared rich sacrifices, such as yellow sugar steamed cake, white sugar steamed cake, roast pig, white meat, white eggs, sugar cane, wine, incense candles and so on.*
>
> *The grave sweeping ceremony began, chaired by Chen Houfu, returned overseas Chinese. People came to forward to pay respect, offering flowers to show their infinite respect for those who contributed a lot for the development of their hometown and died overseas. After the worshipping ceremony, people took pictures together for commemoration.*
>
> (*Xinning Magazine*, January 15, 1957: 89-91)

Conclusion

1) Charitable Spirit

Chinese people have a strong sense of attachment to their hometown. For Chinese laborers who went abroad to earn a living, the concept of "fallen leaves returning to the roots" were all the most important. If they could not return to their hometown during their golden years, it would be their final wish to be buried there after they died. Meanwhile, death was very important to Chinese and the concept of interment was deeply rooted. Under the influence of long standing Chinese culture, Chinese persevere to maintain the traditional burial practice. This, along with the unpleasant experiences of Chinese in overseas countries, gave rise to the custom of bone repatriation which involved a colossal amount of work and lasted much of a century.

The general route of bone repatriation can be summed up as follows: overseas native society and charitable association – Tung Wah Hospital in Hong Kong (temporary deposit in Tung Wah Coffin Home) – Tung Wah Hospital, branches of the native society or charitable association in Hong Kong (repatriation to the deceased's hometown) – charitable association in the deceased's hometown (bone collection and construction of communal free graveyards). From foreign countries to the deceased's hometown, charitable associations were responsible for every leg of the journey. These vast bone repatriation undertakings were not only reflections on bone repatriation itself, but also the Chinese culture and traditions therein. They symbolised the fear for ghosts and deities in traditional Chinese culture, as well as the social and ethical beliefs in Confucian teachings. They were the result of joint efforts by Chinese communities in China and abroad, where a sophisticated charitable network was built through the spirit of benevolence in traditional Chinese culture. This benevolence was blown up in a specific time in history, a special living environment and special cultural beliefs – "The generous, benevolent deed prevents the bones of our deceased friends from being exposed; it is also the responsibility of our generation. As the ancient saying goes, 'benevolent deeds bring good fortune', while we repatriate the bones of our deceased friends, we also build a foundation of blessings." (Advertisement of Quong Fook Tong Benevolent Association of Kaiping, May 16, 1916) (Website of Chinese in Northwest America Research Committee)

Such spirit of benevolence was often exemplified in the rules and regulations in the accounting journal for each bone repatriation undertaking. General committee members were told, "Work together. Do not gang up for personal interests. Do not be complacent. Put public interest before personal gain. Be careful with your speech. Do not practise favouritism. Be diligent and thrifty. Be meticulous and thorough. Do not abuse your position. Thoughts and actions should be consistent. Persevere unremittingly. Be god fearing and uphold the spirit of benevolence." (Clause 1 of the rules and regulations of Chong How Benevolent Association, 23rd year of Qing Emperor Guangxu's reign, 1897)

In order to remind the managers to always keep in mind traditional moral and ethical beliefs as well as uphold the spirit of benevolence, a template for the general committee member's oath (to be burned) was included in the accounting journal (multiple accounting journals of Chong How Benevolent Association). It was widely known that when general committee members took office, they were required to fill their name in the template, offer sacrifice to the gods and burn the oath. In doing this, they asked the deities to be their witnesses. Below is an excerpt of the template.

I, general committee member of Chong How Benevolent Association, have been elected to undertake bone repatriation for our deceased friends. I hereby swear that I will stay true to my conscience, work to the best of my ability and keep clear accounting records. I shall not misappropriate funds to serve my personal interests. If I violate this oath, may ill fortune fall upon me. I ask the gods to be my witness.

Signed by _____ *on* _____ *day of* _____ *month in the year* _____

2) Further Insights

With regard to the custom of bone repatriation, a closer look at the archives of Tung Wah Group of Hospitals will reveal that the bones from the Americas far outnumbered those from Southeast Asia – which had a larger Chinese population. I believe there were at least three reasons why bone repatriation was not as widely practised in Southeast Asia than in North America:

First of all, the political climate in Southeast Asia was less tense than that in North America and Australia. There were no exclusion laws. Many Chinese people had families, and there were Chinese schools perpetuating Chinese culture. Chinese compatriots did not have to worry about not having anyone visiting their graves after they died. Meanwhile, in North America and Australia, where Chinese people were discriminated against, it was difficult for most Chinese people to start a family. Supporting their parents as well as their wives and children at home became the spiritual support and motivation for their work. They regarded the foreign countries as temporary places of residence, where they made money to support their families. *The Chinese Times*, a Chinese newspaper in Vancouver, Canada, published an advertisement of Quong Fook Tong Benevolent Association of Kaiping on 16 May 1916, stating the reason for the bone repatriation, "Sending the bones of our deceased friends to their hometown mean they will not be buried in a foreign country. They will have no regrets" (Website of Chinese in Northwest America Research Committee).

Secondly, there were specific laws in Southeast Asian countries such as Malaysia and Singapore that restricted the transport of human bones. In 1934, Tung Wah Hospital wrote in its reply to Singapore's Kwong Wai Shiu Hospital, "We are aware of your government's intention to loosen bone repatriation laws. We are, however, obliged to follow the existing laws in Hong Kong. In response to your request, we have enclosed Chinese and English versions of Hong Kong's bone repatriation laws, so that you can submit them to your government. We are most delighted to offer our assistance in this charitable deed." In 1935, the volunteer manager of Kwong Tong Cemetery in Kuala Lumpur wrote in a letter to Tung Wah Hospital, "Many overseas Chinese compatriots repatriate the bones of deceased Chinese persons to China for burial. Due to hygiene concerns, however, our government has imposed strict regulations on bone repatriation. The procedures are complicated, resulting in increased costs. Even though we want to repatriate the bones, it is very difficult to carry out the process" (Yip, 2009: 250-251). As a matter of fact, there were also bone transportation laws in the United States, and the application procedure was rather cumbersome.

In different political environment, the same restrictions on bone transportation and the same cumbersome procedures produced different psychological effects.

Thirdly, in Hong Kong, Tung Wah Hospital had built a coffin home, offered free coffins for Chinese persons who passed away at sea and took delivery of bones repatriated from abroad. These benevolent deeds, along with

Hong Kong's international shipping network, meant the city was unique as a port-of-exit for Chinese people leaving China. Most of the Chinese in the Americas, Australia and New Zealand originated from Guangdong Province. Their native societies abroad maintained close connections with counterparts in Hong Kong to make sure that the bones reach the deceased's hometown. The trading companies specialising in trade with China, Southeast Asia and North America in Hong Kong which had their business locally played an important role in the charitable bone repatriation network. To them, bone repatriation was both a business opportunity and a benevolent act (Sinn, 2013; Yip, 2009).

3) Other than Bone Repatriation...

As far as the development history of the hometown of overseas Chinese is concerned, it is worthwhile to look into the family and society behind. Chinese making a living abroad often carried the weight of their families on their shoulders. They were totally devoted to their families and the development of their hometown. Yet, once they died, their families would change and the women behind them would see their lives change completely. Most of the stories about "chaste women" found in county records involve a "husband who died abroad":

> *Chen was betrothed to Li Beidou. They were not yet married when Beidou died abroad. When Chen heard the news, she was devastated. She adopted a son and cared for him for more than ten years. People in the village all thought she was a virtuous woman. When her son was old enough, she found him a wife. After that, she said, "I have done what I should do, and can now go see my husband." She threw herself into the sea and died.*
>
> *Huang was betrothed to Chen Chunping. They were not yet married*

when her husband went abroad. Huang went to live with her husband's family.
Her husband died abroad, and Huang was devastated. She adopted a son and
cared for him until he was grown-up. People in the village thought she was a
virtuous woman.

(*Xinning Xianzhi*, 19th year of Qing Emperor Guangxu's reign,
1968: 896-898)

In the magnificent diaolou, buildings and villas in the hometown of
overseas Chinese often lived women who spent their whole lives waiting for
their husbands. After their husbands died abroad, it was customary for them to
raise the children they had with their husbands, or adopt children.

Looking back on the bone repatriation undertakings, which lasted most
of a century, the lives of the Chinese who died abroad can be described with
two lines in the renowned lyrical poem *Man Jiang Hong* by Yue Fei, "At the
age of thirty, my deeds are nothing but dust, my journey has taken me over
eight thousand *li* [approximately 4,000 km] away". Whether the Chinese were
successful or not, all that was left of them in the end was a coffin or a set of
bones repatriated to their hometown. In 1902, the remains of Choie Sew Hoy,
a wealthy Chinese merchant tycoon in New Zealand, as well as those of 500
Chinese laborers affiliated with Cheong Shing Tong, sank to the bottom of the
sea along with the *SS Ventnor*. (Zhou, 1995: 17). And as Professor Marlon K.
Hom said, "The bone repatriation service provides a fair chance for all fallen
leaves return to their roots" (Hom, 2002: 38, cited in Yip, 2009: 24).

Today, more than a hundred years after the cultural tradition of "fallen
leaves returning to the roots" prevailed among overseas Chinese, the world has
undergone a reverse development. With the abolition of the Chinese Exclusion
Act and the change of contemporary immigration policy, overseas Chinese can

be naturalized, marry and have children in their country of residence, take root and live and work in peace and contentment. Overseas Chinese began to worry that their parents were too lonely in the graves of their hometown – there would be no future generations worshipping them. As a result, quite some Chinese immigrants returned to their home village in China and brought their parents' ashes to overseas for burial – for easier care and worshiping. In fact, this is also due to the consideration of traditional cultural thinking – take roots in a place, and bring blessings to the future generations.

The correspondences from the Tung Wah Coffin Home archives published in this volume reflect the yearning of overseas Chinese to return to their roots. They also illustrate how native societies and charitable associations in overseas countries, Hong Kong and the Mainland China uphold a spirit of mutual assistance and benevolence when working together to repatriate the bones of deceased Chinese to their hometown for burial. Today, the Tung Wah Group of Hospitals of Hong Kong is committed to preserving Tung Wah Coffin Home and its historical archives, which act as silence witnesses to the history of overseas Chinese.

– END –

中文（按中文筆劃排序）

一、政府檔案

《大同日報》，民國 37.12（14），省立圖書館藏。

《至孝篤親月刊》，民國 37.11（1），頁 44，台山檔案館藏。

《新寧雜誌》，1957（02），頁 89－91，台山檔案館藏。

《新寧雜誌》，民國 38.1（1），頁 28－29，台山檔案館藏。

《新寧雜誌》，民國 38.1（15），頁 51－52，台山檔案館藏。

《溫邊月刊》，民國 37.11（15），頁 9－10，台山檔案館藏。

二、地方志 / 機構內部刊物

台山縣衛生志編寫組：《台山縣衛生志》，廣州：廣東人民出版社，1988，頁 82－
　　85。

余定邦：〈新加坡甯陽會館曹家館二三事〉，《台山文史》第八輯，廣東台山縣政協
　　文史委員會編，1987－1988。

東華三院檔案及歷史文化辦公室：《源與流的東華故事》，2014。

《金山昌後堂徵信錄》，光緒廿九年歲次癸卯鐫，美國軒佛三邑公所藏，吳瑞卿博士
　　提供。

香港台山商會志編纂委員會：《台山：香港台山商會志》（非正式發行），2000。

《新寧縣志（清光緒十九年刊本）》，《新修方志叢刊——廣東方志之七》，台北：
　　台灣學生書局，1968。

福建民族本志辦公室：《福建省志・民族志》，廈門：鷺江出版社，2013。

廣東台山華僑志編纂委員會：《廣東台山華僑志》（非正式發行），2005。

廣東省地方史志辦公室編：《歷代東方志集成——民國開平縣志》，廣州：嶺南美術
　　出版社，2014。

歐濟霖：《新會華僑義塚》（新會地方史志叢書第八輯），江門市新會區史志辦公室編印，2005。（包括：廣東新會的華僑義塚，自「華僑華人研究（第三輯）」，暨南大學華僑華人研究所和香港中文大學華僑華人研究社編，1995；〈華僑義塚碑刻考〉，《新會報》，2001。

三、專著／論文

丁新豹：《善與人同——與香港同步成長的東華三院（1870－1997）》，香港：三聯書店（香港）有限公司，2010。

丁蘭蘭：〈略論鄭洛地區仰韶文化成人瓮棺二次葬〉，《四川文物》，2008年3月。

孔飛力著，李明歡譯：《他者中的華人——中國近現代移民史》，南京：江蘇人民出版社，2016。

王衛平：〈明清時期江南地區的民間慈善事業〉，《社會學研究》，1998年1月，頁84－97。

令狐萍：《美國華僑華人史》，北京：中國華僑出版社，2017。

仲富蘭：〈入土為安和葬俗形式演變〉，《國風》，第一卷（2004）。

仲富蘭：《我們的國家：風俗與信仰》，上海：復旦大學出版社，2012。

列維·布留爾著，丁由譯：《原始思維》，北京：商務印書館，1985。

艾瑞克·羅斯著，張威譯：《澳大利亞華人史（1888－1995）》，廣州：中山大學出版社，2009。

亨利·簡斯頓著，楊于軍譯：《四邑淘金工在澳洲》，北京：中國華僑出版社，2010。

何佩然：《源與流——東華醫院的創立與演進》（東華三院檔案資料彙編系列之一），香港：三聯書店（香港）有限公司，2009。

《佛說盂蘭盆經（附供儀、附幽冥戒儀）》，北京：八大處靈光出版寺，1999。

吳尚鷹：《美國華僑百年紀實（附加拿大）》，香港：香港嘉羅印刷有限公司，1954。

吳信如：《地藏經法研究》，北京：中醫古籍出版社，1998。

李永球：《魂氣歸天——馬來西亞華人喪禮考論》，馬來西亞：漫延書房，2012。

李恩涵：《東南亞華人史》，台北：東方出版社，2015。

周耀星：《紐西蘭華僑史略》，紐西蘭雙星出版社，1996。

武曄卿：〈寒食節，上巳節與清明節合流考〉，《時代文學》，2008年第10期。

胡娟：〈古代「招魂」習俗探討〉，《戲劇之家第》，09（上）期，2016，頁259－260。

倫海濱：〈解放前新會城的慈善機構〉，《新會文史資料選輯》，第23輯（1986年6月）。

凌純聲：《中國邊疆民族與環太平洋文化》，台北：聯經出版社，1979。

唐力行：《商人與中國近世社會》，台北：台灣商務印書館，1997。

時國強：〈先唐的魂魄觀念及招魂習俗〉，《山西師大學報（社會科學版）》，第39期第1卷（2012年1月），頁91－94。

高添強：〈喪葬服務與原籍安葬〉，載冼玉儀，劉潤和主編《益善行道—東華三院135周年紀念專題文集》，香港：三聯書店（香港）有限公司，2006，頁80－112。

高添強：《高山景行——香港仔華人永遠墳場的建立與相關人物》，香港：香港華人永遠墳場管理委員會出版（非正式出版），2012。

陳淑君、陳華文：《民間喪葬習俗》，北京：中國社會出版社，2008。

楊安堯：〈華工與秘魯華人社會〉，《華僑華人歷史研究》，2000年第3期，頁47－53。

楊鏡初：《金衣箚記彙編》（加拿大維多利亞內部發行），維多利亞，1997年6月。

萬建中：《喪俗》，北京：中國旅遊出版社，2004。

葉漢明：《東華義莊與寰球慈善網絡——檔案文獻資料的印證與啟示》（東華三院檔案資料彙編系列之三），香港：三聯書店（香港）有限公司，2009。

劉伯驥：《美國華僑史》，台北：黎明文化事業公司，1976、1982、1984。

廣東省博物館等：〈廣東曲江石峽墓發掘簡報〉，《文物》，1978年7月。

歐濟霖、陳漢忠：《新會華僑華人史話》，北京：中國縣鎮年鑑社，2004。

黎全恩：《加拿大華僑移民史（1858－1966）》，北京：人民出版社，2013。

龐炳庵：《中國人與古巴獨立戰爭》，北京：新華出版社，2013。

四、報刊文章

〈山東半島發現新石器時代早期多人二次合葬墓〉，《新華網》，2007年5月9日。

林震宇：〈新會城西仁安醫院、義莊在哪裏？〉，《江門日報》，2016年1月1日。

〈河南靈寶發現仰韶文化早期大型二次葬合葬墓〉，《新華網》，2007年11月10日。

五、學位論文

王文豔：〈安徽嶽西二次葬俗研究〉，安徽大學碩士論文，2010。

武宇嬙：〈禮與俗的演繹〉，北京師範大學博士論文，2007。

張醜平：〈上巳、寒食、清明節日民俗與文學研究〉，南京師範大學博士論文，2006。

六、古籍

[宋]衛湜：《禮記集說》（卷一百一），北京：國家圖書館出版社，2003。

[唐]魏徵：《隋書》卷三十一〈地理志下〉，北京：中華書局，1997。

[清]《聖祖仁皇帝——日講禮記解義》（卷四、卷三十六），長春：吉林出版集團，2005。

[清]黃遵憲：《上鄭欽使稟文》第十八號（2），光緒八年七月二十三日，載吳振清、徐勇、王家祥編校《黃遵憲集》下卷《文集·公牘》，天津：人民出版社，2003。

[清]顧炎武：《天下郡國利病書》卷一百〈廣東四〉，上海：上海古籍出版社，2012。

七、展覽

《香江有情──東華三院與華人社會》（香港康樂及文化事務署與東華三院合辦，香港歷史博物館與東華三院文物館策劃的展覽），2010。

八、網頁

澳華博物館網頁：https://chinesemuseum.com.au

英文（按英文字母排序）

一、專著／論文

Abraham, Terry and Wegars, Priscilla. "Urns, Bones and Burners: Overseas Chinese Cemeteries." *Australasian Historical Archaeology*, 21 (2003), pp. 58-69.

Amanik, Allan and Fletcher, Kami (eds.). *Till Death Do Us Part: American Ethnic Cemeteries as Borders Uncrossed*. University Press of Mississippi, April 2020.

Arkush, R. David and Lee, Leo O. (trans. and eds.). *Land Without Ghosts: Chinese Impression of America from the Mid-nineteenth Century to the Present*. Berkeley, CA: University of California Press, 1989.

Bromley, Isaac Hill. *The Chinese Massacre at Rock Springs, Wyoming Territory, September 2, 1885*. Boston: Franklin Press, 1886.

Chinn, Thomas W. (ed.). *A History of the Chinese in California: A Syllabus*. San Francisco: Chinese Historical Society of America, 1969.

Chow, Lily Siewsan. *Blood and Sweat Over the Railway Tracks: The Chinese Labourers in the Canadian Pacific Railway Construction (1880-1885)*. Vancouver, BC: Chinese Canadian Historical Society of British Columbia, 2014.

Chung, Sue Fawn and Wegars, Priscilla (eds.). "The Chinese Have a Vault in Which They Deposit Those Corpses Which Are To Be Sent to China." *(Daily Alta California, 6 January 1858), Chinese American Death Rituals: Respecting the Ancestors.* Walnut Creek, CA: Altamira Press, 2005.

Chung, Sue Fawn. *Chinese in the Woods: Logging and Lumbering in the American West.* Urbana, IL: University of Illinois Press, 2015.

Cox, Thomas R. *Mills and Markets: A History of the Pacific Coast Lumber Industry to 1900.* Seattle: University of Washington Press, 1974.

Gyory, Andrew. *Closing the Gate: Race, Politics and the Chinese Exclusion Act.* Chapel Hill, NC: University of North Carolina Press, 1998.

Harrod, Ryan P. and Crandall, John J. "Rails Built Of The Ancestor's Bones: The Bioarchaeology of The Overseas Chinese Experience." *Journal of Historical Archaeology*, 49:1 (February 2015), pp. 148-161.

Hing, Bill Ong. *Making and Remaking Asian America through Immigration Policy, 1850-1990.* Stanford: Stanford University Press, 1993.

Hsu, Madeline Yuan-yin. *Dreaming of Gold, Dreaming of Home: Transnationalism and Migration between the United States and South China, 1882-1943.* Stanford, Calif. : Stanford University Press 2000.

Lai, David Chuenyan. *Chinatowns: Towns within Cities in Canada.* Vancouver: The University of British Columbia Press, 2011.

Lee, Erika. *The Making of Asian America: A History.* New York, NY: Simon and Schuster, 2015.

Ma, Laurence J. C. and Cartier, Carolyn L. *The Chinese Diaspora: Space, Place, Mobility, and Identity.* Lanham, Md.: Rowman & Littlefield, 2003.

MacKay, Donald. *The Lumberjacks.* Toronto: McGraw-Hill Ryerson, Ltd., 1978.

Price, Charles. "Asian and Pacific Island Peoples of Australia," in James T. Fawcett and Benjamin V. Cariño (eds.). *Pacific Bridges: The New Immigration from Asia and the Pacific Islands.* New York: Centre for Migration Studies, 1987.

Quimby, George I. "Culture Contact on the Northwest Coast, 1785-1795." *American Anthropologist*, New Series, 50:2 (April-June 1948).

Scott, Janet Lee. *For Gods, Ghosts, and Ancestors: The Chinese Tradition of Paper Offerings*. Hong Kong : Hong Kong University Press, 2007.

Shelton, Tamara. "Understanding Historic Spaces: Urban Progress and the San Francisco Cemetery Debate, 1895-1937." *California History*, 85:3 (2008), pp. 26-47, 69-70.

Sinn, Elizabeth. *Pacific Crossing: California Gold, Chinese Migration, and the Making of Hong Kong*. Hong Kong: Hong Kong University Press, 2013.

Sinn, Elizabeth. Power and Charity: *A Chinese Merchant Elite in Colonial Hong Kong*. Hong Kong: Hong Kong University Press, 2003.

Skelton, Robin. *They Call It The Cariboo*. Victoria, BC: Sono Nis Press, 1980.

Watson, James and Rawski, Evelyn (eds.). *Death Ritual in Late Imperial and Modern China*. Berkeley: University of California   Press, 1988.

Yalom, Marilyn. *The American Resting Place: Four Hundred Years of History Through Our Cemeteries and Burial Grounds*. Boston: Houghton Mifflin Co., 2008.

Yu, Henry. *A Journey of Hope*. Vancouver, BC.: The University of British Columbia Press, 2018.

Zesch, Scott. *The Chinatown Wars: Chinese Los Angeles and the Massacre of 1871*. New York: Oxford University Press, 2012.

二、報刊文章

"Chinese Laborers Finally Rest in Peace." *Los Angeles Times*, September 5, 2010.

三、學位論文

Briggs, Andrew Ryall. "Feng Shui and Chinese Rituals of Death across the Oregon Landscape." M.A. Thesis. Portland State University, 2002.

Merritt, Christopher W. "The Coming Man from Canton, Chinese Experience in Montana (1862-1943)." Ph. D Dissertation. University of Montana, Missoula, 2010.

Narvaez, Benjamin Nicolas. "Chinese Coolies in Cuba and Peru: Race, Labor, and Immigration, 1839-1886." Ph.D. Dissertation. The University of Texas at Austin, 2010.

Schmidt, Ryan. "The Forgotten Chinese Cemetery of Carlin, Nevada: A Bioanthropological Assessment." M.A. Thesis. University of Nevada, Las Vegas, 2001.

Zhang, Juwen. "Falling Seeds Take Root: Ritualizing Chinese American Identity Through Funerals." Ph.D. Dissertation. University of Pennsylvania, 2001.

四、網頁

Chin, Philip. "The China Trade and the Mystery of the First Chinese in the United States." Retrieved from: http://www.chineseamericanheros.org.

Chinese in Northwest America Research Committee (CINARC): https://www.cinarc.org.

落葉歸根

——東華三院華僑原籍安葬檔案選編 下冊

Fallen leaves returning to their roots :

A selection of archives on the bone repatriation service
of Tung Wah Group of Hospitals for overseas Chinese
(Book B)

東華三院檔案及歷史文化辦公室　編

中華書局

中南美洲西歸先友

隴西慈善會辦事處用箋 *
LONG SAI LI

東華醫院列位執事先生鈞鑒

　　謹復者茲奉　惠書領悉一是本會籌運先
　　友歸國前因儎乸留滯今復因先友名不備稽
　　延時日致勞
　　執事諸先生費神心殊忐忑但本会此次蒙友人委
　　託代办者数拾合计多至壹佰式十六具所捐善款無多
　　前付上港銀僅及仟員以支應各費餘捐
　　貴院惟款甚微薄耳茲付上先友名冊一乸到祈
　　檢收代為妥办不勝感謝此復仰候

佳安

　　　　　　　　　　（印章：古巴灣京隴西商旅自治講習所）慈善會會長 沾聖耀棠 謹復

　　　　　　　　　　一九二九年五月式号晚

---

* 信件中文釋文格式與字形均以原件為依據，部分字型與現今不同，釋文未予更改。本書 300 封信件均以此原則處理。

From the Office of Long Sai Li Benevolent Association, Cuba

Dear Managers of Tung Wah Hospital,

This is a reply to your last letter. Earlier on there were hiccups regarding the bill of lading in the transportation of our deceased friends' remains. Then the incomplete name list further delayed the arrangement and we are worried to have strained the mind of you sirs.

This time we have been entrusted by our friends to repatriate dozens of remains totaling 126 sets. We enclose a small amount of funds we have raised, in the sum of 1,000 Hong Kong dollars, to pay for the repatriation. Please accept any remainder as a small donation to your esteemed hospital. Also enclosed is a list of the deceased friends. We shall be most grateful if you could check the shipment against the list and take care of this matter on our behalf.

Yours sincerely,
Chim-sing *(Zhansheng)* & Yiu-tong *(Yaotang)*
Chairmen of Long Sai Li Benevolent Association
(Stamp: Long Sai Li Merchants Autonomy Learning Office, Habana, Cuba)

Evening of 2 May 1929

安定堂自治所用箋
ON TEN TONG

東華醫院總理

羅文錦曁執事諸先生鑒敝堂起運　先友壹百具

　　　囘籍案塟由本處九月卅日附輪歸國寄交

貴醫院代收煩將各　先友之姓名籍貫分別按址寄

　　　寄囘併轉知各　先友之親屬領歸以安窀穸

　　　而妥幽魂敝堂昆仲不勝感激想　先友居于九泉之下

　　　亦當銘感　貴院之恩德矣茲付上港銀六佰伍拾

　　　元如　先友親屬到領煩將此款每名代交港銀伍

　　　元俾他以作案塟之費餘存微貲謹奉

貴院為香油之資希乞笑納莫嫌錙銖敝堂不勝

　　　存幸矣　先友之姓名籍貫另抄付上希為知之

並祝

近安

　　　　　　　　　　十八、十、十八　古巴灣城安定堂慈善会處長胡俊首頓

　　　　　　　　　　　　　　　　（印章：古巴灣城安定堂慈善會）

另一人註：十月十四梁禹公收仄六百五十元

另一人註：十二月廿六日囘信

Letter from Sociedad On Ten Tong, Habana, Cuba, to Tung Wah Hospital on 18 October 1929

From the Office of On Ten Tong

Dear Director Lo Man-kam and Managers of Tung Wah Hospital,

We have repatriated 100 sets of remains of our deceased friends by sea on 30 September. Please take delivery of the remains when they arrive in Hong Kong and send them to the deceased's hometown according to their names and native counties. Please also inform the families of the deceased to collect the remains, so that they can be laid to rest. We, as well as our deceased friends, will be forever grateful to you for your kindness.

We have enclosed 650 Hong Kong dollars. Please give the family of each deceased friend 5 dollars to cover burial costs when they come to collect the remains and keep any remainder as oil-money. We would like to make a donation to your esteemed hospital, however small it is.

Please find on a separate sheet the names and native counties of the deceased friends.

Yours sincerely,
Wu Chun (*Wu Jun*)
Chairman, Sociedad On Ten Tong, Cuba
18 October of the 18th year of the Republic of China

(Stamp: Sociedad de On Ten Tong, Habana, Cuba)

Another person's remarks: Leung Yu-kung (*Liang Yugong*) acknowledged receipt of 650 dollars on 14 October

Another person's remarks: Replied on 26 December

隴西商旅自治講習所用箋
Long Sai Li

東華醫院列位執事善長仁翁統鑒

　　敬啓者本所慈善會客歲付寄先生遺
　　骸囬國请託
　　貴院分批各縣交先友家人收領安葬兩
　　次皆云收妥今將經年現接新会霞路鄉趙
　　昭和先生來函称云其家父（趙信華）之遺骸仍未收
　　更有京梅陳先生亦云未有報及料係分派
　　之误或派交附近各義庄伊等不知查收茲
　　特函達佈
　　執事復按前派發手續　示知或就地付函
　　通知指導其收領安葬則獲福無疆矣此請
　　仰候

公安

慈善会書記處李杏壇敬啓

中民十八年十月廿号

另一人註：去函新会商会詢問十月廿六新会商会覆函　該骨殖
　　　　　已將原函繳覆前途　十一月初二日復　　已交仁
　　　　　　　　　　　　　　　　　　　　　　育善堂

Letter from Long Sai Li Benevolent Association, Cuba, to Tung Wah Hospital on 20 October 1929

From the Office of Long Sai Li Benevolent Association, Cuba

Dear Managers and benevolent Directors of Tung Wah Hospital,

When we repatriated the remains of our deceased friends back to China last year, we asked your esteemed hospital to deliver the remains to the deceased's hometown by batches, so that their families could collect them and lay them to rest. For two repatriations, we were told that the remains were safely delivered. However, after almost a year, we just received a letter from Chiu Chiu-wo (*Zhao Zhaohe*) of Ha Lo Township (*Xialu Xiang*), Sun Wui (*Xinhu*i), who claimed he had not yet received the remains of his father Chiu Shun-wah (*Zhao Xinhua*). Furthermore a Mr Chan of King Mui (*Jingmei*) had not got any news. Presumably there had been an error in the delivery, or the remains might have been sent to a coffin home nearby and nobody knew. We, therefore, write to inquire about the prevailing procedure of repatriation and delivery of remains, or please let the families know how they can collect the remains for burial.

May you be blessed for your benevolence.

Yours sincerely,
Lee Hang-tan *(Li Xingtan)*
Secretariat, Long Sai Li Benevolent Association

20 October of the 18th year of the Republic of China

Another person's remarks: Enquiry was sent to Sun Wui Commercial Association. Sun Wui Commercial Association replied on the 26th day of the 10th lunar month that the bones had been given to Yan Yuk Sin Tong *(Ran Yu Shan Tang)*.
The reply letter has been forwarded to Long Sai Li Benevolent Association.

Replied on the 2nd day of the 11th lunar month

黃江夏堂用箋
WONG KONG JA TONG

東華醫院执事
羅文錦総理先生 ^{钧鑒}

敬启者^{敝堂}現組織一慈善会执拾先友骨殖
七拾叁具分裝五大箱經扵本月廿八日附船
寄交貴院代收轉運各縣善堂醫院暫貯通
傳各先友　親友收領以正邱首是祷
并夾上滙票壹張伸港銀柒佰伍拾員正煩台
轉交每具先友葬費五員共除去銀叁佰陸拾
五員仍有銀叁佰捌拾五員貴院收作運費香
油可也此乃區區微資貴院諸公慈善為懷
請祈見諒谨此并請

台安
　夾上儀紙至時煩為僱工起卸為盼
　各先友列名表另函

弟 黃 ^{宗伸}
诵芬 等上
^{堃明}

（印章：古巴隴西黃江夏堂慈善會）

中華民國十八年十月廿九日

另一人註：滙票壹張計艮七百五十元
　　　　　己十月卅日梁禹照收
另一人註：己十一月廿六日覆

茲將各先友姓名表列后

台山縣

黃傳鼎	灣頭堡龍蟠村人	收領人黃傳發
黃社全	洞口堡樹下村人	收領人黃社涯
黃寬犖	潮沙堡河朗村人	收領人黃寬棋
黃仁貴	獨岡堡塘口村人	收領人黃宗權
黃長金	大亨和樂村人	收領人黃柏森
黃增玉	大亨牛仔芋人	大亨車站收便合
黃義經	大亨舊村人	大亨車站收便合
黃增顏	大亨舊村人	大亨車站收便合
黃增暢	大亨牛仔芋人	大亨車站收便合
黃隆基	廣海沖傍村人	收領人黃邦仕
黃世澤	三合車咀村人	收領人黃瑞康
黃會烔	洞口堡村頭里人	收領人黃傳義
黃炳滋	洞口堡游魚里人	收領人黃炳周
黃廣興	湖境校椅塘人	收領人黃彩蓮
黃卓峯	三合月角村人	收領人黃柏熙
黃元參	南坑東龍村人	收領人黃日衡
黃崇澤	潮沙河朗福安村人	收領人黃崇偉
黃柏松	海晏沙蘭村人	收領人黃曉良
黃傳保	橫江新龍村人	收領人黃樹勳
黃昶羨（即報運）	潮境大嶺村人	收領人黃茂運
黃雲德	潮境京口嶺村人	收領人黃美旺
黃阿榮	南門永康堡大家塘村人	收領人黃權振
黃增崑	松仔朗新陽村人	收領人黃啓英
陳文藻	五十區李坑村人	收領人陳　莊

新會縣

黃玉海	大澤蟠龍鄉人	收領人黃亞根孔高
黃重溢	大七區京背村人	收領人黃重濟
黃名都	坑口堡山頂里人	收領人黃學靄
黃錦全	黃冲新輝里人	收領人黃仕鎌
黃兆基	古井大朗坡人	收領人黃華琼
黃賢碩	大十區張村鄉人	收領人黃賢永
黃賢銘	大十區張村鄉人	收領人黃齊合
黃孔仁	大十區張村鄉人	收領人黃意女
黃桂枝	杜阮平嶺村人	收領人黃錦堂
林善民	羅坑羅穊里人	收領人林國根

香山縣

黃焯常	斗門大濠冲人	收領人黃舉郁
黃社良	斗門大濠冲人	收領人黃康文
周耀濃	斗門東澳村人	收領人周福恩
黃祥基	斗門大濠冲人	收領人黃有基
黃能立	斗門下村鄉人	收領人黃啓耀
黃華添	松柏堡長洲鄉人	收領人黃錦明
黃華悅	斗門大濠冲人	收領人黃買諒
黃灶榮	斗門大濠冲人	收領人黃藻鴻
黃繽燦	斗門大濠冲人	收領人黃華春
黃盤祥	斗門小赤坎人	收領人黃享信
黃鴻添	斗門大濠冲人	收領人黃松煥
黃求烱	斗門大濠冲人	收領人趙　氏
熊傳晃	斗門大濠冲新村人	收領人熊買達
黃彰基	斗門大濠冲人	收領人黃楊基
黃基達	斗門小赤坎人	收領人黃買為
黃鴻綱	斗門大濠冲人	收領人黃卓斌
黃鴻康	斗門大濠冲人	收領人黃基發
黃錦鴻	斗門大濠冲人	收領人黃漢光

黃華興	增城湖都白水鄉人	收領人黃洪柱
黃橋貴	增城湖都白水鄉人	收領人黃錦位
黃禮光	增城湖都白水鄉人	收領人黃月光
黃紀安	開平顧邊南隆里人	收領人黃紀實
黃柱蘭	開平齊塘堡龍護里人	收領人黃錦灼
黃昂堅	開平顧邊南興里人	收領人黃永年
黃其庚	開平顧邊牛仔山清康村人	收領人胡　氏
吳文植	恩平大五區沙湖堡塘下村人	收領人吳信牛
吳援朝	恩平大五區沙湖堡高園村人	收領人吳濃保
吳作葵	恩平大五區鵬崗里人	收領人吳作彥
吳績楚	恩平沙湖堡鵬崗里人	收領人吳作彥
陳福田	赤溪縣塘磚村人	收領人陳昌堯
岑善柱	順德縣麥朗鄉人	收領人岑慎柱
黃　甜	南海縣九江北方大伸翹南社河坑弍約	收領人黃厚德
黃岑氏	南海縣九江北方大伸翹南社河坑弍約	收領人黃傑良
朱文垣	南海縣九江北方大伸文林里人	收領人朱德康
胡李氏	南海縣九江市龍涌社人	收領人從風草堂
林　鉅	鶴山縣昆華堡址山鄉蒼華里人	收領人林世厚嫂麥氏
鍾熙緝	恩平黃坡白廟堡洞心村人	收領人鍾華欽
駱國權	花縣大五區蓮塘鄉人	收領人駱楚屏
駱宗熙	花縣大五區蓮塘鄉人	收領人駱兆衛

注意駱國權 駱宗熙兩具骨殖暫貯貴院煩去函駱楚屏先生
　　　　來貴院收領免有遺失

古巴灣城黃江夏堂慈善會抄

（印章：古巴灣城黃江夏堂慈善會）

004 Letter from Wong Kong Ja Tong Comision Beneficencia, Habana, Cuba, to Tung Wah Hospital on 29 October 1929

From the Office of Wong Kong Ja Tong Comision Beneficencia, Habana, Cuba

Dear Managers of Tung Wah Hospital and Director Lo Man-kam,

We have set up a charitable association to exhume the bones of 73 deceased friends. The bones have been placed in five large boxes and repatriated by sea on the 28th day of this month. When the bones arrive in Hong Kong, please send them to the deceased's hometown for temporary storage in respective benevolent associations and hospitals and inform their families and friends to claim them for burial.

We have enclosed a money order for 750 Hong Kong dollars. Please give 5 dollars to the family of each deceased friend, 365 dollars in total, to cover burial costs, and keep the remaining 385 dollars as transportation fee and oil money. Your benevolence is well known, we hope you don't mind the small amount of donation.

We wish you well.

Please see enclosed the bill of lading for receiving the bones and a separate list of the deceased's names and native counties.

Yours humbly,
Wong Chung-sun *(Huang Zongshen)*, Chung-fan *(Songfen)* and Kwan-ming *(Kunming)*
(Stamp: WONG KONG JA TONG COMISION BENEFICENCIA, HABANA, CUBA)

29 October of the 18th year of the Republic of China

Another person's remarks: One money order for 750 dollars received by Leung Yu-chiu (Liang Yuzhao) on the 30th day of the 10th lunar month, Year of Gei Zi *(Jisi)*

Another person's remarks: Replied on the 26th day of the 11th lunar month, Year of Gei Zi *(Jisi)*

[Editor's remarks: Name list of the deceased friends is available only in Chinese]

慈善辦事處隴西公所列位公叔宗兄
　　均鑒逕啓者惟有家先叔李才初
　　乃係新会蓮塘興仁里人氏乃係正式隴西公所
　　人捐款購買樓月費堂底各等項年年清
　　結先友才初的確旧歲尾由古巴湾京隴西
　　公所慈善辦事處運返祖國親人的
　　偅保領不料会城仁育堂報紙落李才
　　初無埠名落仁育堂答復不知由何埠運
　　返祖国有三十五名不知由何埠運返祖國係由
　　古巴湾京運返有五元蕹費仁育堂答復
　　云三十五名先友非係由古巴湾京運返三十五
　　名先友蕹費清為烏有為親人者迫不淂
　　已用商庄担保保領若然隴西手續三十五名
　　先友從速追究香港東華医院新会城仁
　　育堂兩處善堂補囬三十五名先友蕹費抑
　　或隴西無蕹費不夠匯香港東華医院会城仁育
　　堂兩處謹得十三名先友有蕹費其餘三十五名
　　無蕹費祈隴西公所列位公叔宗兄　順囬乙音
　　的確滙夠兩處善堂蕹費不防追究責罰大斥
　　特斥司理人員兩處善堂應要補囬蕹費
　　祈列位公叔宗兄　祈即囬復弟順知　並頌

大安

一九二九年十弍月八号

　　　　　　　　　　　　　弟李逢光（即係龍逢）握手
　　　　　　　　　　　　　　　　（吉不用紅）

005 Letter of Lee Fung-kwong to Long Sai Li Benevolent Association, Cuba on 8 December 1929

Dear fellow clansmen of Long Sai Li Benevolent Association, Cuba

My late uncle Lee Choi-ying (*Li Caireng*) was a native of Hing Yan Lane (*Xingren Li*), Lin Tong (*Liantang*), Sun Wui (*Xinhui*). He was a member of the Long Sai Li Benevolent Association and used to pay the regular fees and donate money to the association every year.

Late last year, his remains were repatriated to the hometown by Long Sai Li Benevolent Association, Havana, Cuba. When his nephew went to collect the remains, Yan Yuk Tong (*Ren Yu Tang*) in Sun Wui told him that Lee Choi-ying's name was not on the Cuba repatriation list, and they did not know from where his remains were sent. The same happened to 35 sets of remains. It was not known where they were repatriated from. Burial fees of 5 dollars were used to be offered to each deceased friend repatriated from Havana, Cuba, but Yan Yuk Tong replied that the 35 sets of remains were not transported back from Havana. The deceased's relatives were forced to ask merchants to be their guarantors in order to collect the remains.

If the 35 sets of remains were indeed repatriated by Long Sai Li Benevolent Association, we demand that the Tung Wah Hospital in Hong Kong and Yan Yuk Tong in Sun Wui give the burial fees to the deceased families. Or, is it because the Long Sai Li Benevolent Association did not give enough funds to the Tung Wah Hospital and Yan Yuk Tong that only the families of 13 deceased friends were offered burial fees and the families of the remaining 35 deceased friends were not given any money? Please inform us if enough funds have been given to the two benevolent associations. If enough funds have been given, please condemn the managers of the two benevolent associations and make sure they take responsibility. The two benevolent associations should give the burial fees to the families.

Please reply at your earliest convenience.

Yours humbly,
Lee Fung-kwong, also known as Lung-fung (*Li Fengguang*, also known as *Longfeng*).

8 December 1929

隴西慈善會辦事處用箋
LONG SAI LI

東華醫院院長暨
執事善長仁翁列位先生鈞鑒

　　謹啟者本所慈善會扵民拾七年分二次寄運
　　先友遺骸歸國因湾島迩來工商衰落籌款
　　無多僅付港銀千員以應各方運費懇
　　貴院代為妥办手續經告完竣均無異詞本所同
　　人不勝感激但現接新會縣李逢光先生來函称
　　新會縣屬由本所付歸之先友三十五具均無葬費
　　五員交先友之家人收領觀此或係會城仁育善堂
　　執事人員胡混抑是
　　貴院因本所付囬公費過少未有款項付交各方办
　　理也本所同人未明真相謹此函達如
　　貴院將款付交仁育善堂请移函告知令其照办
　　並希　賜教以釋群疑此请恭祝

公安　不宣

（並將逢光來函夾呈）

民十八年中歷十弍月十四日
民十九年西歷元月十三號
（印章：古巴灣京隴西商旅自治講習所慈善會）
（印章：古巴灣京隴西商旅自治講習所）

慈善會 沾聖 祝南 謹叩

另一人註：庚二月初四覆

Letter from Long Sai Li Benevolent Association, Cuba, to Tung Wah Hospital on 13 January 1930

From the Office of Long Sai Li Benevolent Association

Dear Managers and benevolent Directors of Tung Wah Hospital,

We repatriated two batches of remains in the 17th year of the Republic of China. Since industry and commerce had gone downhill in Havana, we were only able to raise 1,000 Hong Kong dollars to cover the costs of repatriation. It was later reported that your esteemed hospital had successfully sent the remains back to the deceased's hometown, and we are most grateful to you for your efforts. However, we just received a letter from Lee Fung-kwong (*Li Fengguang*) of Sun Wui (*Xinhui*), who claimed that for 35 sets of remains repatriated by our association, the deceased's families had not received the burial fees of 5 dollars as pledged. We would like to know if the managers of Yan Yuk Tong (*Ren Yu Tang*) in Sun Wui created any chaos, or if it was because we did not send enough funds to your esteemed hospital that you could not pay the required sum to all parties. We have yet to find out the truth. If you have given the funds to Yan Yuk Tong, please write to them and tell them once again what to do. Please reply and explain the situation to us to ease our mind.

We wish you well.

Yours humbly,
(Stamp: Long Sai Li Merchants Autonomy Learning Office of Long Sai Li Benevolent Association, Habana, Cuba)
(Stamp: Long Sai Li Merchants Autonomy Learn Office, Habana, Cuba)
Chim-sing & Chuk-nam (*Zhangsheng & Zhunan*)
Chairmen of the benevolent association

14th day of the 12th lunar month of the 18th year of the Republic of China
13 January of the 19th year of the Republic of China

(Letter from Fung-kwong enclosed)

Another person's remarks: Replied on the 4th day of the 2nd lunar month, Year of Gang Ng (*Gengwu*)

僑港新會商會用牋

□□□□□□先生台鑒　去年

貴院交敝會運返外埠先友骨殖嗣因李才

初一具未有領到葬費伍元其親屬遞函古巴

灣隴西慈善會致該慈善會徑函

貴院詰問茲查李才初親屬未有領該葬費

之緣因寔由敝會抄該先友骨殖葬費之憑單

一時疏忽誤將李才初一名混入別埠以致該葬

費未有照交茲由敝會將該緣因備函會城仁

育善堂並請將葬費伍元補交李才初親屬

照領以清手續用將情由函達

台端表白並為道歉希為

察照原諒為荷專泐順頌

台祺唯

照不宣

義務司理劉毓芸（印章：香港新會商會）

中華民國庚午年二月十六日

007

Letter from Sun Wui Commercial Association of Hong Kong to Tung Wah Hospital on 16 February 1930

From the Office of Sun Wui Commercial Association of Hong Kong

Dear Managers of Tung Wah Hospital,

Last year, your esteemed hospital handed over the bones of deceased friends including those of Lee Choi-ying (*Li Caireng*) to us for repatriation. Since the Lee's relatives did not receive the burial fees of 5 dollars, they wrote to Long Sai Li Benevolent Association in Cuba, and the benevolent association wrote to your esteemed hospital to find out why the family of Lee Choi-ying did not receive the burial fees. The fact was that when we recorded the vouchers for our deceased friends' burial fees, we mistakenly put Lee Choi-ying under a different city, resulting that no burial fees were available for his family. We have written to Yan Yuk Sin Tong (*Ran Yu Shan Tang*) to explain the situation and provided the burial fees for them to give to the family of Lee Choi-ying for settling the matter accordingly.

I, hereby, write to you to clarify the matter and apologize to you. Please excuse us.

I wish you well.

Yours sincerely,
Lau Yuk-wan (*Liu Yuyun*), Volunteer Manager
(Stamp: Sun Wui Commercial Association of Hong Kong)

16 February, Year of Gang Ng *(Gengwu)*

新會城仁育善堂用箋

東華醫院
列位善長先生鈞鑒敬啟者頃接古巴灣
城隴西慈善會來函以該會去年運囬之
先友骸骨每具均付有葬費五元內有三
十五具因誤列入別埠以致無葬費交給
請為查明辦理見復等語查去年由港運
囬之各埠先友骸骨係蒙僑港新會商會
司理劉毓芸先生熱心辦理當時之先友
姓名里居及由何處運囬每具葬費若干皆
蒙劉君列明寄下敝堂均依照來單點明始
行刊登告白召人認領至應給葬費若干亦
照原單數目分給歷數十年辦理並無錯誤
此幫先友骨殖由劉君經手着陳洪記運返
計各埠先友骨殖二百四十六具照來人名
單點收有葬費者祇得二百〇一具無葬費
者占四十五具至古巴灣城隴西慈善會先
友葬費照來單列明得十七具每具五元共葬
費八十五元內有李才礽一具照寄來人名單
係列入別埠且未有地名是以此具骸骨由
何處運囬敝堂實不得而知今據該會來函
所稱列入別埠而無葬費者相差至三十五
具之多顯有錯誤亟應函請
示明以便轉致該會知照此帮先友骨殖
敝堂已代墊支運費港銀二百七十七元九毫
而分給葬費均照來單數目分給并無扣
減茲將去年劉毓芸先生經手列來之葬
費進支清結單一紙附呈
察核究竟此項葬費如何差誤務請迅
賜查明詳為

示復以便轉復該會知照望勿有延是

所感盼專函奉懇順頌

公祺

　　　　　　（印章：新會仁育堂）仁育堂同人敬叩

中華民國十九年二月廿八日

另一人註：庚二月初五日覆

　　　謹將劉毓芸先生經手先友骸骨葬費進支清單照列扚後

進東華醫院交來代收飛枝梳活埠中華公所先友骸骨二具　　　　　四八六寸　九元七毫二仙

　　又交來代收暹羅廣華醫院先友骸骨三十二具　　　　　　　　二元寸　　六十四元

　　又交來代收庇李士彬埠四邑積善堂先友骸骨四具　　　　　　六元寸　　二十四元

　　又交來代收墨國磨潯耀埠愛善堂先友骸骨二具　　　　　　　十元寸　　　廿元

　　又交來代收金山砵崙埠中華會館先友骸骨一百四十二具　　　三元寸　四百二十六元

　　又交來代收金山芝城中華会館一具三元雪梨伍根埠一具　　　五元寸　　　八元

　　又交來代收古巴灣城隴西慈善會先友骸骨十七具　　　　　　五元寸　　八十五元

　　　　共來銀六百叁拾六元七毫弍仙

支數列

支陳洪記運先友骸骨二百四十五具艇腳作靈棺計　　　　　　二二二寸　二百二十二元

支陳洪記運內箱棺一具作靈棺半計　　　　　　　　　　　　二二二寸　十一元一毫

支陳洪記運骸骨士担拾具半　　　　　　　　　　　　　　　一六寸　　十六元八毫

支報關十具半　　　　　　　　　　　　　　　　　　　　　二四寸　二十五元二毫

支醫院工費　　　　　　　　　　　　　　　　　　　　　　　　　　二元八毫

　　　　共支銀弍百七十七元九毫

除支實存港銀三百五拾八元八毫二仙申双毛[1]四百八十一元五毫四仙

　　　　　　　　　　八月初四日列

1　民國時期於廣東地區其中一種流通貨幣

Letter from Yan Yuk Tong of Sun Wui, China, to Tung Wah Hospital on 28 February 1930

From the Office of Yan Yuk Sin Tong, Sun Wui *(Xinhui)*

Dear benevolent Directors of Tung Wah Hospital,

We just received a letter from Long Sai Li Benevolent Association in Havana, Cuba, regarding the deceased friends they repatriated last year. 5 dollars should be offered to the family of each deceased friend to cover burial costs, but 35 sets of remains were mistakenly listed under another place and no burial fees were available to the families. They asked us to investigate the matter and reply to them.

We understand that it was Lau Yuk-wan (*Liu Yuyun*), manager of Sun Wui Commercial Association of Hong Kong, generously helped record the names and native counties of the deceased friends, where the remains were repatriated from, and the amount of burial fees offered for each set of remains. After we received the name list and funds from Lau, we checked the remains against the name list and put up advertisements asking the deceased's families to claim the remains. When the remains were collected, we gave out the burial fees according to the list. We have done the same for several decades and there has never been a problem.

The batch of remains in question was sent by Lau through Chan Hung Kee. There were 246 sets of remains from various places and we checked against the name list. We received burial fees for 201 sets of remains; no money was sent for 45 sets. Among the list, we received burial fees from Long Sai Li Benevolent Association Havana, Cuba for 17 sets of remains – 5 dollars for each deceased friend, 85 dollars in total. One of the deceased friends, Lee Choi-ying (*Li Caireng*), was listed under "Other Places" and the name of the place has not been recorded on the list. Therefore, we cannot possibly know where the remains were repatriated from. Meanwhile, according to the letter from Long Sai Li Benevolent Association, Havana, Cuba, 35 sets of remains were listed under "Other Places" and no burial fees were available for them. There is obviously some kind of error. Please investigate and explain to us the situation, so that we can inform the benevolent association accordingly.

As to this batch of remains, we have paid the shipping fees, in the sum of 277.90 Hong Kong dollars (on page 4), in advance. We have also given the burial fees to the families according to the list. We have enclosed the record of income and expenditure for the funds sent by Lau Yuk-wan last year for your reference. Please investigate the shortfall in the burial fees at your earliest convenience, so that we can answer their query.

Thank you for your efforts.

We wish you well.

Yours humbly,
From the fellows of Yan Yuk Tong
(Stamp: Yan Yuk Tong, Sun Wui)

28 February of the 19th year of Republic of China

Another person's remarks: Replied on the 5th day of the 2nd lunar month, Year of Gang Ng (*Gengwu*)

(Enclosed) Record of income and expenditure for burial fees arranged and sent by Lau Yuk-wan (*Liu Yuyun*) is as follows:

Income received from Tung Wah Hospital:

2 sets of remains sent by Chinese Consolidated Benevolent Association of Fresno	4.86 dollars each, 9.72 dollars in total
32 sets of remains sent by Kwong Wah Hospital of Siam	2 dollars each, 64 dollars in total
4 sets of remains sent by Si Yap Jik Sin Tong, Brisbane	6 dollars each, 24 dollars in total
2 sets of remains sent by Oi Sin Tong, San Meteo Atenco, Mexico	10 dollars each, 20 dollars in total
142 sets of remains sent by Chinese Consolidated Benevolent Association of Portland, USA	3 dollars each, 426 dollars in total
1 set of remains sent by Chinese Consolidated Benevolent Association of Chicago , USA, 3 dollars &1 set of remain sent by Hong Hem of Sydney	5 dollars each, 8 dollars in total
17 sets of remains sent by Long Sai Li Benevolent Association, Habana, Cuba	5 dollars each, 85 dollars in total

Total amount received: 636.72 collars

Expenditure

Shipping costs for 245 sets of bones paid to Chan Hung Kee	2.22 dollars each, 222 dollars in total
Shipping costs for 1 coffin paid to Chan Hung Kee (half price)	2.22 dollars each, 11.10 dollars
Stamp fees for 10.5 sets of bones paid to Chan Hung Kee	1.6 dollars each, 16.80 dollars
Customs declaration fees for 10.5 sets of bones	2.4 dollars each, 25.20 dollars
Hospital fees	2.80 dollars

Total expenditure: 277.90 dollars

Balance: 358.82 dollars
Converted to Kwangtung *(Guangdong)* silver coin (20 cents) : 481.54 dollars [local currency]

Record made on 4th day of 8th lunar month

新會城仁育善堂用牋

東華醫院
列位先生鈞鑒敬復者奉讀
鈞函拜悉一切此次古巴先友骸骨未知如何錯誤
致勞古巴隴西慈善會來函責備歉恐萬分又煩
貴院費神調查更為感激茲如
命將原先友姓名表照錄呈上煩為
瞽照懇請詳細調查迅為　示復以明真相曷勝企禱
專函拜懇即頌　公祺

仁育堂同人敬叩
（印章：新會仁育善堂）

中華民國十九年三月六日

另一人註：庚二月十四覆

Letter from Yan Yuk Tong, Sun Wui, China, to Tung Wah Hospital on 6 March 1930

From the Office of Yan Yuk Sin Tong (*Ran Yu Shan Tang*), Sun Wui *(Xinhui)*

Dear Managers of Tung Wah Hospital,

Thank you for your letter explaining the situation with the remains of our deceased friends from Cuba. It is not known what went wrong in the repatriation, such that Long Sai Li Benevolent Association of Cuba wrote to condemn us and we were regretful and worried. Worse still, you have strained your mind to investigate the matter and we are most grateful to your esteemed hospital. Please find enclosed the original list of the deceased friends as you have requested and look into the matter at your earliest convenience. We are indebted to your kindness to find out the truth.

We wish you well.

Yours humbly,
Fellow members of Yan Yuk Tong
(Stamp: Yan Yuk Sin Tong, Sun Wui)

6 March of the 19th year of the Republic of China

Another person's remarks: Replied on the 14th day of the 2nd lunar month, Year of Gang Ng *(Gengwu)*

古巴俞乾羅致李隴西慈善會信件

1930 年 5 月 31 日

李隴西慈善会会長
杏壇先生鑒 1928 年　貴会起運先友骨碿
　　囬藉弟彼時曾托代運先兄俞池兴（花県人）歸國据
　　計有日今始接到家人來書称及先兄骨
　　碿尤未抵步曾在廣州市各善堂查檢亦無下
　　落因念及此殊為掛慮是以特字奉上是否各
　　先友偕同到步抑為途中阻滯祈求詳細賜
　　复以慰遠念俾得函知家人到期接洽則感德
　　無涯矣此請

公安

弟俞乾罗字上

五月卅一号

010

Letter from Yu Kin-law, Cuba, to Long Sai Li Benevolent Association on 31 May 1930

Dear Chairman Hang-tang (*Xingtan*) of Long Sai Li Benevolent Association,

When your esteemed association exhumed and repatriated the remains of deceased Chinese compatriots in 1928, I sought your help in repatriating the remains of my late brother, Yu Chi-hing (*Yu Chixing*) of Fa Yuen (*Huaxian*). I just received a letter from my family saying that the bones of my late brother had not returned yet. They have checked with all benevolent associations in Canton (*Guangzhou*) but there was no trace of my brother's remains. I am very concerned about the matter, thus writing this letter. Did the remains of all the deceased arrive [in Canton] at the same time? Or were there setbacks in the process of repatriation? Please investigate the matter and reply to me in detail to ease my mind. Upon receiving your reply, I will write to tell my family when and how to claim the bones. I will forever be grateful to you for your kindness.

Best wishes,

Yours sincerely,
Yu Kin-law (*Yu Qianluo*)

31 May

隴西商旅自治講習所用箋
Long Sai Li

東華醫院列位執事先生青鑒

　　敬啓者本所前接新會仁育善堂來函與
　　貴院函此事原属李逢光一函質問餘未有谈
　　及者但此等事項在本所同人均以一時之误皆
　　属一笑置之前函經已説明據最迩接來俞乾
　　羅先生函称他先兄俞池興之遺骸仍未有
　　妥收想
　　貴院執事或因時局輸運維艱或因地僻未
　　便留存院中抑因误運別方未能详悉茲將原函
　　呈核恳　代明復　示以免懸掛是為至盼此
　　请敬候

公安

民十九年六月四号

（印章：古巴灣京隴西商旅自治講習所）謹啓

011

Letter from Long Sai Li Merchants Autonomy Learning Office, Cuba, to Tung Wah Hospital on 4 June 1930

From the Office of Long Sai Li Merchants Autonomy Learning Office

Dear Managers of Tung Wah Hospital,

We received letters from Yan Yuk Sin Tong (*Ren Yu Shan Tang*) of Sun Wui *(Xinhui)* and your esteemed hospital regarding an interrogation from Lee Fung-kwong (*Li Fengguang*). We understand there was a slight error and have already put the matter behind us. Our previous letter also explained the situation.

Recently, we received a letter from Yu Kin-law (*Yu Qianluo*) who claimed that he had not yet received the remains of his late brother Yu Chi-hing (*Yu Chixing*). Are the remains still in the care of your esteemed hospital, as a result of difficulties in transportation due to political turmoil or remoteness of the destination? Or have they been sent to the wrong destination? We enclose Yu's letter for your reference. Please investigate the matter. We await your reply to ease our mind.

Yours sincerely,
(Stamp: Long Sai Li Merchants Autonomy Learning Office, Habana, Cuba)

4 June of the 19th year of the Republic of China

Fupau Hermanos y Compañía

東華医院
列位善長 均鑒敬啓者茲有先友胡球濠公彭才添

　　公骨金两具即日護送金山大埠轉船付上拜浼

　　貴医院代運往九江鄉其藉貫另列扵後別日

　　請祈查收并煩傳知　盛埠誠泰金山庄閡翼

　　之先生妥議轉運不勝感戴之致容圖後謝

　　專此即請

鈞安

（印章：□□兄弟公司書）^弟胡仕 謹浼

西六月八号

中五月十二日

胡球濠公　南海九江鄉龍涌市人
彭才添公　南海九江鄉岡咀社人

012 Letter from Wu Sze, Mexico, to Tung Wah Hospital on 8 June 1930

Fupau Hermanos y Compañía

Dear benevolent Directors of Tung Wah Hospital,

The bones of our deceased friends, Wu Kau-ho (*Hu Qiuhao*) and Pang Choi-tim (*Peng Caitian*), have been transported to San Francisco for repatriation to Hong Kong by sea. Please help transport the bones to Kau Kong Township *(Jiujiang Xiang)*. The native counties of the deceased friends are listed at the end of this letter. After you have taken the remains into your care, please contact Kwan Yik-chi (*Guan Yizhi*) of Shing Tai Gold Mountain Firm in Hong Kong and discuss the repatriation arrangements with him.

We are most grateful to you for your kindness.

We wish you well.

Yours sincerely,
Wu Sze (*Hu Shi*)
(Stamp: XX Brothers Company)

8 June
12th day of the 5th lunar month

Wu Kau-ho, native of Lung Chung City *(Longchong Shi)*, Kau Kong, Nam Hoi *(Nanhai)*
Pang Choi-tim, native of Kong Tsui Sei *(Gangzui She)*, Kau Kong, Nam Hoi

Fupau Hermanos y Compañía

東華医院
列位仁翁 均鑒敬啓者西歷月之八號茲有專函奉上付

　　有由金山大埠轉交先友骨金兩具拜凂代運囬

　　鄉斯函想已早達　台端料邀　青盼矣茲特副

　　函夾上請祈复阅恕不贅陳但該船腳未見到

　　收想必在港收理定矣惟船腳若干抵步時祈

　　通知誠泰金山庄　阅翼之兄差他辦理便好

　　謹此奉知餘照未及有勞有勞专此即請

公安

　　　　　　　　　　　　（印章：XX 保兄弟公司書）^弟胡仕頓

　　　　　　　　　　　　西歷六月廿三号

　　　　　　　　　　　　中五月廿七日

013 Letter from Wu Sze, Mexico, to Tung Wah Hospital on 23 June 1930

Fupau Hermanos y Compañía

Dear benevolent Directors of Tung Wah Hospital,

I wrote to you on 8 June to seek your help in sending the bones of my two deceased friends, repatriated from San Francisco, to their hometown. I trust the letter has been delivered to you and you have read it. For your easy reference, I attach herewith a copy of the last letter again. Please be reminded that the shipping fees of sending the bones to their hometown were not included in the letter and the fees shall be settled in Hong Kong. Regarding the amount of the shipping fees, please contact my respected friend, Kwan Yik-chi *(Guan Yizhi)* of Shing Tai Gold Mountain Firm when the bones are received. He will settle the matters accordingly.

Thank you for your efforts. I wish you well.

Yours humbly,
Wu Sze *(Hu Shi)*
(Stamp: XX Brothers Company)

23 June
27th day of the 5th lunar month

古巴灣城黃江夏堂用箋
WONG KONG JA TONG

東華醫院総理
羅文錦暨諸执　事先生均鑒逕啓者敝會去歲

　　籌運第一帮先友骨殖七十三具已起運　貴処義

　　庄暫存又云　貴院定章向未有代運返各

　　縣鄉祇可代通知各縣商會或善堂代領此

　　舉亦善惟未知各県商會善堂辦到否現

　　拠中山縣各先友之親屬來函报告收領妥當

　　其餘各県之先友親屬未有函报知順此查詢

　　茲七月七號由総統船附上先友七十八具共分四大

　　箱到時祈為查收仰即通知各県商會善堂

　　俾得早日收領以正首邱而安先灵則厚望專

　　茲寄上戾紙壹張該港銀陆佰大元到时

　　祈查收除每具交囬銀五元共三百九十元其餘式

　　百壹拾元以作艇脚香油等用是荷希為

　　察納請早示知為盼統請

　均安

　　　并夾先友名单紙一張船紙式張查收可也

（印章：古巴灣城黃江夏堂慈善會）

総理黃诵芬

處長黃宗伸　仝頓

書記黃堃明

中華民國十九年七月七日

另一人註：七月初九日復

（新聞剪報）

■ 江夏堂慈善會啓事

為通告事^本會籌運第二帮先友骨殖回國經已釘
裝妥當原定期六月廿三日附輪歸國旋據該船公
司稱云是期貨物過多不能運儎是以改期於七月
初七日附輪並將各先友籍貫姓名詳列於下惟凡
其親友欲往中華義山致祭者請於初三日（即禮
拜四日）下午一時同往幸勿吝玉為盼此佈

◆ 茲將先友籍貫姓名表列于后

黃傳烈開平厚山堡咀頭村（黃傳權收）　　黃傳信台山大塘堡安盛村（黃百廉收）

朱弼祥中山東鎮西樵鄉人（朱譚氏收）　　林善寶新會北洋北合里人（林華勝收）

洪有德中山東鎮西樵鄉人（洪宏就收）　　黃作矩台山那仁堡東邊頭人（黃炳觀收）

黃華遷新會古井龜頭光龍里（黃承端收）　黃宏意新會第十區張村鄉人（黃宏良收）

黃世濂台山三合銅鑼灣人　　　　　　　　黃泗榮台山三合鵝腔村人（黃保述收）

黃廷宗台山三合銅鑼灣人　　　　　　　　黃雲灼台山口嶺堡人（黃益韶收）

黃初謂台山口嶺堡人（黃英韶收）　　　　黃錫祥台山南坑堡東遂村（黃熾業收）

易子英鶴山玉橋村人（易渭岩收）　　　　黃達遠新會古井大朗坡人（黃根大收）

黃　堯台山企嶺堡永安村人（黃操昌收）　黃和世台山草骨朗盛平村（黃國基收）

黃順傳台山草骨朗盛平村人（黃仲芬收）　黃榮享台山洞口堡甘邊鄉人（黃振銓收）

吳章鑛新會古井文樓鄉人（吳李氏收）　　鍾周美新會大澤鎮龍田鄉人（鍾蓮收）

陸玲蜴鶴山十七堡那水村人（陸金銘收）　鍾德庚新會大八區官田鄉人（鍾閎福收）

王擴皇台山都斛南村山邊里人（王擴萬收）楊紹熹鶴山大凹鄉石橋里人（楊百就收）

楊　濃鶴山大凹鄉永興里人（楊緒環收）　黃傳燒台山籄竹門人（黃劍閙收）

黃金德開平百合風歲朗人（黃炳漢收）　　張　抒新會大七區沙富南薰里（張北照收）

李潤沾鶴山平嶺東頭里人（李振恩收）　　楊社燦鶴山九堡南庄村人（楊社板收）

黃炳松鶴山赤草新村人（黃炳沾收）　　　凌世週新會河村亨美鄉人（凌先銘收）

呂統文新會大澤呂村人（呂洪泮收）　　　呂莪明新會大澤呂村人（呂緒瑞收）

呂北志新會江門水南東海里人（呂永華收）呂家儉新會大澤呂村人（呂家矩收）

呂傳昌新會大澤呂村人（呂緒端收）　　　凌伸佑新會河村亨美鄉人（凌阿旋收）

廖廷光台山公益區長塘舊村人　　　　廖撝光台山沖蔞甫草洋村人

廖燦芳台山沖蔞甫草洋村人　　　　　駱景林花縣蓮塘村人

駱達書花縣蓮塘村人　　　　　　　　黃藉安新會牛灣人（黃牛收）

黃滿誠新會牛灣人（黃棠收）　　　　黃傳展台山洞口潮安村人

楊松榮鶴山大凹鄉石橋里人（楊炳南收）　宋　長鶴山大凹曹坑村人（宋厚收）

楊弈育鶴山大凹鄉坑尾里人（楊忪務收）　黃義德台山企嶺堡永安村人（黃北大收）

楊緒瑞新會仙洞太和里人（楊纘收）　　呂　挽新會大澤呂村人（呂永禎收）

馮天福中山第八區黃梁鎮大蠔沖塘山里人（馮眾享收）　歐陽傍中山東鎮四都蘇子村西堡人（歐陽昌收）

呂登統新會大澤呂村人（呂旺收）　　徐銘禎鶴山小官堡獺山村人（徐兆志收）

黃潤德台山企嶺堡永安村人（黃灶旺收）　黃韶德台山企嶺堡永安村人（黃進昌收）

麥有為台山莘村磐石村人（麥有華收）　麥夢熊台山莘村銀塘村人（麥傑榮收）

黃佐德台山企嶺堡永安村人（黃錦大收）　葉迎藻台山筋坑君子坑人（葉建焯收）

彭榮據台山彭沙坑新龍村人（彭榮倫收）　彭劉氏台山彭沙坑新龍村人（彭榮倫收）

彭家滾台山彭沙坑新龍村人（彭子炎收）　楊陸氏新會仙洞接源里人（楊雲朱收）

彭育民台山彭沙坑新龍村人（彭榮靄收）　徐兆意鶴山小官田堡獺山村（徐兆志收）

何　炎恩平金汎堡錦嶺村人（何立啓收）　黃衍蘭開平魁崗堡石灘村人（凌子鏗收）

趙不標台山海晏都崙定村人（趙士彼收）　何章求鶴山古都芸蓼村人（何如寬收）

楊雲榮鶴山大凹鄉石閘里人（楊緒照收）　黃昭棟台山橫江堡舊村人（黃玉榮收）

呂　後新會大澤呂村人（呂德業收）　　楊弈博鶴山大凹鄉人

　　　　　　　　　　　　　　　　　（交佛山蠻衛里楊東海收注意）

六月三十日　　　　　古巴灣城黃江夏堂慈善會謹啓

另一人註：注意未註收領者因代报者一时忘記收領人

014 Letter from Wong Kong Ja Tong Comision Beneficencia, Habana, Cuba, to Tung Wah Hospital on 7 July 1930

From the Office of Wong Kong Ja Tong Comision Beneficencia, Habana, Cuba

Dear Director Lo Man-kam and Managers of Tung Wah Hospital,

Last year, we repatriated the first batch of the bones of our deceased friends. 73 sets of bones were exhumed and sent back, and they had been placed temporarily in the coffin home of your esteemed hospital. We understand that your esteemed hospital does not directly transport the remains to the deceased's hometown, in accordance with established practices and can only inform the merchant associations or benevolent associations of the respective counties to collect the remains on behalf of the families. This is very kind of you but we wonder if the merchant associations and benevolent associations have done the job properly. Now, the families of our deceased friends from Chung Shan (*Zhongshan*) wrote to us and told us they had received the remains. We have yet to receive words from the families of our deceased friends in other counties. Can you please follow up on the matter?

Meanwhile, we have recently repatriated 78 sets of remains, placed in four large boxes, on a President Lines ship departing on 7 July. After you take delivery of the remains, please inform the merchant associations and benevolent associations of the respective counties to collect them and return them to the deceased's families, so that our deceased friends can be laid to rest.

We enclose a cheque for 600 Hong Kong dollars. Please give 5 dollars to the family of each deceased friend, 390 dollars in total, and keep the remaining 210 dollars to pay for transportation costs and also as oil money to your esteemed hospital.

We look forward to your reply.

We wish you well.

Please refer to the list of deceased friends as well as the two bills of lading enclosed when you take delivery of the remains.

Best wishes,
Wong Chung-sun (*Huang Zongshen*), Chairman
Wong Chung-fun (*Huang Songfen*), Director
Wong Kwan-ming (*Huang Kunming*), Secretary
(Stamp: WONG KONG JA TONG COMISION BENEFICENCIA, HABANA, CUBA)

7 July of the 19th year of the Republic of China

Another person's remarks: Replied on the 9th day of the 7th lunar month

[Editor's remarks: Name list of the deceased friends is available only in Chinese]

古巴灣城安定堂自治所慈善會致東華醫院信件

1930 年 7 月 25 日

安定堂自治所用箋

中華民國十九年七月廿五日

東華医院諸執事先生均鑒　啓者自去年九月卅日由湾
　　附輪先友共五箱合壹百具既蒙函覆收貯發落以
　　為將之妥發今接先友梁景昌家眷來函報称仍未領囙
　　骨殖等語前來據此未曉何故日前經奉函呈上
　　請調查先友伍梓芬台山人亦未領收今未蒙音覆
　　至于梁景昌君亦是台山人見祈合併調查妥當
　　勞為分發免至遺失為幸是否如何仰希便
　　覆以便答先友之家人藉知先友而慰幽魂餘
　　容後叙謹此敬請

群安

安定堂自治所慈善會主任梁裔南

（印章：古巴灣城安定堂慈善會）

另一人註：七月初九日覆

015 Letter from Sociedad On Ten Tong, Habana, Cuba, to Tung Wah Hospital, 25 July 1930

From the Office of On Ten Tong

25 July of the 19th year of the Republic of China

Dear Managers of Tung Wah Hospital,

We repatriated the remains of 100 deceased friends, placed in five boxes, from Havana by sea on 30 September last year. You wrote to us to confirm that you had received the remains and we believe everything had been taken care of. Yet the family of our deceased friend Leung King-cheong (*Liang Jingchang*) recently wrote to inform us that they still had not received his bones. We wrote to you earlier seeking your help in investigating the whereabouts of the remains of Ng Chi-fun (*Wu Zifen*), a native of Toi Shan (*Taishan*). Since we have not yet received your reply and Leung King-cheong is also a native of Toi Shan, can you please investigate the two cases together at once? Please send the bones back to the deceased's hometown, so that they will not be lost.

Please rely to us with any information you may have, so that we can inform the families of the deceased.

We hope the deceased can be laid to rest.

Yours sincerely,
Leung Yui-nam (*Liang Yinan*)
Chairman of Sociedad On Ten Tong
(Stamp: Sociedad de On Teng Tong, Habana, Cuba)

Another person's remarks: Replied on the 9th day of the 7th lunar month

安定堂自治所用箋

中華民國十九年七月廿八日

東華醫院諸執事先生均鑒　啓者本堂慈善會經于
　　去年九月间辦理先友歸國既蒙關顧一切欣慰奚如
　　銘感五中茲因叠接先友伍梓芬梁景昌「俱台山人」
　　梁棕荣「順德倫教人」家屬來函报称該等遺骸
　　骨殖至今日久仍未能收領亦未曉將該等姓
　　名遺骸安置何處抑以撥分各縣商會處理辦之希
　　請追究间或誤會遺失望即調查妥辦先友們
　　得歸原籍安歸樂土以慰幽魂使則含笑九泉
　　吾人等感佩莫名餘容後叙專此即請并候

祺祉

（印章：安定堂印）
（印章：古巴灣城安定堂慈善會）
慈善會主任梁裔南

　　計開
　　伍梓芬台山五十區平安村人莊在大二箱
　　梁景昌台山松仔蓢黃梁村人莊在大二箱
　　梁棕荣順德倫教人莊在大四箱

再者如知先友或未頒發請將先友梁棕荣直寄順德大良懷遠義莊
轉交其家屬收無悮

另一人註：七月初九日復

016   **Letter from Sociedad On Ten Tong, Habana, Cuba, to Tung Wah Hospital on 28 July 1930**

From the Office of On Ten Tong

Dear Managers of Tung Wah Hospital,

We repatriated the remains of our deceased friends in September last year, and are much indebted to you for your kind assistance. Recently, the families of Ng Chi-fan (*Wu Zifen*) and Leung King-cheong (*Liang Jingchang*), both native of Toi Shan (*Taishan*), and Leung Chung-wing (*Liang Zongrong*), a native of Lun Gao (*Lunjiao*), Shun Tak (*Shunde*), wrote to us and informed us that they had not collected the remains of their late relatives yet, and did not know where the remains were kept or if they had been sent to the merchant associations of the respective counties for handling. Please find out whether there is any misunderstanding, or if the remains have been lost. We hope you would give your urgent attention to this matter, so that the remains of our deceased friends can return to their homeland and be laid to rest. The spirits of the deceased will be pleased with what you have done for them.

We are most grateful to you for your kindness.

We await your reply.

Yours sincerely,
Leung Yui-nam *(Liang Ruinan)*, Manager
(Stamp: Sociedad On Ten Tong)
(Stamp: Sociedad de On Ten Tong, Habana, Cuba)

Note:
Ng Chi-fan, native of Ping On Village *(Ping'an Cun)*, District 50 *(Wushi Qu)*, Toi Shan, placed in Box No.2
Leung King-cheong, native of Wong Leung Village *(Huangliang Cun)*, Chung Tsai Long *(Song Zai Lang)*, Toi Shan, placed in box no. 2
Leung Chung-wing, native of Lun Gao *(Lunjiao)*, Shun Tak *(Shunde)*, placed in Box no. 4

If the remains have not yet been repatriated, please send those of Leung Chung-wing directly to Wai Yuen Coffin Home *(Huaiyuan Yizhuang)* in Shun Tak. The coffin home will hand over the remains to the deceased's family.

Another person's remarks: Replied on the 9th of the 7th lunar month

古巴灣城陳穎川堂慈善會致東華醫院信件

1930 年 8 月 14 日

並將此次運回之先友分別開列

陳子鏡台山夾牘村人　交其家人陳裔蕃收

陳滿旋南海九江人　交香港陳寶棧收

陳明旺台山海晏夏春場人　交其家陳初盛收

陳業創台山水南水背村人　交其家人陳天良收

陳連棟台山玉懷黃第園人　交其家陳益培收

陳謀諒新會京梅村人　交其家人陳華燦收

陳滋孫新會京梅村人　交其家陳孫贊收

陳賢雙新會陳冲山咀村人

陳昌泰赤溪田頭鄉人　交其家人陳兆樞收

陳典岳新會山咀村人　交其家人陳社合收

陳海源台山玉懷河洲村人　交其家人陳燦廷收

陳旋明台山長沙坑人　交其家人陳耀坤收

陳玉文台山長沙坑人　交其家人陳育女收

陳文蘭台山冲泮水坑村人　交其家人陳耀俊收

陳　彬恩平潢埗頭人　交其家人陳榮準收

陳文樓台山三合高頭嶺人　交其家人陳保滄收

陳瑞池新會天馬人　交其家人陳懋賴收

陳信沾新會天馬人　交其家人陳捷禮收

陳柏文台山三合牛瀾人　交其家人陳嗣昌收

陳津良台山三合洋瀾大湖塘人　交其家人陳濃洽收

陳合本開平赤坎大朗人　交其家人陳澤瑞收

陳潔蒼番禺鴉湖草塘庄　交其家人陳秋福收

陳光遇台山水南水樓村人　交其家人陳植旋收

陳纘榮（即陳選）台山陳邊新屋村人　交其家人陳百現收

陳進孫新會高沙村人　交其家人陳錫欽收

陳孫美新會高沙人　交其家人陳和順收

陳炳焜中山得都庫充人　交其家人陳生收

陳錦元新會沙堆村人　交其家人陳典泮收

陳認穩台山水南隔水圍人　交其家人陳何穩收

陳煥明台山大塘站洞寧人　交其家人陳仕文收

陳認華台山水南潮陽村人　交其家人陳家熠收

陳元亨廣東省城西關永慶街永慶二巷　交其家人陳阿女收

陳英賢中山東鎮陵岡人　交其家人陳順興收

陳榮崇中山馬山東昇里人　交其家人陳瑞祥收

陳文庚台山三合永勝村人　交其家人陳錫球收

陳文柏台山三合高頭嶺人　交其家人陳良鴻收

陳國羨恩平沙湖堡松塘人 交其家人陳培均收　　陳森彥恩平沙湖堡松塘人 家人陳初瑤收

陳光照台山海晏沙浦汶陽人 家人陳國治收　　陳光添台山沖蔞高咀人 家人陳光槐收

陳光翼台山沖蔞高咀人 交其家人陳松年收　　陳光勝台山都斛東坑村人 交其家人陳典策收

陳垂成台山海晏大担人 交其家人陳瑞杭收　　陳　彬南海九江南方興教社人 家人陳仲收

陳　國台山三合北斗潮勝人 家人陳偉良收　　陳文培台山三合白石塘人 交其家人陳錦植收

陳庭釗南海九江大谷人 交其家人　　葉錦沛台山筋坑順水村人 交其家人葉榮璋收

葉汝平台山君子坑潮龍人 交其家人葉添燦收　　潘騰波順德大良人 交其家人潘釗庭收

潘年初順德大良人 交其家人潘源初收　　何伯懷順德陳村人 交其家人何仲儒收

楊誠堃順德陳村人 交其家人楊賜存收　　趙咸臻台山浮石人 交其家人趙泮槐收

余毓燧台山桂水潮澗人 交其家人余松炳收

以上所列各先友之姓名籍貫仰
祈照他分發並每先友交港銀
五元其家人收以作葬費

劉顯祖之先友無款照交可也

陳潁川堂慈善会付
（印章：古巴灣城陳潁川堂）
（印章：古巴灣城陳潁川堂書柬）
一九三〇年即十九年八月十四號

Letter from Chang Weng Chun Tong, Habana, Cuba, to Tung Wah Hospital on 14 August 1930

We enclose a list of the deceased friends repatriated in this batch.

The list shows the names and native counties of the deceased friends. Please send the remains to the deceased's families according to the list, and give each family burial fees of 5 Hong Kong dollars.

For our deceased friend Lau Hin-cho (*Liu Xianzu*), although no burial fees are provided, please hand over his remains to his family.

From Chang Weng Chun Tong
(Stamp: Chang Weng Chun Tong, Dragones, NUM. 46, Altos, Habana, Cuba)
(Stamp: Chang Weng Chun Tong, Habana, Cuba)

14 August of the 19th year of the Republic of China 1930

[Editor's remarks: Name list of the deceased friends is available only in Chinese]

018 古巴灣城陳頴川總堂慈善會致東華醫院信件

1930 年 8 月 18 日

東華醫院総理執事先生^{鈞鑒}

逕啓者^{敝堂}前月檢運先友已扵八月五
號附輪運回祖國以安先靈而正首邱
亦經先函报及
貴醫院　先生等奉闻如該船到港时
仰　先生命工伴將該四大木箱之先友
起回　貴醫院然後將各先友按址
送回原籍再招其先友家人到領俾
其安葬至扵分送各先友手續料
先生等善為處置毋須別述故付上港
赤一張伸銀五百大元到祈请收並每
先友交其家人收港銀五元計五十
五具共交銀二百七十五元其餘二百二十五元係
為送　貴醫院香油費仰為照收
但^{敝堂}此次所運之先友是為第一期然
以所送　貴院之香油些少此因世难
而捐款有限之故耳如他期或將先
友運回時再行付上香油多些便是
如收到此款後仰即先來字告及俾吾
等办理手續清楚是為公便也
谨此即请

公祺

並將先友籍貫名單
抄錄一紙呈上俾為所知

（印章：古巴灣城陳頴川堂）
（印章：古巴灣城陳頴川堂書束）
陳頴川総堂慈善會
総理　月湖
財政　文献　等仝言
書記　瑛荣
民十九年即一九三〇年八月十八號

另一人註：庚八月初七覆

Letter from Chang Weng Chun Tong, Habana, Cuba, to Tung Wah Hospital on 18 August 1930

Dear Directors and Managers of Tung Wah Hospital,

We exhumed the remains of our deceased friends earlier and they had departed for China by sea on 5 August, in order that our deceased friends can be laid to rest in their hometown. We had also written to inform you of the delivery in our last letter. When the remains, placed in four large wooden boxes, arrive in Hong Kong, please arrange labor to take them into your care and then send them to the deceased's hometown. Please inform the families of the deceased friends to collect the remains for burial. We trust that you can handle the sending of the remains to their families well, so we will not repeat the steps here.

We enclose a cheque for 500 Hong Kong dollars. Please give 5 dollars to the family of each deceased friend, 275 dollars in total, for 55 deceased friends, and keep the remaining 225 dollars as our oil money to your esteemed hospital.

This is the first batch of repatriation of remains of our deceased friends but the oil money we can contribute to your hospital is quite small. Please understand that life is difficult and we have not been able to raise much money. We will donate more oil money to your hospital if we repatriate remains in future.

Please acknowledge receipt of the cheque so that we are able to complete our relevant procedures.

We enclose a list of the deceased's names and native counties for your information.

Yours sincerely,
Yuet-wu *(Yuehu)*, Director
Man-hin *(Wenxian)*, Treasurer
Ying-wing *(Yingrong)*, Secretary
Chang Weng Chun Tong

(Stamp: Chang Weng Chun Tong, Habana, Cuba)
(Stamp: Chang Weng Chun Tong, Dragones, NUM. 46, Altos, Habana, Cuba)

18 August of the 19th year of the Republic of China

Another person's remarks: Replied on the 7th day of the 8th lunar month, Year of Gamg Ng (*Gengwu*) (1930)

旅中美洲掘地孖罅國華僑總會用箋
COLONIA CHINA

東華醫院執事大鑒　逕啓者本
月十九日運返先友骸骨三十四具
經詳前函茲由香港廣東銀
行匯返美金壹百柒拾元请
代支給每具運鄉費金五元
可也　此頌

公祺

　　　　　　（印章：中美洲掘地孖罅華僑總會）華僑總會　謹啓
　　　　　　　　　　　　　　　　　　　一九、八、廿三

另一人註：伸港銀伍佰壹拾捌元一毛七仙
另一人註：庚九月初五复

Letter from Colonia China, Guatemala, to Tung Wah Hospital on 23 August 1930

From the Office of Colonia China, Guatemala

Dear Managers of Tung Wah Hospital,

My previous letter had already detailed the repatriation of 34 sets of bones of our deceased friends on the 19th day of this month. Now we transmit 170 US dollars to you via The Bank of Canton in Hong Kong. Please use the funds to cover the costs of transporting the remains back to the deceased's hometown, 5 US dollars for each set of remains.

Your kindness is much appreciated.

Yours sincerely,
Colonia China
(Stamp: Colonia China, Guatemala)

23 August of the 19th year of the Republic of China

Another person's remarks: 518.17 Hong Kong dollars received
Another person's remarks: Replied on the 5th day of the 9th lunar month, Year of Gang Ng (*Gengwu*)

旅中美洲掘地孖罅國華僑總會用箋
COLONIA CHINA

香港東華醫院大鑒　逕啓者敝處華

　　僑先友骸骨三十四具分裝六箱本

　　月十九日搭「掘地孖罅」船運至金山大埠

　　轉船附歸

　　貴院貯候各該親屬到領除另

　　函通知各先友親屬外謹將儎

　　運船紙二張夾上到請

　　提收另由香港廣東銀行匯上美金作運

　　返鄉費專此奉託敬請

公安

（印章：中美洲掘地孖罅華僑總會）華僑總會謹啓

另一人註：庚九月初五復

Letter from Colonia China, Guatemala, to Tung Wah Hospital in 1930

From the Office of Colonia China, Guatemala

Dear Managers of Tung Wah Hospital,

The remains of our 34 Chinese compatriots, placed in six boxes, were transported to San Francisco on the *Guatemala* on the 19th day of this month. They will then be transferred onto another ship and sent to Hong Kong. Please take them into your care. The deceased's families will come to your esteemed hospital to collect the remains. We have informed the families by post separately. Please take delivery of the remains with the enclosed two bills of lading. We have also transmitted some funds in US dollars to you via the Bank of Canton in Hong Kong to pay for transportation fees to the deceased's hometown.

Your assistance is much appreciated.

We wish you well.

Yours sincerely,
Colonia China
(Stamp: Colonia China, Guatemala)

Another person's remarks: Replied on the 5th day of the 9th lunar month, Year of Gang Ng (Gengwu)

至德慈善會用牋
Chi Tack Tong

逕啓者敝會承各侨梓委
託撿運先友骨殖归國以正首
邱而妥幽灵经於九月一日由輪
船 President Fillmore 號運返　貴院代
收轉交统計二十八具分裝兩大箱
茲由萬寶華办庄滙上港銀三百
五十元內分交各先友內地運費每
具十元共计二百八十元其餘七十
元聊作奉交　貴院香油與搬
運費想　貴院向來熱心办理
慈善事業　仁風遠播無任
欣佩今敝会懇托　貴院關照
辦理伏希　俯賜接納仍請
見覆為荷　此致

東華醫院执事先生

　　　　附件
　　先友姓名籍貫单一紙
　　萬寶華滙单票一張
　　裝運先友骨殖儎紙二張

　　　　　　　　　　会長　蔡仲榮（印章：仲榮）

中華民國十九年九月三日

另一人註：庚十一月初二覆

至德慈善会檢運先友骨殖名单

吳振濃	恩平烏石蔭人
吳奕銘	开平樓冈西頭新屋里人
周集和	中山縣神涌村人
周瑞崇	开平茅冈下洞橫坑里人
周奕棉	中山縣東鎮關塘埔村人
周成忖	开平茅冈西社人
周遵杕	开平茅冈西社人
周家儀	开平周坑網山人
蔡盛煜	台山橫嶺鄉人
蔡英犖	台山和安里人
蔡傑球	台山橫嶺鄉人
蔡維盛	台山双楼村人
蔡鴻鈞	台山橫嶺鄉人
蔡元燦	台山上蓮塘村人
蔡英暢	台山甫草村人
蔡如燦	台山甫草村人
蔡英堯	台山甫草村人
蔡文初	台山沙浦下蓮塘村人
曾孝南	南海九江大谷人
莫福純	恩平那西堡水流坪人
岑祝元	恩平大江堡石塘村人
歐陽汝萬	中山縣大嶺鄉人
張培簡	开平羊路龍山東成里人
李聖鎏	新会西十區河村鎮沙湾鄉人
李福有	新会西十區河村鎮沙湾鄉人
馮汝熾	鶴邑雅瑤羅經坊人
高北樂	新会古井那伏鄉人
關聯太	南海九江北方沙咀四閘人

（印章：至德慈善會）

「內有先友骨殖三具乃曾武城旅所讬西人
釘裝箱內非敝会經手」

曾章番　曾南
曾社信

021

Letter from Chi Tack Tong, Cuba, to Tung Wah Hospital on 3 September 1930

From the Office of Chi Tack Tong

Dear Managers of Tung Wah Hospital,

We have been asked by fellow Chinese compatriots to repatriate the remains of our deceased friends to China, so that they can be laid to rest in their hometown. On 1 September, 28 sets of remains, placed in two large boxes, have been repatriated on the *SS President Fillmore*. Please hand over the remains [to the deceased's families]. We have also remitted 350 Hong Kong dollars to your esteemed hospital via Man Bo Wah trading firm to pay for transportation costs to the mainland: 10 dollars for each set of remains, 280 dollars in total. Please keep the remaining 70 dollars as our oil money to your esteemed hospital and transportation costs. Your continuous work of benevolence is known far and wide, and you are greatly admired by many people. We now seek your assistance in repatriating the remains.

We look forward to your reply.

Enclosed herewith:
List of the names and native counties of the deceased friends
Remittance receipt issued by Man Bo Wah
2 bills of lading for the bones of the deceased friends

Yours sincerely,
Choi Chung-wing (*Cai Zhongrong*), Chairman
(Stamp: Chung-wing)

3 September of the 19th year of the Republic of China

Another person's remarks: Replied on the 2nd day of the 11th lunar month, Year of Gang Ng (*Gengwu*)

[Editor's remarks: Name list of the deceased friends is available only in Chinese]

東華醫院諸先生大鑒敬啓者茲收到
　　掘地孖罅信説及運囬先友一幫內有
　　一先友伍洪調但未知到否如到祈照留
　　在或能轉運來廣州市某某代理処弟
　　收倘無代理者候通知弟到收便是諸
　　事有勞不勝謝謝耑此謹请並候

籌安

^弟伍灼燊上
（弟通信地址）廣州市清水濠 112 号
中華民國十九年十月六日

022 Letter from Ng Cheuk-sun, China, to Tung Wah Hospital on 6 October 1930

Dear Managers of Tung Wah Hospital,

I received a letter from Guatemala which said that the remains of some deceased friends had been repatriated to Hong Kong. Among them were the remains of Ng Hung-diu (*Wu Hongdiao*). I am wondering if the remains have arrived in Hong Kong. If they have, can you please keep Ng's remains, or send them to me via the agent in Canton *(Guangzhou)*? If there is no agent in Canton, please contact me and I will go to collect his remains.

I am most grateful to you for your efforts, and I wish you well.

Yours sincerely,
Ng Cheuk-sun (*Wu Zhuoshen*)

112, Ching Shui Ho (*Qingshui Hao*), Guangzhou (My correspondence address)

6 October of the 19th year of the Republic of China

安定堂自治所用箋
ON TEN TONG
中華民國十九年十月十二日

東華醫院執事先生鑒　屢接大教領悉一是勿念惟
是數月前未得各先友親屬函覆如何故未能裁答現
在台山先友梁景昌伍梓芬之親屬來函亦云收妥該
骨殖矣至于順德籍梁棕荣先友尤未見覆如何據云
候安處置然因無地址是以還處在貴　院義庄候領等
情前來據此吾人日久難達完成工作當月前由敝堂給
与公函一封交其親屬籍作為憑按址前往提領而安
歸土以盡吾人責任如見該函希為接洽是所切盼
耑此致覆

台安

（印章：古巴灣城安定堂慈善會）
（印章：安定堂印）慈善會主任　梁裔南上

023

Letter from Sociedad On Ten Tong, Habana Cuba, to Tung Wah Hospital on 12 October 1930

From the Office of On Ten Tong

12 October of the 19th year of the Republic of China

Dear Managers of Tung Wah Hospital,

Your previous letters were well received and your concern was noted. A few months ago, we had not yet heard from all the families of our deceased friends, so we could not respond to your enquiry. Now we had words from the families of Leung King-cheong (*Liang Jingchang*) and Ng Chi-fun (*Wu Zifen*), both native of Toi Shan (*Taishan*), that they received the bones. With regard to the remains of our deceased friend Leung Chung-wing (*Liang Zhongrong*), a native of Shun Tak (*Shunde*), we still had not heard from his family. We were told that the remains were still kept in your coffin home because there was no receiving address. We were worried that it might be difficult for us to complete the job. So we issued an official letter to the deceased's family a few months ago, and told them they could take the letter to the specified address and collect the remains of the deceased. In case you are presented with the letter, please provide assistance to the deceased's family.

Best wishes,
Leung Yui-nam (*Liang Yinan*), Manager

(Stamp: Sociedad On Ten Tong, Habana, Cuba)
(Stamp: Sociedad de On Ten Tong, Habana, Cuba)

危地馬拉旅中美洲掘地孖罅國華僑總會致東華醫院信件
1930 年 10 月 21 日

旅中美洲掘地孖罅國華僑總會用箋
COLONIA CHINA

東華醫院执事先生大鑒

　　逕啓者本月十四日由巴拿馬郵船
　　公司「委內瑞拉」船運回先友骸骨式
　　十捌具（共廿九箱）合裝五箱茲由金
　　山大埠香港廣東銀行匯上
　　美金壹百四十元正到日请為
　　查收并希　代支交先友每具運
　　鄉費每份五元可也專此奉達
　　即頌

公祺

　　　　　　　　　　　（印章：中美洲掘地孖罅華僑總會）
　　　　　　　　　　　華僑總會謹啓
　　　　　　　　　　　一九、十、廿一

另一人註：436.1 元

Letter from Colonia China, Guatemala, to Tung Wah Hospital on 21 October 1930

From the Office of Colonia China, Guatemala

Dear Managers of Tung Wah Hospital,

On the 14th day of this month, we sent back the remains of our 28 deceased friends (in 29 boxes), placed in five large boxes, on the *Venezuela* of Panama Mail Steamship Company. The remittance of 140 US dollars has been sent to you through The Bank of Canton in San Francisco. Please check and use the funds to cover the costs of transporting the remains back to the deceased's hometown, 5 US dollars for each set of remains.

Your kindness is much appreciated.

We wish you well.

Yours sincerely,
Colonia China
(Stamp: Colonia China, Guatemala)

21 October of the 19th year of the Republic of China

Another person's remarks: 436.1 dollars

古巴灣城劉氏自治所委員會致東華醫院信件

1930 年 11 月 11 日

古巴灣城劉氏自治所
Union De Las Familias Lau

敬啓者卑所同人倡辦慈善籌款執拾先友骸骨弍拾叁具共
載一大箱拎是年西歷九月廿九日由古巴國亞湾拿埠附船運囬
香港素仰
貴院辦理慈善不分畛域茲付昃紙一張该港銀弍佰伍拾大
員寄劉麗堂先生收委其轉交與
貴院請為代運先友囬鄉之資並儎紙一張到祈查收至该船抵
港之日携此儎紙起上閅箱按照名单分發各處指令先友親
屬收領安塟以妥先灵实為德便仍希示覆此請

東華醫院總理暨
列位董事先生均鑒

古巴湾城劉氏自治所委員會 劉和卿 劉希燗 謹啓
（印章：劉氏自治所）

民國十九年十一月十一日

先友名單

鍾德逢	廣東新會古井官田鄉人氏
劉維芳	廣東台山橫水鄉金紫里人氏
劉孔霖	廣東台山橫水鄉橫圳人氏
劉孔安	廣東台山橫水鄉中沙萍人氏
劉貴昌	廣東中山谿角鄉人氏
劉煜維	廣東台山橫水鄉上橫圳人氏
劉維芬	廣東新會牛湾龍蟠里人氏
吳賢鐸	廣東新會古井龍泉鄉人氏
劉維掌	廣東新會牛湾坑頭人氏永昌里
劉栢希	廣東新會牛湾坑頭鄉歧山里人氏
劉希琴	廣東新會牛湾坑頭鄉人氏
劉尊清	廣東台山李拗鄉人氏
劉樹蕃	廣東台山橫水鄉龍塘村人氏
勞經漢	廣東開平長沙塘葹畔堡崗背人氏
劉儒槐	廣東台山白虎頭鄉人氏
劉尊德	廣東台山白虎頭鄉人氏
劉希勺	廣東台山橫水龍安里人氏
劉鋭希	廣東台山橫水鄉石鼓村人氏
劉惠維	廣東新會牛湾坑頭歧山里人氏
吳良晃	廣東新會古井龍泉鄉人氏
吳賢棣	廣東新會古井龍泉鄉人氏
吳煥英	廣東增城雅瑤塘邊坊人氏
劉　生	廣東鶴山城緣合鄉人氏

Letter from the Committee of Union De Las Familias Lau, Habana, Cuba to Tung Wah Hospital on 11 November 1930

From the Office of Union De Las Familias Lau

Dear Directors of Tung Wah Hospital,

We organized a fund raising campaign to exhume and repatriate the remains of 23 deceased friends. The remains have been placed in one large box and sent to Hong Kong from Havana, Cuba, by sea on 29 September. We are aware that the benevolent work of your esteemed hospital extends to every part of the world and have sent a cheque for 250 Hong Kong dollars to you, in the care of Lau Lai-tong (*Liu Litang*), to cover the costs of transporting the remains of our deceased friends to their hometown. We also enclose a bill of lading. Please take delivery of the remains with it. After you have taken the remains into your care, please send them to their respective destinations according to the enclosed list and inform the deceased's families to collect the remains and lay them to rest.

We await your reply.

Yours sincerely,
Lau Wo-hing (*Liu Heqing*)
Lau Hay-cheuk (*Liu Xijue*)
Committee of Union De La Familia Lau
(Stamp: UNION DELA FAMILIA LAU, Calle San Jose No. 35 – B "Altos", HABANA, CUBA)

11 November of the 19th year of the Republic of China

[Editor's remarks: Name list of the deceased friends is available only in Chinese]

026 古巴黎伯熙致東華醫院信件

敬啓者舍弟不幸于古巴国身故生為別世之人死為異域
之鬼白骨長埋黃泉飲恨然每欲運骸返国奈乏舟資設
法無從適偵湾埠劉氏自治所倡辦慈善運骸返国深
蒙該所諸执事允許俾得將舍弟之骸骨附搭于箱內
運囬香港素仰
貴醫院办理慈善無分畛域兹付上戾帋一張該港銀拾
員請為代運囬鄉之資仍望指示其家人認領安瘞以妥先
灵則生死感德無涯矣仍望賜覆此請

東華醫院總理暨
列位董事先生均鑒

^弟黎伯熙　頓首

中華民國十九年十一月十二日

另一人註：先友名黎樂常南海九江人氏
　　　　　　其箱已详細寫明

Letter from Lai Pak-hei, Cuba, to Tung Wah Hospital on 12 November 1930

Dear Directors of Tung Wah Hospital,

My younger brother passed away sadly in Cuba. When he lived, he was a man in a foreign country; after he died, he was a ghost far away from home. He must be very upset being buried in foreign land. I wanted to send his remains back to China, but did not have enough money. Recently I learnt that the Union De Las Familias Lau in Havana, Cuba was offering free bone repatriation service to China. The managers agreed to transport the bones of my late brother to Hong Kong. I have heard about the benevolent work of your esteemed hospital, and how you offer help to Chinese people in every part of the world. I enclose a cheque for 10 Hong Kong dollars. Please send my brother's bones back to our hometown, and inform his family to collect the bones for burial.

My late brother and the family shall be most grateful to you for your kindness.

I await your reply.

Yours sincerely,
Lai Pak-hei (*Li Boxi*)

12 November of the 19th year of the Republic of China

Note: The name of the deceased, Lai Lok-sheung (*Li Lechang*), a native of Kau Kong (Jiujiang), Nam Hoi (Nanhai), has been marked on the box containing his bones.

027 墨西哥協興隆致東華醫院信件

1931 年 1 月 29 日

　　字奉

東華醫院
貴执事先生大鑒

　　敬啟者^{小号}經西十月五号奉上之草函內云有南海西樵
　　藻美鄉吳順高其人骨殖一箱乃由墨國文慎丕堯埠
　　西人船務經紀代理由日本直头輪船轉付返港交
　　貴醫院　代收一節
　　惟是近來因日奴無理進兵強占東省凡属中國內地
　　與外埠之國民無不痛心疾首憤其蠻橫無理之要求
　　者也是以吳順高該箱骨殖改着該西人代理停上由日本
　　輪船而付今改由美國輪船直付返港交　貴醫院代收云云
　　但下日該箱骨殖抵步者祈劳查收是溈特此告知
　　祈為諒諒是荷
　　餘恕不叙專此順頌

　　大安

^弟（印章：墨國粒巴士協興隆書柬）字頓

民廿年一月廿九号

另一人註：該骨殖到港請通知文咸東九十二號
　　　　　孟壽榮　電話 二一五五九號

Letter from Hip Hing Lung Company, Mexico, to Tung Wah Hospital on 29 January 1931

027

Dear Managers of Tung Wah Hospital,

In our letter dated 5 October, we mentioned that the bones of Ng Shun-ko *(Wu Shungao),* Tso Mei Township *(Zao Mei Xiang),* Sai Chiu *(Xiqiao)*, Nam Hoi *(Nanhai)* would be sent from Manzanillo to your esteemed hospital on a Japanese ship through a shipping company run by a foreign agent. However, as the Japanese had recently occupied Manchuria in Northeast China, Chinese people at home and abroad condemned their barbaric and unreasonable demands. We have, therefore, asked the foreign agent not to send the bones on a Japanese ship. Instead the bones will now be transported to your esteemed hospital on an American ship. Please note the arrangement and take delivery of the bones after they arrive in Hong Kong.

We hereby write to inform you of the matter and apologize for any inconvenienced caused.

Thank you for your efforts.

We wish you well.

Yours sincerely,
(Stamp: Hip Hing Lung Company, La Paz, Mexico)

29 January of the 20th year of the Republic of China

Another person's remarks: When the bones arrive in Hong Kong, please inform Mang Sau-wing *(Meng Shourong)* at 92 Bonham Strand; phone number 21559.

東華醫院主席执事先生^{大鑒}逕啟者舊年七月亞湾陳潁川
　　總堂慈善会運囬歸國先友骨殖內有一具係廣東台山海晏
　　都大北村人名陳垂成者據舊年十月已接到　先生囬函云及概
　　帮骨殖与款項均經妥收起好安存在港遲日點交各人領收以安
　　窀穸而慰陰靈現弟家人來函稱説未曾收到骨殖等語弟聞言
　　之餘未知事屬何解故付函懇呈　先生查明于陳垂成骨殖現
　　存在香港抑或錯交他方請速再尋起妥點交與港商馬昌銓兄
　　收轉付交弟家人妥收為禱想　执事先生慈善為怀當仁不讓歷
　　來辦事認真中西同欽死生感德萬里遙遙付歸之骨殖費幾多
　　金錢經幾許手續纔達到港目的務請　諸先生不憚其煩早日
　　查明點交馬昌銓兄領收以慰死者陰魂以矣生者企望是所切
　　盼若妥交後請照住址付囬乙音 Rafael Chong Marchena P. Camagüey Cuba 此请

台祺

　　　　　　　　　　　　　　弍十年三月八号 旅亞湾陳少安奉

另一人註：已复

Letter from Chan Siu-on, Cuba, to Tung Wah Hospital on 8 March 1931

028

Dear Chairman and Managers of Tung Wah Hospital,

In July last year, Chang Weng Chun Tong in Havana repatriated the bones of deceased friends to China. Among them were the bones of Chan Shui-shing *(Chen Chuicheng)*, a native of Dai Pek Village *(Dabei Cun)* Hoi Ngan Dou *(Haiyan Du)*, Toi Shan *(Taishan)*, Kwangtung *(Guangdong)*. We received a letter from you in October last year that the bones and burial fees had arrived in Hong Kong and they would be handed over to the deceased's family so that the deceased's spirit could find eternal peace. However, my family wrote to me recently saying that they had not received the bones yet. I hereby write to you to find out if the bones of Chen Shui-shing are still in Hong Kong, or if they have been sent to the wrong place. Please investigate the matter at your earliest convenience. After you find the bones, please hand them over to Hong Kong merchant Ma Cheong-chuen *(Ma Changquan)*, who will pass them to my family.

Your benevolence is known far and wide, and you never hesitate to offer help to those in need. You are committed in your work and you are respected by people around the world. Both the living and the deceased at home and abroad are grateful to you. A lot of money and efforts had been devoted and complicated procedures had been involved for the bones to arrive in the destination from afar and I hope you do not mind taking the trouble to attend to the matter. Please hand over the bones to Ma Cheong-chuen, so that the spirit of the deceased finds eternal peace and the living eases their mind.

After the bones are handed over, please reply to the following address to let me know.
Rafael Chong Marchena P. Camagüey Cuba.

Yours sincerely,
Chan Siu-on *(Chen Shao'an)* of Havana

8 March of the 20th year of the Republic of China

Another person's remarks: Replied

中國朱澤泉致東華醫院信件

1931 年 3 月 20 日

東華医院列位仁翁均鑒　敬啓者今特字懇求

　　阁下代查有否由掘地子剌國付返之先友

　　骨殖名朱燦祥乃係南海九江東方新安人

　　氏西名 Joee Chuy 輕在箱面寫明唐番籍

　　貫諒無有悮会之虞昨由掘國有信

　　通訊云上数月經由貴院轉交云云故此

　　敢膽求仁翁代為一查示覆為慰至于

　　經費成若干順為指示一切是禱不僃

　　　兹事多劳有費精神草此並頌

善祉均安

　　　　　　　　　　　　　　　　　　　　弟朱澤泉 叩

民廿年三月念日

通訊處　南海九江圩大成押轉交便合

另一人註：辛弐月初七日復

Letter from Chu Chak-chuen, China, to Tung Wah Hospital on 20 March 1931

Dear benevolent Directors of Tung Wah Hospital,

I write to implore you to check whether the bones of Chu Chan-cheung (*Zhu Canxiang*), a native of Dong Fong *(Dongfang), Sun On (Xin'an),* Kau Kong *(Jiujiang),* Nam Hoi *(Nanhai),* had been repatriated from Guatemala. The deceased was known by the English name Joee Chuy. His native township was written in Chinese and English on the box carrying his bones, and there should not have been any mix-up. I received a letter from Guatemala yesterday saying that the bones were repatriated through your esteemed hospital a few months ago. I, therefore, venture to ask your help in investigating the matter. If there are fees that have to be paid, please let me know.

I am most grateful to you for your efforts.

I wish you well.

Yours sincerely,
Chu Chak-chuen (*Zhu Zequan*)

20 March of the 20th year of the Republic of China

Correspondence address: Dai Shing Pawn Shop (*Dacheng Ya*), Kau Kong Market Town, Nam Hoi

Another person's remarks: Replied on the 7th day of the 2nd lunar month, Year of San Mei *(Xinwei)*

030 中國周品南致東華醫院信件

東華醫院執事暨列位先生大鑒

　　敬啓者近日接讀^{敝叔姪}來函称及周集（中山東鎮神涌人）

　　和骨骸已扵九月間由夏湾拿埠運返

　　在貴醫院處至今日久未卜何時轉寄來

　　如果有運过南蓢之便希為一齐運下因^弟不暗

　　規例如且家貧故敢奉告恳據實回音以免

　　企望有勞是荷此致

文祺

^弟周品南手啓

中華民國廿年式月初四日
中華民國廿年三月廿二日

另一人註：已复
另一人註：中山東鎮神涌周品南
另一人註：至德堂庚八月廿九到葬費十元

Letter from Chow Bun-nam, China, to Tung Wah Hospital on 22 March 1931

Dear Managers of Tung Wah Hospital,

I recently received a letter from my uncle and niece saying that the remains of Chow Chap-wo *(Zhou Jihe)*, a native of Sun Chung *(Shenchong)*, Dong Town *(Dongzhen)*, Chung Shan *(Zhongshan)*, have been sent to your esteemed hospital from Havana in September. Many months have passed, I wonder when the remains will be sent here. If you are repatriating remains to Nam Long *(Nanlang)*, I hope you can also send Chow Chap-wo's remains to us. I am not familiar with the regulations and our family is poor. I therefore venture to tell you about our situation. Please reply to me whether you are able to send back the remains to us or not to ease my mind.

I am most grateful to you for your efforts.

I wish you well.

Yours sincerely,
Chow Bun-nam *(Zhou Pinnan)*

4th day of the 2nd lunar month of the 20th year of the Republic of China
22 March of the 20th year of the Republic of China

Another person's remarks: Replied
Another person's remarks: Chow Bun-nam of Sun Chung, Dong Town, Chung Shan
Another person's remarks: Burial fees of 10 dollars were given by Chi Tack Tong *(Zhi De Tang)* on the 29th day of the 8th lunar month, Year of Gang Ng *(Gengwu)*

東華醫院
總理先生鑒啓者^敝堂経於旧年八月五日付寄五拾
　　五個先友骸骨又同月十六日經付上港銀五百元以
　　為香油先友蕐費亦經先後收到
　　貴院付來覆書（報知經已收到先友骸骨及香油費）
　　詎至今日有楊誠塑先友在古之親屬楊斗山先生
　　到來^敝堂報告未經收到楊誠塑先友之骸骨想
　　此情況未知何因爰特函詢勞速些轉交楊家收
　　領安蕐倘若照經付上之（順德縣陳村済義庄代付交新
　　圩晒魚地橋珠酒楼內通知楊賜存收）等字而莫能交到者
　　勞照現寄下述之最近住址可以易於交到是否如何尚希
　　惠覆耑此即请

台安

　　（付交順德縣陳村済義庄代收勞該庄通知陳村
　　旧圩花洲古道內街榮昌錫紙店便於通知楊斗山家收）
　　　　　　　　　　　　　　　陳潁川總堂寄（印章：古巴灣城陳潁川堂書柬）

民廿年五月拾四日

Letter from Chang Weng Chun Tong, Habana, Cuba, to Tung Wah Hospital on 14 May 1931

031

Dear Directors of Tung Wah Hospital,

We repatriated the bones of 55 deceased friends on 5 August last year and remitted 500 Hong Kong dollars as oil money to your hospital and burial fees of the deceased friends on the 16th day of the month. We received your reply acknowledging receipt of the bones and oil money. Yet recently, Yeung Dau-shan *(Yang Doushan)*, relative of our deceased friend Yeung Shing-kwan *(Yang Chengkun)* in Cuba, came to us and said that they had not yet received the bones of Yeung Shing-kwan. We wonder what has happened. We hereby write to urge you to hand over the bones of Yeung Shing-kwan to his family as soon as possible. If you were unable to deliver the bones to the previous address of Yeung Chi-chuen *(Yang Cicun)* at Kiu-chu Restaurant *(Qiaozhu Jiulou)* in Sai Yu Dei *(Shaiyudi)*, Sun Market Town *(Xinxu)*, via Chai Coffin Home *(Ji Yizhuang)* in Chan Village *(Chen Cun)*, Shun Tak *(Shunde)*, please send them to the nearer address below for easier access. Whether you can deliver the bones or not, please reply to let us know.

We wish you well.

(Please send the bones to Chai Coffin Home in Chan Village, Shun Tak and ask them to inform Yeung Dau-shan's family at Wing Cheong Tin Foil Shop in Inner Street, Fa Chau Ku Dou *(Huazhou Gudao)*, Chan Village Old Market Town)

Yours sincerely,
Chang Weng Chun Tong
(Stamp: Chang Weng Chun Tong, Habana, Cuba)

14 May of the 20th year of the Republic of China

東華醫院暨
列位執事先生^電

駐古巴（印章：古巴灣城安定堂）字上

　　啓者本堂年前凂運派各縣之
　　先友骨殖中有迻九江鄉丁鉅年之金
　　箱壹具今伊家人憑函并蓋店圖
　　章到領取自行運籍安塋希為照
　　交该駐港伊之親屬領取是寔諸
　　費　尊神感激復謝并頌

善安

中華民國廿年四月初一日

另一人註：已復

Letter from Sociedad On Ten Tong, Habana, Cuba, to Tung Wah Hospital on 17 May 1931

032

Dear Managers of Tung Wah Hospital,

(Stamp: ON TEN TONG, SALUD NUM, 26 ALTOS, HABANA, CUBA)

We repatriated the bones of deceased friends last year which included the bones of Ting Kui-nin (*Ding Junian*) of Kau Kong Township (*Jiujiang Xiang*). His family would like to collect the bones from your esteemed hospital with a letter bearing the seal of a shop and send them back to his hometown for burial. Please hand over the remains to the deceased's family in Hong Kong.

We are most grateful to you for your efforts.

We wish you well.

Yours sincerely,
1st day of the 4th lunar month of the 20th year of the Republic of China

Another person's remarks: Replied

033 古巴灣城安定堂致東華醫院信件

1931 年 5 月 17 日

東華醫院暨鑒
紳耆先生

古巴國頓啟
夏灣拿

（印章：古巴灣城安定堂）

文啓者年前^{本堂}運返各先友骨殖囬
籍料未尽妥致詎緣南海九江鄉有
丁鉅年金箱壹具伊家人來函稱云
年餘尚未運抵等语想如許日久诚
恐有遺運之虞希為注意一查如何
覆知一慰免兩相盼望是禱并祝

善祺
中華民國廿年四月初一日

并交隨尾艮五元拾他收用

另一人註：已復

Letter from Sociedad On Ten Tong, Habana, Cuba, to Tung Wah Hospital on 17 May 1931

Dear Directors of Tung Wah Hospital,

We repatriated the bones of deceased friends last year. There must have been errors on our part, as the family of Ting Kui-nin *(Ding Junian)* of Kau Kong Township *(Jiujiang Xiang)*, Nam Hoi *(Nanhai)*, wrote to us saying that his bones had not been returned to his hometown. A long time has passed since the repatriation and we are worried that the bones of Ting Kui-nin have been left behind. Please check if the bones are still in your care and reply to us to ease the mind of us and the family.

Thank you for your help.

We wish you well.

Yours sincerely,
(Stamp: ON TEN TONG, SALUD NUM, 26 ALTOS, HABANA, CUBA)
Habana, Cuba

1st day of the 4th lunar month of the 20th year of the Republic of China

5 dollars have been given to him as follow-up fees.

Another person's remarks: Replied

歐陽東致古巴灣城黃江夏堂慈善會信件

1931 年 5 月 23 日

黃江夏堂慈善會

執事諸先生均鑒敬啓者曩日中華義山起先

友骨骸登報通知各親屬具領運囬祖國以正首

邱一事[弟]曾托貴堂運返一具名歐陽傍由貴

書記黃堃儀先生收了運費[弟]諒必妥辦不意

迄今弍年之久接得[弟]之堂兄大東酒店司理歐

陽品來札□及尚未領得盡力調查並無着落向弟

質問實難答復故特修書奉達貴堂是否代

為運返祈復一音示知以免兩望為幸敬叩

羣安

[弟]歐陽東字頓

一九三一年五月廿三

Letter from Au Yeung Tung to Wong Kong Ja Tong Comision Beneficencia, Habana, Cuba, on 23 May 1931

Dear Managers of Wong Kong Ja Tong Comision Beneficencia,

The remains of deceased friends were exhumed from the communal graveyard for Chinese compatriots earlier, and a notice was published in the newspaper calling on the families of the deceased to collect the remains and send them to the mainland for burial. I asked your esteemed association to transport the remains of Au Yeung Pong *(Ouyang Bang)* and paid the shipping fees to Wong Kwan-yee *(Huang Kunyi)*, secretary of your association. I expected that the matter would be well taken care of but now two years had passed, my cousin Au Yeung Bun *(Ouyang Pin)*, who works as manager in Dai Tung Hotel *(Dadong Jiudian)*, informed me that he had not yet collected the remains. He tried to find out the whereabouts of the remains but in vain. He then pushed me for an answer and I had no idea. Now I write to you to ask if your esteemed association has repatriated the remains. I await your reply.

I wish you well.

Yours sincerely,
Au Yeung Tung *(Ouyang Dong)*

23 May 1931

古巴灣城黃江夏堂慈善會致東華醫院信件

1931 年 5 月 29 日

古巴灣城黃江夏堂用箋
Wong Kong Ja Tong

東華醫院

　　執事先生^{鈞鑒}啓者^敝會曾旧年六月

　　间先後付囘先友骨殖多具深蒙　先生

　　按址妥辦感激良多但本堂昨接到

　　由坑上歐陽東兄來函詢及謂曾託本堂代寄

　　歐陽傍一具係中山縣東鎮四都蔴子村西堡

　　其收領人歐陽品先生至今仍未收到等語

　　查歐陽傍号数 707 因此特函請台審查

　　何人收領曾否按址付寄　希祈　示覆此致

勛安

　　　　　　　　　　　　　　　　　（印章：古巴灣城黃江夏堂慈善會）

中華民國廿年五月廿九日

另一人註：已复

Letter from Wong Kong Ja Tong Comision Beneficencia, Habana, Cuba, to Tung Wah Hospital on 29 May 1931

From the Office of Wong Kong Ja Tong Comision Beneficencia, Habana, Cuba

Dear Managers of Tung Wah Hospital,

We repatriated the remains of our deceased friends in June last year and are most grateful to you for your assistance. Yesterday, we received a letter from Au Yeung Tung *(Ouyang Dong)* of Hang Sheung *(Kengshang)* saying that he had asked us to repatriate the remains of Au Yeung Pong *(Ouyang Bang)* to Ma Tsz Chuen Sai Po Village *(Mazicun Xipao Cun)*, Dong Chun Si Dou *(Dongzhen Sidu)*, Chung Shan *(Zhongshan)*, but the recipient, Au Yeung Bun *(Ouyang Pin)*, had not received the remains. Au Yeung Pong should be in Box No. 707, please find out who took delivery of the remains or if they have been sent to the correct address. We await your reply.

We wish you well.

Yours sincerely,
(Stamp: WONG KONG JA TONG COMISION BENEFICENCIA, HABANA, CUBA)

29 May of the 20th year of the Republic of China

Another person's remarks: Replied

古巴灣城陳穎川總堂用箋
Chang Weng Chun Tong

東華醫院主任先生義鑒敬啓者敝

　　堂去歲办回之先友蒙

貴院接收妥當経來字賜教感謝

　　良多諒必按址附回各縣着其親

　　属領收無誤惟現接兄弟來函説

　　其親屬之先友骨石仍未收到來

　　字查問是以據情奉告如尚有

　　在港未運回各縣者請為留心妥办

　　為感肅此並請

義祺

　　　　　　　　　　　　　　陳穎川總堂総理^{月湖}頓

中華民國二十年六月念四日

Letter from Chang Weng Chun Tong, Habana, Cuba, to Tung Wah Hospital on 24 June 1931

From the Office of Chang Weng Chun Tong, Habana, Cuba

Dear Managers of Tung Wah Hospital,

We repatriated the remains of our deceased friends last year. Your letter acknowledging receipt of the remains was well received and we are most grateful to you for taking them into your care. We trust that you had sent the remains to the deceased's families in their hometown according to the addresses given. Yet we recently received a letter from the family of one deceased friend saying that they had not received the bones and made an enquiry to us. We are telling you what has happened and hope you attend to this matter. If the bones of our deceased friend remain in your care in Hong Kong, please send them onto the deceased's hometown.

We are most grateful to you for your benevolence.

We wish you well.

Yours humbly,
Yuet-wu *(Yuehu)*
Director of Chang Weng Chun Tong

24 June of the 20th year of the Republic of China

古巴灣城黃江夏堂用箋
Wong Kong Ja Tong

東華醫院

　　執事先生鈞鑒敬啓者茲據林善寶

　　先友（新會北洋北合里人）伊親屬家函报告

　　伊侄面謂該先友家人未經收到等语隨

　　查^{敝會}存底部確已去年付佃　貴院

　　收但距今彼輩追詢情由故特函詢

　　执事先生在处調查該先友是否按址付

　　寄或仍留港地請台刻示覈諸勞

　　紉感耑此　順候

勛安

（查收領人林華勝）

慈善會啓

（印章：古巴灣城黃江夏堂慈善會）

中華民國廿年六月廿八号

另一人註：已复

　　　　庚七月初三運起

　　　　辛八月十七新會商會領

Letter from Wong Kong Ja Tong Comision Beneficencia, Habana, Cuba, to Tung Wah Hospital on 28 June 1931

From the Office of Wong Kong Ja Tong Comision Beneficencia, Habana, Cuba

Dear Managers of Tung Wah Hospital,

The family of our deceased friend Lam Sin-bo *(Lin Shanbao)*, a native of Bak Hop Lane *(Beihe Li)*, Buk Yeung *(Beiyang)*, Sun Wui *(Xinhui)*, informed us that they had not yet received his remains. We checked our records, and confirmed that the remains were sent to your esteemed hospital last year. But now as the family is asking the whereabouts of the remains, we therefore write to you to find out if the remains have been sent to the address specified, or if they are still in Hong Kong. Please reply to us.

We are grateful to you for your efforts.

We wish you well.

Yours sincerely,
(Stamp: WONG KONG JA TONG COMISION BENEFICENCIA, HABANA, CUBA)

28 June of the 20th year of the Republic of China
To be received by Lam Wah-shing *(Lin Huasheng)*

Another person's remarks: Replied
Sent on the 3rd day of the 7th lunar month, Year of Gang Ng *(Gengwu)*; collected by San Wui Commercial Society on the 17th day of the 8th lunar month, Year of San Mei *(Xinwei)*

038 巴拿馬三邑同善堂致東華醫院信件

1931 年 7 月 15 日

東華醫院執事先生^{英鑒}啓者本堂茲值

第拾弍屆檢運各先友回國之期經扵月

之十四日由英國船公司 Ocean Steam Ship

Company 船名 Tantalus 附寄各先友之骨骸

回港總計共弍拾壹箱內寔共捌拾弍具經

有箱口単列明號数並將籍貫及姓氏詳

明到时祈照侎紙查收並祈代出通告如有

照藉貫及姓名掛号到領收者望乞代為

妥交惟每具依照向例代支給運費港艮五元

至扵徵信錄一節遲日列妥定必寄返拜勞

代為刊印該侎紙各件茲寄返港德興泰號

轉呈如該號將各件交到时求即代為妥办

一切事關慈善公益諒必當仁不讓還頌

公德無量謹此奉托並頌

義安

巴拿馬三邑同善堂

総理拔興號謹啓（印章：巴拿馬埠拔興號書柬）

一九三一年七月十五日

茲將第拾弍屆檢運先友箱口單列呈

第壹號箱內

馮燊球公（同字一號）南海華夏鄉　　　　盧萼凌公（同字五號）南海沙頭堡

龐有志公（同字十二號）南海石灣鄉　　　龐　湛公（同字二十九號）南海石灣鄉

第弍號箱內

蘇　溪公（同字十號）番禺鴉湖　　　　　莫　佳公（同字二號）番禺

曹灼球公（同字五十八號）番禺　　　　　蘇福秋公（同字五十七號）番禺

第叁號箱內

潘純添公（同字八號）順德冲鶴鄉　　　　黃吉甫公（同字四十六號）番禺石基村

黃　加公（同字四十九號）番禺石碁鄉　　黃炳會公（同字四十八號）番禺石碁村

第四號箱內

張西就公（同字六十五號）花縣西門堡十八田會村　　侯天保公（同字十八號）花縣上古嶺村

溫社記公（同字二十六號）花縣西崗頭村　馮東海公（同字二十二號）花縣西壇村

第五號箱內

侯善舉公（同字五十一號）花縣上古嶺村　廖炳乾公（同字二十一號）花縣滿鄉儒村

張石金公（同字十六號）花縣滿鄉儒村　　張運章公（同字二十七號）花縣石子逕村

第陸號箱內

劉德和公（同字二十三號）花縣天心塘　　劉啓沛公（同字三十七號）花縣天心塘

張雲清公（同字五十六號）花縣　　　　　林文標公（同字五十五號）花縣

第柒號箱內

梁月開公（同字三十二號）南海丹灶鄉　　潘　湘公（同字三十八號）南海

崔溶海公（同字三十六號）南海沙頭　　　郭　三公（同字四十二號）番禺

第捌號箱內

區經奎公（同字十五號）南海西樵良埇（辛九月廿九德利招領）　　符汝鑑公（同字二十四號）南海西樵大涡鄉（辛九月十二電器商會）

馮紹文公（同字四十四號）南海胡村　　　馮　耀公（同字四十三號）南海胡村

第九號箱內

譚祥文公（同字六號）台山白水書坑村

譚堯文公（同字五十四號）台山白水書坑村

陳　炳公（同字四十號）台山上澤圩平州村

陳文湛公（同字三十四號）台山上澤圩大塱村

第拾號箱內

勞迺長公（同字四號）開平長沙塘興賢坊
（辛未八月十九新廣合領）

陳貽曉公（同字二十八號）台山上澤圩平州村

陳貽操公（同字六十一號）台山縣

陳　享公（同字三十五號）台山上澤圩牛山村

第十一號箱內

葉　添公（同字四十五號）赤溪田頭堡大口廟村

吳金發公（同字七十六號）寶安鹽田村

陳秉祥公（同字六十九號）寶安全灣村

陳衡章公（同字七十七號）寶安羅方村

第十弍號箱內

吳述宏公（同字十三號）恩平蓮安里

莫瑞介公（同字五十九號）恩平第五區那西現龍里

吳廷娑公（同字三號）恩平永樂村

鄺　培公（同字三十一號）台山第一區蟹村東頭

第十叁號箱內

趙元兆公（同字十九號）新會皋頭村

胡元慶公（同字六十號）新會

葉金發公（同字六十六號）中山良都深灣黃第江村

張　連公（同字六十八號）中山良都石鼓

第十四號箱內

陳洪德公（同字四十一號）台山上澤圩平安村

謝文效公（同字三十九號）開平西門下灣鄉

陳澧元公（同字三十三號）香山石岐

鄧潤炳公（同字四十號）順德水滕塘棣坊多棋杆

第十五號箱內

林　寬公（同字六十三號）中山良都深灣呂魚頭金鐘腳村

蔡天球公（同字七十號）中山良都深灣月角村

伍　保公（同字七十四號）中山隆都南村

陳在好公（同字十一號）中山隆都江背村

第十六號箱內

劉其興公（同字九號）鶴山四堡矮嶺村

鍾北興公（同字七十九號）鶴山縣

丘土榮公（同字七號）鶴山東坑堡東坑村

余鳳昌公（同字六十二號）鶴山四堡小洞村

第十七號箱內

李宗景公（同字五十號）中山谷鎮白石鄉

駱永煇公（同字六十七號）中山谷都白石環八畝村

黃栢卿公（同字五十二號）香山城內拱辰街

黃玉堂公（同字七十三號）中山石岐長州村

第十八號箱內

卓門鍾氏（同字七十五號）中山谷都大布新村

毛學鑑公（同字六十四號）中山谷都大布新村

古廷勝公（同字七十一號）中山恭都教長埔村（辛九月初九日德興行）

鍾　祺公（同字四十七號）香山谷都金釵環村

第十九號箱內

陳母劉氏（同字十七號）香山東鎮杬边圩蒲山鄉

甘天運公（同字七十二號）中山大字都石門爛泥村

梁讓明公（同字十四號）香山犁村

林萬谷公（同字二十號）香山東鎮杬边圩大車鄉

第廿號箱內

杜承基公（同字八十號）鶴山縣

余社福公（同字七十八號）鶴山縣

楊纘鴻公（同字二十五號）鶴山白水帶村

梁象英公（同字五十三號）香山良都沙涌鄉

第二十一號箱內

呂加堯公（同字八十一號）鶴山縣

田寶泉公（同字八十二號）鶴山縣

東華醫院執事先生照

一九三一年七月十五日

巴拿馬三邑同善堂謹上

另一人註：辛七月十二九龍倉

038

Letter from Sam Yap Tung Sin Tong of Panama, to Tung Wah Hospital on 15 July 1931

Dear Managers of Tung Wah Hospital,

This is the 12th bone exhumation and repatriation exercise of our deceased friends and 82 sets of bones, placed in 21 boxes, were sent to Hong Kong on the *Tantalus*, Ocean Steam Ship Company of Britain on 14 July. The boxes were numbered and marked with the native counties and names of the deceased. Please check the shipment against the bill of lading, and issue a notice informing the deceased's families to collect the remains. If someone comes to claim the bones with a receipt indicating county and name of the deceased, please hand over to him and pay each deceased friend's transportation fees of 5 Hong Kong dollars on our behalf. As to the *Zhengxinlu* (accounting journal), we will send you all the information in due course. Please help us publish it. The relevant bills of lading, along with the other documents, will be sent to you through Tak Hing Tai in Hong Kong. Please kindly assist us to settle the matters.

We trust that you will not hesitate in helping us with the charitable act. Your benevolence will be known far and wide.

We wish you well.

Yours sincerely,
But Hing Company, Director of Sam Yap Tung Sin Tong of Panama
(Stamp: But Hing Company, Panama)

15 July 1931

[Editor's remarks: Name list of the deceased friends is available only in Chinese]

古巴灣城陳潁川總堂用箋
Chang Weng Chun Tong

香港東華醫院

　　總理先生大鑒逕啟者去年八月五日経付五拾

　　五副先友之骸骨又遲至十六日経付上港銀

　　五佰元為　貴院收应香油及先友之塋

　　費亦経收到　貴院示覆均皆先後收

　　妥但是現接到幾箇報告均係未曾收到故特

　　函告恳速查交為各該先友之家人收領切

　　勿延遲尚希　惠覆專此即請

台安

　　　　　　　　　　　（印章：古巴灣城陳潁川總堂用東）
　　　　　　　　　　　　古巴灣城陳潁川總堂

中華民國廿年九月十七日

各先友藉貫及各該先友之家人通信處

陳柏文（藉貫）廣東台山縣三合區洋瀾堡牛
瀾村（家人通訊處）付交廣東台山三合圩仁济堂
收交牛瀾村陳嗣昌先生收［另一人註：台山商會領辛五月十三］

陳津良（藉貫）廣東台山縣三合區洋瀾堡
大湖塘村（家人通訊處）付交台山縣三合圩仁济堂
收交大湖塘陳濃洽先生收［另一人註：台山商會領辛五月十三］

陳瑞池（藉貫）廣東新會縣天馬村（家人通
信處）廣東新會天馬村陳懋賴或陳九
先生收［另一人註：辛八月十七新会商会領］

陳寅芳（藉貫）廣東台山縣新昌區冲泮堡水坑村（家人通信處）廣東台山縣新昌區
冲泮水坑村陳耀俊先生收

陳元亨（藉貫）廣東省城永慶二巷陳
誠德堂（家人通信處）廣東省城永慶二巷
陳誠德堂陳阿女先生收［另一人註：辛五月十六金龍相店領］

楊誠堃（藉貫）廣東順德陳村（家人通
信處）付交順德陳村济義庄代收交陳村旧
圩花洲古道內街榮昌錫紙店轉交楊斗山先
生之家人收［另一人註：庚十月廿六順德商会領］

陳煥明（即陳生）（藉貫）廣東台山縣大
塘站洞寧村(家人通信處)付交台山縣大塘
站洞寧村陳仕文先生收［另一人註：辛五月十七台山商会領］

（印章：古巴灣城陳潁川總堂）
（印章：古巴灣城陳潁川總堂用柬）
古巴灣城陳潁川總堂慈善會

中華民國廿年九月十七日

Letter from Chang Weng Chun Tong, Habana, Cuba, to Tung Wah Hospital on 17 September 1931

From the Office of Chang Weng Chun Tong

Dear Directors of Tung Wah Hospital,

We repatriated the bones of 55 deceased friends on 5 August last year and remitted 500 Hong Kong dollars as oil money to your esteemed hospital and burial fees of deceased friends on the 16th day of the month. We received your reply acknowledging receipt of the bones and money. Yet the families of several deceased friends informed us that they had not received the remains of their late family members. We hereby urge you to investigate the matter at your earliest convenience. Please hand over the remains to the deceased's families without delay.

We await your reply.

We wish you well.

Yours sincerely,
Chang Weng Chun Tong, Habana, Cuba
(Stamp: Chang Weng Chun Tong, Habana, Cuba)

17 September of the 20th year of the Republic of China

[Editor's remarks: Name list of the deceased friends is available only in Chinese]

古巴灣城陳穎川總堂致東華醫院信件

1931 年 10 月 5 日

古巴灣城陳穎川總堂用箋
Chang Weng Chun Tong

香港東華醫院
總理先生鑒逕啟者現接陳光槐陳
　松寧兩君函稱陳光添陳光翼兩
　先友之骸骨均未收到故特函報懇
　急轉交上述先友之家人收領是為至
　要專此順請

台安

　　陳光添［藉貫］廣東台山縣沖蔞区高咀村
　付交台山縣沖蔞区高咀村［家人］陳光槐先生收
　　陳光翼［藉貫］廣東台山縣沖蔞區高咀村
　付交台山縣沖蔞區高咀村［家人］陳松寧先生收

　　　　　　　　灣城陳穎川總堂（印章：古巴灣城陳穎川總堂書束）

中華民國廿年拾月五日

Letter from Chang Weng Chun Tong, Habana, Cuba, to Tung Wah Hospital on 5 October 1931

From the Office of Chang Weng Chun Tong

Dear Directors of Tung Wah Hospital,

We received a letter from Chan Kwong-wai *(Chen Guanghuai)* and Chan Chung-ning *(Chen Songning)* saying that they had not yet received the bones of Chan Kwong-tim *(Chen Guangtian)* and Chan Kwong-yik *(Chen Guangyi)*. We hereby urge you to hand over the remains of the abovementioned deceased friends to their families as soon as possible.

We wish you well.

The bones of Chan Kwong-tim, a native of Go Tsui Village *(Gaozui Cun)*, Chung Lau District *(Chonglou Qu)*, Toi Shan County *(Taishan Xian)*, Kwangtung *(Guangdong)*, should be sent to Chan Kwong-wai (his family) in Go Tsui Village, Chung Lau Town, Toi Shan County.

The bones of Chan Kwong-yik, a native of Go Tsui Village, Chung Lau Town, Toi Shan County, Kwangtung, should be sent to Chan Chung-ning (his family) in Go Tsui Village, Chung Lau Town, Toi Shan County.

Yours sincerely,
Chang Weng Chun Tong, Habana
(Stamp: Chang Weng Chun Tong, Habana, Cuba)

5 October of the 20th year of the Republic of China

墨國順省那卡利埠黃江夏分堂用牋
Wong Kong Ja Tong

東華醫院執事先生偉鑒

敬啓者茲將黃桂樸遺骸付上到日希為查收
勞即轉寄開平蜆岗龍口里黃義盛收便妥所
需費用若干祈往德輔道滙生源號黃桂家處
磋商便能妥支諸事有勞幸甚感甚
　　肅此并候

大安

中華民國廿年拾月廿八日

（印章：墨國順省那卡利埠黃江夏堂）字頓

Letter from Wong Kong Ja Tong, Nogales Sonora, Mexico, to Tung Wah Hospital on 28 October 1931

From the Office of Wong Kong Ja Tong, Nogales Sonora, Mexico

Dear Managers of Tung Wah Hospital,

We have repatriated the remains of Wong Kwai-pok *(Huang Guipu)*. Please take the remains into your care after they arrive in Hong Kong and send them onto Wong Yi-shing *(Huang Yisheng)* in Lung Hou Lane *(Longkou Li)*, Hin Kong (Xiangang), Hoi Ping (Kaiping). With regard to the costs incurred, please discuss the matter with Wong Kwai-ga *(Huang Guijia)* of Wui Sang Yuen on Des Voeux Road and the reimbursement will be made.

We are most grateful to you for your efforts.

We wish you well.

Yours sincerely,
(Stamp: Wong Kong Ja Tong, Nogales, Sonora, Mexico)

28 October of the 20th year of the Republic of China

古巴灣城遡源總堂用箋
SUE YUEN TONG

東華醫院執事先生：

　　本會籌辦第三屆先友回籍，經將各
先骸釘封三大箱，共伍拾壹具，抡十一
月九日付寄大來公司船（船名 Qte Hayes）返國，到時請
貴院派人到船起囲，按籍貫寄去，毋
任感感！茲付上港銀壹佰元，為　貴院
香油之用，若妥收，希見覆！

　　並問公安！

古巴
灣城 遡源堂慈善会

（印章：灣城遡源總堂慈善籌辦處印）

中華民國廿年十一月十一日

■ 遡源總堂慈善會啟事

本會經將是屆各先骸一一執妥，定於十一月九日付船歸國，並擬定每先
骸給回葬費十元：「港銀」茲為慎重起見，凡領先骸葬費者，要覓殷商蓋
章擔保，方准領取：

◆ 茲將運歸之先骸姓名籍貫列左

（第一箱）

鄺有廣	台山嶺背長龍村人	鄺敬銓	台山嶺背長安村人
鄺修平	台山沖蔞西龍里人	鄺光仁	台山倉下人
雷學積	台山張良邊人	雷維沛	台山塘面和樂村人
雷維彩	台山塘面和樂村人	雷學滋	台山塘面曹崗人
雷法昌	台山塘面坑尾人	雷從江	台山塘面龍崗村人
雷祥維	台山大崗大洞村人	雷家嵩	台山大崗大洞村人
雷金女	台山大崗大洞村人	雷子榮	番禺鍾村長巷人
鄺乃衍	中山斗門小濠涌人	容　佑	新會官冲鳳鳴里人

（第弍箱）

鄺煜堂	開平泮村太平里人	何永同	開平社邊西頭社寶華里人
方良錫	開平古宅龍岡人	何齊好	開平社邊中心社寶華里人
方富濯	開平沙塘坑口村人	方弈鳳	開平古宅安榮里人
方北海	中山隆都濠涌村人	鄺飛雄	中山斗門小濠涌鄉人
方計來	中山南區人	鄺悅榮	中山斗門斗門村人
鄺挹光	中山斗門小濠涌鄉人	鄺保養	中山斗門小濠涌鄉人
鄺笏修	中山斗門小濠涌鄉人	莫裕興	中山斗門赤水坑村人
譚業駿	中山斗門斜排村人	方　寬	東莞人

（第叁箱）

雷龍廣	台山塘面三家村人	雷有傳	台山塘面棠棣里人
雷道基	台山公益區張邊村人	雷宜斌	台山張良邊龍溪人
雷積勝	台山五十區潤頭人	雷銳良	台山鎮口地羅人
鄺榮顯	台山嶺背人	鄺羣光	台山沖蔞順和人
鄺光韶	台山嶺背同興社人	郭耀林	台山筋坑堡常安村人
黃新活	台山牛山區鳳岡村人	梁百濃	台山吉那區西廓高龍人
關發達	台山都斛豐江村人	許大富	台山大塘橫坑村人

雷　瀚　台山人

方　喜　潮州人
鄺顯敬　台山嶺背籈水村人
鄺烓敬　台山岐背永華村人
方榮佐　恩平沙潮區牛路水村人

（各先友姓名籍貫，如有差錯，仰從速指正。）

◆ 附啓

　　凡屬本堂之先骸，其在山埠者，要在本月三十日以前運出本灣，方
　　得搭是屆運回。（歸落第三箱）遲則保留至第四屆付歸：

茲定於十一月八日下午一點鐘，為公祭先友回籍之期，仰各先友親屬依
期到中華義山虔祭一切，此啓

十月廿三號

　　　　　　　　　　　　　　　　　　　　古京遡源總堂慈善會啓
　　　　　　　　　　　　　　（印章：灣城遡源總堂慈善會籌辦處印）

Letter from Sue Yuen Tong, Habana, Cuba, to Tung Wah Hospital on 11 November 1931

From the Office of Sue Yuen Tong, Habana, Cuba

Dear Managers of Tung Wah Hospital,

We have organized the third bone repatriation exercise of our deceased friends to their hometown, and sent 51 sets of bones, placed in three large sealed boxes, to China on the *Qte Hayes* of the Dollar Shipping Company on 9 November. When the bones arrive in Hong Kong, please take them into your care and send them back according to their native county. We shall be most grateful to you for your assistance. We enclose 100 Hong Kong dollars as oil money to your esteemed hospital. Please acknowledge receipt of the funds.

We wish you well.

Yours sincerely,
Sue Yuen Tong, Habana, Cuba
(Stamp: Sue Yuen Tong Sociedad de Instruccion Y Recreo)

11 November of the 20th year of the Republic of China

[Editor's remarks: Name list of the deceased friends is available only in Chinese]

古巴灣城要明總會所用箋
Yiu Men Chong Woy So, Habana, Cuba

東華醫院列位执事先生大鑒

　　仰慕　高風神情渴注近維　旅祺多吉動定咸

宜以符私祝敬啓者敝會同人等此次籌運先友骨

殖囬國竭盡棉力差幸告成心之所願也因思

先生等見義勇為当仁不讓且平日对扵公益慈善

各種事業莫不為之贊助熱誠毅力無任欽馳故

敝會是次所办之各先友敢請　尊等轉代妥办惟

現謹將先友共壹拾弍具共壹箱已由大來公司輪船寄運

來港但抵埗之日希為接應並祈雇工起上　貴院

暫為停厝後煩順即轉致其他親屬收領是荷茲

并由本埠萬寶華號轉港陳寶棧滙上通用港

銀壹佰大員正到祈檢收作為捐助　貴院香油

之資便是若收妥後統希示覆此請并

　　　　　頌

羣祺　　　　　　　　　　　　　　　　　民國二十年拾一月拾六号

　　　　　　　駐古巴灣京要明總會所慈善會　正會長朱志廣　暨同人等謹啓
　　　　　　　　　　　　　　　　　　　　籌办處長黎蘭清

　　　　　　　　　　　　　　　（印章：古巴灣城要明總會所慈善會）

Letter from Yiu Men Chong Woy Sol, Habana, Cuba, to Tung Wah Hospital on 16 November 1931

From the Office of Yiu Men Chong Woy So, Habana, Cuba

Dear Managers of Tung Wah Hospital,

We admire your high moral status and your benevolence is known far and wide. We have tried our best to devote much time and effort to repatriate the bones of our deceased friends. It is our wish that this act of benevolence can be completed.

We know that your good selves never hesitate to perform righteous deeds, and you have long been dedicated to charity work, offering unwavering support to acts of benevolence. Therefore, we venture to seek your help in the repatriation. We have sent the bones of 12 deceased friends, placed in one box, to Hong Kong on a ship of the Dollar Shipping Company. When the bones arrive in Hong Kong, please arrarge labor to take them into your care for temporary storage and then transport them to the deceased's hometown. Meanwhile, we remit 100 Hong Kong dollars from Man Bo Wah Ho in our city to Chan Bo Chan in Hong Kong as oil money to your esteemed hospital. Please acknowledge receipt of the funds and the bones.

We wish you well.

Yours sincerely,
Chu Chi-kwong *(Zhu Zhiguang)*, Chairman
Lai Lan-ching *(Li Lanqing)*, Organizing Office Director
Yiu Men Chong Woy So, Habana, Cuba
(Stamp: YIU MEN CHON WOY SOL COMISION BENEFICENCIA HABANA, CUBA)

16 November of the 20th year of the Republic of China

古巴旅古京廣肇慈善會致東華醫院信件

1931 年 11 月 17 日

東華醫院列位执事先生鑒

　　啓者茲由大來公司直途船俩上先友骨
骸一大箱到埠勞代妥理感感茲夾付上
炅帋乙張該艮肆拾大元助香油之用祈
照查收示知諸多勞此請

旅安

　　　　　　　　　　　　　　　　旅古京廣肇慈善會
　　　　　　　　　　　　　　　　陳居華付

一九三一年十一月十七号

Letter from Kwong Siu Benevolent Association, Habana, Cuba, to Tung Wah Hospital on 17 November 1931

Dear Managers of Tung Wah Hospital,

We repatriated the bones of our deceased friends, placed in one large box, on a direct ship of Dollar Shipping Company. Please take the remains into your care after they arrive in Hong Kong. We enclose a cheque for 40 dollars as our oil money to your esteemed hospital. Please acknowledge receipt of it.

Thank you for your efforts, and we wish you well.

Yours sincerely,
Chan Gui-wah *(Chen Juhua)* of Kwong Siu Benevolent Association, Habana, Cuba

17 November 1931

香港東華醫院列位先生^{大鑒}敬啓者茲由墨國民成李
　祐水埠扵本年西歷元月廿八号啓行之輪船直头付交
　貴醫院先友骨骸一木箱付骨骸俩紙正張經由該水
　埠代理西人當日隨函付上今將副俩紙套上但到步請照
　查收如蒙代收妥拜冼再轉寄交南海九江萬善堂交錢行
　西街致安祥銀號收便是今夾上香港大通艮行積一張第
　951 號值港艮四拾元到步請照查收將作代收骨骸及轉寄之
　費用但得收妥便笔示慰但來信請照信面西住址付來無惧
　諸事種種費神之致也餘恕未及專此并候

　　另一人註：（此款壬弍月初九日進）
台祺
　　　　　一九三二年弍月拾号　　　　　　　　　注墨国^下_埠關海公司字頓

　　　　　　　　　　　　　　　　　　　　　（印章：墨國關海公司書柬）

^{小號}門牌住址
Jose Juan y Cia
Apartado # 18
Arriaga Chis. Mexico

Letter from Jose Juan Y Cia, Mexico, to Tung Wah Hospital on 10 February 1932

Dear Directors of Tung Wah Hospital,

We repatriated the remains of deceased friends, placed in a wooden box, from the port of Manzanillo, Mexico, by sea on 28 January directly to your esteemed hospital. The original bill of lading had already been sent to you together with the remains by the foreign agent based in the port area. We now enclose a copy of the bill of lading. When the remains arrive in Hong Kong, please take them into your care and send them onto Man Sin Tong *(Wan Shan Tang)* in Kau Kong *(Jiujiang)*, Nam Hoi *(Nanhai)*. From there, remains will be forwarded to On Cheung Native Bank *(Anxiang Yinhao)* in Chin Hang Sai Street *(Qianxingxi Jie)*. We hereby enclose a cheque, Number 951 and issued by the Chase National Bank in Hong Kong for 40 Hong Kong dollars, to cover the costs of receiving and repatriation of bones. Please acknowledge receipt of the funds and send your reply to the address on the envelope.

We are most grateful to you for your efforts and await your reply.

Yours humbly,
Jose Yuan Y Cia, Mexico
(Stamp: Jose Yuan Y Cia)

10 February 1932

Address of our company:
Jose Juan Y Cia
Apartado # 18
Arriaga Chis. Mexico

Another person's remarks: Received on the 9th day of the 2nd lunar month, Year of Yam Sun *(Renshen)*

香港
中華醫院 [1] 總理先生台鑒

敬啓者茲由美國花咭公司轉上　吳如鎏公之骸
骨于　貴院祈查收勞貯下并懇由　貴院致函
于南海九江市太平街公和金鋪內吳如彬俾由鄉派
人到領該　公原藉南海九江鎮南方阜安社人
但弟亦已付函于舍下通知俾到　貴院收領帶囬
安葬并套上大通銀行晸㦬乙張值港銀式拾伍元
祈照查收懇將該項誌弟捐助　貴院之費如
收妥祈示覆諸多有勞感謝感謝专此并
請

鈞安

弟吳如淦 頓
Luis Ung Jr.
Apartado No. 61.
Guaymas Son.,
Mexico

中華民國廿一年三月七号

1　意指東華醫院

Letter from Luis Ung Jr., Mexico, to Tung Wah Hospital on 7 March 1932

Dear Directors of Tung Wah Hospital,

The bones of Ng Yu-lau *(Wu Ruliu)* had been repatriated from the USA to your esteemed hospital. Please take delivery of the bones and send a letter to Ng Yu-bun *(Wu Rubin)* at Gung Wo Goldsmith *(Gonghe Jinpu)*, Tai Ping Street *(Taiping Jie)*, Kau Kong Town *(Jiujiang)*, Nam Hoi *(Nanhai)*, for him to arrange someone from the hometown to collect the bones. The deceased was a native of On Sheh *(Anshe)*, Nam Fong Port *(Nanfang Fu)*, Kau Kong Town, Nam Hoi. I have also written to my family asking them to send someone to collect the bones from your esteemed hospital and take back to the hometown for burial. Please find enclosed a cheque of Chase National Bank for 25 Hong Kong dollars as my donation to your esteemed hospital. Please acknowledge receipt of the cheque.

I am most grateful to you for your efforts. I wish you well.

Yours humbly,
Luis Ung Jr.
Apartado No. 61.
Guaymas Son.,
Mexico

7 March of the 21st year of the Republic of China

中國何根愷致東華醫院信件

1932年6月3日

東華醫院
列位先生 電鑒

^弟何根愷謹上

敬啓者^弟乃南海屬九江人^{胞兄}根耀前十年在古巴
身故去年拾月间得接^{舍姪}桂桐由古巴發囬一函云及
將他先父即何根耀之骨殖执起乘要明邦慈善会運
先友囬籍之便搭運囬港　貴院轉運回九江從風草堂
交^弟收領安蓺大約十一月左右乃可到鄉等語惟至今日久
查问從風草堂未見運到此件如係已経運到　貴院抑或
現下尚未運到請賜一音示知俾^弟候到從風草堂收領或
到　貴院領囬安蓺未定但賜函祈交九江市船欄街廣逢源
海味店收轉^弟可得收九江從風草堂現改為九江救济院
祈為知之信到之下請為即復诸事有勞口當謝謝
謹此并請

大安

夏曆四月廿九日

^陽_曆六月三号

Letter from Ho Gun-hoi, China, to Tung Wah Hospital on 3 June 1932

Dear Directors of Tung Wah Hospital,

I am a native of Kau Kong *(Jiujiang)*, Nam Hoi *(Nanhai)*. My elder brother Gun-yiu *(Genyao)* passed away in Cuba ten years ago. In October last year, I received a letter from my nephew Gwai-tung *(Guitong)* in Cuba saying that he had exhumed the bones of his late father, i.e. Ho Gun-yiu and repatriated them to Hong Kong through a benevolent association of Ko Yiu *(Gaoyao)* and Ko Ming *(Gaoming)* when it repatriated other bones to the hometown. He said your esteemed hospital would transport the bones to me at Chung Fung Cho Tong *(Cong Feng Cao Tang)* in Kau Kong and I should expect the bones to arrive sometime in November. However, according to Chung Fung Cho Tong, the bones have yet to arrive. I should be grateful if you could tell me whether the bones have been delivered to your esteemed hospital, and whether I should collect them from Chung Fung Cho Tong or your esteemed hospital. Please send your reply to me in the care of Kwong Fung Yuen Dried Seafood Shop *(Guang Feng Yuan)*, Shuen Lan Street *(Chuanlan Jie)*, Kau Kong City. Please note that Chung Fung Cho Tong is now called Kau Kong Relief & Shelter Home *(Jiujiang Jiujiyuan)*.

I look forward to your reply at your earliest convenience. Thank you very much for your efforts.

Yours sincerely,
Ho Gun-hoi *(He Genkai)*

29th day of the 4th lunar month
3 June

旅中美洲掘地孖罅國華僑總會用箋
Colonia China
中華民國廿一年七月五日

東華醫院主任先生大鑒

逕啓者昨年十月十四日^{敝会}曾附晨

慎總統船先友骸骨一帮交

貴院代為分發各該所屬親人

領葬茲查內有「林顯」一具新

會人係即林顯揚仰檢出連回港

幣五元交該親屬領取為荷專

此順頌

公祺

旅瓜國華僑總會謹啓
（印章：中美洲掘地孖罅華僑總會印）

Letter from Colonia China, Guatemala, to Tung Wah Hospital on 5 July 1932

From the Office of Colonia China, Guatemala

5 July of the 21st year of the Republic of China

Dear Managers of Tung Wah Hospital,

On 14 October last year, we repatriated the remains of our deceased friends on the *SS President Jackson* and sought the help of your esteemed hospital to distribute the remains to the deceased's families for burial. Among the remains were those of Lam Hin *(Lin Xian)*, also known as Lam Hin-yeung *(Lin Xianyang)*, of Sun Wui *(Xinhui)*. Please pass the remains, along with burial fees of 5 Hong Kong dollars, to his family.

Thank you very much for your efforts.

We wish you well.

Yours sincerely,
Colonia China, Guatemala
(Stamp: Colonia China, Guatemala)

陳潁川總堂
Chang Weng Chun Tong

香港東華醫院諸執事先生均鑒

　　逕啓者本會前経民十九年底運歸先友于

　　貴院收惟是內有一具先友陳昌泰係赤溪

　　縣田頭鄉海龍灣村今據其家人报告未曾收到

　　料必仍在　貴院因未能查察以至擱置故特

　　用函懇請　執事先生細查覓着陳昌泰

　　骨殖從速轉附交其家人收妥以安先灵而正首

　　邱是為至要如何之處請即　示覈為盼此請

均安

　　　　　　　　　　　　　　　　古巴陳潁川堂慈善會謹上

中華民國廿一年七月十一日

Letter from Chang Weng Chun Tong, Cuba, to Tung Wah Hospital on 11 July 1932

From the Office of Chang Weng Chun Tong, Cuba

Dear Managers of Tung Wah Hospital,

We are writing with regard to the remains of deceased friends sent to your esteemed hospital at the end of the 19th year of Republic of China. Among the remains were those of Chan Cheong-tai *(Chen Changtai)*, a native of Hoi Lung Wan Village *(Hailongwan Cun)*, Tin Tau Township *(Tiantou Xiang)*, Chek Kai County *(Chixi Xian)*. His family informed us that they had not yet received the remains of the deceased. We believe the matter has been overlooked and the remains are still in the care of your esteemed hospital. Please find out where the remains of Chan Cheong-tai are and hand them over to his family as soon as possible, so that our deceased friend can be laid to rest. Please reply to us with the finding of your investigation.

We wish you well.

Yours sincerely,
Chang Weng Chun Tong, Cuba

11 July of the 21st year of the Republic of China

駐中美洲葛大李架國泮大連埠華商會館用箋
CLUB WAH SION

東華醫院

值理先生大鑒敬啟者茲拾本月十九日

由「散打‧舌司梨亞」輪船寄運先僑梓遺

骸拾貳具共裝叁大箱囬國到港付交

貴院代暫收存以便各親屬到

貴院收領素仰

貴院執事先生慈善為懷定不以煩瀆

為歉也今將俌紙等件寄呈至希

查照除分函各先僑梓親屬屆時到

貴院請領外謹耑函奉達希代妥辦至

感至盼敬頌

公安

泮大　華商會館　　正會長陳培興
漣埠　　　　　　　書記蘇國慶

（印章：中美洲葛國泮大漣埠華商會館印）

　　　計開

卓玉泉公遺骸一具　　　　　　　　　　　第壹號箱

　廣東中山縣第六區官堂鄉人氏交

　卓展宏　鳥宏二君收

黃慶公遺骸一具　　　　　　　　　　　　第貳號箱

　廣東中山縣谷鎮白石環獺山村人氏煩交

　黃容保　林啟維二君收

黃光奕公遺骸一具　　　　　　　　　　　第叁號箱

　廣東中山縣谷鎮平湖村人氏煩交

　黃畔君收

林陳氏遺骸一具	第肆號箱
廣東中山縣谷鎮白石環獺山村人氏煩交	
林啟維先生收	
余良和公遺骸一具	第伍號箱
廣東台山縣平安村荻海區人氏交	
余里和先生收	
陳杜氏遺骸一具	第陸號箱
廣東中山縣谷都白石環人氏煩交	
陳經鳳　蘭鳳　均鳳三位先生收	
陳燦興公遺骸一具	第柒號箱
廣東中山縣谷鎮白石環下涌人氏煩交	
陳經鳳　蘭鳳　均鳳三君	
李宗德公遺骸一具	第八號箱
廣東中山縣谷鎮白石鄉人氏交	
鄭颮安君收	
陳侨興公遺體一具	第玖號箱
廣東中山縣白石環下涌交	
陳經鳳　蘭鳳　均鳳三君收	
鄭其澄公遺骸一具	第拾號箱
廣東中山縣谷鎮桥头鄉人氏交	
鄭其兆君收	
容達祥公遺骸一具	第拾壹號箱
廣東中山縣谷鎮烏石鄉人氏交	
容益祥君收	
吳帝連公遺骸一具	第拾貳箱
廣東中山縣谷鎮鴉崗鄉人氏交	
吳德如先生收	

中華民國二十一年七月十九日
（印章：中美洲葛國泮大漣埠華商會館印）

050 — Letter from Club Wah Sion Puntarenas, Costa Rica, to Tung Wah Hospital on 19 July 1932

From the Office of Club Wah Sion, Puntarenas, Costa Rica

Dear Directors of Tung Wah Hospital,

We repatriated the remains of 12 deceased friends, placed in three large boxes, on the *Santa Cecilia* on the 19th day of this month. Please take the remains into your care when they arrive in Hong Kong, so that the families of the deceased can collect them from your esteemed hospital. The charitable deeds of your good selves are known far and wide. We are certain you will not mind offering help.

We now send the bill of lading for your reference. We have also sent letters to the families of the deceased and asked them to claim the remains from your esteemed hospital. Please take care of the matter. We are most grateful to you for your help in this matter.

We wish you well.

Yours sincerely,
Chan Pui-hing *(Chen Pei-xing)*, Chairman
So Kwok-hing *(Su Guoqing)*, Secretary
Club Wah Sion, Puntarenas
(Stamp: Club Wah Sion of Puntarenas, Costa Rica, C.A.)

19 July of the 21st year of the Republic of China

[Editor's remarks: Name list of the deceased friends is available only in Chinese]

駐中美洲葛大李架國泮大漣埠華商會館用箋
CLUB WAH SION

東華醫院

值理先生大鑒敬啟者昨於本月十九日從輪寄運

^{本埠}先僑梓遺骸拾貳具共裝叁大箱囬美國

金港公司陳孟霖君代為轉寄

貴院代暫收存以便各親屬到　貴院收領素

仰　貴院執事先生慈善為懷定不以煩瀆

為歉也今將俋紙等件寄呈至希　查收除

分函各先僑梓親屬屆時到　貴院請領外謹崙

函奉達希代妥辦至感至盼敬頌

公安

泮大 華商會館　正會長陈培興
漣埠　　　　　書記蘇國慶

（印章：中美洲葛國泮大漣埠華商會館印）

中華民國二十一年七月二十日

計開

卓玉泉公	廣東中山縣第六區官塘鄉人氏 第壹號箱　交卓展宏　卓鳥宏二君收
黃　慶公	廣東中山縣谷鎮白石環獺山村人氏 第貳號箱　交黃容保　林啟維二君收
黃光奕公	廣東中山縣谷鎮平湖村人氏 第叁號箱　交黃畔先生收
林陳氏	廣東中山縣谷鎮白石環獺山村人氏 第肆號箱　交林啟維先生收
余良和公	廣東台山縣平安村荻海區人氏 第伍號箱　交余里和先生收
陳杜氏	廣東中山縣谷都白石環人氏 第陸號箱　交陳經鳳　蘭鳳　均鳳三君收
陳燦興公	廣東中山縣谷鎮白石環下涌人氏 第柒號箱　交陳經鳳　蘭鳳　均鳳三君收
李宗德公	廣東中山縣谷鎮白石鄉人氏 第八號箱　交鄭賧安君收
陳侨興公	廣東中山縣白石環下涌人氏 第玖號箱　交陳經鳳　蘭鳳　均鳳三君收
鄭其澄公	廣東中山縣谷鎮桥头鄉人氏 第拾號箱　交鄭其兆君收
容達祥公	廣東中山縣谷鎮烏石鄉大圩人氏 第拾壹號箱　交容益祥君府上收
吳帝連公	廣東中山縣谷鎮鴉崗鄉人氏 第拾貳號箱　交吳德如君收

Letter from Club Wah Sion, Puntarenas, Costa Rica, to Tung Wah Hospital on 20 July 1932

From the Office of Club Wah Sion, Puntarenas, Costa Rica

Dear Directors of Tung Wah Hospital,

We repatriated the remains of 12 deceased friends, placed in three large boxes, by sea on the 19th day of this month through Chan Mang-lam *(Chen Menglin)* of Golden Port Company, USA. Please take the remains into your care after they arrive in Hong Kong, so that the families of the deceased can collect them from your esteemed hospital. The charitable deeds of your good selves are known far and wide. We are certain you will not mind offering help.

We now send the bill of lading for your reference. We have also sent letters to the families of the deceased and asked them to claim the remains from your esteemed hospital. Please take care of the matter. We are most grateful to you for your help in this matter.

We wish you well.

Yours sincerely,
Chan Pui-hing *(Chen Pei-xing)*, Chairman
So Kwok-hing *(Su Guoqing)*, Secretary
Club Wah Sion, Puntarenas
(Stamp: Club Wah Sion of Puntarenas, Costa Rica, C.A.)

20 July of the 21st year of the Republic of China

[Editor's remarks: Name list of the deceased friends is available only in Chinese]

駐中美洲葛大李架國泮大連埠華商會館用箋
CLUB WAH SION

東華醫院值理先生英鑒

敬啟者昨扵本月十九日「散打舌司尼亞」輪船寄運^{本埠}
先友遺骸拾貳具共裝叁大箱回國付交　貴院另將各
俉紙等件託　鄭赽安君帶上託代暫收存以便各親屬
到　貴院領收後因手瀆不合故特寄交美國金港
公司提收託　陳孟霖君代為轉寄　貴院各俉紙
等件業經由　陳孟霖君直寄交　貴院諒扲
日間可到至希　查收按名照交各先友親屬收領諸費
清神無任感盼並頌

公安

泮大　華商會館　正會長　陈培興
漣埠　華商會館　書　記　蘇國慶
（印章：中美洲葛國泮大漣埠華商會館印）

中華民國二十一年七月二十日

Letter from Club Wah Sion, Puntarenas, Costa Rica, to Tung Wah Hospital on 20 July 1932

From the Office of Club Wah Sion, Puntarenas, Costa Rica

Dear Directors of Tung Wah Hospital,

We repatriated the remains of 12 deceased friends, placed in three large boxes, to your esteemed hospital, on the *Santa Cecilia* on the 19th day of this month, and asked Cheng Dit-on *(Zheng Die'an)* to bring and keep the bill of lading and other documents with him until the families of the deceased collect the remains from your esteemed hospital. However, this was apparently not the correct procedure. We have now asked Chan Mang-lam *(Chen Menglin)* of Golden Port Company of USA, to send the bill of lading and other documents to you and they should reach you soon. Please hand over the remains to the deceased's families according to the documents.

We are most grateful to you for your efforts.

We wish you well.

Yours sincerely,
Chan Pui-hing *(Chen Pei-xing)*, Chairman
So Kwok-hing *(Su Guoqing)*, Secretary
Club Wah Sion, Puntarenas
(Stamp: Club Wah Sion, Puntarenas, Costa Rica, C.A.)

20 July of the 21st year of the Republic of China

就安號

香港東華醫院諸執事先生^{均鑒}

敬啟者頃接古巴湾京陳潁川總堂慈善會
來函內稱于民国十九年底由湾付囬大批
先友金骸到貴院收照轉交各屬先友家
人領囬但內有^{鄙人}先父金骸一具名陳昌泰
廣東赤溪縣田头鄉人至今日久未見貴執事
來函通知諒亦一时錯悞故今即修函附上懇先
生查明來函示知俾得前往領取為要勿延此請

中華民國廿一年八月廿三日

陳兆樞　托

From the Office of Chau On Ho

Dear Managers of Tung Wah Hospital,

We received a letter from the head office of Chang Weng Chun Tong, Cuba, with regard to a large batch of remains repatriated to your esteemed hospital from Havana at the end of the 19th year of the Republic of China, to be collected by the families of the deceased. Among the remains were those of my late father Chan Cheong-tai *(Chen Changtai)*, a native of Tin Tau Township *(Tiantou Xiang)*, Chek Kai County *(Chixi Xian)* of Kwantung *(Guangdong)*, but I have still not received any letter from you. I think there was probably an oversight, so I now write to ask you to investigate the matter. Please reply to me and tell me when I can collect the remains at your earliest convenience. I hope there will be no further delay.

Yours sincerely,
Chan Siu-shu *(Chen Zhaoshu)*

23 August of the 21st year of the Republic of China

就安號

東華醫院執事先生均鑒
敬啟者近接得古巴陳潁川總堂慈善會囘來
一函內稱于民國十九年底由灣城付囘大帮先
友金骸係交貴院收轉交各先友家屬領收等
云但內有一具係赤溪縣田頭鄉人陳昌泰
事經秋餘之久前未見貴院來函通知亦未見
陳潁川堂來函示知故遲之又久延遲至今
方得悉前經付囘貴院諒貴院先生一時忘錯
未及來函通知今鄙人特此修函奉上懇
貴執事先生見字即查明該陳昌泰骸骨
一具即來函達知俾得前往領囘以安先灵
為荷想貴執事先生皆慈善為懷諒
不以為却伏祈留心是祷謹此並候

財安
　　又者前付上一函內挾灣京慈善
　　會一函諒亦得收無惧

　　　　　　　　　　　　　　　　　陳兆樞托

中華民國廿一年八月廿九日

Letter from Chan Siu-shu, China, to Tung Wah Hospital on 29 August 1932

From the Office of Chau On Ho

Dear Managers of Tung Wah Hospital,

We recently received a letter from Chang Weng Chun Tong, Cuba, with regard to a large batch of remains repatriated to your esteemed hospital from Havana at the end of the 19th year of the Republic of China, to be collected by the families of the deceased. Among the remains were those of Chan Cheong-tai *(Chen Changtai)*, a native of Ting Tau Township *(Tiantou Xiang)*, Chek Kai County *(Chixi Xian)*, Kwangtung *(Guangdong)*. A long time has since passed, but we have not yet received any letter from your esteemed hospital or Chang Weng Chun Tong. We now know that the remains had been sent to your esteemed hospital. There was probably an oversight and you might slip up to reply to us. I now write to ask if you can find out where the remains of Chan Cheong-tai are. Please inform us when we can collect the remains for burial at your earliest convenience so that the deceased will have eternal peace.

Your benevolence is known far and wide. We hope you are not offended and give thoughts to this matter.

We await your reply, and we wish you well.

We enclose the letter from the benevolent association in Havana.

Yours sincerely,
Chan Siu-shu *(Chen Zhaoshu)*

29 August of the 21st year of the Republic of China

中美洲尼架拉瓜國步路飛埠中華會館用箋
CHINESE CLUB, BLUEFIELDS, NICARAGUA, C. A.

東華醫院執事諸公偉鑒逐啓者^敝

^會將歷年先友骸硐共六名裝成壹

箱由總統輪船寄上到祈照收分發各梓

里俾得魂歸黃土骸峀祖國可也素仰

諸公慷慨義舉慈善大懷定能代辦妥當

用再函達（另函夾有出口咭）希為諒照實感公諢為盼

草此并請

善祺

計開　木裝一箱　共六名

郑式琳　　　中山縣谷都平嵐鄉東堡

林維清　　　中山縣谷都平嵐鄉林堡

侯賢祖　　　中山縣谷都白石鄉

鄭文祿　　　中山縣烏石鄉

黃立禮　　　開平縣百合圩齐塘堡

鄭忠休　　　開平縣百合圩白沙窟

中華民國二十一年九月廿四日　　　　　　　　　　中華會館付

Letter from the Chinese Club of Bluefields, Nicaragua, to Tung Wah Hospital on 24 September 1932

From the Office of the Chinese Club, Bluefields, Nicaragua, Central America

Dear Managers of Tung Wah Hospital,

We repatriated the remains of six deceased friends exhumed in the past years. We placed them in one box and send to your hospital on the President Line ship. Please receive and send the remains to the deceased's hometown, so that they can be laid to rest in homeland.

Your generosity and benevolence are known far and wide. We are certain this matter will be well taken care of. We will send to you a separate letter with the bill of lading enclosed. Please check.

We are most grateful to you for your efforts.

We wish you well.

Yours sincerely,
The Chinese Club

24 September of the 21ˢᵗ year of the Republic of China

[Editor's remarks: Name list of the deceased friends is available only in Chinese]

古巴灣城要明公所信箋
Yiu Men Keng Sol

東華醫院 顏成坤 先生 鑒
　　　　　陳廉伯

逕啓者本所慈善會以該帮　先友義屬
同胞誼同桑梓撫白楊而興感念黑塞以
生愁夫在路人猶有瘞之心豈鄉里能無
歸之想乎故本所慈善會有見及此乃今
年冬季着手籌辦此帮　先友的工作現
已手續告竣爰於拾壹月二十八號將此帮
先友骨石十弍具裝成壹大箱附大來輪
船公司運儎囬國直交　貴院代收若該箱
先友骨石到時請　台轉達「永樂街十四號
怡來號暨永和街十三號和興昌」兩號便能
料理轉寄伊親屬妥收也且即日由紐約銀
行購赤壹張值港幣伍拾元滙上乃作要
明公所慈善會捐助　貴院之微忱實不
成敬意用特函達希為查收复達則不勝
銘感矣此致順頌

旅祺

民、廿一、十一月卅日

要明公所慈善會謹上（印章：古巴灣城要明公所印）

另一人註：已复

Letter from Yiu Men Keng Sol, Habana, Cuba, to Tung Wah Hospital on 30 November 1932

From the Office of Yiu Men Keng Sol, Habana, Cuba

Dear Mr Ngan Shing-kwan and Mr Chan Lim-pak of Tung Wah Hospital,

Our association upholds the mission of offering help to fellow Chinese compatriots. We came from the same hometown to earn a living in the same overseas city. Life in a foreign country is not easy. We all miss our homeland and hope to return one day. Therefore, we began to exhume the remains of our deceased friends this winter, so that they could be repatriated to their hometown. We finished exhumation, and have sent the bones of 12 deceased friends, placed in one large box, to your esteemed hospital on a ship of Dollar Shipping Company on 28 November. Please take the bones into your care when they arrive in Hong Kong, and notify Yee Loy Ho at 14 Wing Lok Street as well as Wo Hing Cheong at 13 Wing Wo Street to handle the matters. The above two companies will send the remains to the deceased's families.

We have also sent a cheque for 50 Hong Kong dollars issued by Bank of New York, as a small donation to your esteemed hospital.

Please receive and acknowledge receipt of the cheque.

We are most grateful to you for your assistance.

We wish you well.

Yours sincerely,
Yiu Men Keng Sol
(Stamp: Yiu Men Keng Sol, Habana, Cuba)

30 November of the 21st year of the Republic of China

Another person's remarks: Replied

陳穎川總堂
Chang Weng Chun Tong

香港東華醫院諸執事先生大鑒敬啓者遙想

諸先生福與時增財與時進良可頌也

本會前年首次運送先友歸國已淂

貴院办理妥善今第二次運送先友骨殖

歸國五十二具共弍大箱昨十一月廿八日已

由亞湾拿附輪（直頭船）啓程一俟抵港之時

希祈起妥茲付上昃紙弍張共港銀四佰陆

拾元請為照收內除港銀弍佰陆拾元係奉

囬每具先友為葬費港銀伍元須查交收

領先友者妥收其餘港銀弍佰元壹佰奉與

貴院為香油資壹佰為分送各先友歸各

縣各鄉之費淂以囬籍以正首邱而安先靈

定當獲福靡既矣如收到此銀信仰速示

覆免至遠望是荷餘未細及耑此並候

近祉

并付上往起先友之西文喬弍張祈注意收

古巴灣城陳穎川總堂慈善會謹上

（印章：古巴灣城陳穎川總堂）

中華民國二十一年十二月八日

Letter from Chang Weng Chun Tong, Habana, Cuba, to Tung Wah Hospital on 8 December 1932

From the Office of Chang Weng Chun Tong

Dear Managers of Tung Wah Hospital,

Your benevolence is known far and wide; your blessings have grown over the years.

A couple of years ago, we repatriated the first batch of remains of our deceased friends. The deceased have all been laid to rest in China, thanks to the assistance of your esteemed hospital. We are now sending the second batch of bones to the mainland again. There are 52 sets of bones which are placed in two large boxes. They have been repatriated from Havana by sea (direct vessel) on 28 November. Please take the bones into your care when they arrive in Hong Kong. We enclose two cheques for 460 Hong Kong dollars in total. Of the money, 260 dollars are the burial fees for the deceased's families (5 Hong Kong dollar for each set of remains). As to the remainder, please keep 100 dollars as our oil money to your hospital, and use 100 dollars to pay for repatriation fees to the deceased's hometown. You are blessed with your benevolence.

Please acknowledge receipt of the letter and cheques as soon as you receive them to ease our mind.

We wish you well.

We also enclose two bills of lading in English for your reference.

Yours sincerely,
Chang Weng Chun Tong, Habana, Cuba
(Stamp: Chang Weng Chun Tong, Habana, Cuba)

8 December of the 21st year of the Republic of China

058 尼架拉瓜國步路飛埠中華會館致東華醫院信件
1933 年 2 月 25 日

中美洲尼架拉瓜國步路飛埠中華會館用箋
CHINESE CLUB, BLUEFIELDS, NICARAGUA, C. A.

香港東華醫院執事先生均鑒

　　公啓者得接到去年十弍月卅日賜來大教得知一切
　　再查以前各先梓友之骨殖係由該屬親人經手裝
　　箱今查詢該人據云而鄭式琳鄭文祿二位先友
　　之骨殖係封埋在侯賢祖之礶內因當日寫信之人
　　未知梗概是以未有詳明致令列位費心祈見鄭式
　　琳文祿二位之親屬到領可对他言明在侯賢祖
　　之礶內照此分給各人之親屬領囘安塋以安窀
　　穸不勝費神之至肅此敬頌

公安

（印章：尼架拉瓜
步路飛埠 中華會館）

藍
田 中華會館

西曆一九三十三年二月廿五日

Letter from the Chinese Club, Bluefields, Nicaragua, to Tung Wah Hospital on 25 February 1933

From the Office of the Chinese Club, Bluefields, Nicaragua, Central America

Dear Managers of Tung Wah Hospital,

We received your letter dated 30 December of last year, which showed us the full picture. We then investigated the matter and found out that the bones of the deceased friends were usually placed in the boxes by their clansmen. The bones of Cheng Sik-lam *(Zheng Shilin)* and Cheng Man-luk *(Zheng Wenlu)* have been placed in the container for Hau Yin-cho's *(Hou Xianzu's)* bones. The person who wrote the letter earlier was not aware of this and did not inform you. We are very sorry for the worry this has caused to you. When the family of Cheng Sik-lam and Cheng Man-luk come to collect the bones, please tell them that the bones have been placed in the same container along with Hau Yin-cho's bones. Please distribute the bones to the families so that they can claim the bones and lay them to rest accordingly.

Thank you very much for your efforts.

We wish you well.

Yours sincerely,
The Chinese Club, Bluefields
(Stamp: Chinese Club, Bluefields, Nicaragua)

25 February 1933

陳潁川總堂
Chang Weng Chun Tong

香港東華醫院諸執事先生鑒啓者比維
　　諸执事旅于港地定占佳勝良可頌也本
　　慈善會客岁十一月廿八日運送先友歸國
　　五十弍具共弍大箱已搭直頭船由灣啓行
　　至十弍月初旬寄上港銀四百六十元內除港艮伍元与
　　每具先友為葬費共二百六十元餘二百元一百元為送先友
　　返各縣各鄉之費一佰元奉与　貴院香油費
　　但先友与及銀信料已到步妥收迄今數月久
　　尚未蒙　示覆殊令挂望抑有別故如何之處
　　仰速速報知以釋懷疑不勝感祷之至此請并候

大安

中華民國廿弍年三月十六日

陳潁川總堂慈善會上
（印章：古巴灣城陳潁川總堂）

Letter from Chang Weng Chun Tong, Habana, Cuba, to Tung Wah Hospital on 16 March 1933

From the Office of Chang Weng Chun Tong

Dear Managers of Tung Wah Hospital,

Your benevolent work in Hong Kong is much celebrated.

On 28 November last year, we repatriated 52 sets of remains, placed in two large boxes, from Havana to Hong Kong by direct vessel. In early December, we remitted 460 Hong Kong dollars to you. Of that, 260 dollars, 5 dollars for each deceased friend, were to cover the burial fees for the deceased's family and 100 dollars were for transportation fees to repatriate the deceased from Hong Kong to their hometown. The remaining 100 dollars were our oil money to your esteemed hospital. We believe you received the remains and the remittance letters a few months ago but we have yet to hear from you. We wonder if anything has happened. Please reply to us at your earliest convenience to put our mind at ease. We are most grateful to you for your assistance and await your reply.

We wish you well.

Yours sincerely,
Chang Weng Chun Tong, Habana, Cuba
(Stamp: Chang Weng Chun Tong, Habana, Cuba)

16 March of the 22nd year of the Republic of China

060 中國陳章烈致東華醫院信件

1933 年 6 月 25 日

東華医院商會列位先生青鑒啓者去年先兄陳
章法陳章宇之骨殖由亞灣運回　貴會事理前日
已托陳洪記運返[敝]鄉　曾経日久惟是旅湾僑胞
每副骨殖分派五元塟殮未見　貴會將此款
交來[弟]懸望甚殷如接到此函仰祈從速交來
德輔道中一百一拾九號三樓均和安收入便是矣專此
並祝

公安

中山斗门南山鄉人[弟]陳章烈叩

又五月初三日

Letter from Chan Cheung-lit, China, to Tung Wah Hospital on 25 June 1933

Dear Directors of Tung Wah Hospital,

Last year, the bones of my late brothers, Chan Cheung-fat *(Chen Zhangfa)* and Chan Cheung-yu *(Chen Zhangyu)*, were repatriated from Havana to your esteemed hospital. I have asked Chan Hung Kee to transport the remains to my hometown. Some time has passed and I am aware that burial fees of 5 dollars are offered to the family of each deceased Chinese compatriot from Havana. Yet I have not received the funds which I have been longing for from your esteemed hospital. I would be most grateful if you could pass the funds to me, in the care of Kwan Wo On, 3/F, 119 Des Voeux Road, Central, as soon as you receive this letter.

I wish you well.

Yours sincerely,
Chan Cheung-lit *(Chen Zhanglie)* of Nam Sha Township *(Nanshan Xiang)*, Dou Mun *(Doumen)*, Chung Shan *(Zhongshan)*

3rd day of the 5th leap lunar month

061 古巴灣城中華總會館致東華醫院信件

1933 年 6 月 30 日

古巴灣城中華總會館用箋
CASINO CHUNG WAH

香港東華醫院主席先生大鑒

茲有先友鄺郴光骨殖運回祖國
安葬如到港時希為照料是荷
此致並頌

大安

總理　吳礼林（印章：中華總會館）

中華民國廿二年六月卅日

Letter from Casino Chung Wah, Habana, Cuba, to Tung Wah Hospital on 30 June 1933

From the Office of Casino Chung Wah, Habana, Cuba

Dear Chairman of Tung Wah Hospital,

The bones of our deceased friend Kwong Lau-kwong *(Kuang Liuguang)* are being repatriated to China. When they arrive in Hong Kong, please take them into your care.

Thank you very much for your kindness.

I wish you well.

Yours sincerely,
Ng Lai-lam *(Wu Lilin),* Director
(Stamp: Casino Chung Wah, Habana, Cuba)

30 June of the 22nd year of the Republic of China

金山大埠廣利
Quong Lee & Company

東華醫院
执事先生 大鑒　敬啓者茲由們罗

総統船運与甘堪元公骨灰壹具順夾
入俺乕祈照起上暫存該代支費用若
干俟其親属拈二号俻紙到
貴院承領之時如数收还可也該甘
公乃在墨国身亡因港中無親友
代收故轉託　貴院代收耳手此

即請
善祺

民廿二年十月廿八号（印章：金山大埠廣利號書東）

Letter from Quong Lee & Company, San Francisco, USA, to Tung Wah Hospital on 28 October 1933

From the Office of Quong Lee & Company

Dear Managers of Tung Wah Hospital,

The ashes of Kam Hom-yuen *(Gan Kanyuan)*, together with the bill of lading, have been repatriated on the *SS President Monroe*. Please take the ashes into your care when they arrive in Hong Kong, and pay any expenses incurred first. The family of the deceased will reimburse you when they come to collect the ashes with a copy of the bill of lading. Kam passed away in Mexico. As he has no family or friend in Hong Kong, we seek your esteemed hospital's help in handling the matter.

Thank you for your assistance.

We wish you well.

Yours sincerely,
28 October of the 22nd year of the Republic of China

(Stamp: Quong Lee & Company, San Francisco)

063 瓜地馬拉旅瓜華僑總會通告

1933 年 11 月 30 日

通告　華字第十九號

　　為通告事，查本年所擬檢運回國之先友，
共三十三名，因其手續需時，遂致延至本月廿
八日，乃得辦理完妥，除第三十號陳元瑞因未有
地方官證明書，第三十三號林時佐及孔湘等證明
書到未趕及，迫得留後辦理外，其餘三十箱先
友骨殖，業於本月廿九日付火車寄往散河些
Puerto San Jośe 埠，定十二月六日搭 Santa Lucia
船運往金山，轉付回香港東華醫院候領，
除另函通知各該先友親屬外，特此通告，右
通告

旅瓜國全體僑胞
　　是期運回国之先友骨殖姓名列
　　　左；

陳福榮	順德	譚　銘	北江	容尊樂	新會
簡邱氏	南海	劉　獲	新會	伍洪熤	台山
張　滿	中山	林　增	中山	孔蔭軒	南海
趙　欽	新會	甄滉慶	新會	林勤煜	中山
余贊廷	新會	黃兆賢	南海	黎汪元	南海
梁金銘	順德	容吉祥	中山	吳三珠	南海
梁　興	新會	黃玉濂	南海	馮澤民	南海
黃松深	新寧即台山	梁元敬	順德	關會遠	南海
林焯榮	中山	李　潤	南海	梁福裔	順德
馬　錦	台山	黃贊森	中山	梁潤勝	順德

合共三十名先友

旅瓜華僑總會
（印章：中美洲掘地孖罅華僑總會印）
中華民國二十二年十一月卅日

Letter from Colonia China, Guatemala, to Tung Wah Hospital on 30 November 1933

Notice: Wah No.19

This year, we exhumed the remains of 33 deceased friends for repatriation to the mainland. The lengthy process was finally completed on the 28th day of this month. With the exception of the remains of Chan Yuen-shui *(Chen Yuanrui)* in Box No. 30 which have no local government certificate as well as those of Lam Shi-jor *(Lin Shizuo)* and Hung Sheung *(Kong Xiang)* in Box No. 33 which have yet to receive the local government certificates, the rest of the bones, placed in 30 boxes, were transported to Puerto San José by train on the 29th day of this month. There, they will be taken to San Francisco on the SS *Santa Lucia*, and then to Tung Wah Hospital in Hong Kong for collection by the deceased's families. While the families of the deceased will have been notified by post, this notice serves to inform fellow Chinese compatriots in Guatemala of the repatriation.

Colonia China, Guatemala
(Stamp: Colonia China, Guatemala, Central America)

30 November of the 22nd year of the Republic of China

[Editor's remarks: Name list of the deceased friends is available only in Chinese]

瓜地馬拉旅瓜華僑總會致東華醫院信件

1933 年 12 月 20 日

旅中美洲瓜地馬拉華僑總會
COLONIA CHINA

東華醫院主任先生大鑒

逕啓者本年十一月六日^{敝會}曾搭美國輪船
"Santa Lucia" 號運回先友骸骨三十具分裝八
大箱到舊金山後轉船付返
貴院代為收貯候領茲特檢回正副俉紙二張
通告一紙寄呈到日請
照提收并懇代為安置候各親屬領
取可也至上落搬運費已函上海廣東銀
行匯返
貴院收滬洋柒拾大元正至香油等費
容　日再為付上專此奉達并頌

公祺

旅瓜華僑總會會長何金華

　　附　　　　　　　　　　　（印章：中美洲掘地孖罅華僑總會印）
　　俉紙二張
　　通告一張

中華民國二十二年十二月廿日

Letter from Colonia China, Guatemala, to Tung Wah Hospital on 20 December 1933

From the Office of Colonia China, Guatemala

Dear Managers of Tung Wah Hospital,

We repatriated the remains of 30 deceased friends, placed in eight large boxes, on 6 November. The remains were first taken to San Francisco on the *SS Santa Lucia* and then transferred to another ship bound for Hong Kong to your esteemed hospital for the collection by the deceased's families. We enclose the original bill of lading and a copy, along with a notice for your reference. When the remains arrive in Hong Kong, please take care of them and await the deceased's families to collect. As to the unloading and transportation fees, we have sent mail to the Shanghai branch of the Bank of Canton to remit 70 Shanghai silver dollars to your esteemed hospital. We will send oil money to your esteemed hospital later.

Thank you for your kind attention.

Yours sincerely,
Ho Kam-wah (He Jinhua)
Chairman, Colonia China, Guatemala
(Stamp: Colonia China, Guatemala, Central America)

20 December of the 22nd year of the Republic of China

Enclosed:
2 bills of lading
1 notice

旅中美洲瓜地馬拉華僑總會
COLONIA CHINA

香港東華醫院主任先生鑒

迻啓者茲隨函付上滬洋柒拾大元正係由上
海廣東銀行匯呈到日收妥請
照支撥入旅瓜地馬拉國華僑總會本年
十一月六日搭美国輪船運回先友骸骨三十
具之上落搬運費為荷至香油費会隨
後附上便是专此奉達敬候

公祺

旅瓜華僑総會會長何金華
中華民國二十二年十二月二十日
（印章：中美洲掘地孖罅華僑總會印）

Letter from Colonia China, Guatemala, to Tung Wah Hospital on 20 December 1933

From the Office of Colonia China, Guatemala

Dear Managers of Tung Wah Hospital,

We enclose a remittance of 70 Shanghai silver dollars from the Shanghai branch of the Bank of Canton. Please use the funds to pay the unloading and transportation fees of 30 sets of remains on board the American Line vessel repatriated by Colonia China, Guatemala on 6 November. We will send oil money to your esteemed hospital separately.

Thank you for your kind attention.

We wish you well.

Yours sincerely,
Ho Kam-wah *(He Jinhua)*
Chairman, Colonia China, Guatemala
(Stamp: Colonia China, Guatemala, Central America)

20 December of the 22nd year of the Republic of China

香港廣東銀行用牋
The Bank of Canton, Ltd.

東華醫院

主席先生大鑒茲有梁祐勳君由中美
洲滙來港銀陸拾叁元壹毛柒仙幷函一通
委交　貴院收者茲付上本行第捌叁伍貳
號支票一張到祈查收又夾上空白收条一套
請照簽妥擲囬俾轉前途為荷至該原
函連同奉呈順及此候

善安

關口字
中華民國廿三年元月卅號
（印章：廣東銀行）

Letter from The Bank of Canton Ltd., Hong Kong, to Tung Wah Hospital on 30 January 1934

From the Office of The Bank of Canton, Ltd., Hong Kong

Dear Chairman of Tung Wah Hospital,

Leung Yau-fun *(Liang Youxun)* from Central America has sent 63.17 Hong Kong dollars, along with a letter, to your esteemed hospital. I enclose herewith a cheque, No. 8354, issued by our bank, as well as a blank receipt. After you receive the funds, please sign the receipt and send it back to us. The original letter is also enclosed.

I wish you well.

Yours sincerely,
Kwan X *(Guan X)*
(Stamp: The Bank of Canton, Ltd.)

30 January of the 23rd year of the Republic of China

東華醫院执事先生鑒　敬啓者昨接到友來函
　　云及昨廿二年十弍月六号由大呂宋掘地孖嘑埠運
　　返先友三十具內有一具南海橫江吳三珠未知
　　貴院收到否但收到請即覆一音以得早日到
　　來領回安葬但要如何手續領回祈一并示知
　　為盼特此敬候

列位先生
大安

　　　　　　　　　　　　　通信處三水西南文秀路徐贊記
　　　　　　　　　　　　　　　內徐仲恒收便得

中華民國廿三年二月壹日

Letter from Tsui Chung-hang, China, to Tung Wah Hospital on 1 February 1934

Dear Managers of Tung Wah Hospital,

I received a letter from my friend saying that the remains of Ng Sam-chu *(Wu Sanzhu)*, a native of Wang Kong *(Hengjiang)*, Nam Hoi *(Nanhai),* were among the 30 sets of remains repatriated from Guatemala on 6 December last year. I wonder if your esteemed hospital has received the remains. Please reply to me with any news you may have, so that the remains can be collected and buried in the deceased's hometown soon. Please also notify me of the procedures for claiming the remains.

I await your reply.

I wish you well.

Yours sincerely,
Correspondence address:
Tsui Chung-hang *(Xu Zhongheng)*
c/o Tsui Tsan Kee (Xuzan Ji)
Sai Nam Man Sau Road *(Xinan Wenxiu Lu)*
Sam Shui *(Sanshui)*

1 February of the 23rd year of the Republic of China

陳穎川總堂
Chang Weng Chun Tong

香港東華醫院

總理先生大鑒逕啟者民國廿壹年十壹月廿陆日付

　　寄先友骨殖五十二具经得民国廿二年五月十一日

　　惠函報告收妥并按址通知各先友之親屬往

　　貴院收領矣但據陳恒歡君称陳恒翼先

　　骸尚未收到云查陳恒翼係開平縣浪溪村人

　　為此專函追催務祈急速通知廣東開平赤

　　坎荫浪溪村陳炳輝往

　　貴院收領安葬萬乞勿延是所切祷專此奉瀆并頌

台安

　　　　　　　　　　　　　　亞灣拿陳穎川堂慈善會啟

　　　　　　　　　　　　（印章：古巴灣城陳穎川總堂書束）

中華民國廿叁年叁月七日

Letter from Chang Weng Chun Tong, Habana, Cuba, to Tung Wah Hospital on 7 March 1934

From the Office of Chang Weng Chun Tong

Dear Directors of Tung Wah Hospital,

We repatriated the remains of 52 deceased friends on 26 November in the 21st year of the Republic of China. We received a letter from you dated 11 May in the 22nd year of the Republic of China saying that you had taken the remains into your care and informed the deceased's families to claim them from your esteemed hospital according to the addresses we provided. However, Chan Hang-foon *(Chen Henghuan)* claims that he has not yet received your letter regarding the remains of Chan Hang-yik *(Chen Hengyi)*, a native of Long Kai Village *(Langxi Cun)*, Hoi Ping County *(Kaiping Xian)*. We hereby write to urge you to notify Chan Bing-fai *(Chen Binghui)* of Long Kai Village, Chek Hom *(Chikan)*, Hoi Ping *(Kaiping)*, Kwangtung *(Guangdong)*, to claim the remains for burial from your esteemed hospital without delay.

We wish you well.

Yours sincerely,
Chang Weng Chun Tong, Habana, Cuba
(Stamp: Chang Weng Chun Tong)

7 March of the 23rd year of the Republic of China

古巴灣城羅豫章旅所慈善會致東華醫院信件
1934 年 3 月 14 日

東華醫院諸执事先生暨各善長仁翁青電

　　敬啟者　台等高居盛境玉體康寧福履日
　　綏謀事遂意則予等不勝原望也茲者旅
　　古巴湾城本所同人組織慈善会募捐運
　　費將先昆季遺骸運囬故里安蕚乐土今
　　將先友起妥用大箱裝裹由総統輪船公司輪 6 號
　　付上抵埔之日懇台等代為料理將內铁箱面先
　　友姓名付囬原藉則先友之家人感德無涯矣
　　並死者唧笑于九泉矣茲由萬國寶通銀
　　行付上赤紙一張伸港銀壹佰式拾大元正祈查
　　照收以應運費諸事多勞存没均感　耑此
　　□候　並祝

善安

民国弐拾三年 新歷叁月拾四号 古巴湾城
　　　　　　舊歷正月廿九日

　　　　　　　　　　　　　　羅豫章旅所慈善会同人啟
　　　　　　　　　　　　　（印章：古巴灣城羅豫章旅所）

羅義德 字傳祝先友	乃廣東闹平縣單水口月山堡羅村鄉 金居村人氏
羅宗耀先友	乃廣東台山縣都斛 吉安村人氏
羅莩翔先友	乃廣東闹平縣單水口月山堡羅村鄉 南塘里人氏
羅沛軒先友	乃廣東闹平縣月山堡單水口 羅村鄉南塘里人氏
羅齐盛先友	乃廣東闹平縣單水口月山堡羅村鄉 平岗村人氏
羅連協先友	乃廣東香山斗门田边里人氏　煩勞轉交 香山前山福善堂收代領

羅文篤先友	乃廣東開平單水口月山堡羅村鄉 錦州里人氏
羅烈儀先友	乃廣東開平單水口月山堡羅村鄉 南塘里人氏
羅社勇先友	乃廣東開平單水口月山堡羅村鄉 南塘里人氏
羅祺光先友	乃廣東開平單水口月山堡羅村鄉 錦州里人氏
譚美潤先友	乃廣東開平單水口 后溪新屋坊人氏
伍連登先友	乃廣東台山河冲堡巷裡村人氏 即大江圩左近
伍洪裔先友	乃廣東台山錦被荫堡 錦棠村人氏
麦阿卓先友	乃廣東鶴山麦村木佳頭村人氏 即近單水口龍山圩

以上先友共拾貳名即將付來之款一百二拾元每
名先友發給薘費銀伍元尚有銀五十元作
為運費及香油之用

若先友名下有單水口字請向單水口
愛善堂運囬以便各人領取諸事
多劳

（印章：古巴灣城羅豫章旅所）

069 Letter from Lao Yi Chiang Lay Sol Habana, Cuba, to Tung Wah Hospital on 14 March 1934

Dear benevolent Directors and Managers of Tung Wah Hospital,

I wish you prosperity, good health, abundant blessings and your wishes fulfilled.

We have raised funds to repatriate the remains of our deceased clansmen from Havana, Cuba, to their hometown for burial. The remains were placed in large boxes and sent to Hong Kong on the President Lines departing on 6 March. When the remains arrive in Hong Kong, please take them into your care, and send the remains according to the names of the deceased friends marked on the iron boxes to their hometown. The deceased will have enteral peace and your benevolence will be appreciated by their family members.

We enclose a cheque for 120 Hong Kong dollars issued by the National City Bank, to cover the transportation costs. Please check and receive.

Thank you for your assistance. The deceased and their families should be most grateful for your benevolence.

We wish you well.

Yours sincerely,
Lao Yi Chiang Lay Sol Habana, Cuba
(Stamp: Lao Yi Chiang Lay Sol)

14 March of the 23rd year of the Republic of China
29th day of the 1st lunar month

[Editor's remarks: Name list of the deceased friends is available only in Chinese]

東華大医院执事列先生大鑒啓者去岁西歷十二月廿一号有新会
　　龍泉鄉先友刘獲名骸骨一具経由和地孖鏄鏄永昌隆号上列西文
　　Jesus Leu Y. Chiquimula Guatemala C. A.
　　由輪船付來香港　貴医院代收轉交先友伊家人到
　　領安葬約今数月仰恳
貴医院先生查明該先友有無到否恳早通知委先
　　友家人早日到領為感此請

大安

　　　　　　　　　　　　　　　（印章：香港新益和李希獲書束）
　　　　　　　　　　　　　　　　　　　　　　李聖錦

　　　　　　　　　　　　　（印章：香港新益和康樂道中六十六號）

民國廿三年新歷四月九号

070 Letter from Lee Hey-wok and Lee Shing-kam, Hong Kong, to Tung Wah Hospital on 9 April 1934

Dear Managers of Tung Wah Hospital,

On 21 December last year, the bones of Lau Wok-ming *(Liu Huoming)*, a native of Long Chuen Village *(Longquan Xiang)*, Sun Wui *(Xinhui)*, were repatriated by Wing Cheong Lung Ho in Guatemala (Jesus Leu Y. Chiquimula Guatemala C.A.) by sea to your esteemed hospital in Hong Kong for onward transfer to the deceased's family to claim them for burial. A few months have passed. Can you please find out if the remains have arrived at your esteemed hospital? We are grateful if you could notify the deceased's family to claim them as soon as possible if the remains are with you.

We wish you well.

Yours sincerely,
(Stamp: Li Hay-wok *(Li Xihuo)* and Li Shing-kam *(Li Shengjin)*.
From the desk of Sun Yick Wo, Hong Kong)
(Stamp: Sun Yick Wo, 66 Connaught Road C., Hong Kong)

9 April of the 23rd year of the Republic of China

东華医院值理大鑒^余接旅瓜地孖剌華侨会來
　　函云及于一九三三年十二月運囬先友三十六名其
　　中黃贊森一名乃^余先兄故特奉函詢
　　及此帮先友可曾到達
貴院否届时懇祈
搋函示知為盼也諸多有勞不勝謝謝敬請

大安

　　　　　　　　　　　　　　　　　　　^弟黃贊祥　謹上

一九三四年四月十九号

（通訊处）
本港德付道中四号 A 四楼
太平洋行內
鄭聲泰收交
黃贊祥收入便妥

071   Letter from Wong Chan-cheung, Hong Kong, to Tung Wah Hospital on 19 April 1934

Dear Managers of Tung Wah Hospital,

I received a letter from the Chinese Association of Guatemala saying that the remains of 36 deceased friends have been repatriated in December 1933. The bones of my late brother, Wong Chan-sum *(Huang Zansen)*, are among those repatriated. I am thus writing to enquire if this batch of remains have arrived at your esteemed hospital. I await your reply.

I am most grateful to you for your efforts, and I wish you well.

Yours sincerely,
Wong Chan-cheung *(Huang Zanxiang)*

19 April 1934

Correspondence address:
Wong Chan-cheung
c/o Cheng Sing-tai
Gilman & Co., Ltd.
4A, 4/F, Des Voeux Road, Central, Hong Kong

古巴灣城遡源總堂用箋
SUE YUEN TONG

東華醫院執事先生：

　　敝會所負之使命，凡三年執拾先
骸一次，今經到期，敝會又繼續辦去，
已完成執拾工作，統計先骸四拾捌
具，分裝三大箱，由灣搭大來公司之
們羅總統船於九月十日起程運歸。
至何日到港，請　貴執事派人往輪船
起卸，即按籍貫分寄各處，至深感德！
　　現敝會捐助　貴院香油銀（港銀）
壹百大元，託香港廣英源方富恭君轉
交，請照收！先骸分寄各處之轉運
費，又託方富恭君妥為支給，請與他
接洽無悞。日後辦理情形如何，並希
示覆！

　　並詢善安！

（印章：灣城遡源總堂慈善籌辦處印）
古巴灣城遡源總堂慈善会（印章：古巴灣城遡源總堂書束）

中華民國廿三年九月十二日

072 Letter from Sue Yuen Tong, Habana, Cuba, to Tung Wah Hospital on 12 September 1934

From the Office of Sue Yuen Tong, Habana, Cuba

Dear Managers of Tung Wah Hospital,

Our association exhumes the remains of our deceased friends once every three years. It is time for another batch of remains to be repatriated. We have exhumed 48 sets of remains and placed them in three large boxes. They will be repatriated on the *SS President Monroe* of Dollar Shipping Company on 10 September. Please arrange labor to unload the remains when they arrive in Hong Kong, and distribute them to the deceased's hometown according to their counties. We are most grateful to you for your assistance.

We would like to donate oil money of 100 Hong Kong dollars to your esteemed hospital. The funds will be given to you by Fong Fu-kung *(Fang Fugong)* of Kwong Ying Yuen in Hong Kong. He will also give you money to cover the costs of sending the remains to the deceased's hometown. Please further liaise with him.

Please keep us posted on the progress of repatriation.

We wish you well.

Yours sincerely,
Sue Yuen Tong, Habana, Cuba
(Stamp: Sue Yuen Tong, Habana, Cuba)
(Stamp: Sue Yuen Tong Benevolent Office, Habana, Cuba)

12 September of the 23rd year of the Republic of China

廣東恩平馮永球用箋
FRANCISCO FUNG

東華醫院执事善翁安啓茲者

　　現有先友馮樹畔君遺骸由本月
　　弍十四号在大來公司船總統號附
　　交貴院乃廣東恩平蓮塘洞蓮昌
　　里人今寄上昃紙壹張伸港銀拾元
　　備作各費之用妥收後懇求示覆
　　並貴院運交恩平何院收交其親
　　人請註信內俾淂早日通信其親属
　　至時到領是好並候

均安

弟馮永求字

（印章：古巴 灣城 唐德隆書束）

一九三四年九月廿四号

073 Letter from Francisco Fung, Cuba, to Tung Wah Hospital on 24 September 1934

From the desk of Francisco Fung

Dear benevolent Directors and Managers of Tung Wah Hospital,

The remains of Fung Shue-boon *(Feng Shupan)* have been repatriated to your esteemed hospital on the President Line of Dollar Shipping Company on the 24th day of this month. The deceased friend was a native of Lin Cheong Lane *(Lianchang Li)*, Lin Tong Tung *(Liantang Dong)*, Yan Ping *(Enping)*, Kwangtung *(Guangdong)*. I enclose a cheque for 10 Hong Kong dollars to cover the costs of repatriation. Please acknowledge receipt of the cheque. As to the remains, please send them to Ho Yuen *(He Yuan)* at Yan Ping who will hand over to the deceased's family. Please write to ask him to inform the deceased's family to collect the remains.

I wish you well.

Yours sincerely,
Francisco Fung
(Stamp: From the Office of Tong Tak Lung, Habana, Cuba)

24 September 1934

東華醫院総理先生公鑒逕啓者現茲付

　　上香油伸港銀拾大元到日查收區區微物

　　是属不誠事体奈因環境耳請求見諒

　　弟等現在西人長生店办理先友囬國內属式

　　俱係弟等親属壹俱林立維先友闹平蜆岗

　　堡水背村人壹俱林舉旋先友台山城東南安

　　村人在古巴搭大來公司值頭船西歷九月廿四日

　　啓程到時恳請貴　総理依照該先友箱

　　面縣鄉村名分發代等家人領收按葦祖國

　　以慰死者在天之靈生者亦殊深感謝此請

　　　　並頌

群安

　　　　　　　　　　　　　　旅古巴　闹平人林立惇　仝叩
　　　　　　　　　　　　　　　　　　台山人林德濃

大中華民國廿三年九月廿四日

074 Letter from Lam Lap-dun and Lam Tak-nong, Cuba, to Tung Wah Hospital on 24 September 1934

Dear Directors of Tung Wah Hospital,

We enclose oil money of 10 Hong Kong dollars to your hospital. We understand this is a very small donation, but it is the best we can do given our circumstances. I have arranged a funeral parlour run by foreigners to repatriate two sets of remains of my late relatives, Lam Lap-wai *(Lin Liwei)*, a native of Shui Bui Village *(Shuibei Cun)*, Hin Kong Bo *(Xiangang Bao)*, Hoi Ping *(Kaiping)*, and Lam Kui-shuen *(Lin Juxuan)*, a native of Nam On Village *(Nan'an Cun)*, Toi Shan City East *(Taishan Chengdong)*, direct from Cuba on a ship of Dollar Shipping Company. The ship is set to sail on 24 September. When the remains arrive in Hong Kong, please send them to the deceased's hometown according to the address marked on the boxes, so that their families can collect the remains and bury them. The deceased's spirits will be pacified and the living will be most grateful to you for your benevolence.

We wish you well.

Yours sincerely,
Lam Lap-dun *(Lin Lidun)* of Hoi Ping and Lam Tak-nong *(Lin Denong)* of Toi Shan sojourn in Cuba

24 September of the 23rd year of the Republic of China

古巴李南翘致東華醫院信件

1934 年 9 月 28 日

古巴灣城開明公報
Hoi Men Kung Po

香港東華醫院
總理先生鑒

啓者夾上㚙紙壹張值港銀十五元
希為查收此款係交李祝南李偉
來葉達柏三位先友骸骨寄運費
称依照箱面縣鄉區付交便妥至於
該先友骸骨着西人毛連拿壹同寄
返希為週理壹切不勝感盼之至事
欵為妥順復為荷並候

僑祺

李南翘　謹上　廿三 · 九 · 廿八

075

Letter from Lee Nam-kiu, Cuba, to Tung Wah Hospital on 28 September 1934

From the Office of Hoi Men Kung Po

Dear Directors of Tung Wah Hospital,

I enclose a cheque for 15 Hong Kong dollars. Please use the funds to cover the costs of sending the bones of Lee Chuk-nam *(Li Zhunan)*, Lee Wai-loi *(Li Weilai)* and Yip Tat-pak *(Ye Dabai)* to the designated address marked on the boxes. I have asked a foreigner, Molina to repatriate the bones to Hong Kong. Please take the bones into your care after they arrive.

Thank you for your efforts. I await your reply.

I wish you well.

Yours sincerely,
Lee Nam-kiu *(Li Nanqiao)*

28 September of the 23rd year of the Republic of China

古巴磨連拿致東華醫院信件

1934 年 10 月 3 日

東華醫院諸善長均鑒　久仰
斗山無緣識荊望風怄不盡葵傾比維
　　旅祉吉祥善事崇建為頌為祝敬啟
　　者[僕]雖古巴藉人而與貴國同胞非常
　　親善而對於華友之不幸在古逝世
　　者尤為哀悼不置所謂遠適異國昔
　　人已悲更不幸夙志未酧而埋骨於異
　　鄉其悲哀痛恨為何如耶[僕]雖至愚
　　同是人類寧不悲感故每覩此白楊荒
　　塚啼血鵑聲歲歲寒食化鶴難歸能
　　勿為之傷心哉是以惻然而悲倏然而哀
　　爰有籌運先友骨殖附回貴國之舉
　　俾魂兮之得以归來而生者之得以憑祭
　　而死者亦得正首邱矣此乃意至善也
　　今者業已將办理先友之骨殖落船手續
　　完竣茲將儎紙一張附呈
貴院[僕]素知 貴院專办理慈善事務為
　　宗旨如抵埗之日請即起運先友之骨殖
　　暫时存貯於　貴院計冧各先友之骨
　　殖共弍拾具如費用幾何請向各先
　　友之戚屬收回便妥[僕]業已去函通知
　　各先友之親人到港領收矣臨風佈臆
　　不盡欲言倘逢郵便望惠德音肅此
　　並候

善祺

古巴國人[弟]磨連拿謹上

一九三四年、十、三

Letter from Molina, Cuba to Tung Wah Hospital on 3 October 1934

Dear benevolent Directors of Tung Wah Hospital,

I have long admired your good selves for your gracious acts of benevolence and would love to have the chance to meet you some day. Even though I am Cuban, I am very close to your countrymen. It saddens me when my Chinese friends pass away in Cuba – their wishes unfulfilled, their spirits yearning to return to their homeland. We are all humans. Whenever I see the desolate graves of my deceased Chinese friends, I feel unbearable pain. I learn that arrangements can be made to send the remains of deceased friends back to their hometown through you, so that those living can pay their respects to the deceased and those who have passed away can find eternal peace. These are utter acts of philanthropy. Now I am repatriating the bones of deceased friends and have finished the necessary procedures. The bones of the deceased friends have been loaded on a ship. I also enclose a bill of lading for your reference. I understand performing deeds of benevolence is one of your hospital's missions. Please take the bones, 20 sets in total, into your care after they arrive in Hong Kong, and collect the incurred fees from the deceased's families. I have written to the deceased's families and asked them to come to Hong Kong to collect the bones. I am most grateful to you for your assistance.

I await your reply, and I wish you well.

Yours humbly,
Molina, Cuban

3 October 1934

東華醫院善長执事先生大鑒敬啓者茲接湾城遡源堂慈
　善會通告謂九月十日將湾城先骸付船歸國未悉現在
　抵步否如抵步後未悉貴院代轉与先友原籍各縣慈善機關候親
　屬領囬或要親到貴院領取因[弟]先父遺骸亦由該帮
　運囬係書（黃文禧順德第七區龍山海口埠忠興社）[弟]今
　不在順德居住遷往南海九江落籍故先父遺骸亦欲運囬
　九江安葬如貴院代運各先友囬原籍請將該號骨殖
　運囬南海九江可也切勿運往順德深盼貴院賜函示知俾得明
　白領取手續不勝感銘之至矣專此敬候

台安

　　　　　　　　　　　　　　　[弟]黃植鴻謹上　廿三年十月廿二日

　　通訊處　南海九江大正坊怡昌押交[弟]收可也

077 Letter from Wong Chik-hung, China, to Tung Wah Hospital on 22 October 1934

Dear Managers of Tung Wah Hospital,

I have been notified by Sue Yuen Tong, Havana, Cuba, that the remains of deceased friends have been repatriated by sea on 10 September. I wonder if the remains have arrived in Hong Kong. If they have, will your esteemed hospital send them to the charitable associations in the deceased's hometown for their families to collect? Or is it necessary for the deceased's families to claim the remains from your esteemed hospital in Hong Kong? The remains of my late father Wong Man-hei *(Huang Wenxi)* of Chung Hing Society *(Zhongxing She)*, Lung Shan Hoi Hau Port *(Long Shan Haikou Bu)*, The Seventh District *(Diqi Qu)*, Shun Tak *(Shunde)* are among this batch. I have moved to Kau Kong *(Jiujiang)*, Nam Hoi *(Nanhai)*, and would thus like to lay my father to rest here. If your esteemed hospital will send the remains to the deceased's hometown, please send my late father's remains to Kau Kong, Nam Hoi and do not send them to Shun Tak. I should be most grateful if your esteemed hospital can notify me of the procedures for claiming the remains of my late father. I await your reply.

I am very grateful to you and I wish you well.

Yours sincerely,
Wong Chik-hung *(Huang Zhihong)*

22 October of the 23rd year of the Republic of China

Correspondence address:
Yee Cheong Pawn Shop *(Yichang Ya)*, Dai Ching Fong *(Dazheng Fang)*, Kau Kong, Nam Hoi

旅秘中山會館用箋
SOCIEDAD CHUNG SANG HUY CUN

東華醫院

諸位執事先生大鑒敬啓者茲有先友孫公耀生遺

　　骸一具由^弟經手办妥交是期日本輪船墨洋丸号

　　運返

貴院如該日輪抵步時請即派人將該骸起上代為

　　存下俟孫耀生之子孫培君乘是期美輪隨後到

　　时當來

貴院領取帶返家鄉安葬經另函交孫培君收执

　　如孫培到院時請照交渠收領為荷專此奉瀆

　　敬候

公安

　附載紙一張請查照收入

^弟歐陽安上

一九三四年十月廿四日

078 Letter from Sociedad Chung Sang Huy Cun, Peru, to Tung Wah Hospital on 24 October 1934

From the Office of Sociedad Chung Sang Huy Cun

Dear Managers of Tung Wah Hospital,

I have repatriated the remains of deceased friend Suen Yiu-sang *(Sun Yaosheng)* on the Japanese ship *Bokuyo Maru*. When the ship arrives in Hong Kong, please unload the remains and take them into your care. Suen Pui *(Sun Pei)*, son of Suen Yiu-sang, who is travelling to Hong Kong on an American vessel will take the remains to the deceased's hometown for burial. I have already written a letter to Suen Pui. When he comes to your esteemed hospital, please hand over the remains to him.

Thank you very much for your assistance.

I wish you well.

Please see enclosed bill of lading for your reference.

Yours sincerely,
Au Yeung On *(Ouyang An)*

24 October 1934

林西河堂用箋
SAY JO JON

香港東華醫院

执事先生^{伟鑒}風和日暖夏節祈長人民舒暢草木逢生

　　恭維

諸公時度麗景韶光快怡財源春簡福祉亨泰唯

　　頌唯賀^{同人等}學疎才短貽笑大方憾雲暮之遠

　　隔愧蕪札之未候能不瀚顏引瞻蘭采曷馨葵傾

　　所望者金鍼時賜以闬乎茅塞是有願事

　　逕啓者^{敝堂}籌運先昆仲骨殖回國慈善會經

　　前星期曾將先昆仲骨殖七十具执拾完妥过箱定扵本

　　年六月三號搭大來輪船公司直頭船附上貴院

　　收勞照箱面姓名縣鎮區鄉遞寄到各處慈善会

　　機閞俾該先昆仲之親属淂于就地領回殯塟以安

　　竂歹而妥先靈茲由紐約銀行滙上戝紙壹張伸港銀壹

　　佰四拾元交貴院收作慈善費到祈笑納請勿以少見嫌幸

　　甚至事完妥者請惠德音祈賜指南^{同人等}感德难忘容

　　當酬报扵萬一遙祝諸公前途勝利獲福無量矣草

　　此并達上

仁安

中華民國廿四年西曆六月十一日

^{古巴}^{湾城}林西河堂総理錦沛^{暨仝人等}^謹^上
慈善會會長榮樂

另一人註：已复

079 Letter from Say Jo Jon, Habana, Cuba, to Tung Wah Hospital on 11 June 1935

From the Office of Say Jo Jon

Dear Managers of Tung Wah Hospital,

Under the warm summer breeze, people are comfortable and relaxed while vegetation flourished. May you be blessed with prosperity and longevity. The benevolence of your good selves is known far and wide. Incompetent and inexperienced as we are, we long for the chance to meet you and learn from you.

We are an association handling repatriation of clansmen's bones. We exhumed and packed the remains of our 70 deceased clan brothers into boxes last week and repatriated them to Hong Kong on a direct vessel of Dollar Shipping Company on 3 June this year. When the remains arrive in Hong Kong, please take them into your care, and send them to the charitable associations in the deceased's hometown according to the information on the boxes, so that the deceased's families can collect the remains for burial. In this way, the deceased's spirits can find eternal peace.

We enclose a cheque for 140 Hong Kong dollars, issued by Bank of New York, as our donation to your esteemed hospital. We are sorry for only contributing the small amount.

When you have completed the repatriation, please write to let us know. We are most grateful to you for your kind assistance.

We wish you well.

Yours sincerely,
Kam-pui *(Jinpei)*, Director of Say Jo Jon, Habana, Cuba, Wing-lok *(Rongle)*, Chairman of the benevolent association and fellow members

11 June of the 24th year of the Republic of China

Another person's remarks: Replied

古巴灣城中華總會館用箋
Casino Chung Wah

東華醫院
列位執事先生惠鑒逕啟者本總會舘為旅古巴三

　　萬餘華僑之總機關近以轄屬之中華總義山各

　　先僑遺骨纍纍滿目亟待清理爰特發起籌

　　運各先僑骨殖囬國以安先靈並決定託由

貴醫院在港接收轉發內地各屬慈善機關收領

　　素仰

貴醫院執事先生辦理慈善事業夙具精神與

　　經驗仁風遠播薄海同欽對于本會舘之懇託

　　定能接納茲者第一期先僑骨殖共計四百八十

　　具（分載十二大箱每箱四拾具）定于本月十七日由

　　灣附交大來公司波市總統輪船載返香港到

　　時懇為接收依照箱面所列地址轉附內地各屬

　　附近慈善機關以便其親屬就近領收可也茲

　　凂由陳亮明先生交上港銀九百陸拾員請為察

　　收此欵作為

貴醫院辦理此事搬遷及轉寄各屬等費用（葬

　　費另由各先僑親屬自備）妥收後希為示覆一

　　音並祈迅速轉發各屬以慰各先僑親屬之望

　　為荷諸事多勞不勝銘感盼念之至耑此奉

　　達即頌

台祺

　　　　　　　　　　　　旅古巴灣城中華總會館朱家兆　敬上
　　　　　　　　　　　　　　書記李南翹
　　　　　　　　　　　　　（印章：古巴中華總會館）

中華民國廿四年六月十二日

080 Letter from Casino Chung Wah, Habana, Cuba, to Tung Wah Hospital on 12 June 1935

From the Office of Casino Chung Wah

Dear Managers of Tung Wah Hospital,

Our association serves more than 30,000 Chinese compatriots in Cuba. At the Chinese Communal Graveyard managed by us, there are bones of our deceased friends everywhere. We decided to exhume the bones and repatriate them to the deceased's hometown for burial. We would like to ask your esteemed hospital to take the bones into your care in Hong Kong, and then send them to the charitable associations in the deceased's hometown.

We have long heard about the charitable deeds of your esteemed hospital and admired your benevolence. We are confident that you have vast experiences and would help us with the repatriation. The first batch of bones, 480 sets in total (placed in 12 large boxes; 40 sets per box), will be repatriated to Hong Kong from Havana on the *SS President Pierce* of Dollar Shipping Company on 17th of this month. When the bones arrive in Hong Kong, please take them into your care and send them to the charitable associations in the mainland according to the addresses marked on the boxes, so that the deceased's families can claim and collect the bones. Meanwhile, we have asked Chan Leung-ming *(Chen Liangming)* to hand over 960 Hong Kong dollars to cover the costs of repatriation (the burial fees will be borne by the deceased's families). Please acknowledge receipt of the funds, and please send the remains to the deceased's hometown at your earliest convenience to ease the mind of the families.

We are most grateful to you for your efforts.

Yours sincerely,
Chu Ka-siu *(Zhu Jiazhao)* and Lee Nam-kiu *(Li Nanqiao)*, Secretary
Casino Chung Wah, Habana, Cuba

12 June of the 24th year of the Republic of China

(Stamp: Casino Chung Wah, Centro Principal, AMISTAD 128 2º PISOS, HABANA, CUBA)

中國曹灼才致東華醫院信件

1935 年 8 月 6 日

東華醫院列位先生公鑒啟者現在古
巴国埠運櫬先友曹灼林骨殖回国
未知底步可否或到步之期仰望
先生再運回番禺高唐圩昌後堂
處以便先友家人領取可也說及香
港異地並無兄弟在處謀生愚弟不
識貴地無人倚賴难以到步否特付乙函
希望各位先生着力運回免至
掛念感謝恩德無涯矣接信之後
早日回音可也祝頌

精神

但回信寄廣州番禺龍歸市寿春堂葯店
宝号收轉交柏塘村曹灼才收便合

愚弟曹灼才　付

中華民國廿四年七月初八日

081 **Letter from Cho Cheuk-choi, China, to Tung Wah Hospital on 6 August 1935**

Dear Directors of Tung Wah Hospital,

The bones of Cho Cheuk-lam *(Cao Zhuolin)* were repatriated from Cuba. I wonder if the bones have arrived in Hong Kong. When they arrive, please send them to Chong How Tong *(Chang Hou Tang)*, Ko Tong Market Town *(Gaotang Xu)* at Pun Yu *(Pangyu)* so that they can be collected by the deceased's family. I do not know anyone in Hong Kong. I am also not familiar with your city and have no one to rely on, so it is very difficult for me to come to Hong Kong. I should be most grateful if you can help send the bones back to his hometown. I await your reply.

I wish you well.

Please send your reply to Cho Cheuk-choi of Pak Tong Village *(Botang Cun)*, c/o Sau Chun Tong Herbal Shop *(Shouchun Tang Yaodian)*, Lung Gui City *(Longgui Shi)*, Pun Yu, Canton *(Guangzhou)*.

Yours sincerely,
Cho Cheuk-choi *(Cao Zhuocai)*

8th day of the 7th lunar month of the 24th year of the Republic of China

古巴中華總會舘用箋
Casino Chung Wah

東華醫院諸執事先生均鑒

　　逕啓者本總會舘办理第一期先友骨殖
　　已扵六月间寄由大來輪船公司裝載回
　　國計拾二箱共四百八拾具交　貴院收另凂陳
　　亮明君就近轉交戾紙式張值港銀九百六拾元
　　諒卜抵埠收妥今又办第二期先友骨殖共
　　一百零八具分裝三大箱亦由大來公司们羅船
　　裝載回國八月十二日由啓行又凂陳亮明君
　　轉交戾乕壹張值港銀二百一拾四元至時統希
　　察收此款乃本總會舘捐交　貴院為慈
　　善等費然对扵先友骨殖如抵埠時尚望
　　妥為料理按箱面縣份地址轉運入內地各
　　慈善機関以候其親属收領素仰
　　貴院諸執事先生办理慈善夙具精神仁
　　風遠播薄海同欽對於本總會舘之恳託諒
　　能接納故敢再次矣倘前後二次款項兩期
　　先友骨殖如能收妥迅速覆函以慰先僑在
　　古之親属可也諸多費神不勝感盼之至謹
　　此上達並頌

公祺

中華總會舘　總理朱家兆
　　　　　　書記李南翹

中華民國廿四年八月拾二日

（印章：古巴中華總會舘）

載乕弍張

082 Letter from Casino Chung Wah, Habana, Cuba, to Tung Wah Hospital on 12 August 1935

From the Office of Casino Chung Wah

Dear Managers of Tung Wah Hospital,

We had repatriated the first batch of the bones of our deceased friends to your esteemed hospital on a ship of Dollar Shipping Company in June. There were 480 sets of remains, placed in 12 boxes. We had also asked Chan Leung-ming *(Chen Liangming)* to bring you two cheques for 960 Hong Kong dollars. We believe you have taken delivery of the bones and received the cheques.

We are now repatriating the second batch of bones. There are 108 sets of bones placed in three large boxes. They have been despatched on the *SS President Monroe* of Dollar Shipping Company on 12 August. Chan Ming-leung will bring you another cheque for 214 Hong Kong dollars as our donation to your esteemed hospital. When the bones of our deceased friends arrive in Hong Kong, please take them into your care and send them to the charitable associations in mainland according to the addresses marked on the boxes, so that the deceased's families can collect the bones.

We have long heard about your acts of kindness and we trust you will help us with the repatriation again. Please write to us as soon as possible to acknowledge receipt of the bones and the funds of the two batches, so that the minds of the deceased's relatives in Cuba are eased.

Thank you very much for your efforts.

Yours sincerely,
Chu Ka-siu *(Zhu Jiazhao)*, Director and Lee Nam-kiu *(Li Nanqiao)*, Secretary
Casino Chung Wah, Habana, Cuba

(Stamp: Casino Chung Wah, Centro Principal, AMISTAD 128 2° PISOS, HABANA, CUBA)

12 August of the 24th year of the Republic of China

Two bills of lading enclosed

香港旅港鶴山商會致東華醫院信件

1935年8月12日

旅港鶴山商會用箋

東華醫院
大司理先生台鑒逕復者
來書敬悉至該古巴埠
先友骨殖請即轉知陳
洪代運返鄉交沙坪同善
堂收領便合先此奉復
并請

善祺

會長葉蘭泉（印章：旅港鶴山商會）

乙亥年七月十四日

083 Letter from Hok Shan Chamber of Commerce in Hong Kong to Tung Wah Hospital on 12 August 1935

From the Office of Hok Shan Chamber of Commerce in Hong Kong

Dear Manager of Tung Wah Hospital,

Your letter is well received. Should the bones of our deceased friends from Cuba arrive in Hong Kong, please inform Chan Hung to send them to Sha Ping Tung Sin Tong *(Shaping Tong Shan Tang)* in our hometown.

Yours sincerely,
Yip Lan-chuen *(Ye Lanquan)*
Chairman
(Stamp: Hok Shan Chamber of Commerce in Hong Kong)

14th day of the 7th lunar month, Year of Yuet Hoi *(Yihai)*

香港台山商會用牋

東華医院执事先生^鑒頃接來函內開
　　古巴各埠運囬先友骨殖^{敝邑}着壹佰
　　伍拾具容日着陳洪由^{敝會}具領到
　　貴院点交運入台城義庄召領安葬至
　　外埠有無運費葬金請悉數送來^{敝會}
　　簽收是荷此复并請

善祺

（印章：香港台山商會書束）

中華民國廿四年八月十二日

Letter from Toi Shan Association of Hong Kong to Tung Wah Hospital on 12 August 1935

From the Office of Toi Shan Association of Hong Kong

Dear Managers of Tung Wah Hospital,

We received your letter informing us that the bones of 150 deceased friends from our county had been repatriated from Cuba. We will ask Chan Hung to collect the bones from your esteemed hospital and send them to Toi Shing Coffin Home *(Taicheng Yizhuang)* for the deceased's families to claim. Should there be any transportation and burial fees sending from Cuba, please send to us.

We await your reply, and we wish you well.

Yours sincerely,
(Stamp: Toi Shan Association of Hong Kong)

12 August of the 24th year of the Republic of China

駐港中山僑商會所用箋

逕啟者現准　台函藉悉從古巴運到敝邑籍先
友骨殖五十二具查其中卅具属黃梁都者應運
交斗門億中舘二具属前山者应運交前山福善
堂其餘廿具則運交石岐與善堂当由敝會預函
以上三處知照并代登廣告招領但各先友除支
運費外有無葬費餘存統希闹列清單撥付敝
會以便分發各該家属具領安葬歿存均感矣此致

東華醫院执事先生

（印章：駐港中山僑商會所）程名譽

主席　郭　泉

黃石泉

中華民國廿四年八月十四日

085

Letter from Chung Shan Commercial Association, Hong Kong, to Tung Wah Hospital on 14 August 1935

From the Office of Chung Shan Commercial Association, Hong Kong

Dear Managers of Tung Wah Hospital,

Thank you for your letter informing us that 52 sets of bones had been repatriated to our native county from Cuba. Among them, 30 sets belonged to native of Wong Leung Do *(Huang Liangdu)* and they should be sent to Yik Chung Kwun *(Yizhong Guan)*, Dou Mun *(Doumen)*. Two sets belonged to native of Chin Shan *(Qianshan)* and they should be sent to Fook Sin Tong *(Fu Shan Tang)*, Chin Shan. The remaining 20 sets should be transported to Yu Sin Tong *(Yu Shan Tang)*, Shekki *(Shiqi)*. We will write to the benevolent associations and ask them to publish announcements calling on the deceased's families to claim the bones. Meanwhile, after paying the transportation charges, is there any money left that can be offered to the deceased's families as burial fees? Please provide us with detailed information so that we can hand over to the deceased's families.

The deceased and their families are most grateful to you for your efforts.

Yours sincerely,
Kwok Chuen *(Guo Quan)*, Chairman
Ching Ming-yu *(Cheng Mingyu)*
Wong Shek-chuen *(Huang Shiquan)*
(Stamp: Chung Shan Commercial Association, Hong Kong)

14 August of the 24th year of the Republic of China

駐港開平商務公所用箋
HOI PING COMMERCIAL CHAMBER

東華醫院

執事先生台鑒昨接八月十二号

來函以

貴院接由古巴湾中華會館付囬^敝邑先友骨

殖叄拾叄具应運囬^敝邑某會所或某善堂

接收俾各先友親属就地領取着為函复以便轉

運等語查恩開廣福堂在阓平百合圩設有

廣福堂義祠一所專係辦理接收由外洋運囬恩

平阓平两邑先友骨殖之機関用特函复

貴院請即將此次由古巴湾中華會館付囬^敝邑

之先友骨殖運囬阓平百合圩廣福堂義祠接

收以便各先友親属就近領取是盼專此希复

即頌

公安

（印章：香港開平商務公所）謹復

中華民國廿四年八月十五日

086

Letter from Hoi Ping Commercial Chamber, Hong Kong, to Tung Wah Hospital on 15 August 1935

From the Office of Hoi Ping Commercial Chamber

Dear Managers of Tung Wah Hospital,

Yesterday, we received your letter dated 12 August informing that 33 sets of bones of deceased friends from our county had been repatriated from Casino Chung Wah in Cuba. The bones should be sent to their respective native associations or benevolent associations for the deceased's families to collect. And you were expecting our reply where the bones should be despatched.

As far as we know, the Yan Hoi Kwong Fook Tong *(Enkai Guang Fu Tang)* operates Kwong Fook Tong Communal Ancestral Hall *(Guang Fu Tang Yici)* in Bak Hop Market Town *(Baihe Xu)*, Hoi Ping *(Kaiping)*, to handle the bones of deceased Yan Ping and Hoi Ping native repatriated from abroad. Therefore, we send this letter to advise you to take delivery of the remains sent by Casino Chung Wah, Cuba and send them to Kwong Fook Tong Communal Ancestral Hall at Bak Hop Market Town for the deceased's families to collect.

We await your reply.

We are most grateful to you for your efforts, and we wish you well.

Yours sincerely,
(Stamp: Hoi Ping Commercial Chamber, Hong Kong)

15 August of the 24th year of the Republic of China

僑港新會商會用牋

函复者項准
貴院函闲敝院接古巴灣中華會館來函並于本
年七月初五日用亞丹士輪船運到各邑先友骨殖
共四百八十具委敝院將各邑先友骨殖代運囘各
該鄉以安窀穸查貴邑占壹百六十壹具至应運囘
貴邑某会所或某善堂接收以便各先友親屬
就地領取希為示复俾得代運囘鄉等由准此
查敝邑所占該項骨殖应運囘新会城仁安醫
院接收便妥相应函复即請
查照代運為荷此致

東華醫院

新会商會司理劉毓芸

中華民國廿四年八月十五日（印章：僑港新會商會）

087 Letter from Sun Wui Commercial Association of Hong Kong, to Tung Wah Hospital on 15 August 1935

From the Office of Sun Wui Commercial Association of Hong Kong

For the attention of Tung Wah Hospital,

We received a letter from your esteemed hospital saying that you had received 480 sets of bones repatriated on *SS President Adams* by Casino Chung Wah, Havana, Cuba, on the 5th day of the 7th lunar month this year and were entrusted to send the bones to the deceased's hometown for burial. You were also advised that 161 sets should be transported to their respective native associations or benevolent associations for the deceased's families to collect and asked us to reply to you about the details so that you could send the bones to our county.

In reply to your enquiry, please send the bones to Yan On Hospital *(Ren'an Yiyuan)* in Sun Wui City *(Xinhui Cheng)* at your earliest convenience.

Thank you very much for your efforts.

Yours sincerely,
Lau Yuk-wan *(Liu Yuyun)*
Manager, Sun Wui Commercial Association
(Stamp: Sun Wui Commercial Association of Hong Kong)

15 August of the 24th year of the Republic of China

古巴灣城隴西慈善會辦事處用箋
LONG SAI LI

東華醫院總理执事先生大鑒逕啓者本會

　　扵陽歷八月十弍日已由大來輪船公司付來

　　先昆仲骨殖共計八十具分為弍箱到步

　　祈為收妥分發各處善堂以便其親属收領

　　不勝感激修德必獲報矣茲者因未稔

　　尊址項由康年儲蓄銀行李星衢冕卿

　　兩先生處付上港赤弍張共銀弍佰伍拾元

　　以壹佰五十元為運骨殖費另壹佰元為

　　敬送　貴院以作香油之需到步祈查收希

　　即　賜复以免企望肅此敬祝

貴院諸执事

前途發達

古巴
灣城　李隴西慈善會李瑞生謹上

瑞良
沾聖

（印章：古巴灣京隴西商旅自治講習所）

大中華民國廿四年八月十五日陽歷

088 Letter from Long Sai Li Benevolent Association, Habana, Cuba, to Tung Wah Hospital on 15 August 1935

From the Office of Long Sai Li Benevolent Association

Dear Directors and Managers of Tung Wah Hospital,

We repatriated the bones of 80 deceased friends, placed in two boxes, on a ship of Dollar Shipping Company on 12 August. When the bones arrive in Hong Kong, please send them to the respective benevolent associations of the deceased's hometown for collection by their families. We are most grateful to you for your kind assistance.

As we are not sure about the address of your hospital, we have asked Lee Sing-kui *(Li Xingqu)* and Min-hing *(Mian Qing)* of Hong Nin Bank to send you two cheques for 250 Hong Kong dollars in total – 150 dollars to cover transportation fees of the remains and 100 dollars of oil money to your esteemed hospital. Please acknowledge receipt of the funds immediately to ease our mind.

May you have a prosperous future.

Yours sincerely,
Lee Shui-sang *(Li Ruisheng)*
Lee Shui-leung *(Li Ruiliang)*
Lee Chim-sing *(Li Zhansheng)*
Long Sai Li Benevolent Association, Habana, Cuba

(Stamp: Long Sai Li Merchants Autonomy Learning Office, Habana, Cuba)

15 August of the 24th year of the Republic of China

旅港鶴山商會用箋

東華醫院大執事先生台鑒

敬復者前月得接來諭敬悉
種切至於古巴華僑總會此
次運囬先友之骨殖內有一具
屬於敝邑先友者因是日未
得葉會長吩示辦法以故
未能刻即裁會抱歉之
至隨於即晚轉知運棺人
陳洪君因敝邑有先友骨殖
百餘件候船運返沙坪
同善堂代收着該家屬到
領等情囑陳君將古巴先
友骨殖統希運返并轉達
貴院知照今日將古巴先友名
字抄白請葉會長簽字寄
返矣祈知之此請

善安

書記室謹覆（印章：旅港鶴山商會）

乙年九月廿四日

089

Letter from Hok Shan Chamber of Commerce in Hong Kong to Tung Wah Hospital on 21 October 1935

From the Office of Hok Shan Chamber of Commerce in Hong Kong

Dear Manager of Tung Wah Hospital,

We received your letter informing us that among the bones repatriated by Casino Chung Wah in Cuba, one set of bones should belong to a deceased friend from our county. We did not reply right away as we were awaiting the instruction of our Chairman Yip *(Ye)*. We apologize for that.

We had told Chan Hung *(Chen Hong)*, the person undertaking the repatriation of the bones that, as there were some 100 sets of bones awaiting transportation to Tung Sin Tong *(Tong Shan Tang)* in Sha Ping *(Shaping)*, where they would be collected by the deceased families, the bones of the deceased friends repatriated from Cuba should be sent along with those. We hereby notify your esteemed hospital of this arrangement.

We will send another letter, bearing the names of the deceased friends from Cuba and signed by Chairman Yip, to your esteemed hospital.

We wish you well.

Yours sincerely,
Secretariat
(Stamp: Hok Shan Chamber of Commerce in Hong Kong)

24th day of the 9th lunar month, Year of Yuet Hoi *(Yihai)*

中國中山與善堂致東華醫院信件

1935年10月15日

香港慈善平糶義倉與善堂蔭遠堂追遠堂用箋

東華醫院列位先生鑒啓者頃由陳
洪船運到古巴湾中華會館付返各先友
黃禮容等骨殖共弍拾具已照点明入
院存俟各伊親属到領便是此請

善安

（印章：中山與善堂）

中華民國廿四年十月十五日

090 Letter from Yu Sin Tong, Chung Shan, China, to Tung Wah Hospital on 15 October 1935

From the Office of Rice for Charity of Hong Kong, Yu Sin Tong, Yam Yuen Tong and Chui Yuen Tong

Dear Directors of Tung Wah Hospital,

We have received the bones of 20 deceased friends including those of Wong Lai-yung *(Huang Lirong)*, repatriated by Casino Chung Wah in Havana, Cuba, on a boat operated by Chan Hung *(Chen Hong)*. The bones are now stored in our hospital awaiting collection by the deceased's families.

I wish you well.

Yours sincerely,
(Stamp: Yu Sin Tong, Chung Shan) *(Yu Shan Tang, Zhongshan)*

15 October of the 24th year of the Republic of China

東華醫院

执事先生台鑒昨奉十月十七日

大函拜悉種切查^敝堂向來接到外埠慈善

機關付來先友骨殖名単及葬費即在港付印

先友名單多份連同葬費付回開平百合圩^敝堂義

祠分別給領同時將先友名單分寄開恩兩縣

各圩市當眾地方標貼以便各先友親属週知

到領凡外埠慈善機關並無葬費付回者^敝堂

亦每具發給葬費弍元以安窀穸據

來示所称古巴中華會館付回^敝邑属先友骨殖

六十具經于夏歷七月廿一日交陳洪記運往開平百

合圩^敝堂義祠當時並曾將姓名籍貫分別開

列付去但^敝堂現尚未接到先友名単無從付印

用特函請

貴院即將夏歷七月廿一日運回^敝邑属之先友骨殖

六十具姓名籍貫查抄一份交下俾得付印寄回

^敝邑屬分貼公佈以便各先友親属週知到領是盼

專此奉懇並頌

台安

惠函交德付道中三百一十三號四樓敝堂便得覆

（印章：開恩廣福堂書束）民廿四、十、廿二

091 Letter from Hoi Yan Kwong Fook Tong, Hong Kong, to Tung Wah Hospital on 22 October 1935

Dear Managers of Tung Wah Hospital,

Thank you for your letter dated 17 October and we are able to know more about the matters. In fact, whenever we receive name lists and burial fees for the bones of deceased friends repatriated from overseas benevolent associations, we make several copies of the name lists in Hong Kong and send them, along with the burial fees, to the communal ancestral hall of our association in Bak Hop Market Town *(Baihe Xu)*, Hoi Ping *(Kaiping)*. The name lists would also be sent to various market places in Hoi Ping and Yan Ping *(Enping)*, where they would be put up on public notice boards to inform the families of the deceased to collect their bones. In the case that no burial fees are offered by the overseas benevolent associations, we give 2 dollars as burial fees to the family of each deceased friend.

According to your last letter, the bones of 60 deceased friends from our county, repatriated by Casino Chung Wah in Cuba, have been sent to the communal ancestral hall of our association in Bak Hop Market Town, Hoi Ping on the 21st day of the 7th lunar month through Chan Hung Kee, whereas the lists of the deceased's names and hometown would be sent to us separately. However, we have not received the name lists and cannot make copies. So we write to you again. Please send us the name lists for the 60 deceased friends from our county, whose bones were repatriated on the 21st day of the 7th lunar month. We would like to send copies of the lists to our county, so that they can be put up to inform the families of the deceased to collect the bones.

We are most grateful to you for your kindness.

We wish you well.

Please reply to us at 4/F, 313 Des Voeux Road Central.

(Stamp: Hoi Yan Kwong Fook Tong, Hong Kong)

22 October of the 24th year of the Republic of China

香港開恩廣福堂致東華醫院信件

1935 年 10 月 28 日

東華醫院
执事先生台鑒疊奉
大函並先友人名单二張均經祗悉承
詢古巴中華総會舘運囬[敝]邑屬先友骨殖壹
拾柒具应運囬某會所接收着即函复等語該
帮先友骨殖請照旧運囬開平百合圩[敝]堂義
祠收領以便轉給各先友親属領囬安葬可也專此奉
复即頌

台安

開恩廣福堂謹啟（印章：開恩廣福堂書柬）
廿四、十、廿八

Letter from Hoi Yan Kwong Fook Tong, Hong Kong, to Tung Wah Hospital on 28 October 1935

Dear Managers of Tung Wah Hospital,

We had received your letter and two name lists of the deceased friends. You inquired to which association the 17 sets of bones repatriated by Casino Chung Wah in Cuba should be sent and were waiting for our reply. Please send the remains to the communal ancestral hall of our association in Bak Hop Market Town *(Baihe Xu)*, Hoi Ping *(Kaiping)* as before so that they can be handed over to the families of the deceased for burial.

We wish you well.

Yours sincerely,
Hoi Yan Kwong Fook Tong
(Stamp: Hoi Yan Kwong Fook Tong)

28 October of the 24th year of the Republic of China

僑港新會商會用牋

逕啓者查古巴夏灣中華会館扵乙亥七月初五由亞
丹士船運返之敝邑先友骨殖一百六十一具前承
貴院函詢應寄交何處接收當經函复請交新会
城仁安医院在案現接本港古井達善堂來函請求
將該批骨殖中之屬扵該堂關係各鄉者寄交新会
縣古井達善堂接收較為利便即由加拿大普乐先
律各輪寄到之同樣骨殖亦請寄交該堂接收等語
查所請尚屬可行除函复該堂外相応抄同骨殖名
兩紙函達
貴院查照請將开列之骨殖寄交新会縣古井達
善堂接收至所餘由亞丹士輪運返之骨殖仍請交新
会城仁安医院接收所有運葬費統交敝会具領是
荷此致

東華医院
　　附骨殖名錄兩紙

新会商会司理　劉毓芸
（印章：僑港新會商會）

中華民國廿四年十一月四日

093 **Letter from The San Wui Commercial Society, Hong Kong, to Tung Wah Hospital on 4 November 1935**

From the Office of The San Wui Commercial Society, Hong Kong

To Tung Wah Hospital,

Casino Chung Wah in Havana, Cuba, repatriated the bones of 161 deceased friends of our county on the 5th day of the 7th lunar month in the Year of Yuet Hoi *(Yihai)*. We received a letter from your esteemed hospital asking where the bones should be sent. In our previous reply, we asked you to send the bones to Yan On Hospital *(Ren'an Yiyuan)* in Sun Wui Town *(Xinhui Cheng)*. Now, Kwu Tseng Tat Sin Tong *(Gujing Da Shan Tang)* in Hong Kong informed us that it would be more convenient to send the bones of the deceased friends affiliated with them to Kwu Tseng Tat Sin Tong in Sun Wui County *(Xinhui Xian)*. They also asked for bones repatriated on the Canadian ships be sent to Kwu Tseng Tat Sin Tong in Sun Wui County. We consider this feasible. Apart from writing to them, we have also sent to your esteemed hospital a list of the deceased friends whose bones should be sent to Kwu Tseng Tat Sin Tong in Sun Wui. As to the remaining bones repatriated on the *SS President Adams*, please send them to Yan On Hospital in Sun Wui Town. Please pass all burial fees to us for arrangement.

Two lists of bones of deceased friends are enclosed.

Yours sincerely,
Lau Yuk-wan *(Liu Yuyun)*
Manager, San Wui Commercial Society

(Stamp: The San Wui Commercial Society, Hong Kong)

4 November of the 24th year of the Republic of China

南海縣佛山救濟院方便所用箋

逕覆者頃准
大函以現接古巴灣中華會館運到各邑先友骨殖四百八
十具着即代為遷回各該鄉以安窀穸茲將南邑先友譚
炳祥譚柏祥等骨殖二具着陳洪記運交敝方便所到希
查收并請轉致各先友親屬就地領取等由業經妥為查
收惟來函并未叙述該先友親屬姓名地址無從轉其就
地具領准函前由相應函復
查照希即將該先友譚炳祥譚柏祥等親屬姓名地址函復
過所以憑分別轉知就近領回安塋為荷此致

東華醫院
列位執事

（印章：南海縣佛山救濟院方便所）啓
（即原日佛山方便醫院）

中華民國廿四年十一月七日

094

Letter from Fut Shan Shelter, Nam Hoi, China, to Tung Wah Hospital on 7 November 1935

From the Office of Fut Shan Shelter *(Foshan Jiujiyuan Fangbian Suo)*, Nam Hoi County *(Nanhai Xian)*

Dear Managers of Tung Wah Hospital,

Thank you for your letter informing us that you were transporting the bones of 480 deceased friends repatriated by Casino Chung Wah in Havana, Cuba, for us to send to the deceased's hometown for burial. You also mentioned that among the 480 deceased friends, you had arranged Chan Hung Kee to send the bones of Tam Bing-cheung *(Tan Bingxiang)* and Tam Pak-cheung *(Tan Baixiang)*, who were native of Nam Hoi, to our shelter, and asked us to inform the deceased's families to claim the bones. We have already received the bones in order. However, since your letter did not mention the names and addresses of the deceased's families, we have no way to inform them to collect the bones. Please check and send us the names and addresses of the families of Tam Bing-cheung and Tam Pak-cheung, so that we can inform their families to claim the bones for burial.

Yours sincerely,
Fut Shan Shelter (Former Fut Shan Fong Bin Hospital)*(Foshan Jiujiyuan Fangbian Yiyuan)*

7 November of the 24th year of the Republic of China

鶴邑同善總堂用箋

東華医院総理先生^{鈞鑒}逕啟者茲本日接收到
貴院由陳洪艇運到古巴灣埠先友骨殖鍾大琛等共拾
叄具経即按照列來名冊点收妥當起貯義庄容即
通知各該親屬到領就是耑此復達并候

善安

鶴邑同善総堂啓
（印章：鶴邑同善總堂）

中華民國二十四年十一月十四日

095 Letter from Tung Sin Tong, Hok Shan, China, to Tung Wah Hospital on 14 November 1935

From the Office of Tung Sin Tong *(Tong Shan Tang)*, Hok Shan *(Heshan)*

Dear Directors of Tung Wah Hospital,

We received the bones of 13 deceased friends in order including those of Chung Tai-sum *(Zhong Dachen)*, repatriated from Havana, Cuba, through your esteemed hospital on a boat operated by Chan Hung. According to the name list provided by your esteemed hospital, we have checked the shipment in order. We have placed the bones in our coffin home and informed the deceased's families to collect them.

We wish you well.

Yours sincerely,
Tung Sin Tong, Hok Shan *(Heshan)*
(Stamp: Tung Sin Tong, Hok Shan)

14 November of the 24th year of the Republic of China

中國鶴邑同善總堂致東華醫院信件
1935 年 11 月 15 日

鶴邑同善總堂用箋

東華醫院

列位執事先生^{大鑒}敬啓者昨日接到

貴医院由陳洪記船載運到古巴湾敝邑籍之鍾大琛等先

友骨殖共拾叁具当經收妥函復　貴院知照惟未審該埠

先友骨殖有無隨葬費發給未荷明白声敍茲因急于發給

領葬故用特函達

貴院查照希為查明該埠先友骨殖有無隨葬費交給

與領葬者恳即明白賜示以便照办為荷耑此并候

善安

鶴邑同善総堂啓

（印章：鶴山同善總堂）

中華民國廿四年十一月十五日

再者伏查　貴院列來古巴埠先友姓名单皆無籍
貫里居佈告招領難扵週知恳請查明古巴中華會
館所列來姓名冊扵鍾大琛等先友名冊內抄列籍貫里居
復函示知以便照為佈告招領為祷又及此致

東華醫院先生

鶴邑同善総堂　啓
（印章：鶴山同善總堂）

中華民國二十四年十一月十五日

Letter from Tung Sin Tong, Hok Shan, China, to Tung Wah Hospital on 15 November 1935

From the Office of Tung Sin Tong *(Tong Shan Tang)*, Hok Shan

Dear Managers of Tung Wah Hospital,

We received the bones of Chung Tai-sum *(Zhong Dachen)* and those of other deceased friends from our county, 13 sets in total, repatriated from Havana, Cuba, through your esteemed hospital on a boat operated by Chan Hung Kee. We hereby acknowledge receipt of the bones.

We have no idea if any burial fees are offered to the deceased friends. Therefore, we write to you and ask you to find out if burial fees are offered for the deceased friends repatriated from Havana so that we can give the burial fees to the deceased's families as soon as possible. Please reply to us clearly and we will follow your instructions.

We await your reply and wish you well.

Yours sincerely,
Tung Sin Tong, Hok Shan *(Heshan)*
(Stamp: Tung Sin Tong, Hok Shan)

15 November of the 24th year of the Republic of China

Dear Managers of Tung Wah Hospital,

After further investigation, we found out that the list of deceased friends repatriated from Cuba did not contain any information about the deceased's native county and addresses. This makes it difficult for us to put up notices calling on the deceased's families to collect the remains. Please check with Casino Chung Wah of Cuba and inform us of the native county and addresses of the deceased friends including those of Chung Tai-sum, so that we can put up notices informing their families to collect their bones.

Thank you for your assistance.

Yours sincerely,
Tung Sin Tong, Hok Shan

(Stamp: Tung Sin Tong, Hok Shan)

15 November of the 24th year of the Republic of China

中國鶴邑同善總堂致東華醫院信件

1935 年 12 月 29 日

鶴邑同善總堂用箋

逕啓者茲本日接收到
貴院付交鴻利船運到古巴埠呂發骨殖壹具
經已收妥祈勿介懷為荷此致

東華醫院

鶴邑同善総堂　啓
（印章：鶴邑同善總堂）

中華民國廿四年十二月廿九日

097 — **Letter from Tung Sin Tong, Hok Shan, China, to Tung Wah Hospital on 29 December 1935**

From the Office of Tung Sin Tong *(Tong Shan Tang)*, Hok Shan *(Heshan)*

To Tung Wah Hospital,

This is to inform that we have received in order the bones of Lui Fat *(Lu Fa)*, repatriated from Cuba through your esteemed hospital on the *Hung Lee*. Please rest assured that the bones are in our care.

Yours sincerely,
Tung Sin Tong, Hok Shan
(Stamp: Tung Sin Tong, Hok Shan)

29 December of the 24th year of the Republic of China

北美洲西歸先友

東華醫院大善長执事先生大鑒敬覆者蒙旧歷元月

廿六日函達貴港工商銀行黃香蘭及林天木二位先生將

大善長函闻之件曾三月十四號轉達与^弟知云無名氏者每具

骸骨該医院改葬每具葬費乄七毛連金塔及工艇等費每

具共港乄壹元六毫便可照為办理等語至于己巳年三月廿

九日即西歷五月八號賜來大函內蒙大教指示亦與黃香蘭林天林先生等

前函皆同惟是各会館前日曾附回貴医院代办之事均由各会館

自理大約今日亦是相同旧日之办法所云各先友骸骨到港時均憑

貴医院料理先友去脚費仍每具亦有乄數元付歸家屬收領安

葬等情^弟所知者亦然也此以言有名氏及有縣屬者均歸各会

館支办妥当不用^弟助但^吾思此次之办与別不同亦斷無一人之力以办

中事独力难持因旧歲^弟入坑办事所到者旧地重逢所经見者先友

遺骸橫佈荒野牛羊踐踏闻者見者莫不慘然憐惜是以^弟就地

迫不得已向左右相近之處籌些款項执拾遺骸所望者各有縣属各有姓名將亡魂

有帰永享家人之祭祀但各有名姓者各縣各会館在處自行領回

自办支理妥当無容^弟一人担負惟指实無名氏者無人承領者^弟方敢

直告求請办法而已^弟仍然着人到各處訪尋如稍有所知遺骸之姓名

者仍求各人到來报名及縣属由此在處交各人收領或报有住上址者間有望付

回家人之收領更勝过義地之安葬也此事將实情报上仍然由^弟

一人担負火船載脚及医院代為安葬之費——籌妥時何月何日何船付

回港自当早日付上先友之名冊及無名氏亦当列明何號箱及共具数之

多宗與及箱头號之多宗此时报上懇乞代办感德不忘耑此呈

上並請

公　安

美國由舊金山三藩市奉

^弟梅耀文鞠躬

民國十八年五月初六日即西歷 1929 年六月十二號

Letter from Mui Yiu-man, USA, to Tung Wah Hospital on 12 June 1929

Dear benevolent Directors and Managers of Tung Wah Hospital,

You wrote to Wong Heung-lan (*Huang Xianglan*) and Lam Tin-muk (*Lin Tianmu*) of the Hong Kong Industrial and Commercial Bank on the 26th day of the 1st lunar month. They wrote to me on the 14th day of the 3rd lunar month enclosing your previous letter to them. I was then aware that the burial costs for each set of unidentified remains were 0.7 dollars, whereas the total handling costs for each set of remains were 1.6 Hong Kong dollars if the costs for the urn, labor and shipping were included. Your letter dated 29th day of the 3rd lunar month (8 May), 1929 to me contained instructions same as those mentioned in the letter from Wong Heung-lan and Lam Tin-muk to me. Previously, the benevolent associations made arrangements for the remains of deceased friends to be transported to your esteemed hospital themselves; I believe the same should apply today. It was said that after the remains arrive in Hong Kong, your esteemed hospital would deduct the handling charge [from the funds sent by the benevolent associations], and out of the remaining funds, a few dollars would be given to the family of each deceased friend to help them pay for burial. This is also what I know. The benevolent associations usually take care of the repatriation if the deceased's names and native counties are known, and they do not require my assistance. Now, what I am trying to do is, however, very different. I can hardly accomplish it on my own.

Last year, I revisited a place I used to know and saw the remains of deceased friends scattering across the wilderness, being trampled on by cattle and sheep. It was indeed a heartbreaking sight. They were so pitiable that I thought I had to do something. I raised some funds from people nearby to collect the remains, in the hope that the remains with identified names and native counties could be repatriated to their hometown, where their families would offer sacrifices to them. Nevertheless, while the remains of deceased friends whose names were known would have been repatriated to their hometown by respective benevolent associations, the unidentified remains are eventually left unattended. It is in this light that I write to you to find a solution. I am still trying to find out who the remains belong to. I have asked people to come forward if they know the name and native county of any one of the deceased friends. The remains can be collected from here, or if the deceased's address in their hometown is known, the remains can be repatriated and received by the families. This would be much preferable than burial in a free cemetery.

I am telling you the real situation of these deceased friends. I will pay the shipping charges, as well as any burial fees that may be incurred by your hospital. After I have raised the funds required, I will inform you of the name of the ship taking the remains to Hong Kong and the expected date of arrival as soon as possible. I will also send you a list of the deceased's names together with the unidentified and inform you which boxes they are placed in and how many sets there are as well as the total number of boxes.

Thank you in advance for your great kindness to help. I am grateful to you for your efforts.

I wish you well.

Yours humbly,
Mui Yiu-man *(Mei Yaowen)*, San Francisco, USA

6th day of the 5th lunar month of the 18th year of the Republic of China (12 June 1929)

099 中國中山與善堂致東華醫院信件

1929年7月10日

與善堂用箋

東華醫院
列位善董先生大鑒敬復者前月浔接
覆函敬悉一切據稱去年十月舊金山德善堂有先
友骨殖三十八具搭克利夫蘭船運返業經起卸
貴院義庄妥存本年四月廿一由新全安棧領去
一具餘三十七具現厝庄上又云外埠寄囬先友
骨殖向例並無代運到內地衹係着伊親屬
來港蓋章認領等語敝堂接到該函後當
即將此意轉達各先友親屬知之以便磋商茲
據該親屬又來敝堂談及查各埠先友骨殖
多有付返　貴院轉運敝堂代存義庄候
伊親屬到領安塟今德善堂絕無運費
交帶　貴院轉運內地勢必無從代運今
將　貴院付返原函轉佈該各先友親
屬然後始知德善堂無運費付返
貴院又并非敝堂有意留難阻滯不
肯向　貴院蓋章領囬实情在伊親屬亦
當原諒昨日各先友親屬又到敝堂磋商
情愿自出運費最好請
貴院從中設法從廉代僱運船載返石岐交敝堂
囬春院義庄然後懸紅由該親屬覔店盖
章認領較為妥當若係由伊親屬來港
盖章認領吾恐貧寒之家無以正其邱
首之日倘不設法運囬岐地任其枯骨抛零
不特無以安死者之心則又無以对華僑關懷
之意況千山萬水得以運返港中今距內地
非遙又不設法轉囬岐地將澤及枯骨之謂
何也又恐伊親屬之心有所不安也茲特專函
貴院務懇与　善長列位從中設法磋

商使該善堂付返三十七具先友幽魂可
慰不勝銘感之至現在敝堂集議請
貴院代為一查未審直頭代僱船統運至
岐該價若干抑或由　貴院在港僱船搭石岐渡
尾拖運到敝堂囬春院庄上該價若干并請两
種办法代為一查務以從廉妥訂乞即迅
賜覆音以便轉達各先友親屬知之事
關公益諸費
精神容當面謝此上即請

善安希為
朗照不宣

中山與善堂同人謹啓（印章：中山與善堂）

中華民國十八年七月十日　即旧六月初四

Letter from Chung Shan Yu Sin Tong, China, to Tung Wah Hospital on 10 July 1929

From the Office of Yu Sin Tong

Dear benevolent Directors of Tung Wah Hospital,

We are writing in response to your correspondence received last month.

We know that Tak Sin Tong (*De Shan Tang*) of San Francisco repatriated 38 sets of bones in October last year. The remains were transported on the *SS President Cleveland* and have been placed in the coffin home of your esteemed hospital since their arrival in Hong Kong. On 21 April this year, Sun Chuen On Chan (*Xin Quan An Zhan*) collected one set of bones. The remaining 37 sets are still in the care of your coffin home. We are also aware that it is not customary for you to transport the remains sent from overseas to the mainland; the families of the deceased are expected to come to Hong Kong to acknowledge and collect the remains. Upon receiving your correspondence, we informed the families of the deceased so that arrangements could be made.

Subsequently, the families came to us to discuss the matter. They said your esteemed hospital had previously transported the remains of deceased friends to us, and we placed them in a coffin home until the deceased's families came to collect them. However, since Tak Sin Tong has not provided any funds to pay for shipping costs, it would not be possible for your esteemed hospital to transport the remains to mainland China. We showed your reply letter regarding the bone repatriation to the families of the deceased. It became clear that Tak Sin Tong has not sent any funds to pay for bone repatriation to China, whereas we are by no means not unwilling to acknowledge and claim the remains from your esteemed hospital. The families of the deceased should understand and forgive us.

Yesterday, the families came to us again to discuss the matter. They are willing to pay the shipping costs. It would be much appreciated if your esteemed hospital can hire a boat at a cost as low as possible to transport the remains to Wui Chun Yuen Coffin Home (*Huichunyuan Yizhuang*) in Shekki (*Shiqi*). Notices will then be put up to inform the families and they should find a shop to act as guarantor to claim the remains from the coffin home. We are afraid that the poor families will not be able to afford the travel expenses if they have to come to Hong Kong to collect the remains. If the remains are not sent back to Shekki, there will be no hope for proper burial. It was indeed the final wish of the deceased to be laid to rest in the hometown. The overseas Chinese compatriots were so kind as to have already sent the remains across the oceans to Hong Kong, and taking into consideration the proximity between Hong Kong and mainland China, the deceased as well as the overseas Chinese compatriots would be let down if we do not do our best to transport their remains back to Shekki. The families of the deceased would also be ill at ease.

We, therefore, by sending this letter to your esteemed hospital, seek your further assistance to have the 37 sets of remains sent back to China so that the spirits of the deceased friends can be consoled. And we would be very grateful for your kindness and efforts. We have resolved to put up a request for you to find out the costs of hiring a boat to transport the remains directly from Hong Kong to Shekki; and the costs of having a boat bound for Shekki to tow the remains and transport them to Wui Chun Yuen Coffin Home. Kindly arrange the transportation from the above options at the lowest cost and get back to us at your earliest convenience, so that we can inform the families of the deceased.

We are most grateful to you for your kindness in this charitable act. This has caused you much trouble and we shall express our gratitude in person.

Best wishes and sincerely,
From the fellow members of Chung Shan Yu Sin Tong *(Zhongshan Yu Shan Tang)*
(Stamp: Chung Shan Yu Sin Tong)

10 July of the 18th year of the Republic of China
4th day of the 6th lunar month

100 美國鄧夏利致東華醫院信件

1929 年 7 月 18 日

LIBERTY MARKET
HAM YICK COMPANY

東華醫院諸大值理公鑒啓者

是企李崙船美國運通公司運
回廣東開平属護龍鄉仁慶里
村鄧俊字荐隆靈柩一具但運
到者西人定送到醫院勞諸公收
領遲日仁慶里有人出來運返鄉安
葬

大安

中國通信
澳門海边新街门牌十八號關洪達堂
開平県赤坎埠茂兴号鄧爵
荣或開平県護龍圩均昌
隆鄧爵荣

弟鄧夏利囑

西歷一九二九年柒月十八日

From the Office of Ham Yick Company

Dear Directors of Tung Wah Hospital,

I am writing to inform you that the coffin of Tang Chun *(Deng Jun)*, style name Chin-lung *(Jian-long)*, of Yan Hing Lei Village *(Renqingli Cun)* in Woo Lung Township *(Hulong Xiang)*, Hoi Ping *(Kaiping)*, Kwangtung *(Guangdong)* Province, will be repatriated on a ship of the American Express Company. Upon arriving in Hong Kong, a westerner will take the coffin to your hospital. Please take it into your care. Someone from Yan Hing Lane *(Renqing Li)* will come to take the coffin back to the deceased's hometown for burial in due course.

I wish you well.

Yours humbly,
Tang Ha-lei *(Deng Xiali)*

18 July 1929

Correspondence address in China:
Kwan Hung Tat Tong, 18 Rua Do Guimarães, Macau
Tang Cheuk-wing *(Deng Juerong)*, Mau Hing Shop *(Maoxing Hao)*, Chek Ham *(Chikan)*, Hoi Ping County
or Tang Cheuk-wing, Kwun Cheong Lung *(Jun Chang Long)*, Woo Lung Market Town *(Hulong Xu)*, Hoi Ping County

同茂泰用箋
TONG MOW TAI

東華醫院大鑒敬啓者茲因先友陸長允
　　為遺產承办事法院註冊官（即大葛）
　　要審查運柩囘港日期以資證明
　　查該友遺骸乃係前乙丑年十二月間
　　在　貴院領回托陳洪記運返原籍
　　安葬茲恳將當日由美國抵港船名
　　時期及起運囘鄉日期代為查明詳
　　細繕函　賜复俾作佐證以利進行
　　实紉公誼專此即頌

善安

司理先生
各大善長　　均電

^弟（印章：香港李陞街同茂泰書束）謹啓

中華民國十八年九月十八日　　己八月十六日

另一人註：己八月廿日函覆

Letter from Tong Mow Tai, Hong Kong, to Tung Wah Hospital on 18 September 1929

From the Office of Tong Mow Tai

Dear benevolent Directors and Managers of Tung Wah Hospital,

For verification purpose during the inheritance process, the Registrar of the Hong Kong Supreme Court demands proof of when the remains of our deceased friend Luk Cheung-wun (*Lu Changyun*) arrived in Hong Kong. I understand that the remains were claimed from your esteemed hospital in the 12th lunar month in 1925 and repatriated to the deceased's hometown by Chan Hung Kee. I would be most grateful if you could check the name of the ship which carried the remains from America to Hong Kong, and when the remains were repatriated to the deceased's hometown. Please reply to me with the information in detail, so that proof can be provided to the court.

Thank you for your efforts.

Yours sincerely,
(Stamp: Tong Mow Tai, Li Sing Street, Hong Kong)

18 September of the 18th year of the Republic of China (16th day of the 8th lunar month, Year of Gei Zi (Jizi))

Another person's remarks: Reply letter sent on the 20th day of the 8th lunar month

102 美國抓李𨫼埠華僑致東華醫院信件

1929 年 10 月 1 日

東華醫院執事列位先生[偉鑒] 敬啓者茲由

美國郵船名丕亞市寄來 先友骸骨四拾

叁具抵港查收煩即代為轉寄各縣標紅佈

告俾得各 先友親屬人等所知領囬 先友安

葬于窀穸存歿均感並付上赤帋一張伸港帋

銀壹佰伍拾元正到步照收以為捐貼 貴院之

用如收到此艮之日以及 先友骸骨抵步祈即覆示

以免企翹是所切祷諸事多煩不勝感感 專此

敬悬順候

鈞安

（印章：伍文栩書柬）

民國十八年新曆十月一号 美國抓李抓𨫼埠華僑仝人等謹上

另一人註：已十月初十日覆函

茲將各先友姓名縣鄉列明于後

傅訓賡	台山深井龍田里人氏	黃廷普	台山上閣浮月村人氏
伍元忠	台山下坪村人氏	黃廷純	台山樹下村人氏
黃章任	台山潮境西村人氏	廖烈錦	會邑砂堆人氏
黃添章	台山潮境西村人氏	朱英裘	會城潮溪里內泗沖朱村人氏
何 大	開邑龍塘白龍里人氏	盤醮隆	台山盤屋村人氏
朱子林	台山西光沖村人氏	黃百合	開邑水口人氏
黃學携	會邑坑口村山頂里人氏	胡振和	儒良里龍興里人氏
李宏英	台山密沖文沖村人氏	許 佐	台山水步榮安村人氏
吳三才	恩邑平安堡廣塘村人氏	鍾 孔	會邑古井人氏
許炳桂	台山水步龍安村人氏	蔡 就	台山沙沖人氏
伍于秩	台山斗洞風塘村人氏	馮 乾	陽江人氏
黎 進	鶴山人氏	鄧 茂	鶴山人氏
鍾 欽	會邑古井烟管咀村人氏	李杰衍	台山南村山背里人氏
區洪優	台山廣海橫龍村人氏	薛裔箴	會邑長沙鄉人氏
黃啓胤	台山潮境西村人氏	高振瀼	會邑那伏人氏
李 玉	台山密沖玉枕村人氏	李 積	台山蜜沖玉枕村人氏
李 河	台山蜜沖滙潮村人氏	李 則	台山蜜沖滙潮村人氏
劉社星	台山白石村人氏	劉周易	台山白石村人氏
朱昌華	會城潮溪村人氏	朱昌合	會城潮溪村人氏
朱箕源	會城潮溪村人氏	張苟女	台山蘆溪村人氏
張旺相	台山蘆溪村人氏	張成效	台山蘆溪村人氏
劉尊輝	台山白石村人氏		

102   Letter from the overseas Chinese in Walla Walla, USA, to Tung Wah Hospital on 1 October 1929

Dear Managers of Tung Wah Hospital,

43 sets of remains would be repatriated from America on the *SS President Pierce* of the American Lines. Please send them to the deceased's hometown. People will put up notices to inform families to collect the remains and lay them to rest. The deceased and surviving families will be grateful to you. We have also enclosed a cheque for 150 Hong Kong dollars to cover the costs and donate to your esteemed hospital. Please reply to us as soon as you receive the funds as well as the remains of our deceased friends to ease our mind.

We are most grateful to you for your efforts.

We wish you well.

Yours sincerely,
Chinese compatriots of Walla Walla, USA
(Stamp: Ng Man-hui)*(Wu Wenxu)*

1 October of the 18th year of the Republic of China

Another person's remarks: Replied on the 10th day of the 10th lunar month, Year of Gei Zi (*Jisi*)

Enclosed is the name list of the deceased friends.

[Editor's remarks: Name list of the deceased friends is available only in Chinese]

東華醫院执事先生^{偉鑒}　敬啓者^{敝埠}昨五号由美
　　国郵船名丕亞市寄來　先友骸骨四十一具料近到
　　港惟當時忘記船冧夾入信內付上茲即將寄　先友
　　之船冧一張到步查收如　先友抵步祈即携此船
　　冧提起轉寄各縣可也諸事多煩不勝銘感專此
　　敬請順候

　　均安

　　　　　　　　　　　　　　　　　　（印章：伍文栩書束）
民國十八年十月十四号　　　　美國抓李抓罅埠華僑等仝人謹叩

103 Letter from the overseas Chinese in Walla Walla, USA, to Tung Wah Hospital on 14 October 1929

Dear Managers of Tung Wah Hospital,

41 sets of remains were sent from our city on the *SS President Pierce* of the American Line on 5 October, and they should arrive in Hong Kong soon. Yet we forgot to send the bill of lading to you in our last letter. We, hereby, enclose the bill of lading. Please take delivery of the remains with this document when they arrive in Hong Kong, and transfer them to the respective counties.

We are most grateful to you for your efforts.

We wish you well.

Yours sincerely,
(Stamp: Ng Man-hui)*(Wu Wenxu)*
Chinese compatriots of Walla Walla, USA

14 October of the 18th year of the Republic of China

紐約中華長生有限公司
Chinese Cheung Sang Funeral Corporation

東華醫院主席暨列位善董均鑒敬

啟者茲有先友譚高字彪文 Tom Gow 廣東

台山縣白水堡永和鄉人氏于民國十八年十二月

五號在本埠因病入醫院逝世享壽六十四歲

其屍骸係由本公司製殮裝置妥當付搭

麥頃尼総統船 S. S. President McKinley 寄上

貴院轉運回籍安葬該船係本月廿八號

由舍路開行回港其子譚初隨菡扶柩到時

尚希接済妥為處置实為德便耑此即頌

善祺

総理梁麗天啟

（印章：梁麗天 BVE）

（印章：Chinese Cheung Sang Funeral Corporation, New York）

中華民國十八年十二月廿號

104 Letter from Chinese Cheung Sang Funeral Corporation of New York, USA, to Tung Wah Hospital on 20 December 1929

From the Office of Chinese Cheung Sang Funeral Corporation, New York

Dear benevolent Chairman and Directors of Tung Wah Hospital,

Tom Gow (*Tan Gao*), style name Bill-man (*Biaowen*), was a native of Wing Wo Township (*Yonghe Xiang*), Bak Shui Bo (*Baishui Bao*), Toi Shan (*Taishan*), Kwangtung *(Guangdong)*. He died of illness, at the age of 64, in a local hospital on 5 December of the 18th year of the Republic of China. We have embalmed his body and placed him in a coffin properly, which will be delivered to your hospital on the *SS President McKinley* and then repatriated to his hometown for burial. The ship will depart Seattle on the 28th day of this month. The deceased's son Tom Chor (*Tan Chu*) is travelling with the coffin. When he arrives in Hong Kong with his father's coffin, please offer him any assistance he may require.

May you be blessed for your benevolence.

We wish you well.

Yours sincerely,
Leung Lai-tin (*Liang Litian*)
General Manager
(Stamp: Leung Lai-tin BVE)
(Stamp: Chinese Cheung Sang Funeral Corporation, New York)

20 December of the 18th year of the Republic of China

美國紐約中華公所
Chinese Consolidated Benevolent Association

香港東華醫院院長先生大鑒

　　逕啟者茲有先友譚高^字彪文西字
　　TOM GOW 廣東台山縣白水堡永和鄉人氏于
　　民國十八年十二月五日在本埠醫院逝世
　　享壽六十四歲其屍骸由本埠長生公司
　　付搭麥乾尼總統船 S.S. President McKinley
　　寄回香港　貴院轉運回原籍安葬
　　該船係本月廿八号由舍路埠開行該先
　　友抵港時請求
　　貴執事照料一切寔為德便耑此即頌

公祺　并候
年安

（印章：紐約中華公所）主席易綺茜

中華民國十八年十二月二十一日

105

Letter from the Chinese Consolidated Benevolent Association of New York, USA, to Tung Wah Hospital on 21 December 1929

From the Office of Chinese Consolidated Benevolent Association, New York

Dear Chairman of Tung Wah Hospital,

Tom Gow (Tan Gao), style name Bill-man *(Biaowen),* was a native of Wing Wo Township *(Yonghe Xiang)*, Bak Shui Bo *(Baishuibao)*, Toi Shan *(Taishan)*, Kwangtung *(Guangdong)*. He died of illness, at the age of 64, in a local hospital on 5 December of the 18th year of the Republic of China. His body was embalmed and placed in a coffin by a local funeral company. The coffin has been arranged to be sent to your hospital on the *SS President McKinley*. Please repatriate it to his hometown for burial. The ship will depart Seattle on the 28th day of this month. Please take our deceased friend's coffin into your care after it arrives in Hong Kong.

We are most grateful to you for your kindness. We wish you well and have a blessed new year.

Yours sincerely,
Yik Yi-sin *(Yi Qiqian)*
Chairman,
(Stamp: Chinese Consolidated Benevolent Association, New York)

21 December of the 18th year of the Republic of China

美國紐英崙中華公所
The United Chinese Assoication

逕啟者茲據此间西人報告因坟坊記號錯乱

悞执先友一名查該先友名號龔　源是台山

海宴望頭村人前十餘年在波市頓埠逝世經本

公所查訪各埠龔姓僑梓乏人承領祇留此

具骸骨扵殯殮所恐有遺失之悞適遇徐貴

由本埠歸國托他親帶該先友骸骨一具返

港送交

貴院代為收保請轉召該親屬承領以正首丘

而慰幽靈無任感德素仰

貴院乐行功德經理先友能有善權不忖煩

續勞為收發籍恩之施存殁靡忘此致

香港東華醫院諸善長先生

紐英崙中華公所啟（印章：紐英崙中華公所）

　　計開

龔　源先友骸骨壹具

　　台山縣海宴望頭村人係西曆壹千玖百壹

　　拾捌年八月间在美國波市頓埠逝世

大中華民國十九年元月廿九日

Letter from The United Chinese Association, USA, to Tung Wah Hospital on 29 January 1930

From the Office of The United Chinese Association, New England

Dear benevolent Directors of Tung Wah Hospital,

It was reported by a native here that, due to inaccurate cemetery records, the remains of one of our deceased friends were mistakenly exhumed. The deceased, Kung Yuen (*Gong Yuan*), was a native of Mong Tau Village *(Wangtou Cun)*, Hoi Yin *(Haiyan)*, Toi Shan *(Taishan)*, who passed away in Boston more than 10 years ago. We have spoken to Chinese compatriots with the family name Kung *(Gong)* in various cities, but no one has come forward to claim the remains. We are concerned that the remains may be lost if they are left in the funeral home. As Tsui Kwai (*Xu Gui*) is returning to China from Boston, we have asked him to take the remains of the deceased to Hong Kong and hand them over to you. Please take the remains into your care and contact the family of the deceased to collect them, so that the deceased can be laid to rest.

The benevolence of your esteemed hospital is known far and wide. In the past, the deceased sent to your hospital had been taken into good care. Therefore, we seek your help to receive the remains of the deceased and hand them over to his family. The deceased and his family members shall forever be grateful to you for your kindness.

Yours sincerely,
The United Chinese Association, New England
(Stamp: The United Chinese Association, New England)

29 January of the 19th year of the Republic of China

Note:
One set of bones of Kung Yuen, a native of Mong Tau Village, Hoi Yin, Toi Shan, who passed away in Boston, USA, in August 1918

美國金山大埠東莞寶安堂致東華醫院信件

1930 年 2 月 13 日

逕啟者　貴院自成立以來歷行方便
善績卓著中外素仰均賴諸公熱
心樂善主持有方同胞無不讚嘉
茲有敝邑僑梓刘旭階君不幸在
埠逝世經得同人等將其遺骸運
回原屬安葬準於弍月十四日由積臣船
載返其辦法先懇　貴院接理并代
為通達駐港東莞東義堂繼續轉運
回死者家鄉安葬用特函知屆時冀
望帮忙玉成善举同人等感激靡似
矣此致

駐港東華醫院主席暨
列位执事先生均鑒

金山大埠東莞（印章：寶安堂）
主席林承參
書記譚昌

民十九弍月十三日

Letter from Tung Goon Bo On Association, San Francisco, USA, to Tung Wah Hospital on 13 February 1930

Dear Chairman and Managers of Tung Wah Hospital of Hong Kong,

Ever since your establishment, the charitable deeds of your esteemed hospital are well known in China and overseas, whereas your benevolence, enthusiasm and good work are admired by Chinese compatriots all over the world.

Lau Yuk-kai (*Liu Xujie*), a fellow Chinese compatriot, passed away in San Francisco. We shall repatriate his remains on the *SS President Jackson* on 14 February. Please take the remains into your care after they arrive in Hong Kong, and notify Tung Goon Tung Yee Tong *(Dongguan Dong Yi Tang)* in Hong Kong to transport them to the deceased's hometown.

We, hereby, write to inform you of the matter. Please help us accomplish this deed of benevolence. We shall be most grateful to you for your help.

Yours sincerely,
(Stamp: Tung Goon Bo On Association, San Francisco)
Lam Shing-cham (*Lin Chengcan*), Chairman
Tam Cheong (*Tan Chang*), Secretary

13 February of the 19th year of the Republic of China

中國增邑義安堂致東華醫院信件

1930 年 2 月 22 日

東華醫院大總理先生大鑒　啓者前廿二
日由加蘭総統船付上增城沙貝鄉甘涌
坊西約湛錫翰公靈柩壹具並載脚紙
一張到日請為起上代為轉交增城增義堂
值理先生通知其家人到來領家中
安葬為幸　謹此佈達

順安

（印章：增邑義安堂）
黃浩泉　凂

民國十九年弍月廿二日

108 Letter from Yee On Tong, Tsang Shing, China, to Tung Wah Hospital on 22 February 1930

Dear Directors of Tung Wah Hospital,

We write to inform you that on the 22nd day of this month, the remains of Cham Shek-hon *(Zhan Xihan)*, a native of Sai Yeuk *(Xi Yue)*, Kam Chung Fong *(Ganchong Fang)*, Sa Pui Township *(Shabei Xiang)*, Tsang Shing *(Zengcheng)*, have been repatriated on the *SS President Grant*. We have enclosed the bill of lading. Please take the remains into your care after they arrive in Hong Kong, and hand over to the manager of Tsang Yi Tong *(Zeng Yi Tang)* of Tsang Shing, who will inform the deceased's family to claim the remains for burial.

We wish you well.

Yours sincerely,
Wong Ho-chuen *(Huang Haoquan)*, in mourning
(Stamp: Yee On Tong, Tsang Shing) *(Yi An Tang)*

22 February of the 19th year of the Republic of China

中國黃焯致東華醫院信件

1930年3月2日

東華院執事列位先生均鑒　敬啓者[弟]聞先
十年前在英國咸水埠所故身之華
僑各骸骨經前年寄回　貴院轉
發各屬未知是否煩各　先生代
[弟]查看新会古井大朗坡鄉黃植華
之名有無該骨付囬仰祈示知
諸事有勞餘後及此請

台安

三月式號　[弟]黃焯　頓

另一人註：庚二月十四覆

109 Letter from Wong Cheuk, China, to Tung Wah Hospital on 2 March 1930

Dear Managers of Tung Wah Hospital,

I heard that the bones of Chinese compatriots who passed away in Vancouver, Britain ten years ago have been repatriated the year before last to your esteemed hospital, and you have already sent the remains to the deceased's hometown. Is that true? I would like to enquire about the bones of Wong Chik-wah (*Huang Zhihua*) from Dai Long Po Township (*Dalangpo Xiang*), Ku Cheng (*Gujing*), Sun Wui *(Xinhui)*. Can you please find out if his bones have been repatriated?

I look forward to your reply and am most grateful to you for your efforts.

I wish you well.

Yours humbly,
Wong Cheuk *(Huang Zhuo)*

2 March

Another person's remarks: Replied on the 14th day of the 2nd lunar month, Year of Gang Ng *(Gengwu)*

東華醫院諸執事先生雅鑒啓者頌維迪
　　吉諸事如意嗣因^吾先父譚雅興在美
　　國逝世至今十二年已但其骸骨未見寄囬
　　^弟曾追至开平百合愛善堂亦總未見有
　　其名字^吾先父原籍开平秘洞新安里譚
　　雅興乳名炳培希望諸執事先生仁人
　　君子懇煩一些代^弟細查得囬先父之骸
　　骨以留紀念則^弟感恩不忘則諸先生
　　亦獲福不淺矣　　並請

台祺

　　　　　　　　^弟良民　敬上　十九、三、弍

通信処
開平秘洞鼠山墟永隆号交新安里譚良民收

另一人註：庚二月十四覆
另一人註：黃江夏堂、安定堂、廣福堂

110 Letter from Tam Leung-man, China, to Tung Wah Hospital on 2 March 1930

Dear Managers of Tung Wah Hospital,

I hope this letter finds you well. My father Tam Nga-hing (*Tan Yaxing*) passed away in the United States 12 years ago, but his remains have still not been repatriated. I have chased Oi Sin Tong *(Ai Shan Tang)* in Bak Hop *(Baihe)*, Hoi Ping *(Kaiping)* and was told that his name was not on any record. My late father Tam Nga-hing, also known as Bing-pui *(Bingpei)*, was a native of Sun On Lane *(Xin'an Li)*, Bi Dong *(Midong)*, Hoi Ping. I would be most grateful if you charitable managers can help me find out where my late father's bones are, so that I can have them back and lay my father to rest.

I shall forever be grateful to you for your kindness, and may you be blessed for your benevolence.

Yours sincerely,
Leung-man (*Liangmin*)

2 March of the 19th year of the Republic of China

Correspondence address: Tam Leung-man of Sun On Lane, Wing Lung Ho *(Yonglong Hao)*, Shu Shan Market Town *(Shushan Xu)*, Bi Dong, Hoi Ping

Another person's remarks: Replied on the 14th day of the 2nd lunar month, Year of Gang Ng *(Gengwu)*
Another person's remarks: Wong Kong Ja Tong, On Teng Tong, Kwong Fook Tong

中國黃焯致東華醫院信件

1930 年 3 月 12 日

裕華銀號用牋

東華院列位先生均鑒敬啓者前奉
草函料邀青及浼代查前年由
英國咸水埠寄囬新会古井大
葫坡黃植華之骨弟經所聞寄
囬　貴院未知是否仰祈代查
明示覆諸事有勞感感順請

台安

弟黃焯　頓
中華民國十九年三月十弍日

111 Letter from Wong Cheuk, China, to Tung Wah Hospital on 12 March 1930

From the Office of Yue Wah Native Bank *(Yuhua Yinhao)*

Dear Directors of Tung Wah Hospital,

I wrote to you earlier to inquire about the bones of Wong Chik-wah (*Huang Zhihua*), repatriated from Vancouver, Britain the year before last. The deceased was a native of Dai Long Po (*Dalang Po)*, Ku Cheng (*Gujing),* Sun Wui *(Xinhui)*. I heard that his bones were sent to your esteemed hospital. Please advise if you have investigated the matter. I look forward to your reply.

Thank you very much for your efforts. I wish you well.

Yours humbly,
Wong Cheuk (*Huang Zhuo*)

12 March of the 19th year of the Republic of China

美國紐約中華公所
Chinese Consolidated Benevolient Association

香港東華醫院総理先生暨列位善董均鑒

公啟者現據本埠悦來裕號梅景翔君公源號陳

孔滿君面稱有先友梅迺文（西名 Nye Moy）廣東台山

縣端芬扳桂里人于是年三月十七号在紐約公家医

院逝世享壽六十九歲于是日將其灵柩付車出域多

利埠搭亞洲皇后船運回香港東華医院交其子

梅冠襄收領安葬請代函達該医院善董妥為照

料等情據此茲特將情函達

台端俟梅迺文君灵柩到港恳代接済通知其子

梅冠襄君到港收領安葬实為德便耑此即候

善祺

主席李青一

（印章：紐約中華公所）

中華民國十九年三月廿三號

Letter from the Chinese Consolidated Benevolent Association of New York, USA, to Tung Wah Hospital on 23 March 1930

From the Office of Chinese Consolidated Benevolent Association, New York

Dear benevolent Directors of Tung Wah Hospital,

Mui King-cheung (*Mei Jingxiang*) of Yuet Loi Yue Ho and Chan Hung-moon (*Chen Kongman*) of Gong Yuen Ho in New York came to us to say that Mui Nai-man (*Mei Naiwen*); English name Nye Moy, a native of Ban Kwai Lane *(Bangui Li)*, Duen Fun *(Duanfen)*, Toi Shan County *(Taishan Xian)*, passed away in a public hospital in New York on 17 March of this year at the age of 69. Today, his coffin has been transported by road to Victoria. From there, the coffin will be taken to the Tung Wah Hospital of Hong Kong on the *Empress of Asia* for his son, Mui Goon-sheung (*Mei Guanxiang*) to collect. They asked me to write to you to take the coffin into your care.

I hereby, write to you to seek your assistance in this matter. Please take the coffin of Mui Nai-man into your care after it arrives in Hong Kong and inform the deceased's son, Mui Goon-sheung, to come to Hong Kong to collect it for burial.

Your benevolence will be much appreciated.

Yours sincerely,
Lee Ching-yat (*Li Qingyi*), Chairman
(Stamp: Chinese Consolidated Benevolent Association, New York)

23 March of the 19th year of the Republic of China

東華醫院
列位仁善長^{均鑒哀啓者竊思家父區聘長}

遠離家鄉為口奔馳故往英屬加拿大省

覓食不料正月十五日在外仙遊于本月

式十日由加拿大皇后船運到香港惟^弟

一介農民不諳外國手續素仰

貴善院慈善為懷所有外僑靈柩運到香

港總由

貴善院轉運內地故特函奉上請

將先父屍骸運到鶴山沙坪圩同善堂

抑或由運柩船侢入內地希為示覆

以便迎柩安葬先人淂歸故土合家沾

恩無既耳謹此奉上

並請

善安

^{孤子}區灝光　泣血稽首（印章：鶴山沙坪奇利勝書束）

庚三月初五日

另一人註：三月十六覆

113

Letter from Au Ho-kwong, China, to Tung Wah Hospital on 3 April 1930

Dear benevolent Managers of Tung Wah Hospital,

My father Au Ping-cheung *(Qu Pinzhang)* left home to earn a living in Canada of the British Empire and died abroad unexpectedly on the 15th day of the 1st lunar month. His remains will be taken to Hong Kong on the 20th day of this month on the *Empress of Canada*. Since I am a farmer, I have no knowledge of the procedures of foreign countries. I heard about the benevolent deeds of your esteemed hospital that the remains of all Chinese compatriots who died abroad were first sent to Hong Kong to your esteemed hospital and then transported to mainland China. I, therefore, seek your help in transporting the remains of my late father either to Tung Sin Tong *(Tong Shan Tang)* in Sha Ping Market Town *(Shaping Xu)*, Hok Shan *(Heshan)*, or sending them to mainland China on a water hearse. Please reply to my letter, so that I can make arrangements for my father's burial.

My entire family and I should be most grateful to you for your kindness. I wish you well.

In mourning,
Au Ho-kwong *(Ou Haoguang)*, son
(Stamp: Kei Lei Shing *(Qi Li Sheng)*, Sha Ping, Hok Shan)

5th day of the 3rd lunar month, Year of Gang Ng *(Gengwu)*

Another person's remarks: Replied on the 16th day of the 3rd lunar month

香港東華醫院执事先生鈞鑒久仰

貴院利濟寬宏

名譽昭著甚佩甚佩^{敝会館}本屆檢起先友

遺骸柒拾捌具分裝拾叁大箱蓋面書明各先

友姓名籍貫於三月初六日由^{敝埠}上車輪運回

國特將載紙呈上請

貴院接理起卸並請按其名籍分送各邑善

堂以便各先友之家眷收領現付上仄乔一張

伸港幣玖佰叁拾陸元內除交每位先友灵骸葬

費伍元外餘存伍佰肆拾陸元統交

貴院為轉運之需遲日寄上各先友名冊一本

及証根柒拾捌條此等証根懇同時轉寄各善

堂為对照領者收條之用手續雖繁惟較慎

重依據辦理至為感荷專此敬頌

公祺

美國珠卜中華會館 必卜　主席余錫中敦禮 謹達
　　　　　　　　書記余寶三

（印章：必珠卜中華會館）

民國十九年三月初六日寄

114

Letter from the Chinese Consolidated Benevolent Association of Pittsburg, USA, to Tung Wah Hospital on 4 April 1930

Dear Managers of Tung Wah Hospital,

We greatly admire your esteemed hospital. Your benevolent deeds are known far and wide.

Our association has exhumed the remains of 78 deceased friends and placed them in 13 large boxes, each attached with a list of the names and native counties of the deceased. The remains have been repatriated from our city on the 6th day of the 3rd lunar month. We have enclosed the bill of lading in this letter. Please collect the remains and take them into your care when they arrive in Hong Kong and transport them to the benevolent associations of the deceased's native counties, so that their families can collect the remains accordingly. We have also enclosed a cheque for 936 Hong Kong dollars. Please give the family of each deceased friend burial fees of 5 dollars and keep the remaining 546 dollars to cover the transportation costs to mainland China. We will send a list of the deceased friends, as well as 78 certification slips [to proof the identity of the deceased] later. Please send the slips to the benevolent associations in mainland China by post, so that the identity of those who come forward to claim the remains can be verified. The procedures are complicated but the precautions are necessary.

We are most grateful to you for your efforts. We wish you well.

Yours sincerely,
Yu Shek-chung (*Yu Xizhong*) & Yu Dun-lai (*Yu Dunli*), Chairmen, and Yu Bo-sam (*Yu Baosan*), Secretary of the Chinese Consolidated Benevolent Association of Pittsburg, USA
(Stamp: Chinese Consolidated Benevolent Association of Pittsburg)

Posted on the 6th day of the 3rd lunar month of the 19th year of the Republic of China

加拿大域多利恩平同福支堂用牋
HONG FOOK TONG SOCIETY

東華□□□事先生鈞鑒

逕啟者^敝邑先友生則淪落他邦死則葬身異域一坏黃
土憑弔其誰青塚孤魂渺無所依本支堂^{同人}為妥先
靈而安先骸計特僱人將先骸妥為執拾計共七
十四具茲由太平洋輪船付歸用特函懇
執事先生於^敝邑先骸到達香港之時煩代起運轉
寄至恩平聖堂墟新錦綸寶號同福堂司事徐瑞華
君收發并夾上炅紙一張寸港銀捌拾元到祈查收
以应支搬運各費便是諸事有勞無任感激
樂善如
執事先生等定当妥為办理矣先友在天有靈
亦為之含笑矣耑此特託並候

福安

（印章：域多利埠同福堂支部）
総理聶習槐謹上
十九年四月十九日

115 Letter from Hong Fook Tong Society, Victoria, Canada, to Tung Wah Hospital on 19 April 1930

From the Office of Hong Fook Tong Society, Victoria

Dear Managers of Tung Wah Hospital,

Fellow Chinese compatriots had passed away in our city. They left their hometown to earn a living in a foreign country; after they died, they were buried on foreign land. Far from their homeland, they yearn for their families and their spirits are desolate. In order to soothe the spirits of the deceased, we have exhumed the remains, 74 sets in total, and they have been repatriated on a ship of the Pacific Lines.

Please take delivery of the remains when they arrive in Hong Kong, and send them to Sun Kam Lun (*Xin Jin Lun*) in Sing Tong Market Town *(Sheng Tang Xu)*, Yan Ping *(Enping)*, in the care of Tsui Shui-wah *(Xu Ruihua)*, manager of Hong Fook Tong Society. We enclose a cheque for 80 Hong Kong dollars to pay for the costs of repatriation.

We are most grateful to you for your efforts. Your benevolence is known far and wide, and we are confident this matter will be taken care of. The deceased will also be pleased with what you have done for them.

We wish you well.

Yours sincerely,
Lip Chap-wai *(Nie Xihuai),* Director
(Stamp: Hong Took Tong Society, Victoria)

19 April of the 19th year of the Republic of China

美國紐約中華公所
Chinese Consolidated Benevolent Association

東華醫院院長暨列位善董均鑒

敬啓者茲有先友黃道銳 Wong Do You
廣東台山縣松蓢東盛村人于民國十八年十月
廿七號在本埠逝世享壽四十五歲茲由其次
子黃守權扶柩回籍安葬該灵柩付搭美
國普利市総統船該船六月十四號由舍路埠開
行該柩將來抵港時尚希　貴院善董照料
一切並代運回台山原籍藉安窀穸功德無量
謹此上達即候

善祺

（印章：紐約中華公所）
紐約中華公所主席李青一　十九年六月七號

116 Letter from Chinese Consolidated Benevolent Association of New York, USA, to Tung Wah Hospital on 7 June 1930

From the Office of Chinese Consolidated Benevolent Association, New York

Dear Chairman and benevolent Directors of Tung Wah Hospital,

Our deceased friend, Wong Do You (*Huang Daorui*), a native of Dong Shing Village *(Dongsheng Cun)*, Chung Long *(Songlang)*, Toi Shan *(Taishan)*, Kwangtung *(Guangdong)*, passed away in New York on 27 October in the 18th year of the Republic of China, at the age of 45. His second son, Wong Sau-kuen (*Huang Shouquan*), will accompany his coffin back to his hometown for burial. The coffin will be repatriated on the *SS President Pierce*, departing Seattle on 14 June. When the coffin arrives in Hong Kong, please take it into your care and help transport it to our deceased's friend hometown in Toi Shan.

Your virtue and benevolence are without boundaries. We wish you well.

Yours sincerely,
Lee Ching-yat (*Li Qingyi*), Chairman of the Chinese Consolidated Benevolent Association of New York
(Stamp: Chinese Consolidated Benevolent Association of New York)

7 June of the 19th year of the Republic of China

中國馮登致東華醫院信件

1930 年 6 月 8 日

東華醫院主值列位先生大鑒

　　寅啓者茲由大來公司總統輪船運
　　囬貴院代收馮良先友棺柩壹
　　具並夾信內俀紙三張到步蒙為
　　照料馮良先友乃係南海九江鄉人
　　氏其村名拜石里其子馮煊到領
　　該輪船大約七月十二三日到港矣故特
　　奉字通知諸廢神馳感德莫忘

謹此奉達

　　　　　　　　　　　　　　弟南海九江 馮登　拜涴

中華民國十玖年六月八日　　　　　　　（印章：喜報平安）

117   Letter from Fung Deng, China, to Tung Wah Hospital on 8 June 1930

Dear Managers of Tung Wah Hospital,

The coffin of deceased friend Fung Leung (*Feng Liang*) has been repatriated on the vessel of the President Line of Dollar Shipping Company to your hospital. I have enclosed three bills of lading. Please take the coffin into your care after it arrives in Hong Kong. The late Fung Leung was a native of Bai Shek Lane *(Baishi Li)*, Kau Kong Township *(Jiujiang Xiang)*, Nam Hoi *(Nanhai)*. His son will come to Hong Kong to collect the coffin. The ship is expected to arrive in Hong Kong on the 12th or 13th day of July. I, hereby, write to inform you of the matter.

May you be blessed for your benevolence. Your kindness will always be remembered.

Yours sincerely,
Fung Deng (*Feng Deng*) of Kau Kong, Nam Hoi
(Stamp: with joy and peace)

8 June of the 19th year of the Republic of China

美國紐約中華公所
Chinese Consolidated Benevolent Association

東華醫院院長暨列位善董均鑒敬啟者現據

梁子康君面称其胞弟梁声寧別字雲階于本月

廿一日在紐約身故五十三歲茲將其灵柩附搭夏利慎

総統船運回香港東華醫院轉運南海九江原籍安塋

該船本月卅一日由紐約啟程預計九月廿日到港請代函懇

東華医院善董等屆時妥為照料等情前來用特據情函達

台端俟先友梁声寧抵港時希為照料轉運原籍

安葬以妥先灵實為德便耑此即頌

義祺

（印章：紐約中華公所）主席李青一

中華民國十九年七月廿七日

118 Letter from Chinese Consolidated Benevolent Association, New York, USA, to Tung Wah Hospital on 27 July 1930

From the Office of Chinese Consolidated Benevolent Association, New York

Dear Chairman and benevolent Directors of Tung Wah Hospital,

Leung Chi-hong (*Liang Zikang*) came to us to say that his younger brother Leung Shing-ling (*Liang Shengning*), also known as Wan-kai (*Yunjie*), passed away in New York on the 21st day of this month at the age of 53. His coffin will be taken to Tung Wah Hospital in Hong Kong on the *SS President Harrison* and then repatriated to Kau Kong *(Jiujiang)*, Nam Hoi *(Nanhai)* for burial. The ship will depart New York on the 31st day of this month and is expected to arrive in Hong Kong on 20 September. We therefore earnestly request your esteemed hospital to take the coffin of our deceased friend Leung Shing-ling into your care when it arrives in Hong Kong, and send it to the deceased's hometown for burial.

We are most grateful to you for your kindness.

Yours sincerely,
Lee Ching-yat (*Li Qingyi*)
(Stamp: Chinese Consolidated Benevolent Association, New York)

27 July of the 19th year of the Republic of China

紐約中華長生有限公司
Chinese Cheung Sang Funeral Corporation

東華醫院總董暨列位善董均

鑒敬啓者先友梁声寧南海九

江人氏于七月卅一日由本埠搭夏利慎

總統船寄運回港轉運原籍安葬

預計九月廿号可以抵步茲將儀紙

付上希為查收俟該先友灵柩到

時煩為照料一切不勝感德之至耑

此即頌

善祺

（印章：紐約中華長生有限公司）

紐約中華長生公司總理梁麗天

（印章：梁麗天 BVE）

民國十九年八月二號

119 — Letter from Chinese Cheung Sang Funeral Corporation, New York, USA, to Tung Wah Hospital on 2 August 1930

From the Office of Chinese Cheung Sang Funeral Corporation, New York

Dear benevolent Directors of Tung Wah Hospital,

The remains of our deceased friend Leung Shing-ling (*Liang Shengning*), a native of Kau Kong *(Jiujiang)*, Nam Hoi *(Nanhai)*, have been repatriated from our city to his hometown by way of Hong Kong on the *SS President Harrison* on 31 July, and are expected to arrive in Hong Kong on 20 September. We enclose the bill of lading. Please take the remains into your care when they arrive in Hong Kong.

We are most grateful to you for your kindness.

Yours sincerely,
Leung Lai-tin (*Liang Litian)*,
General Manager of Chinese Cheung Sang Funeral Corporation, New York
(Stamp: CHINESE CHEUNG SANG FUNERAL CORP. NEW YORK, N.Y., USA)
(Stamp: Leung Lai-tin BVE)

2 August of the 19th year of the Republic of China

東華醫院列位仁翁先生均鑒敬啓者^弟之叔

    母黃罗氏即中山長洲雲開之媳婦因窮困在美國自

    盡其柩由梓友義捐於二月初四運到香

    港寄入　貴院处置然先人以归土為

    安不忍其暴露但其家貧欲運回原籍

    安厝而乏經済費無所出傳聞積存一

    帮為善堂出資办理載回原籍未悉

    然否如是者何日可以運回或不然如

    何手續可以運回請示其詳想

列位先生以善為怀諒不我却也賜函請

    交中山石岐大馬路誠信孚收入可也

    並頌

時祉

                  庚又月十三日 ^弟黃偉 上言

120

Letter from Wong Wai, China, to Tung Wah Hospital on 7 August 1930

Dear benevolent Directors of Tung Wah Hospital,

My aunt, Madam Wong-Law (*Huang-Luo Shi*), wife of Wong Wan-hoi (*Huang Yunkai*) of Cheung Chau (*Zhangzhou*), Chung Shan *(Zhongshan)*, committed suicide in America to escape poverty. Friends of our hometown donated money to pay for the repatriation of her remains. They arrived in Hong Kong on the 4th day of the 2nd lunar month and have been placed in the care of your esteemed hospital. We want to lay her to rest, but since her family is very poor, they cannot afford the costs of transporting the remains to her hometown. We heard that you have sponsored remains repatriation in the past, is that true? If you can help, when will my aunt's remains be repatriated? If you cannot help, what do we need to do to have her remains repatriated? Please reply to me with detailed instructions.

Your benevolence is known far and wide. I trust you will help and thus venture to write to you.

Please send your reply to Shing Shun Fu (*Chengxin Fu)*, Shekki Dai Ma Lo (*Shiqi Da Malu)*, Chung Shan.

I wish you well.

Yours sincerely,
Wong Wai (*Huang Wei*)

13th day of the leap 6th lunar month, Year of Gang Ng *(Gengwu)*

加拿大域多利寧陽餘慶堂用箋
Ning Young Yee Hing Tong

逕啓者本総堂奉各邑善堂命执行辦理是
屆此間加拿大屬我僑　先友事宜自十五年
年頭開首以至于今方行結束本屆手續現
計連年檢起箱裝　先友遺骸共有千八百
具間之數屬于廣府人氏居多公定近欲
整理附返
鈞醫院起收如前辦理相應先行呈報
鈞醫院查知預為照料希速示機宜
遵行為荷　此致

香
港東華醫院大董事先生

（印章：域多利甯陽餘慶堂印）
総理李堯
書記林寿民

中華民國十九年十月十六日

121

Letter from Ning Young Yee Hing Tong of Victoria, Canada, to Tung Wah Hospital on 16 October 1930

From the Office of Ning Young Yee Hing Tong, Victoria

Dear Directors of Tung Wah Hospital,

We have been entrusted by various benevolent associations in China to undertake repatriation of the remains of Chinese compatriots who passed away in Canada. The work began in the 15th year of the Republic of China and we have just finished exhuming and collecting the remains for this batch. We have exhumed a total of 1,800 sets of remains and placed them in boxes. Most of the deceased friends were native of Kwangtung *(Guangdong)* province. We would, therefore, like to transport the remains to your esteemed hospital. Please take them into your care as you did before. We hereby write to you to enquire about the relevant procedures for the repatriation. Please reply to us at your earliest convenience, and we shall act according to your instructions.

Yours sincerely,
Lee Yiu (*Li Yao*), Chairman
Lam Sau-man (*Lin Shoumin*), Secretary
(Stamp: Ning Young Yee Hing Tong, Victoria)

16 October of the 19th year of the Republic of China

美國紐約中華公所
Chinese Consolidated Benevolent Association

東華醫院院長暨列位善董均鑒公啓者

茲有先友鍾進字倬超（John Jung）鶴山縣萊蘇鄉人于是

年十月廿八号在本埠逝世享壽七十歲由本埠中

華長生有限公司办理製殮事宜經于本月六号

付寄打礮公司亞尖總統船 S.S President Adams 託　貴院轉運原

籍安葬約計十二月廿七号抵港到时尚希妥為

接運实為德便耑此即候

善祺

（印章：紐約中華公所）主席李青一

（印章：紐約中華公所）

民國十九年十一月十二號

122 Letter from the Chinese Consolidated Benevolent Association of New York, USA, to Tung Wah Hospital on 12 November 1930

From the Office of Chinese Consolidated Benevolent Association, New York

Dear benevolent Directors of Tung Wah Hospital,

Our deceased friend Chung Chun *(Zhong Jin)*, John Jung, style name Chuek Chiu *(Zhuochao)*, a native of Loi So Township *(Laisu Xiang)*, Hok Shan *(Heshan)*, passed away in New York on 28 October of this year, at the age of 70. His funeral was undertaken by Chinese Cheung Sang Funeral Corporation in New York, and his coffin was repatriated on 6 November on the *SS President Adams* of Dollar Shipping Company. Please send our deceased friend's coffin to his hometown for burial. The coffin is expected to arrive in Hong Kong around 27 December. Please take it into you care and send it to his hometown.

Your benevolence shall be much appreciated. We wish you well.

Yours sincerely,
Lee Ching-yat (*Li Qingyi*)
(Stamp: Chinese Consolidated Benevolent Association, New York)
(Stamp: CHINESE CONSOLIDATED BENEVOLENT ASS'N 16 MOTT ST. NEW YORK, N.Y, U.S.A.)

12 November of the 19th year of the Republic of China

美國紐約中華長生有限公司致東華醫院信件

1930年11月13日

紐約中華長生有限公司
CHINESE CHEUNG SANG FUNERAL CORP.

東華醫院列位善鑒敬啓者茲有
先友鍾進[字]倬超廣東鶴山縣萊蘇
人現由本公司办理喪事付來 貴
醫收轉運囬原籍其子鍾大道
安葬已于本月六日搭亞泵総統船
約于十弍月廿七日到步屆时仰祈妥為
處理实為德便茲將儎帋付來
希祈照收是幸耑此即請

善祺

（印章：中華長生有限公司）
総理梁麗天　啓（印章：梁麗天 BVE）

民國十九年十一月十三日

123 Letter from Chinese Cheung Sang Funeral Corporation of New York, USA, to Tung Wah Hospital on 13 November 1930

From the Office of Chinese Cheung Sang Funeral Corporation, New York

Dear benevolent Directors of Tung Wah Hospital,

We undertook the funeral of our deceased friend Chung Chun *(Zhong Jin)*, John Jung, style name Chuek Chiu *(Zhuochao)*, a native of Loi So Township *(Laisu Xiang)*, Hok Shan *(Heshan)* County, Kwangtung *(Guangdong)*. We have transported his remains to your esteemed hospital. Please send them onto the deceased's hometown, where his son Chung Tai-to *(Zhong Dadao)* will lay him to rest. The remains were repatriated on the *SS President Adams* on 6 November and expected to arrive in Hong Kong around 27 December. Please take the remains into your care and handle the matter properly.

We are most grateful to you for your kindness. We also sent the bill of lading for your kind information. Please check if it is in order.

Thank you for your kind assistance. I wish you well.

Yours sincerely,
Leung Lai-tin *(Liang Litian)*
(Stamp: CHINESE CHEUNG SANG FUNERAL CORP., 22 MULBERRY ST. NEW YORK, N.Y.)
(Stamp: Leung Lai-tin BVE)

13 November of the 19th year of Republic of China

東華醫院值理曁諸執事先生偉鑒：

敝会館月前運歸之先友遺骸　請求
貴院接收办理未見下復諒亦早已妥
為轉運各邑以督各善堂按照手續分
給安不至有所錯漏也惟敝会館近接
各先友家眷屢報知各善堂只發先友遺骸
葬費銀式元恰与各先友家眷報告書
預告之五元葬費相差大半殊為驚異
始亦不以為深信也至昨閱樓岡月刊
第七年第九卷之族聞欄所載該處之
先友遺骸葬費確是式元致令各侨
胞向敝会館办事人執問原委無以
明澈之苔話復對然其中情形想
貴院執事先生定能明白今特修
函請詢希為早日詳復以釋群
疑是幸順候

公安

必珠卜中華會館　謹上
（印章：必珠卜中華會館）

民國十九年十一月十五日

124 Letter from the Chinese Consolidated Benevolent Association of Pittsburgh, USA, to Tung Wah Hospital on 15 November 1930

Dear Directors and Managers of Tung Wah Hospital,

We repatriated the remains of our deceased friends in earlier months, and have asked your esteemed hospital to take them into your care. We have yet to receive your reply, but we understand that the remains have already been transported to the deceased's hometown and the respective benevolent associations have handed over the remains to the deceased's families.

We believe everything is in order. Nevertheless, the families of the deceased recently informed us that the benevolent associations only gave each family burial fees of 2 dollars. This was less than half of the 5 dollars we previously informed each family. We were taken by surprise, but were initially sceptical about what the deceased's families said. Yesterday, however, we read in the "Clan News" column of *Low Kong Monthly Magazine* (Issue 9, Year 7) that the burial fees for each deceased friend were indeed 2 dollars. Various Chinese benevolent associations asked the managers of our association for details about the situation, but we had no clear explanation for them. We believe the managers of your esteemed hospital must know what has happened, and thus write to you to enquire about the matter. Please reply to us at your earliest convenience to clear all doubts.

We wish you well.

Yours sincerely,
Chinese Consolidated Benevolent Association of Pittsburgh
(Stamp: Chinese Consolidated Benevolent Association of Pittsburgh)

15 November of the 19th year of the Republic of China

紐約中華長生有限公司
CHINESE CHEUNG SANG FUNERAL CORP.

東華醫院執事先生大鑒敬啓者茲有先友
　余國慶 Yee On 廣東台山縣荻海慶和里
　人于民國十九年十一月十七号在紐約布埒街醫
　院因病逝世享年四十九歲是日其親屬扶柩
　由本埠搭車出舍路趕乘昃慎総統船該船
　定本月廿七号由舍路動輪運回香港請
　貴院代收妥為轉運原籍埋葬藉安窀穸
　而妥先靈實為德便耑此即候

善祺

　　　　　　　　　　　　紐約中華長生有限公司総理梁麗天
　　　　　（印章：中華長生有限公司）（印章：梁麗天 BVE）

中華民國十九年十二月廿日

125 Letter from Chinese Cheung Sang Funeral Corporation, New York, USA, to Tung Wah Hospital on 20 December 1930

From the Office of Chinese Cheung Sang Funeral Corporation, New York

Dear Managers of Tung Wah Hospital,

Yee On *(Yu Guoqing)* was a native of Hing Wo Lane *(Qinghe Li)*, Dik Hoi *(Dihai)*, Toi Shan *(Taishan)*, Kwangtung *(Guangdong)*. He died of illness, at the age of 49, in Bradford Street Hospital, New York, on 17 November in the 19th year of the Republic of China. Today, his family took his coffin to Seattle by car to catch the *SS President Jackson*. The ship will set sail for Hong Kong from Seattle on the 27th day of this month. When it arrives in Hong Kong, please take the coffin into your care and repatriate the remains to his hometown, so that he can be laid to rest.

We are most grateful to you for your efforts.

Yours sincerely,
Leung Lai-tin *(Liang Litian)*
General Manager, Chinese Cheung Sang Funeral Corporation, New York
(Stamp: CHINESE CHEUNG SANG FUNERAL CORP. 22 MULBERRY ST. NEW YORK, N.Y.)
(Stamp: Leung Lai-tin BVE)

20 December of the 19th year of the Republic of China

東華醫院列位總理先生大鑒本月初二日由泗益棧交來

大函內開美國必珠卜中華會館是屆運回之先友骨殖開平籍吳亦楨

等十二具查係由寶號代領轉運回內地當時敝院經照每具給以葬費五

元共六十元一統送上寶號盖章收妥茲敝院接到必珠卜中華會館來函

云敝館近接各先友親屬屢報知各善堂祇發先友遺骸葬費銀式元恰

與各先友家眷報告書預告之五元葬費相差大半殊為驚異始亦不以

為深信也至昨閱樓岡月刊第七年第九卷之族聞欄所載該處之先友

遺骸葬費確是式元致令各僑胞向敝會館辦事人执問原委無以明澈答

復等語特此函達請為代查示復以便轉復前途等因奉此查敝堂向例對

於外洋各埠運回之先友骨殖凡由敝堂辦理運回四鄉不論滙回葬費多

少均將該款先行撥歸敝堂然後由敝堂支辦運費另每具發給葬費式

元以歸劃一此次美國必珠卜中華會館運回開平先友吳亦楨等骨殖十二

具由

貴院代該會館交泗益棧轉交敝堂收銀六十元經敝堂司理吳堅潤君

如數收妥進入敝堂數內支辦此係依照向例辦理以免紛歧用特函達

台端尚希　轉覆前途以釋羣疑實紉公誼耑此即頌

善祺

中華民國十九年十二月廿三日　　　　　　　　（印章：開恩廣福堂書束）

Letter from Kwong Fook Tong of Hoi Ping and Yan Ping, China, to Tung Wah Hospital on 23 December 1930

Dear Directors of Tung Wah Hospital,

We received a letter from the Si Yik Chan *(Siyi Zhan)* on the 2nd day of this month regarding the bones of 12 native of Hoi Ping *(Kaiping)* including those of Ng Yik-ching *(Wu Yizhen)* repatriated from the Chinese Consolidated Benevolent Association of Pittsburg through your esteemed hospital. They were claimed and transported by Si Yik Chan to the mainland. At that time, you gave burial fees of 5 dollars for each deceased friend, 60 dollars in total, to Si Yik Chan and the shop acknowledged receipt of the funds with its official stamp.

However, you later received a letter from the Chinese Consolidated Benevolent Association of Pittsburg saying that the families of the deceased recently informed them that the benevolent associations [of their native counties] only gave each family burial fees of 2 dollars. This was less than half of the 5 dollars previously pledged to each family. The Chinese Consolidated Benevolent Association of Pittsburg was taken by surprise, but was initially sceptical about what the deceased's families said. However, they read in the "Clan News" column of *Low Kong Monthly Magazine* (Issue 9, Year 7) earlier on that the burial fees for each deceased friend were indeed 2 dollars. As such, various Chinese associations have asked the managers of the Chinese Consolidated Benevolent Association of Pittsburg for details about the situation, but they have no clear explanation for them. Therefore, they asked your esteemed hospital to investigate the matter and reply to them.

After our investigation, we learn that it has been our usual practice to send all bones repatriated from overseas to the deceased's hometown through our association. We will inject the burial fees, irrespective of the amount, sent from abroad into our pool first. We then pay the transportation costs with the funds and give burial fees of 2 dollars to the family of each deceased friend to align with our usual arrangement. For the 12 sets of remains of Hoi Ping including those of Ng Yik-ching, repatriated by the Chinese Consolidated Benevolent Association of Pittsburg, your esteemed hospital gave 60 dollars to us through Si Yik Chan. Our manager, Ng Kin-yun *(Wu Jianrun)* received the funds and entered the sum into our books. We then handled the funds according to our usual practice. To avoid misunderstanding, we hereby write to you so that you could explain to the relevant people if needed.

Thank you for your efforts.

Yours sincerely,
(Stamp: Kwong Fook Tong of Hoi Ping and Yan Ping)

23 December of the 19th year of the Republic of China

荻海宏濟醫院用牋

焯生家先生暨
香港余風采堂諸公　公鑒頃接十一月初六日大函

及轉錄香港東華醫院大函称楼岡月刊

第七年第九卷載称該处之先友塋費確是

弎元着速在楼岡月刊更正等語查敝院

經埋之先友俱是余姓大埠寄來之先友

原無塋費由香港余風采堂每具支給双毛

銀叁元必珠卜方面寄來之先友係由

貴處先支妥由港運敝院之運費尚餘之

欵滙回敝院連水計每具尚照交双毛銀 4.74 元（水

單粘後）各経手領骸及銀人俱有簽據或商

店盖章隨时可以跟據也復核東華醫院函

內轉錄楼岡月刊所載「該处之先友遺骸塋

費確是弎元」該月刊所載係指該處所謂

該处者实与敝院無關因敝院所經理者不

是楼岡先友委速在楼岡月刊更正一節

似不应辦也此事除在風采月刊登載

外兹特函覆

台端恳請據情轉報東華醫院可也此覆

并候

善祺

庚和手啓

（印章：余庚和印）

（印章：台山荻海宏濟醫院）

民國十九年十二月卅一日

蒙

十九年八月十八号

　　滙來双毛銀 198 元　　　　內大埠方面先友廿一具每三元寸共計 63 元

　　　　　　　　　　　　　　內必珠卜方面先友 45 具每三元寸計共 135 元

十九年九月廿九号

　　滙來港紙銀 59.88 元 3.14 寸

　　　　　　　　　　伸双毛艮 78.4 元係必珠卜先友蜇費

　　　　　　　　　　先後兩次必珠卜先友每具蜇費双毛 4.74 元

焯生家先生暨
香港余風采堂　公鑒

十九年十二月卅一號

　　　　　　　　　　　　　　　　　　宏濟醫院抄（印章：余庚和印）

Letter from Wang Chai Hospital, Dik Hoi, Toi Shan, to Yee Fung Toy Association of Hong Kong on 31 December 1930

From the Office of Wang Chai Hospital *(Hongji Yiyuan)*, Dik Hoi *(Dihai)*

Dear Mr Cheuk Sang-ka *(Zhuo Shengjia)* and Directors of Yee Fung Toy Association of Hong Kong,

We received your letter dated the 6th day of the 11th lunar month, in which you also attached the letter from Tung Wah Hospital with regard to the announcement published in *Low Kong Monthly Magazine* (Issue 9, Year 7) that the burial fees for each deceased friend should be 2 dollars. You also requested us to contact the magazine to publish amendment swiftly.

The truth is, all the remains we handled came from San Francisco with the family name Yu *(Yu)* and no burial fees were available to the deceased's families. It was the Yee Fung Toy Association of Hong Kong which offered 3 Kwangtung silver dollars to the family of each deceased friend. For the remains repatriated from Pittsburg, the shipping fees from Hong Kong to our hospital were settled by your association first. When we received the remitted funds, we deducted the shipping fees and paid the family of each deceased friend 4.74 Kwangtung silver dollars. The persons who handled the remains and money have all signed on the relevant documents or obtained necessary company stamps. The records can be checked and verified anytime. Regarding the *Low Kong Monthly Magazine* attached in the letter from Tung Wah Hospital mentioning that the burial fees for each deceased friend were 2 dollars, we would like to clarify that the remains handled by our hospital were not the ones mentioned in *Low Kong Monthly Magazine*. It seems that we are not in the right position to ask the magazine to make rectification.

Please be informed that in addition to writing to you, we have also published an announcement in *Fung Toy Monthly Magazine*.

We hereby reply to your letter. Please share this message with Tung Wah Hospital.

We wish you well.

Yours sincerely,
Geng-wo *(Genghe)*
(Stamp: Yu Geng-wo)
(Stamp: Wang Chai Hospital, Dik Hoi, Toi Shan)

For your kind information,

We received remittance of 198 Kwangtung silver dollars on 18 August in the 19th year of the Republic of China.

There were 21 sets of remains from San Francisco. The burial fees for each set of remains were 3 dollars, 63 dollars in total.

There were 45 sets of remains from Pittsburgh. The burial fees for each set of remains were 3 dollars, 135 dollars in total.

On 29 September of the 19th year of the Republic of China, we received remittance of 59.88 Hong Kong dollars, in the conversion rate of 3.14 dollars, which ended up to 78.4 Kwangtung silver dollars as burial fees for the deceased friends from Pittsburg.

For the two batches of remains from Pittsburgh, the family of each deceased friend received burial fees of 4.74 Kwangtung silver dollars.

For the attention of Mr Cheuk Sang-ka and Directors of Yee Fung Toy Association of Hong Kong,

Copied by Wang Chi Hospital
(Stamp: Yu Geng-wo)

31 December of the 19th year of the Republic of China

加拿大域多利寧陽餘慶堂用箋
NING YOUNG YEE HING TONG

東華醫院總理先生大鑒　逕啓者^{本堂}自成立以來
　　向以办理僑界慈善事業為主旨即執先友遺骸
　　駐加各邑善堂歷屆均推舉^{本堂}办理亦荷蒙
　　貴院鼎力劻勷湛恩汪濊沒存均感現屆經去年
　　年執拾完竣共計有一千八百餘具亟待運回故
　　土俾正首丘前年十月十六日曾具蕪函呈報
　　貴院請　示機宜祇遵办理乃望眼將穿未蒙
　　示覆想前函定為洪喬所誤茲特虔修寸楮奉
　呈
　　貴總理等可否依照前屆辦法將先友遺骸附回
　　貴院查收再勞分發各縣慈善機關查收分領是
　　否可行仍懇迅賜
　　示復以策進行是所切盼想
　　貴院為嶺表最大善慈機關亦即僑界慈善之
　　明星定必有以饜我海外十三邑僑梓之渴望不讓申
　　叔獨美於前也耑此奉懇祇頌

道祺鵠候
環章不宣

　　　　　　　　　　　　　　　總理李覺世
　　　　　　　　　　　　　　　書記羅振覺
　　　　　　　　　　　　　（印章：域多利寧陽餘慶堂印）

中華民國二十年二月七日

另一人註：辛元月十七日復

128 Letter from Ning Young Yee Hing Tong, Victoria, Canada, to Tung Wah Hospital on 7 February 1931

From the Office of Ning Young Yee Hing Tong, Victoria, Canada

Dear Directors of Tung Wah Hospital,

Since the founding of our society, we are dedicated to the welfare of fellow Chinese compatriots. For many years, we have been elected by the benevolent associations in various cities across Canada to oversee the exhumation and repatriation of our deceased friends' remains. Meanwhile, your esteemed hospital has offered your assistance to us unreservedly over the years, both the deceased and their family members are extremely grateful to you.

Last year, we exhumed the remains of some 1,800 deceased friends and the remains are awaiting repatriation to their hometown. We wrote to you on 16 October of last year to inform you of this and seek your guidance in handling the matter, but have yet to receive your reply. We believe our correspondences have been lost in the post. We now write to you again to ask if we should repatriate the remains of our deceased friends following past procedures, that we send the remains to your esteemed hospital and you help hand them over to the benevolent associations in various counties in mainland so that the remains could be checked and claimed. Please reply to us at your earliest convenience to let us know if this is feasible, so that we can start the process as soon as possible.

Your esteemed hospital is the largest charitable association in the Ling Nam *(Lingnan)* – the star of Chinese charities. We trust that you will help fulfil the wishes of Chinese compatriots from 13 cities in Canada.

We await your reply and are most grateful to you for your benevolence.

Yours sincerely,
Lee Kok-sai *(Li Jueshi)*, Chairman
Law Chun-kok *(Luo Zhenjue)*, Secretary
(Stamp: Ning Young Yee Hing Tong, Victoria)

7 February of the 20th year of the Republic of China

Another person's remarks: Replied on the 17th day of the 1st lunar month, Year of San Mei *(Xinwei)*

香港四邑商工總局用箋
THE SZE YUP INDUSTRIAL & COMMERCIAL UNION

東華醫院
主席先生曁
列位総理先生均鑒頃接加拿大域多利寗
陽餘慶堂総理李覺世先生來函云該堂経理
执拾僑加先友一事擬援照前屆办法請
貴院帮忙接理分發各邑業經一再有函奉商
貴執事想此等慈善事務
貴院定必樂意帮忙应如何發还望早日畁其数行
指示一切俾該餘慶堂李総理等安心寄運以妥各
先友之幽魂实為德便專此敬頌

善祺萬福

當年主席譚煥書
（印章：香港四邑商工總局書束）

中華民國二十年三月弍號

另一人註：辛元月十七日復

129 Letter from The Sze Yup Industrial and Commercial Union of Hong Kong, to Tung Wah Hospital on 2 March 1931

From the Office of The Sze Yup Industrial and Commercial Union of Hong Kong

Dear Chairman and Directors of Tung Wah Hospital,

We received a letter from Chairman Lee Kok-sai *(Li Jueshi)* of Ning Young Yee Hing Tong Benevolent Association in Victoria, Canada, saying that their manager intended to follow past procedures for exhuming the bones of deceased friends who passed away in Canada, and would like to seek the assistance of your esteemed hospital in handing over the bones to various Chinese counties. We trust that your esteemed hospital would be willing to assist them in this charitable endeavour. Please reply to them at your earliest convenience and give detailed instructions. Chairman Lee and others of Ning Young Yee Hing Tong could then ease these mind and send back the deceased friends to their hometown for eternal peace.

We are most grateful to you for your benevolence. May your benevolence bring you abundant blessings.

Yours sincerely,
Tam Woon *(Tan Huan)*
Chairman
(Stamp: The Sze Yup Industrial and Commercial Union of Hong Kong)

2 March of the 20th year of the Republic of China

Another person's remarks: Replied on the 17th day of the 1st lunar month, Year of San Mei *(Xinwei)*

美國舍路中華會舘用箋
Chong Wa Benevolent Association

東華醫院執事大鑒

　　為去年尾月本會館由處運歸國先友共叁百五十五俱
　　同時滙歸香港戾紙銀壹千八百三十五元概交与　貴醫院
　　執事先生代為办理一切迄今數月未見
　　貴醫院执事　示覆本會館董事殊深渴望迫
　　得再函托陳月峯先生就近代轉致
　　貴醫院执事是否有此斑先友及有此款收
　　到否懇　公留意示覆藉慰渴望感佩
　　餤想未及專此特候

公祺

　　　　　　　　　　　　　　　　　　　主席曾詩傳
　　　　　　　　　　　　　　　　　　　書記胡　均頓

　　　　　　　　　　　　　　　　　　（印章：舍路中華會舘）

中華民國二十年五月十六日泐

另一人註：已覆

130   Letter from Chong Wa Benevolent Association, Seattle, USA, to Tung Wah Hospital on 16 May 1931

From the Office of Chong Wa Benevolent Association, Seattle

Dear Managers of Tung Wah Hospital,

Late last year, we repatriated the remains of 355 deceased friends and sought your help in handling the matter. We also sent a cheque for 1,835 Hong Kong dollars to your good selves. A few months have passed, but we have yet to hear from you. The directors of our association are quite eager to know the status of repatriation. We thus wrote to Chan Yuet-fung (*Chen Yuefeng*) who is near you and asked him to transfer our letter to you to clarify if your esteemed hospital had received the remains of our deceased friends as well as the funds. Please reply to us at your earliest convenience.

We are most grateful to you for your updates.

We wish you well.

Yours sincerely,
Tsang Sze-chuen (*Zeng Shichuan*), Chairman
Wu Kwan (*Hu Jun*), Secretary
(Stamp: Chong Wa Benevolent Association, Seattle)

16 May of the 20th year of the Republic of China

Another person's remarks: Replied

義興隆機器廠用箋
GNEE HENG LONG

東華醫院執事先生大鑒敬啓者^家在暹京

　經商多年原籍廣東番禺有子逢盖

　留學美國波士頓市麻省工程大學不幸

　於去年八月間因駕車不慎遇險畢命

　現托其同學林植豪君料理將灵柩運

　囬計時不日林君當有電報通知何日由

　美啟程寄付何輪何時可以抵港一俟接浔

　佈告自當詳細奉知今特專函預報請

　於棺柩抵港之時格外注意妥為照料

　并請暫寄　貴莊秋间當派親屬囬

　港運囬省城安葬至代墊各項費用當

　即如數歸趙諸費

　清神存没均感專此即請

公安

　　　國廿年六月十号（印章：暹羅唝叻義興隆書柬）周鏡泉上

131 Letter from Chow Keng-chuen, Siam, to Tung Wah Hospital on 10 June 1931

From the Office of Gnee Heng Long

Dear Managers of Tung Wah Hospital,

My family, originally from Pun Yu *(Panyu)*, Kwangtung *(Guangdong)*, have operated a business in Siam for many years, whereas my son, Fung-koi *(Fenggai)*, studied in the Massachusetts Institute of Technology in Boston, USA. In August last year, my son tragically died in a traffic accident while driving his car. I have asked his school friend, Lam Chik-ho *(Lin Zhihao)*, to bring his coffin back. Lam should inform me by telegraph soon when he will depart America, which ship he will be sailing on and when he will arrive in Hong Kong. Once I have further information, I will pass it onto you. I now write to you in advance to seek your help. Please pay special attention and take my son's coffin into your care and store it in your coffin home after it arrives in Hong Kong. I will arrange for my relative to come to Hong Kong in Autumn to collect the coffin and transport it back to Pun Yu for burial. I shall reimburse you for all expenses incurred.

Thank you for your kind assistance. My late son and my family members are most grateful to you for your kindness.

I wish you well.

Yours sincerely,
Chow Keng-chuen *(Zhou Jingquan)*
(Stamp: Gnee Heng Long, Siam)

10 June of the 20th year of the Republic of China

加拿大域多利台山寧陽總會館用箋
HOY SUN NING YUNG BENEVOLENT ASS'N HEAD OFFICE

香港東華醫院
顏成坤董事先生曁列位執事先生鑒

　　遞啓者現加拿大域多利埠台山寧陽總會館是
　　屆執拾各邑先友骸骨統計合共一千一百一十具現由
　　詩丕亞公司俄国皇后輪船裝載囬港煩
　　貴善院僱工起收並將各邑先友轉運囬各該邑
　　善堂安置以候先友家屬領收安葬以慰靈爽
　　功德無量矣兹付囬港仄旀壹張值銀伍百大元
　　請查照收以應支需惟是本總會館職員遞年
　　更換恐對于办理难免人生路不熟之感或有未
　　能的當之處尚希賜函指敎是所感盼

此致

　　　　　　　　　　　　　　　　　　總理李覺世
　　　　　　　　　　　　　　　　　　書記黃世鈜
民國二十年七月廿八日　　　　　（印章：駐利維城台山寧陽總會館）

另一人註：已复

132 Letter from Hoy Sun Ning Yung Benevolent Association Head Office, Victoria, Canada, to Tung Wah Hospital on 28 July 1931

From the Head Office of Hoy Sun Ning Yung Benevolent Association, Victoria, Canada

Dear Chairman Ngan Shing-kwan and Managers of Tung Wah Hospital,

We, Hoy Sun Ning Yung Benevolent Association of Victoria, Canada, have exhumed the bones of 1,110 deceased friends of various counties. The bones will be repatriated to Hong Kong on the *Empress of Russia* of the Canadian Pacific Steamship Company. Please take the bones into your care and send them onto the benevolent associations of the deceased's hometown, so that the families can collect the bones and lay our deceased friends to rest. You kindness is boundless. We enclose a cheque for 500 Hong Kong dollars to cover the expenses incurred. Please check accordingly. As we have new staff every few years, we may not be aware of the necessary procedures. If we have done anything inappropriately, please let us know.

We are most grateful to you for your help.

Yours sincerely,
Lee Kok-sai *(Li Jueshi)*, Chairman
Wong Sai-wang *(Huang Shihong)*, Secretary
(Stamp: Hoy Sun Ning Yung Benevolent Association Head Office, Victoria)

28 July of the 20th year of the Republic of China

Another person's remarks: Replied

加拿大域多利台山寧陽總會館用箋
HOY SUN NING YUNG BENEVOLENT ASS'N HEAD OFFICE

東華醫院
顏成坤先生曁各董事先生鑒

　　逕啓者早月呈函曾經商量運寄先友辦
　　法幸蒙示復照准辦理現查執拾骸骨統
　　計合共一千八百一十九具准期于八月一日由詩丕亞公司俄
　　國皇后輪船載運囬港相應函達
　　貴院屆時雇工起收代為分發各邑善堂俾
　　骸親收領安葬是則豈惟幽魂各得其所
　　貴院為善之熱誠當亦積德無量矣此致

崇安

　　　　　　　　　　　　　　　　總理李覺世
　　　　　　　　　　　　　　　　書記黃世鉉
　　　　　　　　　　　　（印章：駐利維城台山寧陽總會館印）

中華民國二十年七月廿八日

133

Letter from Hoy Sun Ning Yung Benevolent Association Head Office, Victoria, Canada, to Tung Wah Hospital on 28 July 1931

From the Head Office of Hoy Sun Ning Yung Benevolent Association, Victoria, Canada

Dear Chairman Ngan Shing-kwan and Managers of Tung Wah Hospital,

We wrote to you several months ago to enquire about the procedures for repatriating the bones of deceased friends. Thank you very much for your reply, and we have followed your instructions. We exhumed the bones of 1,819 deceased friends and will repatriate them to Hong Kong on the *Empress of Russia* of the Canadian Pacific Steamship Company. When you receive the bones and letter, please take the bones into your care and send them onto the benevolent associations of the deceased's hometown, so that the families can collect the bones and lay our deceased friends to rest.

May the deceased's spirits find eternal peace.

The benevolence of your esteemed hospital will be known far and wide.

We wish you well.

Yours sincerely,
Lee Kok-sai *(Li Jueshi)*, Chairman
Wong Sai-wang *(Huang Shihong)*, Secretary
(Stamp: Hoy Sun Ning Yung Benevolent Association Head Office, Victoria)

28 July of the 20th year of the Republic of China

東華醫院执事先生台鑒啓者

　　前由金山囬唐在船中逝世之李
　　業金現係在　貴院否若係在
　　貴院又用如何手續方能運囬
　　安塟希為詳細示復台山新
　　昌埠明信銀號^{收交}李禹民收
　　便可諸事有勞不勝感德之至
　　專此并請

台安

^侄禹民謹上

弍十年八月廿八号

134 Letter from Lee Yu-man, to Tung Wah Hospital on 28 August 1931

Dear Managers of Tung Wah Hospital,

I am writing to find out if the remains of Lee Yip-kam *(Li Yejin)*, who passed away onboard a ship bound for China from San Francisco, are in your esteemed hospital. If they are, what procedures do I need to complete in order to have the remains sent back to the hometown for burial? Please reply to me, Lee Yu-man *(Li Yumin)*, c/o Ming Shun Native Bank *(Mingxin Yinhao)*, Sun Cheong Port *(Xinchang Bu)*, Toi Shan.

I am most grateful to you for your assistance.

I wish you well.

Yours sincerely,
Lee Yu-man

28 August of the 20th year of the Republic of China

香港廣東銀行用牋
The Bank of Canton, Ltd.

東華醫院
列位總理先生台鑒敬啓者項接中
　　山縣東鎮隔田鄉陸滿函稱伊叔陸
　　世樵在美國金山大埠逝世其遺柩
　　業於本年國曆六月間由該埠開來之
　　某總統船運港由
　　貴院代轉計程諒已抵埗等語等情前
　　來用特函達
　　台端如有上述遺柩曾否抵港抑或在途
　　敢煩　示知以便由^弟函禀得以着人前來
　　領收回鄉安葬有勞至感專此敬候

台安

　　　　　　　　　　　　　　　陸榮光　拜啓

中華民國廿年九月壹號

Letter from Luk Wing-kwong, Hong Kong, to Tung Wah Hospital on 1 September 1931

From the Office of The Bank of Canton Limited, Hong Kong

Dear Directors of Tung Wah Hospital,

I received a letter from Luk Moon *(Lu Man)* of Gut Tin Township *(Getian Xiang)*, Dong Town *(Dong Zhen)*, Chung Shan County *(Zhongshan Xian)*, saying that his uncle Luk Sai-chiu *(Lu Shiqiao)* passed away in San Francisco, USA. His coffin had been sent back from San Francisco to Hong Kong on a ship of the American President Lines in June. It was said that your esteemed hospital would repatriate the coffin and that it should have arrived in Hong Kong. I hereby write to find out if the coffin has reached you or if it is still on the way. Please reply to me, so that arrangements can be made for the remains to be taken to the deceased's hometown for burial.

We are most grateful to you for your efforts.

We wish you well.

Yours sincerely,
Luk Wing-kwong *(Lu Rongguang)*

1 September of the 20th year of the Republic of China

中國鄭鏡祥致東華醫院信件

1931 年 9 月 23 日

啓者東華醫院大總理顏成坤善長
先生鑒邇來東干勝埠諸事皆吉為
祝之慰啓者余父在花旗仙遊去世由
西正月初十日由美國搭秩父丸運返香港
東華医院轉交仍尚未到余經已在香港
查問办事人員言及有收經已交中山
囬春院為弟在中山查問與善堂総
理言及新舊両年未有收到亦再半
年之久未有交到但望総理得接此
信望先生寫明運費洗用銀多寡
与余交□善長為□自繫囬音中山石
岐南基路廣信海味店收轉交余便□
即鄭賞字昌鴻靈柩無悮可也餘無別及
即請

列位先生鈞安

辛八月十弍日　弟鄭鏡祥叩禀

136

Letter from Cheng Keng-cheung, China, to Tung Wah Hospital on 23 September 1931

Dear Chairman Ngan Shing-kwan and Managers of Tung Wah Hospital,

I wish you well.

My father passed away in the USA. His coffin was back from the USA on the *Chichibu Maru* on the 10th day of the 1st lunar month this year and should be repatriated through the Tung Wah Hospital of Hong Kong, but it had not arrived in Chung Shan *(Zhongshan)* yet. I made an enquiry in Hong Kong, and was told that my father's coffin had been received and sent to Wui Chun Yuen *(Huichun Yuan)* at Chung Shan. Wui Chun Yuen then asked the director of Yu Sin Tong *(Yu Shan Tang)* on my behalf and was told that my father's coffin had not been received either around the Western or Chinese new year. Since then, another six months had passed, the coffin had still not arrived. When you receive this letter, please inform me how much the repatriation fees are and I will settle the payment. Please send your reply to me, in the care of Kwong Shun Dried Seafood *(Guangxin Haiwei Dian)*, Nam Kei Road *(Nanji Lu)*, Shekki *(Shiqi)*, Chung Shan. I write to you with regard to the coffin of Cheng Sheung *(Zheng Shang)*, style name Cheong-hung *(Changhong)*.

I await your reply. May you all be blessed.

Yours humbly,
Cheng Keng-cheung *(Zheng Jingxiang)*

12th day of the 8th lunar month, Year of San Mei *(Xinwei)*

東華醫院^暨院長經理執事先生^{偉鑒}敬啓者茲聞英屬咸水埠中華會館將加
　拿大各埠仙友骨石在咸水埠八月一号托船寄囬香港　貴醫院接收然後轉派各
　縣之説但有弍月餘仍無見報登載因先父亦在其內故特函奉告求懇　貴
　院賜复俾明真相易办理也至於到港　貴院該如何轉派或該縣人轉派該
　県或着人到港　貴院領取其須如何手續請　貴院賜教為盼
　餘未細及仰复是荷專此敬請

醫安

新會
第五區　桐井陸蔚南字頓

（印章：廣州市高第街西華鞋廠書東）

民廿年十月七日

「回信地址請寄省城高第中路門牌一百五十八號西華鞋廠轉交陸蔚
南收便妥有勞」

137

Letter from Luk Wai-nam, China, to Tung Wah Hospital on 7 October 1931

Dear Chairman and Managers of Tung Wah Hospital,

I heard that the Chinese Consolidated Benevolent Association in Vancouver, Britain, repatriated the bones of deceased friends who passed away in various cities of Canada from Vancouver to Hong Kong by sea on 1 August. The bones were supposed to be sent to your esteemed hospital first and then transported to various native counties. However, more than two months have passed but no notice has been published in the newspaper yet. Since the bones of my late father are among those repatriated, I would be most grateful if you could reply to tell me the situation, so that I could make necessary arrangement. After the bones arrive in Hong Kong, how do you transport them to their hometown? Will you help transport the bones to the respective counties or a representative of the respective county should come to Hong Kong to collect the bones? Please kindly let me know the procedures. I await your reply.

I wish you well.

Yours humbly,
Luk Wai-nam *(Lu Weinan)* of Tung Cheng *(Tongjing)*, the Fifth District *(Diwuqu)*, Sun Wui *(Xinhui)*
(Stamp: From the Office of Sai Wah Shoe Factory *(Xihua Xiechang)*, Ko Dee *(Gaodi)* Street, Canton)

7 October of the 20th year of the Republic of China

"Please send your reply to Luk Wai-nam, c/o Sai Wah Shoe Factory, 158 Ko Dee Chung Road, Canton."

加拿大域多利台山寧陽總會館用箋
HOY SUN NING YUNG BENEVOLENT ASS'N HEAD OFFICE

東華醫院列位善董先生鑒

逕啓者本總會館前八月一日由俄国皇后船付畀
各先友起落費銀伍佰大元諒已妥收並各邑先友壹
仟捌佰餘具想亦妥為安置惟轉駁運返各邑
善堂一切費用歸各邑善堂自行料理但經兩閱月餘
未得　貴院囘音賜敎本總會館執事等殊
為焦慮望　貴院善董從速賜函指示俾得
領教而免縈懷是所切盼此致

並候
文祺

總理李覺世
書記黃世鋐

民國二十年十月十日　　　　　　　（印章：駐利維城台山寧陽總會館印章）

兹將各邑先友開列

台山餘慶堂	六百七十九具	箱头六百六十四只 鐵箱四个合共六百六十八箱 付交台城東門外義庄祠起收
中山福善堂	一百二十一具	箱头 一百一十八只 另鐵箱一个
岡州福慶堂	二百四十具	箱头 二百三十二只 付交會城新盛街仁安醫院起收
開平廣福堂	二百六十具	箱头 二百五十七只
增城仁安堂	二十二具	箱头 十七只
恩平同福堂	八十一具	箱头 八十只
番禺昌后堂	一百六十三具	箱头 二百五十七只
東莞保安堂	九具	箱头 九只
南海縣口堂	九具	箱头 九只
順德行安堂	八具	箱头 八只
鶴山縣口堂	四十四具	箱头 四十四只
新安縣口堂		

Letter from Hoy Sun Ning Yung Benevolent Association Head Office, Victoria, Canada, to Tung Wah Hospital on 10 October 1931

From the Head Office of Hoy Sun Ning Yung Benevolent Association, Victoria, Canada

Dear benevolent Directors of Tung Wah Hospital,

We trust that you had received the 500 dollars we sent to you to cover the costs of unloading the remains of our deceased friends repatriated on the *Empress of Russia* on 1 August. We also believe that you had taken the 1,800 sets or so remains of our deceased friends of various counties into your care. However, the costs of transportation from Hong Kong to mainland China should be paid by the benevolent associations of the deceased's hometown.

It has been more than two months since we sent the funds and the remains back, but we have yet to hear from your esteemed hospital. Please reply to us at your earliest convenience as our managers are worrying about the matters.

We await your reply and we wish you well.

Yours sincerely,
Lee Kok-sai *(Li Jueshi)*, Chairman
Wong Sai-wang *(Huang Shihong)*, Secretary
(Stamp: Hoy Sun Ning Yung Benevolent Association Head Office, Victoria)

10 October of the 20th year of the Republic of China

[Editor's remarks: Name list of the deceased friends is available only in Chinese]

139 香港梁芸軒致東華醫院信件

1931 年 10 月 12 日

香港永安有限公司
THE WING ON CO., LTD.

東華醫院總理
顏成坤先生偉鑒敬啓者茲有敝友
郑賞兄[字]昌鴻在美國不幸仙遊經
鄉友將該靈柩於元月內搭秩父丸
交　貴院轉交中山東鎮鰲溪鄉他
子郑鏡祥收惟至今日久未見該棺
運到未知　貴院有收到否敢請
代為一查如何之處請早示覆是所
厚望也耑此奉托即請并頌

时祺

[弟]梁芸軒上言

中華民國一九三一年陽曆十月十二號
辛年陰曆九月初二日

倘有信回覆請交
永安公司西文寫字楼
梁芸軒收可也

另一人註：已复

Letter from Leung Wan-hin, Hong Kong, to Tung Wah Hospital on 12 October 1931

THE WING ON CO., LTD.

Dear Chairman Ngan Shing-kwan of Tung Wah Hospital,

My friend, Cheng Sheung *(Zheng Shang)*, style name Cheong-hung *(Changhong)* passed away in the USA. Fellow townsmen sent his coffin on the *Chichibu Maru* in January to his son Cheng Keng-cheung *(Zheng Jingxiang)* in Ngo Kai Village *(Aoxi Xiang)*, Tung Town *(Dong Zhen)*, Chung Shan *(Zhongshan)*, through your esteemed hospital. However, the coffin has yet to arrive in Chung Shan. Can you please advise if your esteemed hospital has received the coffin? Please reply to me at your earliest convenience.

Thank you for your efforts.

I wish you well.

Yours sincerely,
Leung Wan-hin *(Liang Yunxuan)*

12 October 1931
2nd day of the 9th lunar month, Year of San Mei *(Xinwei)*

Please send your reply to me through the foreign language office of Wing On Company.

Another person's remarks: Replied

香港東華医局

列位執事先生大鑒　謹啓者敝善堂是屆议

　　　決舉辦檢運先骸事務目下經已着手檢集妥

　　　竣大小合共式十具擇準扵本月十一日由此間附搭

　　　胡佛總統 S. S. Pres. Hoover 轉運东歸直寄交

貴局暫為收存故用特預函告達屆时如該先骸等

　　　運抵　貴處時希即代為妥存並請發函下列地

　　　址俾得前往提領為盼附夾上載紙乙張仰祈查

　　　照是荷諸費清神謝謝耑此預達并頌

公安

　　　　　　　　　　　　　　　　上
　　　　　　　　　　中山恭集善堂謹啓（印章：集善堂）
　　　　　　　　　　　　　　　　都

民國廿一年三月十一日

候領人通信地址如下（中山縣下柵圩茂昌號轉交 卓篤先 收）
梁厚晃

另一人註：Pxxx Sin Tong Assn San Francisco
c/o 819 Grant Ave. San Francisco. Calif., USA

Letter from Chap Sin Tong, Chung Shan, China, to Tung Wah Hospital on 11 March 1932

Dear Managers of Tung Wah Hospital,

We decided to repatriate our deceased friends to their hometown. We exhumed 20 sets of remains and had made arrangements for them to be sent to your esteemed hospital on the *SS President Hoover* on the 11th day of this month. Please take them into your care when they arrive in Hong Kong, and send a letter to the recipient in the following address requesting him to collect the remains. We enclose the bill of lading for your reference.

We are most grateful to you for your efforts. We wish you well.

Yours sincerely,
Chap Sin Tong *(Ji Shan Tang)*, Sheung Kung Do *(Shanggong Du)*, Chung Shan *(Zhongshan)*
(Stamp: Chap Sin Tong) *(Ji Shan Tang)*

11 March of the 21st year of the Republic of China

Address of the recipient:
Leung Hau-fong *(Liang Houhuang)* & Cheuk Tuk Sin *(Zhuo Duxian)*
c/o Mau Cheong Ho *(Maochang Hao)*
Ha Jat Market Town *(Xiazha Xu)*
Chung Shan

Another person's remarks: Pxxx Sin Tong Assn San Francisco
c/o 819 Grant Ave. San Francisco. Calif., USA.

特字

東華醫院大执事鑒啓者茲今一千九百三十二

年新曆三月十九号啓行太平洋公司

總統船旋國運來尸棺一具乃係

廣東省番禺縣慕德里司南村宏

仁里人周義和名由英屬域多利埠

儎囬有勞先生祈查到步請查收領

代為駁運番邑城北高塘墟俟他鄉

親屬領囬安葬就可惟是医院運駁費

用若干請來香港滙安公司滙兑店門

牌干諾道西九十三號祈為交妥諸事多勞

請備覆音

　　　順請

善安

一九三二年三月十九号　　　　　　　　周鏡{輝/如} 拜託

Letter from Chow Keng-fai and Chow Keng-yu to Tung Wah Hospital on 19 March 1932

Dear Managers of Tung Wah Hospital,

On 19 March 1932, the coffin of Chow Yee-wo *(Zhou Yihe)*, a native of Wang Yan Lane *(Hongren Li)*, Sze Nam Village *(Sinan Cun)*, Mo Tak Lane *(Mude Li)*, Pun Yu County *(Panyu Xian)*, Kwangtung *(Guangdong)*, has been repatriated to Hong Kong from Victoria, British Columbia, Canada, on the President Lines ship. Please take the coffin into your care when it arrives in Hong Kong and send it to Ko Tong Market Town *(Gaotang Xu)*, city north of Pun Yu for his family to claim. With regard to the costs for sending the coffin from Hong Kong to Pun Yu, please collect the money from Wui On Foreign Exchange at 93 Connaught Road West.

Thank you very much for your efforts. We await you reply.

We wish you well.

Yours sincerely,
Chow Keng-fai *(Zhou Jinghui)*, Chow Keng-yu *(Zhou Jingru)*

19 March 1932

東華醫院諸大执事^{尊鑒}敬啓者窃思□遊異域覓
　　食番邦無非仰奉腑蓄然運乖時蹇思□期而嘆不
　　得以致老死番邦曷勝浩嘆今有宗□伯黃賢興
　　者在美國高老砂埠与世長辭^{敝姓}將其灵柩運歸
　　恳諸大執事代為照料遲一二礼拜伊家親知情定
　　然出港領囘安蜇以正首邱伊乃廣東台山縣白
　　沙新圲牛角龍村人氏今特字告知貴院灵柩由
　　林肯船運裝五月六号由美國大埠開行到步恳
　　為料理所謂福田廣種異培富貴之花心地宏開
　　定报平安之竹理所宜言也福星載道　并祝

諸大执事萬事勝意

　　　　　　　　　　　　　　　　　　美國高老砂埠黃江夏堂上

民國式拾一年西曆五月式号

Letter from Wong Kong Har Tong of Colusa, USA, to Tung Wah Hospital on 2 May 1932

Dear Managers of Tung Wah Hospital,

Chinese compatriots leave their homeland to make a living in a foreign country. They long to return to their hometown but many of them tragically die abroad. Our deceased friend, Wong Yin-hing *(Huang Xianxing)* passed away in Colusa, USA and we had repatriated his coffin to Hong Kong. Please take the coffin into your care for one or two weeks and his family will come to Hong Kong to collect his remains for burial. The deceased is a native of Ngau Kok Lung Village *(Niujiao Long Cun)*, Pak Sha New Market Town *(Baisha Xin Xu)*, Toi Shan County *(Taishan Xian)*, Kwangtung *(Guangdong)*.

We hereby write to inform you that the coffin will be repatriated from San Francisco, USA on the *SS President Lincoln* on 6 May. Please take it into your care after it arrives in Hong Kong. Your benevolence is far reaching and you will be blessed for your kindness.

We wish you well.

Yours sincerely,
Wong Kong Har Tong of Colusa, USA

2 May of the 21st year of the Republic of China

143

香港王棠致東華醫院信件

1932年5月12日

五華實業信託銀行香港分行
NG WAH TRUST & INDUSTRIAL BANK HONG KONG BRANCH

東華醫院
司理先生大鑒茲有香山濠涌鄉方可照之妻何
氏在美國裴士那埠逝世靈柩日間運來香港到步
入義莊後希向電話示知為盼　此致并頌

台安

王棠

廿一年五月十二日

From the Office of Ng Wah Trust & Industrial Bank, Hong Kong Branch

Dear Managers of Tung Wah Hospital,

Madam Ho, the wife of Fong Ho-chiu *(Fang Kezhao)* from Ho Chung Township *(Haochong Xiang)*, Heung Shan *(Xiangshan)*, passed away in Frensno, USA. Her coffin had been repatriated to Hong Kong and should arrive soon. Please give me a call after it has reached your coffin home.

I wish you well.

Yours sincerely,
Wong Tong *(Wang Tang)*

12 May of the 21st year of the Republic of China

東華醫院諸执事先生敬啓者素聞　諸执事慈善為怀惻憫為

心久聞盛　名如雷貫耳独惜[弟]寄跡他邦緣慳乎瞻韓飄蓬異

域面鮮於識荆恨何如之惟有仰天遙　祝諸执事　先生百鹿延

釐千羊緝慶繁庥益集嘉祉咸臻而已耳兹有哀懇者[弟]有胞

[弟]名劉錫廣乃順德県騰冲鄉人氏向寄居美洲砵崙埠时遭不

幸痛於本年五月下旬身故今將其灵柩運囬祖國以正首坵准於

五月廿八日由他輔總統船運囬計时下月約　等日可以抵港但抵港之

後定必漸停厝扵於東華醫院候親傳人等到來領收帶囬家鄉安

塟[弟]亦有傳寄歸囑託劉錫建劉源湘兩人到　貴院與諸执事

先生商量領收帶歸安塟以慰幽魂　伏乞　貴院諸执事先生驗

明俾他兩人早日帶歸妥窀沒存均感至於柩內并無夾帶違禁

物品如有不妥之处隨时可以通訊查究[弟]為完全負責之人素

仰　貴院諸执事　先生嚴明慈善常為各地僑胞所乐道[弟]不揣

冒昧故敢特字哀告藉助一臂諸事有勞容当拜謝

[弟]劉錫堅　哀上

一九三二年五月廿六号晚

Letter from Lau Shek-kin, USA, to Tung Wah Hospital on 26 May 1932

Dear Managers of Tung Wah Hospital,

Your benevolence and kindness are known far and wide. I have always admired your good work, but since I live in a foreign country, I have yet to meet you in person. Nevertheless, I pray that you have good health and a life full of blessings.

My younger brother, Lau Yeung-kwong *(Liu Yangguang)*, a native of Tang Chung Township *(Tengchong Xiang)*, Shung Tak County *(Shunde Xian)*, passed away tragically in Portland, USA, in late May. His coffin will be repatriated on the *SS President Taft* on 28 May, and is expected to arrive in Hong Kong next month. After it arrives in Hong Kong, it needs to be placed in Tung Wah Hospital until our family comes to take it to our hometown for burial. I have asked Lau Yeung-kin *(Liu Yangjian)* and Lau Yuen-sheung *(Liu Yuanxiang)* to go and discuss the repatriation procedures with the managers of your esteemed hospital. It is hoped that my brother can be laid to rest in our hometown. When the two men come to your esteemed hospital, please check and let them collect the coffin as soon as possible. The deceased and the living will be grateful to you. Also, please be assured that there are no restricted articles in the coffin. If there are any problems, please do not hesitate to write to me. I will take full responsibility of the matter.

I have long heard of your benevolence. Fellow Chinese compatriots all over America admire your good selves very much, so I venture to seek your help.

I am most grateful to you for your efforts.

Yours sincerely,
Lau Shek-kin *(Liu Shijian)* in mourning

Evening of 26 May 1932

敬懇者廣東開平橫石鄉家父周憲芹前經
商美之小埠不幸身故曾托敝兄弟撿拾先骸
完妥附出大埠轉回家鄉隨接復函報知為時已
久未得拜領安葬誠恐忙中錯附別處去沒
存含恨迫得函達
　台端敬懇檢查簿據有無先父骸砸附到
貴院乞即示復実為德便此呈

東華醫院值理董事先生暨各执事先生照

　　通訊處德輔道中二百四十三號三樓廣裕荣

　　民國式十一年六月十一号

　　　　　　　　　弟周章達謹上（印章：香港廣裕榮）

Letter from Chow Cheung-tat, Hong Kong, to Tung Wah Hospital on 11 June 1932

Dear Directors and Managers of Tung Wah Hospital,

My father, Chow Hin-kan *(Zhou Xianqin)* of Wang Shek Township *(Hengshi Xiang)*, Hoi Ping *(Kaiping)*, Kwangtung *(Guangdong)*, ran a business in a small town in America and passed away there. I had asked our fellow townsmen to exhume my late father's bones and send them to San Francisco for repatriation to our hometown. I received a reply later saying that a long time had passed, and no one was informed to collect the bones for burial. I am concerned that the bones may have been mistakenly sent to another place as you were heavily preoccupied. I therefore urge you to check your records to see if the bones of my late father have been sent to your esteemed hospital. I await your reply.

Thank you very much for your kindness.

Correspondence address: Kwong Yu Wing, 3/F, 243 Des Voeux Road Central

Yours sincerely,
Chow Cheung-tat *(Zhou Zhangda)*
(Stamp: Kwong Yu Wing, Hong Kong)

11 June of the 21st year of the Republic of China

東華醫院諸報事先生鑒逕啓者茲有^{兄弟}蔡熠奕係
台山縣公益區大江沙浦中羌村人昨六月初旬在雲哥華埠
逝世茲將其遺骸壹具由亞洲皇后船六月十八号船期運囬
香港另死者有夾碼箱壹只內有旧衣物亦是同船寄來用是函
達　貴院查收懇為料理運其柩囬原籍安塟至
於夾碼箱勞通知香港上環西街荣德豬油鋪領回俾
交其妻子收領是荷素仰　貴醫院慈善為懷办理諸
事妥当今蒙妥理此事存歿均感耑此佈達即詢

義安　　　　　　　　　　　旅雲哥華埠沙浦房^{同人}蔡 傑夫 仝啓
　　　　　　　　　　　　　　　　　　　　　　英錦

民國廿一年六月十五号泐

Letter from Choi Kit-fu & Choi Ying-kam, Canada, to Tung Wah Hospital on 15 June 1932

Dear Managers of Tung Wah Hospital,

Our deceased friend Choi Jap-yik *(Cai Yiyi)*, a native of Chung Keung Village *(Zhongqiang Cun)*, Tai Kong Sha Po *(Dajiang Shapu)*, Kung Yat District *(Gongyi Qu)*, Toi Shan County *(Taishan Xian)*, passed away in Vancouver in early June. His remains will be repatriated to Hong Kong on the *Empress of Asia* on 18 June, along with a suitcase containing his old clothes. Please take delivery of the remains when they arrive in Hong Kong, and send the coffin to the deceased's hometown for burial. As to the suitcase, please inform Wing Tak Lard Shop at Sai Street, Sheung Wan, Hong Kong, to collect it and hand over to his widow.

The benevolence of your hospital is known far and wide. We trust that this matter will be taken care of by your good hands. The deceased and the family are grateful to you.

We wish you well.

Yours sincerely,
Choi Kit-fu *(Cai Jiefu)*, Choi Ying-kam *(Cai Yingjin)* and all the Sha Po Fong fellow clansmen residing in Vancouver

15 June of the 21st year of the Republic of China

147

中國前山福善堂致東華醫院信件

1932年7月5日

前山福善堂用箋

東華醫院
列位執事先生大鑒逕啟者由五月有
斗门人氏先友任鍇錦名華好由域多
利埠運囬現有斗门人路經本堂因搭
斗门渡不及來本堂邀求將該先友
骨箱一具暫停一天至今念餘日仍未
見其人來携囬茲特函懇求
貴院代查在港时領該先友担保者
追究該帶先友親屬早日來本堂
領囬免延至日久本堂葬于義地
請勞代查如何之處懇答复為
盼專函奉達此請

善安

（印章：前山福善堂）拜啓

民國廿一年七月五日

另一人註：鴨巴甸街十八號美新鞋廠

Letter from Fook Sin Tong of Chin Shan, China, to Tung Wah Hospital on 5 July 1932

From the Office of Fook Sin Tong *(Fu Shan Tang)* of Chin Shan *(Qianshan)*

Dear Managers of Tung Wah Hospital,

The remains of Yam Kai-kam *(Ren Kaijin)*, also known as Wah-ho *(Huahao)* and a native of Dou Mun *(Doumen)*, were repatriated from Victoria in May. Someone from Dou Mun passed by our association and asked us to take the bones of the said deceased friend into our care temporarily for one day, as he had missed the boat bound for Dou Mun. It is now more than twenty days but the remains are still in our care. We write to seek your help in finding out the name of the deceased friend's relative who collected the bones from you in Hong Kong through the guarantor. We would like to locate that person to claim the bones from our association as soon as possible, so that we need not bury the bones in our communal graveyard. Please reply to us with the information.

We wish you well.

Yours sincerely,
(Stamp: Fook Sin Tong, Chin Shan)

5 July of the 21st year of the Republic of China

Another person's remarks: Mei Sun Shoe Factory, 18 Aberdeen Street

東華醫院執事善長鈞鑒^{鄙人}有胞弟

　　梁瑞賢字朗焯年五十六歲係赴鄙市輪船當

　　廚工由六月中旬開行將近至檀香山不幸身故

　　近聞該骸已囬　貴院未卜其人有無行李銀

　　兩等物但因其妻年僅三十歲其子十弍歲其

　　女八歲吾為伯父年已六十四歲在其妻當此

　　痛哀地位难以舉步在吾又屬老弱难以出入

　　如果屬在困窮不能備敷出入費用爰特

　　修函呈請　貴院查核懇為細查有無

　　行李祈照此列住址賜音示知為盼

^{鄙人}梁瑞德謹呈

有音賜來照此
廣東開平縣沙溪市
廣昌荣店梁瑞德收入便妥

中華民國廿一年九月六日

Letter from Leung Shui-tak, China, to Tung Wah Hospital on 6 September 1932

Dear Managers of Tung Wah Hospital,

My younger brother, Leung Shui-yin *(Liang Runxian)*, style name Long-cheuk *(Langzhuo)* and aged 56, worked in the kitchen of the *SS President Pierce*. The ship set sail in mid-June, but my brother died onboard when the ship was near Honolulu. I heard that his remains had been taken to your esteemed hospital, and wonder if he had any luggage or valuables such as money left behind. He is survived by a wife of only 30 years old, as well as a son and a daughter aged 12 and 8 respectively. I, their uncle, am 64 years old. My brother's widow is heartbroken and it is hard for her to come to Hong Kong. Meanwhile, as I myself am old and weak, I can come neither. Also, we do not have the money to make the trip. I therefore write to ask you to find out if my late brother had left behind any luggage. Please send your reply to the address below. I look forward to hearing from you.

Yours humbly,
Leung Shui-tak *(Liang Ruide)*

Please send your reply to:
Leung Shui-tak, Kwong Cheong Wing shop *(Guang Chang Rong Dian)*, Sha Kai City *(Shaxi Shi)*, Hoi Ping County *(Kaiping Xian)*, Kwangtung *(Guangdong)*

6 September of the 21st year of the Republic of China

Letter from Dollar Steamship Lines and American Mail Line to Tung Wah Hospital on 19 October 1932

DOLLAR STEAMSHIP LINES
AND
AMERICAN MAIL LINE

PO 352 JWM

Hongkong,
October 19, 1932

File: C-3-C

Tung Wah Hospital,
Hongkong

Gentlemen: -

On the arrival of our ss "President Monroe" V-27, on May 14th, 1932, the remains of one of our steerage passengers, Francisco Lee Soon, age 33, was delivered to you.

Francisco Lee Soon died on board our "President Monroe" on May 6th, while that steamer was enroute to Hongkong. The cause of death was tuberculosis. Francisco Lee Soon was a passenger on board the "President Monroe" from Havana and was destined to Hongkong, and the body was embalmed and delivered to the Tung Wah Hospital on arrival of the "President Monroe" at this port.

Will you please be good enough to address to me a letter confirming that the remains of Francisco Lee Soon was turned over to you and also advising us as to what disposition was made of the remains?

Very truly yours,

J. W. MORRIS
Passenger Agent

JWM: MC

美國郵船公司及金元輪船公司致東華醫院信件
1932 年 10 月 19 日

（原信件中文翻譯本）

本年五月十四日门罗總統船抵港时有搭客李宣者年三十三歲

留下各物經已交付貴院

李宣於五月六日因肺癆傷死於船中而當时本

船亦在途次囬港之时也

李宣是由夏灣拿來港者他的尸體已於船

□时交付貴院矣

請貴院　示禀証明李宣之遺物確已交付

貴院及如何處置此等遺物

金山大埠岡州總會館用箋
KWONG CHOW ASSOCIATION

逕啓者前蒙代為照拂敝會館第一批先
骸運回原籍实深感佩茲再付上第式
批請為按址分發以妥先灵尤為感激
計開新會城西仁安医院收廿七箱鶴
山沙坪圩同善堂收三箱另一箱係
易時臻由其羊城親屬到
貴医院自行收領就是為此相應
函達即希
查照為荷謹致

東華医院主席

（印章：金山大埠岡州會館）袁鄉愚弟名另肅

民國廿一年十一月七号

另一人註：士担报関一元　一五四 什七具計一百六十九元四毫

Letter from Kwong Chow Association, San Francisco, USA, to Tung Wah Hospital on 7 November 1932

From the Office of Kwong Chow Association, San Francisco

Dear Chairman of Tung Wah Hospital,

Thank you very much for your assistance in the repatriation of the first batch of remains from our association. Now we are repatriating the second batch of remains. Please send them to the deceased's hometown according to our list, so that our deceased friends can be laid to rest. I shall be most grateful to you for your efforts.

Among them, 27 boxes should be sent to City West Yan On Hospital *(Chengxi Ren'an Yiyuan)* in Sun Wui *(Xinhui)*; three boxes should be sent to Tong Sin Tong *(Tong Shan Tang)* in Sha Ping Market Town *(Shaping Xu)*, Hok Shan *(Heshan)*. One box contains the remains of Yik Si-chun *(Yi Shizhan)* and his family from Canton *(Guangzhou)* will come to your esteemed hospital to collect the remains. Please check and follow up accordingly.

Your humble brother,
Yuen Ling-shuk *(Yuan Lingsu)*
Kwong Chow Association, San Francisco

7 November of the 21st year of the Republic of China

Another person's remarks: 1 dollar for customs stamp, 154, 17 sets of remains, 169.40 dollars in total

151 美國金山大埠岡州會館致東華醫院信件

1932 年 11 月 8 日

金山大埠岡州總會館用箋
KWONG CHOW ASSOCIATION

逕啓者昨草上一函為敝會館第二
批先友之運輸回籍請代為按址分發
因一時忘却夾入提貨紙故即補行
付上以利搬運焉至此次工錢若
干連前次共該幾何仰即見示
以便归趙实所至盼且感也為
此再瀆　清聽希即
查照謹致

東華医院主席

袁鄉愚名另肅（印章：金山大埠岡州會館）

民國廿一年十一月八号午

Letter from Kwong Chow Association, San Francisco, USA, to Tung Wah Hospital on 8 November 1932

From the Office of Kwong Chow Association, San Francisco

Dear Chairman of Tung Wah Hospital,

I wrote to you yesterday to seek your assistance in the repatriation of the second batch of remains of the deceased friends from our association. I asked you to send the remains to the deceased's hometown according to the addresses on our list but forgot to send you the bill of lading.

I am sending it to you now, so that you can take delivery of the remains. Please inform us how much the transportation fees are, for this repatriation and the previous one.

We await your reply.

Thank you very much for your efforts.

Your humble brother,
Yuen Ling-shuk *(Yuan Lingsu)*
(Stamp: Kwong Chow Association, San Francisco)

In the afternoon of 8 November of the 21st year of the Republic of China

152 中國新會城西仁安醫院致東華醫院信件

1932 年 12 月 19 日

新會城西仁安方便醫院用箋

東華醫院執事先生大鑒逕啓者昨國歷十
二月十五日頃接陳洪先生有信到來稱説舊金山
大埠岡州會館撿運先友骸骨壹百五拾四具經
已運到　貴院是以[敝]院派戴心海君到港轉運
回邑待各處先友親屬早日領取安葬以妥先魂
实紉公誼　此請

善安

東華醫院執事先生鈞鑒　　（印章：新會城西仁安醫院書柬）

中華民國二十一年夏歷十一月廿二日

Letter from City West Yan On Hospital of Sun Wui, China, to Tung Wah Hospital on 19 December 1932

From the Office of City West Yan On Hospital *(Chengxi Ren'an Yiyuan)*, Sun Wui *(Xinhui)*

Dear Managers of Tung Wah Hospital,

We received a letter from Chan Hung *(Chen Hong)* dated 15 December, saying that the Kwong Chow Association in San Francisco has exhumed and repatriated 154 sets of bones of our deceased friends, and the bones have arrived at your esteemed hospital. We have, therefore, sent Tai Sum-hoi *(Dai Xinhai)* to Hong Kong to repatriate the bones to the deceased's families in their hometown, so that our deceased friends can be laid to rest as soon as possible.

We wish you well.

Yours sincerely,
(Stamp: City West Yan On Hospital, Sun Wui)

22nd day of the 11th lunar month of the 21st year of the Republic of China

中國荻海杏春堂致東華醫院信件

1932 年 12 月

東華醫院列位先生^{大鑒}啟者^弟先父

　　浩中骸骨係光緒卅四年由金山運囬

　　貴院理应連時取囬安塟妥当方為

　　合式因^弟出外洋故此阻延至今祈各

　　位先生代為查明在何处蒙　列位通

　　知^弟即來取囬可也此事諸費精神容

　　日叩謝此請

大安　　　　　　　　　　　　　　　　如有信寄荻海杏春堂湯收

廿一年十二月□日

　　　　　　　　　　　　　　　　　　　　^弟光和_頓
　　　　　　　　　　　　　　　　　　　　　板和

　　　　　　　　　　　　　　　　　　　　（印章）

Letter from Dik Hoi Hang Chun Tong, China, to Tung Wah Hospital in December 1932

Dear Directors of Tung Wah Hospital,

The bones of our late father, Ho-chung *(Haozhong)*, were repatriated from San Francisco to your esteemed hospital in the 34th year of the Guangxu's reign. We should have collected our late father's bones for burial immediately, but since we had been abroad, we were not able to come sooner. Please find out the whereabouts of our late father's remains and notify us. We shall come to collect them immediately.

We are most grateful to you for your efforts.

We wish you well.

Please send your reply to Hang Chun Tong *(Xing Chun Tang)*, Dik Hoi *(Dihai)*

Yours sincerely,
Kwong-wo *(Guanghe)* and Ban-wo *(Banhe)*
(Stamp)

X December of the 21st year of the Republic of China

紐約中華長生有限公司
CHINESE CHEUNG SANG FUNERAL CORP.

東華醫院総理善長先生^{均鑒}敬啟者現有一梓理張

祥輝 CHONG CHUNG FAI 廣東南海縣西樵

人氏在本埠仙遊由本公司製殮于新歷十

弍月廿九日將其灵柩寄総統船 S. S. President

Adams 運囬香港該船約弍月十八九日可能到

港恳煩　貴院执事妥為照料祈預早

日通知香港皇后大道中門牌五十號德祥

寶號伊子張裔先生帮助料理付囬南

海西樵原籍安塟实為感德　耑此即候

善安

　　　　　　內夾儀紙一張請查照收

　　　　　　　　　（印章：紐約中華長生有限公司）總理梁麗天

　　　　　　　　　　　　　（印章：梁麗天 BVE）

民國廿二年元月七日　　　　　　　　　　紐約中華長生公司付

Letter from Chinese Cheung Sang Funeral Corporation of New York, USA, to Tung Wah Hospital on 7 January 1933

From the Office of Chinese Cheung Sang Funeral Corporation of New York

Dear benevolent Directors of Tung Wah Hospital,

Chong Chung Fai *(Zhang Xianghui)*, a clansman of Sai Chiu *(Xiqiao)*, Nam Hoi County *(Nanhai Xian)*, Kwangtung *(Guangdong)*, passed away in our city. Our company is responsible for his funeral service. We have repatriated his coffin to Hong Kong on the *SS President Adams* on 29 December. The ship is expected to arrive in Hong Kong on 18 or 19 February. Please take the coffin into your care and inform his son, Cheung Yui *(Zhang Yi)* at Tak Cheung Company, 50 Queen's Road Central, Hong Kong in advance, and assist him to send the remains to Sai Chiu, Nam Hoi, for burial.

We are most grateful to you for your benevolence. We wish you well.

Please find enclosed the bill of lading.

Yours sincerely,
Leung Lai-tin (Liang Litian),
General Manager
(Stamp: Leung Lai-tin BVE)
(Stamp: Chinese Cheung Sang Funeral Corporation of New York)

7 January of the 22nd year of the Republic of China

KUO MIN TANG CHINESE NATIONALIST LEAGUE OF CANADA HEAD QUARTERS

中國國民黨駐加拿大總支部執行委員會公函第五三號

逕啟者案查^{敝部}第六次代表大會主席團之一伍若泉同志歷年
為黨宣勞在職病故當經^{敝部}決議舉行黨葬典禮運柩回原籍廣
東省台山縣海晏那馬新寨村安葬以表隆重而資闡揚伍代表靈
柩及附運花箱等共七件已附三月二十五日由此間啟行之詩丕亞公
司輪船日本皇后號赴香港相應將伍代表病故及運柩附輪啟行
日期函達
貴院查照希煩照拂至紉公誼此致

香港東華醫院諸執事先生

　　　附錄伍若泉駐港親屬姓名如下

　　　　　　　　伍頤學
　　　萬國旅店　伍時贊
　　　　　　　　伍于梧

（印章：中國國民黨駐加拿大總支部執行委員會印）
（印章：中國國民黨加拿大總支部執行委員會常務委員）
陳辯惑（印章：陳辯惑）
侯民一（印章：侯民一）
關崇穎（印章：關崇穎）

中華民國廿二年三月廿三日

Letter from Kuo Min Tang Chinese Nationalist League of Canada Headquarters, Vancouver, Canada, to Tung Wah Hospital on 23 March 1933

Official correspondence no. 53 of the Executive Committee of Kuo Min Tang Chinese Nationalist League of Canada Headquarters

Dear Managers of Tung Wah Hospital,

Comrade Ng Yeuk-chuen *(Wu Ruoquan)*, Co-chairman of the 6th Congress of our organisation devoted great efforts to the League over the years and passed away while in office. To show our utmost respect, we decided to repatriate his remains to his hometown, Sun Chai Village *(Xinzhai Cun)*, Na Ma *(Nama)*, Hoi An *(Haiyan)*, Toi Shan County *(Taishan Xian)*, Kwangtung *(Guangdong)*, for burial after his party funeral. Seven items, including the coffin of Chairman Ng and cases, will be sent to Hong Kong on the *Empress of Japan* of Canadian Pacific Steamship Company on 25 March. We hereby write to inform you of Chairman Ng's passing due to sickness and the date of departure of the vessel carrying his coffin. Please take the remains into your care.

We are most grateful for your kind assistance.

Please see below the names of Ng Yeuk-chuen's relatives in Hong Kong:
Ng Yi-hok *(Wu Yixue)*, Ng Sze-chan *(Wu Shi-zan)* and Ng Yu-ng *(Wu Yuwu)* of Man Kwok Inn

(Stamp: Standing Committee Members, Executive Committee, Kuo Min Tang Chinese Nationalist League of Canada Headquarters)
(Stamp: Chan Bin-wak) *(Chen Bianhuo)*
(Stamp: Hau Man-yat) *(Hou Minyi)*
(Stamp: Kwan Sung-wing) *(Guan Chongying)*

23 March of the 22nd year of the Republic of China

156 加拿大梁燕謀致東華醫院信件

1933 年 4 月 22 日

東華醫院善長先生鈞鑒

弟梁燕謀字上

敬啓者　弟有先兄弟灵柩一具寄運到
貴醫院轉交新會縣屬棠下圩善堂仰祈
從早發落俾得其家人就近領受回家安葬
存殁均感謹此並頌

康祺

民廿二四月廿二号

L. J. Kee
Webb, Saok
Canada

Dear Directors of Tung Wah Hospital,

The coffin of my late friend was sent to your esteemed hospital for repatriation to the benevolent association in Tong Ha Market Town *(Tangxia Xu)*, Sun Wui County *(Xinhui Xian)*. Please handle the matter at your earliest convenience, so that his family can collect the remains for burial.

The living and the deceased are most grateful to you for your benevolence.

I wish you well.

Yours humbly,
Leung Yin-mau *(Liang Yanmou)*
22 April of the 22nd year of the Republic of China

L. J. Kee
Webb, Saok
Canada

香港東華醫院大鑒啓者聞得

美國紐約埠中華公所將执檢先友係

西曆七月十四日由紐約埠將先友落船運

囬香港約于西曆九月式号到港^吾胞弟

方松大先友一名到港之时未知親往港

東華醫院領囬否抑或醫院置理

運囬各鄉收領否勞煩貴院院長註明到

來通知彼得知情預備領囬先友可也

特此請候

大安

　　通信處佛山咸魚街生昌柴舖方富湘

　　收入無悞

中華民國廿二年六月十七日　　　　　　　　　　　　　　　^愚方富湘手書

Letter from Fong Fu-sheung, China, to Tung Wah Hospital on 17 June 1933

Dear Mangers of Tung Wah Hospital,

I heard that the Chinese Consolidated Benevolent Association, New York would repatriate the remains of deceased friends from New York to Hong Kong on 14 July, and the remains are expected to arrive in Hong Kong on 2 September. The remains of my late younger brother, Fong Chung-dai *(Fang Songda)*, are among this batch. After the remains arrive in Hong Kong, do I need to collect them from the Tung Wah Hospital in person? Or will you send them to our hometown? Please reply to me and let me know, so that I can make preparation for claiming my brother's remains.

I await your reply and wish you well.

Correspondence address:
Fong Fu-sheung *(Fang Fuxiang)*
Sang Cheong Firewood *(Shengchang Chaipu)*, Ham Yu Street *(Xianyu Jie)*, Fat Shan *(Foshan)*

Yours humbly,
Fong Fu-sheung *(Fang Fuxiang)*

17 June of the 22nd year of the Republic of China

逕啓者敝邑旅美仙友茲由敝堂代執骸骨共三十七具分載七箱內第一
號箱至第六號箱每箱六具箱之內外均將仙友姓名分別註明定期於
本月廿五日由林肯總統船載運囬港茲將載紙一張付上如該船抵港時
請飭人起運并希轉知德輔道西七十五號厚德祥金山庄轉增義堂
領囬運返原籍安葬仍希見復為荷此致
東華醫院列位先生大鑒

　　　　　　　　　　　　　旅美增城義安善堂總理　黃浩泉
　　　　　　　　　　　　　　　（印章：增邑義安堂）

中華民國廿二年八月廿四日

Letter from Tsang Shing Yee On Association in America, USA, to Tung Wah Hospital on 24 August 1933

Dear Directors of Tung Wah Hospital,

We have exhumed the bones of deceased fellow townsmen. 37 sets of bones have been placed in seven boxes – six sets each in Box No. 1 to 6 – and the names of the deceased have been marked on the inside and outside of the boxes. The bones will be repatriated to Hong Kong on the *SS President Lincoln* on the 25th day of this month. We enclose the bill of lading for your reference. Please take delivery of the bones when they arrive in Hong Kong, and inform Hau Tak Cheung Gold Mountain Firm, at 75 Des Voeux Road West, to send the bones to Tsang Yee Tong *(Zeng Yi Tang)*, so that the deceased's families can collect the remains for burial.

Thank you very much for your assistance. We await your reply.

Yours sincerely,
Wong Ho-chuen *(Huang Haoquan)*
Director, Tsang Shing Yee On Association in America

(Stamp: Tsang Shing Yee On Association)

24 August of the 22nd year of the Republic of China

159 中國方富湘致東華醫院信件

1933年9月3日

東華醫院鑒敬啓者得接來函聞
美国紐約埠中華公所执先友寄田香港東
華醫院因予胞弟方松大先友一名地
步南海蟠崗堡巒衛里約于九月弍號
運到港未知自親人往港東華醫院收領
否抑或醫院置理轉運各鄉收領勞
貴院來函通知如何办法順字通知此請

大安

通信處佛山咸魚街生昌號方富湘收

中華民國廿二年九月三日　　方富湘手書

Dear Managers of Tung Wah Hospital,

I received a letter saying that the Chinese Consolidated Benevolent Association of New York has repatriated the remains they exhumed to Tung Wah Hospital in Hong Kong. My late younger brother, Fong Chung-dai *(Fang Songda)*, is among the deceased, and his address is Po Luen Wai Lane, *(Baoluanwei Li)*, Lui Kong Po *(Leigang Bao)*, Nam Hoi *(Nanhai)*. His remains are expected to arrive in Hong Kong around 2 September. I wonder if we should collect the bones in person from the Tung Wah Hospital, or if the hospital would send the bones to the deceased's hometown. Please reply to me and let me know the procedures.

I wish you well.

Correspondence address:
Fong Fu-sheung *(Fang Fuxiang)*
Sang Cheong Ho *(Sheng Chang Hao)*, Ham Yu Street *(Xianyu Jie)*, Fat Shan *(Fo Shan)*

Yours sincerely,
Fong Fu-sheung

3 September of the 22nd year of the Republic of China

萬春榮華記用箋
MAN CHUN WING WAH KEE

逕啓者近日由紐約埠運回先友
有下列一名否仰祈代查何時到
港何時運入內地統希 示知
俾^弟通知其家人預備領葬感
德實深此候

台祺

東華大醫院
執事先生鈞鑒

　　　癸酉八月初二日

　　　　　　　　　　（印章：香港南北行街萬春榮華記書束）
　　　　　　　　　　　　　　　^弟黃得仁　頓

　　　　　由紐約運回先友
黃文銓　台山縣松蒽合和村人

Letter from Wong Tak-yan, Hong Kong, to Tung Wah Hospital on 21 September 1933

From the Office of Man Chun Wing Wah Kee

Dear Managers of Tung Wah Hospital,

The remains of a deceased friend as stated below have recently been repatriated from New York. Can you please check when the remains will arrive in Hong Kong and when they will be sent to mainland China? Please notify me so that I can ask the deceased's family to prepare to claim the remains for burial.

I am most grateful to you for your benevolence.

2ⁿᵈ day of the 8ᵗʰ lunar month, Year of Gwai Yau *(Guiyou)*

(Stamp: Man Chun Wing Wah Kee, Nam Pak Hong Street, Hong Kong)

Yours sincerely,
Wong Tak-yan *(Huang Deren)*

Repatriated from New York:
Wong Man-chuen *(Huang Wenquan)*, native of Hop Wo Village *(Hehe Cun)*, Chung Long *(Songlang)*, Toi Shan County *(Taishan Xian)*

161 letter from the Wong Fook Sui, Hong Kong, China, to Wong Zane Fook on 15 October 1933

October 15, 1933
Hong Kong, China

Zane Fook

Dear Cousin:

I received a letter from Shin You saying that my
son Wong Ah You is coming to Hong Kong on the S. S. Coolidge.
When she arrived I didn't find him, but later I received a
letter from you saying he did come on that ship, so I went in
more details. Next I find him dead on ship and was taken care
of at Dung Wai Yee Yan, undertaker. I am taking his belongings
and trunk. Do you know how much cash he took along, so I can
claim it here and take his body back to the village to bury.

Wong Fook Sui
Sin Kai
Hong Kong   Sar Tan

（原信件譯本）

曾福兄鑒前接　辛有來信云
^{小兒}黃亞有乘哥列治総統船
來港但係接船不見踪跡及
後再淂接兄函云他实搭該
船來港經詳細調查後始悉
他在船上身故遺柩由東華醫
院辦理其遺下行李等件已
由^弟收領但未悉他有無現款
遺下如　兄知其詳請為示
悉以便在此仝時收妥然後將
其遺柩運回鄉間安葬

一九三三年十月十五号　黃福瑞
新階沙田

駐美台山寗陽總會館
HOY-SUN NING YUNG BENEVOLENT ASSOCIATION
IN AMERICA

逕啟者茲於十一月十七日由丕
亞士總統船付囬先友四十七具
并港艮壹佰五十元到祈查收
轉寄囬台山城義莊候領每具
請代給囬葬費双毛艮四元除
支尚餘多少留作
貴院办理該事手續費有費
精神無任感激并希示覆為
荷此致

香港東華醫院總理^暨
列位执事先生

台山寗陽総會館
主席譚光中

中華民國廿二年十一月十七日
（印章：駐美洲台山寗陽總會館之印）

另一人註：每具給二元七角四十七具共一百二拾六元九角尚餘二十三元一角撥作工艇費

Letter from Hoy Sun Ning Yung Benevolent Association in America, San Francisco, USA, to Tung Wah Hospital on 17 November 1933

From the Office of Hoy Sun Ning Yung Benevolent Association in America

Dear Directors and Managers of Tung Wah Hospital,

We repatriated the remains of 47 deceased friends on the *SS President Pierce* and remitted 150 Hong Kong dollars to you on 17 November. Please send the remains to the coffin home in Toi Shan City *(Taishan Cheng)* and give the family of each deceased friend burial fees of 4 Kwangtung silver dollars. Please use the remaining funds to cover other expenses incurred during repatriation.

We are most grateful to you for your assistance and await your reply.

Yours sincerely,
Tam Kwong-chung *(Tan Guangzhong)*
Chairman, Hoy Sun Ning Yung Benevolent Association

17 November of the 22nd year of the Republic of China

(Stamp: Hoy Sun Ning Yung Benevolent Association in America)

Another person's remarks: 2.70 dollars for each set of remains, 126.90 dollars in total for the 47 sets; remaining 23.10 dollars to cover the transportation fees

東華医院執事先生大鑒逕啓者茲有一位曾發
　　先友在美國金山二埠去世其棺骸運囬本港本医院代理
　　祈台見字如何指示照料^弟着曾發家眷周妹
　　面议運囬惠陽約塘学布村人氏此棺骸搭於
　　门羅総統船準十月初七日到即陽歷十一月廿四号到港
　　謹此先為卦号此致

台安

　　　　　　　　　　　　十月初二日　　^弟翁榮彬上呈
　　　　　　　　　　　（印章：香港油麻地砵倫街義和堂書柬）

Letter from Yung Wing-bun, Hong Kong, to Tung Wah Hospital on 19 November 1933

Dear Managers of Tung Wah Hospital,

A deceased friend Tsang Fat *(Zeng Fa)* passed away in Sacramento, California, and his coffin is being sent to us in Hong Kong. When you receive this letter, would you please advise me of the repatriation procedure? I will ask Chow Mui *(Zhou Mei)*, wife of Tsang Fat, to talk to you in person with regard to sending the coffin to the deceased's hometown at Hok Po Village *(Xuebu Cun)*, Yeuk Tong *(Yuetang)*, Wai Yeung *(Huiyang)*. The coffin is being taken to Hong Kong on the *SS President Monroe*, and is expected to arrive on the 7th day of the 10th lunar month, i.e. 24 November.

I am informing you in advance on the coffin's arrival. Please take note of the matter.

I wish you well.

Yours sincerely,
Yung Wing-bun *(Weng Rongbin)*
2nd day of the 10th lunar month
(Stamp: Yee Wo Tong, Portland Street, Yaumatei, Hong Kong)

Letter from McKENNA & McKENNA Attorneys, USA, to Tung Wah Hospital on 24 November 1933

McKENNA & McKENNA
ATTORNEYS AT LAW
NOTARY PUBLIC
440 WILCOX BUILDING

November 24, 1933.
Dung Wai Yee Yan,
Undertakers
Hong Kong, China

In re: death of Wong Ah You , on or
About October 15, 1933.

Gentlemen:

I am retained by Wong Ah You to administer on his
estate, and we are informed by a letter written on
October 15th, by the father of Wong Ah You that you
took charge of the body and conducted the funeral
of his son who died on the President Coolidge of the
Dollar Line, about two days before reaching port at
Hong Kong. I am enclosing to you a copy of the
letter that was sent by the father.

Please check over your records and determine for me
whether you handled such a case, and have any record
of the funeral of Wong Ah You. Any information that
you may give me on this subject will be greatly appreciated and if you can furnish us a death or burial
certificate, please send same forthwith, and if there
are any charges in connection with this certificate,
we will gladly defray same.

Very truly yours,
Jimmy Mckenna

JIM:a

美國麥堅拿律師致東華醫院信件

1933 年 11 月 24 日

（原信件譯本）

東華醫院先生鑒

对於黃亞有身故事（時間約于一九三三年十月十五号）弟經被聘為黃亞有
之承辦人現接黃亞有之父于十月十五号來函説及其子黃亞有於哥列治總統船到港前二天
在船上身
故其喪葬事由 貴院料理一切現將其父來函另抄一份夾呈祈為 核閲並請
貴院調查有無理及黃亞有之喪葬事倘能將其出殯証書寄來則深為感謝所有費用当如
數奉還此請

大安

律師麥堅拿上 一九三三年十一月廿四号 美國罗省埠

The Garden Hotel

東華醫院諸善士先生鑒敬啟者茲有廣東省台山
縣馬洞田心堡田洋村人馬能聰在外國身故現承
其遺命運柩囬國安葬今付由坎那大船十二月二号
離云埠揚帆囬港托交東華醫院代理轉交其
子馬念籌領歸安葬以慰故魂事屬善事
勞执事先生通告其在香港親屬知之
「親屬住址香港海傍廣兆榮中環一百一拾五號」「馬念彬先
生处」自可轉告其子馬念籌知之蒙諸
先生妥為照办則不僅其家人感恩感
德而先生等亦獲福無彊矣謹此

順頌
福安

鄉弟馬能友敬字

民二十二年十一月廿八号

The Garden Hotel

Dear benevolent Directors of Tung Wah Hospital,

Ma Nang-chung *(Ma Nengcong)*, a native of Tin Yeung Village *(Tianyang Cun)*, Tin Sum Bo *(Tianxin Bao)*, Ma Don *(Madong)*, Toi Shan County *(Taishan Xian)*, Kwangtung *(Guangdong)*, passed away abroad. I will arrange for repatriation of his coffin to the Mainland for burial according to his last wish. The coffin will be transported to Hong Kong on the *Canada* departing Vancouver on 2 December. Please take the coffin into your care when it arrives in Hong Kong, and arrange to hand it over to the deceased's son Ma Nim-chau *(Ma Nianchou)*, so that the deceased can be laid to rest in his hometown.

This is an act of benevolence. Please inform the deceased's family in Hong Kong after the remains arrive and they will notify the deceased's son Ma Nim-chau. Please contact Ma Nim-bun *(Ma Nianbin)* at Kwong Siu Wing, No. 115 Central Waterfront.

Not only will the deceased's family be grateful to you, but your good selves will also be rewarded for your benevolence.

I wish you well.

Yours sincerely,
Ma Nang-yau *(Ma Nengyou)*

28 November of the 22nd year of the Republic of China

166 美國檀香山隆都從善堂致東華醫院信件

1933年11月30日

檀香山隆都從善堂用牋
Lung Do Chung Sin Tong

東華醫院
列位善長鄉先生均鑒
伏處海壖雲霄迴隔瞻言
台曜驤首為勞辰維
勳福光昭
聲華卓越綜持公益擘畫精深大力囬旋美
無不舉宜乎中外聞風群相引重善界中
當僂一指矣弟寄跡檀嶠徒滋塵累自維才
短莫展一籌乃蒙梓僑不棄公舉主持從善堂
事務綆短汲深時虞叢脞但弟等之與諸公地
雖非李郭之同舟而志甚切良平之借箸
諸公閎才卓識其將何以教之也茲有懇者是
年敝堂檢執先友數凡九拾六名準於十二月十
五日附乘朴總統輪嵐返歸葬宗邦以免飄泊異
域查素來在港主其事全仗
貴院諸公獨力勇為庶畢乃事固已頌聲載道
有口皆碑且
諸公對於此舉尤屬駕輕就熟一措一施自當
有條不紊加以茲事體大斷不能驟易生手致
有舛岐用特肅函匄諸左右務望代援一臂力
成此舉屆時旅骨到埗萬請妥為買舟付返
石岐與善堂權為安放並請代篆一書力託該
堂董事諸公出紅登報招人到領俾得先友得
正首丘則雲天高誼不獨身受者感戴已也茲

付返港銀壹佰大員以資代办之用敬乞照信檢

收除支各用之外其餘盡送

貴院以作善費倘蒙妥办之後尚祈賜楮

示知有瀆

清神歉仄莫可舉似統希

鑒恕臨穎禱馳並伸謝臆專此敬頌

崇安

（印章：檀埠隆都從善堂書柬）隆都從善堂　總理　黃官信
　　　　　　　　　　　　　　　　　　　秘書　林仲池

　　　　　　　　　　　　　　　　（印章：林仲池印）

中華民國二十二年十一月三十日

166 Letter from Lung Do Chung Sin Tong, Honolulu, Hawaii USA, to Tung Wah Hospital on 30 November 1933

From the Office of Lung Do Chung Sin Tong, Honolulu, Hawaii

Dear benevolent Directors of Tung Wah Hospital,

Your charitable deeds are far reaching, while your benevolence is known far and wide. We are sojourners in Honolulu. Although we are not very capable, we have earned the support of fellow townsmen and have been elected to run the benevolent society. Meanwhile, your good selves and we may be in different parts of the world, but we share the same aspiration to serve people. You are knowledgeable and experienced, and we would love to learn from you.

This year, we have exhumed the remains of 96 deceased friends. The remains will be repatriated to Hong Kong on the *SS President Polk* on 15 December. As your experience in bone repatriation is well celebrated, we would like to seek your help in sending the remains of deceased friends to their hometown. We believe you will handle the matters orderly. When the remains arrive in Hong Kong, please take them into your care and send them to Yu Sin Tong *(Yu Shan Tang)* in Shekki *(Shiqi)*. Please also ask the Directors of Yu Sin Tong to publish a notice on the newspaper to inform the deceased's families to claim the remains. Thanks to your benevolence, the lonely spirits of the deceased will find eternal peace. We are remitting 100 Hong Kong dollars to you to cover the expenses incurred. Please keep the remaining funds as our donation to your esteemed hospital.

Thank you very much for your kindness. We wish you well.

Yours sincerely,
Wong Kwun-shun *(Huang Guanxin)*, Director, and Lam Chung-chi *(Lin Zhongchi)*, Secretary of Lung Do Chung Sin Tong
(Stamp: Lam Chung-chi)
(Stamp: Lung Do Chung Sin Tong, Honolulu)

30 November of the 22nd year of the Republic of China

美國舊金山梅州應福堂致東華醫院信件

1933年12月21日

香港東華醫院執事先生鈞鑒逕啟

者茲由敝堂寄上助費艮紙壹張該

港銀伍拾大圓信到查收後請先生即

將收據寄囬弟可將據呈明於眾之知

特此并祝

烈位精神

大中華民國廿二年歲次癸酉十一月初五日

弟鍾志雲寄（印章：舊金山梅州屬應福堂）

另一註：已復并付收條

167 Letter from Mui Chow Ying Fook Tong, San Francisco, USA, to Tung Wah Hospital on 21 December 1933

Dear Managers of Tung Wah Hospital,

We have sent you a donation of 50 Hong Kong dollars by cheque. Please send us a receipt after you have received the cheque, so that we can show it to our fellow clansmen.

We wish you good health.

Yours sincerely,
Chung Chi-wan *(Zhong Zhiyun)*
(Stamp: Mui Chow Ying Fook Tong, San Francisco)

5th day of the 11th lunar month, Year of Gwai Yau *(Guiyou)*
22nd year of the Republic of China

Another person's remarks: Replied with receipt

東華醫院諸执事先生均鑒敬禀者

　　迩因本族昆仲甄平字明述于一九三四年
　　元月廿八号在山地把罢埠仙遊同人
　　等將他運囬祖國安葬以尽同人
　　之職　甄平字明述係廣東台山縣新昌區
　　　　　石海风陽里人
　　久聞执事先生办事妥当故特先字
　　禀明勞為轉運不特死者心安其家人
　　亦感恩不淺矣諸事有勞同人等
　　不勝謝謝矣

　　　　　　　　　　　　　　　　中山堂字頓

一九三四年弍月七号

168 Letter from Chung Shan Tong, China, to Tung Wah Hospital on 7 February 1934

Dear Managers of Tung Wah Hospital,

Our fellow clansman Yan-ping *(Zhenping)*, style name Ming-shut *(Mingshu)*, passed away in Santa Barbara on 28 January 1934. We consider it our responsibility to repatriate his remains to our hometown.

Yan-ping, style name Ming-shut, was a native of Fung Yeung Lane *(Fengyang Li)*, Shek Hoi *(Shihai)*, Sun Cheong District *(Xinchang Qu)*, Toi Shan County *(Taishan Xian)*, Kwangtung *(Guangdong)*.

We have long heard that your good selves handle these matters smoothly. Therefore, we write to you to seek your help in repatriating the remains. Both the deceased and his family will forever be grateful to you for your benevolence.

Thank you very much for your assistance.

Yours sincerely,
Chung Shan Tong *(Zhong Shan Tang)*

7 February 1934

MODERNIZE TAILORS

東華醫院諸执事先生大鑒

　　現有一位兄弟不幸在此处身故
　　其遺骸預備下水船俄國皇后
　　運回到時請　諸位善長料理
　　其遺骸起上貴院將來轉運
　　回鄉下現籌些費用由俄國皇
　　后船付回謹此先達並請

公祺

^弟黃撰傳頓首

民國廿三年四月十四日

Letter from Wong Chan-chuen, Canada, to Tung Wah Hospital on 14 April 1934

MODERNIZE TAILORS

Dear Managers of Tung Wah Hospital,

My brother passed away here, and his remains would be repatriated on the *Empress of Russia*. When the remains arrive in Hong Kong, please take them into your care, and send them back to his hometown later. I am trying to raise some funds now, and will send the funds to you through the *Empress of Russia*.

I hereby write to inform you of the matter.

I wish you well.

Yours sincerely,
Wong Chan-chuen *(Huang Zhuanchuan)*

14 April of the 23rd year of the Republic of China

東華醫院貴执事鑒 逕啟者本埠現执口口
　二拾九具分裝八箱已寄喜市船付返該船于四
　月十九號由紐約開行他時到港祈為查收以便
　轉寄寧陽義庄代為分發可也茲付來港銀
　弍百元敬托李津南先生送上到日檢收煩代
　支寄各先友歸寧船車費之外餘存多寡
　作本公所簽題于貴院以助慈善為荷　若該
　欵妥收請便囬文以慰眾望耑此上請並頌

公祺
　　　廿三年三月初五日

　　　　　　　美京中華公所（印章：美京中華公所）謹上
　　　　　　　　　主席李珠廼

Letter from the Chinese Consolidated Benevolent Association of Washington, D.C., USA, to Tung Wah Hospital on 18 April 1934

Dear Managers of Tung Wah Hospital,

We have exhumed 29 sets of remains and will repatriate them by sea in eight boxes. The ship will depart New York on 19 April. When the remains arrive in Hong Kong, please take them into your care and send them onto Ning Yeung Coffin Home *(Ningyang Yizhuang)*, so that they can be handed over to the deceased's families. We have asked Lee Chun-lam *(Li Jinnan)* to bring 200 Hong Kong dollars to you. Please use the funds to cover the costs of repatriation to the deceased's hometown, and keep the remainder as our donation to your esteemed hospital.

Please acknowledge receipt of the funds to ease our mind.

We wish you well.

Yours sincerely,
Lee Chu-nai *(Li Zhunai)*
Chairman, Chinese Consolidated Benevolent Association of Washington, DC, USA
(Stamp: Chinese Consolidated Benevolent Association of Washington, DC, USA)

5th day of the 3rd lunar month of the 23rd year of the Republic of China

MODERNIZE TAILORS

東華醫院諸执事先生大鑒

　　茲付囬港艮五十元請祈查收為運
　　吾兄接傳遺骸返入內地之費用
　　棺木現由俄國皇后船運囬到
　　時請　公等料理將棺木起囬
　　貴院何日運囬鄉下祈由　公等
　　定之先水船弟曾有函報告料
　　已知之謹此並請

公祺

弟黃撰傳上

民國廿三年四月廿日

MODERNIZE TAILORS

Dear Managers of Tung Wah Hospital,

I have sent 50 Hong Kong dollars to you to cover the costs of sending the remains of my late elder brother Chip-chuen *(Jiechuan)* to the mainland. Please acknowledge receipt of the funds. The coffin is being taken to Hong Kong on the *Empress of Russia*. Please take the coffin into your care after it arrives in Hong Kong. I rely on you to decide when to repatriate the remains to the hometown and I presume you have got the updated shipment details that I have sent to you in another letter earlier on.

I wish you well.

Yours sincerely,
Wong Chan-chuen *(Huang Zhuanchuan)*

20 April of the 23rd year of the Republic of China

中山與善堂啓事用箋

逕啓者去年夏曆十一月初八日接枱山隆都從善堂來函
內及在埠檢扸先友骨骸九十六具於十二月十五日附乘朴総統
輪船遄返　貴院轉運敝堂分發各親屬領回安葬云云現因
各親屬頻來查問有無到否茲特函達懇將情形及
落船日期運上如何　示知俾得各親屬領囬安
葬為是此致即頌

時祺

東華醫院執事先生

（印章：中山與善堂）

中華民國廿三年五月十五日

Letter from Chung Shan Yu Sin Tong, China, to Tung Wah Hospital on 15 May 1934

From the Office of Chung Shan Yu Sin Tong *(Zhongshan Yu Shan Tang)*

Dear Managers of Tung Wah Hospital,

On the 8th day of the 11th lunar month last year, we received a letter from Lung Do *(Longdu)* Chung Sin Tong *(Cong Shan Tang)* in Hawaii saying that they exhumed the remains of 96 deceased friends, which would be repatriated on the *SS President Polk* on 15 December. The letter also mentioned that when the remains arrived in your esteemed hospital, you would send them to us, so that we could hand over to the deceased's families for burial. Now the families of the deceased friends have come to us frequently to find out if the remains have arrived. We therefore write to you to inquire about the shipping details and arrival time of the remains. Please reply to us and we will inform the deceased's families to collect the remains.

We are most grateful to you for your efforts. We wish you well.

Yours sincerely,
(Stamp: Chung Shan Yu Sin Tong)

15 May of the 23rd year of the Republic of China

金山正埠合和總會館
HOP WO BENEVOLENT ASSOCIATION

香港東華医院

列位執事先生善鑒茲由固列芝總統船

運回敝堂各先友遺骸四百七十四具共捌拾

箱交台山荻海宏済医院收者廿壹箱交闸

平百合墟善堂收者五十九箱所有運費

均已交楚至於運入內地（運回荻海及百合圩）

之運費未知是否由內地善堂支給抑或由

貴医院支給懇依照向來手續辦理之

是所盼禱茲坿入俵紙壹張祈

察收為荷耑肅即頌

善祺

合和會館主席兼廣福堂值理余鑄秋啓
（印章：廣福堂）

中華民國廿叁年十一月廿九日

另一人註：荻風采堂
　　　　　交廣福堂

173

Letter from Hop Wo Benevolent Association, San Francisco, USA, to Tung Wah Hospital on 29 November 1934

Hop Wo Benevolent Association, San Francisco, USA

Dear Managers of Tung Wah Hospital,

We have repatriated the remains of 474 deceased friends, placed in 80 boxes, on the *SS President Coolidge*. Among them, 21 boxes are to be sent to Wang Chai Hospital *(Hongji Yiyuan)*, Dik Hoi *(Dihai)*, Toi Shan *(Taishan)* and 59 boxes to the benevolent association at Bak Hop Market Town *(Baihe Xu)*, Hoi Ping *(Kaiping)*. Kindly note that the shipping charges have been paid in full. As to the costs of sending the remains to the mainland (Dik Hoi and Bak Hop Market Town), please advise if they should be paid by the benevolent associations in mainland China or your esteemed hospital. Please handle the matter according to the usual practice. We also enclose a bill of lading for your action.

We are most grateful to you for your kindness.

We wish you well.

Yours sincerely,
Yu Chu-chau *(Yu Zhuqiu)*
Chairman of Hop Wo Benevolent Association and General Committee Member of Quong Fook Tong Benevolent Association
(Stamp: Quong Fook Tong Benevolent Association)

29 November of the 23rd year of the Republic of China

Another person's remarks: Hand over to Kwong Fook Tong through Fung Toy Tong *(Feng Cai Tang)* in Dik Hoi

（借用）張良邊鄉公所用箋

東華醫院執事先生公鑒敬啓者現聞
　余家兄雷學秀之骸硾近日由美國運囬
貴院如到收時切勿運交台城因台城距離
　甚遠携帶艱难煩將該骸硾運囬公益
　埠交福寧醫院收存余家鄉與公益埠
　毗連而居領取便捷請予照准不勝感
　佩　耑此并請

公安

台山縣公益區張良边東華村雷述周敬上

中華民國廿四年夏歷七月十七日

174 Letter from Lui Shut-chau, China, to Tung Wah Hospital on 15 August 1935

(Borrowed) From the Office of Cheung Leung Bin Village Communal Hall
(Zhang Liangbian Xianggongsuo)

Dear Managers of Tung Wah Hospital,

The remains of my brother Lui Hok-sau *(Lei Xuexiu)* are being repatriated to your esteemed hospital from the USA. When the remains arrive in Hong Kong, please do not send them to Toi Shing *(Taicheng)*, as it is far away and difficult to be transported to where I live. Please send the remains to Fook Ning Hospital *(Funing Yiyuan)* in Kung Yik Port *(Gongyi Bu)*. As my hometown is adjacent to Kung Yik Port, I can collect the remains easily.

I hope you accede to my request. I am most grateful to you for your kindness.

I wish you well.

Yours sincerely,
Lui Shut-chau *(Lei Shuzhou)*
Tung Wah Village *(Donghua Cun)*, Cheung Leung Bin *(Zhang Liang Bian)*, Kung Yik District *(Gongyi Qu)*, Toi Shan County *(Taishan Xian)*

17th day of the 7th lunar month of the 24th year of the Republic of China

美國金山大埠番禺昌後堂致東華醫院信件
1935 年 11 月 8 日

東華醫院执事先生^{大鑒}

　　逕啟者^{本善堂}檢执先友向例拾年壹次是屆檢
　　执經已完妥准於西曆拾壹月捌號由美大埠開
　　行之夏利臣總統船運囬到港時請
　　执事先生等留意煩為料理駐港^{敝邑}継善堂當
　　事若到領取各先友運囬邑屬各地尤望
　　貴执事協助壹切為感耑此並頌

善祺希為
電鑒不備

金山大埠番禺昌後堂謹啓
（印章：金山番禺昌後堂）

計開

番禺先友	大棺四具	中棺五具	小童九具	白骨五十一具
花縣先友		中棺壹具	小童七具	白骨二十一具

共九十八具

中華民國廿四年拾壹月捌日

175 Letter from Pon Yup Chong How Benevolent Association, San Francisco, USA, to Tung Wah Hospital on 8 November 1935

Dear Managers of Tung Wah Hospital,

It is our usual practice to exhume and repatriate the bones of our deceased friends once every ten years. We have recently finished exhuming the bones of our deceased friends and repatriated them from San Francisco on the *SS President Harrison* on 8 November. When the bones arrive in Hong Kong, please take them into your care. Representatives of Kai Sin Tong *(Ji Shan Tang)*, the charitable association of our county in Hong Kong, will collect the bones and send them to the deceased's hometown. Your assistance is very much appreciated.

We wish you well.

Yours sincerely,
Pon Yup Chong How Benevolent Association, San Francisco
(Stamp: Pon Yup Chong How Benevolent Association, San Francisco)

List of deceased friends:
Deceased friends from Pun Yu *(Panyu)* – 4 big coffins, 5 medium coffins, 9 sets of children's remains, 51 sets of bones
Deceased friends from Fa Yuen *(Huaxian)* – 1 medium coffin, 7 sets of children's remains, 21 sets of bones, 98 sets of remains in total

8 November of the 24th year of the Republic of China

東華醫院總理^暨

列位执事^{均鑒}逕啟者前呈粗函並各項要件想

　　先生等定必收妥茲屆^{敝善堂}檢執先友運囘祖國

　　蒙

　　先生等妥為料理沒存甚為感激今將夏利臣船倆

　　紙兩張付俾得易於起運上落仰祈

　　查收為盼餘未細述耑此並候

善祺希為

察照不備

金山番禺昌後堂緘

（印章：金山番禺昌後堂）

中華民國廿四年拾一月拾弍日

Letter from Pon Yup Chong How Benevolent Association, San Francisco, USA, to Tung Wah Hospital on 12 November 1935

Dear Directors and Managers of Tung Wah Hospital,

We sent a letter to you earlier, along with the documents you might require, and believe you have received them. Thank you for taking care of the bones of our deceased friends and arranging for repatriating the bones to the mainland. The deceased and the living are grateful to you.

We hereby enclose the bill of lading of the *SS President Harrison* for your follow up action. When the bones arrive in Hong Kong, please collect and take them into your care.

We wish you well.

Yours sincerely,
Pon Yup Chong How Benevolent Association, San Francisco
(Stamp: Pon Yup Chong How Benevolent Association, San Francisco)

12 November of the 24th year of the Republic of China

廣東紡織廠用牋

東華醫院諸執事先生大鑒：現聞美
國芝加哥埠運囘一批逝世華僑骸
骨，查有吳澤垂 吳業合兩名亦在其
內，該批骸骨已否運抵
貴院？何時可以領囘？及有無須備具領
手續？請為詳細見示，至盼至感，專
此拜託，並候

公祺

^弟吳公義頓

中華民國廿四年十二月廿七日

177 Letter from Ng Kung-yee, China, to Tung Wah Hospital on 27 December 1935

Kwang Tung Weaving Factory *(Guangdong Fangzhi Chang)*

Dear Managers of Tung Wah Hospital,

I heard that a batch of bones of deceased Chinese compatriots were repatriated from Chicago, USA and the bones of Ng Chak-shui *(Wu Zechui)* and Ng Yip-hop *(Wu Yehe)* were among them. Have the bones arrived at your esteemed hospital? When can the bones be claimed? What are the procedures for claiming the bones? Please give me detailed instructions. I appreciate your help and await your reply.

I wish you well.

Yours sincerely,
Ng Kung-yee *(Wu Gongyi)*

27 December of the 24th day of the Republic of China

廣東紡織廠用牋

東華醫院諸執事先生惠鑒：前接到
美國芝加哥埠 Chicago 通訊，謂該埠有身
故僑胞骸骨數百具，內有新會縣人吳澤垂
吳業合兩人骸骨同時寄返，轉知屆時前赴
領囘等語；弟即於去年十二月底函詢
貴院，对於上列骸骨，何時運抵
貴院，及具領手續如何，請予查明詳細
見示，迄未奉復，茲特再為函詢，務請
查明荅復，以便赴港具領，想慈祥如
執事等，定樂為指示也。專此拜託，並候
春祺。

弟吳公義頓
（印章：吳公義）

中華民國廿五年一月六日

178 Letter from Ng Kung-yee, China, to Tung Wah Hospital on 6 January 1936

Kwang Tung Weaving Factory *(Guangdong Fangzhi Chang)*

Dear Managers of Tung Wah Hospital,

I received a message from Chicago, USA, saying that the bones of a few hundred Chinese compatriots would be repatriated to your esteemed hospital. Among the bones were those of Sun Wui *(Xinhui)* native Ng Chak-shui *(Wu Zechui)* and Ng Yip-hop *(Wu Yehe)*. I was advised to claim them from your hospital.

Then I wrote to you in late December last year to find out when the bones would arrive in Hong Kong, as well as the procedures for claiming the bones. Since I have not yet received your reply, I am writing to you again. Please reply to me, so that I can come to Hong Kong to collect the bones. I am sure your good selves would be kind enough to help me.

I wish you well and await your reply.

Yours sincerely,
Ng Kung-yee *(Wu Gongyi)*
(Stamp: Ng Kung-yee)

6 January of the 25th year of the Republic of China

中國吳公義致東華醫院信件

1936年1月21日

廣東紡織廠用牋

東華醫院諸執事先生惠鑒關於美國
芝加哥埠（或稱芝加高或稱市卡咕英文原名 Chicago）
有逝世華僑骸骨一批內有吳澤垂吳業合两人
亦在其內前經函請
貴院查明運抵日期及具領手續示知以便办理
旋奉一月八日
大函以該批骨殖未有接到該埠來函未能預先
告知具領手續則須本港商店或商會盖章担保
方能領囬等語查上述吳澤垂係本人胞兄
吳業合係堂兄茲為避免在港覔商店商
會担保蔴煩起見擬請
貴院准予通融办理由本人派舍侄賫函赴
港直接領囬吳澤垂吳業合骨殖两具運
返新會縣原籍安葬以歸簡便想
貴院慈善為懷當予人以便利也再該批
骨殖雖屬芝加哥逝世華僑惟出口時必經
金山大埠或舍路埠誠恐用該两埠中
華會館名義運返亦未可料仍請
詳為查明示復倘確未運到俟運抵時
乞為見示無任感荷專此即候

台祺

（印章：廣東紡織廠會計課）課長吳公義
（印章：吳公義印）

中華民國廿五年一月廿一日

179 Letter from Ng Kung-yee, China, to Tung Wah Hospital on 21 January 1936

Kwang Tung Weaving Factory *(Guangdong Fangzhi Chang)*

Dear Managers of Tung Wah Hospital,

Ng Chak-shui *(Wu Zechui)* and Ng Yip-hop *(Wu Yehe)* were among the Chinese compatriots who passed away in Chicago, USA. I wrote to you earlier to enquire when their bones would arrive in Hong Kong as well as what the procedures for claiming the bones were. In your reply to me on 8 January, you mentioned that you had not yet received news from Chicago and could not tell me when the bones would arrive. As to the procedures for claiming the bones, you said that I needed a shop or merchant association in Hong Kong to act as my guarantor.

The deceased Ng Chak-shui is my elder brother, whereas Ng Yip-hop is my cousin. In order to save my trouble of finding a shop or merchant association in Hong Kong to act as my guarantor, I hereby seek your permission for me to send my nephew to Hong Kong to collect the bones of Ng Chak-shui and Ng Yip-hop for burial with my letter. The benevolence of your esteemed hospital is known far and wide. I hope you could simplify the procedures in this instance. Meanwhile, although the bones are repatriated from Chicago, they must pass through San Francisco or Seattle when they leave the USA. Thus it is possible that the bones are repatriated under the name of the Chinese Consolidated Benevolent Associations in these two cities. Please investigate the matter again and reply to me. If the bones haven't arrived, please notify me when they will arrive in Hong Kong.

I await your reply.

I wish you well.

Yours sincerely,
Ng Kung-yee *(Wu Gongyi)*, Head of Department
(Stamp: Account Department, Kwangtung Weaving Factory)
(Stamp: Ng Kung-yee)

21 January of the 25th year of the Republic of China

亞洲西歸先友

會安黃雲居用箋

东華醫院大值理^{偉鑒}敬啓者^{敝埠}廣仁堂

　　歷年運先友遺骸回籍深蒙　貴善堂代

　　為轉運各處甚屬妥当今^{敝堂}当第七屆之

　　期例应開運現已開辦約明年二三月可能運

　　囬到時定拜勞　貴善堂代理轉運計^{敝堂}

　　上屆開運至今已有十年之久但未知　貴善

　　堂照旧辦法抑有改行新例章程如何希

　　為復示俾得知所遵從謹此并請

善安

列位善長^{均鑒}

　　　　　　　　己年六月初六（印章：會安峴港廣仁堂）頓

　　復函祈交永樂街昆茂行轉來便妥

Letter from Kwong Yan Tong, Hoi An, Da Hang, Annam, to Tung Wah Hospital on 12 July 1929

From VANCU FAIFOO

Dear Directors of Tung Wah Hospital,

We are very much indebted to you for your kind help and proper arrangement in repatriating the remains of the deceased friends of Kwong Yan Tong *(Guang Ren Tang)* to their hometown over the years. Now we are going to send the 7th batch and preparation work has begun. We expect the remains to arrive in Hong Kong in the 2nd or 3rd lunar month next year, and would like to bother you to send them onto the deceased's hometown. Ten years have passed since the last repatriation. We would like to confirm whether your past procedures still stand, or if you have new rules and regulations in place. Please enlighten us with your reply, and we will follow your guidelines.

We wish you well.

Yours sincerely,
(Stamp: Hoi An, Da Nang, Kwong Yan Tong)

6th day of the 6th lunar month, Year of Gei Zi *(Jisi)*

Please send your reply to Kwan Mau Hong, Wing Lok Street.

181 新加坡李亞雲致東華醫院信件

1929 年 7 月 13 日

中華醫院^{执事先生}鑒启者^{氏夫}黃南生旧年五月初旬在埠

　身故棺柩停留貴院本欲領囘大東方保險之銀携囘故

　鄉安葬詎料^{氏夫}之女黃亞惹女壻熊福文心懷不良胆敢

　在英政府控呈在案保險之欵於^氏無干不得已与其夫婦交

　涉爭頌一年有餘用費銀数仟元案情此行解決該保險

　之欵終被其夫婦奪去大半矣今氏人財兩空昔日之志實無力挽

　囘故特飛函前來乞貴院將棺柩在埠暫歸黃土以慰死

　者之瞑目則幽明均感臨札神馳不勝企慕

　　　并頌

鈞安

　　又批囘信處寄星架坡小坡蔴里街門牌四十九号捷興塩店收

　　　　　　　　　　　李亞雲　上言　己巳陆月初七日寄

　　　　　　　　　　　　　　　　　（印章：捷興圖書）

Dear Managers of Chung Wah [Tung Wah] Hospital,

My husband Wong Nam-sang (*Huang Nansheng*) passed away in your city in early May last year, and his coffin had been under the care of your hospital. I intended to take his remains back to his hometown for burial after I had received the payment from Great Eastern Insurance Company. However, my husband's daughter Wong Ah-ye (*Huang Yare*) and son-in-law Hung Fook-man (*Xiong Fuwen*), with evil intentions, filed a lawsuit in the British court to claim the insurance compensation. I have no choice but to sue them. The lawsuit went on for over a year, and I spent several thousand dollars on it. Eventually, the case was settled but the couple took most of the insurance compensation, while I have to carry on with no husband and no money. I could no longer accomplish what I intended to do.

Therefore, I write this letter to you. I implore you to bury my husband's coffin in Hong Kong temporarily, so that he can be laid to rest in peace.

I am most grateful to you for your kindness.

Yours humbly,
Lee Ah-wan *(Li Yayun)*
(Stamp: Jit Hing Books)

Sent on the 7th day of the 6th lunar month, Year of Gei Zi *(Jisi)*

P.S. Please send your reply to Jit Hing Salt Shop, 49 Siu Por Mari Street, Singapore.

暹羅廣肇別墅用箋

東華醫院
列位先生大鑒敬啓者現敝別墅於本
月五號附佳東輪船儎回各姓先友靈
柩式百四拾壹具并夾呈儎唔壹張各
姓先友名籍冊壹本到時懇照查收
如照收妥順希見復為荷專此敬請

善安

（印章：暹京廣肇別墅書柬）主席　黃求標　上

弍拾年元月五日

另一人註：已复

From the Office of Kwong Siew Villa, Siam

Dear Managers of Tung Wah Hospital,

We repatriated the coffins of 241 deceased friends on the 5th day of this month on the *Kaitung* with a bill of lading and a list of names and native counties of the deceased friends. Please take the remains into your care and notify us of their safe arrival.

We wish you well.

Yours faithfully,
Wong Kau-biu (*Huang Qiubiao*), Chairman
(Stamp: Kwong Siew Villa, Siam)

5 January of the 20th year of the Republic of China

Another person's remarks: Replied

183 暹京廣肇別墅致東華醫院信件

1931 年 1 月 5 日

暹羅廣肇別墅用箋

東華醫院
列位先生大鑒敬啓者現敝別墅於本月五號
附佳東輪船儎回各姓先友靈柩弍百四拾壹
具除隨輪呈上儎帋壹張各姓先友名籍冊
壹本外茲由郵局寄上振盛行滙票壹張計
港幣柒佰叁拾員到時懇照查收所有領
取手續除照舊例每名發給葬費銀弍員
外尚存之欵作為費用支銷便是諸費
精神順希見復為盼專此敬請

善安

（印章：暹京廣肇別墅書柬）主席　黃求標　上

弍拾年元月五日

另一人註：已復

Letter from Kwong Siew Villa, Siam, to Tung Wah Hospital on 5 January 1931

From the Office of Kwong Siew Villa, Siam

Dear Managers of Tung Wah Hospital,

We sent back the coffins of 241 deceased friends on the 5th day of this month on the *Kaitung* with a bill of lading and a list of names and native counties of the deceased friends. We had also sent a money order for 730 Hong Kong dollars, issued by Chun Shing Hong, by post. Please check when you receive it. The procedures for claiming are the same as before. Please give burial fees of 2 dollars to the family of each deceased friend and use the remaining funds to cover any expenses incurred.

We await your reply, and are most grateful to you for your efforts.

Yours sincerely,
Wong Kau-biu (*Huang Qiubiao*),
Chairman (Stamp: Kwong Siew Villa, Siam)

5 January of the 20th year of the Republic of China

Another person's remarks: Replied

BUREAU CIMETIÈRE DE CANTON
穗義祠公事用箋

香港東華醫院执事鄉先生^暨
　列位董事善長諸公^{均鑒}　公啓者
　^{敝埠}是屆又當例撿執先友白骨囘
　東之期経扵國歷一月結日完竣統約
　計南圻西堤金边六省共六仟二百余具之譜
　経昨会議头帮約在三月中俵返二帮
　約在四月中俵返每帮叁仟餘具如
　定期囘港到時先電奉知俾得
　預便駁船俵埋義庄存貯至於搬運
　工費每件該艮若干請祈　示知以便滙
　上餘事後詳此請

公安

（印章：安南穗義祠執先友白骨圖章）字頓

中華民國廿年二月十三日

另一人註：辛元月十七復

Letter from Bureau Cimetiére de Canton, Cholon, Annam, to Tung Wah Hospital on 13 February 1931

From the Office of Bureau Cimetiére de Canton

Dear Managers and Directors of Tung Wah Hospital,

It is time for the bones of deceased friends to be repatriated to their hometown. We finished exhumation by the end of January, and had exhumed a total of some 6,200 sets of bones from six provinces of Cochinchina, Cholon and Phnom Penh. At a meeting of our society yesterday, we decided that the first batch of bones would be repatriated in the middle of March, and the second batch middle of April. There are approximately 3,000 sets of bones in each batch. We will inform you by telegraph once we confirm the date of repatriation, so that you can make arrangements for boats to take the bones to your coffin home. Please let us know how much the transportation costs are and we will remit the funds to you.

We wish you well.

Yours sincerely,
(Stamp: Seal of Remains Exhumation and Repatriation of Bureau Cimetiére de Canton, Annam)

13 February of the 20th year of the Republic of China

Another person's remarks: Replied on the 17th day of the 1st lunar month, Year of San Mei *(Xinwei)*

穗義祠公事用箋
BUREAU CIMETIÈRE DE CANTON

香港東華醫院执事諸君^暨

列位大董事善長鄉先生^{均鑒}公啓者前由

郵政局付上片函料為洞悉詳及^{本帮}是

年又屆执運先友白骨囬东之期头帮約在

夏歷本年元月廿左右俻大廣西輪船返港三千零六具

弍帮約在弍月中約二千九百具之譜如大廣西動輪返

港定当電聞如到時請祈預俻駁船運俻義

庄候各県鄉到領諸費精神專此敬請

公祺

（印章：安南穗義祠执先友白骨圖章）頓

中華民國廿年三月四日

辛元月十六

Letter from Bureau Cimetière de Canton, Cholon, Annam, to Tung Wah Hospital on 4 March 1931

From the Office of Bureau Cimetière de Canton

Dear Managers and benevolent Directors of Tung Wah Hospital,

We sent a letter to you by post earlier to inform you that it was time for us to repatriate the remains of our deceased friends this year. We trust you are aware of that. The first batch of remains, 3,006 sets in total, will be transported to Hong Kong on the *Guangxi* around the 20th day of the 1st lunar month, whereas the second batch of remains, 2,900 sets in total, will be transported in the middle of the 2nd lunar month. We shall inform you by telegraph when the ship sets sail. After the remains have arrived in Hong Kong, please arrange boats to take them to the coffin home and wait for various counties' representatives to claim the remains.

We are most grateful to you for your efforts.

We wish you well.

Yours sincerely,
(Stamp: Seal of Remains Exhumation and Repatriation of Bureau Cimetière de Canton, Annam)

4 March of the 20th year of the Republic of China
16th day of the 1st lunar month, Year of San Mei *(Xinwei)*

穗義祠公事用箋
BUREAU CIMETIÈRE DE CANTON

東華醫院列位执事先生暨

顏成坤董事先生均鑒　敬覆者

　　昨奉到元月十六复來　大教知悉一切

　　內詳十具以上者每具收工艇費艮三毛寸

　　各等前來敝埠歷屆撿運先友回东

　　均蒙　貴醫院代收代發歷屆撿执

　　骨殖回東有別帮答附回港親自帶

　　返汕头或福州但有敝等公函與之連根

　　對號者请祈將該骨箱交來手携

　　去并交每具葬費例艮式元头帮由

　　陳東亞行大廣西輪俒回三千零六具該輪約

　　在本月廿六七動輪返港如定期啓行

　　當由電奉聞至於工艇費俟式帮

　　啓程然後將工艇費及津助葬費一齊

　　滙上茲因正期公司輪返港之便特為敬

　　告諸多勞神不勝感感专此敬請

善安

　　　　　　　　　　　穗義祠执運先友総協理字啓

　　　　　　　　　（印章：安南穗義祠执先友白骨圖章）

　　　　　　　　　　　　　　　辛未元月廿四日泐

中華民國廿年三月十二日

Letter from Bureau Cimetière de Canton, Cholon, Annam, to Tung Wah Hospital on 12 March 1931

From the Office of Bureau Cimetière de Canton

Dear Chairman Ngan Shing-kwan and Managers of Tung Wah Hospital,

We received your reply on 16 January and noted that for more than ten sets of remains, the cost of sending each set of remains to China by boat is 30 cents etc.

Over the years, your esteemed hospital had taken the bones we exhumed and repatriated into your care, and transported them to the mainland. This time, some of the remains will be handled directly by their families and transported to Shan Tau *(Shantou)* or Fook Chau *(Fuzhou)*. If people present our letter and the corresponding receipt, please hand over the bones of the deceased to them, along with burial fees of 2 silver dollars. Now, 3,006 sets of bones will be transported on the *Guangxi*, and is scheduled to depart for Hong Kong on the 26th or 27th day of this month. When the ship sets sail as scheduled, we shall inform you by telegraph. As to the shipping charges from Hong Kong to China and the burial fees, we shall transmit the funds to you when the second batch of the bones sets sail.

We are most grateful to you for your efforts. We wish you well.

Yours sincerely,
Manager for Remains Exhumation and Repatriation of Bureau Cimetière de Canton
(Stamp: Seal of Remains Exhumation and Repatriation, Bureau Cimetière de Canton, Annam)

24th day of the 1st lunar month, Year of San Mei *(Xinwei)*
12 March of the 20th year of the Republic of China

187 安南堤岸穗義祠致東華醫院信件

1931 年 3 月 13 日

穗義祠公事用箋
BUREAU CIMETIÈRE DE CANTON

東華醫院執事諸公暨
列位董事善長均鑒公啓者茲
由陈东亞行大廣西輪船偁返先
友骨骸三千零六具如到請祈委駁
偁上義庄夾上偁紙等请祈查
收办理余公函詳此请

公安

（印章：安南穗義祠执先友白骨圖章）頓
辛元月廿五日

中華民國廿年三月十三日

Letter from Bureau Cimetière De Canton, Cholon, Annam, to Tung Wah Hospital on 13 March 1931

From the Office of Bureau Cimetière De Canton

Dear Managers and benevolent Directors of Tung Wah Hospital,

We repatriated the bones of 3,006 deceased friends on the *Guangxi* of Chan Tung Ah Hong Shipping. After the bones arrive in Hong Kong, please check and take them to your coffin home. Enclosed is the bill of lading for checking.

We wish you well.

Yours sincerely,
(Stamp: Seal of Remains Exhumation and Repatriation of Bureau Cimetière De Canton, Annam)

25th day of the 1st lunar month, Year of San Mei *(Xinwei)*
13 March of the 20th year of the Republic of China

188 中國廣州城西高崗方便醫院致東華醫院信件

1931 年 3 月 18 日

城西高崗方便醫院用牋

香港東華醫院
列位先生大鑒逕啓者現接到越南東京海防河內
廣善堂普濟醫局運囬第十二期先友骸骨総共
叁百弍拾五具敝院暫代收貯候各該親屬到領
貴醫院占弍具用特函請
通知各先友親屬携帶由越南原發凴單到院查
對給領實紉厚誼并頌

善祺 附先友姓名单乙紙

廣州城西方便醫院啓
（印章：城西高崗方便醫院書柬）

中華民國二十年三月十八日

越南東京海防廣善堂普濟醫局運回第十二
　期先友骸骨

　計開
陳周氏^{番禺人}　　　　　　海防四十六号
鄧黃氏　　　　　　　　河字三十八号
　以上弍具請

東華醫院查傳各親屬携同原發溤单來省到院
　查對給領為荷

民國二十年三月十八日　　　　　　（印章：城西高崗方便醫院書柬）

Letter from City West Ko Kong Fong Bin Hospital, Canton, China, to Tung Wah Hospital on 18 March 1931

From the Office of City West Ko Kong Fong Bin Hospital *(Chengxi Gaogang Fangbian Yiyuan)*

Dear Directors of Tung Wah Hospital,

We have received the 12th batch of bones of 325 deceased friends, repatriated by Po Tsai Clinic *(Pu Ji Yiju)* of Kwong Sin Tong *(Guang Shan Tang)* in Hanoi, Vietnam. The bones will remain in our care until they are collected by the deceased's families. Among them, two sets of bones are listed under your esteemed hospital. Please inform the families of the deceased friends to collect the remains. They should present the original letters issued in Vietnam so that we can verify their identities and hand over the bones to them.

We are most grateful to you for your assistance.

A list of the deceased friends is enclosed.

Yours sincerely,
City West Ko Kong Fong Bin Hospital, Canton *(Guangzhou)*
(Stamp: City West Ko Kong Fong Bin Hospital)

18 March of the 20th year of the Republic of China

[Editor's remarks: The name list is available only in Chinese]

穗義祠公事用箋
BUREAU CIMETIÈRE DE CANTON

东華醫院諸善長先生^{台鑒}前由郵局

　　付上公函內有二連根四張又廿八早特電奉

　　聞由大廣西輪付返先友骨箱三千零六具料

　　必妥办該□費脚等懇祈代支俟本月

　　中付第二帮骨殖時一齐滙返茲夾

　　上秋字一十八号陽江潘宝^{即保}公二連根一張如

　　該親屬到領請祈对號交箱诸

　　費精神容後叙及并請

善安

　　　　　　　　　　　　（印章：安南穗義祠执先友白骨圖章）字頓

辛未弍月初一日

Letter from Bureau Cimetière de Canton, Cholon, Annam, to Tung Wah Hospital on 19 March 1931

From the Office of Bureau Cimetière de Canton

Dear Directors of Tung Wah Hospital,

We sent a letter to you by post earlier, enclosed with four receipts. On the 28th day, we sent a telegram to inform you that 3,006 sets of bones of our deceased friends had been repatriated on the *Guangxi*. We trust that you would handle the matter properly. As to the costs for transporting the remains [to the mainland], please pay first. We shall remit the funds to you together with those of the second batch of bones repatriated in the middle of this month.

Please find enclosed the receipt for the bones of Poon Bo *(Pan Bao)* of Yeung Kong *(Yangjiang)*, placed in Box "Chau 18". If his relatives come to collect the bones, please hand over the relevant box to them.

We are most grateful to you for your efforts.

We wish you well.

Yours sincerely,
(Stamp: Seal of Remains Exhumation and Repatriation of Bureau Cimetière de Canton, Annam)

1st day of the 2nd lunar month, Year of San Mei *(Xinwei)*

日本長崎廣東會所致東華醫院信件

逕啓者遠隔天涯睠懷故土人之情也我僑居先友羈旅

　孤魂十年飄泊不有善後無以慰先靈而盡友道^{同人}等

　因此擬將義地先塋重加整理綜計能起運者約七十

　名一律函封骸骨欲扵國曆五月底附北野丸安裝囬

　籍擬權厝　貴院托為照料一切素仰

貴院見義勇為當仁不讓定能敬恭桑梓善与人

　同但辦理程序如何未諗　貴院章程用敢就

　教伏祈詳示俾便遵行附呈通知先友関系人

　告白一㕑祈為代登省港報各二份各登一星期

　并請將登載者每惠寄一份俾得存案為幸

　所支款項容當璧還諸事有勞毋任感謝

　此致

东華醫院大総理

　　　　　　　　　　　　　　　　^{日本長崎}廣东会所　謹啓

　　　　　　　　　（印章：日本長崎市廣馬場一番廣東會所）

中華民國二十年三月廿七日

日本長崎廣東義地起遷先友

本會所自置之廣東義地原為便利本帮僑民暫時寄
塟之需向例凡塟淺滿十年者即湏起遷囘籍俾得騰
出餘地以供淺來者之湏要茲経本會同人議決定於三
月底興工起遷先友約於本年五月底裝運囘粤托由香港
東華医院按置仰各先友親属届時到港查明領塟特此
通告

日本長崎廣東會所　啓

Letter from Kwang Tung Association of Nagasaki, Japan, to Tung Wah Hospital on 27 March 1931

Dear Directors of Tung Wah Hospital,

Even though we are thousands of miles away, we hold our hometown close to our hearts. The spirits of our deceased friends have been drifting for ten years. If nothing is done for them, we cannot lay them to rest and fulfill our moral obtigation for clansmen. We, therefore, plan to reorganize the local communal graveyard and expect to exhume and repatriate the remains of about 70 deceased friends, and intend to send them back on the *Kitano Maru* towards the end of May in this year. We now seek the help of your esteemed hospital in handling the remains. We are well aware of the benevolent acts of your esteemed hospital and believe you would be kind enough to offer your help. We trust that you share our love for our country and fellow countrymen, and our wish to extend benevolence to those in need. However, we do not know the relevant procedures. We would thus like to ask your esteemed hospital what we should do and we shall follow your instructions. We enclose a notice to the families or relatives of the deceased friends. Please publish it in two newspapers each in Canton *(Guangzhou)* and Hong Kong for one week, and send one copy of each printed notice to us for our record. We shall reimburse you for the costs incurred.

We are most grateful to you for your efforts.

Yours sincerely,
Kwang Tung Association, Nagasaki, Japan
(Stamp: Kwang Tung Association of Nagasaki, 1 Hirobaba-machi, Nagasaki, Japan)

27 March of the 20th year of the Republic of China

Remains of Deceased Friends Exhumed from Kwang Tung Communal Graveyard in Nagasaki, Japan

Kwang Tung Communal Graveyard, run by our association, offers a temporary burial place for deceased Chinese compatriots. It is our usual practice that after ten years, the bones will be exhumed and repatriated to make room for other deceased friends. We have resolved to begin exhuming the bones of our deceased friends in end of March. The bones will be repatriated to Kwangtung *(Guangdong)* through Tung Wah Hospital in Hong Kong in end of May.

Would families of our deceased friends please travel to Hong Kong then to claim the bones of the deceased.

Kwang Tung Association, Nagasaki, Japan

安南堤岸穗義祠致東華醫院信件

1931 年 4 月 23 日

穗義祠公事用箋
BUREAU CIMETIÈRE DE CANTON

東華医院董事諸公台電啓者前由港和發成
賈和興公司報効由陸賈輪船俩運第弍帮
先友骨殖箱二千八佰一十五具如到請祈委盆艇古尼搬
入　貴義庒俟各県個人到領余由滙单信函
詳專此敬請

善安

（印章：安南穗義祠执先友白骨圖章）頓

中華民國廿年四月廿三日

另一人註：辛三月初六

Letter from Bureau Cimetière de Canton, Cholon, Annam, to Tung Wah Hospital on 23 April 1931

From the Office of Bureau Cimetière de Canton

Dear Directors of Tung Wah Hospital,

We sent a telegram earlier to inform you that Wo Fat Shing and Ka Wo Hing Company had helped repatriate the second batch of 2,815 sets of bones on the *Luk Gah*. Please arrange coolies to take the remains to your coffin home when they arrive in Hong Kong. The families of individual deceased friends will come from various counties to collect them. Please refer to the remittance letter for the detailed arrangement of the remaining bones.

Thank you for your assistance. We wish you well.

Yours sincerely,
(Stamp: Seal of Remains Exhumation and Repatriation of Bureau Cimetière de Canton, Annam)

23 April of the 20th year of the Republic of China

Another person's remarks: 6th day of the 3rd lunar month, Year of San Mei *(Xinwei)*

日本長崎廣東會所致東華醫院信件

1931 年 4 月 24 日

逕啓者前奉蕪函諒登
大覽茲敝所廣東義莊起遷先友総数
約有七十名約扵國暦五月底由北野丸
載運囬粵屆時擬托
貴院暫代安置俾各先友親屬隨时到
領事関慈善諒蒙　贊助為此先函
奉達如蒙將托办手續先行
示知尤為感祷此致
東華医院大総理公鑒

日本長崎廣東会所簡肖藜啓（印章：簡肖藜印）

中華民國二十年四月廿四日

Letter from Kwang Tung Association of Nagasaki, Japan, to Tung Wah Hospital on 24 April 1931

Dear Directors of Tung Wah Hospital,

We have exhumed the remains of about 70 deceased friends from Kwangtung Coffin Home here, and plan to repatriate them to Kwangtung *(Guangdong)* on the *Kitano Maru* at the end of May. We would like to ask your esteemed hospital to take the remains into your care after they arrive in Hong Kong. The families of the deceased will come to collect the remains. We hope you would assist us in this charitable act.

We, hereby, write to you about this in advance. If you can assist us, please inform us what we should do.

We shall be most grateful to you for your kindness.

Yours sincerely,
Kan Siu-lai *(Jian Xiaoli)*
Kwang Tung Association, Nagasaki, Japan
(Stamp: Kan Siu-lai)

24 April of the 20th year of Republic of China

穗義祠公事用箋
BUREAU CIMETIÈRE DE CANTON

東華醫院执事暨

大董事主席先生^{台鑒}公啓者初七午

電闻謂由陸賈輪佮返骨骸二千八百一十五具料必脩

便駁盆工力起上義庄候人到領每具津

助省毛艮式元料必代為買省毛时價核

寸但办妥請祈列单來俾札徵信彔以供

眾覽方昭大信茲夾上公定津助省毛艮

傳遞数十張如有人问及何以是屆津

助省毛等情請祈將該傳遞發

交他看便得了然明白^{敝等}經通佈

各縣鄉領骨骸囬鄉之办事員知照

諸多費神不勝感謝之致此請

公安

（印章：安南穗義祠执先友白骨圖章）頓　三月初九

津助莛運費陸續滙返但到時照時價办理

為荷又及

陸賈佮返二千八百一十五具骨骸隨押医生放行紙水陸衙放行紙請

祈將此紙代買保家付來該郵費入來往数為荷

中華民國廿年四月廿六日

193 Letter from Bureau Cimetière de Canton, Cholon, Annam, to Tung Wah Hospital on 26 April 1931

From the Office of Bureau Cimetière de Canton

Dear Chairman and Managers of Tung Wah Hospital,

We sent a telegram to you in the afternoon of the 7th day [of the 3rd lunar month] to inform you that we had repatriated 2,815 sets of remains on the *Luk Gah*. We trust you will arrange labor to take them to your coffin home and await the deceased's families to come to collect them. The family of each deceased friend should be given burial fees of 2 Kwangtung silver dollars. Please keep a record of the funds distributed and send it to us for our compilation of *Zhengxinlu* (accounting journal) for public information and display of our accountability. We also enclose several dozens of information sheets with details of the burial fee subsidy. If you receive enquiries about the burial fees and other matters, please give one to the enquirer. It would explain everything. We have already informed the families in various counties and villages to collect the remains.

We are most grateful to you for your efforts.

We wish you well.

Yours sincerely,
(Stamp: Seal of Remains Exhumation and Repatriation of Bureau Cimetière de Canton, Annam)

9th day of the 3rd lunar month

The burial fees will be sent to you in due course, please distribute according to the exchange rate.
2,815 sets of remains have been repatriated on the *Luk Gah*, along with exit permits issued by a doctor and the marine police department. Please arrange insurance coverage and the postage fee is also attached.

26 April of the 20th year of the Republic of China

香港和發成啓事用箋

東華醫院
執事先生大鑒啓者陸賈船今早由越
　　南到港俻來　貴院所收之骨殖二千八百一十五箱蒙
　　已放艇開船起卸甚慰□今將安南寄
　　來过關會照及信共三紙夾此奉上祈照
　　察存為荷此請

大安

（印章：香港和發成書柬）

中華民國辛未年三月十弍日

Letter from Wo Fat Shing, Hong Kong, to Tung Wah Hospital on 29 April 1931

From the Office of Wo Fat Shing, Hong Kong

Dear Managers of Tung Wah Hospital,

It is gratifying that the *Luk Gah* carrying 2,815 sets of remains from Vietnam to your hospital has arrived this morning. Thank you for taking delivery of them. We hereby enclose the exit permits issued by the Vietnamese authorities and a letter, three pages in total for your kind attention and retention, please.

Thank you.

Yours sincerely,
(Stamp: Wo Fat Shing, Hong Kong)

12th day of the 3rd lunar month, Year of San Mei *(Xinwei)*

麗興金鋪用箋

逕啓者現據
安南穗義祠來函畧謂是屆執運先友骨
殖^{敝邑}該壹佰肆拾玖具每具津助葬費省
毛銀弍元計共弍佰玖拾捌元経已一應運寄
貴院義庄寄厝候領等情來社經^{敝社}去
函^{敝邑}矜育堂着派人到港具領故特函達
貴院但^{敝邑}矜育堂派員到領時請照骨殖
數及隨助費二百九十八元一應交与具領素仰
貴院熱心慈善故特函奉託並附骨殖號数
單計共壹佰四十九號到時請按照號數姓氏
察對交領專此奉懇袛請

善安
東華大醫院列位执事先生台鑒

旅越四會公益社啓

中華民國廿年五月五日

旅越四會各先友骨殖號数単

壹号	李　彬	三十一	錢陈氏大
式号	黃門邝三	三十式	吳　富
三号	邱門黃瑞	三十三	呂　帝
四号	梁　貴	三十四	莫　正
五号	潘門凌式	三十五	梁　心
六号	林梁氏好	三十六	陈　祥
七号	梁耀文	三十七	趙丕球
八号	刘張氏式	三十八	冼　森
九号	梁門陈葵	三十九	李　有
十号	巨　德	四十	黃　紹
十一号	窜　士	四十一	曾　灶
十式	朱門黃意	四十二	羅　金
十三	陳　泉	四十三	丁　三
十四	譚　熙	四十四	李　懷
十五	李　通	四十五	羅　芳
十六	梁　錦	四十六	吳林氏愛
十七	梁張氏鳳	四十七	吳　貴
十八	區　根	四十八	鄧　生
十九	謝　德	四十九	林張氏花
式十	盧李氏細妹	五十	梁駱氏娇
二十一	顧　公	五十一	阮潘氏喜
二十二	謝李氏妹	五十二	郭　帶
二十三	梁　洪	五十三	陈　四
二十四	丁　蘇	五十四	馮　利
二十五	許　妹	五十五	郭　昌
二十六	許黃氏五	五十六	丁　科
二十七	嚴　德	五十七	巫　可
二十八	徐　桂	五十八	嚴　堂
二十九	鄭　榮	五十九	窜　中
三十	陈吳氏大	六十	謝　華

六十一	謝陈氏	九十七	邵丁氏
六十二	鄧曾氏金	九十八	吳　福
六十三	吳榮昇	九十九	張　凌
六十四	莫　釗	一〇〇	黃志年
六十五	歐　登	一〇一	吳　貴
六十六	李　煜	一〇二	黃　可
六十七	譚　祥	一〇三	蕭　祖
六十八	陈　錦	一〇四	潘邰氏
六十九	刘志祥	一〇五	何黃氏
七十	李葉氏金	一〇六	張廷德
七十一	譚陈氏妹	一〇七	潘葉氏
七十二	盧周氏蘭	一〇八	潘李氏
七十三	葉　九	一〇九	潘緒九
七十四	葉　成	一一〇	李东玲
七十五	雷　威	一一一	沈英公
七十六	鄧　文（此具留葬未運）		
七十七	黃　成	一一二	林周氏可娣
七十八	譚何氏弍	一一三	周梁氏
七十九	陈李氏意	一一四	徐　坤
八十	陈均垣	一一五	梁邝氏
八十一	封丁氏顏	一一六	吳碧林
八十二	丁　四	一一七	梁奕公
八十三	刘氏奀	一一八	賴　華
八十四	譚秀氏	一一九	罗刘氏
八十五	罗麥氏	一二〇	林均庭
八十六	曾沅氏	一二一	趙黃氏
八十七	陳昌公	一二二	封　松
八十八	鄧　珍	一二三	刘周氏美
八十九	鄧　金	一二四	李　秀
九十	梁　球	一二五	刘萬公
九十一	范　才	一二六	嚴石公

九十二	胡　苟	一二七	黃任公
九十三	雷　星	一二八	梁　安
九十四	葉　有	一二九	吳　桂
九十五	邵罗氏	一三〇	陸大公
九十六	張　公	一〇〇一	何才公
一〇〇二	謝氏月		
一〇〇三	廖氏娇	一〇一三	梁新公
一〇〇四	賴蘭氏（原李蘭）	一〇一四	梁氏弍
一〇〇五	梁坤公	一〇一五	嚴氏三
一〇〇六	郑　慶	一〇一六	陈氏帶
一〇〇七	黃氏桂妹	一〇一七	歐林氏蓮
一〇〇九	張水德（原名張德）	一〇一八	徐氏帶
一〇一〇	黃氏□五	一〇一九	伍門曾氏
一〇一一	葉　唐（原曾帶）	一〇二〇	陈东初公
一〇一二	林寿公	一〇二一	張炳公

總共一百四十九具

东華大医院查对

Letter from Sei Wui Kung Yick Society, Annam, to Tung Wah Hospital on 5 May 1931

Dear Managers of Tung Wah Hospital,

We received a letter from Bureau Cimetière de Canton in Annam with regard to repatriation of the bones of deceased friends who were native of our county. We were told that 149 sets of remains, along with burial fees of 2 Kwangtung silver dollars for each deceased friend (298 dollars in total), had been sent to the coffin home of your esteemed hospital, awaiting collection by the deceased's families. We had already written to Ging Yuk Tong *(Jin Yu Tang)* in our county and asked them to send a representative to Hong Kong to collect the remains. We, hereby, write to your esteemed hospital to inform you of this. When the representative of Ging Yuk Tong arrives, please hand over the bones, together with burial fees of 298 dollars, to him. We are well aware of your esteemed hospital's benevolent work, and therefore write to you seeking your assistance in this matter. Please see the enclosed list of 149 deceased friends and the corresponding numbers, and hand over the bones to the representative of our county accordingly.

We wish you well.

Yours sincerely,
Sei Wui Kung Yick Society of Annam

5 May of the 20th year of the Republic of China

[Editor's remarks: Name list of the deceased friends is available only in Chinese]

東華医院大総理鑒逕啓者昨奉　大函敬悉
現^{敝所}義莊起迁先友業已竣事定扵本年五
月十八日（即舊曆四月初一日）將先友骸砠附北野丸輪
船運港到達时務懇代為安置以便各先友親属隨
時到領各先友親屬早経發函通知似可不用登
報茲寄上先友名冊一紙（詳細名冊容再奉上）烦
轉致各属公共团体以便轉達各處鄉村週知十八
日隨船滙上港幣五百元以应
貴院代办一切之需如有殘餘請撥交
貴院慈善之用至先友親属領葬補助費每名發
給港幣五元俟查明实数亦扵同日滙上嵩此奉托
袛请

公安

日本長崎廣東会所簡肖藜　啓（印章：簡肖藜印）

中華民國二十年五月十日

Letter from Kwang Tung Association of Nagasaki, Japan, to Tung Wah Hospital on 10 May 1931

Dear Directors of Tung Wah Hospital,

We have finished exhuming the remains of our deceased friends from our coffin home, and will repatriate them on the *Kitano Maru* on 18 May (1st day of the 4th lunar month) this year. When the remains arrive in Hong Kong, please take them into your care for the families to claim them. We have already informed the deceased's families by post to claim the remains, so it seems that there is no need to publish notices in the newspaper. We enclose a brief list of the deceased (a detailed list will be sent to you later) in this letter. Please forward this to the respective public organizations, so that they inform various villages. We will send 500 Hong Kong dollars to you together with the shipment on 18 May, to cover the handling costs incurred. Please use the remaining funds to support the charitable work of your esteemed hospital. The family of each deceased friend should be given burial fees of 5 Hong Kong dollars. After we have worked out the total amount, we will also send the funds on the same day.

We are most grateful to you for your efforts.

Yours sincerely,
Kan Chiu-lai (*Jian Xiaoli*)
Chairman, Kwang Tung Association, Nagasaki, Japan
(Stamp: Kan Siu-lai)

10 May of the 20th year of the Republic of China

197 香港和發成致東華醫院信件

1931 年 5 月 20 日

香港和發成啟事用箋

東華醫院

執事先生大鑒敬啓者去月陸賈船由越南運來之

骨殖曾扵去月十二日將其过關護照弍張信一封統

呈　貴院收存矣刻接越南穗義祠辦事所

來函着將該護照寄还該處以為下屆作指南

之需云云今將原函抄上仰希將此護照撿齊擲

交敝處俾淂轉寄前途為荷專此即頌

台祺

（印章：香港和發成書柬）

中華民國辛未年四月初四日

另一人註：已复

茲將越南穗義祠辦事所來函抄錄

和興大公司執事諸鄉先生大鑒公啓者前報効由陸賈船
　　偁返港之骨殖其衛生師与西貢水陸警廳放行紙由
　　貴輪押偁返港此紙是否交東華医院抑或交港和發成
　　行收茲字奉達　貴執事祈通函返港將該放行医生紙
　　統附返來俾得存據下屆西堤帮長依樣葫芦因五年一屆
　　該任帮長定不知頭緒故收囬存貯以便着手往西提各衙簽
　　字是否有當請祈留意通函港埠求為付來諸多費神不勝
　　感謝之致也餘後詳此請

台安

穗義祠办事所
設提岸廣肇公所內　三月廿八日

Letter from Wo Fat Shing, Hong Kong, to Tung Wah Hospital on 20 May 1931

From the Office of Wo Fat Shing, Hong Kong

Dear Managers of Tung Wah Hospital,

We sent two exit permits and a letter regarding the bones transported on the *Luk Gah* to your esteemed hospital on the 12th day of last month for your kind reference and retention. However, we received a letter from Bureau Cimetière De Canton of Vietnam, asking us to send the permits back to them so that they could keep them as reference for the next repatriation. We enclose a copy of the letter from Bureau Cimetière De Canton. Please pass the permits to us and we will send them to Bureau Cimetière De Canton.

Thank you for your efforts.

Yours sincerely,
(Stamp: Wo Fat Shing)

4th day of the 4th lunar month, Year of San Mei *(Xinwei)*

Another person's remarks: Replied

A copy of the letter from Bureau Cimetière de Canton of Vietnam:

Dear Managers of Wo Hing Company,

With regard to the bones repatriated to Hong Kong on the *Luk Gah*, please advise if the exit permits issued by the doctor and the marine police department of Saigon have been passed to Tung Wah Hospital or Wo Fat Shing in Hong Kong. We would appreciate it very much if you could return the permit of the doctor and other documents to us, so that our next chairman can use as reference to follow suit. Since each of our chairman serves a five-year term, the chairman responsible for the next repatriation would foreseeably have no idea about the necessary procedures. We shall keep the permit for our future chairman's reference, so that he will know which government departments in Cholon he should approach. Please kindly assist us in this matter.

We are most grateful to you for your efforts.

Yours sincerely,
Office of Bureau Cimetière de Canton, Cholon

28th day of the 3rd lunar month

東華醫院義庄

列位執事先生大鑒敬啓者茲聞日本長崎埠有大

帮先人骨石運回原籍交　貴院義庄分派^弟有先

母扵光緒拾七年在日本長崎埠逝世至今骸石

尚未運回但此次未知有先母骨石在內否倘有陳盛

祥或用開富或開記等字樣之妻黃氏骸石在內伏乞

通知南海平洲鄉村頭龍元坊四拾叁号陳進光俾

得前來領取是為德便草此拜懇敬请

均安

^弟陳進光叩
四月廿四日

另一人註：辛四月廿八覆

Letter from Chan Chun-kwong, China, to Tung Wah Hospital on 13 June 1931

Dear Managers of Tung Wah Coffin Home,

I heard that a large batch of bones had been repatriated from Nagasaki, Japan, to the deceased's hometown through your coffin home. My mother passed away in Nagasaki, Japan, in the 17th year of the Guangxu's reign. Her bones are yet to be repatriated. I wonder if my mother's bones have been included in this batch of remains. Please check if there are bones under the name "Madame Wong" *(Huang)*, wife of Chan Shing-cheung *(Chen Shengxiang)* or Hoi Fu/Hoi Kee *(Kaifu/ Kaiji)*. If there are, please inform me, Chan Chun-kwong *(Chen Jinguang)*, at No. 43, Lung Yuen Fong *(Longyuan Fang)*, Ping Chow Township *(Pingzhou Xiang)*, Nam Hoi *(Nanhai)*. I will then come to collect the remains.

I am most grateful to you for your help and I wish you well.

Yours humbly,
Chan Chun-kwong

24 April

Another person's remarks: Replied on the 28th day of the 4th lunar month, Year of San Mei *(Xinwei)*

199 暹京廣肇別墅致東華醫院信件

1931 年 6 月 23 日

暹羅廣肇別墅用箋

逕啓者近疊據張告元函稱先弟張卓元有骸骨
壹具経由本別墅運到
貴院再三在港請領未蒙允許等情前來想或
因手續未合一時未便給予爰將前情函達
台端倘張卓元親屬再到請領骨殖時懇按照
向章准予具領如本別墅或有未合之手續伏
希　示悉以便備办一切為荷此致

東華醫院執事先生

主席　黃求標上
（印章：暹京廣肇別墅書柬）

二十年六月廿三日

Letter from Kwong Siew Villa, Siam, to Tung Wah Hospital on 23 June 1931

From the Office of Kwong Siew Villa, Siam

Dear Managers of Tung Wah Hospital,

We recently received a letter from Cheung Ko-yuen *(Zhang Gaoyuan)* saying that the bones of his late younger brother, Cheung Cheuk-yuen *(Zhang Zhuoyuan)*, were sent to your esteemed hospital through us, but his family had not been able to collect his remains in Hong Kong despite great efforts. This was presumably because the relevant procedures had not been completed. We hereby write to you with regard to this matter. When the relatives of Cheung Cheuk-yuen comes to collect his bones, please let them claim according to your regulations. If there are procedures we need to complete, please inform us and we will do so.

Yours sincerely,
Wong Kau-biu *(Huang Qiubiao)*, Chairman
(Stamp: Kwong Siew Villa, Siam)

23 June of the 20th year of the Republic of China

200 日本長崎廣東會所致東華醫院信件

1931 年 6 月 23 日

逕啓者　案查前五月十八日將先友骸
硒六十七件附北野丸日輪運囬香港
托由
貴院安置并托香港恒豐号滙上
港幣八百五十元以应
貴院代办各項之費想
貴院早經妥辦惟至今未蒙
賜覆不識真相何若為此再函
奉達希即
查覆為荷此致

東華医院大総理鑒

長崎廣東會所簡肖藜（印章：簡肖藜印）

二十年國暦六月廿三日

另一人註：四月初九　五百元捐　三百三十五元葚費

Letter from Kwang Tung Association, Nagasaki, Japan, to Tung Wah Hospital on 23 June 1931

Dear Directors of Tung Wah Hospital,

We repatriated the remains of 67 deceased friends on the Japanese ship *Kitano Maru* on 18 May and asked your esteemed hospital to take them into your care. We also remitted 850 Hong Kong dollars to you through Hang Fung Ho in Hong Kong to cover the costs of handling. We believe you have already taken care of the matter but we have not received your reply yet. We hereby write to you again. Please investigate and reply to us.

Yours sincerely,
Kan Siu-lai *(Jian Xiaoli)*
Kwang Tung Association, Nagasaki, Japan
(Stamp: Kan Siu-lai)

23 June of the 20th year of the Republic of China

Another person's remarks: Received donation of 500 dollars and burial fees of 335 dollars on the 9th day of the 4th lunar month

虎門太平溥善堂用牋

東華醫院
執事諸公^{大鑒}

敬啟者前閱報紙得悉安南各先友金
骸經已裝運到　貴院已有月餘惟今
日久未蒙分發寄運^{敝堂}虎門鄰鄉一
帶茲今各鄉先友親屬携領金骸紙到^{敝堂}
問及茲故專函奉達請祈示覆為禱此頌

善祺

（印章：太平溥善堂）

中華民國弍拾年七月拾日

另一人註：已复

Letter from Tai Ping Po Sin Tong, Fu Mun, China, to Tung Wah Hospital on 10 July 1931

From the Office of Tai Ping Po Sin Tong, Fu Mun

Dear Managers of Tung Wah Hospital,

We read in the newspaper that the bones of deceased friends who passed away in Annam were repatriated to your esteemed hospital. It is now more than a month, but the bones had not yet been sent to us for distribution to the villages near Fu Mun *(Humen)*. The families of the deceased friends recently brought the letters for bone collection to us to inquire about the matter. We, hereby, write to you and await your reply.

We are most grateful to you for your benevolence.

Yours sincerely,
(Stamp: Tai Ping Po Sin Tong)*(Taiping Pu Shan Tang)*

10 July of the 20th year of the Republic of China

Another person's remarks: Replied

202 安南堤岸廣肇公所致東華醫院信件

1931 年 8 月 14 日

堤岸廣肇公所用牋

逕啓者于夏曆五月廿五日滙港怡興隆交

貴院收港幣叁千元是次六月卅日由法郵船又滙港怡興隆交

貴院收港幣五千元連三月初五日滙交銀五千元三共交銀一萬三千元

頭帮付先僑骸骨三千零六具二帮付先僑骸骨二千八百一十五具二共付骸骨

五千八百二十一具

应支每具上落艇脚費三毛寸該艮一千七百四十六元三毛每具助港幣二元寸該銀一萬

一千六百四十二元

二共支港銀一萬三千三百八十八元三毛除滙交之外尚欠銀三百八十八元三毛如有別項應支过総

共欠若干求為示知俾得如數照滙交足但求早日分送各

縣之骸骨与慈善机關收以得各親属領葬因各縣之

親属早已由越旋鄉候領日久且各縣慈善機関屢屢來

信追問之故請祈見諒多費精神不勝深感恭此並頌

善祺
東華醫院
主席先生
列位善長

代理 堤岸 廣肇帮長馮燦（印章：堤岸廣肇公所）

中華民國廿年八月十四日

Letter from Bureau Cimetière de Canton, Cholon, Annam, to Tung Wah Hospital on 14 August 1931

From the Office of Bureau Cimetière de Canton, Cholon

Dear Chairman and Directors of Tung Wah Hospital,

On the 25th day of the 5th lunar month, we remitted 3,000 Hong Kong dollars to your esteemed hospital through Yee Hing Lung in Hong Kong. On the 30th day of the 6th lunar month, we remitted 5,000 Hong Kong dollars to you again through Yee Hing Lung. Together with the 5,000 Hong Kong dollars sent to you on the 5th day of the 3rd lunar month, we had remitted a total of 13,000 Hong Kong dollars to you. We have sent to you the bones of 3,006 deceased Chinese compatriots in the first batch and 2,815 sets of bones in the second batch, 5,821 sets of bones in total. Burial fees of 2 dollars each should be paid, whereas the transportation fees for each set of bones are 30 cents. The transportation costs and burial fees for the bones should be 1,746.30 Hong Kong dollars and 11,642 Hong Kong dollars respectively. The two sums add up to 13,388.30 Hong Kong dollars. As we have sent 13,000 dollars to you already, we still owe your esteemed hospital 388.30 dollars. If there are any other expenses incurred, please let us know and we will remit the funds to you. We hope that the bones can be sent to the corresponding benevolent associations as soon as possible. The families of the deceased have traveled from their villages to the benevolent associations in the hope of collecting the remains, and they have waited for quite some time. The benevolent associations have written to us repeatedly to enquire about the repatriation. We, therefore, write to you with regard to the matter.

Thank you very much for your understanding, and we are most grateful to you for your efforts.

Yours sincerely,
Fung Chan *(Feng Can)*
Acting Chairman, Bureau Cimetière de Canton, Cholon
(Stamp: Bureau Cimetière de Canton, Cholon)

14 August of the 20th year of the Republic of China

203 香港駐港東莞工商總會致東華醫院信件

1931 年 9 月 17 日

駐港東莞工商總會用箋

東華醫院
列位執事先生大鑒敬啓者本年夏曆
二月初三日由大廣西輪船載囬安南埠先友
骨殖叁佰叁拾柒具三月十二日由陸賈輪船
載囬安南先友骨殖五百五拾弍具合共捌佰
捌拾九具除各親屬自赴
貴院領去十一具外实存捌佰柒拾捌具另七月
初六日由俄國皇后輪船載囬域多利埠先友
骨殖九具共計捌佰捌拾柒具均寄厝
貴院義庄茲敝會定於本月初七日全数代運
囬鄉招屬領瘗為此函達请
飭知義庄管理人照交至所感禱專此即頌

台祺

（印章：駐港東莞闔邑工商總會書柬）

辛未年八月初六日

Letter from General Chamber of Commerce & Industry of Tung Kun District in Hong Kong, to Tung Wah Hospital on 17 September 1931

From the Office of the General Chamber of Commerce & Industry of Tung Kun District in Hong Kong

Dear Managers of Tung Wah Hospital,

We repatriated from Annam the bones of 337 deceased friends on the *Guangxi* on the 3rd day of the 2nd lunar month this year, and those of 552 deceased friends on the *Luk Gah* on the 12th day of the 3rd lunar month. There were 889 sets of bones in total. After the bones of 11 deceased friends were collected from your esteemed hospital by their relatives, 878 sets of bones were left in your custody. Meanwhile, the bones of nine deceased friends were repatriated from Victoria, on the *Empress of Russia* on the 6th day of the 7th lunar month. As such, a total of 887 sets of bones are placed temporarily in the coffin home of your esteemed hospital. We shall send all of the remains to the deceased's hometown on the 7th day of this lunar month. Please inform the caretaker of the coffin home to hand over the bones to us then.

We are most grateful to you for your efforts.

Yours sincerely,
(Stamp: General Chamber of Commerce & Industry of Tung Kun District in Hong Kong)

6th day of the 8th lunar month, Year of San Mei *(Xinwei)*

駐港東莞工商總會用箋

東華醫院

列位执事先生台鑒敬啓者昨承

貴院發給領单前赴義庄領囬辛未年

二月初三日大廣西船運囬安南埠骸骨三百三十七具

又辛未年三月十二日陸賈船運囬安南埠骸

骨五百四十一具二柱合計捌佰柒拾捌具均已起運

清楚兹將義庄發囬滮单二張繳請

察收銷號并懇核明應給葬費若干如

數送交大道西第八號門牌全安公司周鎰

畚君妥收以便分發各先友親属具領为

盼又^{敝會}駁運骸骨係用東義堂名義經

理交款時取囬東義堂收條即可無誤合

併奉陳專此順頌

公祺

（印章：駐港東莞闔邑工商總會書柬）

附呈義庄滮單弍紙

辛未年八月初九日

Letter from General Chamber of Commerce & Industry of Tung Kun District in Hong Kong, to Tung Wah Hospital on 20 September 1931

From the Office of General Chamber of Commerce & Industry of Tung Kun District in Hong Kong

Dear Managers of Tung Wah Hospital,

Yesterday, we collected 337 sets of bones repatriated from Annam on the *Guangxi* on the 3rd day of the 2nd lunar month, Year of San Mei *(Xinwei)*, and 541 sets of bones repatriated from Annam on the *Luk Gah* on the 12th day of the 3rd lunar month, Year of San Mei, from your coffin home with the letter issued by your esteemed hospital. A total of 878 sets of bones had been repatriated [to the mainland].

We hereby enclose the two receipts issued by the coffin home. Please verify the receipts and work out the total amount of burial fees to be given. The funds should be sent to Chow Yat-yu *(Zhou Yishe)* of Chuen On Company at No. 8 Queen's Road West, so that the burial fees can be distributed to the deceased's families. Meanwhile, we oversee repatriation of the bones to China in the name of Tung Yee Tong *(Dong Yi Tang)*, so please expect a receipt issued by Tung Yee Tong when you send the funds.

We are most grateful to you for your efforts.

Yours sincerely,
(Stamp: General Chamber of Commerce & Industry of Tung Kun District in Hong Kong)

Two receipts issued by coffin home enclosed

9th day of the 8th lunar month, Year of San Mei *(Xinwei)*

東華醫院列位先生 ^{大鑒}

　　敬啓者前日由
貴醫院運來高要第七區永安安南先友骨
　　箱経已到步第七區团局问及小店該葬費
　　由何處滙上 ^弟 当時説他滙香港皇后道嘉
　　華駁廣东肇慶慎成銀号代永安順昌收銀
　　若干今接慎成來函云及無与嘉華來往
　　故特草函奉上該項懇求
貴醫院直滙到肇慶慎成代小店收妥請列
　　收条并求示复諸事有勞
清神不勝銘感容當叩谢并請

台安

　　　　　　　　　　　　　　　　　（印章：永安順昌號）
　　　　　　　　　　　　　　　　　^弟羅幹生頓

廿年六月七號

Letter from Law Gon-sang, China, to Tung Wah Hospital on 7 June 1931

Dear Directors of Tung Wah Hospital,

The bones of deceased friends from Annam, repatriated to Wing On *(Yung'an)*, the 7th District of Go Yiu *(Gaoyao)*, by your esteemed hospital, had arrived. The community police office of the 7th District asked our shop how the burial fees would be sent to them, and I replied that the funds would be remitted to Wing On Shun Cheong by Ka Wah [Bank] on Queen's Road in Hong Kong via Sun Shing Native Bank *(Shencheng Yinhao)* in Shiu Hing *(Zhaoqing)*, Kwangtung *(Guangdong)*.

Yet I received a letter from Sun Shing that they do not have any business connection with Ka Wah. So I write to ask your esteemed hospital to send the funds directly to our shop with the receipt in the care of Sun Shing Native Bank in Shiu Hing. Please reply to let us know if this is possible.

I am most grateful to you for your efforts.

I wish you well.

Yours sincerely,
Law Gon-sang *(Luo Gansheng)*
(Stamp: Wing On Shun Cheong Ho)

7 June of the 20th year of the Republic of China

暹京廣肇別墅用箋

香港東華醫院
列位善長先生大鑒逕啓者茲有台山縣人陳君子超
於本月四日搭江蘇輪船運他先父新保先生靈柩回
國因陳君年少無知及久居異域沿途生疏用特函達
貴院執事先生如陳君道經香港時請為指示一切想
貴院一視同仁定能樂意　垂顧也專此并頌

公祺

　　　　　　　　　　　　　　主席黃求標　謹啓
　　　　　　　　　　　　（印章：暹羅廣肇醫局書束）

中華民國二十年十二月三日

From the Office of Kwong Siew Villa, Siam

Dear benevolent Directors of Tung Wah Hospital,

Chan Chi-chiu *(Chen Zichao)*, a native of Toi Shan County *(Taishan Xian)*, will bring the coffin of his late father Sun-po *(Xinbao)* to China on the *Jiangsu* on the 4th day of this month. Since Chan is young and not very knowledgeable, and there are many things he – who has been living in a foreign country for so long – does not know, we hereby write to ask you to give him guidance when he arrives in Hong Kong. We believe your esteemed hospital would help him, as you treat everyone equally.

We are most grateful for your kindness.

Yours sincerely,
Wong Kau-biu *(Huang Qiubiao)*, Chairman
(Stamp: Kwong Siu Clinic of Siam)

3 December of the 20th year of the Republic of China

中華僑務公所用箋
安南峴港
CONGREGATIONS CHINOIS
ANNAM TOURANE

東華大醫院鈞鑒

敬啓者前詢執運華僑先友靈骸事
宜經蒙指迷甚感而各先友灵骸今経執
竣決於下期松江船運返香港煩
貴醫院代為收發并祈先將各先友姓名
登錄報章俾該親屬淂其先知預備迎
接免延擱時日有所不便幸甚諸勞清
神泥首遠謝即此敬荷

鈞安

　　　　茲將各先友姓名錄呈于后

　　　　　　　　　　　　中華僑務公所　夏七月廿六日
　　　　　　　　　　　　（印章：峴港中華僑務公所書束）

中華民國廿一年八月廿七日

茲將運返香江諸先友列

廿八	關友謙	九江	四十九	陈景隆	潮州
廿九	黎炳芬	九江	五十	歐阳為	福建
三十	黎梁氏	九江	五十一	歐阳樹	福建
三十一	黎蘇氏	九江	五十二	謝瑞屏	防城
三十二	刘周南	鶴山	五十三	楊善初	防城
三十四	呂北樂	鶴山	五十四	倫輔樓	三水
三十五	林遠公	台山	五十六	何元球	杏市
三十六	謝喜賢	南海	五十七	謝泽公	福建
三十七	李傳寬	三水	六十	張成章	福建
三十八	李胡氏	三水	六十三	吳榕生	香港
三十九	易口楨	省城	六十四	吳鈺堂	香港
四十一	何孔氏	杏市圩	六十五	何兆槐	高要
四十二	甘鳳祥	中山	六十六	吳卓華	澳門
四十三	郑应楦	中山	六十七	刘观德	中山
四十四	陈有芳	中山	六十八	刘余氏	中山
四十五	張泰安	中山	六十九	刘伍氏	中山
四十六	吳遜初	中山	七十	吳寶鑾	南海
四十七	陈宗詠	中山	七十四	黃余氏	中山
四十八	陈郑氏	中山	七十五	黃朝韓	中山

合共三十八具

Letter from Congregations Chinois of Turance, Annam, to Tung Wah Hospital on 27 August 1932

From the Office of Congregations Chinois, Turance, Annam

Dear Managers of Tung Wah Hospital,

Thank you for your reply and advice with regard to the repatriation of the remains of our deceased friends. Now, we have finished exhuming the remains and will send them to Hong Kong on the next shipment of *Chung Kong*. Please take the remains into your care when they arrive in Hong Kong. Please also publish a list of the deceased friends in the newspaper in advance, so that their families can prepare to collect the remains and will not cause any delay.

We are most grateful to you for your efforts.

I wish you well.

Yours sincerely,
Congregations Chinois

26th day of the 7th lunar month
27 August of the 21st year of the Republic of China
(Stamp: Congregations Chinois, Danang)

The name list is on the next page.

[Editor's remarks: Name list of the deceased friends is available only in Chinese]

蘇洛粵僑同鄉執行委員會用箋
Yokow Tiong Hieng Woi

逕啓者^{敝處}第二批先友骨殖計

有九具^{同人}等擬定一交冬季

即將其分別運返原籍安葬

以慰幽魂惟將來各骨殖到港

時欲拜勞

貴院代收暫貯義庄候其

親屬到領至費用若干手

續如何仰即

示知以便籌俻素仰

貴院乐善為怀此項善舉

必不見卻却也專此并候

台祺

東華医院
执事先生

中華民國廿一年九月廿三日

^{常務}梁緝熙（印章：蘇洛粵僑同鄉執行委員會印）

Letter from the Executive Committee of Yokow Tiong Hieng Woi of Sulu, Philippines, to Tung Wah Hospital on 23 September 1932

From the Office of Yokow Tiong Hieng Woi, Sulu

Dear Managers of Tung Wah Hospital,

We will repatriate the second batch of bones of our deceased friends, nine sets in total, in early winter, so that the deceased can be laid to rest. When they arrive in Hong Hong, please keep the bones in your coffin home until the families of the deceased come to Hong Kong to collect them. Also, please notify us of the costs and the procedures of handling the matter so that we can make the necessary arrangements. Your benevolence is known far and wide, we trust you will not decline to help.

We await your reply.

Yours sincerely,
Leung Chap-hei *(Liang Qixi)*
Executive Committee Member
(Stamp: Executive Committee of Yokow Tiong Hieng Woi, Sulu)
23 September of the 21st year of the Republic of China

逕啓者茲查何明軒即文炷又名何明扵民國
八年即舊歷己未年三月廿九日在南洋吉隆波
身故係葬在南洋吉隆波廣東義山壹號地第
九〇四四號至今十四年該遺骨未悉有運囘
貴院否相應函達请煩
查明至到領手續如何統希
見覆為盼此致

東華醫院执事鈞鑒

　　　函覆：廣州市中華中路學宮街總醫院

　　　　　　　　　何伯偉上言（印章：何伯偉印）

廿一年十一月廿五日

Letter from Ho Pak-wai, China, to Tung Wah Hospital on 25 November 1932

Dear Managers of Tung Wah Hospital,

I understand that Ho Ming-hin *(He Mingxuan)*, also known as Man-chu *(Wenzhu)* and Ho Ming *(He Ming)*, passed away in Kuala Lumpur on the 29th day of the third lunar month, Year of Gei Mei *(Jiwei)*. He was buried in No. 9044, Lot 1 of Kwong Tong Cemetery in Kuala Lumpur. 14 years had passed and I wonder if his bones had been sent back to your hospital. Please investigate the matter for me and notify me of the procedures for claiming the bones. I await your reply.

Yours sincerely,
Ho Pak-wai *(He Bowei)*
(Stamp: Ho Pak-wai)

25 November of the 21st year of the Republic of China

Please send your reply to: Hok Gung Street General Hospital *(Xuegong Jie Zong Yiyuan)*, Chung Wah Chung Road *(Zhonghua Zhonglu)*, Canton (Guangzhou).

廣肇醫院
KWONG SIU HOSPITAL

東華醫院主席先生台鑒敬啓者查

敝院（前稱醫局）於民十六年十月間

運囬先友骨殖一帮內有鍾炳

芳一具據其親屬來報至今

仍未收到不知現在是否尚在

貴院義庄敬祈代為一查該

鍾炳芳係東莞城豬仔墟人氏

如已查獲請囬函示知不勝感

盼之至此頌

台祺

（印章：暹京廣肇醫院）啓
廿一、十二、七日

Letter from Kwong Siu Hospital, Siam, to Tung Wah Hospital on 7 December 1932

From the Office of Kwong Siu Hospital, Siam

Dear Chairman of Tung Wah Hospital,

Our hospital (formerly Kwong Siu Clinic) repatriated a batch of remains of our deceased friends in October of the 16th year of the Republic of China. Among the remains were those of Chung Bing-fong *(Zhong Bingfang)*. His relatives reported to us that they had not yet received the bones. Would you please find out if the remains are still in your coffin home? Chung Bing-fong was a native of Chu Tsai Market Town *(Zhuzai Xu)*, Tung Koon City *(Dongguan Cheng)*. If you find his remains, please write to let us know.

We are most grateful to you for your efforts.

We wish you well.

Yours sincerely,
(Stamp: Siam Kwong Siu Hospital)

7 December of the 21st year of the Republic of China

國民革命軍第一集團軍總司令部總醫院用牋

逕啓者前懇
貴院代查「何明軒」即「文炷」又名「何明」於民國八年即
「舊歷己未年」三月廿九日在南洋吉隆波身故係葬扵
廣東義山一號地第九千〇〇四號現拟查囘該何明
軒遺骨未知有無寄存
貴院相應再為函達請煩
費神查明仍希
見覆並請註明往運手續如何為感此上

香港東華醫院执事台鑒

何伯偉謹啓（印章：何伯偉印）

中華民國廿二年一月八日

另一人註：已复

Letter from Ho Pak-wai, China, to Tung Wah Hospital on 8 January 1933

From the General Hospital of the Command Centre of the 1st Group Army of the National Revolutionary Army

Dear Managers of Tung Wah Hospital,

I wrote to your esteemed hospital earlier to enquire about Ho Ming-hin *(He Mingxuan)*, also known as Man-chu *(Wenzhu)*, or Ho Ming *(He Ming)*, who passed away in Kuala Lumpur, Nanyang on 29 March in the 8th year of the Republic of China (Year of Gei Mei *(Jiwei)*) and was buried in No. 9004, Lot 1, Kwong Tong Cemetery. I would like to find out if his bones have been stored in your esteemed hospital. Please investigate the matter for me and give me a reply. Grateful if you could also notify me of the procedures for repatriating the bones.

Yours sincerely,
Ho Pak-wai *(He Bowei)*
(Stamp: Ho Pak-wai)

8 January of the 22nd year of the Republic of China

Another person's remarks: Replied

蘇洛粵僑同鄉執行委員會用箋
Yokow Tiong Hieng Woi

東華医院
列位先生大鑒敬啓者^{敝埠}

　現有先友骨殖十具左右
　亟欲寄交　貴院義庄
　貯候諸先友親属到領
　現在办法如何昨年
　曾経奉函请教未蒙見
　復念念茲特再函奉恳
　務望　貴院將办理手續
　賜示以便遵照办理是
　所切禱并请

善安

　　　　　　　　　　　　　　　蘇洛粵侨同鄉会謹啓
　　　　　　　　　　　　（印章：蘇洛粵僑同鄉執行委員會印）

中華民國二十二年二月八日

Letter from the Executive Committee of Yokow Tiong Hieng Woi, Sulu, Philippines, to Tung Wah Hospital on 8 February 1933

From the Office of Yokow Tiong Hieng Woi, Sulu

Dear Directors of Tung Wah Hospital,

We would like to send approximately ten sets of bones to your coffin home for temporary storage for the families of the deceased to claim. Would you please advise us of the prevailing procedures for repatriation? In fact, we wrote to you to seek your advice last year, but have yet to hear from you. We now write to you again. Please reply to us and we will follow your instructions to handle the matter.

We await your reply.

We wish you well.

Yours sincerely,
Yokow Tiong Hieng Woi, Sulu
(Stamp: Executive Committee of Yokow Tiong Hieng Woi, Sulu)

8 February of the 22nd year of the Republic of China

日本橫濱中華會館致東華醫院信件

1933 年 2 月 10 日

日本橫濱中華會館

香港（印章：日本橫濱中華會館通信印章）
東華醫院執事先生鈞鑒逕啟者茲據本埠華
僑鮑應彪到稱擬將其先伯鮑焜及其先伯母
鮑孔氏遺骸兩具准於本月十三日由橫濱搭乘美
國大來公司汽船哥力芝總統經由香港運回原
籍中山縣安葬為此特請敝會館轉懇
貴院於該船抵港時代其起上設法暫厝待該
僑函着其堂兄鮑明常（已故者之子）前赴
貴院領取所有代墊費用祈向領取者索回等
情到館相應專函
貴院懇祈准予辦理實為慈便專此并頌

善安

代理慈務理事　黃焯民
（印章：日本橫濱中華會館慈務理事印）

中華民國二十二年二月十日
（印章：日本橫濱中華會館通信印章）

Letter from Yokohama Chinese Association, Japan, to Tung Wah Hospital on 10 February 1933

From the Office of Yokohama Chinese Association, Japan

Dear Managers of Tung Wah Hospital,

Bau Ying-biu *(Bao Yingbiao)*, a Chinese compatriot in our city, would like to send the remains of his late uncle, Bau Kwan *(Bao Kun)*, and late aunt, Madam Bau-Hung *(Bao-Kong Shi)*, from Yokohama to Hong Kong on the *SS President Coolidge* of Dollar Shipping Company on the 13th day of this month. The remains will be repatriated to Chung Shan *(Zhongshan)*, the deceased's hometown, for burial through Hong Kong. We, therefore, write to ask you to unload the remains and take them into your care after they arrive in Hong Kong. Bau Ying-biu will write to his cousin Bau Ming-sheung *(Bao Mingchang)*, the deceased's son, to collect the remains from your esteemed hospital. Please pay any expenses incurred first and ask the person who collects the remains for reimbursement. He will present a proper letter to you. Please hand over the remains to him.

We are most grateful to you for your kindness.

We wish you well.

Yours sincerely,
Wong Cheuk-man *(Huang Zhuomin)*
Acting Charitable Affairs Manager
(Stamp: Charitable Affairs manager, Yokohama Chinese Association, Japan)

10 February of the 22nd year of the Republic of China
(Stamp: Correspondence of Yokohama Chinese Association, Japan)

澳門鏡湖醫院致東華醫院信件

1933 年 2 月 17 日

澳門鏡湖醫院用牋

東華醫院
列位先生大鑒現有鮑煒昭鮑梁孔氏靈柩弍具由日本赴麥
堅尼総統輪船俹至香港托
貴院代轉來澳茲承事主之托特委庶務員伍全晉謁
台端奉商轉運辦法務希
指示一切俾便遵行為盼此頌

台祺

（印章：澳門鏡湖醫院書柬）

癸酉年元月廿三日

Letter from Kiang Wu Hospital, Macau, to Tung Wah Hospital on 17 February 1933

From the Office of Kiang Wu Hospital, Macau

Dear Directors of Tung Wah Hospital,

The coffins of Bau Wai-chiu *(Bao Weizhao)* and Madam Bau-Hung *(Bao-Kong Shi)*, have been repatriated from Japan to Hong Kong on the *SS President McKinley*, and you have been asked to send them to Macau. As entrusted by the family of the deceased, we have appointed General Attendant Ng Chuen *(Wu Quan)* to come to you to discuss the repatriation procedures. Please tell him what we should do so that we can follow through.

Thank you for your kind assistance.

We wish you well.

Yours sincerely,
(Stamp: Kiang Wu Hospital, Macau)

23rd day of the 1st lunar month, Year of Gwai Yau *(Guiyou)*

澳門鏡湖醫院致東華醫院信件

1933 年 2 月 22 日

澳門鏡湖醫院用牋

東華醫院
列位先生大鑒前上片函關於鮑煒昭鮑孔氏靈柩由日赴麥
堅尼総統輪抵港請
代轉運來澳一節諒達
台鑒據前途電訊麥堅尼輪于月之十九號可抵港現因逾期数天
用特專函奉達務請
代查該輪已否抵港有無該两柩付到詳為　開示俾便辦理勿延
至盼此頌　　　　　公祺

（印章：澳門鏡湖醫院書柬）

廿二年二月廿二日

Letter from Kiang Wu Hospital, Macau, to Tung Wah Hospital on 22 February 1933

From the Office of Kiang Wu Hospital, Macau

Dear Directors of Tung Wah Hospital,

We trust you have received our last letter informing you that the coffins of Bau Wai-chiu *(Bao Weizhao)* and Madam Bau-Hung *(Bao-Kong Shi)* would be transported to Hong Kong from Japan on the *SS President McKinley*, and asking you to send the remains onwards to Macau. Previously, we have been informed by telegram that the *SS President McKinley* would arrive in Hong Kong on the 19th day of this month. A few days have passed, and we now write to seek your help in checking if the ship has arrived in Hong Kong and whether the two coffins are there. Please reply to us with detailed information, so that we can handle the matter.

Please follow up as soon as possible. We are most grateful to you for your assistance.

We wish you well.

Yours sincerely,
(Stamp: Kiang Wu Hospital, Macau)

22 February of the 22nd year of the Republic of China

澳門鏡湖醫院致東華醫院信件

1933年2月25日

澳門鏡湖醫院用牋

東華醫院
列位先生大鑒現有鮑煒昭鮑孔氏靈柩弍具由日本
赴麥堅尼総統輪船抵港屆時希
代接收俾其親屬到港領運幸勿
見却為盼此頌

公祺

鏡湖醫院主席范潔朋

民廿二年二月廿五日

Letter from Kiang Wu Hospital, Macau to Tung Wah Hospital on 25 February 1933

From the Office of Kiang Wu Hospital, Macau

Dear Directors of Tung Wah Hospital,

I am writing to inform you that the coffins of Bau Wai-chiu *(Bao Weizhao)* and Madam Bau-Hung *(Bao-Kong Shi)* have been repatriated from Japan to Hong Kong on the *SS President McKinley*. Please take the coffins into your care when they arrive in Hong Kong. The family of the deceased will come to Hong Kong to collect them.

Please accede to our request.

Thank you very much for your kindness.

We wish you well.

Yours sincerely,
Fan Kit-pang *(Fan Jiepeng)*
Chairman, Kiang Wu Hospital

25 February of the 22nd year of the Republic of China

澳門鏡湖醫院致東華醫院信件

1933年2月26日

澳門鏡湖醫院用牋

東華醫院
列位先生大鑒接奉
大函敬聆一是承
代接收鮑煒昭鮑孔氏靈柩二具足感
高誼現着庶務員伍全持具領證趋赴
貴院領收該柩轉運來澳唯希
俯賜接納為盼此復順頌

公祺

（印章：澳門鏡湖醫院書柬）

癸酉年二月初三日

Letter from Kiang Wu Hospital, Macau, to Tung Wah Hospital on 26 February 1933

From the Office of Kiang Wu Hospital, Macau

Dear Directors of Tung Wah Hospital,

Thank you very much for your letter.

We are most grateful to you for taking the coffins of Bau Wai-chiu *(Bao Weizhao)* and Madam Bau-Hung *(Bao-Kong Shi)* into your care. We are sending our General Attendant Ng Chuen *(Wu Quan)* with bone collection document to claim the remains from your esteemed hospital so that they could be transported to Macau.

Thank you very much for your efforts. We wish you well.

Yours sincerely,
(Stamp: Kiang Wu Hospital, Macau)

3rd day of the 2nd lunar month, Year of Gwai Yau *(Guiyou)*

澳門鏡湖醫院用牋

現向
東華醫院領囬鮑煒昭鮑孔氏靈柩弍具
即轉運囬中山原藉安葬　此據

（印章：澳門鏡湖醫院書柬）

癸酉年二月初三日

218 Letter from Kiang Wu Hospital, Macau to Tung Wah Hospital on 26 February 1933

From the Office of Kiang Wu Hospital, Macau

This is to confirm that we have claimed the coffins of Bau Wai-chiu *(Bao Weizhao)* and Madam Bau-Hung *(Bao-Kong Shi)* from Tung Wah Hospital. The coffins will be transported to Chung Shan *(Zhongshan)*, the deceased's hometown, for burial.

Yours sincerely,
(Stamp: Kiang Wu Hospital, Macau)

3rd day of the 2nd lunar month, Year of Gwai Yau *(Guiyou)*

澳門鏡湖醫院致東華醫院信件

1933 年 3 月 3 日

澳門鏡湖醫院用箋

東華醫院
列位先生大鑒前因領運鮑氏靈柩沵荷
貴院代為照料至紉
高誼唯據庶務伍全囬説云湏[敝]院主席補函
貴院方合手續等语茲特將[敝]主席署名函一件送達即希
察存為盼此頌

公祺

（印章：澳門鏡湖醫院書柬）

民廿二年三月三月

Letter from Kiang Wu Hospital, Macau, to Tung Wah Hospital on 3 March 1933

From the Office of Kiang Wu Hospital, Macau

Dear Directors of Tung Wah Hospital,

We collected the coffins of our deceased friends Bau and his wife from your esteemed hospital earlier. Thank you very much indeed for your kind assistance.

Our General Attendant Ng Chuen *(Wu Quan)* mentioned that there should be a letter (from our chairman) to your esteemed hospital in order to complete the procedure. Hence, we send you a letter from our chairman for your kind retention.

Thank you.

We wish you well.

Yours sincerely,
(Stamp: Kiang Wu Hospital, Macau)

3 March of the 22nd year of the Republic of China

新興商會用箋

東華醫院列位先生大鑒

敬啟者茲據新興縣興賢社來函称有
安南侨商陳殿臣到局面稱辛年由安
南運回香港東華醫院寒字先友白骨
卅餘具經久停在香港今擬設法運回本
邑未知如何手續等情 敝會 情關桑
梓責任所在理合函達
貴院請將起運应有手續詳為指示
俾淂照覆遵行实為德便專此並
詢

崇祺

駐港新興商會梁展文上

（印章：香港新興商會圖章）（印章：梁展文）

民國廿二年三月九日

220 Letter from Sun Hing Commercial Association, Hong Kong, to Tung Wah Hospital on 9 March 1933

From the Office of Sun Hing Commercial Association, Hong Kong

Dear Directors of Tung Wah Hospital,

We received a letter from Hing Yin Society *(Xingxian She)* in Sun Hing County *(Xinxing Xian)* saying that Chan Din-sun *(Chen Dianchen)*, a Chinese merchant in Vietnam, visited them and informed them about 30 sets of remains which were sent to Hong Kong from Vietnam in the Year of San Mei *(Xinwei)* have been placed in Tung Wah Hospital for quite some time. The society would like to repatriate the remains to our county, but is not sure about the necessary procedures. We are obliged to help out of fraternity care and responsibility and thus write to your esteemed hospital. Please tell us the necessary procedures and we will follow your instructions.

Thank you very much for your kindness. We wish you well.

Yours sincerely,
Leung Chin-man *(Liang Zhanwen)*
Sun Hing Commercial Association, Hong Kong
(Stamp: Sun Hing Commercial Association, Hong Kong)

9 March of the 22nd year of the Republic of China

東華医院諸执事先生電鑒啓者昨接到小呂宋

　蘇洛埠彭毓英毓芬弍位先生來信內及前期船

　由該埠運付彭其聰骸骨係廣東台山桥頭村人

　氏該骸係用木箱裝載箱面天字號係第壹

　號数同日並付港銀叁拾元以葬費之用亦係付

　寄貴院收轉付寄今見久矣未見有到如近日

　到煩貴院执收轉運返廣東台山四九區四九站永

　興市永興隆收轉交与橋頭村彭來盛收

　便是抑或手續不合或貴院規則更改以

　船車等費不能代支煩將叁拾港銀扣除余

　有多少之費將該由四九區住址付來轉交為妥

　倘或有何件不合若办法如何亦恳求貴院

　諸执事先生指示囬字報告小号收到

　　　諸事有劳容日沾恩不顕請祈見諒勿介

二十二年六月十六日　　　　　　　　　　四九永興隆付

　　　　　　　　　　　　　　　　　　　　林德錦

221 Letter from Wing Hing Lung, China, to Tung Wah Hospital on 16 June 1933

Dear Managers of Tung Wah Hospital,

I received a letter from Pang Yuk-ying *(Peng Yuying)* and Pang Yuk-fun *(Peng Yufen)* from Sulu in the Philippines saying that the bones of Pang Kei-chung *(Peng Qicong)*, a native of Kiu Tau Village *(Qiaotou Cun)*, Toi Shan *(Taishan)*, Kwangtung *(Guangdong)*, had been repatriated to Hong Kong. The bones were placed in wooden Box No. 1. Burial fees of 30 Hong Kong dollars were also sent on the same day through your esteemed hospital.

It has been quite a while since then, but there is no trace of the bones and the money yet. I hope they will soon arrive. When you receive the bones, please send to Pang Loi-shing *(Peng Laisheng)* of Kiu Tau Village through Wing Hing Lung *(Yong Xing Long)*, which is located at Wing Hing City *(Yongxing Shi)*, Sei Kau Station *(Sijiu Zhan)*, Sei Kau District *(Sijiu Qu)*, Toi Shan, Kwangtung. If this arrangement does not comply with your prevailing procedures, or if you have changed your rules and can no longer pay the transportation fees in advance, please deduct the amount from the burial fees of 30 Hong Kong dollars and send the remaining funds to the address in Sei Kau area. If our request cannot be entertained, please notify us and we will follow your instructions.

We are most grateful to you for your efforts. Thank you very much for your understanding.

Yours sincerely,
Lam Tak-kam *(Lin Dejin)*
Wing Hing Lung, Sei Kau

16 June of the 22nd year of the Republic of China

蘇洛粵僑同鄉執行委員會用箋
Yokow Tiong Hieng Woi

敬啟者曡接 大函聆悉一是^{敝埠}先友
骸骨業經着手檢執共計十具約在日內
完竣定期夏歷閏五月廿七日運往英屬
山打根埠候船轉俉將來由山打根附俉
之日随函奉告茲滙上港紙銀叁百陆
拾元至希查收每具附帶港紙叁拾元
待各先友親屬到領仰將港紙一併發
給所餘之欵充作各項費用諸多
勞
神曷勝感謝耑此並頌

公安

東華醫院

列位先生鈞鑒

（印章：蘇洛粵僑同鄉執行委員會印）

中華民國癸年又五月廿日

附件：1933 年 7 月 21 日菲律賓關其灼致東華醫院滙票通知書

[東華醫] 院
[列位先] 生均鑒敬啓者茲承本島茉
　　□埠粵侨同鄉会委滙返貴
　　醫院收港艮叁百陸拾元正今
　　即夾入函內港字第八百七拾九號滙票
　　壹張該艮叁百陸拾元正到步
　　請祈携票往德輔道西廿六號向建
　　源收領如蒙收妥请將貴收条直
　　付粵侨同鄉会以淂銷號為盼
　　专此并請
公安

　　　　　　　　　　　　　　　　　^弟關其灼啓
　　　　　　　　　　　　　　　　　七月廿一日
　　　　　　　　　　　　　（印章：小呂宋□和祥書束）

東華醫院收單

　　　　憑单收到

　蘇洛粵侨　喜助經費銀陆拾員正
　同鄉會捐

　　　　　　　　　　　　　　　　　張霜永收
　　　　　　　　　　　　　　　（印章：東華醫院）
　　　　　　　　　　　　癸酉年六月初九日董理值事發

Letter from the Executive Committee of Yokow Tiong Hieng Woi of Sulu, Philippines, to Tung Wah Hospital on 12 July 1933

From Yokow Tiong Hieng Woi, Sulu

Dear Directors of Tung Wah Hospital,

Thank you for your letter.

We have begun exhuming the bones of approximately 10 deceased friends and the exhumation is expected to finish soon. We plan to transport the bones to British Sandakan on the 27th day of the 5th lunar leap month, and depart for Hong Kong by sea. We shall write to you again to inform you when the bones leave Sandakan for Hong Kong. In this letter, we have also remitted 360 Hong Kong dollars to you. Please give 30 dollars to the families of each deceased friend when they collect the bones, and use the remaining funds to pay for any expenses incurred.

Thank you very much for your efforts. We wish you well.

Yours sincerely,
(Stamp: Executive Committee of Yokow Tiong Hieng Woi of Sulu)

20th day of the 5th lunar leap month, Year of Gwai Yau (Guiyou)

Appendix:
Remittance advice from Kwan Kei-cheuk, Philippines, to Tung Wah Hospital on 21 July 1933

Dear Directors of Tung Wah Hospital,

The Executive Committee of Yokow Tiong Hieng Woi of Sulu, Philippines, has remitted 360 Hong Kong dollars to your esteemed hospital. Please find enclosed a money order No. 879 for 360 Hong Kong dollars in total. When the funds arrive, please collect the funds with the money order at Kin Yuen Company at 26 Des Voeux Road West and send the receipt directly to Yokow Tiong Hieng Woi.

We wish you well.

Yours sincerely,
Kwan Kei-cheuk *(Guan Qizhuo)*
21st July 1933
(Stamp: From the Office of ×××, Manila)

Receipt of Tung Wah Hospital

Tung Wah Hospital has received a donation of 60 dollars from Yokow Tiong Hieng Woi.

Signed by: Cheung Sheung-wing (*Zhang Shuangyong*)
(Stamp: Tung Wah Hospital)
Issued by: Director of Tung Wah Hospital

9th day of 6th lunar month, Year of Gwai Yau *(Guiyou)*

菲律賓蘇洛粵僑同鄉執行委員會致東華醫院信件

1933年7月19日

蘇洛粵僑同鄉執行委員會用箋
Yokow Tiong Hieng Woi

東華醫院
列位先生大鑒
敬啟者昨奉蕪函并滙上港銀叁百陸
拾元想荷收妥矣茲附顯生船偶返先
友骨殖十具共裝式大箱偶紙夾斯函
內抵埗之日祈照提收并祈登報以待
各先友親屬到領可也耑此即敬

大安

字啟（印章：蘇洛粵僑同鄉執行委員會印）

中華民國癸年又五月廿七日

茲將各先友姓氏籍貫列後

第一號箱	彭毓傑公	新寧縣石堡桥头村人
第二號箱	潘　璧公	南海橫機鄉三中人
第三號箱	羅樹華公	台山荻海大井傍村人
第四號箱	余聯庚公	台山荻海庙边村人
第五號箱	關津成公	南海九江上西村賢和社人
第六號箱	陳門文氏	新会陳沖人
第七號箱	劉認志公	新會澤湄鄉人
第八號箱	梁兆霖公	南海九江沙咀人
第九號箱	張　生公	中山谷都堡鴨山村人
第拾號箱	黃　柱公	台山華安圩康樂里人

合共十具每具箱面均有列明號碼

東華醫院^照

癸年又五月廿七日

每具箱內亦有名姓单

Letter from the Executive Committee of Yokow Tiong Hieng Woi of Sulu, Philippines, to Tung Wah Hospital on 19 July 1933

From the Yokow Tiong Hieng Woi, Sulu

Dear Directors of Tung Wah Hospital,

We wrote to you earlier and remitted 360 Hong Kong dollars to you. We hope both the letter and the funds have reached you safely. The bones of 10 deceased friends, placed in two large boxes, have been repatriated on the *Hinsang*. We enclosed the bill of lading in this letter. When the remains arrive in Hong Kong, please take them into your care and publish an announcement in the newspaper notifying the families of the deceased to claim the bones.

Thank you for your assistance. We wish you well.

Yours sincerely,
(Stamp: Executive Committee of Yokow Tiong Hieng Woi of Sulu)

27th day of the 5th lunar leap month, Year of Gwai Yau *(Guiyou)*

[Editor's note: The name list is available only in Chinese]

東華醫院賬房先生鑒 敬啓者弟之先父黎炳芬及南妾
　　黎梁氏黎蘇氏共骨殖三副　黎炳芬天字廿九号
　　黎梁氏天字卅号　黎蘇氏天字卅一号
　　係去年八月経由安南會安埠善堂值理雲居
　　号黃金代為付交　貴醫院代收但至今未見報告
　　或有賣新聞紙而內地新聞与外埠新聞不同弟自
　　前年民國廿年経有接得領骨殖憑单三張但當
　　時寫信訪問概無踪跡今有友人自會安返鄉始
　　知旧年廿一年捌月経有付交　貴醫院代收
　　如果屬実今仍貯在　貴医院者最好代為付交九江
　　鳴珂里救濟院轉交弟收其隨函交九江太平街中和
　　首飾店轉弟收領至骨殖三副暫留救濟院待弟到
　　取可也或　貴院不能代付必要弟親到港領或托親友
　　携憑证到取方合手續者祈即示知該憑单雖有
　　寫明有贈送返家安塟每副五元但該埠有款付到
　　貴院一定照交如無則作罷論祈為
　　查照示覆荷之覆函交九江圩太平街中和号
　　轉交弟收可也專此敬頌

善安

弟黎灼臣謹啓

廿二年七月廿八日

To the accountant of Tung Wah Hospital:

The bones of my late father, Lai Bing-fun *(Li Bingfen)* and his concubines Madam Lai-Leung *(Li-Liang Shi)* and Madam Lai-So *(Li-Su Shi)* – Lai Bing-fun in Box No. 29, Madam Lai-Leung in Box No. 30, Madam Lai-So in Box No. 31 – had been sent to your esteemed hospital in August last year by Wan Gui *(Yunju)*, also known as Wong Kam *(Huang Jin)*, manager of a benevolent association in Hoi An, Annam. However, I have not seen any notice or newspaper announcement about the repatriation yet. After all, news publishing in the mainland is different from that abroad.

I received three bone collection documents in the 20th year of the Republic of China. I had written to enquire about the bones, but did not receive any reply from you. A friend of mine recently returned to our hometown from Hoi An, and I was told that the bones had been sent to your esteemed hospital in August in the 21st year of the Republic of China. If this is true and the bones are still in the care of your esteemed hospital, please send them to me, in the care of Ming Or Lei Shelter *(Ming Ke Li Jiujiyuan)*, Kau Kong *(Jiujiang)*. As to the relevant documents, please send them to me through Chung Wo Jewellery *(Zhonghe Shoushi Dian)*, Tai Ping Street *(Taiping Jie)*, Kau Kong. The three sets of bones can be placed in the shelter temporarily and I will go and collect them. If your esteemed hospital cannot send back the bones or if I or my relatives or friends must come to Hong Kong to collect the remains with the documents, please notify me of the procedures.

The documents specify that burial fees of 5 dollars will be offered for each set of bones. If you have received the funds from Hoi An, please give them to me; otherwise, please leave it. Please reply to me at Chung Wo Ho *(Zhonghe Hao)* at Tai Ping Street, Kau Kong Market Town.

Thank you very much for your help. I wish you well.

Yours sincerely,
Lai Cheuk-son *(Li Zhuochen)*

28 July of the 22nd year of the Republic of China

東華醫院諸执事先生台鑒啓者蒙昨初一
　覆來專函指教一二不勝感謝謝對于函内言
　蘇洛埠運囬先友之骨殖祇有彭毓傑姓名
　云云經已^弟查明过彭毓傑即係彭其聪姓氏也
　惟^弟現有些務賤未能親至貴港及覓一商
　號盖章領該骨殖及卅元葬費^弟欲訪
　一親朋到領及帶囬原籍今有多日未能得到
　況且敝处属于口尾地方往貴港地人物十分太
　少以及大小事務似乎十分為难最好者求貴院
　諸执事先生可以做到代為办妥亦另在处代覓
　一襯实知己或可以迁于我敝地之帶客人煩
　执此字為據代領囬彭毓傑之骨殖及先友
　会撥囬之葬費交他帶囬敝境或照住址由
　北街付火車寫明台山四九區四九站永興市^{永興隆}
　收轉交橋頭村彭府收領安葬字懇求貴院
　諸执事先生代做些的善事脩陰積福功德
　無量也又字順問貴院向來所有外洋運囬各
　先友之骨殖有限期收領否亦請求諸执
　事先生賜字囬^弟收望對于貴院代办及覆
　函郵費及毓傑之骨殖船脚車費及帶客
　人之帶工以及貴院諸執事先生出街覓親朋
　領帶該骨殖街口等等完全懇將叁拾元港
　幣內扣除余有多少亦劳寫港幣寄囬^弟收轉交
　彭府收以应安葬之需　　並請

祝安
二十二年七月初十號

永興隆
林德錦仝謹啓
（印章：永興隆）

Letter from Lam Tak-kam, China, to Tung Wah Hospital on 30 August 1933

Dear Managers of Tung Wah Hospital,

Thank you for your reply on the 1st day of this month. You mentioned there was only one person in the name of Pang Yuk-kit *(Peng Yujie)* among those repatriated from Sulu. I have looked into the matter, and discovered that Pang Yuk-kit was in fact Pang Kei-chung *(Peng Qicong)*. Meanwhile, since I am quite occupied these days, I cannot come to Hong Kong in person and find a shop to act as gurantor and collect the bones and the 30-dollar burial fees with their company stamp. I have intended to ask a friend or relative to bring the bones back to our hometown, but no such person is available yet. In addition, I live in a remote place and it is quite difficult for me to handle this matter. Therefore, I would like to ask your esteemed hospital to help. Please find a trustworthy person or someone in Hong Kong who will pass by my town to collect the bones and the burial fees given to the deceased's family by the Chinese association of Pang Yuk-kit with this letter. Please ask the person to bring the bones back or send them by train to the Pang Family at Kiu Tau Village *(Qiaotou Cun)* in the care of Wing Hing Lung *(Yong Xing Long)* in Wing Hing City *(Yongxing Shi)*, Sei Kau Station *(Sijiu Zhan)*, Sei Kau District *(Sijiu Qu)*, Toi Shan *(Taishan)*. I implore you to help me handle this matter. Your immense benevolence is far reaching.

In addition, I would like to ask if there is a time limit for collecting the remains repatriated from abroad. Please write back to me. Kindly deduct the administrative and postage fees, the costs of transporting the bones of Yuk-kit, the money paid to the person taking the bones to my town and the costs incurred to look for that person from the 30 dollars burial fees. Please send any remaining funds to me so that I can pass them to the Pang Family to pay for burial.

I wish you well.

Yours sincerely,
Lam Tak-kam *(Lin Dejin)* of Wing Hing Lung
(Stamp: Wing Hing Lung)

10th day of the 7th lunar month of the 22nd year of the Republic of China

226 日本橫濱中華會館致東華醫院信件

1933 年 11 月 15 日

香港東華醫院
主席先生鈞鑒逕啓者茲有敝埠故僑李琪遺
骸壹具經駐日公使館證明搭乘加力芝總統於十
一月十七日由橫濱運回原藉廣東新會七堡鄉安
葬懇於該輪抵泊香港時請由
貴院代為起上待遲日該故僑親族李耀北君
親赴　貴院領取轉鄉耑此奉懇并頌

善安

（印章：橫濱中華會館慈務理事）鮑博公（印章：鮑博公）

中華民國二十二年十一月十五日

（印章：日本橫濱中華會館通信印章）

Letter from Yokohama Chinese Association, Japan, to Tung Wah Hospital on 15 November 1933

Dear Chairman of Tung Wah Hospital,

We are handling the remains of Lee Kei *(Li Qi)* who passed away in our city. The Chinese Embassy in Japan certified the remains and they have been repatriated from Yokohama on the *SS President Coolidge* on 17 November. The remains will eventually be sent to the deceased's hometown at Chat Bo Township *(Qibao Xiang)*, Sun Wui *(Xinhui)*, Kwangtung *(Guangdong)*. When the remains arrive in Hong Kong, please unload and take them into your care. The deceased's relative, Lee Yiu-pak *(Li Yaobei)*, will collect the remains from your esteemed hospital later on and take them back to his hometown.

We are most grateful to you for your assistance.

Yours sincerely,
Bau Pok-gung *(Bao Bogong)*
(Stamp: Charitable Affairs Manager, Yokohama Chinese Association)
(Stamp: Correspondence of Yokohama Chinese Association, Japan)
(Stamp: Bau Pok-gung)

15 November of the 22nd year of the Republic of China

中華會館用箋

香港東華醫院
主席先生鈞鑒逕啟者前日因敝埠故
僑李琪君遺骸運回粵東懇托
貴院暫代安置各情經由函達想已早
經洞悉矣現該故僑親族李耀北君
擬扵本月二十五日由神戶動程歸里前赴
貴院領取俾便轉回原籍用特專函
介紹請其持函親謁
台端務望予以便利賜以指導至為感
禱耑此敬頌

善祺

（印章：橫濱中華會館慈務理事）鮑博公（印章：鮑博公）

中華民國二十二年十一月二十一日
（印章：日本橫濱中華會館通信印章）

Letter from Yokohama Chinese Association, Japan, to Tung Wah Hospital on 21 November 1933

From the Office of Yokohama Chinese Association, Japan

Dear Chairman of Tung Wah Hospital,

The remains of our deceased friend Lee Kei *(Li Qi)* are being repatriated to eastern Kwangtung *(Guangdong)*. We asked you earlier to take the remains into your care temporarily when they arrive in Hong Kong. I believe you have received our letter and should be well aware of the matter. Now Lee Yiu-pak *(Li Yaobei)*, relative of the deceased, will depart Kobe on the 25th day of this month to collect the remains from your esteemed hospital for burial in the deceased's hometown. We hereby write to inform you of his arrival. He will visit your esteemed hospital with our reference letter. Please support him and provide him necessary guidance.

We are most grateful to you for your assistance.

We wish you well.

Yours sincerely,
Bau Pok-gung *(Bao Bogong)*
(Stamp: Charitable Affairs Manager, Yokohama Chinese Association)
(Stamp: Bau Pok-gung)

21 November of the 22nd year of the Republic of China

(Stamp: Correspondence of Yokohama Chinese Association, Japan)

逕啓者：

　　於民貳拾壹年七月拾壹日吾弟名文安不幸因病而逝世
於船上芝山達尼號後運至貴醫院裡請貴醫院料理一切不
料貴醫院來函申明関於在港葬禮之規則即非有親戚來
至該處是不可埋葬蓋地方甚遠且家務甚忙之故為此未克
親自赴港甚感不樂請問先生究竟其死屍是不尚保存
在貴醫院裡呢还是已経埋葬起來　　此請先生來信通告

為何

李文泉上
民貳貳年十一月卅日

吾之通信處：

Mr. Lee Wen Chuan
c/o Mr. Lee Hie Tiang
Tambakbojo,
Djatirogo;
Java. D. E. I.

Letter from Lee Wen-chuan, Indonesia, to Tung Wah Hospital on 30 November 1933

To Whom It May Concern

My younger brother, Man On *(Wen'an)* unfortunately died of illness on the vessel on 11 July in the 21st year of the Republic of China. His remains were subsequently sent to your esteemed hospital under your care. However, I have received a letter from your esteemed hospital saying that only the relatives of the deceased could claim the remains for burial under the law of Hong Kong. Since I live far away from Hong Kong and am very busy with family affairs, I feel sad that I cannot come to Hong Kong at the moment. I would like to find out if my late brother's remains are still in your esteemed hospital or if they have been buried. I would be grateful if you could give me your reply.

Yours sincerely,
Lee Wen Chuan *(Li Wenquan)*

30 November of the 22nd year of the Republic of China

My correspondence address:
Mr. Lee Wen-chuen
c/o Mr. Lee Hie Tiang
Tambakbojo,
Djatirogo;
Java. D. E. I.

229 中國屈宅致東華醫院信件

1933 年 12 月 23 日

執事先生大鑒茲聞暹埠運回骸骨付到

貴院發落茲有修函奉告祈見字若收到一百七拾四

屈應球骸骨之号請　尊處勞駕來字省

城三府前三十四号三樓林三益堂處以得他

之家人來港到　貴院領取為盼切切

此致

執事先生等

省屈宅托

中華民國廿二年十二月廿三日

Letter from Wat Family, China, to Tung Wah Hospital on 23 December 1933

Dear Managers of Tung Wah Hospital,

I heard that the bones of deceased Chinese compatriots had been transported from Siam to your esteemed hospital. I would like to find out if you have received the bones of Wat Ying-kau *(Qu Yingqiu),* Box No. 174. If you have, please notify me at Lam Sam Yik Tong *(Lin San Yi Tang)*, 3/F, 34 Sam Fu Chin *(Sanfu Qian),* Canton *(Guangzhou)*, so that I can inform the deceased's family to go to Hong Kong to collect the remains from your esteemed hospital.

Thank you for your kindness.

Yours sincerely,
Wat *(Qu)* Family
Canton

23 December of the 22nd year of the Republic of China

暹京
廣肇公學及廣肇醫院總辦事處用牋

逕啓者敝院所屬廣肇墳場每三年運寄同鄉先友

骸骨一次向蒙

貴院在港接收代轉各屬敝院同人淂此互相扶持永

感勿忘茲又逢運期於本月三日由暹寄付亞東輪船共

先友骸骨式佰五拾壹具並由暹恆豐米行滙去香港榮

豐行收轉交

貴院收港銀柒佰陸拾元正戝紙一張如各骸骨到步請

為僱工起上代轉各屬俾各同鄉領囬安塟欵項一節

除每具給囬式元塟費外餘則為

貴院僱工艇及香油等之需諸事多勞不勝感祷此致

東華醫院
執事先生

暹京廣肇総辦事處

（印章：廣肇公學及廣肇醫院總辦事處）主席黃求標

中華民國廿三年三月三日

Letter from Kwong Siew Association General Office, Siam, to Tung Wah Hospital on 3 March 1934

From the General Office of Kwong Siew School and Kwong Siu Hospital, Siam

Dear Managers of Tung Wah Hospital,

The remains of deceased friends are exhumed from Kwong Siew Cemetery, run by our hospital, once every three years. Your esteemed hospital always take the remains into your care after they arrive in Hong Kong and send them back to the deceased's hometown. We are most grateful to you for your help.

It is about time for repatriation of bones again. We have repatriated the bones of 251 deceased friends from Siam on the *Ah-tung* today and have asked Hang Fung Rice Shop in Siam to send a cheque for 760 Hong dollars to your esteemed hospital through Wing Fung Hong in Hong Kong. When the remains arrive in Hong Kong, please hire workers to unload them from the ship and transport them to the deceased's hometown for burial. Please give burial fees of 2 dollars to the family of each deceased friend, and use the remainder to pay the workers and transportation fees. Please keep any funds left as our oil money to your esteemed hospital.

We are most grateful to you for your efforts.

Yours sincerely,
Wong Kau-biu *(Huang Qiubiao)*, Chairman
Kwong Siew Association General Office, Siam
(Stamp: General Office of Kwong Siew School and Kwong Siu Hospital)

3 March of the 23rd year of the Republic of China

暹京
廣肇公學及廣肇醫院總辦事處用箋

逕啓者三月三日^敝處由暹向亞東輪運上各同
鄉先友骸骨共式佰伍拾壹俱抵步時請代為
僱件工起貯以便各同鄉領囘是荷此致

香港東華醫院
執事先生

暹京廣肇總辦事處
主席　黃求標
（印章：廣肇公學及廣肇醫院總辦事處印章）

附各同鄉先友姓名表一紙
中華民國廿三年三月三日

Letter from Kwong Siew Association General Office, Siam, to Tung Wah Hospital on 3 March 1934

From the General Office of Kwong Siew School and Kwong Siu Hospital, Siam

Dear Managers of Tung Wah Hospital,

We repatriated the bones of 251 deceased friends on the *Ah-tung* from Siam today. When the bones arrive in Hong Kong, please hire workers to unload them from the ship and take them into your care. Please send them to their hometown so that their families can collect them.

Thank you very much for your assistance.

Yours sincerely,
Wong Kau-biu *(Huang Qiubiao)*, Chairman
Kwong Siew General Office, Siam

(Stamp: General Office of Kwong Siew School and Kwong Siu Hospital)

Please find enclosed a list of the deceased friend's names.

3 March of the 23rd year of the Republic of China

三水公會用牋

東華醫院總理先生大鑒敬啓者^敝会現接旅暹同鄉來函称旅暹
　　回鄉先友骸骨已於三月三日運港　东華醫院請接洽轉運廣州城西方便
　　醫院以便轉運三水西轉太和義院招領安葬等情查此種善舉關係公益
　　^敝會自応照办茲將旅暹回鄉先友骸骨名籍另紙抄列請
　　賜查核此批骸骨已否到達　貴院及現在曾轉城西方便醫院否
　　如何務請　詳細見覆以便办理是所盼祷專此即頌

公祺

　　　　　　　　　　　　　　　　　　　　（印章：三水公會辦事處）啓

中華民國廿三年四月十日

三水旅暹同鄉先友骸骨姓名籍貫一覽

梁乃讓	三水　崗頭	鄧雲禧	三水伏戶塘口坊
梁方氏	三水　崗頭	潘耀輝	三水周灶
麥　永	三水蘆苞麥街	陳楊氏	三水西南東閘
麥盧氏	三水蘆苞麥街		

　　以上所列之骸骨已于三月三日運港
　　東華大醫院收

中華民國廿三年四月十日　　　　　　　　　（印章：三水公會辦事處）抄列

Letter from the Office of Sam Shui Association, China, to Tung Wah Hospital on 10 April 1934

From the Office of Sam Shui Association

Dear Directors of Tung Wah Hospital,

We received a letter from the native association of our county in Siam saying that the bones of deceased friends had been repatriated to Hong Kong on 3 March. Please receive the bones and arrange to send them to City West Fong Bin Hospital (*Chengxi Fangbian Yiyuan*) in Canton *(Guangzhou)*, so that they can be further transported to Tai Wo Yi Yuen *(Taihe Yiyuan)*, west of Sam Shui (*Sanshui*) for the deceased's family to collect and bury. We are most willing to do our part in such a benevolent deed. Please find enclosed a list of the deceased's names and native counties. Kindly check if the bones have arrived and whether you have transported the bones to City West Fong Bin Hospital. Please reply to us in detail so that we can follow up.

Thank you very much for your assistance.

We wish you well.

Yours sincerely,
(Stamp: Office of Sam Shui Association)

10 April of the 23rd year of the Republic of China

越南東京華僑廣善堂啟事用箋

逕啓者案查本年迺東京廣善堂起運先友遺骸回籍之期
河內為行政中樞所有與居留政府接洽各事均歸河內總
其成現屆其期理合照例舉辦茲寄上長紅式拾張敬煩查
照代為張貼四方俾該親屬依期呈報開執為荷此致

香港東華醫院
列位鄉先生台鑒

    收到此紅条希　示复為荷

　　　　　　　　　　　　　　　　附設在河內粵東會館內
　　　　　　　　　　（印章：越南東京廣善堂運先友辦事所書柬）

中華民國廿三年八月十五日

233 Letter from the Bone Repatriation Office of Kwong Sin Tong, Tonkin, Vietnam, to Tung Wah Hospital on 15 August 1934

From the Office of Kwong Sin Tong, Tonkin, Vietnam

Dear Directors of Tung Wah Hospital,

It is time for us, Kwong Sin Tong, Tonkin, to repatriate the remains of our deceased friends this year. Since Hanoi is the administrative centre of the country, all matters regarding immigration are handled by the Hanoi authorities. We are repatriating the remains according to our usual practice. We enclose herewith 20 notices in this letter. Please arrange to put them up at public places so that the families of the deceased can come to collect the remains.

Please acknowledge receipt of the notices.

Yours sincerely,
(Stamp: Bone Repatriation Office of Kwong Sin Tong, Tonkin, Vietnam, in the Eastern Kwangtung Association of Hanoi)

15 August of the 23rd year of the Republic of China

南洋雪蘭莪林賀致東華醫院信件

1934年10月23日

Lam Ho
林賀

東華醫院執事先生大鑒啓者茲由南洋雪蘭莪吉隆坡埠郵局
內包裹部寄上骨石弍箱到祈代暫為收貯俟陳国祥李順景先生到
貴院領收運回原籍就是除函呈外経先另函轉達前途想
伊等不日當到貴院領收也諸費精神不勝銘感專此奉達

并候

計開

牌照四十号之箱乃李門黃氏仲好之骸骨
由其子李順景到院領收（籍貫新會江門人）

牌照四十一号之箱乃陳容先生之骸骨
由其親屬陳国祥到院領收（籍貫新會江門人）

公祺

弟林賀上　廿三、十、廿三

（關于領收先人骨石事）

東華醫院执事先生均鑒啓者玆有 ^{陳国祥}_{李順景} 两君乃新

會江門人到貴院領收前由南洋雪蘭莪属吉隆坡埠郵

局內包裏部寄囬先人骨石弍箱牌照四十号四十一号見字煩

与伊等接洽為盼感感專此奉達并候

公祺

　　　　　　　　　　　　　　　　弟林賀上　廿三．十．廿三．

Letter from Lam Ho, Selangor, Nanyang, to Tung Wah Hospital on 23 October 1934

From the desk of Lam Ho

Dear Managers of Tung Wah Hospital,

I have sent two boxes of bones from a post office in Kuala Lumpur, Selangor, Nanyang, to your esteemed hospital. Please provide temporary storage when they arrive. Chan Kwok-cheung *(Chen Guoxiang)* and Lee Shun-king *(Li Shunjing)* will claim them from your esteemed hospital and take the bones to the deceased's hometown for burial. Apart from this letter, I have also written to the Chan and Lee. They will come to your esteemed hospital to collect the bones soon. I am most grateful to you for your assistance.

For your kind attention, please.

Note:
Box No. 40 contains the bones of Madam Lee Wong Chung-ho *(Li Huang Zhonghao)*, a native of Kong Mun *(Jiangmen)*, Sun Wui *(Xinhui)*. Her son, Lee Shun-king, will collect the bones from your esteemed hospital.

Box No. 41 contains the bones of Chan Yung *(Chen Rong)*, a native of Kong Mun, Sun Wui. His relative Chan Kwok-cheung will collect the bones from your esteemed hospital.

I wish you well.

Yours sincerely,
Lam Ho *(Lin He)*

23 October of the 23rd year of the Republic of China

(Re: Collection of Bones)

Dear Managers of Tung Wah Hospital,

Chan Kwok-cheung and Lee Shun-king of Kong Mun, Sun Wui, will come to your esteemed hospital to collect the bones, placed in Box No. 40 and Box No. 41, sent from a post office in Kuala Lumpur, Selangor, Nanyang. Please get in touch with them.

I am most grateful to you for your assistance.

I wish you well.

Yours sincerely,
Lam Ho

23 October of the 23rd year of the Republic of China

東華大善院列位先生鈞鑒逕啓者茲有
　　邑人梁文軒昨日到敝堂調查事因伊父
　　梁容扵光緒年間往嗊哩埠經營不
　　幸在該埠身故後由該埠華僑慈善
　　者將外亡僑胞遺骸合帮寄返分送
　　各原藉招領查該梁容字燦垣廣東
　　中山石岐張溪鄉人係扵民十一年三月間
　　該帮由嗊埠寄返當時因其家人
　　完全不知其事時至今日茲有由該
　　埠回唐梓里向其查问始發覺該
　　死者係扵上述年間寄運回港由
貴院分送各該藉招領安葬昨日該梁
　　某到查已由敝堂理事人將歷年各
　　埠寄運回邑之亡骸名姓清查偏查
　　各部并無此人而由该埠回里之亡者
　　梓友則証明已扵此時寄運回港想或由
貴院妥葬義莊未有寄回敝堂招領未定
　　今該亡者之子念父情切且事屬慈
　　善特由敝堂代為函達
貴院查照素仰
貴院各执事先生慈善為怀懇請將
　　大冊代為檢查示覆敝堂轉知其子
　　領回安葬則生者死者永感大恩
　　無既矣謹此佈達并請

公祺

中華民國廿四年六月四日

（印章：中山與善堂）啓

Letter from Yu Sin Tong, Chung Shan, China, to Tung Wah Hospital on 4 June 1935

Dear benevolent Directors of Tung Wah Hospital,

Yesterday, our fellow townsman Leung Man-hin *(Liang Wenxuan)* came to our association to enquire about the remains of his late father Leung Yung *(Liang Rong)*, who was doing business in Penang during Guangxu's reign in the Ching *(Qing)* dynasty and unfortunately passed away. Then his remains were, together with the remains of other deceased friends, repatriated by a Chinese charitable organization in Penang in March of the 11th year of the Republic of China to their respective hometown. However, the family of Leung Yung, style name Chan-woon *(Canyuan)*, a native of Cheung Kai Township *(Zhangxi Xiang)*, Shekki *(Shiqi)*, Chung Shan *(Zhongshan)*, did not know about the repatriation until a fellow townsman returning from Penang asked them about the matter. They were told that the remains of the deceased were transported to Hong Kong in the above-mentioned year and subsequently sent to the deceased's hometown by your esteemed hospital. When Leung came to us to investigate the matter, the manager of our association went through all the names of deceased friends repatriated to our county from various cities over the years, but could not find his name. Meanwhile, the fellow townsman who returned from Penang confirmed that the deceased's remains had indeed been sent to Hong Kong at that time. Maybe the remains are still in the care of your coffin home and have not been sent back to us for his family to claim. The deceased's son misses his father deeply. Considering that this is a matter of charity, we therefore write to enquire about the whereabouts of the remains on his behalf.

The benevolence of your good selves is well known. We are grateful if you could check your records and reply to us. We will notify the deceased's son to collect his father's remains. Both the living and the deceased will be forever grateful to you for your kindness.

We await your reply.

We wish you well.

Yours sincerely,
(Stamp: Yu Sin Tong, Chung Shan) *(Yu Shan Tang)*

4 June of the 24th year of the Republic of China

香港東華醫院庄租部执事先生鑒

　　逕啓者茲付去港紙叁拾壹元正由香港榮昌轉交以叁拾
　　元完納仁寿経手新庄大堂四號張榮翁庄租
　　十個月以壹元為执事先生禀信之費用
　　禀信時祈將該庄租單掛號寄來以
　　免遺失是為至祷茲將禀信地址列下

中英文地址
英屬嘭哼宜蘭突大街十八號　張通手收
Mr. Chong Thong, 18, Main Street, Jerantut, Pahang F. M. S.

　　　　　　　　　　　　　廿四年七月十號 弟張通啓

Letter from Chong Thong, Federated Malay States, to Tung Wah Hospital on 10 July 1935

Dear Manager of Rental Department of Tung Wah Hospital,

I asked Wing Cheong Company in Hong Kong to give you 31 Hong Kong dollars to settle the 10 months' rent of 30 Hong Kong dollars for the coffin of Cheung Wing *(Zhang Rong)* which was arranged by Yan Sau Funeral Service, placed in No. 4, New Hall [of Tung Wah Coffin Home]. The amount also includes 1 dollar to cover your costs of replying to my letter. Please send your reply, along with the rental note, by registered post to the following address.

Chinese and English address:
英屬嘭哼宜蘭突大街十八號 張通手收
Mr. Chong Thong, 18, Main Street, Jerantut, Pahang, F. M. S.

Yours sincerely,
Chong Thong *(Zhang Tong)*

10 July of the 24th year of the Republic of China

謙昌金鋪
HIM CHEONG & CO.

東華医院暨
大值理列位先生均鑒敬啓者弟茲有敝戚謝十
　　章係廣東南海西樵丹灶鄉人氏因前数年
　　不幸在南洋峇株巴轄埠去世刻下弟盡親戚
　　之情稟準當地政府將其之骨石拾埋藏
　　成一小箱由郵局付上　貴院請到時祈為
　　收下并劳通知貴埠皇后大道西二百二十八号
　　生昌金鋪謝金先生到領帶囬返鄉安葬
　　諸事有劳不勝感謝耑此即請

大安

弟劉六英字

中華民國廿四年九月廿三日

Letter from Lau Luk-ying, Federated Malay States, to Tung Wah Hospital on 23 September 1935

From the Office of Him Cheong & Co.

Dear Directors of Tung Wah Hospital,

My relative, Tse Sap-cheung *(Xie Shizhang)*, a native of Dan Jo Township *(Danzao Xiang)*, Sai Chiu *(Xiqiao)*, Nam Hoi *(Nanhai)*, Kwangtung *(Guangdong)*, passed away in Batu Pahat, Nanyang, a few years ago. With the goodwill of being a relative, I have obtained permission from the local government to exhume his bones and send them to your esteemed hospital in a small box by post. Please take delivery of the bones and inform Tse Kam *(Xie Jin)* of Sang Cheong Goldsmiths at 228 Queen's Road West to collect the bones and take them back to the deceased's hometown for burial.

I am most grateful to you for your efforts.

I wish you well.

Yours sincerely,
Lau Luk-ying *(Liu Liuying)*

23 September of the 24th year of the Republic of China

大洋洲西歸先友

238 澳洲新山正埠同昌號致東華醫院信件

1929年5月10日

Leong Hoong Cheong

10 May 1929

東華醫院執事善長先生大鑒敬啓者

茲由敝堂公司之聖丫路濱船運上先友骸骨叁具并倆帋一張抵步時請查照收着人起上可也該叁位先友者一名梁桂字澤培一名梁池字廷藩一名潘筹字標榮該三位具是廣東開平單水口人氏也小店亦早有信报知他等之家人如他等之親人若來港領帶煩　貴院給一执護照証據交他帶归便是倘他等親人若以水陸遙遠轉運為艰則　貴院何时運入百合則路經單水口埠煩着人通傳單水口埠中山路（永茂杉行）收領可也以免運到百合圩时又多費手續見字請祈留意是荷若此豈只該三位先友者之感恩而已而弟等亦載德矣　專此并請

公安

（印章：新山正埠同昌號）字頓

Letter from Leong Hoong Cheong, Melbourne, Australia, to Tung Wah Hospital on 10 May 1929

From the Office of Leong Hoong Cheong

10 May 1929

Dear Manager and benevolent Directors of Tung Wah Hospital,

Our company has repatriated the remains of three deceased friends, along with the bill of lading, on the Saint Aubine Line ship. Please check and receive and hire workers to unload after they arrive [in Hong Kong]. The names of the deceased are Leung Kwai (*Liang Gui*), style name Chak-pui (*Zepei*), Leung Chi *(Liang Chi)*, style name Ting-fan (*Tingfan*), and Poon Chau (*Pan Chou)*, style name Biu-wing *(Biaorong)*. They are all native of Dan Shui Hau (*Danshuikou*) in Hoi Ping (*Kaiping*), Kwangtung (*Guangdong*). We have already written to the families of the deceased. Should they come to Hong Kong to claim the remains, please issue a pass [confirming the identity of the remains] to them. If the deceased's families consider it difficult to transport the remains through water or land routes, please help bring them back when you send other bones to Bak Hop (*Baihe*) passing by Dan Shui Hau. In this case, please help inform Wing Mau Fir Company on Chung Shan Road (*Zhongshan Lu*) in Dan Shui Hau to collect the remains. This will save you the trouble of sorting out the shipment in Bak Hop Market Town (*Baihe Xu*). Please expect the arrival of the remains. Not only our three deceased friends, but we shall also be very grateful to you for your kindness.

We wish you well.

Yours respectfully,
(Stamp: Leong Hoong Cheong, Melbourne)

東華醫院
列位仁慈先生 均鑒遙想福祉時申德祺

　　並進翹仰景慕且祝且頌茲者小号
　　現在雪梨埠起出先友骨骸壹拾
　　四具每具庄作壹小箱共成壹拾四
　　箱該箱面經註明付交貴院查收
　　並經有註明該先友名字籍貫地址
　　於箱面処矣今由太古船行彰德
　　輪船運囘祖國茲特函奉達
　　台端　並附返該先友壹拾四具內俪紙
　　壹張到日煩劳提收妥之後再劳
　　將該先友代運上中山石歧與善堂收
　　入希代轉函該善堂先生按照該先
　　友名字發函通知其家人收領至祷
　　諸多有劳存没均感

福緣善慶
福有攸歸

茲隨函附上仄笠帋一張該司零艮
六磅正到日請照提收煩將該項作
為該先友十四位運費用也多多有劳感感

一九二九年 五月十八号
　　　　　　四月初九日

　　　　　　　　　　　　　（印章：雪梨合昌公司書束）

　　　　　　　　　　　　小號 雪
　　　　　　　　　　　　　　 梨 合昌公司

茲今將各先友人名列開

中山良都恆美李茂德先骸壹具

李應祥先骸壹具

李帝芬先骸壹具

李鈺基先骸壹具

李潤基先骸壹具

李樹洪先骸壹具

李伍維先骸壹具

李意昌先骸壹具

李達昭先骸壹具

李喬南先骸壹具

李錦廷先骸壹具

李新和先骸壹具

李亞計先骸壹具

隆都
龍頭環　候世昌先骸壹具

合共先骸壹拾四具

東華醫院大善堂

慈善执事先生大鑒

民十八年四月十三日　雪梨合昌

239

Letter from Hop Cheung Company of Sydney, Australia, to Tung Wah Hospital on 18 May 1929

Dear benevolent Directors of Tung Wah Hospital,

Your acts of benevolence are noble and admirable.

We have exhumed the bones of 14 deceased friends in Sydney. Each set of bones has been placed in a small box. There are 14 boxes in total and they are addressed to your esteemed hospital. Each box is marked with the name, native county and address of the deceased friend, and the boxes are repatriated on the *Changte* of China Navigation Company. We, hereby, write to inform you of the repatriation. Enclosed is a bill of lading for the 14 sets of bones. Upon their arrival, please take delivery and transport them to Yu Sin Tong (*Yu Shan Tang*) in Shekki (*Shiqi*), Chung Shan (*Zhongshan*). The manager of the association will inform the family of each deceased friend to claim their bones.

We thank you for your efforts. The deceased and the families will be grateful to you.

May you be blessed for your benevolence.

Please also find enclosed a cheque for 6 pounds sterling to cover the transportation costs for the remains of our 14 deceased friends.

Yours humbly,
Hop Cheung Company of Sydney
(Stamp: Hop Cheung Company of Sydney)

18 May 1929
9th day of the 4th lunar month

Enclosed is the name list of the deceased friends.

[Editor's remarks: Name list of the deceased friends is available only in Chinese]

澳洲劉贊廷致東華醫院信件

1929年6月19日

東華大醫院執事先生大鑒敬啓者茲

由太平輪船付上先友一箱並夾上俩嗧

到步祈照查收請代交趙能讓先生收

台山縣浮石村人氏候他到領就是諸事

劳餘多少及專此並頌

大安

（印章：谷當正埠協安書柬）

弟劉贊廷字頓　一九二九年六月十九号

Letter from Lau Chan-ting, Australia, to Tung Wah Hospital on 19 June 1929

Dear Managers of Tung Wah Hospital,

The remains of our deceased friend, contained in a box with the bill of lading attached, will be repatriated on the *Taiping*. After the remains arrive [in Hong Kong], please send them to Chiu Nun-yeung (*Zhao Nengrang*), who is a native of Fou Shek Village (*Fushi Cun*), Toi Shan (*Taishan*).

I am most grateful to you for your efforts.

I wish you well.

Yours humbly,
Lau Chan-ting (*Liu Zanting*)
(Stamp: Cook Town Hip On)

19 June 1929

東華醫院^{大善長暨}
列位先生^{均鑒}

　　敬啓者^弟等向在澳洲昆省加剌孖剌埠經營
　　西人生意今各伴囘唐將生意賣去惟思華
　　友壽終于本埠者十有餘名^弟等去後深
　　慮先友骸骨永留外域不無違感故逐一
　　執起而搭是渡彰德船寄返乃托　貴院
　　代收但誠恐 先友親人未知故今由郵付呈
　　滙票銀壹拾伍磅祈照提收敢懇　先生
　　用特登報俾得　先友家屬領囘安塟
　　除代登報費之外餘項乃作運　先友囘屬
　　之用諸費清神即此敬頌

公安　　　　　　該滙票三百二十九号
　旅澳洲昆時欄省
　加剌孖剌埠

　　　　　　　　　　　　　　　　　^弟差厘贊記袁德梅
　　　　　　　　　　　　　　　　　　鄭維壽仝涴
一九二九年七月廿三号　　　　　　　　陳　贊
如蒙示覆請直接
通知香港金生泰号金山庄
門牌德輔道西七十五號是因^弟等亦搭下渡返港

　　計開先友名列
鄭惠珊　香山谷都烏石人
陳綿創　香山人　　　　　楊　勝　香山人
譚兆海　香山人　　　　　蕭載寬　香山良都深灣人
吳　財　香山得都張家边人　賴長嬌　歸善人
陳肇英　香山人　　　　　張　欽　歸善人
陳　文　南海人　　　　　袁　桐　新安人
許　好　潮州人　　　　　馬門萬女氏　香山良都深灣人
各先友^弟等在本澳洲經用特登報

241 Letter from Cha Li Chan Kee, Australia, to Tung Wah Hospital on 23 July 1929

Dear benevolent Directors of Tung Wah Hospital,

We are merchants in Greymare, Queensland. We have decided to sell our business and return to China. There were a dozen of Chinese friends who died here years ago. As we go home, we are reluctant to leave the remains of them in a foreign country, so we have exhumed the remains and repatriated them on the *Changte*. We would like to ask your esteemed hospital to take the remains into your care [when they arrive in Hong Kong]. Since the deceased's relatives may not be aware of the repatriation, please place notices on newspapers so that they know and come to claim the remains. We have also enclosed a money order for 15 pounds sterling to cover the costs of the newspaper notices and repatriation [to the deceased's hometown].

We are most grateful to you for your efforts.

The money order amounts to 329 dollars.

Yours humbly,
Yuen Tak-mui *(Yuan Demei)*, Cheng Wai-sau *(Zheng Weishou)* and Chan Chan *(Chen Zan)* of Cha Li Chan Kee
Greymare, Queensland, Australia
23 July 1929

As we are also returning to Hong Kong by sea, please send your reply directly to Kam Shan Tai Ho Gold Mountain Firm, 75 Des Voeux Road West, Hong Kong.

The name list of the deceased friends is enclosed.

[Editor's remarks: Name list of the deceased friends is available only in Chinese]

東華大醫院列位　先生鑒

　　敬啟者旧歲伍根所付先友六具昨接到來音所存貯先
　　友医院云未付囬各鄉之話是以茲付來鑒司連艮肆磅
　　大醫院著艮壹磅移叁磅將六具先友分發每具先友
　　艮半磅以為付囬先友各鄉親屬收囬葬費劳醫院列
　　位先生將六具先友付囬各鄉伍海勳伍成文伍阿欽張
　　阿慶羅宏欵蔡阿福劳醫院　先生尽力代為付囬各
　　安葬可也旧歲各葬費实系忘記錯愳如列位先生收
　　艮代祈為之註囬乙音報之

伍根字付
己巳七月初八日
Hong Hem
Gardener Narrandera
N. S. W.

照將各字付囬各縣
義庄各親屬收葬

另一人注：己八月廿五覆
　　　　　照此門牌付無愳

Letter from Ng Gun, Australia, to Tung Wah Hospital on 12 August 1929

Dear Managers of Tung Wah Hospital,

Please be informed that I (Ng Gun) repatriated the remains of six deceased friends last year. Yesterday I received a reply that the remains were still in the care of your hospital and yet to be sent to the deceased's hometown. Therefore, I enclose 4 pounds sterling in this letter. 1 pound is for your hospital. As for the remaining 3 pounds, half a pound is provided for each set of remains for repatriation and burial in the deceased's hometown.

Could you please send the six remains of Ng Hoi-fun *(Wu Haixun)*, Ng Shing-man *(Wu Chengwen)*, Ng Ah-yum *(Wu Aqin)*, Cheung Ah-hing *(Zhang Aqing)*, Law Wang-foon *(Luo Hongkuan)* and Choi Ah-fook *(Cai Afu)* to their hometown for burial? I am sorry that I forgot to send the funds last year. Please repatriate the remains after you have received the funds, so that the deceased friends can be laid to rest in their hometown. Please also send us a reply.

Please send the name lists to the coffin homes of the deceased's hometown so that the relatives can collect the remains for burial.

Yours sincerely,
Ng Gun *(Wu Gen)*
8th day of of the 7th lunar month, Year of Gei Zi *(Jisi)*

Please send your reply to:
Hong Hem
Gardener Narrandera
N. S. W.

Another person's remarks: Replied on 25th day of the 8th lunar month, Year of Gei Zi *(Jisi)*

243 澳洲容蔭祥致東華醫院信件

1929 年 9 月 16 日

東華醫院暨

列位善長大鑒敬啓者今日由亞拿夫拿船運

棺囲港乃係中山谷都烏石鄉人郑煒和公

西名 Charlie Howe 祈知之有銀付上　貴院

由金山庄代交到日請照收入可也

耑此並請

大安

代理人　容蔭祥上言

（印章：庇厘時彬孫祖祐公司書柬）

己巳八月十四日

243 Letter from Yung Yam-cheung, Australia, to Tung Wah Hospital on 16 September 1929

Dear benevolent Directors of Tung Wah Hospital,

The coffin of Cheng Wai-wo (*Zheng Weihe*), also known as Charlie Howe, of Wu Shek Township (*Wushi Xiang*), Guk Doh (*Gudu*), Chung Shan (*Zhongshan*), has been repatriated on the *Arafura*. I will send funds to cover the costs of repatriation to your esteemed hospital through a gold mountain firm. Please receive the funds in due course.

I wish you well.

Yours sincerely,
Yung Yam-cheung *(Rong Yinxiang)*
On behalf of (Stamp: S. Jue Yow & Co., Brisbane)

14th day of the 8th lunar month, Year of Gei Zi *(Jisi)*

東華医院暨
列位善長台均鑒敬啓者今奉上司零單四鎊正到日祈
　照查收可也以助貴院費用茲於亞拿夫拿船有運棺一副回來交
　貴院代收係中山谷都烏石鄉　郑煒和祖　西名差兒好
　今特字達知敬煩　貴院行信以其家人知之寄信
　處交　中山谷都烏石鄉人氏　郑惠敏收入可也
　餘言不尽　　耑此　並請

大安

（印章：庇里時彬孫祖祐公司書柬）
代理人容蔭祥上言

　　　　己巳八月十六日由彰德船
通信處　　（印章：庇厘時彬孫祖祐公司）

另一人註：九月廿八回信

來港艮四十四元　九月廿一日由永安太來
　　　　　　　　梁禹□收給收條

244   **Letter from S. Jue Yow & Co., Brisbane, Australia, to Tung Wah Hospital on 18 September 1929**

Dear benevolent Directors of Tung Wah Hospital,

I am sending 4 pounds sterling to cover the costs of repatriating a coffin on the *Arafura*. Please take the coffin, which belongs to Cheng Wai Wo Jo *(Zheng Weihe)*, English name Charlie Howe of Wu Shek Township *(Wushi Xiang)*, Guk Doh *(Gudu)*, Chung Shan *(Zhongshan)*, into your care, and inform his family. Please send the letter to Cheng Wai-man *(Zheng Huimin)* of Wu Shek Township, Guk Doh, Chung Shan.

Thank you very much for your kindess.

Yours sincerely,
Yung Yam-cheung *(Rong Yinxiang)*
On behalf of (Stamp: S. Jue Yow & Co., Brisbane)

On the *Changte* on the 16th day of the 8th lunar month, Year of Gei Zi *(Jisi)*

Please send your reply to:
(Stamp: S. Jue Yow & Co., 20 Roma St., Brisbane, QLD.)

Another person's remarks: Replied on the 28th day of the 9th lunar month
44 Hong Kong dollars received from Wing On Tai *(Yung An Tai)* on the 21st day of the 9th lunar month

Receipt issued by Leung Yu-X *(Liang Yuzhao)*

澳洲伍俊之致東華醫院信件

1929年10月1日

東華醫院司理先生偉鑒敬啓者

現十月弍号由鉄行公司丹呥船
付囬伍文懌先叔之骸骨是以
修字敬告煩 先生代為照收
暫存醫院延下其家人或其
親屬到來收領可也而吾亦
另有信通知其家人矣諸事
多勞銘感五內耑此即頌
并請

台安

中華民國十八年十月一号

由雪梨伍俊之上言

Letter from Ng Chun-chi, Australia, to Tung Wah Hospital on 1 October 1929

Dear Managers of Tung Wah Hospital,

I write to inform you that the bones of my late uncle, Ng Man-yick (*Wu Wenyi*) will be repatriated on the *SS Delta* of Peninsula and Oriental Steam Navigation Company on 2 October. Please keep the remains in your hospital until the deceased's family or relatives come to collect. I have already notified them of the repatriation by mail.

I am most grateful to you for your efforts.

I wish you well.

Yours sincerely,
Ng Chun-chi (*Wu Junzhi*)
Sydney

1 October of the 18th year of the Republic of China

東華醫院^{善長}先生^鑒茲者拎是日由丹打船付返
　　东東中山石岐長洲村黃社根祖骸骨一具茲今
　　將儎紙隨函付上到日請提收勞即轉駁船寄至中山石
　　岐交与善堂代收轉交其親人認領是日並由本港
　　廣和豐金山庄付返鑒司令單艮壹磅正料不日派
　　到祈照查收將作該事之費佣可也諸多有勞
　　感恩戴德餘不細及此草　並請
列位善長先生

福安

　　　　　　　　　　　　　^弟黃善餘等仝頓
　　　　　　　　　　己十二月初九日付丹打船
　　　　　　　　　　民國十八年一九三〇年元月八号

再者此儎紙載骸骨二具中山渡头村雷姓順荅寄一具他另函呈達云云

246 Letter from Wong Sin-yu, Australia, to Tung Wah Hospital on 8 January 1930

Dear benevolent Directors of Tung Wah Hospital,

The bones of Wong She-gun (*Huang Shegen*) of Cheung Chau Village (*Changzhou Cun*), Shekki (*Shiqi*), Chung Shan (*Zhongshan*), Kwangtung *(Guangdong)*, have been repatriated on the *SS Delta*. I have enclosed the bill of lading for the shipment. After the bones arrive in Hong Kong, please send them onto Yu Sin Tong (*Yu Shan Tang)* in Shekki, Chung Shan by boat. The benevolent association will hand over the remains to the deceased's family. Also, Kwong Wo Fung Gold Mountain Firm in Hong Kong will send you 1 pound sterling to cover the costs of repatriation. Please expect the funds soon.

We are most grateful to you for your kindness.

I wish you well.

Yours sincerely,
Wong Sin-yu (*Huang Shanyu*) & fellow brothers

Sent on the SS *Delta* on the 9th day of the 12th lunar month, Year of Gei Zi (*Jisi*)

8th day of the 1st lunar month of the 18th year of the Republic of China

Bill of lading for two sets of bones is attached.
One set of bones is sent back by Lui (*Lei*) of To Tau Village (*Dutou Cun*), Chung Shan (*Zhongshan*), he will write to you separately.

東華醫院^{貴善長}先生^{台鑒}料卜安居迪吉諸事
　　如意為頌矣茲者於是日由丹打輪船付返廣
　　東中山縣長洲村黃社根祖骸骨一具該儀紙
　　另由郵政寄上今隨函付返鑒司令單艮壹磅正
　　到日請查收煩^{貴善長}即着人往船查收即轉
　　駁船付返中山石岐交與善堂代收着其親人認
　　領便是諸事有劳功德無量不勝感激
　　餘不細及　　此草　順候

列位貴善長仁翁
福安

（印章：澳洲雪梨黃善餘緘）
^弟黃善餘等仝謹上

一九三〇年元月十一号
己民國十八年十二月十二日

247 Letter from Wong Sin-yu, Australia, to Tung Wah Hospital on 11 January 1930

Dear benevolent Directors of Tung Wah Hospital,

I hope this letter finds you well. The bones of Wong She-gun (*Huang Shegen*) of Cheung Chau Village (*Changzhou Cun*), Shekki (*Shiq*i), Chung Shan (*Zhongshan)*, Kwangtung *(Guangdong)*, have been repatriated on the SS *Delta*. The bill of lading was sent by post separately.

I enclose 1 pound sterling with this letter. Please arrange someone to receive the remains from the ship after they arrive in Hong Kong and send them onto Yu Sin Tong (*Yu Shan Tang*) in Shekki, Chung Shan by boat immediately. Please also arrange to inform the deceased's family to collect the remains.

We are most grateful to you for your kind arrangement and efforts.

I wish you well.

Yours sincerely,
Wong Sin-yu (*Huang Shanyu*)
(Stamp: Wong Sin-yu of Sydney, Australia)

11 January 1930
12th day of the 12th lunar month of the 18th year of the Republic of China, Year of Gei Zi *(Jisi)*

東華大醫院
善長先生鑒現接新金山尾利畔埠勝利隆
雷炎学先生函称去年四月十二号由外付返請
貴院轉付交台山縣大塘村雷舉傳先友家人
所收司令單壹拾磅正未曉有無妥付如未請
交弟代為具保代收轉交雷舉傳家人收入之話
相應函達如何之处請照函示順請

善安

　　　　　　　雷熙傳字上（印章：香港永樂街均安和雷熙傳書東）

民國十九年三月十一日　庚午二月十二日

另一人註：庚二月十四覆

248 Letter from Lui Hei-chuen, Hong Kong, to Tung Wah Hospital on 11 March 1930

Dear benevolent Directors of Tung Wah Hospital,

I received a letter from Lui Yim-hok (*Lei Yanxue*) of Shing Lee Lung, Melbourne, with regard to a sum of money, in the amount of 10 pounds sterling, sent from abroad on 12 April of last year for the family of Lui Gui-chuen *(Lei Juchuan)* of Dai Tong Village *(Datang Cun)*, Toi Shan *(Taishan)* through your hospital. Would you please advise if the money had been handed over to the family? If not, please pass the money to me, and I will give it to the family of Lui Gui-chuen.

I await your reply.

I wish you well.

Yours sincerely,
Lui Hei-chuen (*Lei Xichuan*)
(Stamp: Lui Hei-chuen, Kwan On Wo, Wing Lok Street, Hong Kong)

11 March of the 19th year of the Republic of China
12th day of the 2nd lunar month, Year of Gang Ng *(Gengwu)*

Another person's remarks: Replied on the 14th day of the 2nd lunar month, Year of Gang Ng

澳洲鳥修威祖密埠四邑會館致東華醫院信件

1930 年 4 月 16 日

東華醫院先生大鑒敬啓者本會館經已撿
拾先友仙骸五具用鉄箱分裝外共裝一木箱即買
保險由太古輪船之太平輪船付囬貴醫院收
入以便付囬各縣也至船抵港時請照起卸以便
按名分發囬縣先友親屬領收安塟成斯善
舉功德無涯矣至於　貴醫院經費已
由香港陸怡董先生處付囬也耑此順請

大安

　　　　　一九三〇年四月十六号 澳洲（印章：鳥修威祖密埠四邑會館）頓

Letter from See Yap Association of New South Wales, Australia, to Tung Wah Hospital on 16 April 1930

Dear Managers of Tung Wah Hospital,

We had exhumed the remains of five deceased friends and placed them separately in five iron cases. They were then put into a large wooden box, insured and repatriated on the *SS Taiping* of the Australian Oriental Line for burial in the deceased's hometown. Please take the remains into your care when they arrive in Hong Kong and transport them to the deceased's families in their hometown according to the name list, so that our deceased friends can be laid to rest. Your assistance in this matter demonstrates great benevolence. Meanwhile, Luk Yee-tung (*Lu Yidong*) of Hong Kong has paid the fees to your hospital.

We wish you well.

Yours humbly,
(Stamp: See Yap Association, New South Wales, Australia)

16 April 1930

香港東華醫院先生^{電鑒}敬啓者今日由傳館掛號處呈
　上儀吊一張諒妥收矣今吳冲煥呈上先友拾位
　捐助銀伍磅正另壹磅正乃係^弟二位同義捐與
　貴醫院經費二柱共艮陸磅正妥收後懇祈　賜
　回一音是盼　專此敬請

大安

　　　　　　　　　　　　　　　　　　^弟吳^{冲煥}_{煥然}仝呈上

　　　　　　　　　　　　　　　　　（印章：吳煥然書柬）

一九三〇年六月十六号　由利羅船付返
庚午年五月廿日

回信：W. SHOW PAN, 724 ANN ST, VALLEY, BRISBANE,
QUEENSLAND, AUSTRALIA
傳交吳煥然收入照此門牌賜覆無悞

250

Letter from Ng Chung-woon and Ng Woon-yin, Australia, to Tung Wah Hospital on 16 June 1930

Dear Managers of Tung Wah Hospital,

Today we have sent a bill of lading to you by registered post and trust that you receive it in order. Here, 5 pounds sterling have been donated by Ng Chung-woon (*Wu Chonghuan*) for repatriation of 10 deceased friends, whereas another 1 pound sterling is a small donation from us to support the operation of your esteemed hospital. The total amount of the two donations is 6 pounds sterling.

Please acknowledge receipt of the donation. We await your reply.

I wish you well.

Yours sincerely,
Ng Chung-woon
Ng Woon-yin *(Wu Huanran)*
(Stamp: Ng Woon-yin)

16 June 1930

20th day of the 5th lunar month, Year of Gang Ng *(Gengwu)*
Sent on the *SS Nellore*

Please send your reply to Ng Woon-yin at this address:
W. Show Pan.
724 Ann St Valley, Brisbane, Queensland, Australia

紐西蘭黃梓致東華醫院信件

1930 年 11 月 22 日

東華医院列位先生鑒啓者茲由彰德船付回方
富榮先君灵柩乃以運回內地到時祈勞為
收殮之是為至祷諸事有勞感感並頌

大安

弟黃梓　字上

一九三〇年十一月廿二号

（印章：紐絲崙托崙埠　黃梓號　唐山雜貨發客）

251 Letter from Wong Tsz, New Zealand, to Tung Wah Hospital on 22 November 1930

Dear Managers of Tung Wah Hospital,

The coffin of Fong Fu-wing (*Fang Furong*) has been sent back (to Hong kong) for repatriating to the mainland on the *Changte*. Please take the coffin into your care when it arrives in Hong Kong.

I am most grateful to you for your efforts.

Yours sincerely,
Wong Tsz (*Huang Zi*)

22 November 1930

(Stamp: T. W. DOO Merchant and Importer. PHONE 42 – 715, 109 VICTORIA ST., WEST, AUCKLAND, N.Z.)

紐西蘭黃梓致東華醫院信件

1932年2月5日

東華医院列位先生大鑒敬恳者兹有[弟]
先兄黃沐昭不幸在外仙遊現將其灵
柩由太平船運回中國安葬屆時有勞　先生暫
為收殮遲日該死者之子名黃毛到來
貴院查收運回內地安葬矣諸事多勞感感並
頌

大安

[弟]黃梓　字奉

（印章：紐絲崙托崙埠 黃梓號 唐山雜貨發客）

一九三二年二月五号

Letter from Wong Chi, New Zealand, to Tung Wah Hospital on 5 February 1932

Dear Directors of Tung Wah Hospital,

My elder brother, Wong Muk-chiu *(Huang Muzhao)*, passed away abroad tragically. His coffin is being sent back on the *Taiping* and will eventually be repatriated to China for burial. Please take the coffin into your care after it arrives in Hong Kong. My late brother's son, Wong Mo *(Huang Mao)*, will collect the coffin from your esteemed hospital and take it back to the mainland for burial.

Thank you very much for your efforts.

I wish you well.

Yours sincerely,
Wong Chi *(Huang Zi)*

(Stamp: T.W. DOO Merchant & Importer. PHONE 42-715, 109 VICTORIA ST. WEST. AUCKLAND, N.Z.)

5 February 1932

東華大醫院^暨

大善長青鑒敬啓者茲由南京船付返雷学闲

仙骸一具到請查收代為轉寄中山縣與善堂

轉交中山良都渡頭鄉雷宜樂收入安葬茲付返

司連單銀半磅到請查收以資費用專此即請

并頌

善安

^弟雷学快上（印章：竹報）民廿一·二·十七日

通信門牌於後

（印章：YET SHING & CO 日昇號 GENERAL MERCHANTS 82 HABOUR ST. SYDNEY）

另一人註：壬二月初四進

253

Letter from Lui Hok-fai, Australia, to Tung Wah Hospital on 17 February 1932

Dear benevolent Directors of Tung Wah Hospital,

The remains of Lui Hok-hoi *(Lei Xuekai)* have been repatriated on the *Nankin*. When the remains arrive in Hong Kong, please take them into your care and send them to Lui Yee-lok *(Lei Yile)* of Do Tau Township *(Dutou Xiang)*, Leung Do *(Liang Du)*, Chung Shan *(Zhongshan)*, through Yu Sin Tong *(Yu Shan Tang)*, so that the deceased can be laid to rest. I am sending you half pound sterling to cover the costs of repatriation.

Thank you for your assistance.

I wish you well.

Yours sincerely,
Lui Hok-fai *(Lei Xuekuai)*
(Stamp: Chuk Po)

17 February of the 21st year of the Republic of China
(Stamp: Yet Shing & Co., General Merchants, 82 Harbour St. Sydney)

Another person's remarks: received on the 4th day of the 2nd lunar month, Year of Yam San *(Renxin)*

澳洲庇厘時浜東邑公義堂致東華醫院信件

1932 年 3 月 24 日

東華醫院列位值理大鑒啓者茲由彰德船付返^{敝邑}先友
　遺骸玖具至日祈為查收会仝^{敝邑}駐港商会办理按
　址代為運返原藉俾得歸塋故鄉即歿存均感功
　德無量矣隨函夾上船行傤帋乙張又司連票乙張
　該民伍鎊正祈為詧收以作費用專此□懇順頌

善安

　　　　　　　　　　　　　　　壬申二月十八日
　　　　　　　　　　　　　　　一九三二年三月廿四号
　　　　　　　　　　　　　　（印章：庇厘時浜東邑公義堂）
　　　　　　　　　　　　　　（印章：庇厘時浜利秋號書柬）
　　　　　　　　　　　　　　（印章：庇厘時浜麗記號）仝啓

另一人註：Kong Yee Tong c/o Lee Chow 92 Albert St.
　　　　　　Brisbane Q, d Aust

　　　茲將先友姓名鄉藉列左

葉　安 東莞道滘村	任　佛 東莞峽內常平金美村
謝　容 東莞峽內東坑井美村	袁藉恩 東莞峽內常平員山貝村
袁观諾 東莞峽內常平員山貝村	黃观林 東莞峽內東坑隔嶺村
陳連錫 東莞峽內常平郎貝村	陳　泰 東莞峽內常平郎貝村
吳日光 東莞峽內常平橫瀝水边村	

254 Letter from Kong Yee Tong, Brisbane, Australia, to Tung Wah Hospital on 24 March 1932

Dear Directors of Tung Wah Hospital,

The remains of nine deceased friends who were native of our county were repatriated on the *Changte*. Please check and take them into your care when they arrive in Hong Kong and work with the commercial association of our county in Hong Kong to send them to the deceased's hometown for burial. The deceased and the living will be grateful to you. Your benevolence is far reaching.

We enclose the bill of lading and a cheque for 5 pounds to cover the costs of repatriation.

Thank you very much for your efforts. We wish you well.

Yours sincerely,
From (Stamp: Kong Yee Tong, Brisbane),
(Stamp: Brisbane Lee Chow Ho) &
(Stamp: Brisbane Bong Lai Kee Ho)

28th day of the 2nd lunar month, Year of Yam San *(Renshen)*
24 March 1932

Another person's remarks: Kong Yee Tong
90 Lee Chaw
92 Albert St.
Brisbane Q.d Aust

Names and native counties of deceased friends are listed.

[Editor's remarks: Name list of the deceased friends is available only in Chinese]

三盛昌用箋

東華醫院鈞鑒敬啓者茲接堅士 Cairns 埠
　　^{敝友}沈景林先生來函據稱曾託西人名
　　Headrick 由太平船 Taiping 付返羅貴遺
　　骸一箱交　貴院代收屆時代支佣腳等費
　　用若干祈賜列清單^{小號}定當如數璧
　　還多瀆　清神曷勝銘感此達即頌

公祺
　　民廿一・十弍月六日

　　　　　　　　弟（印章：香港德輔道西三盛昌）謹上

另一人註：此具骨殖現存太古倉未有提單

Letter from Sam Sing Chong, Hong Kong, to Tung Wah Hospital on 6 December 1932

From the Office of Sam Sing Chong

Dear Managers of Tung Wah Hospital,

We received a letter from our friend, Sham King-lam *(Shen Jinglin)* of Cairns, saying that he had asked a westerner named Headrick to send the remains of Law Gwai *(Luo Gui)*, placed in one box, to your hospital on the *Taiping*. Please take delivery of the remains. If there are any costs incurred, please pay the fees on our behalf and send a detailed invoice to us and we will reimburse you for all the costs.

We are most grateful to you for your efforts.

Yours sincerely,
(Stamp: Sam Sing Chong, Des Voeux Road West, Hong Kong)

6 December of the 21st year of the Republic of China

Another person's remarks: This set of bones is now stored at the Swire Warehouse without a bill of lading.

東華醫院　先生大鑒　敬啓者[氏]先夫楊

　　邦榮舊歲由澳洲堅时埠運回

　貴院貯候收領奈[氏]乃一庸俗村婦女流其

　　时未便到院領取且[氏]向未明瞭其事以致

　　日久迁延茲月前曾托友人將先夫邦荣

　　之骸具帶抵鄉間叨蒙

　貴院之慈善為懷[氏]等感激無涯矣但由外

　　埠運回之先友每有遷塟費英金壹磅助

　　以領骸者作塟殮費之用等例是以函達

　　該欵如係貯下　貴院仰

先生等祈照後列門牌地址付來轉交與[氏]俾

　　得塟資有賴感恩不淺矣耑此

並候
　　　　　　貴院諸先生公安　廿弍年夏曆三月念七日

　　　　　　　　　　　　　　　　　楊邦荣妻阮氏襝袵

通訊处
中山石歧鳳鳴路
永福利大寶号收下轉與
西鄉區隆圩
楊占微先生收啓
或寫楊占微家母阮氏收啓亦可

另一人註：已复

Letter from Madam Yeung-Yuen, China, to Tung Wah Hospital on 21 April 1933

Dear Directors of Tung Wah Hospital,

The remains of my late husband, Yeung Bong-wing *(Yang Bangrong)*, were repatriated from Cairns, Australia, last year and placed in your esteemed hospital awaiting collection. Since I am an uneducated village woman not knowing what to do, I did not go to your esteemed hospital to collect the remains and caused the delay. It was not until earlier on that I entrusted my friend to bring the remains of my late husband back to our hometown. I am most grateful to you for your kindness. I understand that burial fees of 1 pound sterling are usually offered to the deceased's family. I therefore write to ask if your esteemed hospital has kept the money for me. If yes, please send the money to the address below, so that it can be passed onto me.

I thank you once again for your great kindness.

I await your reply and wish you well.

With best wish & humble greetings,
Madam Yuen *(Ruan Shi)*, wife of Yeung Bong-wing

27th day of the 3rd lunar month of the 22nd year of the Republic of China

Correspondence address:
Yeung Chim-mei *(Yang Zhanwei)* or Madam Yuen, mother of Yeung Chim-mei *(Yang Zhanwei)*
Lung Market Town *(Long Xu)*, Sai Township *(Xi Xiang)*
c/o Wing Fook Lei Company *(Yong Fuli Da Baohao)*,
Fung Ming Road *(Fengming Lu)*, Shekki *(Shiqi)*, Chung Shan *(Zhongshan)*

Another person's remarks: Replied

W. SHOWPA□

21st April 1933

香港東華醫院先生電鑒敬啟者 弟 於旧
　　歲十一月十四號由南京船付返中山縣東鎮
　　張家边鄉先友骨骸三名馬佐寬 公 馬
　　經聯 公 陳仲 公 又中山縣得都庫充新
　　村鄉連理 公 字贊光一名共四名同時呈上
　　滙單乙乭該鑒單貳磅正另船行儌乭距
　　今数月未蒙　賜覆未悉曾照前致蕪函办事
　　否便恳　示知不勝感戴無既矣專此
　　敬請

大安

弟 吳煥然　手啟

一九三三年四月廿壹號□由太平船付返

257 Letter from Ng Woon-yin, Australia, to Tung Wah Hospital on 21 April 1933

From the Desk of W. Sttowp PA X

21 April 1933

Dear Directors of Tung Wah Hospital,

I repatriated the remains of four deceased friends, Ma Jor-foon *(Ma Zuokuan)*, Ma King-luen *(Ma Jinglian)* and Chan Chung *(Chen Zhong)* of Cheung Ka Bin Township *(Zhangjiabian Xiang)*, Tung Town *(Dong Zhen)*, Chung Shan County *(Zhongshan Xian)*, as well as Lin Lei *(Lian Li)*, style name Chan-kwong *(Zanguang)* of Tak Dou Fu Chong Sun Chuen Township *(Dedu Kuchong Xincun Xiang)* of Chung Shan County, on the *Nankin* on 14 November of last year together with a copy of money order for 2 pounds sterling and a bill of lading. However, a few months have passed and I have yet to hear any news from you. I am not sure whether the matter has been settled. Please reply to me to let me know.

I am most grateful to you for your assistance.

I wish you well.

Yours sincerely,
Ng Woon-yin *(Wu Huanran)*

Repatriated on the *Taiping* on 21 April 1933

新甯鐵路會計課銀業股用箋

啓者^弟前年六月廿日由澳洲美利澳埠付
上　貴院收勅台山冲蔞福新里唐翔福先友
骸骨一副仝日付有司令單一張英金弍鎊正以
為轉運費用之需但今經一年之久茲據翔
福先友家人到稱云未見　貴院將其先人骸
砢付返未曉何故是否失漏或係貴人事
繁忙覺辦理但^弟當日在處經許多繁难
乃得办妥該先友返國以為　貴院办理迅
速諸事定必妥善豈料貴院收到該款
及先骸一切均無半字囘复今成年久仍未
代其運返家鄉此中是否或有別情請
煩　貴總理飭役查明該先骸下落從快函
至唐翔福家人領取或從速付返以便其
家人淂早日安塟先人此是公德两便請留
心办理是所切盼此上

東華医院総理先生鑒

　　　　　　　　　　　　　　　　　　　　　　陳仲恒上

中華民國廿二年七月十八日

Letter from Chan Chung-wun, China, to Tung Wah Hospital on 18 July 1933

From the Office of the Accounting Department of Sun Ning Railway Company

Dear Directors of Tung Wah Hospital,

On 20 June last year, I repatriated the bones of Tong Cheung-fook *(Tang Xiangfu)*, a native of Fook Sun Lane *(Fuxin Li)*, Chung Lau *(Chong Lou)*, Toi Shan *(Taishan)*, from Maryborough, Australia. I have also sent 2 pounds sterling to cover repatraition costs. A year had passed but the family of Cheung-fook said they had not yet received the remains. I wonder if there was a mistake, or if you were too busy to take care of the matters. I hope you understand that in order to send the deceased friend back to his hometown, I had overcome a lot of difficulties. I thought your esteemed hospital would handle the matter quickly and properly, yet you did not reply to me after you received the funds and the bones. It has been one year long, but the remains of the deceased have still not been repatriated to his hometown. Has something wrong happened? Would you please ask someone to investigate the matter and find out where the remains are? Please write to Tong Cheung-fook's family as soon as you can. Please ask them to collect his remains, or send the remains to his hometown, so that the deceased can be laid to rest. Your benevolence is much appreciated. Please handle the matter carefully.

Yours sincerely,
Chan Chung-wun *(Chen Zhongheng)*

18 July of the 22nd year of the Republic of China

東華醫院列位先生^{台電}　　敬啓者今有先骸壹
　　具係廣東中山隆都疊石鄉余捷標^名泗崧人氏
　　曾由是浚彰德船俦返但到抵港煩勞起回安在
　　醫院處容日運上石岐回春院內与其親人承領
　　諸多有勞感感另有寄先骸俦乑一張分函付上
　　茲付返司零銀單壹磅正以作起工運費等事
　　祈查收入就是草此
　　並候

善安

　　　　　　　　　　　　　　　　　癸酉年六月初八日由彰德船寄
　　　　　　　　　　　　　　　南方澳洲湯時威盧埠^弟余祥上言

如或有信回音照此門牌　Tin Yuen & Co
　　　　　　　　　　　P.O. Box 318
　　　　　　　　　　　Towns Ville
　　　　　　　　　　　Australia
　　　　　　　　　　　信寄澳洲湯時威盧埠
　　　　　　　　　　　天元號轉交
　　　　　　　　　　　余祥收啓

259 Letter from Yu Cheung, Australia, to Tung Wah Hospital on 30 July 1933

Dear Directors of Tung Wah Hospital,

The remains of Yu Chit-biu *(Yu Jiebiao)*, also known as Sei-sung *(Sisong)*, a native of Deep Shek Village *(Dieshi Xiang)*, Lung Doh *(Longdu)*, Chung Shan *(Zhongshan)*, Kwangtung *(Guangdong)*, have been repatriated to Hong Kong on the *Changte*. After the remains arrive in Hong Kong, please arrange labor to unload and take them into your care, and then send them to Wui Chun Yuen *(Huichun Yuan)* in Shekkei *(Shiqi)*. The deceased's family will collect the remains.

Thank you very much for your assistance. There will be another letter enclosing the bill of lading and a money order for 1 pound sterling. Please use the funds to cover transportation costs.

I await your reply and wish you well.

Sent on the *Changte* on the 8th day of the 6th lunar month, Year of Gwai Yau *(Guiyou)*

Yours sincerely,
Yu Cheung *(Yu Xiang)*
Towns Ville, Australia

Please send any correspondence to me at Ting Yuen & Co, P.O. Box 318, Towns Ville, Australia.

澳洲雪梨永安菓欄致東華醫院信件

1933 年 11 月 11 日

澳洲雪梨永安公司
WING ON & CO., LTD.

香港
東華醫院
執事先生台鑒敬啓者先人郭社桂原籍
廣東中山縣竹秀園鄉人由南京船運棺
回國昨奉上之函請為照料今將船行俌
紙付上到日並懇知照
香港漢臣洋行委人料理為盼耑此再及

並頌
台祺

（印章：雪梨正埠永安菓欄書柬）頓

中華民國廿二年十一月十一日

260

Letter from Wing On & Co., Ltd., Sydney, Australia, to Tung Wah Hospital on 11 November 1933

From the Office of Wing On & Co., Ltd., Sydney

Dear Managers of Tung Wah Hospital,

The coffin of Kwok She-kwai *(Guo Shegui)*, a native of Chuk Shau Yuen Township *(Zhuxiuyuan Xiang)*, Chung Shan County *(Zhongshan Xian)*, Kwangtung *(Guangdong)* will be repatriated on the *Nankin*. I wrote to you earlier asking you to take the coffin into your care when they arrive in Hong Kong. I now enclose the bill of lading in this letter. Please inform Hong Kong Hon Sun Company to arrange a representative to take care of this matter.

Thank you very much for your assistance.

Yours humbly,
(Stamp: From the Office of Wing On & Co., Ltd., Sydney)

11 November of the 22nd year of the Republic of China

東華醫院　院主暨列位　仁翁台鑒　敬啓者茲由元月

十三号開行天打輪船付返先兄洪耀骨骸一副到

希代為妥收存下侍家叔康祺^{現在先施公司}到院

酌落再行轉付石岐或請代為貯下下年到領總

之侍家叔康祺到院酌奪就是茲付返司令

單壹 P 到希收存為幸專此敬頌

均安

　　　　　　　　　　　　　　　民國廿三年新歷元月拾号^{香邑}關鴻光敬叩

旅住址
Hong Sing & Co
Stanthorpe Queensland
Australia

另付返載紙壹張

261 Letter from Kwan Hung-kwong, Australia, to Tung Wah Hospital on 10 January 1934

Dear benevolent Chairman and Directors of Tung Wah Hospital,

The bones of my late elder brother, Hung-yiu *(Hongyao)*, have been repatriated on the *SS Tanda* on 13 January. When the bones arrive in Hong Kong, please take them into your care. Please wait for my uncle Hong-kei *(Kangqi)* who works in the Sincere Company to come to your esteemed hospital to discuss whether the bones would be sent to Shekki *(Shiqi)* or to be kept under your good care for another year for the bones to be claimed. Anyhow, my uncle Hong-kei will come to you to further discuss the details. I enclose a money order for 1 pound sterling as well.

I wish you well.

Yours humbly,
Kwan Hung-kwong *(Guan Hongguang)* of Heung Shan *(Xiangshan)*

10 January of the 23rd year of the Republic of China

Please also see enclosed a bill of lading.

Correspondence address:
Hong Sing & Co.
Stanthorpe, Queensland, Australia

東華医院

执事諸公惠鑒者^{敝邑}有先友金骸七大箱共伍拾叁具□

六箱每庄八具但壹箱庄五具箱外嘜 TWHHK 由是渡太平船付

回交

貴医院收之暫貯義庄隨函夾呈俩紙壹張煩照提收^{敝堂}

已有信交^{敝邑}旅港商會諸人詳明此事料有登門拜候然該

先友決運入新塘圩寶善堂收存以便先友親人到領但如何

運法敬求指

示一切甚幸^{敝堂}托厚德祥代送

貴医院港紙叁拾員惟些少之款不成事體萬望原宥耑此

敬候
大安

英一九三四年弍月十号　　　　　　　　　　　葉炳南（印章：雪梨增城聯福堂）

262 Letter from Luen Fook Tong, Sydney, Australia, to Tung Wah Hospital on 10 February 1934

Dear Managers of Tung Wah Hospital,

The remains of 53 deceased friends, eight sets in six boxes and five sets in one box all marked with "TWHHK", have been repatriated on the *Taiping*. Please take delivery of the remains and place in the coffin home of your esteemed hospital temporarily. We enclose the bill of lading for claiming the remains. Meanwhile, we have notified the commercial association of our county in Hong Kong of this matter. They will visit your esteemed hospital and make arrangements for the remains to be transported to Bo Sin Tong *(Bao Shan Tang)* in Sun Tong Market Town *(Xintang Xu)* for the deceased's families to collect. We would be most grateful if you could notify us of the relevant procedures. We have also asked Hau Tak Cheung to send 30 Hong Kong dollars to your esteemed hospital. Please accept our small donation.

I wish you well.

Yours sincerely,
Yip Bing-nam *(Ye Bingnan)*
(Stamp: Luen Fook Tong, Sydney)

10 February 1934

紐西蘭楊朝利致東華醫院信件

1934 年 9 月 8 日

東華醫院执事先生台鑒

啓者家父靈柩由舍弟錦
堂親自跪送返國乘章德
輪船由雪梨九月二十二號啓程
屆時抵港希祈派人下船
照料諸多感激謝謝餘未
細述謹此
并頌
公祺

（印章：新西蘭金山卡賴左治埠楊朝利號）
西一九三四年九月八号
弟楊錦波字頓（印章：卡賴左治朝利楊書柬）

Letter from Chew Lee Young, New Zealand, to Tung Wah Hospital on 8 September 1934

Dear Managers of Tung Wah Hospital,

The coffin of my late father will be taken back to China by my younger brother Kam-tong *(Jintang)* on the *Changte* in person. The ship will depart Sydney on 22 September. Please send someone to the ship to assist my brother when the ship arrives in Hong Kong.

I am most grateful to you for your kindness. Please accept my apology on the brief account of the matter.

I wish you well.

Yours humbly,
Young Kam-bor *(Yang Jinbo)*
8 September 1934

(Stamp: Young Chew Lee, Christchurch)

(Stamp: CHEW LEE YOUNG, CHINESE MERCHANTS, G.P.O. BOX 822, 8 FERRY ROAD CHRISTCHURCH, N. Z.)

東華醫院司理先生大鑒
敬启者特函奉來懇悉久聞香港東華醫院
　　保障民權為海外內侨胞謀幸福同事以庇
　　陰德不淺者矣茲者現下七月十三日由澳洲
　　芝葫埠先友一名黃華添全体金骨裝一箱
　　直付彰德輪船返港交東華醫院收入係寫明白
　　箱面交廣東台山懸南坑堡龍昇村人氏勞煩
　　先生等見此字及收到者侯他日交囬黃起銳先生收
　　領返囬本境安葬以享受家人遞年拜墓留為紀念也
　　如遲他日黃起銳先生携來由外边付返彰德公司
　　船票載紙為憑據祈為照交起銳收領就是耳
　　諸凡多勞謝謝請順收妥請順字囬覆音也
　　會面有期敬候

大安

　　　　　　　　　　　　　由澳洲芝葫埠華人醫生黃華衮上

中華民國廿四年七月十五日
（印章：W. QOON, CHINESE HERBALIST, 116 YARRA STREET
(OFF LITTLE RYRIE STREET) GEELONG, VICTORIA, AUSTRALIA)

Letter from Wong Wah-kwan, Australia, to Tung Wah Hospital on 15 July 1935

Dear Managers of Tung Wah Hospital,

I have long heard of the benevolent work of Tung Wah Hospital of Hong Kong. You safeguard the rights of our people and serve Chinese compatriots at home and abroad. Your virtues are immense.

I have repatriated the bones of a deceased friend, Wong Wah-tim *(Huang Huatian)*, from Geelong, Australia, to your esteemed hospital on the *Changte* on 13 July. The remains have been placed in a box marked with "Native of Lung Sing Village *(Longsheng Cun)*, Nam Hang Bo *(Nankeng Bao)*, Toi Shan County *(Taishan Xian)*, Kwangtung *(Guangdong)*". After you take delivery of the remains, please wait for Wong Hei-yui *(Huang Qirui)* to come to collect. He will take them to the deceased's hometown for burial so that his family can pay respect to him forever. When Wong Hei-yui comes to your esteemed hospital to collect the remains with the bill of lading issued by the *Changte*, please hand over the remains to him.

Thank you for your kind efforts. I await your reply to my letter, and look forward to meeting you in person.

I wish you well.

Yours sincerely,
Wong Wah-kwan *(Huang Huagun)*
W. Qoon, Chinese herbalist
Geelong, Australia

15 July of the 24th year of the Republic of China

(Stamp: W. Qoon, CHINESE HERBALIST, 116 Yarra Street (off Little Ryrie Street), Geelong, Victoria, Australia.)

東華醫院
執事先生大鑒謹啟者今由彰德輪寄
返陳耀培遺骸一箱隨函奉呈俩紙一件
至懇代為提收并請函知彼之家屬
領回安葬俾安窀穸是所至盼付上司
零單銀壹磅到祈照收以作費用便
請賜覆一音無任深感專此奉託敬

頌
台祺

弟陳壽培頓

一九三五年十一月廿号

陳耀培名阿三廣東中山縣隆鎮象角鄉人氏
如覆函祈照下列門牌轉弟收便妥

(印章：　KWONG WAR CHONG & CO.
　　　　　P. O. BOX 48 HAYMARKET,
　　　　　SYDNEY, N. S. W.）

另一人註：14.65 元

265   Letter from Chau Sau-pui, Australia, to Tung Wah Hospital on 20 November 1935

Dear Managers of Tung Wah Hospital,

I repatriated the bones of Chan Yiu-pui *(Chen Yaopei)* on the *Changte* today and now enclose the bill of lading in this letter for your follow up. Please take delivery of the bones and inform the deceased's family to collect them for burial and lay the deceased to rest. I have also sent you 1 pound sterling to cover any costs incurred. Please reply to us.

I am most grateful to you for your benevolence. I wish you well.

Yours humbly,
Chan Sau-pui *(Chen Shoupei)*

20 November 1935

Chan Yiu-pui, also known as Ah Sam *(Asan)*, was a native of Cheung Kok Township *(Xiangjiao Xiang)*, Lung Town *(Long Zhen)*, Chung shan County *(Zhongshan Xian)*, Kwangtung *(Guangdong)*.

Please send your reply to the following address:

(Stamp: KWONG WAR CHONG & CO., P. O. BOX, 48 HAYMARKET, SYDNEY, N. S. W.)

Another person's remarks: 14.65 dollars

内地及香港西歸先友

中國旅鄂中山會館致東華醫院信件

1930年3月14日

中山會館籌備檢運先友委員會用箋

東華醫院

列位紳董先生惠鑒逕啓者日前奉蕪函

備詳^{敝邑}旅鄂同鄉運送先友囬籍道經

盛埠敢請代為照料轉運囬鄉等情諒邀

台閱到時必

允為所請也今有先友骸棺兩副一副運往中

山下柵壚金山學堂收一副運往石岐與善堂

收另有骸骨拾壹大箱分陸箱運往下柵壚金

山學堂收分四箱運往前山福善堂收分一箱

運往石岐與善堂收可也^{敝處}業經派有譚益

照君隨船押送該先友來港到時請與該押儎人

接洽便知其詳細也今由國民銀行滙上香港通用

紙銀叁百陸拾元請照

察收以備代為僱艇轉運各鄉接收之需此次先

備送之款乃按照去年^{敝地}四大兩都運送先友經

過約略之數而已查去年^{敝地}四大兩都運送先友亦由

貴醫院代為轉運云云然年月變遷搬運手續

或有出入固不能一概而論將來辦理完竣所需

費用或超過所按之類數或有餘剩統請向

貴埠泰安棧程名譽君接洽可也今將正副

儎紙各壹張請照

查收煩飭人照料一切專此拜托有費

清神曷勝銘感之至臨風佈意不盡區區順頌

公安

旅漢（印章：中山會館檢運先友委員會）

蕭鏡心先生　鞠躬上言

中華民國十九年三月十四日

另一人註：

運費　182.40元

工艇費　46.70元

除支存　130.90元

Letter from Lui Ngog Chung Shan Association, China, to Tung Wah Hospital on 14 March 1930

From the Office of Lui Ngog Chung Shan Association *(Lu E Zhongshan Huiguan)*

Dear Directors of Tung Wah Hospital,

You must have received our earlier letter regarding the repatriation of the remains of our late friends who resided in Wu Pek *(Hubei)* province to their hometown through Hong Kong. We trust you would agree to help take care of the remains and transport them to the deceased's hometown. Now we are repatriating two coffins, one to Kam Shan School *(Jinshan Xuetang)* in Ha Shan Market Town *(Xiazha Xu)*, Chung Shan *(Zhongshan)*, the other to Yu Sin Tong *(Yu Shan Tang)* in Shekki *(Shiqi)*. There are also 11 large boxes of bones, six boxes to Kam Shan School, four boxes to Fook Sin Tong *(Fu Shan Tang)* in Chin Shan *(Qianshan)* and one box to Yu Sin Tong. Our representative, Tam Yik-chiu *(Tan Yizhao)* will travel with the remains of the deceased friends to Hong Kong by boat. Please get in touch with him when he arrives, and he will provide you with more details.

We have remitted 360 Hong Kong dollars to you through the National Bank to cover the costs of transporting the remains to the deceased's hometown by boat. The amount is based on the costs of repatriation from the two areas in our county in the past. We are also aware that your esteemed hospital helped us send the remains of our deceased friends to their hometown at our county from Hong Kong last year. We understand the procedures may have changed. If the costs incurred exceed the amount of funds we have sent, or if there is any remainder, please get in touch with Ching Ming-yu *(Cheng Mingyu)* of Tai On Chan in Hong Kong. We have also enclosed the original and copy of the bill of lading. Please take the remains into your care.

We seek your help in this matter and shall be most grateful to you for your kindness. Words cannot describe our gratitude to you.

We wish you well.

Yours respectfully,
(Stamp: Committee for Repatriation of Remains, Lui Ngog Chung Shan Association)
Siu Geng-sum *(Xiao Jingxin)*
14 March of the 19th year of the Republic of China

Another person's remarks:
Transportation costs: 182.40 dollars
Labour and boat charges: 46.70 dollars
Balance: 130.90 dollars

東華醫院列位善長惠鑒頃接

雲南河口商會寄來函（并附憑單一張）稱於本年七月四日

附回^{亡弟}雷沛華遺骨一具托交廣州

廣仁善堂收轉給領并塟費二元着^弟

具領自行安塟者等由當即往詢廣仁善堂

詎知廣仁善堂早已停辦無法查領轉詢

諸方便醫院亦茫無頭緒據其當事者相告

云凡自雲南寄回廣東之一般遺骨其必

經香港由

貴院轉船運穗自來如此飭^弟函請

貴院查照办理云云用是函請

貴院究竟此事內容如何乞即

查明賜淰俾淂照行則存歿均感

大德於無既矣敬請

公安并希

示淰為盼

雷鯤池手啟（印章：雷鯤池章）

中華民國十九年七月廿一日

　　　寓廣州市泰康路五十四號三樓

Letter from Lui Kwan-chi, China, to Tung Wah Hospital on 21 July 1930

Dear benevolent Directors of Tung Wah Hospital,

I received a letter from Wan Nam Ho Hou Merchant Association *(Yunnan Hekou Shanghui)* (with receipt enclosed) which stated that the remains of my late brother Lui Pui-wah (*Lei Peihua*) had been handed over to Kwong Yan Sin Tong *(Guang Ren Shan Tang)* in Canton *(Guangzhou)* on 4 July this year, along with burial fees of 2 dollars. I was told to collect my brother's remains for burial.

I immediately went to Kwong Yan Sin Tong only to find that it had ceased operation for quite some time, and I could not claim my brother's remains. I checked with various Fong Bin Hospitals *(Fang Bian Yiyuan)* and they could not provide me with any information either. The managers told me that all remains repatriated from Wan Nam to Kwangtung *(Guangdong)* passed through Hong Kong, and your esteemed hospital would transport them to Canton by boat. They advised me to check with you. Therefore, I write to seek your help in investigating the matter. Please reply to me with any information you may have so that I can follow up.

My late brother and my family will forever be grateful to you for your kindness.

I wish you well and await your reply.

Yours sincerely,
Lui Kwan-chi (*Lei Kunchi*)
(Stamp: Lui Kwan-chi)

21 July of the 19th year of the Republic of China

From 3/F, 54 Tai Hong Road *(Taikang Lu)*, Canton

268 香港泰安棧長記致東華醫院信件

1932 年 6 月 29 日

民國庚午十九年弍月廿三日支兩次士担共八仙

旅鄂中山會館運柩如下
　　東華醫院款壹佰八拾元左右
　　着滙囬漢口旅鄂中山會館未交
　　今經蕭鏡心經理人囬來問此款項

東華醫院主任先生鑒

壬申五月廿六日（印章：香港中環泰安棧長記書柬）字

Letter from Tai On Chan Cheung Kee, Hong Kong, to Tung Wah Hospital on 29 June 1932

Two stamps of 8 cents bought on the 23rd day of the 2nd lunar month, Year of Gang Ng *(Gengwu)* (19th year of the Republic of China, 1930)

Dear Managers of Tung Wah Hospital,

Some coffins were repatriated by Lui Ngog Chung Shan Association *(Lu E Zhongshan Huiguan)*.

Approximately 180 dollars should be sent to Lui Ngog Chung Shan Association at Hon Hau *(Hankou)* by Tung Wah Hospital but the funds had not been received yet. We now ask our agent, Siu Geng-sum *(Xiao Jingxin)*, to inquire about the funds.

Yours sincerely,
26th day of the 5th lunar month, Year of Yam San *(Renshen)*
(Stamp: Tai On Chan Cheung Kee, Central, Hong Kong)

東華醫院善長鈞鑒敬啓者兹有先父
　　盧俊文靈柩一具係在　貴院身故終
　　扵本月廿六日今拟將該柩搭夜輪上省
　　到河南起岸安葬伏祈
　　貴院轉求
　　廣済醫院代為報關保領至起岸手
　　續如何指示一切實為
　　德便之至專此并矣

善安
　　　　壬申年六月廿七

　　　　　　　　　　　　　　　　　　弟盧瑞廷拜啓
　　　　　　　　　　　（印章：香港中環聯昌號書柬）租卑利街十二号

Letter from Lo Shui-ting, Hong Kong, to Tung Wah Hospital on 30 July 1932

Dear benevolent Directors of Tung Wah Hospital,

My late father, Lo Chun-man *(Lu Junwen)*, passed away in your esteemed hospital on the 26th day this month. I would like to have his coffin repatriated to Ho Nam *(Henan)* through Canton *(Guangzhou)* by boat in the evening. Please help ask Kwong Chai Hospital *(Guangji Yiyuan)* in Canton to handle customs clearance for my late father's remains. Please also advise the repatriation procedures, from collection of the remains to unloading.

I am most grateful to you for your benevolence.

I wish you well.

Yours humbly,
Lo Shui-ting *(Lu Ruiting)*
(Stamp: Luen Cheong Ho, Central, Hong Kong) 12 Jubilee Street

27th day of the 6th lunar month, Year of Yam San *(Renshen)*

270 香港福壽殯儀致東華醫院信件

1932 年 9 月 10 日

敬啓者茲有先友張振佳因老咳成病在本
港身故運回廣州省城安葬担保人店啟
泰源在高陞街報運人張柏何養桥船名民興船
牌五〇五七號懇求函知廣済醫院代為報關俾
得放行实為德便此上

東華醫院
列位先生均鑒

壬八月初十日（印章：福壽書柬）

Letter from Fook Sau Funeral Service, Hong Kong, to Tung Wah Hospital on 10 September 1932

Dear Managers of Tung Wah Hospital,

Cheung Chun-kai *(Zhang Zhenjia)* died of chronic respiratory disease in Hong Kong. His remains will be repatriated to Canton *(Guangzhou)* for burial. The guarantor, Kai Tai Yuen, is located in Ko Shing Street. The shippers are Cheung Pak *(Zhang Bo)* and Ho Yeung-kiu *(He Yangqiao)* and the remains will be carried on the *Man Hing* with registration number 5057. Please inform Kwong Chai Hospital *(Guangji Yiyuan)* to handle the customs clearance with the above information.

Thank you very much for your efforts.

Yours sincerely,
10th day of the 8th lunar month, Year of Yam San *(Renshen)*
(Stamp: Fook Sau Funeral Service)

敬啟者茲有先友黃氏群因咳症病在本港
　身故運囬廣州省城安葬担保店熾記在
　保良新街报運人張佳^弟黃輝船名民
　興船牌五〇五七號懇求函知廣濟醫院代為
　报關俾淂放行实為德便此上

東華醫院
列位先生^{均鑒}

　　　　　　　　　　　　　　壬八月初十日（印章：福壽書柬）

Letter from Fook Sau Funeral Service, Hong Kong, to Tung Wah Hospital on 10 September 1932

271

Dear Managers of Tung Wah Hospital,

Mrs Wong Kwan *(Huang Qun)* died of respiratory disease in Hong Kong. Her remains will be repatriated to Canton *(Guangzhou)* for burial. The guarantor, Chee Kee, is located in New Street. The shippers are Cheung Kai *(Zhang Jia)* and me, Wong Fai *(Huang Hui)* and the remains will be carried on the *Man Hing* with registration number 5057. Please inform Kwong Chai Hospital *(Guangji Yiyua*n) to handle the customs clearance with the above information.

Thank you very much for your efforts.

Yours sincerely,
10th day of the 8th lunar month, Year of Yam San *(Renshen)*
(Stamp: Fook Sau Funeral Service)

272 香港福壽殯儀致東華醫院信件

1932 年 9 月 10 日

敬啓者茲有先友陳明因咳病在本港身
故今運回廣州省城安葬担保店織記号
在保良新街报運人黃叔陳益船名民興船牌五〇五七号
懇求函知廣济醫院代為報關俾得放
行实為德便此上

東華醫院
列位先生均鑒

壬八月初十日（印章：福壽書柬）

Letter from Fook Sau Funeral Service, Hong Kong, to Tung Wah Hospital on 10 September 1932

Dear Managers of Tung Wah Hospital,

Chan Ming *(Chen Ming)* died of respiratory disease in Hong Kong. His remains will be repatriated to Canton *(Guangzhou)* for burial. The guarantor, Chee Kee, is located in New Street. The shippers are Wong Shuk *(Huang Shu)* and Chan Yik *(Chen Yi)* and the remains will be carried on the *Man Hing* with registration number 5057. Please inform Kwong Chai Hospital *(Guangji Yiyuan)* to handle the customs clearance with the above information.

Thank you very much for your efforts.

Yours sincerely,
10th day of the 8th lunar month, Year of Yam San *(Renshen)*
(Stamp: Fook Sau Funeral Service)

建發機器船澳有限公司

東華醫院

陳主席先生台鑒啟者先父徐炳南逝世後靈
　柩寄寓東華醫院義庄本擬覓地在本港新
　界安葬後因罷工風潮發生生意不前各兄弟東
　奔西走各自謀生鄉中雖有產業惟須各兄弟齐集
　簽字方能变賣似此因循負担更巨現擬於是年重陽
　節將先父安葬但積欠義庄庄租達壹千捌百餘元如
　此巨欵無法籌錯特託黃克競公將实在情形轉達
　台端懇求將庄租盡力減少則沒存均感矣耑此即候

時安

中華民國廿一年十月四日

弟徐周謹上

Letter from Chui Chow-kan, Hong Kong, to Tung Wah Hospital on 4 October 1932

273

From the Office of Kin Fat Machinery and Shipyard Company Limited

Dear Chairman Chan of Tung Wah Hospital,

After my father Chui Bing-nam *(Xu Bingnan)* passed way, his remains were temporarily placed in Tung Wah Coffin Home. We had intended to lay him to rest in the New Territories. However, due to the strike, our family business went downhill and my brothers and I tried to make a living in different places. Although we have family properties in our hometown, all of us have to gather and sign the documents in order to sell them. If we make arrangement for this, our burden becomes even heavier. I now hope to bury my father on Chung Yeung Festival this year, but we owe the Coffin Home a rental fee of more than 1,800 dollars. Since I cannot come up with such a large sum of money, I have asked Mr Haking Wong to tell you my situation, in the hope that you can reduce the rent as much as possible. My late father and I shall be most grateful to you for your kindness.

I wish you well.

Yours humbly,
Chui Chow-kan *(Xu Zhoujin)*

4 October of the 21st year of the Republic of China

274 香港馬煒譜致東華醫院信件

1933 年 3 月 25 日

東華醫院

列位善長仁翁鈞鑒敬啟者未同而言其色赧

赧仲氏子曾譏之矣^僕於各

善長素未識荊何敢無端請託惟念慈善為懷濟死

濟生仁恩廣被見善勇為夙所欽佩因不揣顓蒙

謬作微生之乞茲有馬耀者^僕同姓昆弟也前在港病

故停柩於東華義庄迄今歷有七年矣人念故鄉鬼思

故土理想當然蜀帝寄吳尤思親昭君葬胡常思漢

^僕憐馬耀遊魂無依擬作運柩還鄉之想第積欠庄費

數十元加以運柩費營葬費為數甚鉅^僕一介寒士力小任

重是用隱憂迫得函達

台端乞破格施　恩減收庄費倘允如所請^僕當備洋蚨拾

元停庄紙一張統為獻上伏乞早日執行俾庄地不至阻碍

魂魄得返家鄉真歿存均感矣昔范式送喪姬昌埋骨

古人行善澤及枯骸諸

善長何多讓焉如何之處希為示復^僕寓中環德忌笠街

三十號二樓

尊函照寄可也耑此順請

善安諸維

霽照不備

^僕馬煒譜上言

（印章：煒譜學校書束）

中華民國廿二年三月廿五日

另一人註：已復 不能減

Letter from Ma Wai-po, Hong Kong, to Tung Wah Hospital on 25 March 1933

Dear benevolent Directors of Tung Wah Hospital,

I am blushing with shame as I write this letter. I have never met your good selves before. How can I ask for your help? Yet since I have long heard of your far-reaching benevolence, I venture to seek your help.

My friend Ma Yiu *(Ma Yao)* died of illness in Hong Kong. We share the same last name and he was like a younger brother of me. His remains have been placed in Tung Wah Coffin Home for seven years. It is natural for man to miss his hometown and the spirits long to find eternal peace in the home soil. I pity on Ma Yiu's unsettling soul and would like to repatriate his remains to his hometown for burial. However, I cannot afford to pay back the accumulated coffin home rent for several dozen dollars, nor could I afford to pay the costly transportation and burial fees of the coffin. Therefore, I beg your exceptional kindness to reduce the rent. If you could accept my request, I will send 10 dollars and the coffin deposit certificate to you, so that the remains of the deceased can be repatriated to his hometown for burial as soon as possible and the storage space can be made avaitable for others. Both the living and the deceased shall be grateful to you for your great kindness.

Please reply to me at 2/F, 30 D'Aguilar Street, Central.

I wish you well.

Yours humbly,
Ma Wai-po *(Ma Weipu)*
(Stamp: Wai Po School)

25 March of the 22nd year of the Republic of China

Another person's remarks: Replied, rent cannot be reduced

275 中國北海市廣仁善社致東華醫院信件
1933 年 9 月 14 日

敬啓者現^{敝堂}是年係運先友骸壜之期茲議
繞道由港轉省敬浼　貴院代為轉運弟未
知肯為代勞否想　貴院慈善為懷澤及
枯骨諒毋見却可否之處乞即示聞俾得
僱輪照運前來可也餘未別陈肅此敬頌

公安

東華醫院
列位善長

（印章：北海市廣仁善社書柬）

中華民國廿二年九月十四日

Letter from Kwong Yan Sin Sei, Pek Hoi, China, to Tung Wah Hospital on 14 September 1933

Dear benevolent Directors of Tung Wah Hospital,

It is time to arrange for the repatriation of the remains of our deceased friends to their hometown this year and we decided to take an indirect route to send them back through Hong Kong. Would you please advise if your esteemed hospital could help send the remains to Canton *(Guangzhou)*? Your benevolence is known far and wide. Your care extend to the deceased so we trust you will not decline our request. Please notify us if you can help repatriate the remains, and we will hire a ship to take the remains to Hong Kong.

We are most grateful to you for your kindness.

We wish you well.

Yours sincerely,
(Stamp: Kwong Yan Sin Sei, Pek Hoi) *(Guangren Shanshe, Beihai)*

14 September of the 22nd year of the Republic of China

276 香港大來洋行辦房致東華醫院信件
1933 年 9 月 26 日

東華醫院
列位總理先生　均鑒逕啓者前日　貴院發交

　　　敝公司林肯總統船之緣部現查該部經已遺

　　失用特來函奉及請由　貴院另發給緣部壹本

　　即着　貴□於今日送落船可也手此即頌

善安

廿二年九月廿六號

　　　　　　　　　　　　　弟（印章：香港大來洋行辦房書柬）謹啓

Letter from the Comprador's Office of Robert Dollar & Co., Hong Kong, to Tung Wah Hospital on 26 September 1933

Dear Directors of Tung Wah Hospital,

With regard to the donation registry for the *SS President Lincoln* which you sent to us earlier on, we have investigated the matter and found that the registry is lost. I, hereby, write to notify you of this. Please be kind enough to issue a new registry to us and deliver it on board today.

Thank you very much for your assistance. I wish you well.

Yours sincerely,
(Stamp: Comprador's Office of Robert Dollar & Co., Hong Kong)

26 September of the 22nd year of the Republic of China

277 中國北海廣仁善社致東華醫院信件

1933 年 10 月 21 日

敬啓者前月奉呈草函諒邀　台覽未　蒙示覆

現因^{敝社}是年係運先友骸壜之期茲議繞道

由港轉省各鄉等處敬浼　貴院代為轉運

弟未知肯否想　貴院慈善為懷澤及枯骨

諒毋見却可否之處乞即示聞俾得僱輪照運

前來可也餘未別陳肅此敬頌

公安

東華醫院
列位善長^{鈞電}

（印章：北海市廣仁善社書柬）

中華民國廿二年十月廿一日

另一人註：起程請先行通知在港覓定商店担保領囘運費並請列明先友姓名地址及運往何
處

Letter from Kwong Yan Sin Sei, Pek Hoi, China, to Tung Wah Hospital on 21 October 1933

Dear Directors of Tung Wah Hospital,

We wrote to you earlier seeking your help, but have yet to hear from you.

It is time we repatriate the remains of our deceased friends to their hometown this year. We plan to send them to various townships of Canton *(Guangzhou)* through Hong Kong instead of sending them from here direct. We would like to ask if you could help send the remains from Hong Kong to the hometown. Your benevolence is known far and wide. Your care extend to deceased so we trust you will not decline our request. Please notify us if you can help repatriate the remains. If you can, we will hire a ship to take the remains to Hong Kong.

We are most grateful to you for your kindness.

We wish you well.

Yours sincerely,
(Stamp: Kwong Yan Sin Sei, Pek Hoi)*(Beihai)*

21 October of the 22nd year of the Republic of China

Another person's remarks: Before repatriation, it is necessary to provide the name of a shop in Hong Kong that can act as guarantor for the transportation fees. The name and address of the deceased as well as where the remains should be delivered to have to be specified.

粵港達美電機織造廠香港總廠用箋

公啓者 茲有陸尹卿灵柩六十二歲南海人
商由福州啓興隆托廣東義庄招運至
港 貴院收轉省方便醫院交省光復路啓興
隆收請求 貴院于抵步时查照收轉為
荷此上

東華醫院
大總理 鈞鑒

（印章：粵港達美織造廠香港總廠緘）呈

中華民國廿弍年十弍月廿弍日

Letter from Hong Kong-Canton Tat May Weaving Factory, Hong Kong, to Tung Wah Hospital on 22 December 1933

From the Office of Hong Kong-Canton Tat May Weaving Factory

Dear Directors of Tung Wah Hospital,

The coffin of Luk Wan-hing *(Lu Yinqing)*, a native of Nam Hoi *(Nanhai)* who passed away at the age of 62, has been sent to your esteemed hospital by Kwangtung Coffin Home, commissioned by Kai Hing Lung *(Qi Xing Long)* in Fook Chow *(Fuzhou)*. Please check and take delivery of the coffin when it arrives in Hong Kong and send it to Kai Hing Lung on Kwong Fook Road *(Guangfu Lu)*, Canton *(Guangzhou)* through Fong Bin Hospital *(Fangbian Yiyuan)*.

Thank you very much for your assistance.

Yours sincerely,
(Stamp: Hong Kong Headquarters of Hong Kong-Canton Tat May Weaving Factory)

22 December of the 22nd year of the Republic of China

潤安祥豬油廠
YUN ON CHEUNG LARD FACTORY

逕啓者前於壬申年五月有^{先妻}佘
唐氏靈柩壹具寄存　貴院義庄丙寅
三楼第壹壹叁號茲擬於本月念九日
遷運下柵本鄉安葬惟路經澳門須
經过境手續鄙人以對於澳門人地生
疎殊感隔膜敢請　貴院轉函該處
鏡湖醫院代辦一切应有手續以利進行
實為德便此懇

東華醫院
貴總理先生

佘伯才上
（印章：香港潤安祥豬油莊書柬）

中華民國甲戌年正月念四日

Letter from Yun On Cheung Lard Factory, Hong Kong, to Tung Wah Hospital on 9 March 1934

From the Office of Yun On Cheung Lard Factory, Hong Kong

Dear Directors of Tung Wah Hospital,

The coffin of my late wife, Madam Shea-Tong, was placed in the coffin home of your esteemed hospital, at No. 113, 3/F of Bing Yan Hall, in the 5th lunar month of the Year of Yam San *(Renshen)*. Her remains will be repatriated to our hometown for burial on the 29th day of this month, but they will need to pass through the customs of Macau. I am not familiar with Macau, can you please write to Kiang Wu Hospital in Macau and ask them to handle the matter for me?

I am most grateful to you for your kindness.

Yours sincerely,
Shea Pak-choi *(She Bocai)*

(Stamp: Yun On Cheung Lard Factory, Hong Kong)

24th day of the 1st lunar month, Year of Gaap Seot *(Jiaxu)*

中國瓊州海口海南醫院致東華醫院信件

1934 年 6 月 30 日

瓊州海口海南醫院用箋

逕啟者茲有梁炳坤靈柩一具由瓊州海口運囬香
港轉至廣州小欖鎮抵港時煩請
貴院代為照料一切為荷此致

東華醫院

海口 海南醫院啓
弟 陳昌運

中華民國二十三年六月卅日
（印章：海口海南醫院圖印）

Letter from of Hoi Nam Hospital, Hoi Hau, King Chau, China, to Tung Wah Hospital on 30 June 1934

From the Office of Hoi Nam Hospital *(Hainan Yiyuan)*, Hoi Hau *(Haikou)*, King Chau *(Qiongzhou)*

Dear Tung Wah Hospital,

The coffin of Leung Bing-kwan *(Liang Bingkun)* has been repatriated from Hoi Hau, King Chau through Hong Kong for onward transportation to Siu Lam Town *(Xiaolan Zhen)*, Canton *(Guangzhou)*. When the coffin arrives in Hong Kong, please take it into your care.

Thank you very much for your assistance.

Yours sincerely,
Chan Cheong-wan *(Chen Changyun)*
Hoi Nam Hospital, Hoi Hau

30 June of the 23rd year of the Republic of China

(Stamp: Hoi Nam Hospital, Hoi Hau)

香港譚國安致東華醫院信件

1934 年 8 月 10 日

東華醫院賑房執事先生大鑒敬啓者^弟之家母
　譚黎氏（名黎靈枝）昨年十二月去世經於是月廿一日寄厝東
　華義庄寧字第一號一边每月庄租艮四元正斯时已交報效
　銀叁十元另先交首月租銀四元以上兩款由仁壽寿板店代
　交領囘收據惟以後所欠之庄租待至運柜返鄉定然交足
　便是^弟前居干諾道中六十二號四楼今經搬迁現居中環云咸
　街十三號三楼倘蒙　賜教按址寄來是幸此候

善安　　甲七月初一日

　　　　　　　　（印章：中環雲咸街十三號三樓自動電話叁一七八零號）
　　　　　　　　　　　　　　　　　　　　^弟譚國安頓

Letter from Tam Kwok-on, Hong Kong, to Tung Wah Hospital on 10 August 1934

Dear Account Manager of Tung Wah Hospital,

My mother, Madam Tam-Lai *(Tan-Li shi)*, maiden name Lai Ling-chi *(Li Lingzhi)*, passed away in December last year. On the 21st day of that month, her remains were placed on one side of No. 1, Ning Rooms of the Tung Wah Coffin Home. The rent was 4 dollars per month. I had donated 30 dollars to your hospital and paid the first month's rent of 4 dollars. The funds had been sent to you through Yan Sau Funeral Service which collected a receipt on my behalf. As to the rent I owe you since then, I will pay the amount in full when my mother's coffin is repatriated to our hometown.

My previous address was 4/F, 62 Connaught Road Central; I have now moved to 3/F, 13 Wyndham Street, Central. Please send your reply to me at this address.

I wish you well.

Yours humbly,
Tam Kwok-on *(Tan Guo'an)*

(Stamp: 3/F, 13 Wyndham Street, Central. Telephone 31780)

1st day of the 7th lunar month, Year of Gaap Seot *(Jiaxu)*

中國新會愛群善院致東華醫院信件

1934 年 9 月 30 日

東華大醫院總理暨

列位執事台鑒敬啓者敝院善董陸焯南君所開陸豪勝葵扇庄

向來貨運鎮江發售適去年五月間該庄店伴陳伯伊（新會城人）

在鎮染病身故現該庄將伯伊靈柩經由鎮付怡和公司吉和號

長江輪船運申轉港所有運柩一切手續已接據函報妥辦想該柩

不日運到

貴處素仰

貴醫院博愛為懷辦事完善用特具函佈達如先友陳伯伊靈柩

運到時務懇

貴執事妥為照料並希

賜發護照證書俾得轉運回籍歸葬用慰幽魂不勝感禱之至專

此並候

善安餘唯

荃照不備

（印章：廣東新會城內愛群善院）謹上

中華民國廿三年九月三十日

Letter from Oi Kwan Sin Yuen, Sun Wui, China, to Tung Wah Hospital on 30 September 1934

Dear Directors and Managers of Tung Wah Hospital,

Luk Ho Shing Palm Leaf Fan Shop *(Lu Haosheng Kuishan Zhuang)*, owned by our Director Luk Cheuk-nam *(Lu Zhuonan)*, used to ship its products to Chen Kong *(Zhenjiang)* for sale. In May last year, the shopkeeper Chan Pak-yee *(Chen Boyi)*, a native of Sun Wui City *(Xinhui Cheng)*, died of illness in Chen Kong. Now the shop is repatriating the coffin of Pak-yee on a ship of the Jardine, Matheson & Co. by way of Hong Kong. The necessary procedures have been completed and the coffin should arrive in Hong Kong soon.

We have long admired your benevolence and flawless actions and would like to seek your kind assistance in this matter. When the coffin of our deceased friend Chan Pak-yee arrives in Hong Kong, please take it into your care and issue a pass for the coffin to be repatriated to his hometown for burial. Your kindness will help the deceased find eternal peace. Thank you very much for your assistance.

We wish you well.

Yours sincerely,
(Stamp: Oi Kwan Sin Yuen, Sun Wui City, Kwangtung) *(Aiqun Shanyuan, Xinhui Cheng, Guangdong)*

30 September of the 23rd year of the Republic of China

283 中國新會愛群善院致東華醫院信件

1934 年 10 月 13 日

敬復者現奉

大函敬悉一切先友陳伯伊靈柩經蒙

貴院料理停厝義庄至深紉感敝院已轉飭該親屬赴港覓商店

蓋章擔保請領惟查伯伊後嗣幼穉港中又無相熟商店一時未

能前來覓保據該親屬苦請代為設法救濟情殊可憫用特具函

奉懇

貴院俯賜矜憐可否於

貴院下次有先友骨砠運到敝院時順將伯伊靈柩一併附回俾

簡手續至該柩附運一切費用當由敝院如數奉還想

貴院善與人同當邀曲允如何仍希

見復切盼切禱此致

香港東華醫院

執事先生台鑒

（印章：廣東新會城內愛群善院）謹啓

中華民國廿三年十月十三日

Letter from Oi Kwan Sin Yuen, Sun Wui, China, to Tung Wah Hospital on 13 October 1934

Dear Managers of Tung Wah Hospital,

Thank you for your letter informing us that the coffin of Chan Pak-yee *(Chan Boyi)* has been put under your care and placed in your coffin home. We are grateful to you and have asked the family of the deceased to go to Hong Kong and find a shop there to act as their guarantor for claiming the coffin. However, since the children of Pak-yee are quite young and they do not know any shops in Hong Kong, they are not able to go to Hong Kong to find a guarantor. The poor family beg for our help and we consider that the circumstances are unusual and they are pitiable. We hope you sympathize with the family and help them with the repatriation.

Is it possible to send Pak-yee's coffin to our association next time when the bones of other deceased friends are transported through your esteemed hospital to us? Our association will reimburse you for the transportation costs. Benevolence is for all. We hope you offer Pak-yee's family a helping hand.

We await your reply.

Yours sincerely,
(Stamp: Oi Kwan Sin Yuen, Sun Wui City, Kwangtung) *(Aiqun Shanyuan, Xinhui Cheng, Guangdong)*

13 October of the 23rd year of the Republic of China

284 香港仍昌和生藥行致東華醫院信件

1934年11月28日

仍昌和生藥行用箋
YING CHEONG WOO

東華大醫院
執事先生大鑒　逕啓者孔翰墀公之寄
櫬庄租由本年起不歸[敝號]負担
所欠之庄租請追問其承辦人孔憲炯君
該承辦人現寓「本港湾仔軒利詩道四百六拾七號
四樓」敬希知照辦理為荷專泐並頌

善釐

（印章：香港文咸東仍昌和奇記書柬）敬啓

甲戌年拾月廿弎日

Letter from Ying Cheong Woo, Hong Kong, to Tung Wah Hospital on 28 November 1934

From the Office of Ying Cheong Woo Herbal Shop, Hong Kong

Dear Managers of Tung Wah Hospital,

Please be informed that from this year onwards, our shop will not take responsibility for the rent of the remains of Hung Hon-chi *(Kong Hanchi)* in the coffin home. Please collect any outstanding payment from his undertaker, Hung Hin-kwing *(Kong Xianjiong)*, whose address is 4/F, 467 Hennessey Road, Wan Chai.

Please take note of the matter and follow up.

I wish you well.

Yours sincerely,
(Stamp: Ying Cheong Woo, Bonham Strand East, Hong Kong)

22nd day of the 10th lunar month, Year of Gaap Seot *(Jiaxu)*

箇舊天福昌用箋

東華醫院總理鈞鑒敬啓者茲因為^{先叔}楊秀峰早

年係在香港棄世彼時將靈柩借存在

東華貴義庄又有^{先嬸母}楊孫氏之靈柩一併均停在

貴義庄早年原有^{舍弟}楊孝修在港照料應交

貴義庄租銀想已照章呈繳近因一二年未接獲楊孝

修來函報及對於應繳 貴義庄之租銀曾否按月繳

清特函奉達煩

總理查照如按月繳清則已倘未繳清者請查明

示知自當照數呈繳至於^{先叔父}楊秀峯^{先嬸母}楊孫氏

兩付靈柩敬懇

總理轉飭東華義庄管理人妥為保存若有欠少租金

^{榮升}一律負擔甘認滙來繳清決不能欠少分毫諸事

叩

光容當後報餘事未詳專肅敬請

鈞安并請

東華醫院諸公 台安

楊榮升鞠躬

（印章：箇舊天福昌書束）

外批回示祈帶至雲南箇舊縣綠沖花街天福昌

錫號交楊榮升收

民國二十四年七月二十三日

另一人註：云南省

Letter from Tin Fook Cheong, Ku Kau, Wan Nam, China, to Tung Wah Hospital on 23 July 1935

From the Office of Tin Fook Cheong, Ku Kau, Wan Nam

Dear Directors of Tung Wah Hospital,

My late uncle, Yeung Sau-fung *(Yang Xiufeng)* passed away in Hong Kong, and his coffin was placed in the coffin home of your esteemed hospital along with that of my late aunt, Madam Yeung-Suen *(Yang-Sun Shi)*.

My younger brother, Yeung Hau-sau *(Yang Xiaoxiu)*, used to attend to this matter in Hong Kong. He should have paid the rent according to your rules and regulations. However, I have not heard from Yeung Hau-sau in the past one or two years and am therefore not sure if the rent has been paid up-to-date monthly. I hereby write to enquire about the matter. Please find out if all the rent has been paid. If there is any outstanding rent, please notify me of the amount and I will settle the payment accordingly.

As to the coffins of my late uncle Yeung Sau-fung and my late aunt Madam Yeung-Suen, please advise the caretaker of the Tung Wah Coffin Home to take good care of them. I will be responsible for all outstanding rent and settle the payment in full.

I await your reply and I wish you well.

Yours sincerely,
Yeung Wing-shing *(Yang Rongsheng)*
(Stamp: Tin Fook Cheong, Ku Kau) *(Tian Fu Chang, Gejiu)*

Please send your reply to Yeung Wing-shing, c/o Tin Fook Cheong Tin Shop, Luk Chung Fa Street *(Luchonghua Jie)*, Ku Kau County, Wan Nam *(Yunnan)*.

23 July of the 24th year of the Republic of China

Another person's remarks: Wan Nam Province

不知先友西歸地

旅港順德商務局用箋

東華醫院

列位總理均鑒徑啓者現聞^{敝邑}有先友

骨殖多具存貯東華義莊爰用函懇

列公飭司事人將所有順德籍之骸骨及大

棺全數開列姓名統交^{敝局}俾得尅日搭卦

笋艇運返大良寄厝懷遠義莊遍貼長紅招

其親屬就近領葬如逾期一年無人認領則

由懷遠義莊妥為編葬義地代為祭掃使千

里遺骸得歸故土魂兮有知定感

大德於靡既矣專此并敬

善安唯

照不宣

旅港順德商務局主席辛聖三上

己巳年五月十一日

Letter from Hong Kong Shun Tak Overseas Business Bureau to Tung Wah Hospital on 17 June 1929

From the Office of Hong Kong Shun Tak Overseas Business Bureau

Dear Directors of Tung Wah Hospital,

We are aware that the remains of a number of deceased friends of our county have been kept at Tung Wah Coffin Home. We therefore write to your good selves in the hope that you could ask the manager [of the coffin home] to compile a list of the names of all deceased native of Shun Tak (*Shunde*), whose bones or coffins have been placed with you, and send them to us, in order that we could make arrangements for the remains to be returned to Da Leung (*Daliang*) by boat in due course. The remains will be placed in Wai Yuen Coffin Home (*Huaiyuan Yizhuang*) and notices will be put up calling on the relatives of the deceased to claim the remains. If after one year the remains are still unclaimed, Wai Yuen Coffin Home will bury them in the free cemetery and make offerings to them. In this way, our deceased friends, once far away from home, could return to the hometown where they would not be desolate. The deceased will be grateful for your benevolent act.

With great respect and best wishes,

Yours sincerely,
Sun Shing-sam (*Xin Shengsan*), Chairman
Hong Kong Shun Tak Overseas Business Bureau

11ᵗʰ day of the 5ᵗʰ lunar month, Year of Gei Zi *(Jisi)*

287 香港天草堂致東華醫院信件

1929 年 7 月 22 日

敬啓者昨由法国皇后船運囬由^{小號}轉停

新庄大座梅宗民之靈柩今其親屬來

港闹棺驗看特字懇求　貴院發給人情

俾得凴字到庄開棺驗看是盼切祷并請

善安

東華医院

列位善長　　台鑒

己六月十八日

弟（印章：香港西環天草堂書束）字頓

另一人註：經文錦翁批準

Letter from Tin Cho Tong of Hong Kong
to Tung Wah Hospital on 22 July 1929

Dear benevolent Directors of Tung Wah Hospital,

Our company repatriated the coffin of Mui Chung-man *(Mei Zongmin)* on the *Empress of France*, and the coffin has been transferred to the new hall of your coffin home. The deceased's family is coming to Hong Kong to identify the remains. We write to request that when they arrive at the coffin home with a proof, please let them open the coffin and identify the remains. We hope you will consider our request.

I wish you well.

Yours humbly,
(Stamp: Tin Cho Tong) *(Tian Cao Tang)*

18th day of the 6th lunar month of 1929

Another person's remarks: Approved by Mr (LO) Man-kam

288 中國黃焯致東華醫院信件

1930年2月16日

裕華銀號用牋

東華院列位先生均鑒敬啓者頃接
大函拜悉一切蒙代查妥並無
黃植華之骨寄回料弟悞聞耳
勞查之事殊深銘感特此修
函奉謝專此並請

台祺

弟黃焯　頓

中華民國十九年弍月十六日

Letter from Wong Cheuk, China, to Tung Wah Hospital on 16 February 1930

Dear Directors of Tung Wah Hospital,

Thank you for your reply and your assistance in investigating the whereabouts of the bones of Wong Chik-wah (*Huang Zhihua*). I understand that the bones have not been repatriated. I must have been misinformed. I am very grateful to you for taking time to investigate the matter. I, hereby, write to extend my gratitude to you.

I wish you well.

Yours humbly,
Wong Cheuk (*Huang Zhuo*)

16 February of the 19th year of the Republic of China

289 中國前山福善堂收先友骨殖收據

1930年5月2日

茲收到
廣安船主楊泗由港俩運先友骨
殖共四十九具此據

前山福善堂發（印章：前山福善堂）

民國十九年夏曆四月初四日

Acknowledgement of receipt of remains issued by Fook Sin Tong of Chin Shan, China, on 2 May 1930

This is to acknowledge receipt of 49 sets of remains delivered by Yeung See (*Yang Si*), owner of the *Kwong On*, from Hong Kong.

Issued by,
Fook Sin Tong (*Fu Shan Tang*), Chin Shan *(Qianshan)*
(Stamp: Fook Sin Tong, Chin Shan)

4th day of the 4th lunar month of the 19th year of the Republic of China

東華醫院諸执事先生鈞鑒敬託者^弟為先父多年身故
　　　起見所对于遺骸尚未運囬家鄉安葬^弟甚為惆悵之至再
　　　思^{吾父}既終于異國者昔人所共悲以此如論之^弟豈無憾焉因此
　　　已決意循例將^{先父}之遺骸運囬　貴院轉交中山縣得都大
　　　牛溪朗鄉郑^{品復}式位兄長接收俾他覓吉地安葬以惠先父
　　　在天之灵惟^弟素知　貴执事之仗義施恩樂善為怀故敢
　　　以下情上達伏祈為^弟代勞幸勿見却則先人幸甚^弟銘感無
　　　忘也邇者^弟已並內夾之壹鎊送囬費用銀壹磅正伏祈照收
　　　為祷耑函奉達敬請

公安
　　　　再者先父名郑美容

　　　　　　　　　　　　　　　　　　　^弟郑望源頓首

一九三一年元月念八日

Letter from Cheng Mong-yuen to
Tung Wah Hospital on 28 January 1931

Dear Managers of Tung Wah Hospital,

My father passed away many years ago, but his remains had yet to be repatriated to our hometown for burial. I had been despondent about this. My father's death in a foreign country was indeed tragic and a big loss to me, so I decided that I should have his remains sent to my elder brothers Cheng Bun *(Zheng Pin)* and Cheng Fook *(Zheng Fu)* in Da Ngau Kai Long Township *(Niu Xilang Xiang)*, Tak Dou *(Dedou)* Chung Shan County *(Zhongshan Xian)* through your esteemed hospital. My brothers will lay our late father to rest in a plot of blessed land so that his spirit can be soothed.

Since I am well aware of your benevolence, I venture to seek your help in this matter. I hope you will not turn down my request. Both the deceased and I will forever be grateful for your kindness. I enclose 1 pound sterling to cover the costs of transportation. Please check.

I wish you well.

P.S. My late father's name is Cheng Mei-yung *(Zheng Meirong)*.

Yours humbly,
Cheng Mong-yuen *(Zheng Wangyuan)*

28 January 1931

291　中國何根楦致東華醫院信件

1932 年 7 月 9 日

東華醫院^{均鑒}
列位先生

^弟何根楦謹上（印章：九江廣運源書柬）

壬六月初六日

敬啓者日前得接　貴院五月廿四日發來大扎
內及^{先兄}何根耀之骨殖已經運到存在義庄
得悉之下实深銘感^弟理宜親自踵院領囬
安塟緣因些賤事未得果臨是以茲凟港馬
鄧汝兄到來領取見字祈將該骨殖交他帶
返^弟亦可得收矣至于盖章具領已求得香港
大有銀號請着該港馬到該号盖章便可得也
諸事有劳容當致謝謹此并請

均安

Letter from Ho Gun-huen, China, to Tung Wah Hospital on 9 July 1932

Dear Directors of Tung Wah Hospital,

I received a letter from your esteemed hospital, dated 24 May, with regard to the bones of my late elder brother Ho Gun-yiu *(He Genyao)*. I understand that the bones had been sent to the coffin home of your esteemed hospital, and am most grateful to you for taking them into your care. I intended to come and collect the bones and lay my late brother to rest in our hometown in person, but cannot make the trip due to personal matters. I have asked Tang Yu *(Deng Ru)* in Hong Kong to collect my brother's bones. Please hand over the bones to him and he will bring the bones back to me. I have also asked the Tai Yau Native Bank in Hong Kong as the guarantor. Please advise Tang Yu to obtain the necessary stamp from the bank.

Thank you very much for your efforts. I wish you well.

Yours sincerely,
Ho Gun-huen *(He Genxuan)*
(Stamp: From the Office of Kwong Wun Yuen *(Guang Yun Yuan)*, Kau Kong *(Jiujiang)*)

6th day of the 6th lunar month, Year of Yam San *(Renshen)*

香港駐港中山僑商會所致東華醫院信件

1934 年 5 月 5 日

駐港中山僑商會所用箋

東華醫院

執事先生大鑒敬啓者各埠運返先友骨殖属於

敝邑者共有若干具運葬費幾何何名何姓請即

逐一查明分別

示复以便具領運回原籍傳属安葬俾正丘首而慰

幽魂至為感禱專此并頌

台安

馬应彪

主席　杜澤文

程名譽

中華民國廿三年五月五日

Letter from Chung Shan Commercial Association of Hong Kong to Tung Wah Hospital on 5 May 1934

From the Office of Chung Shan Commercial Association of Hong Kong

Dear Managers of Tung Wah Hospital,

Of the remains repatriated from various cities, kindly notify us how many sets belong to deceased friends of our county. Please also let us know the amount of transportation and burial costs as well as the names of the deceased friends. I am grateful if you could investigate and provide us the information, so that we can collect the remains and send to the deceased's hometown for burial and let them rest in peace.

We are most grateful to you for your benevolence.

We wish you well.

Yours sincerely,
Ma Ying-biu *(Ma Yingbiao)*
To Chak-man *(Du Zewen)*,
Ching Ming-yu *(Cheng Mingyu)*
Chairmen

5 May of the 23rd year of the Republic of China

駐港中山僑商會所用箋

東華醫院
執事先生台鑒敬啓者頃蒙將各先友姓名及運
葬費等逐一列示遇會甚感
高誼惟其中工艇費一項不知出自何處何方徵收
收費是否一律抑或多寡不一各有參差內中有
註明免收者又何以故所列運葬費銀碼是實
數抑須尚待扣抵凡此諸端深愧未能了了爰將
原單繳請再加註釋並希查明先友譚帶係^敞
邑何鄉人士分別
示知俾得提出會議補助運費及招領安葬以
妥先靈瑣瑣瀆

神伏祈
鑑諒即頌
大安

　　　附繳原列先友姓名單一紙

　　　　　　　　　　　　　　　　　　馬应彪
　　　　　　　　　　　中山僑商會所主席杜澤文
　　　　　　　　　　　　　　　　　　程名譽

　　　　　　　　　　　中華民國廿三年五月十七日

Letter from Chung Shan Commercial Association of Hong Kong to Tung Wah Hospital on 17 May 1934

From the Office of Chung Shan Commercial Association of Hong Kong

Dear Managers of Tung Wah Hospital,

Thank you for sending us the list of deceased friends' names and native counties, as well as records of the transportation and burial fees. However, we are not sure what the item "transportation cost" is and who is going to settle the payment. We also have doubts on whether the same amount would be charged for each set of remains or different rates are applied. According to the remarks on the list, the charges are waived for the remains of some deceased friends. We would like to know the reasons for the exemption as well. Meanwhile, we don't know if the amount on the records reflects the actual transportation and burial fees or further adjustments will be made. We regret not being able to understand the full picture. Please make clarifications on the original list you previously sent to us. Also, please find out which township in our county our deceased friend Tam Tai *(Tan Dai)* belongs to.

Please reply to us with regard to these queries, and we will convene a meeting to discuss the subsidies for transportation and burial fees, and also the arrangements for remains collection and burial, so that the spirits of our deceased friends could be soothed.

Thank you very much for your understanding.

We wish you well.

We enclose your original list of deceased friends' names.

Yours sincerely,
Ma Ying-biu *(Ma Yingbiao)*
To Chak-man *(Du Zewen)*,
Ching Ming-yu *(Cheng Mingyu)*
Chairmen of Chung Shan Commercial Association of Hong Kong

17 May of the 23rd year of the Republic of China

294 中國黃梓相致東華醫院信件

1934 年 12 月 12 日

東華醫院列位先生大鑒敬啓者我
　　先父黃仁獲由紅毛付囬台山城
　　義庄不料庄錯號数付交于開平
　　城多勞有字示知于我奈因路
　　途隔遠故此達字到來懇請
　　列位　先生勞代轉付台山城
　　義庄取囬免至企望也並請

近安

　　如交到義庄勞字示知可也
　　地址台山都伏大綱郵政無悞

民國廿三年十一月初陸日　　　　　　　　　　　　黃梓相付

Letter from Wong Chi-sheung, China, to Tung Wah Hospital on 12 December 1934

Dear Directors of Tung Wah Hospital,

The remains of my late father, Wong Yan-wok *(Huang Renhuo)*, were supposed to be repatriated from abroad to the coffin home at Toi Shan *(Taishan)*, but they had been mistakenly sent to Hoi Ping *(Kaiping)*. Thank you for letting me know the situation. However since it is difficult for me to travel a long way to Hoi Ping, I venture to seek your help in sending my father's remains to the coffin home at Toi Shan, so that I can collect them as soon as possible.

I wish you well.

If you can send my father's remains to the coffin home, please write to me at Tai Kong Post Office *(Dagang Youzheng)*, Dou Fok *(Dufu)*, Toi Shan.

Yours sincerely,
Wong Chi-sheung *(Huang Zixiang)*

6th day of the 11th lunar month of the 23rd year of the Republic of China

箇舊天福昌用箋

冼總理鈞鑒頃奉

示書各情敬悉原為前函拜託懇請代查^{先叔}楊秀

峯^{先嬸}楊孫氏兩付靈柩前寄停在東華義庄壹

節承蒙調查確實方知自辛未年六月二十二日寄入

至乙亥年七月二十一日止共計伍拾個月該銀伍百元以限

壹月清繳奉命之下自當遵諭籌備趕一月期滙港

決不致遷延惟是辦廠營業錫礦現因正值淘洗礦砂

之際故籌款維艱緩後礦出照數滙來繳清誠恐稍

有耽延尚祈

總理通融寬限數月萬不致效前番^{舍弟}之拖延耳想

總理鴻度海量寬仁厚德諒能俯賜從寬殁存均感

實叨恩便餘事未詳專肅敬請

鈞安并請

東華醫院執事諸公^{台安}

（印章：箇舊天福昌書柬）楊榮升 覆

民國二十四年八月十七日

另一人書：已复

Letter from Tin Fook Cheong, Ku Kau, Wan Nam, China, to Tung Wah Hospital on 17 August 1935

From the Office of Tin Fook Cheong *(Tian Fu Chang)*, Ku Kau *(Gejiu)*

Dear Director Sin,

I wrote earlier to enquire about the coffins of my late uncle Yeung Sau-fung *(Yang Xiufeng)* and my late aunt Madam Yeung-Suen *(Yang-Sun Shi)*, which were temporarily placed in Tung Wah Coffin Home. After investigating the matter, you notified me that the rent for the 50 months from the 22nd day of the 6th lunar month in the Year of Sun Mei *(Xinwei)* to the 21st day of the 7th lunar month in the Year of Yuet Hoi *(Yihai)* totalled 500 dollars and demanded that I should pay the rent up to date within one month. I will certainly try my best to send the funds to Hong Kong before the one-month deadline. However, since we are currently washing the ore at the tin mine I operate, I do not have any extra money to pay at the moment. I will send the money right after the tin has been shipped, but payment may be slightly delayed. I would thus be very grateful if you extend the payment deadline by a few months. Please be assured that I have no intention to delay payment, as my younger brother did previously.

I have long heard about your generosity and benevolence and hope you would approve my request.

The deceased and the living are most grateful to you for your kindness.

I wish you well.

Yours sincerely,
Yeung Wing-sing *(Yang Rongsheng)*
(Stamp: From the Office of Tin Fook Cheong, Ku Kau)

17 August of the 24th year of the Republic of China

Another person's remarks: Replied

茲收到廣安船楊四交來先友
　　共陸拾具此據

民國廿四年拾月五日

（印章：開平百合開恩鄉約圖記）

Receipt from Hoi Ping Bak Hop Hoi Yan Rural Administration, China, to Tung Wah Hospital on 5 October 1935

This is to certify that we have received the bones of 60 deceased friends from the *Kwong On* by Yeung Sei *(Yang Si)*.

5 October of the 24th year of the Republic of China

(Stamp: Hoi Ping Bak Hop Hoi Yan Rural Administration) *(Kaiping Baihe Kai'en Xiangyue)*

297 中國中山福善堂致東華醫院信件

1935 年 10 月 13 日

前山福善堂用箋

東華醫院
列位執事先生大鑒逕復者
茲收周裔炳先友骨殖壹具為
未知交何鄉請煩查明該先友
何鄉人俾得通知該親屬到領
為要此請

善安

（印章：中山縣第五區福善堂緘）拜啟

中華民國廿四年十月十三日

Letter from Fook Sin Tong, Chung Shan, China, to Tung Wah Hospital on 13 October 1935

From the office of Fook Sin Tong *(Fu Shan Tang)*, Chin Shan *(Qianshan)*

Dear Managers of Tung Wah Hospital,

We received the bones of Chow Yui-bing *(Zhou Yibing)* but do not know to which village we should send them. Please check and notify us of the deceased's native village so that we can ask his family to claim the bones.

We wish you well.

Yours humbly,
(Stamp: Fook Sin Tong, Area No. 5, Chung Shan County)

13 October of the 24th year of the Republic of China

台山商會用箋

TOISHAN CHAMBER OF COMMERCE

東華醫院执事^鑒啓者^{敝會}交仁

壽艇具領之先友骨殖共二百八十具

懇即檢查該葬金運費彙送

來^{敝會}以便每具應得若干登

載招領告白幸勿延緩除禮拜

外每日十二句鐘送來便妥此請

善祺

司理黃月樵謹啓

（印章：香港台山商會書東）

中華民國廿四年十月廿三號

Letter from Toishan Chamber of Commerce, Hong Kong, to Tung Wah Hospital on 23 October 1935

From the Office of Toishan Chamber of Commerce, Hong Kong

Dear Managers of Tung Wah Hospital,

We asked Yan Sau Funeral Service to arrange a boat to collect 280 sets of bones from your esteemed hospital. Please check if burial and transportation fees are offered for the deceased's families and send the funds to us, so that we can put up notices to announce the amount of burial fees and inform the families of the deceased to claim the bones. Please take care of this matter at your earliest convenience. Our office is open for 12 hours a day except Sundays.

We wish you well.

Yours humbly,
Wong Yuet-chiu *(Huang Yueqiao)*
Manager
(Stamp: From the Office of Toishan Chamber of Commerce)

23 October of the 24th year of the Republic of China

中國曾興邦致東華醫院信件

1935 年 11 月 14 日

東華醫院列位大善長台鑒　敬啓者即日由廣安船
　　運來本鄉先友骨殖共壹拾九具經已照点收妥安
　　貯義塜內即日佈告鄉中該親屬人等速即領
　　回安塟歸土相安恕不多叙草此并覆

大安

　　　　　　　　　　　　　　　九江闔鄉義塚办事人曾興邦頓

乙十月十九早發

Letter from Tsang Hing-bong, China, to Tung Wah Hospital on 14 November 1935

Dear benevolent Directors of Tung Wah Hospital,

We have received in order the bones of 19 deceased friends of our township repatriated on the *Kwong On* and placed them in the communal graveyard. We will put up a notice in the township so that the deceased's families can claim the bones for burial as soon as possible.

Please take note of this.

We wish you well.

Yours sincerely,
Tsang Hing-bong *(Zeng Xingbang)*
Manager, Kau Kong Communal Graveyard *(Jiujiang Hexiang Yizhong)*

In the morning of the 19th day of the 10th lunar month, Year of Yuet Hoi *(Yihai)*

中國九江救濟院致東華醫院收據

1935 年 12 月 9 日

　　茲收到香港

東華醫院由四合船運囬骨殖壹拾壹箱此據（印章：救濟院）

民國二十四年　十二月九日

（印章：九江救濟院）收条

九江救濟院用牋

Receipt from Kau Kong Relief Shelter, China, to Tung Wah Hospital on 9 December 1935

This is to certify that we have received 11 boxes of bones sent by Tung Wah Hospital in Hong Kong on the *Sei Hop*. (Stamp: Relief Shelter)

(Stamp: Kau Kong Relief Shelter) *(Jiujiang Jiuji Yuan)* Receipt

9 December of the 24th year of the Republic of China

From the Office of Kau Kong Relief Shelter

詞彙表
Glossary

1. Names of Vessels（輪船名稱）

英文 / 外文 / 拼音	中文
Arafura	亞拿夫拿船
Ah-tung	亞東輪船
Bokuyo Maru	墨洋丸號
Canada	坎那大船
Changte	彰德輪 / 彰德船 / 章德輪船
Chichibu Maru	秩父丸
Empress of Asia	亞洲皇后船
Empress of Canada	加拿大皇后船
Empress of France	法國皇后船
Empress of Japan	日本皇后號
Empress of Russia	俄國皇后船
Guangxi	大廣西船
Guatemala	掘地孖礴船
Hinsang	顯生船
Kaitung	佳東輪船
Kitano Maru	北野丸
Kwong On	廣安船

（續表）

英文／外文／拼音	中文
Luk Gah	陸賈輪
Nankin	南京船
Santa Cecilia	散打舌司梨亞輪船
SS Delta	丹吔船／丹打船
SS Nellore	利羅船
SS President Adams	亞泵總統船／亞當斯總統船
SS President Adams	阿丹氏輪船／阿丹氏總統船／阿丹氏總統士
SS President Cleveland	克利夫蘭船／企李侖船
SS President Coolidge	哥列治總統船／固列芝總統船
SS President Fillmore	菲爾莫爾總統船
SS President Grant	加蘭總統船
SS President Harrison	夏利慎總統船
SS President Hoover	胡佛總統船
SS President Jackson	積臣船
SS President Lincoln	林肯船／林肯總統船
SS President McKinley	麥乾尼總統船／麥項尼總統船／麥堅尼輪
SS President Monroe	門羅總統船
SS President Pierce	普利市總統船／丕亞士總統船／波市總統船／鄙市總統船
SS President Polk	朴總統輪船
SS President Taft	他輔總統船
SS Taiping	太平輪船／太平輪
SS Tanda	天打輪船
Venezuela	委內瑞拉船

2. Names of Places, Organizations & Others（地名、機構及其他名稱）

英文／外文／拼音	中文
Auckland, New Zealand	紐絲綸托綸埠（新西蘭奧克蘭）
Australia	新金山（澳洲）
Bak Hop Market Town *(Baihe Xu)*	百合墟
Batu Pahat, Malaysia	馬來西亞峇都巴轄（馬來西亞峇株巴轄）
Bluefields, Nicaragua	尼架拉瓜國步路飛埠（尼加拉瓜布盧菲爾茲）
Bo Sin Tong *(Bao Shan Tang)*, Sun Tong Market Town *(Xintang Xu)*	新塘圩寶善堂
Bone Repatriation Office of Kwong Sin Tong, Tonkin, Vietnam	越南東京廣善堂運先友辦事所
Brisbane, Australia	庇厘時彬／庇厘時浜／庇李士彬埠（布里斯本）
Bureau Cimetiére de Canton	穗義祠辦事所／穗義祠
Canadian Pacific Steamship Company	詩丕亞公司輪船
Canton *(Guangzhou)*	廣州
Carins, Australia	澳洲堅時埠（澳洲凱恩斯）
Casino Chung Wah, Cuba	古巴中華總會館
Cheong Shing Tong *(Chang Shan Tang)*	昌善堂
Chan Hung Kee	陳洪記
Chang Weng Chun Tong, Habana, Cuba	古巴灣城陳潁川堂／古巴灣城陳潁川總堂／古巴灣城陳潁川總堂慈善會
Chap Sin Tong *(Ji Shan Tang)*	集善堂
Chase National Bank	大通銀行（大通國家銀行）

英文／外文／拼音	中文
Chi Tack Tong	至德慈善會
Chin Shan Fok Sin Tong *(Fushantang, Qianshan)*	前山福善堂
China Navigation Company	太古船行
Chinese Club, Bluefields, Nicaragua	尼架拉瓜國步路飛埠中華會館（尼加拉瓜）
Chinese Consolidated Benevolent Association of Pittsburg	必珠卜中華會館
Chinese Consolidated Benevolent Association of Washington, DC, USA	美京中華公所
Chinese Consolidated Benevoment Association, New York	紐約中華公所
Chong How Tong *(Chang Hou Tang)*, Ko Tong Market Town *(Gaotang Xu)*, Pun Yu *(Pangyu)*	番禺高唐圩昌後堂
Chong Wa Benevolent Association, Seattle, USA	美國舍路中華會館
Christchurch, New Zealand	金山卡賴左治埠（新西蘭基督城）
Chui Yuen Tong *(Zhui Yuan Tang)*	追遠堂
Chung Shan Commercial Association of Hong Kong	駐港中山僑商會所
Chung Shan Tong *(Zhongshan Tang)*	中山堂
Chung Shan Yu Sin Tong *(Zhongshan Yu Shan Tang)*	中山與善堂
City West Ko Kong Fong Bin Hospital *(Chengxi Gao Gang Fangbian Yiyuan)*	城西高崗方便醫院
Club Wah Sion, Puntarenas	泮大連埠華商會館
Colonia China, Guatemala	旅中美洲掘地孖罅國華僑總會／瓜地瑪拉旅瓜華僑總會
Colusa, USA	美國高老砂埠（美國科盧薩）

英文 / 外文 / 拼音	中文
Comprador's Office of Robert Dollar & Co., Hong Kong	香港大來洋行辦房
Congregations Chinois, Turane, Annan	安南峴港中華僑務公所
Cooktown, Australia	谷當（澳洲庫克敦）
Costa Rica	葛大李架國（哥斯達黎加）
Dollar Shipping Company	大來輪船公司
Executive Committee of Yokow Tiong Hieng Woi, Sulu	蘇洛粵僑同鄉執行委員會
Fook Sau Funeral Service	福壽
Fook Sin Tong (Fu Shan Tang)	福善堂
Fresno, USA	美國飛枝梳活埠（美國弗雷斯諾）
Fu Mun Tai Ping Po Sin Tong (Humen Taiping Pu Shan Tang)	虎門太平溥善堂
Geelong, Australia	澳洲芝葛埠（澳洲吉朗）
General Chamber of Commerce & Industry of the Tung Kun District in Hong Kong	駐港東莞工商總會
Ging Yuk Tong (Jin Yu Tang)	矜育堂
Greymare, Queensland, Australia	澳洲昆時欄省加剌孖剌埠
Guatemala	掘地孖喇國 / 掘地孖罅國 / 瓜地孖罅國 / 和地孖罅 / 瓜地馬拉（危地馬拉）
Hang Chun Tong, Dik Hoi (Dihai Xing Chun Tang)	荻海杏春堂
Havana/Habana	夏灣拿 / 亞灣拿 / 灣城 / 亞灣（哈瓦那 / 夏灣拿）
Hing Yin Society (Xingxian She)	興賢社
Hoi Men Kung Po	開明公報

英文 / 外文 / 拼音	中文
Hoi Ping Bak Hop Hoi Yan Village Administration *(Kaiping Baihe Kai'en Xiangyue)*	開平百合開恩鄉約
Hoi Ping Commercial Chamber	駐港開平商務公所
Hoi Yan Kwong Fook Tong	開恩廣福堂
Hok Shan Chamber of Commerce in Hong Kong	旅港鶴山商會
Hong Fook Tong Society, Victoria, Canada	加拿大域多利同福堂
Hong Kong Hok Shan Commercial Association	旅港鶴山商會
Hong Kong Shun Tak Overseas Business Bureau	旅港順德商務局
Hong Kong Toi Shan Association	香港台山商會
Hong Kong-Canton Tat May Weaving Factory	香港粵港達美織造廠
Hop Wo Benevolent Association, San Francisco	金山正埠合和總會館
Hoy Sun Ning Yung Benevolent Association Head Office	台山甯陽總會館
Hoy Sun Ning Yung Benevolent Association Head Office, Victoria, Canada	加拿大域多利台山甯陽總會館
Hoy Sun Ning Yung Benevolent Association In America	駐美洲台山甯陽總會館
Jerantut, Pahang, F. M. S.	英屬嘜哼宜蘭突（馬來西亞彭亨而連突）
Jose Yuan Y Cia, Mexico	墨國關海公司
Kiang Wu Hospital, Macau	澳門鏡湖醫院
Kong Yee Tong, Brisbane	庇厘時浜東邑公義堂
Kwang Tung Association, Nagasaki	長崎廣東會所
Kwangtung *(Guangdong)*	廣東
Kwangtung Weaving Factory *(Guangdong Fangzhi Chang)*	廣東紡織廠
Kwong Chai Hospital *(Guangji Yiyuan)*	廣濟醫院

（續表）

英文 / 外文 / 拼音	中文
Kwong Chow Association, San Francisco	金山大埠岡州會館
Kwong Chow Association, San Francisco	金山大埠岡州總會館
Kwong Siew Villa, Siam	暹羅廣肇別墅（泰國）
Kwong Sin Tong, Tonkin, Vietnam	越南東京華僑廣善堂
Kwong Siu Benevolent Association, Havana, Cuba	古巴旅古京廣肇慈善會
Kwong Siew Association, Siam	暹羅廣肇會館 / 暹京廣肇會館
Kwong Siu Clinic, Siam	暹羅廣肇醫局
Kwong Siu Hospital, Bangkok	暹羅廣肇醫院
Kwong Tong Cemetery, Kuala Lumpur	吉隆玻廣東義山
Kwong Wo Fung Gold Mountain Firm	廣和豐金山莊
Kwong Yan Sin Sei	廣仁善社
Kwong Yan Tong, Hoi An, Da Hang, Vietnam	會安峴港廣仁堂（越南）
Kwu Tseng Tat Sin Tong	古井達善堂
La Paz, Mexico	墨國粒巴士（墨西哥拉巴斯）
Lam Sam Yik Tong (Nin San Yi Tang)	林三益堂
Lao Yi Chiang Lay Sol	羅豫章旅所慈善會
Lao Yi Chiang Lay Sol Benevolent Association of Havana	古巴灣城羅豫章旅所慈善會
Long Sai Li Benevolent Association, Cuba	古巴隴西慈善會 / 古巴灣城李隴西慈善會
Long Sai Li Merchants Autonomy Learning Office, Cuba	古巴隴西商旅自治講習所
Long Sai Li Merchants Autonomy Learning Office, Habana, Cuba	古巴灣京隴西商旅自治講習所
Luen Fook Tong, Sydney, Australia	澳洲悉尼增城聯福堂
Lung Do Chung Sin Tong, Hawaii	檀香山隆都從善堂
Man Bo Wah Ho	萬寶華號

（續表）

英文 / 外文 / 拼音	中文
Man Sin Tong (Wan Shan Tang)	萬善堂
Maryborough, Australia	澳洲美利澳埠（澳洲瑪麗伯勒）
Melbourne	新山正埠／尾利畔埠（墨爾本）
Ming Shun Native Bank (Mingxin Yinhao)	明信銀號
Mui Chow Ying Fook Tong, San Francisco	三藩市梅州屬應福堂
New South Wales, Australia,	鳥修威祖密埠（澳洲新南威爾士）
New York Chinese Cheung Sang Funeral Corporation Ltd.	紐約中華長生有限公司
Nicaragua	尼架拉瓜國（尼加拉瓜）
Ning Yeung Coffin Home (Ningyang Yizhuang)	寧陽義莊
Ning Young Yee Hing Tong of Victoria, Canada	加拿大域多利寧陽餘慶堂
Office of Rice for Charity of Hong Kong	香港慈善平糶義倉
Oi Kwan Sin Yuen (Aiqun Shanyuan)	愛群善院
Oi Sin Tong (Ai Shan Tang)	愛善堂
Oi Yuk Tong (Ai Yu Tang)	愛育堂
On Cheung Native Bank (Anxiang Yinhao)	安祥銀號
Penang	庇嘮埠（馬來西亞檳城）
Peninsula and Oriental Steam Navigation Company	鐵行公司
Po Tsai Clinic of Kwong Sin Tong (Guang Shan Tang Pu Ji Yiju)	廣善堂普濟醫局
Po Tsai Clinic of Kwong Sin Tong, Hanoi	越南東京海防廣善堂普濟醫局
Pon Yup Chong How Benevolent Association, San Francisco	金山番禺昌後堂
Puerto San Josè	散河些埠（瓜地馬拉聖荷西港）
Puntarenas	泮大連埠／泮大漣埠（蓬塔雷納斯）

英文/外文/拼音	中文
Quong Fook Tong Benevolent Association (San Francisco)	廣福堂（三藩市）
Quong Lee & Company, San Francisco, California	金山大埠廣利號
Saint Aubine Line	聖丫路濱船
Sam Shui Association *(Sanshui Gonghui)*	三水公會
Sam Yap Tung Sin Tong of Panama	巴拿馬三邑同善堂
Santa Barbara, USA	美國山地把罷埠（美國聖巴巴拉）
Say Jo Jon, Havana, Cuba	古巴灣城林西河堂
Seattle	舍路（美國西雅圖）
See Yap Association, New South Wales, Australia	澳洲鳥修威祖密埠四邑會館
Selangor, Nanyang	南洋雪蘭莪（馬來西亞雪蘭莪）
Siam (Thailand)	暹羅/暹京（泰國）
Sociedad Chung Sang Huy Cun	旅秘中山會館
Sociedad On Ten Tong	安定堂/安定堂自治所
Sonora, Mexico	墨國順省那卡利埠（墨西哥索諾拉州）
Sue Yuen Tong, Havana, Cuba	古巴灣城遡源總堂/古巴灣城遡源總堂慈善會
Sulu	蘇洛（菲律賓蘇祿）
Sun Wui Commercial Association of Hong Kong/ The San Wui Commercial Society, Hong Kong	僑港新會商會
Sze Yap Ming Sin Hospital *(Siyi Mingshan Yiyuan)*	四邑明善醫院
Tai Ping Po Sin Tong *(Taiping Pu Shan Tang)*	太平溥善堂
Tak Sin Tong *(De Shan Tang)*	德善堂
The Sze Yup Industrial and Commercial Union of Hong Kong	香港四邑商工總局
The United Chinese Association, USA	美國紐英崙中華公所

英文 / 外文 / 拼音	中文
Tin Cho Tong	天草堂
Toi Shan Association, Hong Kong/ Toishan Chamber of Commerce of Hong Kong	香港台山商會
Tonkin, Vietnam	越南東京（越南河內）
Townsville, Australia	澳洲湯時威靈埠（澳洲湯斯維爾）
Tsang Shing Tsang Yi Tong *(Zeng Yi Tang)*	增城增義堂 / 增義堂
Tsang Shing Yee On Association in America	旅美增城義安善堂
Tung Goon Bo On Association, San Francisco	金山大埠東莞寶安堂
Tung Sin Tong *(Tong Shan Tang)*, Hok Shan *(Heshan)*	鶴邑同善總堂
Tung Yee Tong *(Dong Yi Tang)*	東義堂
Union De Las Familias Lau	劉氏自治所
Vancouver	雲哥華埠 / 英國咸水埠 / 雲哥華（溫哥華）
Walla Walla, USA	美國抓李抓鑊埠
Wei Yuen Coffin Home *(Huaiyuan Yizhuang)*	懷遠義莊
Wo Fat Shing, Hong Kong	香港和發成
Wong Kong Har Tong of Colusa, USA	高老砂埠黃江夏堂
Wong Kong ja Tong, Nogales, Sonora, Mexico	墨西哥順省那卡利埠黃江夏分堂
Wong Kong Ja Tong, Habana, Cuba	古巴灣城黃江夏堂
Wong Kong Ja Tong Comision Beneficencia, Habana, Cuba	古巴灣城黃江夏堂慈善會
Wui Chun Yuen Coffin Home *(Huichunyuan Yizhuang)*	回春院義莊
Yam Yuen Tong *(Yin Yuan Tang)*	蔭遠堂
Yan Sau Funeral Service	仁壽 / 仁壽壽板店

英文 / 外文 / 拼音	中文
Yan Yuk Tong *(Ren Yu Tang)*/Yan Yuk Sin Tong *(Ran Yu Shan Tang)*	仁育堂 / 仁育善堂
Yee On Tong, Tsang Shing *(Yi An Tang)*	增邑義安堂
Yiu Men Chong Woy So Comision Beneficencia, Habana, Cuba	古巴灣城要明總會所慈善會
Yiu Ming Wui Ning Commercial Association	要明會寧工商局
Yokohama Chinese Association, Japan	日本橫濱中華會館
Yu Sin Tong *(Yu Shan Tang)*	與善堂
Yue Wah Native Bank	裕華銀號

東華三院文物館檔案

　　1870 年，香港第一間為華人而設的慈善機構東華醫院成立。箇中有兩個原因，一是當時華人領袖展現傳統中國文化中的慈善精神，另一是殖民地政府欲與東華醫院的董事局合作，加強與本地市民溝通。東華醫院逐步擴展，為市民和海外華人提供各類服務。在政府的支持下，東華其後成立廣華醫院及東華東院，三間醫院於 1931 年統一管理，是為東華三院。東華隨着歲月發展而成的環球慈善網絡與香港的政治、經濟和社會轉變密不可分，它的歷史也是香港史、中國史及一定程度上世界史的重要組成部分，因此記錄東華行事的檔案是獨特和非常珍貴的。為讓機構作內部參考和與公眾分享，東華一直致力保存及開發其檔案。

　　東華三院於 1970 年一百周年時成立東華三院文物館，收集、維護、研究和展示機構文化資產。文物館的館藏檔案來自各行政部門、服務單位、前任董事局成員、公眾人士及其他機構。類別包括徵信錄（早期年報）、東華與市民及政府的來往函件、董事局及小組委員會會議紀錄、期刊、印刷品、剪報、相片及紀念品等，現時保存最早的檔案是《1873 年東華醫院徵信錄》。

　　文物館館藏其中一項最重要的是東華義莊文獻。東華義莊成立於 1899 年，半個多世紀以來努力不懈地為在香港或海外去世的華人提供一項需求很大的服務；服務跨越時間和地域，為的是履行將棺骨運回家鄉安葬的重要中國傳統。今天，義莊留下的不單是特別的歷史建築，還有 234 項由 1910 至 1970 年代上萬頁的檔案，記錄華人透過很多人的慈善行為而最後得以落葉歸根的歷史，數量之多和內容之廣令人驚嘆。這批檔案包括來自世界各地組織和個人的函件、出入莊保證書、入莊申請書、暫存棺骨合約、棺骨登記冊、收據、接骨提單等。由於早期檔案已經消失，現存的紀錄格外珍貴。它們展現東華 19 世紀末至 20 世紀初在環球慈善網絡中舉足輕重的角色，所記錄的一段時期華人遷徙歷史緊扣香港和中國內地的發展。我們由此知道東華一方面與海外組織密切聯絡接收棺骨，暫存在東華義莊；另一方面聯絡亡者在內地或香港的親友或相關慈善組織安排領回，甚至不畏重重困難運送棺骨回鄉。檔案反映原籍安葬服務的獨特性和東華為華人服務的承擔。

文物館最新接收的檔案是 1,249 項廣華醫院的醫療紀錄。廣華醫院於 1911 年在九龍油麻地成立，是東華醫院的延伸。該批檔案包括第一本早至 1917 年的醫院總冊、1935 年開始的產房紀錄、死亡總冊及手術室紀錄。這是一個關於市民大眾的醫療資料群，這些人曾在廣華醫院享用中西醫療服務，大部分是免費的。檔案由 1917 年開始，直到 1991 年東華三院加入由香港政府成立的醫院管理局，讓屬下五間醫院的日常管理移交該局。檔案反映中西文化的衝突、政府和東華的合作和分歧以及香港醫療的發展。對於研究香港醫療史來說，這是很重要的資料。

現在，東華三院文物館的館藏檔案約 300 延米。東華三院於 2010 年成立檔案及歷史文化辦公室發展其歷史文化及於 2016 年成立一所檔案及文物中心存放及整理文化資產。我們的檔案會繼續增長，訴說中國人在香港及其他地域的故事。

The Tung Wah Museum Archives

In 1870, the Tung Wah Hospital, Hong Kong's first charitable organization for its Chinese population was founded, thanks to the inherent benevolence in the traditional Chinese culture demonstrated by the then Chinese leaders and the policy of the colonial government to work with the Board of Directors of Tung Wah Hospital in enhancing communication with the local community. The hospital expanded to provide various services for the local community and Chinese of other parts of the world. It was amalgamated with the Kwong Wah Hospital and Tung Wah Eastern Hospital which were also established by Tung Wah with Government support to form the Tung Wah Group of Hospitals in 1931. As the development of Tung Wah's global charitable network was inextricably linked with Hong Kong's political, economical and social changes, and its story is an important component of that of Hong Kong, China and to a certain extent the world, the archives recording its activities are unique and invaluable. Tung Wah is committed to preserving them for its own reference and public good.

The Tung Wah Group of Hospitals established the Tung Wah Museum in 1970, centenary of the Group, to collect, preserve, research and exhibit the cultural heritage of the Group. The archival collections of the Tung Wah Museum are formed by original documents either transferred or received from internal administrative departments, service centres, former Tung Wah Board Members, the general public and other organizations. The rich collections consist of *Zhengxinlu* (early annual reports), correspondences amongst Tung Wah, the public and the Government, board meetings and committee meetings minutes, journals, publications, news clippings, photos, souvenirs, etc. The earliest record preserved by the Museum is the *Zhengxinlu* of the Tung Wah Hospital in 1873.

One of the most important collections is the Tung Wah Coffin Home archives. Founded in 1899, the Tung Wah Coffin Home persevered to provide a much-needed service for people who died in Hong Kong or overseas for more than half a century. It fulfilled a significant Chinese burial tradition of repatriating remains to hometown beyond time and geographic boundaries. Today, in addition to the special historic buildings, the Tung Wah Coffin Home has passed down an archival collection of 234 items, in tens of thousands of pages dated from the 1910s to 1970s. The archives are awe-inspiring because they are of a large size and great variety focusing on the history of Chinese returning to the roots through acts of benevolence of many. There are letters sent to Tung Wah from Chinese organizations and individuals all over the world, coffin home guarantee certificates and application forms, temporary coffin depository contracts, coffins and bones registers, receipts and bills of lading for receiving remains. As most of the earliest archives are missing, the remaining records become extremely precious. The archives demonstrate Tung Wah's crucial role in the global Chinese charitable network in the late 19th and 20th century and depict the Chinese migration history of an era closely tied with the development of Hong Kong and China. From them, one could realize that Tung Wah on one hand developed close connections with overseas organizations to receive remains and provide them a temporary depository at the coffin home, and on the other hand contacted the deceased's families, friends or associate charitable organizations in Hong Kong or the mainland for them to claim the remains or even send the remains to the deceased's hometown despite immense difficulties. The archives speak of the uniqueness of the service and Tung Wah's commitment in serving Chinese.

The most recently acquired significant archival collection is 1,249 items of medical records of the Kwong Wah Hospital which was established in 1911 in Yaumatei of Kowloon as an extension of the Tung Wah Hospital. The collection contains hospital registries, the first one of which was in 1917, labor room records dated from 1935, death registries as well as operating theatre records. Together they form a medical heritage of ordinary people who enjoyed Chinese and Western medicine care in the Kwong Wah Hospital, mostly free of charge, for a period from 1917 to 1991 when Tung Wah joined the Hospital Authority established by the Hong Kong Government and handed over to it the daily management of its five hospitals. The archives reflect tension between the Chinese and Western cultures, collaboration and disagreement between the Government and Tung Wah as well as the development of medical care in Hong Kong. They are essential research materials for the academic study of Hong Kong's health care system.

At present, the quantity of the Tung Wah Museum archives is about 300 linear meters. With the establishment of the Records and Heritage Office in 2010 to look after Tung Wah's cultural heritage and an archives and relics centre in 2016 to house and manage the Group's cultural assets, the archives continue to grow and tell the stories of Chinese people in Hong Kong and beyond.

鳴 謝
Acknowledgement

本書得以順利出版，有賴各方人士一直以來的協助、支持及鼓勵，在此謹向下列個人及
單位致謝：

東華三院檔案及歷史文化委員會
五邑大學廣東僑鄉文化研究中心
譚金花博士
東華三院文物館義工團隊
譚福基先生

We are deeply indebted to the following individuals/group for their assistance, support and
encouragement in producing the book:

TWGHs Records and Heritage Committee
Guangdong Qiaoxiang Cultural Research Center, Wuyi University
Dr. TAN Jinhua
Tung Wah Museum Voluntary Workforce
Mr. TAM Fook-kei

□ 責任編輯：吳黎純
□ 裝幀設計：霍明志
□ 排　版：霍明志　陳先英
□ 協　力：林曉娜　李洛霖
□ 印　務：劉漢舉

落葉歸根
——東華三院華僑原籍安葬檔案選編

Fallen leaves returning to their roots:
A selection of archives on the bone repatriation service
of Tung Wah Group of Hospitals for overseas Chinese

□
編
東華三院檔案及歷史文化辦公室

□
出版
中華書局（香港）有限公司
香港北角英皇道 499 號北角工業大廈一樓 B
電話：（852）2137 2338　傳真：（852）2713 8202
電子郵件：info@chunghwabook.com.hk
網址：http://www.chunghwabook.com.hk

□
發行
香港聯合書刊物流有限公司
香港新界大埔汀麗路 36 號
中華商務印刷大廈 3 字樓
電話：（852）2150 2100　傳真：（852）2407 3062
電子郵件：info@suplogistics.com.hk

□
印刷
美雅印刷製本有限公司
香港觀塘榮業街 6 號 海濱工業大廈 4 樓 A 室

□
版次
2020 年 2 月初版
© 2020 中華書局（香港）有限公司

□
規格
16 開（270 mm×195 mm）

□
ISBN：978-988-8674-97-8